Everett E. (Everett Ellsworth) Truette

The Organ

Everett E. (Everett Ellsworth) Truette

The Organ

ISBN/EAN: 9783742832863

Manufactured in Europe, USA, Canada, Australia, Japa

Cover: Foto ©Thomas Meinert / pixelio.de

Manufactured and distributed by brebook publishing software
(www.brebook.com)

Everett E. (Everett Ellsworth) Truette

The Organ

THE ORGAN

VOLUME I.

MAY, 1892—APRIL, 1893.

INDEX.

INDEX.

MAY, 1892.

No. 1.

BACH

YEARLY SUBSCRIPTION $2.00.

SINGLE COPIES 25 CTS.

THE ORGAN

DEVOTED TO

A MONTHLY JOURNAL

THE KING OF INSTRUMENTS

GUILMANT

BUXTEHUDE

BEST

·EVERETT·E·TRUETTE·

EDITOR & PUBLISHER
149 A. TREMONT ST. BOSTON.

HANDEL

CIPHERINGS.

What is the difference between a dentist and an organist? Ans. A dentist manipulates the forceps, draws the ivories, and stops considerable pain. An organist draws the stops, and takes considerable pains in manipulating the ivories.

* * *

Organist. No! the swell of an organ cannot be reduced by a milk poultice. — *Song.*

* * *

A Frenchman, once giving a description of a fugue, said it was a composition in four parts, where one part rushed in after the other, and where the audience rushed out before any of them rushed in. To understand a fugue, it must be listened to intelligently and attentively. — *Music.*

* * *

Church organists in the Pine Tree State are very mercenary. They are always looking after the Maine chants. — *Boston Score.* We will inchoir into this. — *Steubenville Herald.* Give him a good blowing up, and pump hymn for the facts.

* * *

The organ-blower in a London church recently fell asleep during the service, of which fact the audience soon became conscious by the vigorous blowing of his own organ. — *Ex.*

* * *

DIALOGUE IN A CHICAGO DEPOT.

First Old Lady: "Yes know that Timothy Brown, who used to be our organist, has graduated from the Conservatory in Boston, don't yer?"
Second Old Lady: "Why, yes."
F. O. L.: "Wall, I read in a Boston paper that he was wedded to his Alma Mater."
S. O. L.: "Well, I do declare! It is shocking that he should marry Almy what's-her-name, after the way he carried on with that Nipper gal, who sang in his choir last summer."

* * *

R. V. HEARSE'S GREAT MAGICAL DISCOVERY

Stops "cipherings," squeaking, and groaning of the bellows action; in fact, every known (or unknown) disorder of the organ. Put up in pound bottles. $1.00 per bottle.
Directions: Sprinkle one tablespoonful of the discovery on the bellows, and add one pint of kerosene. Apply a lighted match. Repeat the dose every five minutes, till the cipher stops. No case ever known to withstand more than three doses of the Discovery. Agents wanted.

THE ORGAN.

VOL. 1.   BOSTON, MAY, 1892.   No. 1.

THE ORGAN.

A MONTHLY JOURNAL

DEVOTED TO THE KING OF INSTRUMENTS.

EVERETT E. TRUETTE, EDITOR AND PUBLISHER.

CONTENTS:

AUGUSTUS HAUPT.

AUGUSTUS HAUPT, who for the last forty years has been the most distinguished organist of Germany, was born August 25, 1810, at Cunau, in Silesia. His musical studies were directed by A. W. Bach, Bernhard Klein, Siegfried Wilhelm Dehn, and somewhat later by Friedrich Johann Schneider and Johann Gottlob Schneider. He made such a marked progress, that, at the age of twenty-two, he received an appointment at the French Convent in Berlin. Not satisfied, he continued his progress till, in 1849, he succeeded Louis Thiele in the parish church of that city.

His reputation spread abroad, and many organists visited Germany to hear his remarkable execution. In 1854 he was consulted by a number of English organists, who were appointed a committee to draft the plans for a large organ for the Crystal Palace near London. In 1870 he was elected Director of the Königliche Hochschule für Kirchenmusic in Berlin, succeeding his old master Bach, which position he held till his death.

When Professor Haupt was in the prime of life, his performance of the organ music of Bach, Mendelssohn, and Thiele was remarkable for its clearness, breadth, and absolute correctness, while his improvisations, in the style of J. S. Bach, were inimitable. Of late years his advancing age had reduced his energy to such an extent that he rarely played any concerted music, confining himself to *extempore* playing, which even then was unsurpassed.

Professor Haupt told me in 1883, that, up to that time, over a hundred and fifty Americans had studied with him and that over a hundred and seventy-five of his pupils held governmental positions in Germany. He also said that he was "always pleased to have American pupils, as they worked with so much determination and energy, while their mental capacity was admirable."

How fondly I look back to my early morning lessons with Professor Haupt, when he would meet me at the old Parochial Kirche, take out of his bag the enormous key (not less than nine inches long), and, after placing it in the lock and turning it round with his two hands *twice*, take out another key, somewhat smaller, and unlock the second lock by turning that key round *twice*, after all of which we could enter the dark, bare vestibule of the church. On our way up stairs several doors had to be unlocked and locked again, till finally we stood before the old organ.

This instrument had three manuals and forty-two registers. The color of the keys was the reverse of the modern custom, those keys which we call the black keys being white, and *vice versa*. The stops worked on the ratchet principle, and each one, when being drawn, had a squeak peculiar unto itself. There was no low C-sharp in the Pedal-clavier, and a Combination-pedal or a Swell would have been a luxury.

Notwithstanding the barren surroundings, the lessons were always instructive and intensely interesting. After playing a couple of Preludes and Fugues of Bach, which were interspersed with various squeaks, whenever the Professor took

a notion to change the registration, he would take a pinch of snuff and finally say, "*Ach yeh! sehr gut, sehr gut.*" After a number of suggestions from him we would converse a large part of the forenoon on topics connected with the organ, he relating numerous experiences with Mendelssohn, Thiele, Bach, and foreign organists. At home on Oranienberger Strasse, he was equally interesting and always sociable. The representation given above of Professor Haupt is a perfect likeness of him as he appeared in those days, when he would sit by the hour, with his snuff-box on his left and his poodle-dog on his right, and talk about his early days, in which he practised Bach's Trio Sonatas by candle-light, at 5 A.M., *on a piano*, notwithstanding all the crossing of hands which was thus necessary. No matter how long a call one made, on departing it was always, "*Adieu auf wiedersehen.*"

There are many organists in this country who will sigh with me at the thought of never seeing the good old Professor here again. He died the 6th of last July at the ripe age of 81.

HISTORY OF THE ORGAN.

I.

THE actual origin of the organ, notwithstanding laborious research, is enveloped in obscurity; although it is generally conceded that the "Pandean Pipes," which consisted of seven or eight reeds, culled from some brook, fastened together in a straight line by wax, and played by means of the breath being forced into them, was the first kind of organ-building. The honor of inventing this first principle of the organ — pipes placed in a row and sounded by wind — has been ascribed to Pan, the mythical god, but the simple *pipe* (a single reed) was, according to the Scriptures, invented by Jubal, the son of Lamech.

The reeds of the "Pandean Pipes" (known also as "Pan's pipe," "Syrinx," or "Mouth-organ") were gathered from the meadows, and cut off just below the knot, which knot prevented the wind escaping at that end, causing it to return to the end at which it entered (in reality, a *stopped pipe*). The length of the reed, from the knot to the end which was placed at the mouth, regulated the pitch. These reeds were fastened together, so that the open ends made a straight line, with the longest reed at the left, and the closed ends formed an oblique line below.

The mode of playing this primitive instrument was exceedingly tiresome, as either the mouth was kept in constant motion, to and fro, over the tubes, or the tubes had to be incessantly shifted to the right or left, under the mouth; and the tone, while passably agreeable at a distance, sounded coarse and braying when near. Centuries passed before any other method of sounding the pipes, than directly from the mouth, was discovered; but at length an air-tight box came into use, into which the ends of the pipes were inserted through small holes which were cut for that purpose. A small tube, at one end of the box, was placed in the mouth, and the box thus filled with wind which caused the pipes to sound. As all the pipes sounded at once, it was necessary to place the fingers over the openings of those pipes which one did not wish to speak.

When the number of pipes increased to such an extent that the fingers could not control their speech, a small slider, attached to a lever, was placed in the box, under the opening for each pipe, whereby the wind could be shut off from the pipes at pleasure.

To increase the power, a second row of pipes of the same pitch was added; and a rude form of bellows was invented to supply the wind, as human lungs were no longer capable of furnishing the necessary amount.

No precise date can be ascribed to these inventions, but it can be stated with certainty that they date from a period before the birth of Christ.

The next step, in the evolution of the organ, was the so-called "*Hydraulic*" or "*Water Organ*," supposed to have been invented by the celebrated mechanic, Ktesibius, of Alexandria (twenty years before Christ). In order to produce an equal flow of wind for all the pipes, this man used several vessels which were connected with each other and filled with water. The lids closely fitted in the openings of the vessels and could be pressed down by the foot, thus forcing the water from one vessel to another. By this pressure upon the water, and by the corresponding counter-pressure, an equal supply of wind was produced, which was conducted to the pipes.

The hydraulic organ proved to be a costly and defective instrument; and a return was made to the *pneumatic* organ, in which the wind was supplied directly from bellows which were worked by manual labor. The bellows were enlarged, and two of them so connected that in pressing one down the other simultaneously rose, giving a suggestion of the feeders of to-day. This important invention dates from the seventh century.

The introduction of the organ in the churches occurred sometime between the fourth and seventh centuries. Platina tells us that Pope Vitalian I., A.D. 666, first employed the organ for religious worship; but a Spanish bishop, named Julianus, gives an account of their use in the churches of Spain at least two hundred years earlier. Constantine VI., by a special deputation, presented to the church of St. Cornelius, at Compiègne, "a huge organ of lead pipes," in 755 or 756; and Charles the Great caused an organ to be built in Aix-la-Chapelle in 812. This last organ is said to have been the first which acted without water; and Walafrid Strabo, in one of his works, wrote that its softness (?) of tone caused the death of a female.

Organs came into use in English churches about this time, and were constructed by English builders, with pipes of

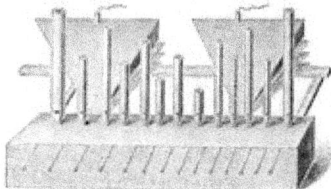

copper fixed in gilt frames. St. Dunstan, in the reign of Edgar, erected an organ with brass pipes. Count Elwin presented an organ to the convent of Ramsey, on which it is said, "The Earl devoted thirty pounds to make copper pipes of organs, which, resting with their openings in thick order on the spiral winding in the inside, and being struck on feast days with a strong blast of bellows, emit a sweet melody and a far resounding peal."

At the end of the tenth century, many churches in Germany possessed organs, notably the Paulina Church at Erfurt, St. James Church at Magdeburg, and the Cathedral at Halberstadt; and nearly all the churches were striving to possess the instrument which was so conspicuous in attracting a congregation.

(*To be continued next month.*)

To the Editor of The Organ:

THE EVOLUTION OF THE SWELL-BOX.

IS A DUPLICATION OF THIS FEATURE COMPATIBLE WITH THE HIGHEST STANDARD OF ORGAN CONSTRUCTION?

THERE are many innovations which owe their existence to *imitation* rather than true merit. We see something new created by some one for a purpose, and do not ask "Why is this done?" but "Who did it?" If the name is acceptable the thing is copied. When an analysis of the subject provokes a controversy, the projectors or introducers of the fashion are brought to the front.

A persistence in advertising a profusion of swell-boxes would bring as great return as an abundance of other things. Also in manufacturing, it is natural that competition should err on the side of too much of a thing rather than a higher grade of a less quantity. Couple this with a desire to secure a contract by catering to a professional "fad" rather than a defence of excess, or to introduce some new and advertising point, largely mechanical, because better understood by the real purchasers, who are not acquainted with the musical requirements of the instrument, and it is plain to see how there may be an over production of mechanical appliances for varying the expression, etc. To a purchasing committee with musicless souls, the statement that a Trumpet of 16 ft. throughout in the Swell-organ, or a 32 ft. stop in the Pedal, will increase the dignity and grandeur of the instrument to an extent which cannot be accomplished by any other pipe addition, is a tonal matter which may not be clearly understood, but upon an explanation of a system of mechanism by which the entire register action can be operated by simply pressing a knob, it is at once adopted as a desirable scheme. Midway between these extremes of tone and mechanism, or a combination of both, stands the organ-swell. The light and shade is easily recognizable by all, and an increase of this effect is thought desirable to any extent (ignoring the ancient proverb) — a good thing, there cannot be too much of it.

The fact that a few prominent organists have indorsed the method of placing the Choir and additional parts of the manual in a Swell-box, expressing themselves publicly to that effect, is no proof that the rank and file of educated musicians believe in it. Doctors of music as well as medicine will disagree; and it is the more significant when they do so, for the subjects in the former case are far less complex than in the latter. Nor is the name-plate upon an instrument constructed in this way a guarantee of indorsement by the builder. It was likely with him, "Hobson's choice," or a matter of gain or loss of the contract. He knows full well that he possesses few rights the middle man is bound to respect, a servant to the profession as far as detail is concerned, and but few of whom can *afford* to maintain an independent position with the eagle eye of competition upon them.

When in the year 1712 the Jordans, father and son, constructed a four-manual organ for St. Magnus Church, London, "one of which is adapted to the art of emitting sounds by swelling the notes, *which never was in any organ before*," they gave to England the honor of introducing the Swell-organ to the world. Her conservative position has doubtless restrained the growth of this feature beyond a reasonable point; but to America must be given the palm (?) for carrying the Swell from the insignificant specimen at "fiddle G" to tenor F, to 4 ft: C, to C C, the reeds of the Choir, "the entire Choir," and now a generous portion of the Great, while we may soon learn of an organic Alexander taking the remainder of it.

Let us look at the subject from a pecuniary point. There are Swells and Swells. The writer has seen a Swell set up against the wall, which was made to serve as a back to the box. Supposed to be tight when new, the sagging of the structure in front carried the Swell off until wall and box had parted company to the extent of one and a half inches. This Swell (?) was used in the regular service, the organist moving the pedal, and the imagination "doing the rest." Examples without number could be quoted, showing the careless manner in which Swell-boxes are constructed. An increase in the number of this sort would not deplete the appropriation to any considerable degree; but the point we wish to make is, that to construct an *effective Swell*, time, money, and skill are necessary.

For a box (Swell-manual) ten feet square, from seven hundred to eight hundred feet of planed one and a half inch plank, not counting waste, are used by the conscientious builder. With two sets of louvers, material throughout, with labor, total cost say a hundred and fifty dollars. For a tight box the louvers must be made to shut and *fit* and to remain fitted. In all, twenty or more pieces of seasoned material from six to eight inches wide, six feet long at least, must be made to move without noise or any appreciable friction; they must be moved, you may say, unconsciously by the player, and this mechanical perfection must continue until *worn out*, to be acceptable. The connecting mechanism to move this double train of louvers by a slight motion of the foot, and without distracting the player, is continued from the box through devious ways, ending with the pedal or "shoe" which has the "right of way" at the desk — other mechanism often being carried round to accommodate it.

The construction of this Swell-pedal action is really a mechanical feat, as the leverage is not in favor of the organist: he must move the pedal *less* than the movement of the louvers, thus there is greater call for perfect mechanism.

It is estimated that the second or inner set of louvers adds to the effectiveness of the *crescendo* and *diminuendo* thirty-three per cent. If this set is omitted, and the number of louvers in the remaining one is reduced by increasing their width, and weight, by shortening, the force of the above statement is lost, *i.e.*, nothing to do — no mechanical feat. Now, this system which we have considered for the Swell cannot be enlarged to include the Choir if it is to be placed in a box, but must be duplicated *in its entirety*. It must have its own box, louvers, and operating mechanism. We cannot add more ears to the train, but must provide an entire new train. There is therefore the cost of such duplication, with much contingent expense in furnishing room, by transposing and rearranging other parts.

Again, in the interior arrangement of an organ, the best plan, if possible, would be to place *all* manual chests upon the same level. All would then receive the same degree of temperature, and be in tune one with the other; the farther we go away from this uniformity, the more "swinging" of the tone under the influence of artificial heat, foul air, etc., and, as the space over the organ decreases, this defect increases. The interior arrangement of the old Music Hall (Boston) organ was a notable example of inequality in this respect. It was never in tune, could not be put in tune, *in toto*. The best location for the Swell would be on a level with the Great. The worst, at the top of the room near the ceiling. This Choir-box must occupy the post of honor, level with the Great; and the Swell, the true and rightful heir, must be forced higher up into the foul atmosphere, to make room for the interloper. Of necessity then the case or screen must be correspondingly elevated, so that we must have more case in addition to the other expense. Four or five feet would be a fair estimate of the additional height required to hide the interior work and extra box.

Here, then, the question is pertinent. Would it not be better to donate the sum required to make the Choir-organ a Swell-organ, to manual or, better, pedal pipe work? and would not one superlative Swell-organ with this extra tonal re-enforcement be more desirable than otherwise?

But let us take another look at the interior. One of the known faults of Church-architects of our time is the reluctance with which floor space and height are allotted to the organ-room. This has been winked at by the committee; and builders, who are accessory to this fault, make it a matter of pride to be able to *stow away* an instrument in the least available space. A following out of this policy has led up to the consideration of a *minimum* instead of a *proper* amount of room for the organ. Beyond a certain proportion, all material placed in the interior is an obstruction to resonance. This principle is well known to all established builders, but it is practically a dead letter under the usual limit of space set apart for their use. On page 290, ¶ 1212, Hopkins & Rimbault, Ed. 1877, may be found the following: "It is a fact worth the remembrance of those who would limit an organ-builder too strictly in regard to space, that one of the secrets of the good effect of many old instruments is their *comparative emptiness*. They have not only pipes to produce tone, but breathing-room to improve it."

Again on page 294, referring to the situation for the bellows — "In German organs they are more frequently put outside the case, as they were indeed in many old English instruments. Where the necessary additional room can be spared, the latter arrangement is the most advantageous; as it allows so much more space for the convenient distribution of the mechanism, as well as admitting of more ready means of access to its several parts for purposes of regulation, repair, etc., besides which the free space then left is *beneficial to the resonance of the organ*."

Now, if removing the bellows from the *bottom* of the organ, the region of mechanism, improves the resonance, how much greater benefit would accrue from the removal of 500 or 700 feet of plank put together in the most bulky form which could be devised, and that too in the *centre* of the organ, and the region of *tone*. But the imposition does not stop here; the box is often extended by adding more plank, until it is large enough to encompass a generous portion of the Great; and yet again, peradventure the architect provides a *room* for this organ, which encloses it upon all sides, leaving but one

(*Concluded on Page 17.*)

THE ORGAN.

BOSTON, MAY, 1892.

THE ORGAN is published the first of every month. Subscription price $1.00 per year; foreign countries $1.50, payable in advance. Single copies, 25 cents.

Subscribers will please state with which number they wish their subscriptions to begin.

The paper will be sent to all patrons till the editor is notified by letter to discontinue.

Subscribers wishing the address of their paper changed must give the old as well as the new address.

Remittances should be made by registered letter, post-office order, or by check payable to Everett E. Truette.

Programmes of organ concerts, with press notices of the same, specifications of new organs, and items of general interest to the subscribers, will be gratefully received.

Correspondence, to secure notice, must in all cases be accompanied by the name and address of the writer, not for publication, but as a guarantee of good faith.

Advertising rates sent on application.

Address all communications.

The Organ, 149 A Tremont Street, Boston, Mass.

☞ An active agent in every city is desired to whom a liberal cash commission will be allowed.

SALUTATORY.

In making our bow to the public, with the presentation of the initial number of THE ORGAN, we would state that we are deeply sensible of the fact that the field of usefulness for a publication in the interest of the organ exclusively is, in this country at least, a matter of doubtful limit. That there is a contingent among musical students, lovers of organ music, and the people, who have a clear understanding of the construction and uses of this peer among instruments, may be believed; but the educational avenues to this knowledge are narrow and circumscribed, forming a domain which seems to be rather avoided until some one is brought face to face with a matter where judgment or an opinion is required, when a lamentable amount of ignorance is displayed or confessed, even among many of the so-called *students of the instrument*. What, then, can be expected from committees or purchasing agents?

Without any intention to encroach upon the right or territory of others, our aim is but to educate, by publishing information regarding the construction of notable organs of this and other countries, in detail as well as in general matters, photographic representations of cases and mechanisms, selections of organ music, a bureau of information upon points of technical or tonal question, and general news concerning organ concerts, new organs, new organ music, and the sayings and doings of prominent persons who are associated with the instrument, which will be instructive to the student and entertaining to all who are interested in this branch of instrumental music.

THE ORGAN will not be in any way a partisan or trade journal, or devoted to the specialties or methods of any person or persons; but its columns will be open for the discussion of any question which may exist or arise, relating to matters constructive, tonal, or educational.

It is evident that progress in any form of art feeds on the appreciation and demand of the people for its products; and if by our efforts we can diffuse among the public some of the knowledge which is now possessed principally by the builders of the organ, and remove to any extent the "veil of mystery" which hangs about the construction and *assembly* of this continually heard and continually misunderstood scion of the church, ours will not be a fruitless mission.

If but a fraction of the admirers of the organ will give their support, this journal will rapidly become what the editor aims to make it, — a pleasure to the professional, a companion to the amateur, and a necessity to the student.

MIXTURES.

(FOUR RANKS.)

Mr. OTTO PFEFFERKORN recently gave an organ recital in the Trinity Church, Denver, Col.

Mr. Minor C. Baldwin gave an organ concert in Chickering Hall, New York, March 31.

Miss Caroline D. Rowley has been engaged to teach in the De Pauw School of Music.

Mr. Samuel A. Baldwin played a number of organ pieces at a miscellaneous concert in the First Baptist Church, Minneapolis, March 30.

Mr. S. B. Whitney gave an organ recital at the Unitarian Church, Concord, N. H., March 24.

The death is announced of Mr. Charles Dubois, at the age of seventy, who was the organist of the Moulins Cathedral.

Mr. Harrison M. Wild has been giving a series of organ recitals in the Unity Church, Chicago.

Mr. E. M. Lott, organist of St. Sepulchre's Church, London, has been in Boston this month, on his way to Toronto.

Mr. F. Blakley Higginson has been giving a series of organ concerts on Sunday afternoons at the South Place Institute, London.

Drs. E. H. Turpin and C. Pearce and Mr. W. S. Hoyte have given a series of recitals at the factory of Mr. H. Wedlake, London.

Messrs. Bishop and Son have recently enlarged the organ in the Church of St. John the Evangelist, Angel Town, England, which now contains ten stops in the Great, twelve in the Swell, nine in the Choir, and four in the Pedal.

Mr. Walter E. Hall recently gave an organ concert in The Auditorium, Chicago, playing compositions of Smart, Berlioz, Händel, and Bennett.

Mr. F. V. McIntyre, pupil of E. M. Bowman, has been engaged as organist of the Second Baptist Church, St. Louis. This church has the largest organ in St. Louis.

Miss Madge Cameron gave an organ recital in Kent Road U. P. Church, Glasgow, on January 28. A large audience was present.

We understand that Thomas Harding, manufacturer of organ-pipes at Mills, Mass., has gone out of business.

We learn from an English contemporary that "the quality of —— & ——'s pipes is considered delicious." Are they T. D. pipes?

"The Raconteur," in the *Musical Courier*, tells us that "Rubinstein plays Beethoven and Bach superbly, and with what a *touch* and with what a *rich organ tone*." (?)

Mr. S. B. Whitney, organist and director of the choir at the Church of the Advent, Boston, has written an article on "Surpliced Boy Choirs in America," which has appeared, with illustrations, in the *New England Magazine* for April.

Mr. Charles William Melville, said to be the oldest organist in this country, died March 8, at his home in Brooklyn. Mr. Melville was eighty-three years old, and was a native of Scotland. He came to New York in 1832, and has played in a great many Catholic churches in New York and Brooklyn.

The new Hope-Jones electric system has been adopted by the firm of W. G. Vowles, in reconstructing and enlarging the organ at All Saints' Church, Bristol, England. By this system the Great and Swell with the Pedal Open Diapason are placed under the tower, and the Choir and Pedal Bourdon are located in the chancel. The desk is so placed that the organist can hear both parts of the organ as well as the choir in a satisfactory manner.

ORGAN MUSIC IN PROVIDENCE, R. I.

This city has a number of fine and large organs, the most noteworthy being the Grace Church, Central Cong., Union Cong., St. Stephen's (Episcopal), and the Cathedral (Roman Catholic). There are also two large organs in public halls; viz., in Infantry Armory and in the Music Hall. In the way of recitals on the "king of instruments" there has been comparatively little done. Some fifteen years ago Henry Carter gave recitals on the then new organ in Music Hall. Mr. A. A. Stanley also gave several series of recitals three or four years ago in Grace Church. Soon after this church had its new Hutchings organ (the largest in the city), Mr. Stanley was called to the professorship of music in the University of Michigan, and was succeeded by Mr. N. B. Sprague, who has for two years given a series of Lenten recitals. These are well attended, and occur immediately after evening prayer. I append the last programme:—

1. Allegro, (from Sonata),	Müller.
2. Largo (requested),	Händel.
3. Nocturne,	Chopin.
4. Processional March,	Whitney.

Mr. H. C. Macdougall has for several years given a series of free recitals in the Central Baptist Church on Saturday afternoons from five to six. The organ is a three-manual Hook & Hastings. These recitals have been very well attended, although no attempt has been made to give "popular" programmes. Mr. N. L. Wilbur, Associate of the College of Musicians, has given a series of recitals, preceding the Star Course entertainments, which, from the judicious programmes and solid interpretations, have been lifted above the ordinary lecture-course recital. Mr. George H. Lomas, A. C. M., is to give a series of recitals in the fall on the large three-manual Hook & Hastings organ in the Beneficent Cong. Church.

H. C. M.

SORGMARSCH.

HUGO BEYER.

1.
2.
Sw.
(open) Gt.
Coup. off
Sw.
Gt.
Sw.
Sw.
Gt.
Coup.
Full
ff
TRIO.
Sw. with Cornopean.
Gt.
poco rit.
(Reduce Gt. to Op. Disp.)
(Coup. off.)
FINE.

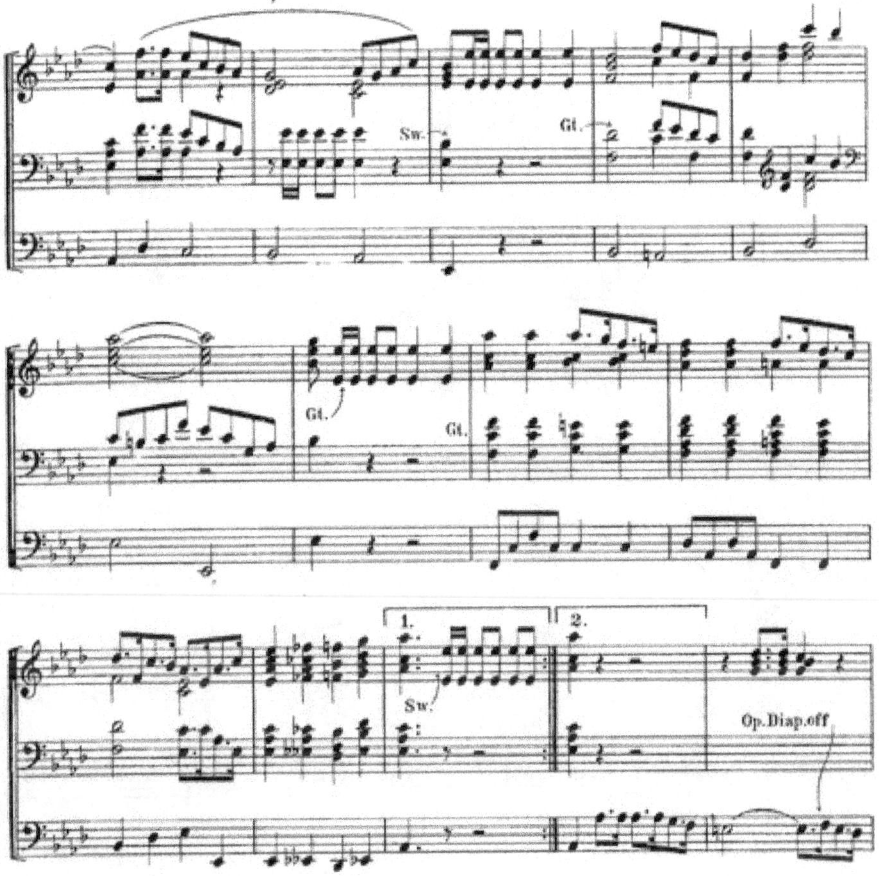
Sw.
Gt.
Gt.
Gt.
1.
2.
Sw.
Op.Diap.off
Sw.
Coup.off
D.C.al Fine.

INTERLUDE.

A. P. F. BOËLLY.

Andante.

Sw.St.Diap.& Flute 4 Ft.

Sw.

Ch. (or Gt.) Melodia.

Ped. Bourdon.
Sw. to Ped.

Ch.

Sw.

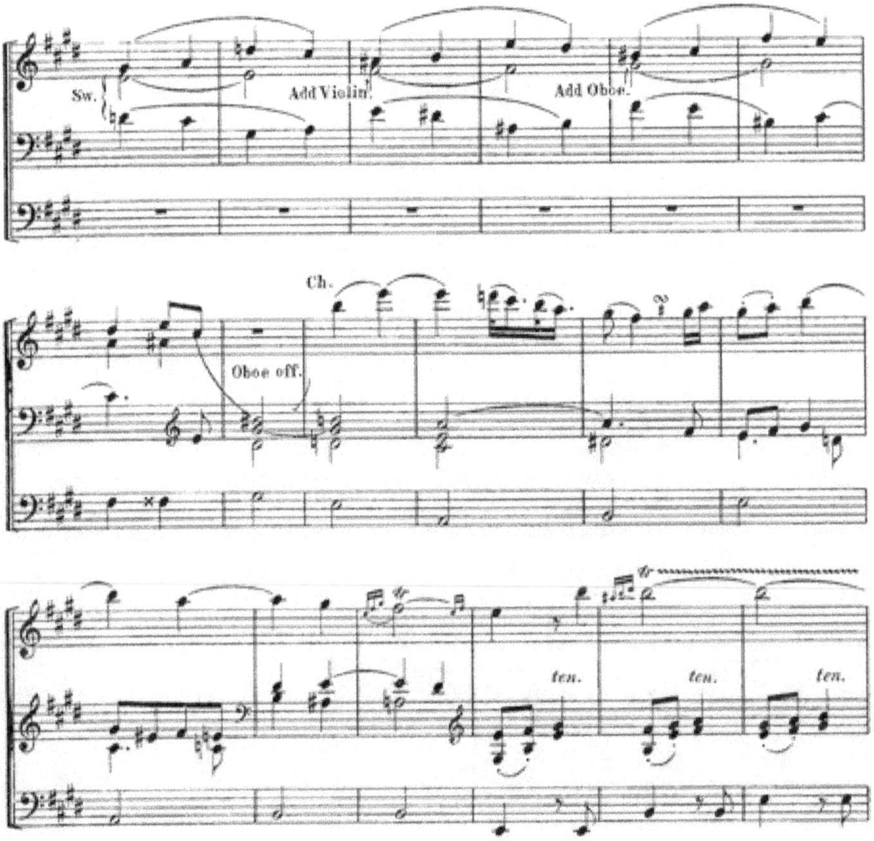
Sw.
Add Violin.
Add Oboe.
Ch.
Oboe off.
ten.
ten.
ten.
rall.

VERSET.

Allegretto.

THEO. SALOME.

Sw. 8 & 4 Ft. with Oboe.

Ch. (or Gt.) Melodia & Dulciana.

Ped. 16 & 8 Ft.

Ch.

Sw. (partly open.)

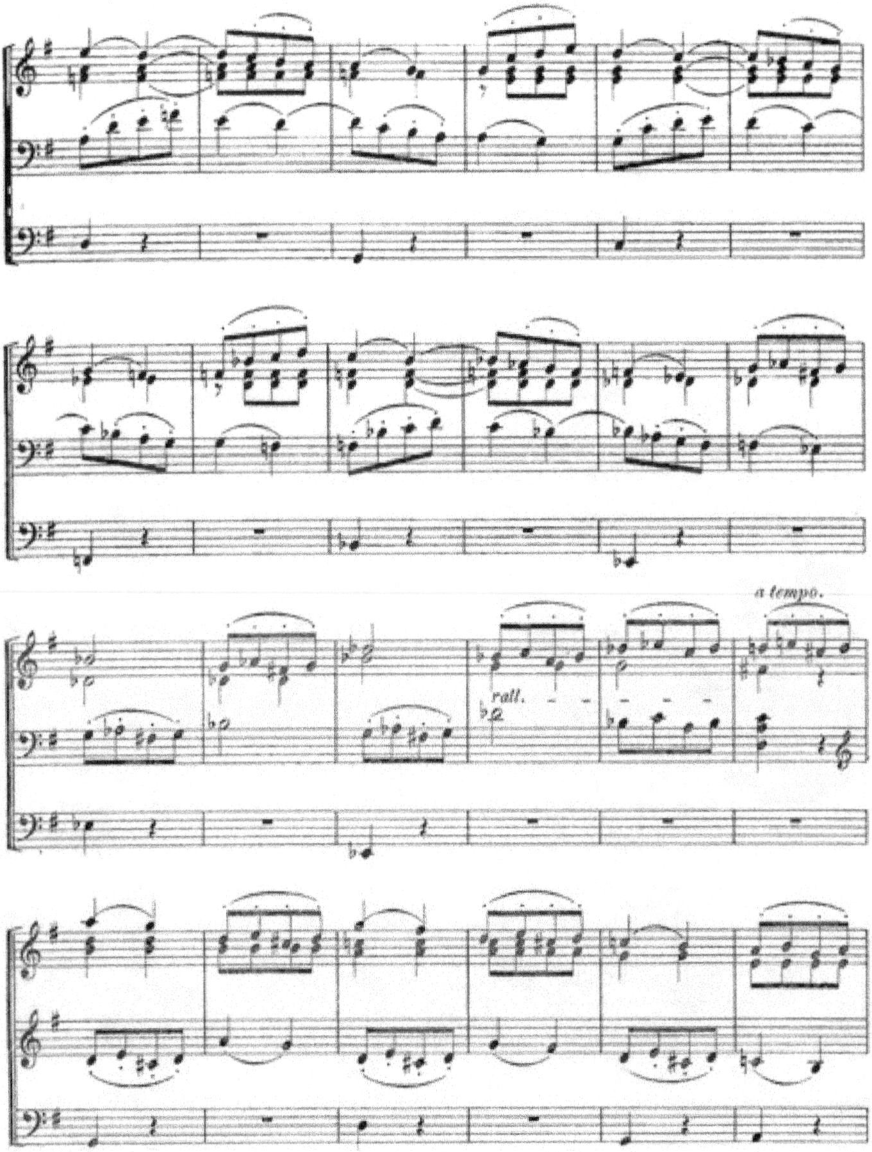
a tempo.
rall.

ri   tar   -   dan   -   do.   -   -

THE EVOLUTION OF THE SWELL-BOX.

(*Continued from Page 7.*)

which receives the "case," the decorated pipes filling the office of the stone, which at last closes up the door and makes of the organ-room an organ-tomb.

In the matter of *manual variety*, it seems that the duplication of the Swell is much the same in tonal effect as the repetition of a member in architecture ; renders the instrument monotonous, and practically reduces a three- to a two-manual organ, and where part of the Great is included, not only in variety, but in power. There is the "magnitude of the *crescendo*," but no "full organ" in the best sense of the term, with five-sixths of the pipe-work covered. Let us look still deeper into the tonal effect of the organ Swell.

It is well known that legitimate *crescendo* and *diminuendo* are produced in all orchestral instruments by degrees of force, and that this effect is produced alone in the organ species by *smothering*, that the treatment of a tone by reducing it in this manner is naturally detrimental to its delicacy, that under a closed Swell the distinctive quality of a pipe, the *bouquet*, if the term may be allowed, is in a more or less degree lost, and which at the point of piano is neutralized so that we do not attempt to analyze it except in the way of pitch and quantity, and only in the *crescendo* do we begin to recognize the beauty of its quality, which would be still further augmented by a removal of the Swell-box, if such a thing were possible, with the pedal. Nothing could be more unsatisfactory than a violin solo by a master, the light and shade controlled by the louvers of a Swell-box. We are therefore forced to admit, that, when considered strictly from a tonal and orchestral standpoint, the organ-Swell is at best an imperfect method of varying the force of sound which cannot be accomplished by reducing or increasing the pressure of wind, and that the superlative effect of the pipe is modified when played in the Swell-box, either alone or collectively. We must therefore accept the inevitable in this case, and will make it as perfect as possible. It is, in the absence of the orchestra, our only method of expression, the companionable portion of the organ; but if this smothering process is extended *ad lib*, this effort repeated on every manual, like a long visit its welcome will be worn out.

It is a fact well known that only a certain amount of pure tone can be obtained from a pipe; any attempt to increase it will result in wind and noise. Now, if the voicing is strained to obtain power to compensate for the wholesale blanketing of the manual, the entire tonal structure is unfavorably affected. The power of the full organ cannot be restored by such an expedient.

Again, paradoxical as it may seem, although the Swell-box is not an improver of pure tone — because it cannot be improved, as pure gold cannot be refined — a coarse and unsympathetic tone can be screened by it, and escape the sunlight of criticism under its cover. A simple instance : Given two stops of equal scale and pitch, say Principals, one voiced by the artist (there are artists), the other by the novice, and both to be used in the same instrument, there is no question where the intelligent builder would place the latter. It would not be in the Great, but in the retirement of the Swell, where the defects would be less noticeable. This would seem an insinuation that the Swell-box might be a refuge for cheap or careless voicing. The opportunity is the incentive. The greater amount of covering the less necessity for the artist. Of all calamities this is the greatest and most to be deplored. It is a poniard-thrust at the heart of the instrument, and we are loath to give the thought a place here ; but our progress in search of light has brought us to it.

We believe, in conclusion, that a careful investigation of the subject by an unprejudiced mind will result in the opinion that the excess of Swell is a fashion, an exaggeration, false in principle, and therefore not compatible with the highest standard of organ construction. The protection of this unparalleled instrument rests with those who know it best ; and they will not see its artistic character dragged down or insulted by tricks of expression, or methods fatal to its tonal life and purity.

GAMBETTE.

ORGAN CONCERTS.

ORGAN RECITAL BY MR. SAMUEL P. WARREN.

At Mr. Warren's two hundred and fifteenth Organ Recital (fourteenth of the present season), in Grace Church, New York, April 7th, the following programme was given : —

Fantasia in B, Op. 10	Schellenberg
Adagio in B flat } from "Ariana"	Guilmant
March in E }	
Sonata in C minor (ninety-fourth Psalm)	Reubke

A programme which, under ordinary circumstances, would be voted dry in the extreme ; but Mr. Warren managed to infuse a little of his own personality into the first and last numbers, which, with the peculiar resources of this particular organ, really proved more interesting ; than was anticipated. The Fantasia is in itself very uninteresting, but by means of the two organs (connected by electricity) at opposite ends of the church, many effects were introduced which aroused one's enthusiasm, and made the number quite enjoyable. The two selections from "Ariana" were charming and very tastefully registered, making one wish that concert-hall privileges might be borrowed to allow one to demand a repetition. The Sonata of Reubke has never been a favorite of ours, but Mr. Warren's presentation of the work was more interesting than any of which we remember. The influence of Wagner seems to be very prominent, and the Sonata as a whole is devoid of form. Mr. Warren is one of the pioneers in giving organ concerts, and the catholicity of his programmes has always commanded our admiration.

The programme of the preceding recital is appended.

Prelude and Fugue in E	Buxtehude.
Largo in G	Handel.
Sonata No. 14, in D	Rheinberger.
Romanza in F (transcription)	Clara Schumann.
Organ Symphony No. 6	Widor.

ORGAN RECITAL BY MR. WM. C. CARL.

We attended the second of a series of organ recitals given by Mr. Carl, in the First Presbyterian Church, New York, when the following programme was given : —

Toccata in F	J. S. Bach.
Pastorale — *L. Rose* (new)	Georges MacMaster.
Noël Espagnole	Alex. Guilmant.
Aria "Entreat me not to leave thee" (Mrs. H. H. Sawyer)	Ch. Gounod.
Prelude	Louis Nicolas Clerambault (1676-1749).
Symphony V.	Ch. M. Widor.
Allegro Vivace — Allegro Cantabile — Toccata.	
Aria, "O God have mercy" (Mr. Carl E. Dufft)	Mendelssohn.
Marche Nuptiale	F. de la Tombelle.

In the Toccata, Mr. Carl showed himself to be the possessor of a brilliant pedal-technique ; and, while we prefer to hear the piece played a little less Vivace, it was well played. In playing the two eighth-notes of the theme staccato, one certainly adds character to it, and renders it more readily recognized in its recurrence, though it is purely a modern interpretation.

The Pastorale of MacMaster is a gem which was exquisitely registered, and Guilmant's Noël Espagnole showed the performer at his best.

If Mrs. Sawyer's intonation had been a little more correct, the Aria would have been very enjoyable. Mr. Dufft was perfectly at home in Mendelssohn's Aria, and sang exceedingly well. If the concert had ended in the middle of the programme, it would have been one of the most satisfactory performances of organ music which we have heard of late ; but, for some unaccountable reason, Mr. Carl seemed to lose control of himself at the beginning of the Symphony, and perhaps the less said of the rest of the programme the better. The wholesale cut which was made in the second movement of the Symphony was unwarrantable. It were better to omit the whole movement than to play but one-third of it.

We regret very much not being able to attend the third concert, April 13th, as, at times, Mr. Carl's playing is extremely interesting.

ORGAN AND HARP MATINEES BY MR. GEORGE W. MORGAN AND MISS MAUD MORGAN.

A SERIES of organ and harp *matinées* was given by the above artists, in Chickering Hall, New York, on March 8th, 15th, 22d, 29th, and April 5th. We were able to attend only the last *matinée*, in which the following programme was performed:—

Septette — Harps and Organ — Manhattan March	Morgan.
Organ Solo — Selections from "Tannhäuser"	Morgan.
Harp Solo — Andante	Alvars.
Vocal { a Liebesgluck	Spicker.
{ b Ho May	Blach.
Harp Solos { a Bercewse	Hasselmans.
{ b Patrouille }	
Organ — Grand Triumphal March (from "Aïda")	Verdi.
Solo and Chorus — Benedictus from St. Cecilia Mass, with six Harps and Organ	Gounod.

Five of Miss Morgan's pupils assisted in the first and last numbers, Mr. Francis Fischer Powers (Baritone) was the vocalist, and the Choir of male voices from the Church of St. Mary the Virgin sang the chorus.

The Septette for Organ and Harps would have been very effective if the ladies had only kept with the organist; but, as it was, about every chord on the harps was a half-beat before that on the organ. Between the first and second numbers Mr. Morgan begged the indulgence of the audience by saying (as near as we could understand him), that "the organ has never been tuned." The condition of the instrument really did seem to warrant such a sweeping statement. We should have preferred to hear Mr. Morgan play at least one piece of legitimate organ music, though the arrangements were effective, and the audience evidently enjoyed them. Miss Morgan played the harp very *prettily*, and Mr. Powers displayed a good voice which he used very effectively. The audience was large and enthusiastic.

INAUGURAL Recital by Mr. R. Huntington Woodman, St. John's P. E. Church, Stamford, Conn., February 25.

PROGRAMME.

Sonata No. 1 (First movement)	Mendelssohn
a. Gavotte	Thomas
b. Minuet and Trio	Calkin
c. Spring Song	Mendelssohn
Overture in D	Smart
a. Cantilene Pastorale }	Guilmant
b. Marche Religieuse }	
Fugue in G minor	Bach
a. Wolfram's Star Song }	Wagner
b. Pilgrim's Chorus }	
Prayer	Lemaigre
Toccata	Dubois
Improvisation	
a. Bridal Song	Jensen
b. Dance of the Bayadères }	Rubinstein
c. Wedding Procession }	

THE new organ (gift of Mr. John P. Langmaid) in the Wesley M. E. Church, Salem, Mass., was inaugurated March 17, by Messrs. J. Frank Donahoe and Charles Albion Clark, Organists, assisted by Mrs. Edwin R. Biglow, Soprano, when the following programme was given:—

Overture, "Occasional Oratorio."	Händel
Mr. Donahoe.	
a. March from Sonata, Op. 35	Chopin-Eddy
b. Grand Chœur	Salomé
c. On the Wings of Song	Mendelssohn
Mr. Clark.	
Salve Regina	Dana
Mrs. Biglow.	
Sonata, Op. 98	Rheinberger
Mr. Donahoe.	
Fear not ye, O Israel	Buck
Mrs. Biglow.	
a. Andante Cantabile	Widor
b. Theme and Variations	Buck
c. Coronation March	Svendsen
Mr. Clark.	
March. "La Reine de Saba"	Gounod

INAUGURAL Recital by Dr. A. H. Mann, Trinity Chapel, Wolverhampton, England.

PROGRAMME.

Toccata and Fugue in D minor	Bach
Fantasia in C	Tours
Chorus, "They that sow in Tears"	Gaul
Barcarolle in F	Bennet
Sonata No. 1 in F	Mendelssohn
Adagio from "Moonlight Sonata"	Beethoven
Chorus, "No Shadows Yonder"	Gaul
Concerto in G minor	Coolidge

THE following programme was given in the Grace M. E. Church, Bloomington, Ill., by Mr. Clarence Eddy, assisted by Miss Electa Gifford, Soprano, March 14.

Sonata in C minor, Op. 70	Oscar Wermann
a. Allegretto	Volkmann
b. Pilgrims' Chorus	Wagner
Aria "Bel Raggio"	Rossini
a. "Ave Mer"	Schubert-Eddy
b. Fugue in G minor (the greater)	Bach
a. "Harvest Home"	Spinney
b. Gavotte	Martini
Variations on the "Old Folks at Home"	Flagler
Song, "Jesus, Lover of My Soul",	Campion
Concert Fantasia	Lux
St. Cecilia Offertory, No. 3	Batiste
Song, "Thou Brilliant Bird"	David
Overture to "Stradella"	Flotow-Buck

INAUGURAL Concert on the new organ in SS. Peter and Paul's Church, Pittsburg, Pa., by Clarence Eddy, assisted by Mrs. Geneva Johnstone-Bishop, Soprano, February 26.

Sonata in C minor, Op. 70	Wermann
"Harvest Home"	Spinney
Gavotte	Martini
Christmas Chimes	Gade
Song, "Salve Regina"	Dana
Toccata and Fugue in D minor	Bach
Allegretto	Volkmann
Pilgrims' Chorus	Wagner
Funeral March and Seraphic Song	Guilmant
Theme, Variations and Finale	Thiele
Aria "Hear ye, Israel"	Mendelssohn
Concert Fantasia	Lux
The Storm Fantasia	Lemmens
Overture to "Stradella",	Flotow-Buck

JUST before going to press we received programmes of a series of organ recitals which Dr. Henry G. Hanchett has been giving in The Marble Collegiate Church, New York City. The programme of the sixth recital, April 11, is given below:

Tannhäuser March	Wagner
Pastorale in F	Kullak
Fanfare in D	Lemmens
"So shall the Lute and Harp"	Händel
Mrs. Anna Burch.	
Polonaise, Op. 70, No. 5	Hummel
Allegretto Grazioso	Tours
Elevation in A flat	Guilmant
Scherzo (Reformation Symphony)	Mendelssohn
Cradle Song	Klein
Mrs. Burch.	
Jubilee Overture	Weber

REVIEW OF NEW ORGAN MUSIC.

FROM NOVELLO, EWER, & CO., N.Y.

FANTASIA	E. SILAS.
ALLEGRETTO PASTORALE	H. W. WAREING.
SONATA IN D MINOR	ALFRED ALEXANDER.
MARSH IN C	H. ELLIOT BUTTON.
NOS. 145-146 OF "ORIGINAL COMPOSITIONS FOR THE ORGAN.

The Fantasia was written for the Opening of the new organ in Blenheim Palace, and does not seem quite so spontaneous as most of the compositions of this writer. However, there is much to be admired in it, notwithstanding several "dry moments," and it will find a place on many concert programmes. Toward the end the composition seems more interesting leading into the March of James the Second (1690), which works up to an effective climax.

The Allegretto Pastorale is melodious and interesting, but we fail to see why it is called a Pastorale. With the exception of a few open fifths held by both feet in the pedal part on the second page, there does not seem to be any suggestion of a Pastorale. These fifths might occur in a Fugue as well as in a Pastorale. We like the composition as a piece, but we would prefer to think of something besides a Pastorale when listening to it.

There are three movements in the Sonata, the first of which (Allegro) is the most interesting, opening with a dignified theme in double-dotted quarter-notes and sixteenth-notes. The counterpoint in triplets which follows lacks spontaneity and does not flow freely, but the movement ends in the same dignified manner in which it begins. The second movement (Adagio) would have pleased us more if it had formed a better contrast to the first movement. The Sonata ends with an Introduction and Fugue. No. 146 is a March which many organists as well as students will welcome. Not difficult, and easily played on a two-manual organ, it will be found very useful.

MEDITATION
WEDDING PROCESSIONAL MARCH } . . . JAMES SHAW.

The former is an excellent piece for students, quite easy (except a running accompaniment in the left hand near the end), and very melodious.

The Wedding Processional March seems to have been written with an eye to the order which we once heard the head usher give to the organist at a large wedding, viz.: "Keep the organ going till the guests are all out." The pertinacity with which the composer has stuck to the original key (E♭), through the first nine pages, is a little monotonous, but the piece is effective, and will be popular with many organists.

FROM ARTHUR P. SCHMIDT, BOSTON.

GOTHIC MARCH
PRAYER
PASTORALE RHAPSODY } TH. SALOMÉ.
SCOTTISH ECLOGUE
FUGUE

Five of a set of ten pieces by this well-known composer, published only by this house. A set of pieces which should be in every organist's library, and which will be valuable to every student. The Scottish Eclogue is the gem of these five, and is a charming bit of writing in the modern French organ-school — a school in which the leading feature is melody, and in which the melody is clothed in rich and ever-varying harmony. This Scottish Eclogue starts off in the key of C, with a solid combination on the Great, presenting the theme in eight bars. Then a repetition (somewhat modified) of the same theme on the Swell, with a similar combination, subdued by the Swell-box. An imitative passage between the Swell and Choir, in the key of the relative minor of the dominant, leads to the theme again on the Great, with staccato counterpoint added in the left hand. Then follows a *quasi* Trio, partly in triplets, in the key of the subdominant — an Oboe solo accompanied on the Choir — which is complete in itself. The first theme is repeated on the Great with a new accompaniment in the left hand, interspersed with fragments of the Trio theme, and the ending is made up of various transpositions and alterations of the first and second motives of the first theme.

The Gothic March has some quaint harmonies, the principal of which is the substitution of a *minor* triad in the place of the usual dominant major triad in the cadences. Students wishing a novelty in which the pedal part is not difficult, and a piece which can be easily registered on a two-manual organ, should look at this piece.

The Pastorale Rhapsody is a little more difficult, and calls for a larger variety of stops to carry out the indicated registration.

FROM G. SCHIRMER, N.Y.

ADAGIO IN F
FUGUE IN G MINOR } Op. 183 . . POLIBIO FUMAGALLI.

Both these compositions have the registration carefully indicated, and will be useful additions to the *repertoire* of organists. The Adagio is a gem, and will be a novelty with students. Two misprints in the Fugue will be puzzling. One in the second measure of the first entrance of the subject, where the half-note should be g instead of a. The other, if not a misprint, is the most harsh dissonance we ever heard. On page four, lower brace, third measure, the f-sharp being a half-note and tied over to an eighth-note in the next measure, makes five parts for a count and a half, while there are but four parts before and after. We think that the half-note (f-sharp) should have been a quarter-note, and the tie and following eighth-note should have been omitted. Students with weak eyes will appreciate these clear pages which are so easily read.

SUNSHINE AND SHADOW
ON THE COAST } DUDLEY BUCK.
THE HOLY NIGHT

Three of a set of "Tone Pictures" composed expressly for the organ. The first is bright and "sunny" with just enough "shadow" interspersed, and on an organ large enough to use the registration indicated will be very effective.

"On the Coast" is intended to represent

> "Dash high, roaring surf,
> On the rockbound coast of Northland!" etc.
>
> . . . .
>
> "O list to the Angelus blest,
> And the chant which floats over the deep." *

After a short *Recitative*, the piece begins with a rolling-up of chords suggestive of the incoming waves and dashing surf. Later on the composer has made use of the old "Vesper Hymn," which is both ingenious and effective.

The review of a number of other compositions is unavoidably delayed till next month.

NEW ORGANS.

CHRIST CHURCH CATHEDRAL, ST. LOUIS, MO.

New Organ built by Frank Roosevelt, N.Y.

GREAT ORGAN.

1 Double Op. Diapason	16 Ft.	7 Octave	4 Ft.
2 First Op. Diapason	8 "	8 Hohl Flöte	4 "
3 Second Op. Diapason	8 "	9 Octave Quint	2⅔ "
4 Viola di Gamba	8 "	10 Super Octave	2 "
5 Gemshorn	8 "	11 Mixture	4 Rks.
6 Doppel Flöte	8 "	12 Trumpet	8 Ft.

(Stops 4 to 12 in the Choir Swell-box.)

SWELL ORGAN.

13 Bourdon	16 Ft.	21 Salicet	4 Ft.
14 Open Diapason	8 "	22 Flute Har.	4 "
15 Violin Diapason	8 "	23 Flageolet	2 "
16 Spitz Flöte	8 "	24 Cornet	3, 4 & 5 Rks.
17 Æoline	8 "	*25 Contra Fagotto	16 Ft.
18 Vox Celestis	8 "	26 Cornopean	8 "
19 St. Diapason	8 "	27 Oboe	8 "
20 Octave	4 "	28 Vox Humana	8 "

CHOIR ORGAN.

(Enclosed in a separate Swell-box.)

*29 Contra Gamba	16 Ft.	*35 Fugara	4 Ft.
*30 Open Diapason	8 "	*36 Piccolo Har.	2 "
*31 Salicional	8 "	*37 Dolce Cornet	5 Rks.
*32 Concert Flute	8 "	*38 Orchestral Oboe	8 Ft.
*33 Quintadena	8 "	*39 Clarinet	8 "
*34 Flute d'Amour	4 "		

PEDAL ORGAN.

40 Open Diapason	16 Ft.	44 Quint	10⅔ Ft.
*41 Violone	16 "	45 Violoncello	8 "
42 Dulciana	16 "	*46 Flute	8 "
43 Bourdon	16 "	*47 Trombone	16 "

Swell to Great Octaves in addition to the usual Couplers.
Swell and Choir Tremulants.

* Pipes of the stops marked (*) are not in the organ at present.

PEDAL MOVEMENTS.

Three, affecting Great and Pedal Stops with Couplers.
Three, " Swell " " " "
Two, " Choir " " " "
Full Organ Pedal (without throwing out the knobs).
Pedal Organ Ventil.
Great to Pedal (Reversible).

The organ is divided into two parts, the parts being 33 ft. apart. The "Roosevelt Patent Wind-Chests" are used throughout the organ and the Combination Action is Automatic and Adjustable. Blown by a Water Motor.

(See Dept. of Organ Concerts for opening Concert.)

SWEDISH LUTHERAN IMMANUEL CHURCH, CHICAGO, ILL.

New Organ built by Geo. S. Hutchings, Boston.

GREAT ORGAN.		SWELL ORGAN.	
1 Open Diapason	16 Ft.	11 Bourdon Treble } 12 Bourdon Bass }	16 Ft.
2 Open Diapason	8 "	13 Violin Diapason	8 "
3 Viola di Gamba	8 "	14 Salicional	8 "
4 Melodia	8 "	15 Æoline	8 "
5 Octave	4 "	16 St. Diapason	8 "
6 Flute Har.	4 "	17 Flauto Traverso	4 "
7 Octave Quint	2⅔ "	18 Fugara	4 "
8 Super Octave	2 "	19 Dolce Cornet	3 Rks.
9 Mixture	3 Rks.	20 Cornopean	8 Ft.
10 Trumpet	8 Ft.	21 Oboe	8 "

CHOIR ORGAN.		PEDAL ORGAN.	
22 Geigen Principal	8 Ft.	28 Open Diapason	16 Ft.
23 Dolcissimo	8 "	29 Bourdon	16 "
24 Flute d'Amour	4 "	30 Violoncello	8 "
25 Violina	4 "		
26 Piccolo Har.	2 "		
27 Clarinet	8 "	The usual Couplers.	

PEDAL MOVEMENTS.

Great Organ Forte Combination.	Swell Organ Forte Combination.
" " Mezzo "	" " Piano "
" " Piano "	Great to Pedal (Reversible).
	Swell Tremolo.

ST. JOHN'S P. E. CHURCH, STAMFORD, CONN.

New Organ built by Frank Roosevelt, N.Y.

GREAT ORGAN.

1 Double Op. Diapason	16 Ft.	7 Hohl Flöte	4 Ft.
2 First " "	8 "	8 Octave Quint	2⅔ "
3 Second " "	8 "	9 Super Octave	2 "
4 Viola di Gamba	8 "	10 Mixture	4 Rks.
5 Doppel Flöte	8 "	11 Trumpet	8 Ft.
6 Octave	4 "		

(*Continued on Page 23.*)

QUESTIONS AND ANSWERS.

All questions must be accompanied by the full name and address of the writer, and, if returned by the 20th of the month, will usually be answered in the following number of THE ORGAN.

Only such questions as refer to the organ, its organists, organ-builders, or to organ-music, will be answered.

Correspondents are requested to write their questions in a clear and concise manner, writing on only one side of the paper.

G. W. Please explain the meaning of the signs which indicate the pedaling in the Litolf Ed. of Mendelssohn's Sonatas.

Ans. 1. Toe of right foot.
2. Heel " " "
a. Toe of left foot.
b. Heel " " " .

Robt. K. B. Will you be so kind as to name a few compositions for violin and organ?

Ans. Fantasia for Organ and Violin Op. 26, by Fisher, Prayer in F, for Organ, Violin, and Piano, Op. 16, Guilmant.

Miss M. E. H. Is there an arrangement for two hands of Merkel's First Sonata, in D-minor, which was originally written for four hands?

Ans. Merkel's Sonata in D-minor, Op. 30, has been arranged for two hands by Otto Türke and published by Kahnt in Zwickau.

X. Is Merkel dead? If so, when did he die?

Ans. Gustav Merkel died October 30, 1885.

G. Who publishes the following compositions?
1. Paraphrase on an Air of Rode, by Best.
2. Symphonies for Organ, by Widor.
3. Grand Chœur by Dubois.

Ans. 1. Augener & Co., London.
2. J. Hamelle, Paris.
3 "Dix Pièces" by Le Duc, Paris.

E. B. L. What is the English equivalent of (1) Prestant and (2) Tibia Major?

Ans. 1. Principal. 2. Bourdon.

F. E. S. What is the composition of spotted metal as used in organ pipes?

Ans. Generally 40 per cent tin and 60 per cent lead. The variation of the spotting is regulated by the quality of the metals used.

J. T. E. Which is the largest organ in the world?

Ans. The organ erected a few years ago by Messrs. Hill & Son of London has the largest number of stops of any organ ever constructed, having 126 speaking stops, five manuals, and pedal clavier.

J. S. B. Please give me the dates of the birth and death of J. S. Bach.

Ans. Born March 21, 1685; died, July 30, 1750.

H. A. P. How many kinds of Manual-Couplers are in use?

Ans. The most common Manual-Couplers are the Unison Couplers between any two manuals, and the Super-Octave and Sub-Octave between Swell (or Choir) and Great, though there are examples of Super-Octave and Sub-Octave

" on its own clavier." In the large organ which is in the Town Hall, Leeds, England, may be found the following mechanical stops, which give the effect of couplers without coming under that classification of stops:—
1. Clarinet and Flute, in Octaves.
2. Oboe and Flute, in ditto.
3. Clarinet and Bassoon, in ditto.
4. Oboe and Bassoon, in ditto.
5. Clarinet and Oboe, in ditto.
6. Flute, Clarinet, and Bassoon, in Double-Octaves.
7. Flute, Oboe, and Bassoon, in ditto.

These are all in the Solo organ, and if any one of these stops is drawn, No. 5, for instance, every key which is held down sounds the Clarinet of that note and the Oboe an octave higher. If No. 6 were drawn, and middle-C held down, the result would be tenor-C of the Bassoon, middle-C of the Clarinet, and the C above of the 8-ft. Flute.

E. One of my pupils, who is studying the fourth book of Rink, is unable to play the pedal part of most of the studies up to *Allegro*. What would you recommend?

Ans. Try "18 Studies in Pedal Phrasing" (two books) by Buck.

Frank. Who invented the Pneumatic Action?

Ans. The Pneumatic Action was invented by an Englishman named Charles S. Barker, between 1837 and 1841, and was first applied by Cavaillé-Coll, in the organ of St. Denis, near Paris.

Enthusiast. Please give me the name of a good treatise on the organ.

Ans. "The Organ," by Hopkins and Rimbalt, is the most comprehensive, though it does not contain the most modern improvements.

Student. What is meant by a C-organ and a G-organ?

Ans. A C-organ is one in which the lowest note of the manuals is great-C; and, likewise, the compass of a G-organ begins at great-G.

E. K. Please tell me the meaning of "Doppel Float."

Ans. "Doppel" is a German word meaning double, and "Float" is an English word sometimes meaning a little contrivance used by country fishermen as a signal when a fish bites. This is a good illustration of the ridiculous custom, which is practised by some organ-builders, of indiscriminately combining foreign and English terms in labelling draw-stops. The principle that "anything will do for a name, inasmuch as the player always tries the stop to find out the quality of tone," is pernicious. One might as well put "Kangaroo" on the stop which draws the Vox Humana. To return to the question, Doppel Flöte, or Floete (erroneously called Doppel Float, Doppel or Dopple Flute, or Doppel Float), is a double-mouthed flute — a stopped pipe made of wood, having two mouths (on opposite sides), giving a large, thick tone of a flute quality.

B. J. A. What studies or pieces would you recommend to follow Leummens's Organ School?

Ans. Selections from "Best's Arrangements," and Mendelssohn's Six Organ Sonatas.

To the Editor of The Organ:

"IF the manufacturers of church or pipe organs would arrange with the representative dealers of the various sections to control the possible pipe-organ business in their respective territories, they could extend their trade and make their arrangements for furnishing organs more promptly and satisfactorily than they now are as a general rule. The first pipe-organ manufacturer who gets up a comprehensive circular to dealers in pianos and organs, inviting co-operation, or who will visit the leading firms and appoint them if possible as agents, will open up new and unexplored fields for the development of the pipe-organ trade." — *Musical Courier.*

The writer of the foregoing suggestion apparently knows little of the possibilities or impossibilities of the pipe-organ business, either in the manner in which it is conducted in securing contracts, or the small margin of profit there is to the manufacturer. There can be no co-operation with either music dealers or representative commission agents.

The leading firms do not, and will not, employ the services of dealers or musical agents to work up their trade. A church organ is built by a legal contract with a church committee direct, after their correspondence with various builders in regard to details and price. In some cases where the committee do not possess sufficient intelligence, an expert is employed by them to supervise the specification, and to pass judgment on the fulfilment of the details of construction, in which case his services are paid for by the committee, according to agreement between them and the expert, and not by the organ-builder. There is no necessity of an expert being employed where a builder of established reputation is selected, and whose scheme of details is according to the conventional standard.

In the value of a pipe-organ, there is no retail and wholesale price, therefore there is no financial margin for a dealer or commission agent to take from the actual value of an instrument. There is an approximate standard of price among leading manufacturers, for organs of equal schedules of registers. The prices vary when a builder decides to lower his price, and receive less profit, in competition with other builders, when the award is to be given to the lowest bidder.

Pipe organs are not made in advance of contracts, each instrument being built for the position it is to occupy. Therefore organs cannot be cheapened by being made in quantity, as with pianos and reed organs, and the contracts are not worked up by dealers, for any profit, or by extensive advertising in the public prints.

The margin of profit on a pipe-organ is comparatively small to the builder when the amount invested in mental, musical, and mechanical labor, added to the material and general expenses is summed up. A wealthy organ-builder, made rich from the business itself, is a rare specimen among the musical fraternity. And if there are any organists who have been in the habit of soliciting commissions on pipe-organs without rendering an equivalent in actual time and labor, could they but cease to importune the harassed organ-builder for *bakhshish*, it might be possible for them to cease to make themselves bores to the art.

No! The pipe-organ business will not in future years be controlled by any combination of syndicates, trusts, music dealers, agents, or organists, and the first pipe-organ manufacturer who gets up a comprehensive circular to dealers in pianos, inviting co-operation, will never open up new and unexplored fields, excepting among the dealers and churches in Alaska and Patagonia.   C. H. W.

THE legacy of $5,000 left by Emma Abbott to the Trustees of a Brooklyn church, in the choir of which she was first engaged, has been paid over, and will be used in repairing and improving the organ in the church. One trustee was in favor of repairing and improving the choir with the money.
— *Boston Times.*

NEW ORGANS.

(*Continued from Page 19.*)

SWELL ORGAN.

12 Bourdon	. . . . 16 Ft.	18 Octave	. . . .	4 Ft.
13 Open Diapason	. . . 8 "	19 Flute Har.	. . .	4 "
14 Spitz Flöte	. . . 8 "	20 Flageolet	. . .	2 "
15 Salicional	. . . 8 "	21 Dolce Cornet	3, 4 & 5 Rks.
*16 Aoline	. . . 8 "	22 Cornopean	. .	8 Ft.
17 St. Diapason	. . . 8 "	23 Oboe	. . .	8 "

CHOIR ORGAN.

24 Geigen Principal	. . . 8 Ft.	28 Flute d'Amour	. . .	4 Ft.
25 Dolce	. . . 8 "	29 Fugara	. . .	4 "
26 Concert Flute	. . . 8 "	30 Piccolo Har.	. . .	2 "
27 Quintadena	. . . 8 "	31 Clarinet	. . .	8 "

PEDAL ORGAN.

32 Open Diapason	. . . 16 Ft.	35 Violoncello	. . .	8 Ft.
33 Bourdon	. . . 16 "	36 *Trombone	. . .	16 "
34 Quint	. . . 10⅔ "			

Swell to Great Octaves in addition to the usual Couplers.
Swell and Choir Tremulants.

*Pipes of stops marked (*) are not in the organ at present.

PEDAL MOVEMENTS.

Three, affecting Great and Pedal Stops with Couplers.
Three, " Swell " " " "
Full Organ Pedal (without throwing out the knobs).
Great to Pedal (Reversible).
Extended action. Water motor.

FIRST CONGREGATIONAL CHURCH, WAKEFIELD, MASS.

New Organ built by Geo. H. Ryder & Co., Reading, Mass.

GREAT ORGAN.

1 Open Diapason	. . . 8 Ft.	5 Twelfth	. . .	3 Ft.
2 Viola di Gamba	. . . 8 "	6 Fifteenth	. . .	2 "
3 Doppel Flöte	. . . 8 "	7 Trumpet	. . .	8 "
4 Octave	. . . 4 "			

SWELL ORGAN.

8 Bourdon Bass }	16 Ft.	13 Flute Harmonique	.	4 Ft.
9 " Treble }		14 Violin	. .	4 "
10 Open Diapason	. . 8 "	15 Flautina	. .	2 "
11 Aeoline	. . 8 "	16 Oboe	. .	8 "
12 St. Diapason	. . 8 "	17 Bassoon }	

CHOIR ORGAN.

18 Violin Diapason	. . 8 Ft.	21 Flute Céleste	. .	4 Ft.
19 Dulciana	. . 8 "	22 Piccolo	. .	2 "
20 Melodia	. . 8 "			

PEDAL ORGAN.

23 Open Diapason	. . 16 Ft.	25 Violoncello	. .	16 Ft.
24 Bourdon	. . 16 "			

The usual Couplers.
Pedal Movements.
Forte and Piano for Great Organ.
" " " Swell "
Reversible Great to Pedal. Swell Tremolo.
Water Motor.
(See Dept. of Organ Concerts for opening recital.)

NEW ORGAN IN THE RESIDENCE OF THEO. HARRIS, ESQ., LOUISVILLE, KY.

Built by Hook & Hastings, Weston, Mass.

GREAT ORGAN.

1 Open Diapason	. . . 16 Ft.	9 Bourdon	. . .	16 Ft.
2 "	. . . 8 "	10 Open Diapason	. .	8 "
3 Doppel Flöte	. . . 8 "	11 Viola	. .	8 "
4 Octave	. . . 8 "	12 St. Diapason	. .	8 "
5 Twelfth	. . . 3 "	13 Quintadena	. .	8 "
6 Fifteenth	. . . 2 "	14 Flauto Traverso	. .	4 "
7 Mixture	. . . 3 Rks.	15 Violina	. .	4 "
8 Trumpet	. . . 8 Ft.	16 Flautina	. .	2 "
		17 Oboe & Bassoon	. .	8 "
		18 Vox Humana	. .	8 "

CHOIR ORGAN.

19 Geigen Principal	. 8 "			
20 Dulciana	. . 8 "			
21 Melodia	. . 8 "			
22 Flute d'Amour	. . 4 "			
23 Piccolo	. . 2 "			
24 Clarinet	. . 8 "			

PEDAL ORGAN.

25 Open Diapason	. . 16 "			
26 Bourdon	. . 16 "			
27 Violoncello	. . 8 "			

The usual Couplers.
Tremolo to Swell Organ.
Forte and Piano Combination Pedals to Great Organ.
" " " " " Swell "
Reversible Great to Pedal Coupler.
The Case is built of Red Birch, and the Front Pipes are decorated in gold and white.
Water Motor.

PROSPECT STREET CONGREGATIONAL CHURCH, CAMBRIDGEPORT, MASS.

New Organ built by George S. Hutchings, Boston.

GREAT ORGAN.

1 Open Diapason	. . 16 Ft.			
2 Open Diapason	. . 8 "			
3 Dulcissimo	. . 8 "			
4 Viola di Gamba	. . 8 "			
5 Melodia	. . 8 "			
6 Octave	. . 4 "			
7 Flute d'Amour	. . 4 "			
8 Octave Quint	. . 2⅔ "			
9 Super Octave	. . 2 "			
10 Mixture	. . 3 Rks.			
11 Trumpet	. . 8 Ft.			

SWELL ORGAN.

12 Bourdon Bass }	16 Ft.			
13 Bourdon Treble }				
14 Violin Diapason	. . 8 "			
15 Salicional	. . 8 "			
16 Aeoline	. . 8 "			
17 St. Diapason	. . 8 "			
18 Flute Har.	. . 4 "			
19 Violina	. . 4 "			
20 Flautina	. . 2 "			
21 Dolce Cornet	. . 2 Rks.			
22 Cornopean	. . 8 Ft.			
23 Oboe }	8 "			
24 Bassoon }				

PEDAL ORGAN.

25 Open Diapason	. . 16 Ft.			
26 Bourdon	. . 16 "			

The usual Couplers.

PEDAL MOVEMENTS.

Forte Great Organ.
Piano "
Forte Swell Organ.
Piano "
Great to Pedal (Reversible).
Tremolo.

TRINITY CHAPEL, WOLVERHAMPTON, ENGLAND.

Organ enlarged by Nicholson & Lord, of Walsall.

GREAT ORGAN.

1 Open Diapason	. . 8 Ft.	11 Bourdon	. . .	16 Ft.
3 St. Diapason	. . 8 "	12 Open Diapason	. .	8 "
3 Gamba	. . 8 "	13 St. Diapason	. .	8 "
4 Wald Flöte	. . 4 "	14 Viol d' Amour	. .	8 "
5 Octave	. . 4 "	15 Voix Céleste	. .	8 "
6 Twelfth	. . 2⅔ "	16 Gemshorn	. .	4 "
7 Fifteenth	. . 2 "	17 Octave	. .	4 "
8 Mixture	. . Rks.	18 Fifteenth	. .	2 "
9 Trumpet	. . 8 "	19 Hautboy	. .	8 "
10 Clarion	. . 4 "	20 Horn	. .	8 "

CHOIR ORGAN.

21 Lieblich Gedact	. 8 Ft.	25 Open Diapason	. .	16 Ft.
22 Dulciana	. . 8 "	26 Bourdon	. .	16 "
23 Octave	. . 4 "	27 Octave	. .	8 "
24 Piccolo	. . 3 "	28 Trombone	. .	16 "

PEDAL ORGAN.

The usual Couplers.
Three Composition Pedals to Great Organ.
" " " " " Swell "

The organ is enclosed in two cases, one of which (containing Great and Swell) is placed on the left, and the other (with the Choir and Pedal) on the opposite side. The action is extended.
(See Dept. of Organ Concerts for opening recital.)

WESLEY METHODIST EPISCOPAL CHURCH, SALEM, MASS.

New Organ (gift of Mr. John P. Langmaid) built by Woodberry & Harris, Boston.

GREAT ORGAN.

1 Open Diapason	. . 16 Ft.	11 Bourdon Bass }	16 Ft.
2 "	. . 8 "	12 " Treble }	
3 Dulciana	. . 8 "	13 Violin Diapason	. . 8 "
4 Melodia (St. Bass)	. 8 "	14 Salicional	. . 8 "
5 Flute d'Amour	. . 4 "	15 Aeoline	. . 8 "
6 Octave	. . 4 "	16 St. Diapason	. . 8 "
7 Octave Quint	. . 2⅔ "	17 Flute Harmonique	. 4 "
8 Super Octave	. . 2 "	18 Violina	. . 4 "
9 Mixture	. . 3 Rks.	19 Flautina	. . 2 "
10 Trumpet	. . 8 Ft.	20 Oboe	. . 8 "
		21 Bassoon }	

PEDAL ORGAN.

22 Open Diapason	. . 16 Ft.	The usual Couplers.
23 Bourdon	. . 16 "	

PEDAL MOVEMENTS.

Forte and Piano Great. Forte and Piano Swell.
Reversible Gt. to Ped. Coupler. Swell Tremolo.
Water Motor.
(See Dept. of Organ Concerts for opening concert.)

FIRST BAPTIST CHURCH, MERIDIAN, MISS.

New Organ built by Hook & Hastings, Weston, Mass.

GREAT ORGAN.

1 Bourdon	. . 16 Ft.	8 Viola	. . .	8 Ft.
2 Open Diapason	. . 8 "	9 St. Diapason	. .	8 "
3 Dulciana	. . 8 "	10 Aeoline	. .	8 "
4 Melodia	. . 8 "	11 Flute Har.	. .	4 "
5 Octave	. . 4 "	12 Oboe	. .	8 "
6 Twelfth	. . 3 "	13 Bassoon }	
7 Fifteenth	. . 2 "		

SWELL ORGAN.

The usual Couplers.

PEDAL ORGAN.

14 Bourdon	. . 16 "	

Forte and Piano Combination Pedals to Great Organ.
Water Motor.

YEARLY SUBSCRIPTION $2.00.

SINGLE COPIES 25 CTS.

THE ORGAN

DEVOTED TO

A MONTHLY JOURNAL

THE KING OF INSTRUMENTS

RHEINBERGER

FRESCOBALDI

MERKEL

· EVERETT · E · TRUETTE ·

EDITOR & PUBLISHER

149 A. TREMONT ST. BOSTON.

HANDEL

THE ORGAN.

VOL. I.   BOSTON, JUNE, 1892.   No. 2.

THE ORGAN.

A MONTHLY JOURNAL

DEVOTED TO THE KING OF INSTRUMENTS.

EVERETT E. TRUETTE, EDITOR AND PUBLISHER.

CONTENTS:

THOMAS APPLETON,

AN EARLY NEW ENGLAND ORGAN-BUILDER.

BY WM. HORATIO CLARKE.[1]

THOMAS APPLETON, one of the most noted organ-builders of his day, descended from the first settler of that name in Ipswich, Mass. He was born in Boston, in Prince Street, December 26, 1785. His father was a house-builder and contractor, and died when the son was thirteen years of age. The mother then supported the family by keeping what was then considered the best boarding-house in Boston, taking the old family mansion of Gov. Bowdoin on Beacon Street. She had for guests many of the most noted men of the country, — governors, judges, and members of Congress and the Legislature. (On his removal from Portsmouth, N. H., Daniel Webster and his family boarded with her for a number of years.) When a boy he frequently visited his grandfather in Haverhill, Mass., where also lived his uncle Daniel, a hatter, and the father of Daniel Appleton, the founder of the publishing house of the Appletons, of New York.

Thomas Appleton was apprenticed to Elisha Larned, a cabinet-maker whose shop was on the corner of Salem and Cross Streets, in Boston. When he was twenty years of age, he became acquainted with William Goodrich of Templeton, Mass. (whose sister he afterward married), and sold him a turning-lathe which his mother had imported for him. At the expiration of his apprenticeship, he went to work with William Goodrich, building organs in a shop on Chambers Street, near the corner of Cambridge Street. Mr. Goodrich was a man of extraordinary skill and ingenuity. He was the son of a Templeton farmer. He went to Boston at the age of twenty-one, and began building organs from his own inventive talent, studying such English instruments as he could find in various cities.

He changed the spelling of his name from Goodridge to Goodrich, and also adopted the middle name of Marcellus. He became first interested in organs from a small instrument he had seen in Templeton, which had been built there by a man named Bruce. Soon after his removal to Boston, he became acquainted with Benjamin Crehore of Milton, a very ingenious maker of musical instruments, and went there to

[1] For the historical facts in this article the writer is indebted to Mr. Edward Appleton, son of the subject of this sketch.

work with him. He then went to Boston and began building organs on his own account. In 1809 William Goodrich engaged with Maelzel, the inventor of the metronome, to travel about the country exhibiting the panopticon, a combination of wind instruments played by machinery, after the manner of the modern orchestrina. The original panopticon was lost at sea, and Mr. Goodrich built another like it, which, after having been exhibited for some time in Boston, was sent to a foreign country. His first organ was built for the old Roman Catholic Church on Franklin Street. He afterwards moved to East Cambridge, and had constant employment as an organ-builder until his death in 1833.

Ebenezer Goodrich, a younger brother of William, also went to Boston when he was of age, and learned his trade

from his brother. They had a disagreement, and he set up business for himself. It is said that the brothers never after exchanged words. He turned his attention chiefly to the manufacture of parlor pipe organs, having a fair amount of business. He died in 1841.

At about the year 1809 Lewis and Alpheus Babcock were making pianofortes, having learned their trade from Benjamin Crehore of Milton, who had been making violoncellos, guitars, and other musical instruments, and who had become a pianoforte maker from copying an English instrument.

In 1810 Thomas Appleton joined the Babcocks and Hayts, dealers in music and instruments, in putting up a brick building in Milk Street, on the site of the birthplace of Benjamin Franklin, for the manufacture of pianos and organs under the firm name of Hayts, Babcock, and Appleton. Benjamin Crehore, then an old man, worked for them.

John Osborn learned the business of piano-making there,

and afterward carried it on at Pantheon Hall, next south of the old Boylston Market; and of him both Jonas Chickering and Timothy Gilbert learned the trade from which an extensive business was afterwards developed.

Thomas Appleton remained in this firm two years, when the business failed on account of the general depression of affairs resulting from the war of 1812. In due time Mr. Appleton took up the manufacture of organs by himself. Bryant P. Tilden, an eminent merchant of those times, was one of the leading men of the old Brattle Street Church, and gave him free access to copy from the organ which had been imported from England.

Thomas Appleton stood at the head of his art for many years. He built thirty-five organs for Boston, many of them having three manuals. His first instrument was built for the church at Church Green, on the corner of Summer and Bedford Streets, the same instrument being in use as late as 1872 in a Baptist church in Providence, R. I. Another organ in the same year, first used in St. Paul's Church, was afterward sent to New Orleans. He also built more than one hundred organs for other places, in Bangor, Portland, New York, Philadelphia, Baltimore, Charleston, Savannah, Columbia, S. C., New Orleans, St. Louis, Cincinnati, Buffalo, Rochester, and in many smaller places over the United States.

He built a three-manual organ for the Handel and Haydn Society, which was used by them in the Boston Music Hall until the large German organ was purchased. This instrument was sent to San Francisco. His last organ was built for the Warren Street Baptist Church, Boston, in 1868. For many years his factory was located over the old Parkman Market, on the corner of Cambridge and North Grove Streets. Here he noted players and musical professors of the day assembled and showed their skill in drawing forth the good qualities of what were then considered the best organs in the country; and when the most delicately awakened strains touched the sympathetic nature, the old builder would exclaim, "Beautiful! Beautiful! Beyond description!" Fugues and organ sonatas did not then belong in the repertoire of the organists of this country, and the players gave the inspiration which their own inherent natures dictated.

In his later days, the venerable organ-builder always looked back to the organ built for the Bowdoin Street Congregational Church, in Boston, as his favorite. This instrument was built at the Cambridge Street factory in 1831, under the supervision of Lowell Mason, who was then the musical director in Bowdoin Street Church, and was considered the masterpiece of Thomas Appleton. It had three manuals, with a pedal open diapason running down to GGGG. The workmanship throughout was of excellent construction. The wind-chests were large, mahogany being freely used. Many of the manual wood pipes were of red cedar and pear tree. The metal pipes were as finely made as at the present day, although much lighter in weight. The reed pipes were of unusually good quality.

The workmen of this past generation have left nothing to be ashamed of in their skill in the use of tools; and our ancestors, with their lack of modern machinery and facilities, knew how to make good joints, and were more faithful in minor details than the young man who "knows it all" after working at the bench for six months. The use of brains is not peculiar to this generation, although at the present day the art of organ building is far beyond the conception of those who did their best in their circumstances and surroundings to furnish all that the times and attainments then demanded.

The last years of the life of Thomas Appleton were spent in Reading, Mass., where he carried on the business for a few years. He died in Reading, July 11, 1872, over eighty-six years of age, and was interred in Mt. Auburn. During the later years he took much interest in musical matters, and often visited the factories of other builders, and frequently was seen at the exhibition of new instruments, when every good point presented would be quickly and generously recognized.

HISTORY OF THE ORGAN.

II.

One of the most important steps in the advancement of the organ was the invention of the key-board, which occurred near the close of the eleventh century. The cathedral of Magdeburg had the honor of receiving the first organ with a key-board, which was erected about this time. The keys were between two and three feet long, three inches wide, and about an inch and a half deep, shaped as shown in the cut, and the key-board consisted of sixteen keys. The mechanism, or "action," was about as cumbersome as could be imagined. Ropes and strings connected the keys with the slides (pallets, of course, had not been invented), and the player, who was called "organ beater," had to pound the keys down nearly a foot with his fists.

Most of the organs contained only from nine to eleven keys, necessarily limiting the compass of the old hymn tunes which were used, while harmony was impossible, as the player could beat down but one key at a time, producing only a melody of the most crude character.

The bellows which supplied the wind in these early organs were equally imperfect and clumsy. They were still made of the "household pattern," with sides or folds of "white horses' hides," and were constantly giving out, necessitating a large outlay of money to keep them in repair. As each individual bellows was capable of supplying but a small quantity of wind, it was necessary to have twenty or thirty of them for an ordinary-sized organ. Prætorius writes of an organ in Manchester, England, which had twenty-six bellows, and required seventy strong men to manage them. These "blowers" placed their feet in wooden shoes which were on top of the bellows, and, by holding on to a transverse bar which was placed above, worked the bellows up

An Organ of the XII. Century, from a MS. in Cambridge, England.

and down. It is obvious that the pressure of wind was unsteady, being controlled only by the strength of the "blowers," and naturally the tone was sometimes strong and frequently weak, while the organ was rarely in tune.

In the twelfth century, after increasing the number of keys, two or three pipes were added to each key. These additional pipes were generally tuned to the fifth and octave, though occasionally to the third and tenth; and, as the pipes had not yet been classified and separated into registers, all the pipes belonging to a key sounded at once, making the whole organ a *mixture*.

The *regal*, also called *portative*, was a small organ (as shown in the cut), which it is supposed was used in processions and in Catholic churches; but antiquarians do not agree in their description of this instrument, nor its usage.

The *positive* (*positif*), in contradistinction to the *portative*, was a larger instrument, with a key-board of the full compass of that period. Both the *portative* and the *positive* could be transported from place to place; but the former could be blown with one hand and played with the other, while the latter had to be set down (*positive* from the Latin word *ponere*, "to set down") on a table or bench, and required the services of a second person to work the bellows.

For many years the *positif* was utilized to accompany the singers or choir, and was placed beside the large organ in the church. When, ultimately, the "great" organ and the *positif* were connected, the key-board of the latter being placed below the key-board of the "great" organ, the *positif* was placed back of the organist, he sitting between the two organs. The *positif* was still used to accompany the choir, and is the origin of our "choir organ." In many French cathedrals the choir organ is still placed behind the organist. It must not be supposed that the expression "a pair of organs" referred to two organs connected in this manner, for the expression has frequently been used to signify a simple *rigal*. Inasmuch as an organ is a *collective* instrument consisting of two or more *sets* of *pipes*, each of which is complete in itself, the word "pair" undoubtedly signified the whole instrument, in the same manner as "a pair of stairs" signifies a flight of stairs, and not two stairs.

Portative Organ XV. Century.

In the thirteenth century the use of the organ in the Greek and Latin Churches was prohibited as being "scandalous and profane," and even to-day the instrument is rarely, if ever, tolerated in the Greek Church.

The size of the keys was gradually reduced by the monks, to whom we are indebted for preserving and improving the organ during the dark ages, till they could be depressed by the fingers, and the compass was extended upwards and downwards till it reached three octaves. The semitones were added, and a priest named Nicholas Faber, in 1360 or 1361, constructed an organ which contained the semitones complete. The invention of the pedal is generally attributed to a German named Bernard, between 1470 and 1480, though there are reasons for believing that pedals were in use at an earlier date. In 1818, when an old organ in the church of Beeskow, near Frankfort, was being taken down the year 1418 was found engraved on the partition of two of the principal pedal pipes.

Undoubtedly Bernard made extensive improvements in the pedal-board and brought it into general usage, which probably caused his name to be associated with its invention.

(*To be continued.*)

ORGAN ARRANGEMENTS.

The following letter from Mr. W. T. Best to the *Musical Opinion and Music Trade Review* of London, will be of interest to our readers.

"My attention has been called to an article on the organ in the lately started *Victorian Magazine* by 'Mr. Walter Parratt, Organist to the Queen,' in which that gentleman maintains a singularly hostile attitude to all 'arranged' music for the organ, singling out for special animadversion my contributions to this class of music, termed by him 'examples of misapplied skill;' — and in lectures delivered in his native town, Huddersfield, he reiterates similar opinions.

"I may here remark that on the only occasion I heard him perform upon the organ he essayed a transcription of Mendelssohn's Overture, 'Ruy Blas.'

"As to question of 'arrangements' of orchestral and other music for an organ is one of some moment, I propose to show that Mr. Parratt's views on this subject are not in accord with highly competent authorities, including the late Mr. Henry Smart, whose article in the *Musical World* (1854) I am fortunate in being able to quote farther on. It is necessary to premise that organ arrangements should exhibit, in

an artistic manner, every important feature of the score, and never be debased for performance on imperfectly constructed instruments by players more or less in a state of pupilage.

"To commence with, the father of all 'arrangers' is no less a personage than Bach, who is well known to have 'accommodated' Vivaldi's violin concertos to the expressionless German organ of his day with its intractable pedal bass. Of all music is arranged form, that for stringed instruments must be truly appalling to purists when 'reduced' — as the French would say — for an organ. Passing to modern German and Continental musicians, — overtures, symphonies, marches, quartets, songs and choruses, etc., have been transferred to the organ by F. Lux, E. Hennig, S. de Lange, E. Silas, R. Salze, F. Liszt, R. Schaab, and Alex. Guilmant, the last named having lately commenced to 'arrange.' In this country we have E. Prout, R. Stewart, G. Cooper, E. J. Hopkins, J. Stainer, G. C. Martin, H. Smart, and F. Archer, all of whom would hardly select music unsuitable for organ effect. Mr. Parrat urges that 'the erection of large concert-hall organs, and the necessity of pleasing the Saturday night audience, has had a disastrous influence over organ music, as in the majority of such programmes two-thirds at least are arrangements of orchestral and choral works.' It must be remembered, however, that in endeavoring to raise the musical taste of the humbler classes, the municipal authorities of our large towns did not intend their concert organs to be restricted to the performance of preludes, and fugues, and somewhat dry sonatas. As is the case with orchestral concerts of a popular character, the higher forms of composition have to be introduced both warily and gradually. As regards the organ, it is beyond cavil that a well known instrumental *adagio* or *andante*, suitably arranged, is infinitely preferable to the frequently dull specimens of modern organ music duly vaunted as being 'original.' Some years ago unfortunate attempts were made (in two organ journals) by utterly unknown men to supply a new stock of music for the most exacting of all instruments, — the organ; but it is melancholy to record that the efforts of these native composers (many of whom had caudal appendages to their surnames) merely served to point a moral as well as excite the risibility of foreign critics.

"It is gratifying to note that a better state of things now prevails; and if we could obtain anything approaching Mozart's great Fantasia in F minor, all would be well. Modern German composers are now timidly adding *crescendo* and *diminuendo* to their organ pieces, the builders being compelled to advance with the times and provide their lifeless stacks of pipes with the means of musical expression common to all English and French organs.

"The works of Mr. Parratt's favorite composers — Herren Merkel and Rheinberger — though in undeniable organ form, are apt to pall upon cultivated ears. Their numerous 'sonatas,' in particular, bear a strong family likeness, the chief themes being encumbered with a wearisome technical development, too often proclaiming the manufactured article rather than the presence of the creative impulse, while the enormous length of many of the movements effectually prevents a frequent performance. The late Mr. H. F. Chorley (for many years the musical critic of *The Athenæum*) made a fierce onslaught (1854) on all adaptations for the organ, calling forth, happily, a speedy rejoinder from Henry Smart of an

(*Concluded on page 41.*)

THE ORGAN.

BOSTON, JUNE, 1892.

THE ORGAN is published the first of every month. Subscription price $2.00 per year (foreign countries $2.50), payable in advance. Single copies, 25 cents.

Subscribers will please state with which number they wish their subscription to begin.

The paper will be sent to all patrons till the editor is notified by letter to discontinue.

Subscribers wishing the address of their paper changed must give the old as well as the new address.

Remittances should be made by registered letter, post-office order, or by check payable to Everett E. Truette.

Programmes of organ concerts, with press notices of the same, specifications of new organs, and items of general interest to the subscribers, will be gratefully received.

Correspondence, to secure notice, must in all cases be accompanied by the name and address of the writer, not for publication, but as a guarantee of good faith.

Advertising rates sent on application.

Address all communications,

The Organ, 149 A Tremont Street, Boston, Mass.

☞ An active agent in every city is desired to whom a liberal cash commission will be allowed.

EDITORIALS.

THE reception which the *Organ* has met with in many localities, and the encouragement which has been voluntarily offered, has proved beyond a doubt that the demand for such a journal had not been over-estimated.

INCONVENIENT PEDAL-BOARDS. — It is announced that Mr. W. T. Best declines for the future to play upon English organs in which the builders place " C under C," as there is much difficulty in reaching the higher Pedal range with any certainty on account of the board being planted too far to the right for the performance of *bona fide* organ compositions.

THE following is from the " Buffalo Budget " in the *Musical Courier:* —

" This reminds me of the action of the Boston Music Hall organ; it was so slow that organist Elson went there Saturday evenings to play the music due Sunday mornings ! "

Will Mr. Elson have the kindness to step forth and inform us when his career as a *" pulsator organum "* ended ? The late Mr. S. A. Emery often spoke of this organ as the one which " spoke day after to-morrow."

THE Critic of the Boston *Transcript* thus expresses his admiration (?) for the organ in the Boston Music Hall, which has been a substitute for the " great organ," removed several years ago.

" One missed, to be sure, the firm bases of the organ pedal, but, considering what the instrument is that usurps the place of an organ (almost) in the Music Hall, one cannot regret that its croup-ridden voice was not brought into play in this psalm."

IN the Chicago *Inter-Ocean,* there appeared, once upon a time, a description of the dedication of the organ in the Auditorium of that city. The following paragraph shows the lofty ambition of the reporter who wrote the article. In speaking of Mr. Clarence Eddy, he tells us that " A master hand swept the seven-storied key-board, a sympathetic foot touched the bass keys, — one thoroughly familiar with the grand instrument, its mechanical intricacies, its musical powers."

We have heard the Chicago foot called all sorts of names before, but it remained for this reporter to discover that it was " sympathetic."

We also learn of the " Harvest Home " that it " opened with a ponderous chord that might have been nature's cannonade precursing a storm, inducing a vibration that would almost seem to sway the structure in unison with the thunderous throb; then came the more peaceful pastoral phrase, in which the music seemed to fall from some Æolian harp, or the sounds that whisper through leafy trees," etc.

What kind of a chord must it have been which suggested " nature's cannonade precursing a storm " ? Was it a chord (?) of the Augmented Ninth with the root, third, fifth, and seventh all suspended in the pedal, and the resolution occurring at the same time in the left hand ? " Sounds that whisper through leafy trees " must have been the pulling of the Tremulant.

A CERTAIN missionary from the heathen countries, who was to preach in a church not many miles from this office, visited the church the afternoon before the Sabbath to confer with the organist in the choice of hymns. After making the selections for the following day, the organist, who intended to try over a few pieces for his preludes, turned on the water for the motor, and as the good missionary noticed the little piece of white ivory, which serves as a wind-indicator, creeping along its little channel, as the wind filled the bellows, he exclaimed in apparent alarm, " There is a white insect crawling on your organ. Will it do any harm ? "

THE following letter from Monsieur A. Wiegand, of Sydney, Australia, to the *Musical Opinion and Music Trade Review,* from which paper we copy it, speaks for itself : —

" As promised, I send you some papers containing accounts of the great successes obtained on Messrs. Hill & Son's great organ. It is really a magnificent one. I have had some necessary alterations made; among other things I have had the balance pedals altered, they were originally on the old system. I can now say, with much pleasure, that I am playing on the greatest organ in the world, and one of the very finest. It is a master-piece. The next greatest organ is that of St. Sulpice in Paris, built by M. Cavaillé-Coll, the well-known organ builder of Paris."

" There were six thousand two hundred people in Sydney Town Hall on August 15th, and more than two thousand were unable to find seats ; yesterday (August 17), there were six thousand five hundred people present at a recital."

When we think of the interest shown in organ concerts in New York (where the organ is probably more popular than in any other city in the United States), and in Boston, where an audience of six hundred is considered large, comparisons are indeed odious.

THE following, from the *Musical Courier,* anent female organists, is *à propos* : —

" ' I tell you it's all nonsense, sir, a woman can't play the organ; it is too complicated and masterful an instrument for her brain, and then — and then — you see — her limbs are not long enough to manipulate the pedals.'

" So spoke the stern committeeman of a conservative church in the West a few years ago. But the girl begged hard to be given a trial ; and when it was further learned that she supported herself and mother, was sending a young brother through Harvard, and, moreover, could read music like lightning, she was allowed to show what, perchance, she might be able to do. On Sunday morning the possessor of ' short limbs ' awoke the echoes of that church as they had never before been awakened, by playing for her show-off piece a magnificent arrangement of ' America,' on which the florid ornamentation was done solely by the pedals ! The man was convinced. The girl remained, married the wealthiest man in the congregation, and to-day is its most shining musical and social light.

" The fact of the matter is, that short limbs are better than long ones to manipulate the movable and melodic trestle-work that forms the floor of the organ-bench. The proper way to ' sit ' an organ-bench is the way a boy sits a rail fence — on the edge, the pendent members swinging free. With this method long limbs will not be found as convenient as short ones. So there !

" I was surprised to learn of three positions held by lady organists in New York. The search for a possible ' one more ' discovered — seventy-five ! "

March from the Third Organ Symphony.

CH. M. WIDOR.

Tempo di Marcia.

Gt. to Octave.

Ch. 8 & 4 Ft. (f)
Sw. 8 & 4 Ft. with Oboe.

Ped. 16 & 8 Ft.
Sw. to Gt. Gt. to Ped.

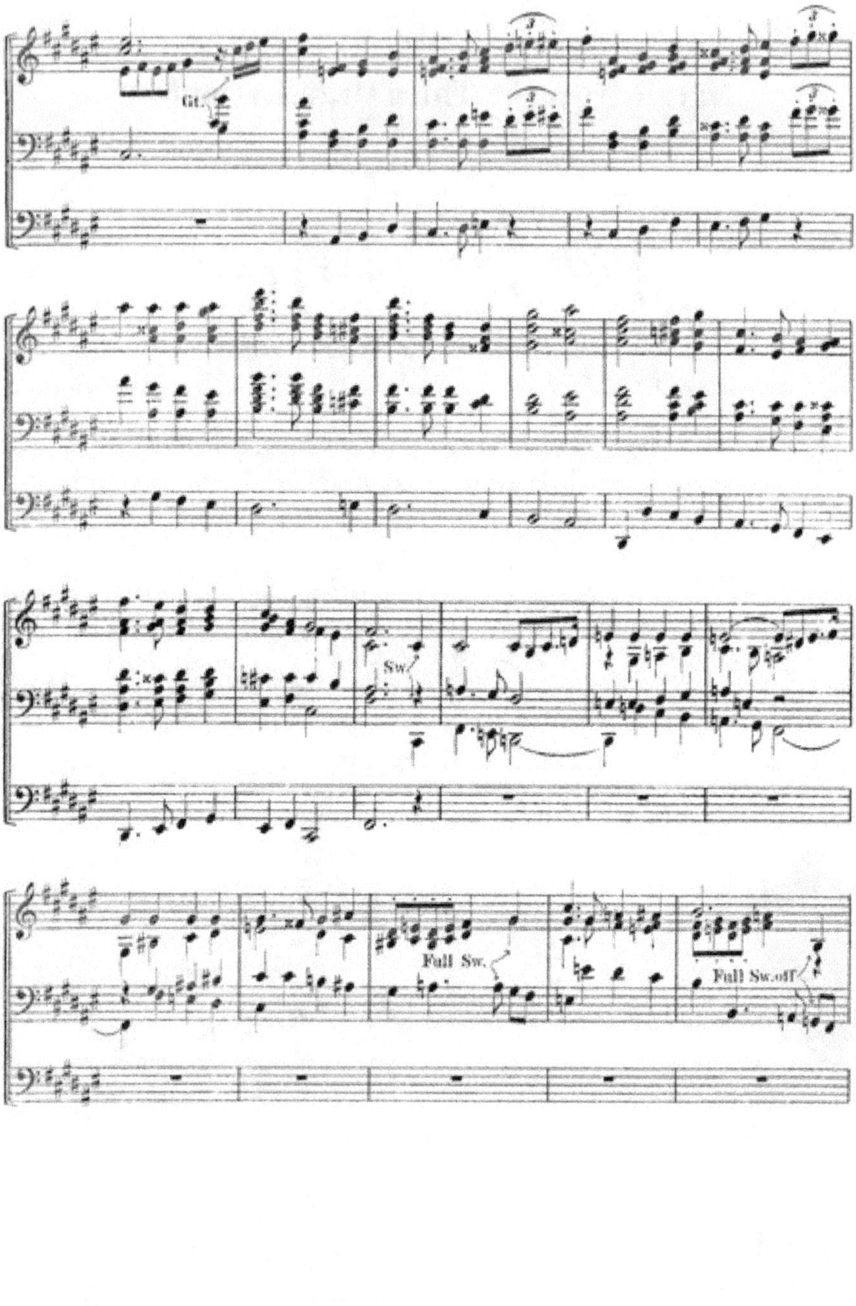
Gt.
Sw.
Full Sw.
Full Sw. off

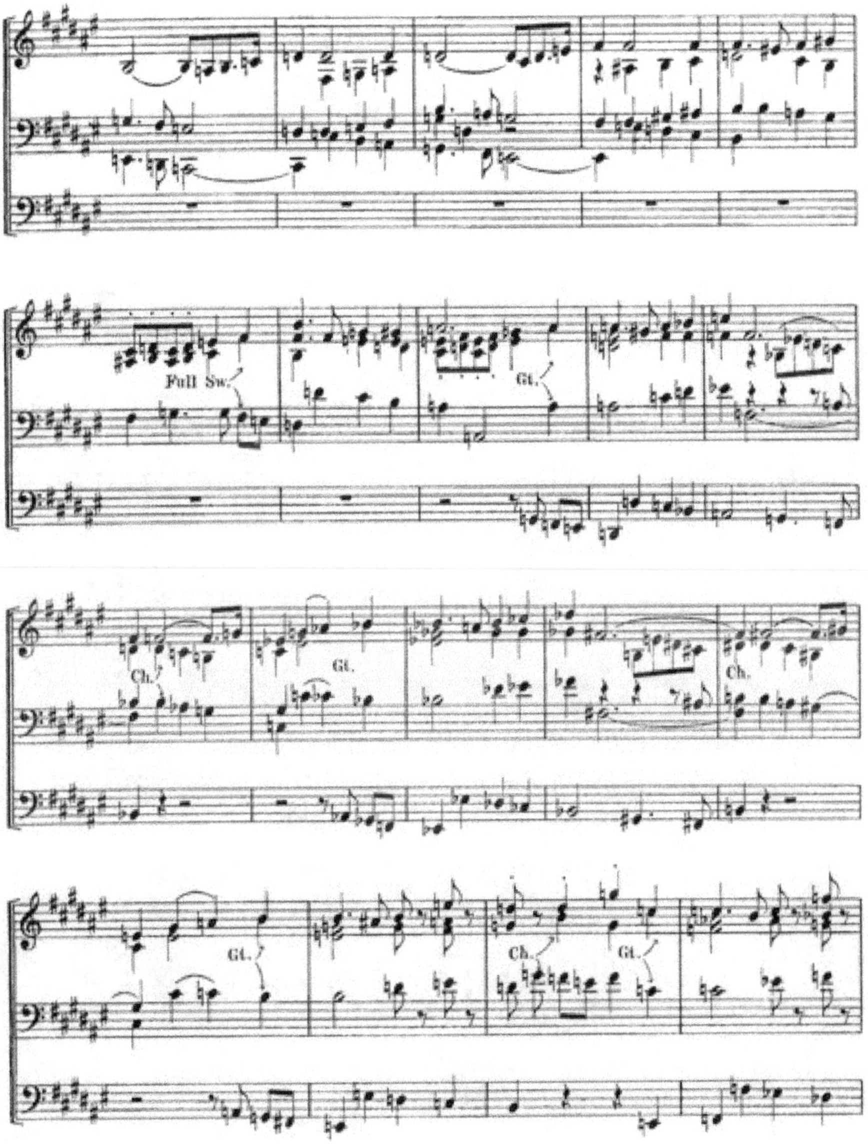
Full Sw.
Gt.
Ch.
Gt.
Ch.
Gt.
Ch.
Gt.

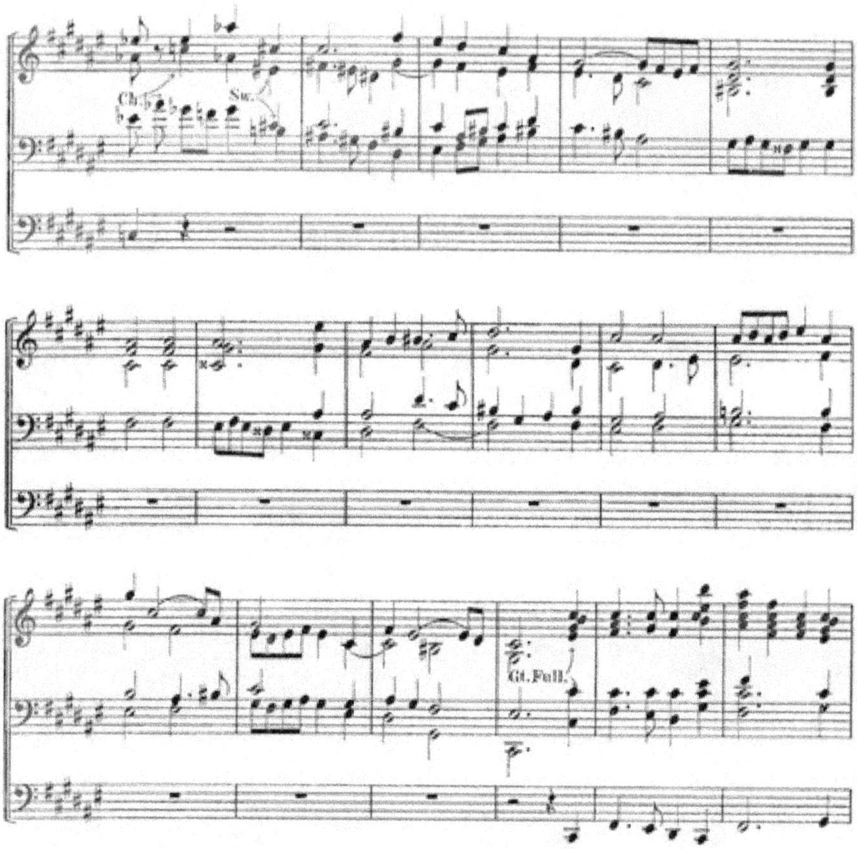
Ch.
Sw.
Gt. Full.
Ch.

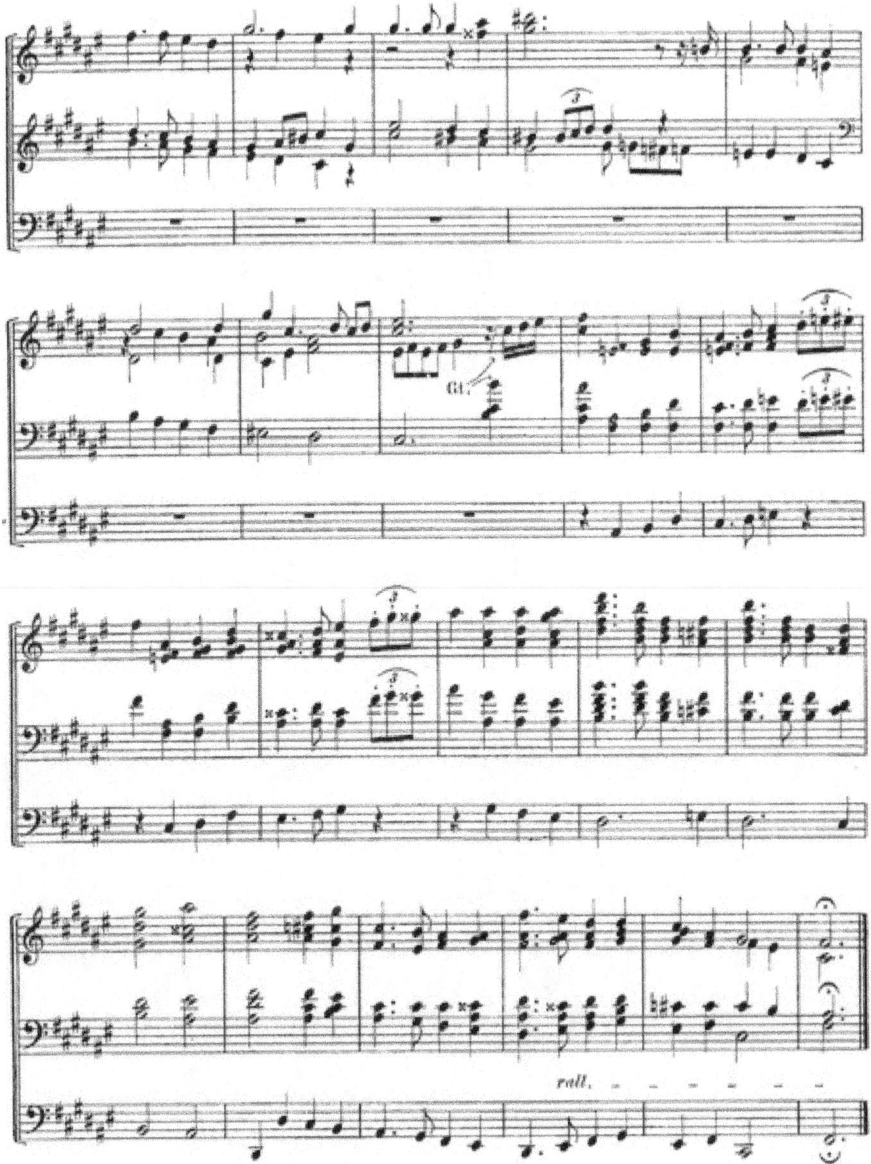
Gt.
rall.

ADAGIO

From SONATA IN G MINOR.

CHRISTIAN FINK.

Adagio ma non troppo.

Sw. St. Diapason.

Ch. (or Gt.)

Ch. (or Gt.) Dulciana.

Sw.

Ped. Bourdon.
Gt. & Sw. to Ped.

Add Oboe.

St Diap. & Trem. only.

Add Oboe.

(Prepare Gt. mf with Op. Diap.)
Sw. to Gt.
Gt.
f
Op. Diap. off.
Sw.
Oboe off.
Salicional only.
molto rit.
Coup. off.
Add Oboe & St. Diap.

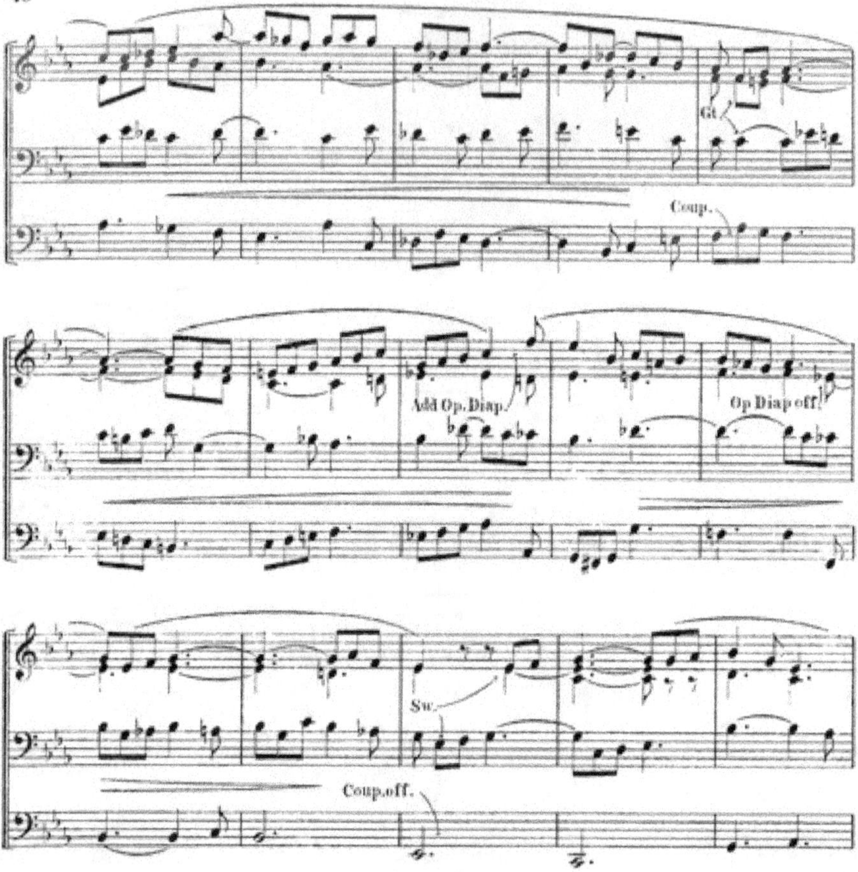
Gt.
Coup.
Add Op. Diap.
Op Diap off.
Sw.
Coup. off.
St. Diap. & Trem only.

ORGAN ARRANGEMENTS.

(Continued from Page 31.)

interesting character, with which I am able to conclude this prolonged letter to your esteemed journal. Mr. Chorley says:—

"'An organist who analyzes an orchestra and its varieties with the view of representing them on the organ, wastes his time, loses his way, and does not know his duties and their limit. The organ can hardly be called an "orchestra in itself" (even of wind instruments), and the fancy of devoting it to arranged music has brought it into low estimation. How shall an orchestra, the basis of which is the brisk and pungent stringed quartet, be represented by its coarser and heavier tones, among which every staccato becomes a "quack," and every rapid arpeggio a yawn or a scream— according as the stops are of wood or of metal — and every chromatic scale a confusion, analogous to the blot of mixed tints on a painter's palette?'"

"To which Mr. Smart replies:—

"'About all this there is, doubtless, some truth; yet so overlaid with misrepresentation, or, rather, non-comprehension of the facts, as to become really valueless. If an organist "analyzes an orchestra," etc., with the view of reproducing on his instrument precisely the effect of the score, for example, of one of Beethoven's symphonies, he certainly "loses his way," and deserves all *The Athenæum* may say of him. And it is, unfortunately, true that many organists, not thoroughly conversant either with the orchestra or their own instrument, do commit this very obvious blunder. If, however, it is intended absolutely to prohibit all adaptations for the organ — however artistically contrived — of modern orchestral and vocal music, we must emphatically dissent from the conclusion. In the first place, such an expurgatorial process must be applied analogously to everything. All "arrangements," of every sort and kind, must be condemned. All "pot pourris" and "selections" for military bands, for instance, must be accounted unrighteous proceedings; for how can clarionets, cornet-à-pistons, alt horns, and the like, represent, better than the organ, the string quality of an orchestra or the voices of the singers? Again, on this principle of rigid exactitude, M. Thalberg and all his fraternity must be summarily interdicted from all further fantasia making for the pianoforte; for an instrument which has only one quality of tone must obviously have less chance of imitating an orchestra than one which has many. And, strangest consequence of all, to carry out the integrity of his views, the critic of *The Athenæum* must straightway forbid a process to which time must have reconciled even him,—namely, the playing of Händel's choruses on the organ; for, if it be a question of exact resemblance of effect, we cannot see the slightest difference of impropriety between the transfer to the organ keys of "For unto us," and a like manipulation of the first movement of the "Eroica" Symphony. The effect of the one will be not an atom more like the orchestra than that of the other. And, indeed, the more modern the music — and, therefore, the more individual the employment of the wind band in its instrumentation — the less will the organ be at fault in the imitation of the score. That an organ is "an orchestra in itself" no one, who values the meaning of words, has ever maintained. But it can be most justly asserted that the organ affords to the performer a command of the extremes of light and shade, of force and delicacy, of variety and qualities, both separately and in combination, which no other single instrument can approach. If it can do nothing towards the "brisk and pungent string quartet," it can boast an unrivalled grandeur in the mass of its tone, an almost unlimited command of gradation and variety of character, and a few individual qualities of sound so nearly resembling their orchestral prototypes as to be sufficient for the exactest purposes of imitation. In fine, without possessing the power of precisely copying, the organ can render more closely a *general* resemblance, or, rather, perhaps, can suggest more forcibly an idea of the effect, of an orchestral

score than any other instrument; and whoever seeks more from it than this, either "loses his way"' in the pursuit, or was a bad judge of his means from the beginning.

"'On the assertion that the "fancy of devoting it to arranged music has brought it into low estimation," we are again completely at issue with *The Athenæum*. There are, doubtless, abundance of instances in which vile taste has been manifested in the selection of music for organ arrangements and in the arrangements themselves; but the habit of cultivating this species of performance in general has, we must maintain, been of the utmost service, both to organs and organists. To the players it has opened an entirely new vista of ideas; without in the least deteriorating their love for, or capability of executing, the music of Bach, it has increased their mechanical accomplishment both in finger skill and the management of their instrument, and has refined and spiritualized their style; while to its urgent demands for improvement, the organ itself is almost indebted for the immense ameliorations in tone and mechanism it has in late years displayed. The English organists are now, undoubtedly, the first in the world, and no long period will elapse, we hope, ere their organs will attain the same supremacy. Whenever this happens, the result will be very mainly due to this "fancy" for "arranged music," in which *The Athenæum* finds so much to censure.

"'In his concluding sentences, the critic from whom we quote, gets wrong in his technics, as most people do who discuss matters with which they are not familiar. The information that "every *staccato* becomes a *quack*," and "every chromatic scale a confusion analogous to the blot of mixed tints on a painter's palette," can only have originated in the writer's exclusive acquaintance with bad instruments and worse players; while the special effects "yawn" and "scream," attributed respectively to wood and metal stops, evince total ignorance of the qualities of either. All this may be very sharp writing, but it is, nevertheless, very flat nonsense.'

"To add to this is quite unnecessary, except to express a hope that Mr. Parratt, as organist to the queen, will add to the list of our composers for the instrument, as befits his high office.   Yours, etc.,

W. T. BEST."

St. George's Hall, Liverpool, April, 23, 1892.

ORGAN CONCERTS.

TWO ORGAN RECITALS BY MR. CLARENCE EDDY.

Trinity Episcopal Church, Alliance, Ohio.

April 30.

Sonata in C minor	Wermann
Andantino	Chauvet
Allegretto	Volkmann
Nuptial Benediction	
Finale	Dubois
Variations on "The Old Folks at Home"	Flagler
Harvest Home	Spinney
Gavotte	Martini
Funeral March and Seraphic Song	Guilmant
Saint Cecilia Offertory	Batiste

April 31st.

Toccata and Fugue in D minor	Bach
Romanza "Evening Star"	Wagner
Pilgrim's Chorus	
Religious Air with Variations	Brewster
March of the Magi Kings	Dubois
Celebrated Largo	Händel-Whitney
Funeral March of a Marionette	Gounod-Archer
Scherzo Symphonique	Guilmant
Concert Fantasia	Lux
Overture to Stradella	Flotow-Buck

(Mrs. Katherine L. Fisk assisted at both recitals.)

At an inaugural recital in the Perkins Street Baptist Church, Somerville, Mass., in which Mr. J. Frank Donahoe was the organist, the following organ selections, in a miscellaneous programme of sixteen numbers, were performed: Sonata, Op. 98, Rheinberger; Marche Célèbre, Lachner, and a "selected" number.

The following selections were performed by Mr. J. Warren Andrews at a miscellaneous concert in the Andrew Presbyterian Church, Minneapolis, May 18th.

Festival Postlude (four hands)	Volkmar
(assisted by Mrs. Andrews)	
Ave Maria d'Arcadelt	Liszt
Marche Militaire	Schubert
Storm Fantasia	Lemmens
Communion in G	Batiste
Gavotte Impériale	Max Schreter
Air	Louis XIII
Auld Lang Syne, Variations (four hands)	Thayer

At Mr. S. P. Warren's Nineteenth Organ Recital in Grace Church, New York, Bach's Toccata and Fugue in F, and Widor's Eighth Symphony were performed.

INAUGURAL RECITAL by Mr. Clarence Eddy, Christ Presbyterian Church, Madison, Wis., May 13.

Grand Festival March	George Carter
Andantino	Chauvet
Allegretto	Volkmann
Overture to Oberon	Weber-Warren
Ave Mer	Schubert
Pilgrim's Chorus	Wagner-Eddy
Funeral March and Seraphic Song	Guilmant
Harvest Home	Spinney
Concert Fugue in G	Krebs
Nuptial Benediction	Dubois
Finale, Laus Deo	Flagler
Concert Variations on "Home, Sweet Home"	Flagler

The above programme was also performed by Mr. Eddy at the opening of a new organ, built by Mr. Frank L. Roosevelt, in the Second Congregational Church, Rockford, Ill., May 6.

An organ recital of the compositions of Alex. Guilmant was given by Mr. Wm. C. Carl, in the First Presbyterian Church, New York, May 7, when the following programme was given :

Fugue in F major (new); Pastorale (Pièces d'Orgue, Bk. 16, new); Marche Réligieuse (first time); Rech. and Aria, "En vain le Flot," from "Belshazzar," first time (Mr. Wm. Dennison) ; Theme, Variations and Finale ; "Aria du Belshazzar," first time (Mr. Albert F. Aveschool) ; Communion, dedicated to Mr. Carl ; Ecce Vasla, with soprano solo by Mrs. Gerrit Smith ; Postlude Nuptiale.

ORGAN RECITAL by Mr. W. T. Best, at the opening of the new organ in the Wesley Chapel, London.

Sonata No. 2, in C minor	Bach
Andante in D (from a Suite for the organ)	Hampton
Toccata in A	Peet
Concertose	Gaudiosi
Fantasia in A minor	Lemmens
Air with variations in A	Haydn
Finale, Alla Marcia in C	Best

Mr. H. O. Farnam of the Wittenberg College, Springfield, Ohio, has been giving a series of monthly organ concerts in the High Street M. E. Church of that city. At the fourth concert, May 7, the following programme was given : —

Toccata and Fugue in D minor	Bach
Intermezzo (Cavalleria Rusticana)	Mascagni
"Behold I Stand at the Door"	Jude
Variations on the Hymn Tune "Beether"	Smith
Impromptu (by request)	Farnam
"Voices of the Woods"	Rubinstein-Watson
Overture to "William Tell"	Rossini

Miss Alice J. Vose, contralto, was the singer. The concluding recital of the series will be given June 3.

ORGAN CONCERT (American Compositions) by Mr. Wm. C. Carl. First Presbyterian Church, New York.

Fantasia, Op. 2,	Frederic Louis Ritter
Andante, Sonata No. 1	William H. Davis
Processional March	Samuel B. Whitney
Song, "Spring Voices",	William C. Carl
Mr. David G. Henderson.	
Varspiel, "Ciello Visconti"	Frederic Grant Gleason
Concert Fantasia	J. F. Petri
Spring Song	Harri Rowe Shelley
Aria, "My Redeemer and My Lord"	Dudley Buck
Mrs. Carl Alvers.	
Variations on a national air	Dudley Buck
Kyrie and Gloria (mass in E minor)	Frank G. Dossert
Quartette and chorus directed by the composer.	

Programme of an organ recital in the Town Hall, Leeds, England, by Mr. J. Herbert England.

Offertoire in F	Wely
Adagio in D	Mozart
Fugue in G minor	Bach
La Cloche du Soir	Chauvet
Gavotte	Martini
Ave Maria	Schubert
Fantasia in F	Best
Adagio Cantabile	Hopkins
Grand Offertoire de Ste. Cécile	Grison

Programme of an organ recital given by Dr. E. H. Turpin in St. David's Church, Merthyr Tydfil, England. Sonata No. 1, Mendelssohn ; Prelude and Fugue, in A minor, Bach ; the "Harmonic Music," Mendelssohn, and works by Molique, Händel, Parry, Spohr, Gounod, Merkel, Beethoven, Gladstone, and Turpin.

MIXTURES.

(FOUR RANKS.)

Mr. George Whiting gave an organ recital at Wellesley College, Monday evening, May 16th.

We understand that the works of the Moline Organ Co., at Moline, Ill., have recently been enlarged.

It is rumored that the Baptist Ecclesiastical Society of Hartford, Conn., desire to purchase an organ.

Mr. Minor C. Baldwin gave a series of daily organ concerts in Association Hall, New York, from May 19th to 28th.

Mr. Gerard Taillandier has been engaged as organist of St. Vincent de Paul's Roman Catholic Church, South Boston.

Messrs. Labagh & Kemp have sold their Organ manufacturing business in New York city, to Messrs. Chapman & Symmes.

Mr. Edward d'Evry gave an organ recital at the Bow and Bromley Institute, London, April 16th, assisted by the Westminster Singers.

M. Alex. Guilmant is giving his annual series of organ concerts at the Paris Trocadéro, the first of which took place on the 13th of April.

A trombone and organ recital was recently given by Mr. R. H. Booth, and Mr. George Dodd, at St. George's Church, Perry Hill, England.

A $25,000 organ was destroyed by fire in the St. Michael's Roman Catholic Church, Thirty-second Street, New York city, a short time ago.

We understand that the upper part of the large building which was constructed principally for Mr. Frank Roosevelt's organ factory, is to let.

A pipe-organ factory is to be established in Des Moines, Iowa, by Messrs. W. W. Witmer, W. H. Lehman, and Wm. Gratian, with a capital of $15,000.

Mr. George Tetley, for twenty-two years honorary organist, and director of the Choir at St. John the Evangelist's, Leeds, England, has resigned his post.

Mr. H. C. Tonking has been giving daily organ recitals at the International Horticultural Exhibition, Earl's Court, London, on an organ built by Messrs. Lewis & Co.

An organist and choirmaster is wanted in Stillwater, Minnesota. Three hundred and fifty dollars is offered to the satisfactory candidate, who must have first-class testimonials, and must be an earnest Churchman and Communicant.

The following item appeared some time ago in the catalogue of a firm of organ-builders : —

No. 363, built in 1872.
2 Manuals, 20 Registers.
Deaf and Dumb Action.
A new, Room,

When Girolamo Frescobaldi was chosen organist of St. Peter's, in Rome, in 1614, thirty thousand people, attracted by his fame, came to listen to his first performance. Such was the enthusiasm for the organ in Italy at that time.

The organ factory of the J. C. Knauff Company, located in Newark, Delaware, is offered for sale. (See ad.)

Mr. George Stevens, who for over fifty years manufactured organs in East Cambridge, Mass., has retired from business, being over ninety years old. Messrs. Gilbert and Butler will continue the business.

Mr. Robert Hope-Jones of Birkenhead, England, has been elected a member of the Institute of Electrical Engineers. Mr. Hope-Jones has made extensive application of electricity to organ building, and points to a complete revolution of organ action which it is claimed will soon be an established fact.

After the inauguration of a large organ in a Western city, the leading daily paper appeared the next morning with the following brief description (?) of the organ : —

"The organ contains 4,680 pipes, weighs 27 tons, and if all the trackers were placed in a straight line they would extend six miles."

We have been informed that the First Unitarian Church of Portland, Me., had water-pipes all laid, to connect with a proposed water-motor for blowing the organ, about twenty years ago, but that only within the last month could they make up their minds to get the motor. They finally purchased and attached a "Whitney Boston Motor."

An excellent portrait of Mr. William C. Carl, organist of the First Presbyterian Church of New York, adorns the title-page of the *Musical Courier* for May 11th. Mr. Carl, not long since, returned from Paris, where he had been studying with Mons. Guilmant for two years, during which time he was special correspondent for the *Musical Courier*.

Arrangements have been perfected by the Brooklyn Institute of Arts and Sciences for a series of organ concerts in this country, by Mr. W. T. Best, of Liverpool, and Mons. Alex. Guilmant, of Paris, the most noted organists of England and France. The concerts will be first given in Brooklyn, and repeated in New York, Boston, Chicago, Philadelphia, Baltimore, Washington, and possibly other cities. No dates are as yet announced.

The prevailing opinion, on this side of the water, that professional organists are short-lived is somewhat weakened by the following facts relating to a few English organists. Dr. Langhurst, of the Canterbury Cathedral, has been in active duty for sixtyfive years. Dr. Done, of the Worcester Cathedral, will celebrate his semi-centenary of active work in 1894. Dr. Hopkins became organist of the Temple Church, London, forty-nine years ago; and Dr. Ford has served for a half century in the Carlisle Cathedral.

NEW ORGAN MUSIC.

G. Flügel Toccata and Fugue, Op. 101.
César Frank. Three Chorals.
A Chrismann. Collection of Organ Pieces, Bk. 1.
Ph. Kuler, Three Pieces for Violin and Organ, Op. 36.
" Adagio for Violoncello and Organ, Op. 34, No. 1.
Alex. Guilmant. Marche Elégiaque   }
              Consolation   }
              Andante Sostenuto   } . . . Bk. 17, Op. 74.
              Communion No. 4.   }
A. H. Walker. Andante with Variations in A.
Charles Vincent. Introductory Voluntaries, Bk. 1.

Mr. Wm. Horatio Clarke, who for many years was a prominent organist in New England, and organ-builder in the West, has been compelled to entirely abandon his profession by a painful attack of rheumatism. Mr. Clarke had located in a charming spot among the hills of Reading, near Woburn, Mass., and was erecting a large four-manual organ, which was to contain many novel features, in a specially constructed "hall" near his house. The instrument was about two-thirds completed when the unfortunate calamity befell Mr. Clarke, which has compelled him to temporarily abandon the project. It was the intention of the projector to establish an organ *sanctum sanctorum* for a limited number of pupils, where, amid the surroundings of nature in her own unique elements, those who wished to fill their lungs with pure air, their hearts with thankfulness to the Giver of all that is beautiful, and their souls with organ music *per se*, could study, practise, and live the life of happy students.

NEW ORGANS.

SPECIFICATION OF THE ORGAN IN THE CATHEDRAL AT EXETER, ENG.

ENLARGED BY MESSRS. H. WILLIS & SONS, LONDON.

(Originally built by Mr. John Loosemore about 1665.)

GREAT.		SWELL.	
Double Open Diapason	16 Ft.	Double Stopped Diapason	16 Ft.
Open Diapason (No. 1)	8 "	Open Diapason	8 "
Open Diapason (" 2)	8 "	Stopped Diapason	8 "
Open Diapason (" 3)	8 "	Echo Gamba	8 "
Stopped Diapason	8 "	Voix Céleste	8 "
Clarabella	8 "	Principal	4 "
Principal	4 "	Celestina	4 "
Harmonic Flute	4 "	Twelfth	3 "
Twelfth	3 "	Fifteenth	2 "
Fifteenth	2 "	Mixture	3 Rks.
Mixture	— Rks.	Contra Hautboy	16 "
Double Trumpet	16 Ft.	Hautboy	8 "
Trumpet	8 "	Cornopean	8 "
Clarion	4 "	Clarion	4 "

SOLO.		CHOIR.	
Gamba	8 Ft.	Lieblich Gedacht	16 Ft.
Dulciana	8 "	Lieblich Gedacht	8 "
Claribel Flute	8 "	Lieblich Gedacht	8 "
Wald-flote	4 "	Lieblich Gedacht	4 "
Gemshorn	4 "	Salicional	8 "
Viola	4 "	Vox Angelica	8 "
Harmonic Flute	4 "	Salicet	4 "
Piccolo	2 "	Vox Humana	8 "
Clarionet	8 "	Orchestral Oboe	8 "
Tuba	8 "	Corno di Bassetto	8 "

(The last three are enclosed in a separate Swell-box.)

PEDAL.		MECHANICAL.	
Double Open Diapason	32 Ft.	The usual Couplers and	
Open Diapason	16 "	Swell Octave	
Violone	16 "	Swell Suboctave	
Bourdon	16 "	Choir fine work (venti)	
Octave	8 "	Choir reeds (venti)	
Violoncello	8 "	Tremulants to Swell and Choir.	
Bass Flute	8 "		

Five Composition Pedals to Great, including Pedal.
Four   "   Swell   "
Great to Pedal, Reversible.
Double acting Venti to take off wind from all Pedal stops except Bourdon.

Both these last two stops can be operated in three ways, viz. : — By thumb pistons placed below the Great keys, by knee pistons placed under the Choir manual, or by pedals for the left foot.

Extra reservoir to the several organs for giving greater steadiness to the tone. The bellows, worked by a gas engine, are placed below in the crypt. The action is tubular pneumatic, and the organ is divided into two parts.

ST. JOHN'S EVANGELICAL LUTHERAN CHURCH, BROOKLYN.

New organ built by Messrs. Geo. Jardine & Son, of New York.

GREAT ORGAN.		SWELL.	
Open Diapason	8 Ft.	Bourdon Treble }	16 Ft.
Doppel Flöte	8 "	Bass }	
Viola di Gamba	8 "	Open Diapason	8 "
Dulciana	8 "	Stopped Diapason	8 "
Principal	4 "	Salicional	8 "
Flûte Harmonique	4 "	Violine	8 "
Twelfth	2⅔ "	Rohr Flute	4 "
Fifteenth	2 "	Fugara	4 "
Trumpet	8 "	Piccolo	2 "
		Dolce Cornet	2 Rks.
PEDAL.		Oboe and Bassoon	8 Ft.
Double Open Diapason	16 Ft.		
Bourdon	16 "		

PEDAL MOVEMENTS.

Forte and Piano Great Organ Combination.
"   "   "   Swell   "
Great to Pedal (reversible).

ACCESSORIES.

Swell to Great	
Ditto in octaves	
Great to Pedal	} Piston Knobs.
Swell to Pedal	
Swell Tremolo	

QUESTIONS AND ANSWERS.

All questions must be accompanied by the full name and address of the writer, and, if received by the 10th of the month, will usually be answered in the following number of THE ORGAN.

Only such questions as refer to the organ, to organists, organ-builders, or to organ music, will be answered.

Correspondents are requested to write their questions in a clear and concise manner, writing on only one side of the paper.

B. J. A. What studies or pieces would you recommend to follow Lemmens' Organ School?

ANS. Selections from "Best's Arrangements" and Mendelssohn's Six Organ Sonatas.

AMATEUR. When an organ key sticks down and sounds all the time, what is the cause and remedy?

ANS. There are various causes which produce ciphering, and the remedies are equally varied. A piece of wood or a pin between two keys will cause one of them to stick down. Damp weather causes parts of the action to swell and prevent the free working of the same. A rusty pivot in a square or in a roller board produces friction which the pallet spring cannot overcome. The wire pull-down under the pallet occasionally gets bent and cannot move freely through the hole made for it. We have known of a dead fly, lodging in the groove through which a tracker moved, producing friction enough to cause a cipher. These are but a few of the causes, and the remedy in each case is self-evident.

A. B. How do you pronounce "Thiele"?

ANS. Tee-ly.

HENRY K. S. Please give me the dates of Buxtehude's birth and death.

ANS. Born, 1637. Died, May 9th, 1707.

CARILLON. In "A Graded List of Studies and Pieces for the Organ," by Truette, is mentioned a piece called "Carillon" by Rousher. To what does "Carillon" allude?

ANS. This composition has for its principal motive an old Carillon or Chime consisting of the following notes:

The Carillon is repeated in the pedal in nearly every measure of the first and last parts of the composition, and a modification of it is used in the middle part.

ORGANIST. Please give me a list of stops for a small two-manual organ, to have three stops on each manual and one on the pedal.

ANS. The following would give general satisfaction.

GREAT.		SWELL.	
Melodia,	8 Ft.	Viola,	8 Ft.
Dulciana,	8 "	St. Diapason,	8 "
Op. Diapason,	8 "	Flauto Traverso,	4 "

PEDAL.

Bourdon,   16 Ft.

Mechanical: Sw. to Gt., Gt. to Ped., Sw. to Ped.

TREMULANT.

B. G. Explain the difference between a "sticker" and a "tracker."

ANS. A "sticker" is a *pushing* connection between parts of organ mechanism, and a "tracker" is a *pulling* connection. It is readily seen that the former must of necessity be larger and stronger than the latter. When one sees a "tracker" of the manual action surprise is usually expressed at its fragile character, as it is of soft pine wood of the straightest grain 1-16 inch in thickness and 1-4 inch in width; but upon an invitation to break one by pulling, a second surprise is expressed at its strength. This apparently flimsy ribbon of wood is the only thing which fills the requirements of organ action; i. e., a minimum of weight with a maximum of strength, combined with unchangeable length either by variations of temperature or "kinking." The length of a "sticker" is limited to a few feet, and that of a "tracker" to the varying demands of the organ action, from a few inches to fifty or seventy-five feet, or until its weight becomes a hindrance to the repetition of a note.

SWELL. Please inform me what the difference is between Swell Organ and Swell Manual.

ANS. Swell Manual indicates only the keyboard of the Swell Organ, but Swell Organ refers to all that part of the instrument which is operated directly by the keys of the Swell Manual. The keys, action, wind-chest, swell-box, and all the pipes in the box. All the mechanism of the swell-pedal is included.

TRAVERS FLUTE. What is the difference in construction between a Travers Flute and a Harmonic Flute?

ANS. The constructive principle of these stops is the same, being usually of 4 Ft. pitch, made double or 8 Ft. length from middle C up, with the two lower octaves of "pitch length." Small holes placed midway in the double length pipes raise the pitch an octave, bringing it up to 4 Ft. pitch and making the whole stop continuous, at the same time producing the harmonic tone of great purity and penetration, from which the name of the stop is derived. In foreign organs one often finds a Harmonic Flute of 8 Ft. pitch. The Harmonic Flute is constructed of metal and is cylindrical, while the Travers Flute is made of wood and square or nearly square. The latter stop is more "windy" and of less power, requiring more standing-room on the wind-chest.

REVIEW OF NEW ORGAN MUSIC.

FROM ARTHUR P. SCHMIDT, BOSTON.

Offertory in E-flat,	
Wedding Hymn,	
Minuet,	Op. 48 . . . . . . Th. Salomé.
Andantino,	
Symphonic Allegro,	

Nos. 6–10 of a set of compositions, the first five of which we reviewed last month. The Symphonic Allegro and the Minuet are the most pleasing and will be popular at once. The ambitious title of the former need not prevent advanced students attempting to play it, as it is a composition which can be readily grasped by any painstaking organist. The Minuet has two well contrasted themes, can be played on two manuals, is not difficult, and will please almost any kind of an audience. The Andantino is one of those compositions which organists like to play when inaugurating a new organ of some size, as the opportunities for showing striking combinations are very numerous. The Wedding Hymn pleases us the least, though skilful handling at the organ would make

it enjoyable. The Offertory is a piece which is useful with pupils whose playing lacks steadiness of tempo. It is melodious and not difficult.

Meditation on the 1=st. Prelude	Bach—Gounod.
Bridal March from "Rebekah"	Barnby.
Serenade	Widor.
Sanctus from Messe Solennelle	Gounod.

Arranged for the Organ by Edwin M. Lott.

The Meditation is an effective, though difficult, arrangement of the celebrated Ave Maria of Gounod. The Serenade is well adapted to interpretation on the organ, though one must have a variety of stops to choose a registration which will not become monotonous on account of the frequent repetitions of the theme.

The Sanctus is well arranged, and will be useful with students who are studying chorus work.

FROM MESSRS. G. RICORDI & CO., LONDON.

Toccata in A . . . . W. T. Best.

A valuable addition to any organist's list of concert pieces. The piece commences with a theme of six bars in the pedal (Allegro molto), followed by the same on the manuals in the key of the dominant, and, with a little thematic treatment, leading to the second theme in the tonic minor, played on the reeds of the swell. A Fughetto on the great (F) follows. After a few massive chords and a pause, a short, *quasi* trio (Religioso), in E major, is given out on the Open Diapason of the great and repeated on the Vox Humana. This theme is very beautiful, and is well contrasted to the preceding passages. The first measure of the first theme is used thematically as a motive, together with a little organ point, in returning to the first theme in the pedal, after which the first twenty-two bars of the piece are repeated. On page

eleven we have a powerful climax with the aid of the Tuba, in the key of G, which is repeated, by way of emphasis, Più Allegro, returning to the tonic after a sudden modulation into the key of F, and ending with the full power of the instrument.

FROM NOVELLO EWER & CO., NEW YORK.

Festival March	H. W. Wareing.
Short Offertory	F. Hamilton Clark.

Nos. 147 and 148 of "Original Compositions for the Organ"—an excellent edition of organ works (principally by English composers) which contains many useful pieces for the teacher as well as for the student. The Festival March is light and tuneful, and the Offertory is short and inoffensive, though students fresh from harmony examinations will Oh! and Ah! at the consecutive fifths on page six.

A Dream of Mozart (Minuet in D.) . . . . . James Shaw.

No supper of mincepie, olives, and beer preceded this dream, for the elements of nightmare are entirely absent. The Minuet is melodious, graceful, and suitable to be played on any organ.

FROM G. SCHIRMER, NEW YORK.

Choral March . . . . Dudley Buck.

No. 4 of "Four Tone Pictures," the first three of which we reviewed last month. This March is built up on "*Ein fest Burg ist unser Gott.*" A suggestion of the choral appears in the *quasi* military introduction, and after two pages written in canon form the choral is played in octaves, first in the upper part and later in the lower part, working up to a strong climax with the choral in full harmony.

NEW ORGANS

(*Continued from page 41*)

HOLY TRINITY CHURCH, SCARBOROUGH, ENGLAND.

New Organ constructed by Messrs. Denman & Son, of York.

(*To be opened in July.*)

GREAT.		SWELL.	
Open Diapason	8 Ft.	Bourdon	16 Ft.
Harmonic Claribel	8 "	Geigen Principal	8 "
Gamba	8 "	Kohr Flöte	8 "
Viol d'Orchestre	8 "	Salicional	8 "
(in a swell-box.)		Vox Angelica	8 "
Harmonic Flute	4 "	Gemshorn	4 "
Principal	4 "	Harmonic Piccolo	2 "
Tuba Mirabilis	8 "	Dulciana Mixtures	3 Rks.
(in a swell-box.)		Oboe	8 Ft.
Couplers — Swell to Great Sub.		Trumpet	8 "
" " Unison.		Clarion	4 "
" " Super.		Couplers. — Sub Octave.
Choir to Great Unison.		Super Octave.
" " Super.		Great to Swell second touch.
Tuba second touch.		Choir to Swell "
Swell to Great second touch.		Tremolant.
Three Composition Pedals.		Crescendo Lever.
Suitable Bass and Special Bass		Three Composition Pedals.
Studs.		Suitable Bass and Special Bass
Crescendo Lever.		Studs.
Tremolant.		

CHOIR.	
Open Diapason	8 Ft.
Dulciana	8 "

PEDAL.	
Open Diapason	16 Ft.
" " (partly from Great)	
"	16 "
Bourdon	16 "
Bass Flute	8 "
Viol d'Orchestre	
(partly from Great)	16 "
Ophicleide (partly from Great)	
(in a swell-box)	16 "
Couplers. — Great to Pedal.	
Swell to Pedal.	
Choir to Pedal.	
Open Diapason second touch.	
Ophicleide	
Crescendo Lever.	

CHOIR.	
Open Diapason	8 Ft.
Dulciana	8 "
Lieblich Gedacht	8 "
Zauber Flöte	4 "
Great Tuba	8 "
Couplers. — Super Octave.	
Swell to Choir Unison.	
" " Super.	
" " second touch.	
Two Composition Pedals.	
Suitable Bass and Special Bass	
Studs.	

GENERAL ACCESSORIES.	
Sforzando Pedal { First touch F.	
{ Second " FF.	
Stop switch.	

The Hope-Jones Electric System will be used throughout the organ. The Choir organ, together with one of the Pedal stops, will be mounted on a light open wood screen, and placed beneath the north chancel arch. The Great and main Pedal organs will be bracketed out from the north wall at the west end of the naive. The Swell and Echo organs will be placed in the tower and will speak into the naive of the church through an arch, which may be opened or closed at the will of the performer.

The wind will be supplied by a Hope-Jones Compound Cylinder, connected with the water main, working absolutely silently. The organ will be controlled by electricity from a small movable Console. All the keys will have a "double touch" by means of which expression may be obtained from the fingers somewhat as in the piano. There will be no stop handles, the registers being governed by an additional row of keys.

PLYMOUTH CHURCH, SEATTLE, WASHINGTON.

New organ, constructed by Messrs. Hook & Hastings, of Boston.

GREAT ORGAN.		SWELL ORGAN.	
Bourdon	16 Ft.	Open Diapason	8 Ft.
Open Diapason	8 "	Viola	8 "
Doppel Flöte	8 "	Stopped Diapason	8 "
Octave	4 "	Flauto Traverso	4 "
Twelfth	3 "	Violina	4 "
Fifteenth	2 "	Flautino	2 "
Mixture	3 Rks.	Oboe (with Bassoon)	8 "
Trumpet	8 Ft.		

CHOIR ORGAN.		PEDAL.	
Geigen Principal	8 Ft.	Open Diapason	16 Ft.
Dulciana	8 "	Bourdon	16 "
Melodia	8 "	Violoncello	8 "
Flöte d'Amour	4 "	The usual Couplers.	
Piccolo	2 "	Tremolo to Swell.	
Clarinet	8 "		

Forte Combination Pedal for Great.
Piano " " "
Reversible Great to Pedal Coupler.
Pneumatic action applied to Great and Swell.

Mr. George S. Hutchings, of Boston, has just shipped a new organ for the Sixth St. M. E. Church, Sacramento, Cal., which has six stops in the great, eight in the swell, and two in the pedal.

AFRICAN METHODIST EPISCOPAL CHURCH, NORFOLK, VA.

New organ built by Mr. Geo. S. Hutchings, Boston.

GREAT ORGAN.		SWELL ORGAN.	
Open Diapason	8 Ft.	Bourdon Treble }	16 Ft.
Dulcissimo	8 "	Bourdon Bass }	
Melodia (stopped Bass)	8 "	Violin Diapason	8 "
Octave	4 "	Salicional	8 "
Flûte d'Amour	4 "	Æoline	8 "
Octave Quinte	2⅔ "	Stopped Diapason	8 "
Super Octave	2 "	Flute Harmonique	4 "
Mixture	3 Rks.	Violina	4 "
Trumpet	8 Ft.	Dolce Cornet	3 Rks.
		Oboe	8 "
		Bassoon }	8 Ft.

PEDAL ORGAN.	
Open Diapason	16 Ft.
Bourdon	16 "
The usual Couplers.	

Forte Combination for Great.
Piano " "
Great to Pedal (reversible.)

St. Andrew's Episcopal Church, of Lambertville, N.J., has been presented a two-manual Hook & Hastings organ, having ten stops in the great, eight in the swell, and two in the pedal, with the usual mechanical accessories, and blown by a water-motor.

Messrs. Hook & Hastings, of Boston, have just completed an organ in the Church of the Holy Trinity, Philadelphia. The instrument is built upon very large scales, containing ten stops in the great, eight in the swell, and two in the pedal, and has reversed action and is blown by a water-motor.

An organ for the residence of Mr. W. Cuthbert Quilter, of Bawdsey Manor, England, has just been completed by Messrs. Norman Bros. & Beard. The instrument is elevated on a gallery in the central hall, the console being on the floor and connected by tubular pneumatic action.

A new organ has been placed in the Grace Lutheran Church, Westminster, Md., by Mr. George S. Hutchings, of Boston, having two manuals and nine speaking stops.

A new organ has been erected in St. Paul's Church, Walla Walla, Washington, by Messrs. Hook & Hastings, of Boston, having four stops in the great, four in the swell, and one in the pedal.

A new organ, recently built for the Methodist Protestant Church," Westminster, Md., by Mr. George S. Hutchings, of Boston, contains three 8 ft. stops and one 4 ft. in the great, the same in the swell, and one 16 ft. in the pedal.

A small two-manual organ built by Messrs. Hook & Hastings, of Boston, has been erected in the Church of the Immaculate Conception, Westerly, R.I., and is arranged to show a stained glass window over a depression in the centre of the instrument, making the design very effective in the church.

A two-manual Hook & Hastings organ has just been presented to the Congregational Church of Norfolk, Conn. This instrument has a beautiful casing of solid mahogany, finished in its natural color, without artificial staining.

The M. P. Möller Organ Co., of Hagerstown, have placed a new organ in Lutheran Church, Jefferson, Md.

A two-manual organ, containing eighteen speaking stops, has just been finished by Messrs. Gilbert and Butler, of East Cambridge, Mass., for a church in Roxbury.

A small two-manual Hook & Hastings organ has been placed in the Immanuel M. E. Church, Waltham, the instrument being entirely hidden, except as it fills three arches opening into the auditorium.

The Perkins St. Baptist Church, of Somerville, Mass., have just received a new organ built by Messrs. Woodberry and Harris, of Boston. The organ contains nine speaking stops in the great, eight in the swell, and two in the pedal, with three combination pedals.

A new organ has been placed in the Christ Presbyterian Church, Madison, Wis., having ten speaking stops in the great, eleven in the swell, six in the choir, and three in the pedal, with six pedal movements. Both choir and swell are in swell-boxes. The organ was built by the Lancashire Marshall Organ Co., of Moline, O.

Vol. I. JULY, 1892. No. 3.

BACH

YEARLY SUBSCRIPTION $2.00. SINGLE COPIES 25 CTS.

The ORGAN

DEVOTED TO

A MONTHLY JOURNAL

THE KING OF INSTRUMENTS

RHEINBERGER

GUILMANT

FRESCOBALDI

BUXTEHUDE

MERKEL

BEST

· EVERETT · E · TRUETTE ·

EDITOR & PUBLISHER

149 A. TREMONT ST. BOSTON.

HANDEL

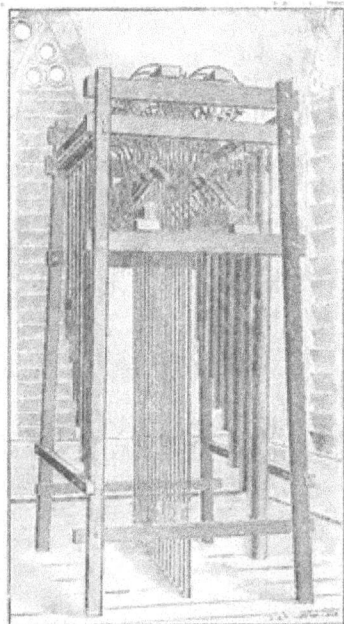

THE ORGAN.

Vol. I.   BOSTON, JULY, 1892.   No. 3.

THE ORGAN.

A MONTHLY JOURNAL.

DEVOTED TO THE KING OF INSTRUMENTS.

EVERETT E. TRUETTE, EDITOR AND PUBLISHER.

(Entered at the Boston, Mass., Post-office as second-class mail matter, June 1, 1892.)

CONTENTS:

W. T. BEST.

IN presenting to the readers of THE ORGAN a sketch of the career of William Thomas Best, who for years has headed the list of great organists, and whose name is undoubtedly familiar to nearly every organist in the world, we cannot do better than to copy the article which appeared in the Liverpool *Daily Post*, the thirteenth of last August, at which time the sixty-fifth birthday of the artist and the thirty-sixth year of his office as organist in St. George's Hall, Liverpool, were duly observed.

"Liverpool has upon her citizen-roll many men in various ranks of life upon whom she looks with pride and pleasure; and among them is one who on Thursday entered upon the sixty-sixth year of his age, and completed his thirty-sixth year of office as organist to the Corporation of Liverpool — Mr. William Thomas Best. We have been warned by Ben Jonson that there is as great a vice in praising as in detracting, and in speaking of Mr. Best's fame as an organist and his services to music, there is a danger of falling into this vice. For not only has he, as far as playing the instrument is concerned, such powers as to have earned him the title of 'Prince of Organists,' with all the many excellences implied in that phrase; but in the improvement of the instrument itself, and in enriching its writings by compositions and arrangements, Mr. Best has done such work as it would be difficult to overpraise. Suffice it to say in explanation of this, and without plunging too deeply into technicalities, that it is in the arrangement of the pedals and pedalling that Mr. Best has made so many and so valuable innovations. Formerly the pedal was used for little more than giving a droning bass, but now the pedal has an organ to itself, leaving the left hand, to which the bass was formerly allotted, free to do the proper work on the key-board.

"William Thomas Best is the son of a solicitor of Carlisle, in which town he was born on August 13, 1826, and where for fourteen years continuously he lived. In those days, as now, the old Cathedral was the centre of musical life in the town, and there the folk would congregate on a Sunday afternoon to hear the anthem and the organ, then played by Young, whose pupil the youth Best became. At this time he was studying for the profession to which his parents intended he should be put, — engineering; but for this he had no liking, and went heartily into the study of his much-loved music. Soon afterwards he paid a visit to Liverpool, and during his stay here received the appointment of organist at Pembroke Chapel. He then went into his studies with renewed zeal, and spent about four hours a day at practice, further developing his technical skill by long and diligent practice on the piano, upon which instrument he for a couple of years played nothing but scales, and exercises founded thereon. His organ practice included Bach's Forty-eight Preludes and Fugues, and of course his pedal work was to him of most interest, and received attention accordingly.

"In 1847 he was appointed organist of the Church for the Blind, and the following year, when but twenty-two years of age, organist to the Philharmonic Society. His name had already become known in London, and in 1852 he was appointed organist to the Royal Panopticon, Leicester Square, which is now the Alhambra. He also held a post at Lincoln's Inn Chapel and St. Martin's-in-the-Fields.

"In 1855 Mr. Best came to Liverpool to preside at the great organ then just completed in St. George's Hall. His salary was fixed by the Corporation at £300 a year, and after some years it was increased to £600, at which figure it now stands. Mr. Best's engagement is for thirty-two weeks in the year, so the remainder is spent, from a musical point of view, by the asides and city sessions, during the sittings of which the organ is silent. This militates greatly against large attendances at recitals, as the public never know when they are certain of a performance. Nevertheless, there are usually good audiences, among them being most of the American and Continental visitors who are continuously passing through the city. The recitals are greatly valued and appreciated by all music-loving people, and the wondrous welcome given to Mr. Best upon his return from his recent Australasian tour show how he is held in the admiration of the people of Liverpool.

"In 1860 Mr. Best was appointed organist to the Wallasey Parish

Church. In 1865 he took the organ at Holy Trinity, Alton Brook, and subsequently was appointed to West Derby Parish Church, where for so many years he made the musical part of the service famous. Here, indeed, many musicians maintain he was heard absolutely at his best, arguing that, whereas at St. George's Hall organ he was expected to demonstrate the excellences of the instrument, in the West Derby Church he would play to suit himself entirely, and his most musicianly feeling had therefore freer scope. After finally settling down here, Mr. Best took to teaching, his name and skill securing him an extensive list of pupils; but the work being distasteful, he gave it up about twenty years ago and devoted himself to compositions and arrangements for the organ and the pianoforte. So famous are many of his arrangements that one is apt to lose sight of original compositions which have proceeded from his prolific pen. Among them are the valuable works, 'Modern School for the Organ' and 'The Art of Organ Playing,' both of worldwide celebrity. Then, too, there are preludes and fugues, sonatas and concert pieces of many kinds. For the orchestra, perhaps his best-known writings are a Festival Overture and Triumphal March. Pianoforte pieces are numerous, and church music, hymns, anthems, and voluntaries occupy a small catalogue, including complete services composed for Carlisle Cathedral and the famous choir of Leeds Parish Church. Arrangements by Mr. Best from the orchestral scores of the great composers are published in thousands of pages, with the intention of familiarizing the public with these works where orchestras are not available to give them as composed. The Handel Album is a particutheir valuable one, containing as it does so many surplices rarely heard, and which might become obsolete but for this subject. One of our organist's great aims has been to let the public know what grand old treasures are locked up in the storehouse of music, and to give them a share in the enjoyment of the greatest works. By means of organ recitals, here and elsewhere, the people have made their first acquaintance with the works of the French school, such as the now well-known offertories of Lefébure Wély and the later compositions of Widor, Saint-Saëns, and Salome.

"During a stay in Italy, Mr. Best edited and arranged for English instruments a selection of pieces by the chief Italian organists, and two folio volumes of this work were issued by the great Italian house of Ricordi. At the present time Mr. Best is engaged upon his *magnum opus*, a complete edition of Bach's organ writings, which he began four years ago, and which is likely to remain in course of publishing for some years yet. The value of this work to organists is inestimable, the copyright, being based upon the podaling, as arranged, and the clearness and novelty of the directing notes. Last year Mr. Best went to Sydney to open the great £10,000 organ (the largest and most expensive in the world), his opinion of which we have already recorded in our columns. It must not be inferred that ten years ago our city organist was offered the honour of a knighthood, which he declined, and was afterward placed on the Civil List, the emoluments of which were substantial because he still enjoys. Of Mr. Best and his playing it needs not to speak, Liverpool people — and, indeed, those within much wider bounds — being quite familiar with him; but the few peeps abroad which we have given above may be of interest to our readers.

"A very crowded audience assembled at St. George's Hall Thursday afternoon, by way of giving a greeting to Mr. W. T. Best on his sixtieth birthday, which was also the day upon which he completed his thirty-sixth year as organist to the Corporation. The audience was the most numerous which has ever gathered in the hall for a Thursday afternoon recital, and when the veteran organist appeared in the organ-gallery he was received with an outburst of the warmest applause, which he acknowledged by bowing twice to the audience. The programme for the afternoon was an exceptionally comprehensive one, including excerpts from composers of very different schools, and serving admirably to illustrate Mr. Best's excellences in all departments. The last number on the programme was Mr. Best's well-known Festal March, which he played magnificently; and at the conclusion of the march the audience would fain have given the organist an ovation, but this he apparently wished to avoid, and, evidently fearsome of the cordiality of his hearers, quickly left the organ-gallery."

Mr. Best's skill in handling the organ is something marvellous. When playing, his two hands perform feats of registration which would require three hands for most any other performer; and those who consider the organ a "cold instrument" have but to listen to his playing to become convinced that one who is so thoroughly skilled in manipulating the resources of an organ can produce effects of expression and tone-coloring which they never thought were possible.

To give a better idea of the style of Mr. Best's programmes we have included in the organ concert department the programmes of the complete cycles (twelve recitals) with which he inaugurated the great organ in the Centennial Hall, Sydney, Australia.

HISTORY OF THE ORGAN.

III.

It is quite evident that organ-building, prior to the middle of the fifteenth century, was confined entirely to the clergy, as no account of a professional organ-builder is to be found. The organs were constructed under the supervision of some monk, who performed the most important and difficult operations, such as the voicing of the pipes, and instructed the laborers how to put the various parts of the instrument together. The earliest known organ-builders by profession were Germans. Heinrich Traxdorf is considered to have been the first professional organ-builder, though this is doubted by some historians. He built an organ in Nuremberg in 1455, and another in Breslau in 1466. Stephen Castendorfer built the organ in the Cathedral at Erfurt in 1483, and also the organ in St. Ulrich's Church, Augsburg, in 1490. The earliest professional organ-builder in England was William Wotton, who constructed an organ for Merton College and one for Magdalen Chapel in 1486-7.

In the sixteenth century several important improvements in organ-building were made, foremost among which may be

mentioned the invention of an improved windchest. The old complicated spring-soundboard, with its labyrinth of springs, was abandoned, and a soundboard having sliding registers was substituted. Whereas, formerly, the slides worked *cross-ways*, admitting or shutting off the wind from all the pipes of any single note, they now worked *lengthway*, separating each set of pipes into a register, which admitted of the pipes being classified according to their tone or pitch. The *stopped pipe* was invented, saving considerable in expense, and giving the pleasing variety of soft tones, which was impossible with open pipes. By the use of a *small scale* a variety of stops having a penetrating tone and imitating a few of the stringed instruments were brought into use, and, by the application of the *large scale* full round tones of a pervading quality were possible. A number of stops with tapering pipes, sometimes with the larger end at the top, as the Dolcan, and frequently with the smaller end at the top, as the Spitz-flöte and Gemshorn were introduced, and added variety to the instrument.

A number of reed stops were invented, with the attempt to imitate the tone of various instruments, and even the voices of men and animals, as Posaune, Trumpet, Shalm, Vox Humana, and Bear's Pipe. The so-called "cheeks" were joined to the lips of some pipes, varying the tone and intonation. The compass was extended to four octaves, though the lowest octave was rarely, if ever, complete, when the instrument was spoken of as "an organ with a short octave."

In 1570 a builder named Lobsinger, of Nuremberg, introduced the bellows with *one fold*, or with *single action*. In 1576 an organ with sixty registers was built by John Scherer in Hermau, Prussia, having forty-eight keys and two octaves of pedals. The bellows (four in all) were twelve feet long and six feet wide.

In 1585 Julius Anton built an organ in St. Mary's Church, Dantzic, which contained the following stops: Stopped Diapason, Flute, Quintatena, Hohlflöte, Gemshorn, Nasat, Singingregal, Violin-regal, and Cremona.

Portative Organ of the XV Century.

In 1596 there was an organ in Breslau having thirty-six registers, three manuals, and pedal, with 1734 pipes, (1367 of metal and fifty-three of wood), and twelve bellows.

In 1665 John Loosemore built a magnificent organ for the Cathedral at Exeter, England, which has been altered and enlarged at various times by Schneider, Jordan, Micheau, Speechly, and recently by Henry Willis and Sons (see The Organ for June for a specification of this organ). One notable feature of the instrument was a Double Diapason, said to be twenty feet in length. In a small organ built for the school connected with the Cathedral, Loosemore placed a "Shaking Stop," which was an attempt at the modern Tremulant. It affected only the lowest octave of the Trumpet, and proved too noisy to be of any service. This organ also contained a wind indicator of novel construction. Two gilt stars were made to revolve in the front of the case, the supply of wind being indicated by the direction of their revolutions.

Among the early English builders one must not fail to mention Thomas Dallam, who constructed the organ for King's College, Cambridge. He closed up his factory in London, and took his whole "establishment" to Cambridge to construct this organ.

In 1644 an ordinance was passed by the House of Lords in England, not only forbidding the use of organs in churches, but ordering their total destruction. Some were purchased by private individuals, and a few were suffered to remain, but most of the instruments were partially or entirely destroyed. The accounts, given in Hopkins and Rimbault's "Treatise on the Organ," of the depredations of the soldiers when destroying the organs in the churches show to what extent the ignorant fanaticism of the puritanical spirit was carried in that country. A few organs escaped destruction by being moved to other localities. The organ in the Magdalen College was conveyed, by order of Oliver Cromwell, to Hampton Court, where it remained in the gallery till after the restoration of the monarchy, when it was returned to the college.

After the restoration, so much difficulty was experienced in procuring organs for churches, to take the places of the instruments which had been foolishly destroyed, that large premiums were offered to induce foreign builders to settle in England. These inducements brought over Bernard Schmidt and Renatus Harris, thus commencing an entirely new epoch in organ-building.

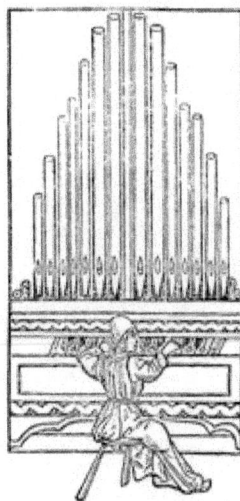

The above cut is a copy of an engraving found in "Theorica Musica" by Franchinus Gaffurius (published in Milan in 1492), showing a monk playing on an ancient organ which had broad keys.

BACH'S ORGAN SONATAS.

BACH, as is well known, composed six sonatas for the organ with two claviers and pedal,—the second of the series being generally regarded as the finest. Though intended for the advancement of his talented son, Wilhelm Friedemann Bach, these works are without graduated difficulty of any kind, and are invariably in contrapuntal form. As a matter of fact, they can only be approached by accomplished players, as the passages for the left hand and pedals present special difficulties; in the former, on account of the high pitch maintained near the right-hand section of the keyboard, while the freely moving pedal-bass appears more suitable for a stringed instrument (violoncello), as, with an exception or two, the bass takes no part in the fugal development of the various movements. A diversified arrangement of the organ stops is often necessary in these three-part sonatas, as opposed to a stereotyped disposition of the registers.

Thus, the highly expressive *Largo* of the second sonata requires special treatment, as well as other movements.

It is also imperative, for a convenient performance of these particular works, that the right hand should play on the clavier immediately below that assigned to the left hand, as the passages for the latter for the most part lie very high, occasionally above the notes for the right hand.— W. T. BEST.

MONSTER ORGANS.

ARE ORGANS WHICH HAVE A HUNDRED OR MORE SPEAKING STOPS COMPATIBLE WITH THE HIGHEST GRADE OF CONCERT PERFORMANCES?

WHAT is the inducement to have an organ of a hundred and twenty-five speaking stops? "The largest organ in the world?" These six words are invariably the cause of all our monster organs. To possess something larger than any one else is, perhaps, but a natural outcome of our age of competition, but how deplorable it is that the words *finer in quality* are rarely substituted for *larger*.

Some years ago an effort was made, here in Boston, to have a large organ reconstructed into a *larger* organ. The projector announced that the organ, when enlarged, would contain a hundred and fifty speaking stops, five manuals, and two pedal-claviers. Why was it to be so large? To have a more perfect and satisfactory performance of the great works for the organ? No! To enable the performers to render their numbers more readily, with a greater variety of coloring and more elaborate registration? No! To have more volume of tone and to be more powerful in *fortissimo* passages? Certainly not! Well, why? Simply to have it heralded all over the globe that "the largest organ in the world" is in Boston.

Suppose this monster had been constructed, would the ambitious residents of Boston have been satisfied? Possibly, for a year or so, but not longer; for about a year after this proposed monarch (not "of the seas," but of the winds) would have been completed (if the scheme had been carried out), the plans for a new organ for the Centennial Hall, Sydney, Australia, were started. The residents of Sydney are just as ambitious as those of Boston, and when they were about to have a large organ, nothing short of "the largest organ in the world" would be sufficient. Consequently, their proposed organ, would contain a hundred and fifty-two speaking stops. Poor Boston! *sic transit gloria mundi*. What would be the advantage of the extra stops? Were they omitted in the Boston organ through oversight? Oh, no! Those two extra stops are Flutes. There are but fifteen in the Boston organ, and a couple more will give greater variety, and then, you see, they will make the Sydney organ "the largest organ in ——," etc.

Why was the project of the Boston organ never carried out? Principally because the wherewithal was not forthcoming. Let us be truly thankful that the scheme, *as planned*, was abandoned. It may here be remarked that the Sydney organ, as completed, has a hundred and twenty-six speaking stops. As that number renders it "the largest organ in the world" (there being no Boston competitor) a larger number was unnecessary.

Now, let us suppose that, instead of patching up the stops which were already in the organ, and adding enough more to bring the number up to a hundred and fifty, the projector had proposed to remove the inferior stops and put perfect ones in their places; to strengthen the weak parts of the organ by substituting similar stops of a larger scale; to soften the harsh stops; to retain such of the reeds as were satisfactory, and to substitute perfect ones for the others; to remove the bellows which were insufficient and cumbersome, putting larger bellows of a modern pattern in their places; to put entirely new windchests and action in place of the old; in short, let us suppose that *quality* instead of *quantity* had been the object, would not the result (if the scheme had been carried out) have proved more satisfactory and permanent?

(Concluded on page 63.)

THE ORGAN.

BOSTON, JULY, 1892.

THE ORGAN is published the first of every month. Subscription price $2.00 per year (foreign countries $2.50), payable in advance. Single copies, 25 cents.

Subscribers will please state with which number they wish their subscription to begin.

The paper will be sent to all patrons till the editor is notified by letter to discontinue.

Subscribers wishing the address of their paper changed must give the old as well as the new address.

Remittances should be made by registered letter, post-office order, or by check payable to Everett E. Truette.

Programmes of organ concerts, with press notices of the same, specifications of new organs, and items of general interest to the subscribers, will be gratefully received.

Correspondence, to secure notice, must in all cases be accompanied by the name and address of the writer, not for publication, but as a guarantee of good faith.

Advertising rates sent on application.

Address all communications,

The Organ, 179 A Tremont Street, Boston, Mass.

☞ An active agent in every city is desired to whom a liberal cash commission will be allowed.

ANNOUNCEMENT.

In response to the request of several organ builders and organists, a large photograph of the Boston Music Hall organ (built by Walker & Sons, of Germany) has been prepared, copies of which we offer for sale. No respectable photograph of this organ was taken while the instrument was standing, owing to the fact that the case, with its abundance of detail, was mostly in shadow, while the burnished pipes were brilliantly illuminated from windows above. When the instrument was being removed several years ago, about twenty-five photographs were taken of various parts of the instrument, — the panels, key desk, one of the towers, etc. Having purchased these negatives, we placed five of the photographs, together with such photographs of the whole instrument as could be secured, in the hands of an artist, who made a large drawing, with all the detail of this grand organ front. From this drawing the woodcut shown on the title-page of this journal was made, and a large photograph has been taken. We have had a number of these photographs printed and mounted on heavy card-board ready for framing. The size is 12 x 14 inches, and the price is $2.00.

It is related by the *Echo* how that the lamented musician, Henry Smart, one day played as a voluntary a selection from Mozart's Twelfth Mass, and afterwards had to listen to a protest from the churchwardens against such "jiggy stuff," and how he subsequently turned the tables on them by performing "Jump, Jim Crow" in slow time, which gave them entire satisfaction until he told them what it was. Somewhat similar complaint has been received by the organist of a church not one hundred miles from Regent Street, where, on a recent Sunday, the Communion Office was sung to an adoption of the said Twelfth Mass. A gentleman, who had apparently been one of the congregation, wrote thus: "In the responses to the commandments, viz., 'Lord have mercy upon us, and incline our hearts to keep this law,' you have a musical flourish between the word 'us' and the word 'and.' I beg respectfully to ask if this is appropriate. It appears to me too light and airy for a solemn response." The organist made answer as follows: "In reply to your note, I can only say that the passage from Mozart's Twelfth Mass, described by you as a 'flourish,' is so written by the composer. As to whether it is appropriate or not, I offer no opinion. I am only a harmless drudge engaged by the vicar of this church to play accompaniments to the singing of the choir, and my duties do not extend beyond endeavoring to play the music placed before me as correctly as I can." — *Musical Opinion.*

This is the time when every organist should review his work for the past season, and lay out a comprehensive plan for the coming season, making a note of the failures as well as the successes of the past. Those who can look back with pride on a successful year, in which the advancement has been steady and sure; in which a number of concerts have been given, presenting novelties as well as selections from the standard works, the performance of which has been more praiseworthy than heretofore; in which the church work has been of a higher grade, including a better class of preludes and postludes, with fewer *improvised apologies*; in which they have attended the recitals of other organists, recognizing and profiting by the good as well as the bad points, thus broadening their minds and extending their ideas: those who can look back on all this are truly ready for a summer of absolute rest and recreation. A trip abroad, or a season at the mountains, lakes, or seashore, is a fitting reward for the bodies of those who have accomplished all this, and would prove the cheapest possible investment of part of the money accumulated during the past year.

The Rev. J. Baron, a former rector of the village church of Upton Scudmore, England, wrote a little pamphlet which he published in 1858, in which he enlarged on the principle of having only a few stops in an organ, but to have them made of the finest materials and with the most superior workmanship. This principle will commend itself at once to every one who is a lover of quality in preference to quantity; but the reverend gentleman rode his hobby into the ground, and buried out of sight the good which was in it by overdoing the matter. So carried away was he with what he considered his original idea, that he caused an organ to be built for his village church which was to illustrate his glorious principle. "Quality! *Quality! QUALITY!*" quoth he, and straightway he had this model organ built. It contained just one stop, — a would-be perfect open diapason of eight feet, all the pipes of which were exposed and well-arranged, so that they had the best possible "speaking-room." The key-board was reversed, and the accompaniments of the village choir were ground out on this singular instrument. It may have been the most perfect open diapason which could be conceived; but imagine the effect of a service the musical portion of which was expressionless and monotonous, with the prelude *mezzo-forte*, the anthem *mezzo-forte*, the hymns *mezzo-forte*, the amens *mezzo-forte*, and the postlude *mezzo-forte*; never more or less than *mezzo-forte*. Verily the clergyman's application of his worthy principle was a *reductio ad absurdum.*

At the final rehearsal before a recent concert in the Mechanics' Building, Boston, in which a large chorus was to be accompanied by orchestra and organ, it was discovered that the pitch of the organ was about a quarter of a tone above that of the orchestra. Neither organ nor orchestra could be spared at the concert, and neither could be tuned to the pitch of the other. The chairman of the Music Committee, being a genius, equal to almost any emergency, boldly guaranteed that the organ should be with the orchestra in the evening. Accordingly chorus and orchestra were dismissed, after which the chairman ordered the fires to be put out and all the windows around the organ to be opened (the thermometer out of doors was a little above zero). Then for two solid hours did Mr. Chairman blow cold air through all the pipes by playing on the full organ, after which the doors were thrown open, and audience, chorus, and orchestra took their places. The organ was found to be exactly with the orchestra, and the battle was won. As the hall grew warmer of course the organ grew sharper, and by the end of the concert the organ was back to its original pitch, making poor harmony (?) with the orchestra, but every one was in good humor, and no one complained.

ALLEGRETTO.

Edited by W. T. BEST.

FILIPPO CAPOCCI.

Gt. Doppel Flöte &
Viola di Gamba.

Sw. St. Diapason, Salicional & Flute 4 Ft.

Ped. 16 & 8 Ft.
Sw. to Gt. & Gt. to Ped.

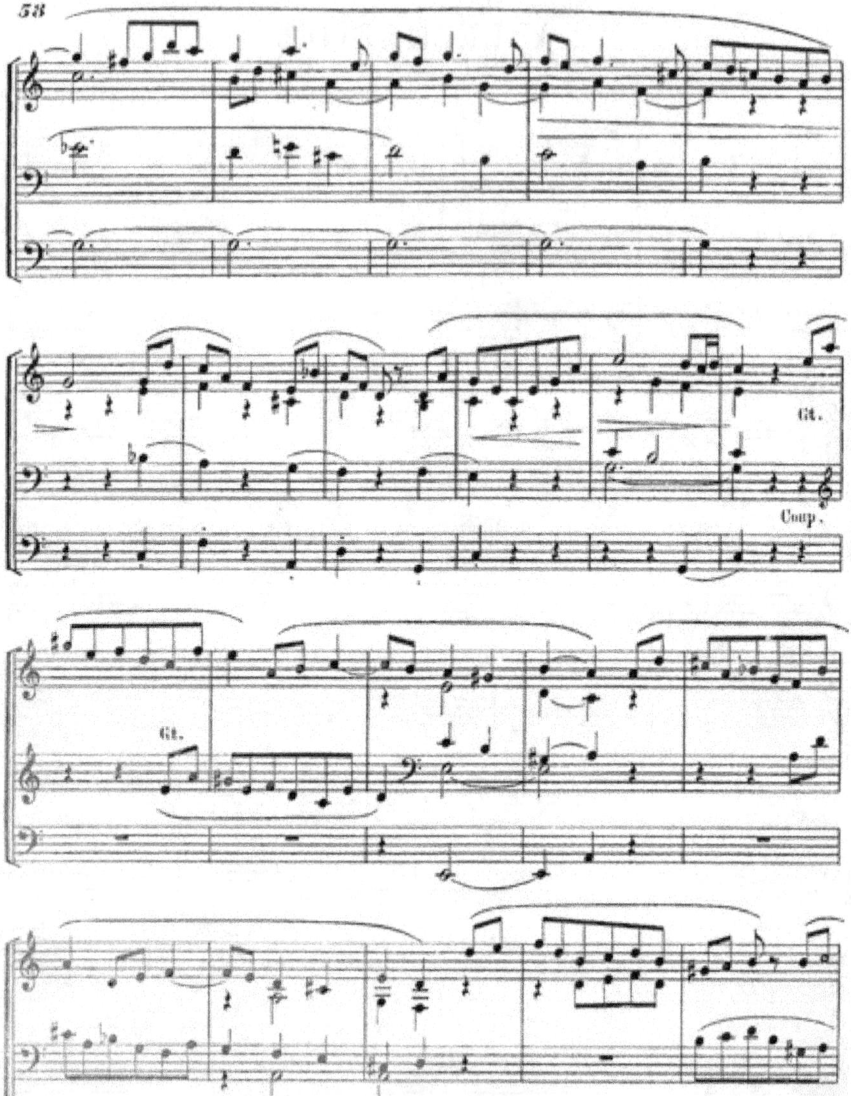
Gt.
Coup.
Gt.

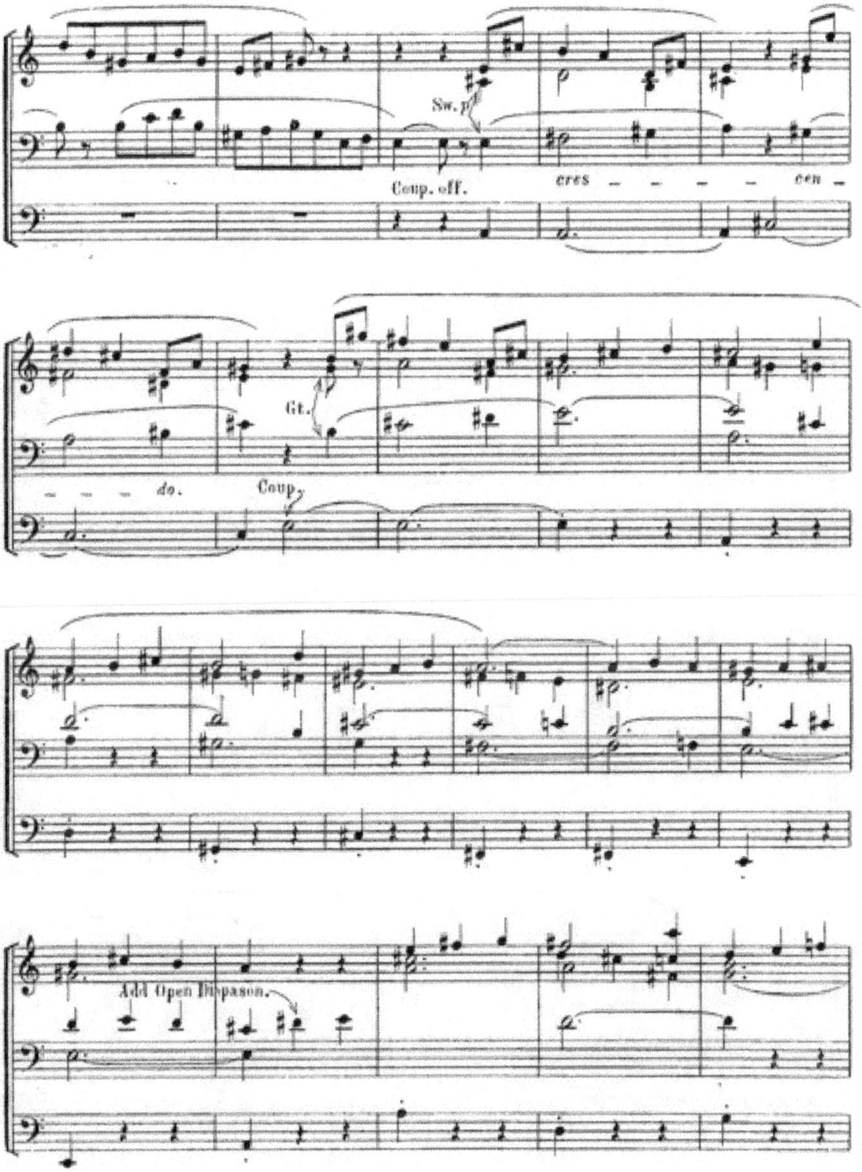
Sw. p
Coup. off.
cres - - - - - cen -
- - - do.
Gt.
Coup.
Add Open Diapason.

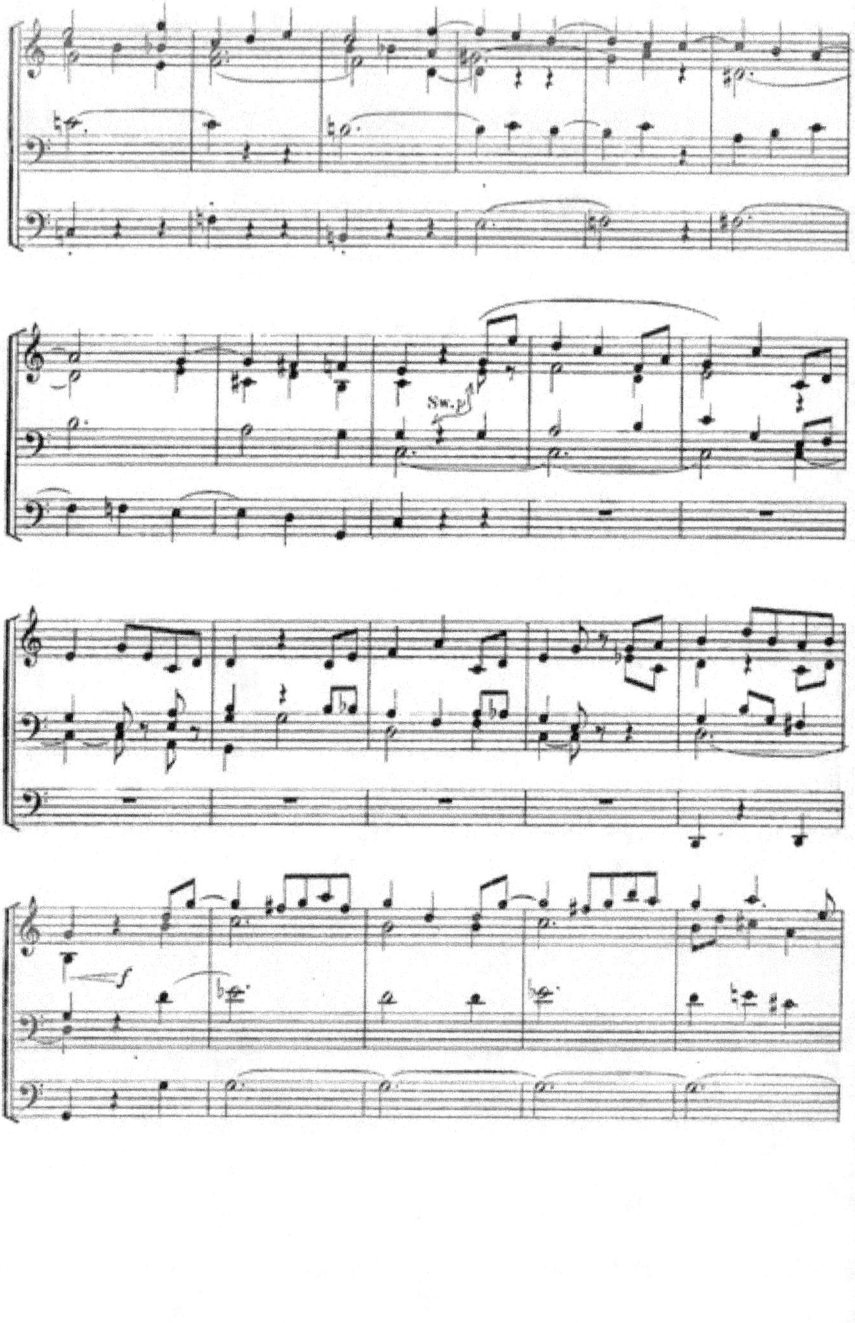
Sw. p
f

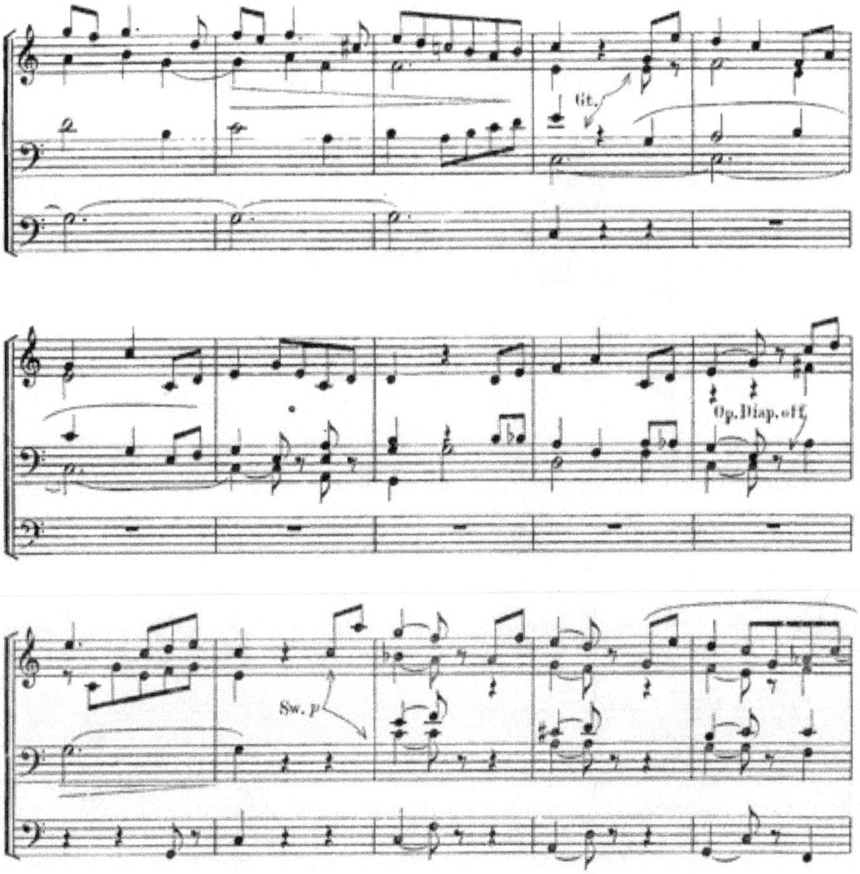
Gt.
Op. Diap. off
Sw. p
Oboe off.
rit.

PRELUDE IN F.

Allegro Moderato.

GUSTAV MERKEL

Gt. to Op. Diap.

Gt.

Sw. n & 4 Ft. with Oboe.

Ped. 16 & 8 Ft.
Sw. to Gt. & Gt. to Ped.

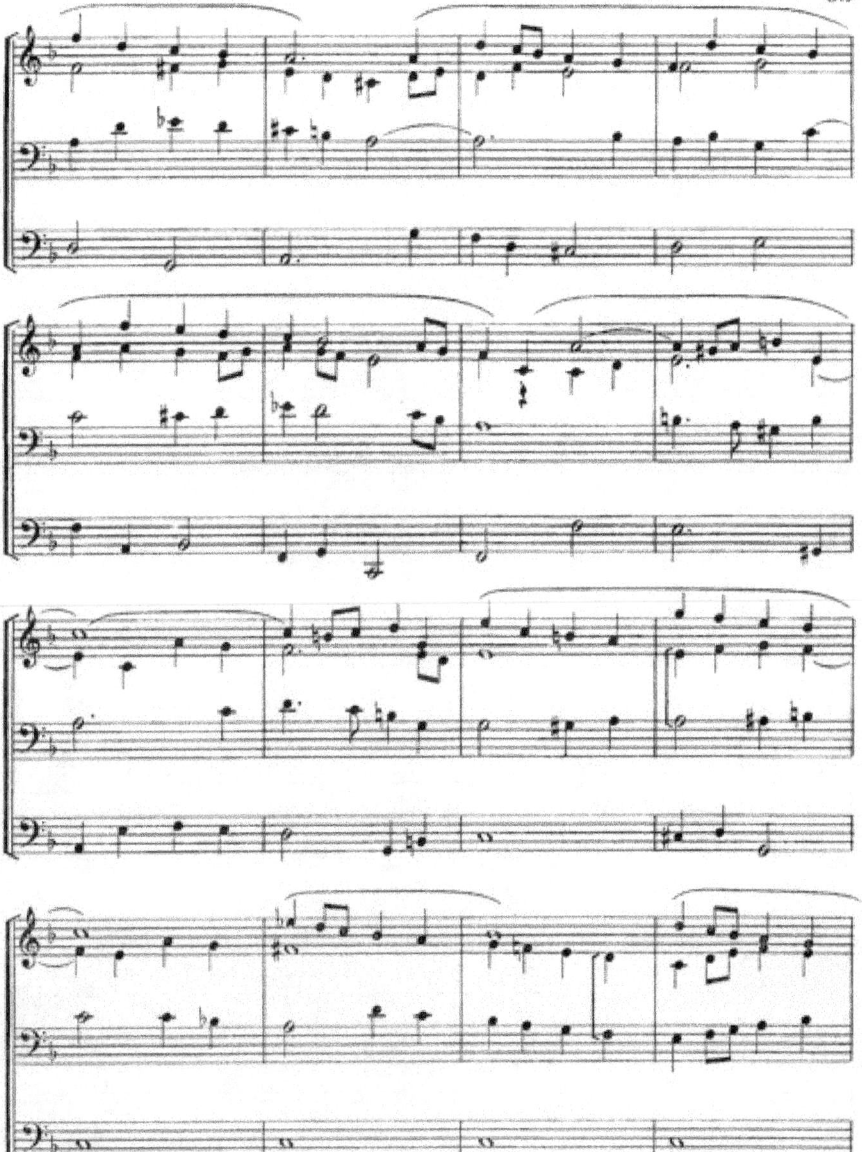

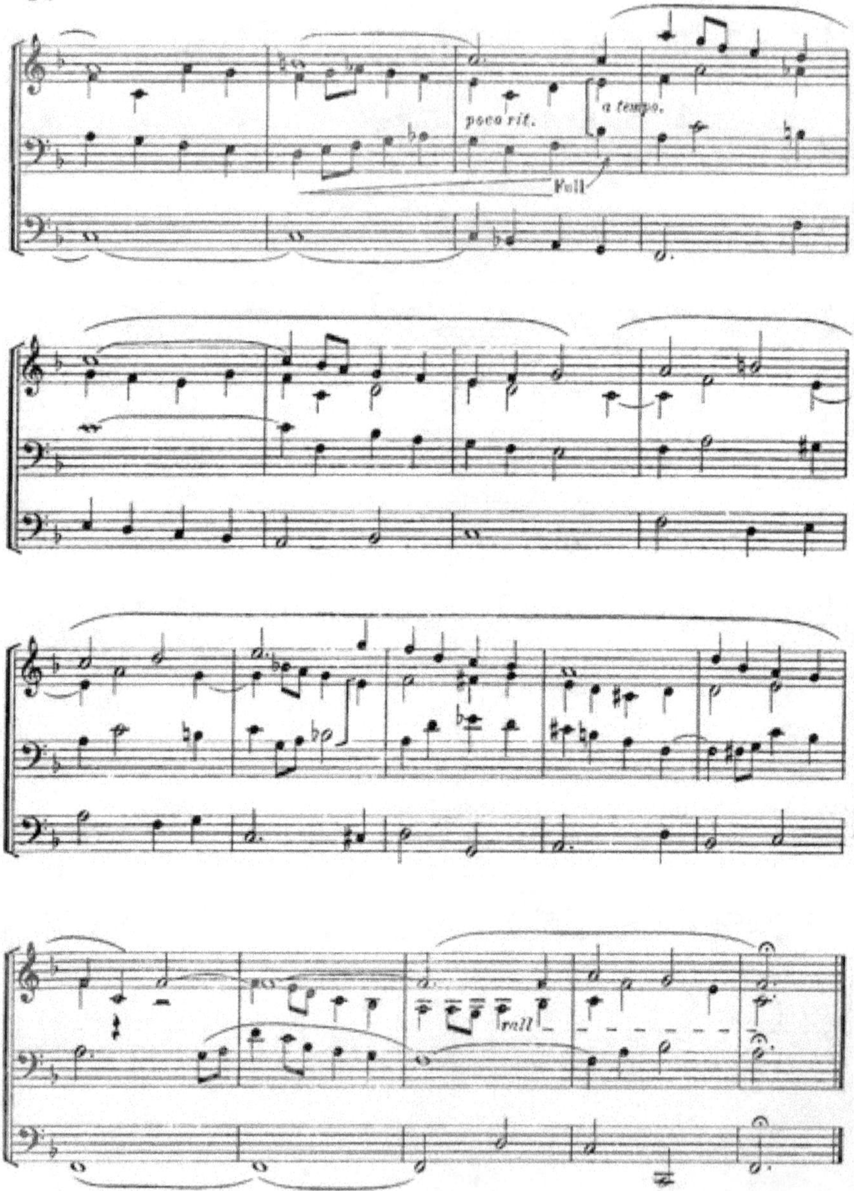
poco rit.
a tempo.
Full
rall

MONSTER ORGANS.

(*Continued from Page 55.*)

Let us consider some of the requisites of a large concert organ. There must be sufficient power to meet every possible demand, and yet stops which produce the softest *pianissimo* must be present. The doubles must be numerous enough to give body without any tendency toward "muddiness." There must be a sufficient number of eight, four, and two feet stops in the manuals, and sixteen and eight feet stops in the pedal (with a proper relative proportion of each), to build up an even volume of tone, and mixture stops enough to add the required brilliancy to that volume of tone. The complement of reeds must be capable of giving the "backbone" to the tone of the instrument, without which every organ is unsatisfactory; and lastly, every desired variety of stops must be present. All these requirements can be obtained in an organ of about eighty stops, and when there are more than that number nearly all the additional stops are duplicates, which do not add one iota to the value of the instrument as a concert organ, but, instead, are superfluous, taking up valuable space, and requiring so much additional attention from the performer.

Of course there are many other things, besides the list of stops, which are necessary to render the instrument satisfactory; in fact, there are many organs which contain about eighty speaking stops, which are anything but satisfactory, but the conditions which make them unsatisfactory would have the same effect in an organ of a hundred and eighty stops. As every organist and organ-builder knows, on the voicing of the pipes depends the success of every individual stop, as well as the effect of the whole organ; but, while every reputable builder claims to do good, and undoubtedly does give, special attention to the voicing of the pipes, the fact that the Oboe in one organ is a success and that in another organ is a flat failure, when both stops were voiced by the same man, is sufficient proof that not enough attention is given to the final resting-place of the organ, when the pipes are being voiced. If our imaginary organ of eighty stops is to be placed in a large concert hall, and the pipes are made with the same scales and voiced the same as they would be for a similar organ which was to be placed in a medium-sized church, it is obvious that one of these organs would not be a success. The organ-builders all say that they take into consideration every condition which will have any influence on the tone of the organ in its final-resting place, and generally intrench themselves behind the argument that they know better than any one else how the pipes should be made and voiced. This may be all true, but it is not emphasized by the fact that the great open diapason in a certain organ, which was built by Messrs. X. & Y. has a rich and full tone, giving body to every combination in which it is used, while the same stop in another organ, also built by Messrs. X. & Y., is a *proxy*. An organ of about eighty stops, having a well-balanced specification, and being properly voiced for the place which is to receive it, would be more effective and more satisfactory to both player and audience than if it contained a hundred or a hundred and twenty-five stops.

In the mechanical accessories, particularly the facilities for changing combinations, it may be a matter of taste which one of the several distinct systems is adopted, or whether two or more are combined, but if a third more of these facilities were added to organs of the size named than is customary, the one advantage of the monster organs would be secured without adding any of the numerous disadvantages. The usual excuses are, that these accessories are expensive, and that, when there are so many, some of them would be out of order all the time. Would they be any more expensive in this organ, or get out of order any sooner, than in a larger organ?

The fact is, if $40,000 is to be expended for a large organ, the corporation or committee endeavor to obtain $39,000 worth of *quantity*, being satisfied with $1,000 worth of *quality*. If an organist or any one else should endeavor to convince the corporation or committee that by selecting the specification of an organ which ordinarily would cost about two-thirds

of that sum, and expending the balance in finer mechanism, more "speaking-room," more attention to the voicing, greater number of accessories, etc., they would obtain a finer instrument, one which could not be improved, he would be sneered at as a fit subject for some asylum. Notwithstanding this state of things at present, the more advanced the art of organ playing becomes, the more the matter will be studied, and the more evident it will be that the best performances of the great organ works, whether ancient or modern, cannot be obtained on the monster organs.

In conclusion, notice what Mr. W. T. Best, than whom no greater authority exists, has written on this very subject in a letter to Mr. T. Casson, which was printed in the *Musical Opinion and Musical Trade Review* of London, last January:—

"I return the specification, which shows little enterprise; in fact, the days of these monster organs are numbered. No organ need have more than fifty stops. The varieties of organ tone are few, and the repetitions of the organ-builders are simply a nuisance to the player, though very useful to the builder from the white elephant point of view after erection."

ORGAN CONCERTS.

In connection with the sketch of the career of Mr. W. T. Best (Q.V.), we present to our readers the programmes of the cyclus of recitals with which he inaugurated the new organ in the Centennial Hall, Sydney, Australia.

OPENING RECITAL.

Toccata and Fugue in D minor	Bach
Andante Cantabile (G Major, No. 2)	Wesley
Fantasia in B major	Best
Overture to "William Tell"	Rossini
Organ Sonata, No. 4	Mendelssohn
Allegretto in B minor	Guilmant
Concert Overture in C	Best

SECOND RECITAL.

Festival Prelude on "Ein feste Burg"	Thomas
Air with Variations in A	Haydn
Gavotte, from Sixth 'Cello Sonata	Bach
Fugue in G minor, No. 3	
Pastorale Symphony, "Bethlehem"	Sullivan
Fantasia in C minor	Hatton
Allegro Cantabile in F minor	Wider
March in D major	Best

THIRD RECITAL.

Overture to "Zampa"	Harold
Air "Angels ever Bright and Fair"	Händel
Prelude and Fugue in C minor	Bach
Concertone in G	Gambini
Andante "The Surprise"	Haydn
Marche Hongroise	Liszt
Concert Fantasia on Old English Airs	Best

FOURTH RECITAL.

Allegro Moderato in A	Smart
Allegretto, from the "Lobegesang"	Mendelssohn
"Honor and Arms scorn such a foe"	Händel
Selections from "Jeanne d'Arc"	Gounod
Fuga — Con Moto perpetuo	Bach
Offertoire in D flat	Salomé
War March	Horsley

FIFTH RECITAL.

Wedding March	Mendelssohn
Variations on "O Sanctissima"	Lux
Toccata	Dubois
Selections from "Robert le Diable"	Meyerbeer
Bell Rondo	Morandi
Introduction and Fugue on a Trumpet Fanfare	Best
Andante from First Organ Sonata	Mailly
"See! the Conquering Hero Comes"	Händel

SIXTH RECITAL.

Sonata No. 5	Mendelssohn
Rêverie Religieuse	Best
Fanfare of Trumpets	Lemmens
Organ Concerto in G	Händel
Triumphal March, "Siege of Corinth"	Rossini
Pastorale in C	Salomé
Grand Chœur in G	

SEVENTH RECITAL.

Overture to Henry VIII	Hatton
Andante con Variazioni	Beethoven
Prelude and Fugue in D	Bach
Funeral March	Best
Cantilène Pastorale	Grison
Andante in G	Smart
Marche du Sacre, "Le Prophète"	Meyerbeer

EIGHTH RECITAL.

Overture "Les Diamants de la Couronne" . .	Auber
Air "The Lost Chord"	Sullivan
Andantino "La Cloch du Soir"	Chauvet
Concert Fantasia on a Welsh March	Best
Selections from "I Puritani"	Bellini
Air and Chorus, "Bai tno stellato soglio" . .	Rossini

NINTH RECITAL.

Overture to "Samson"	Händel
Duett, "Quis est homo"	Rossini
Sonata in F minor	Mendelssohn
Christmas Pastorale	Best
Triumphal March	Costa
Rhapsodie sur Cantiques Bretons (No. 2) . .	Saint-Saëns
"The Heavens are Telling"	Haydn

TENTH RECITAL.

Offertoire	Morandi
Andantino in E	Schubert
Air with Variations	Best
Fuga — Con Moto perpetuo	Bach
Andante Cantabile in A flat	Guiraud
Selection from the "Water Music"	Händel

ELEVENTH RECITAL.

Overture, "The Siege of Corinth"	Rossini
Serenade, "When the Moon is Brightly Shining"	Mellque
The Dead March in Saul	Händel
Fantasia in F minor, "The Storm"	Lemmens
Military March, "La Gazed Passe"	Best
Selection from "Les Huguenots"	Meyerbeer

TWELFTH RECITAL.

Hungarian March, "Rakoczy"	Liszt
The Mermaid's Song, "Oberon"	Weber
Marche Funèbre et Chant Séraphique . . .	Guilmant
Andante in F	Wesley
"The Bell Fugue"	Benfield
Selection from "Il Trovatore"	Verdi
The National Anthem with Variations and Finale .	Best

A SERIES of five monthly organ recitals, given by Mr. Allen W. Swan, in the Unitarian Church, New Bedford, Mass., closed with the following : —

"SPECIAL REQUEST PROGRAMME."

Nuptial March	Guilmant
Allegretto from Fourth Symphony	Mendelssohn
Lied	Gigout
Toccata and Fugue in D minor	Bach
Andante from String Quartette	Tschaikowsky
Religious Melody and Variations	Whiting
Abbenma	Karina
Grand Fantasia (The Storm)	Lemmens
Pastorale	Klein
Festival March	Dunham

Among the other compositions included in the programmes of the series may be mentioned the following : —

Benediction Nuptiav	Saint-Saëns
Adagio	Bourgault-Ducoudray
Sonata No. 2	Guilmant
Variations from the Septuor	Beethoven
Allegro in B flat	Whiting
Sonata No. 5	Mendelssohn
Fantasia, "March of the Men of Harlech" . .	Best
Gavotte	Rameau
Sonata No. 6	Mendelssohn

ORGAN CONCERT in the New York Avenue M. E. Church, by Mr. I. V. Flagler, May 26.

Prelude and Fugue in A minor	Bach
Larghetto from 2d Symphony	Beethoven
Selection from "Lohengrin"	Wagner
Idylle and Toccatto	Rheinberger
Minuetto, Op. 48	Salome
Scene in the Alps	Flagler
Invocation, Laus Deo and Wedding Music . .	Dubois
Pastorale	Guilmant
Marche Solennelle	Tombelle
Variations and Fugue on "America"	Flagler

AT the South Church, Madison Avenue, New York, Mr. Gerrit Smith gave his last recital for the present season on June 6, presenting the following programme, in which he was assisted by Mrs. Gerrit Smith, Soprano, Mr. Francis Fischer Powers, Baritone, and Mr. Adolf Hartdegen, Cellist.

Fugue in E minor, Op. 48, No. 5	Salomé
(Dedicated to Mr. Smith.)	
Andante Sostenuto ed Allegro Giocoso . . .	Guilmant
(Autograph copy sent for the occasion.)	
Agnus Dei	Bizet
(Accompaniment of Cello, Piano, and Organ.)	
Vision, D major } Op. 32, Nos. 2 and 3 . . .	H. W. Parker
Scherzo, D minor }	
(Ms. written for this recital.)	
Offertoire Religieuse	H. B. Hess
(Ms. written for this recital.)	
Grand Fantasia, Op. 417, No. 3	H. N. Bartlet
(Ms. written for this recital.)	
Romanza, Op. 27, No. 2, Cello and Organ . .	J. H. Brewer
(Ms. written for this recital.)	
Recitation and Aria from "Song of Solomon" .	Gerrit Smith
Concert sketch, D minor	Gerrit Smith
(Ms. written for this recital.)	
Theme and Variations, Op. 37	Arthur Bird
(Arranged by W. B. Payas.)	
"God is love"	E. H. Goss
Marche Nuptiale, E major	Tombelle
(Autograph copy.)	

ORGAN RECITAL at the First Baptist Church, Elmira, N.Y., June 6, given by Prof. D. D. Wood, on a new organ (the gift of Mrs. J. Sloat Fassett), which has recently been erected by Messrs. William King & Son of Elmira, N.Y. (See New Organs for specification.)

Toccata in F	Bach
Larghetto from Quintette Op. 163	Mozart
"These are they that shall shine"	Gaul
Miss McGuire	
Scherzo Op. 16	Guilmant
Offertoire St. Cecilia	Batiste
Pilgrims	Adams
Miss McGuire	
Night Song	Schumann
Spring Song	Mendelssohn
Minuet and Chorus	Händel
Fear ye not, O Israel	Buck
Serenade, Op. 15	Beethoven
Overture to Semiramide	Rossini

THE following, from the *Elmira Gazette*, speaks well of the recital : —

"The circumstances surrounding the occasion were all favorable; the organ was new and the organist capable. More than that, the organ was superb and the organist a master. Each was well adapted to the other. Professor Wood is the organist at St. Stephen's P. E. Church and Grace Baptist Church in Philadelphia. He is blind, but in his soul there is the sunlight of musical genius that diffuses its rare throughout his whole existence. His execution is that of a master, whose conception is intuitive by nature, embellished with the thoroughness of careful and diligent study."

INAUGURAL RECITAL in St. Agnes Chapel, Trinity Parish, New York, by Dr. Walter B. Gilbert.

Prelude and Fugue	Händel
Andante	Mendelssohn
Larghetto	Gilbert
Adagio	Spohr
"The Horse and His Rider"	Händel
Largo	Haydn
Bewerk	Rossini
Andante	Mozart
Choral Fugue	Händel
Larghetto	Beethoven
Allegretto	Haydn
Aria	Wesley
Fugue	Gram
"Angels Ever Bright and Fair"	Händel
Slow Movement	Mozart
"Fixed is His Everlasting Seat"	Händel
Aria	Weber
Organ Concerto	Gilbert

NOTE: We would recommend more explicitness in programmes than is here shown. Andante for Mendelssohn is as vague as "Fish" on a menu at a dinner. One would like to know beforehand whether it is to be salmon or herring.

THIRD RECITAL of the present season given by Mr. William C. Hammond, in the Second Congregational Church, Holyoke, Mass., May 24th.

Pièce Symphonique, Op. 14, No. 2	Grieg-Allen
Adagio in A flat	Diend
Pastorale Sonata	Rheinberger
Cantabile in B flat	Rossi
Marche Nuptiale	Guilmant
Benediction Nuptiale	Saint-Saëns

FIFTH Organ Recital in the High-street M. E. Church, Springfield, O., by Mr. H. O. Farnham, assisted by Mrs. W. R. Wilder, soprano, and Miss Anna M. Hollenbeck, pianist.

(REQUEST PROGRAMME.)

Concert Piece in E flat	Parker
Intermezzo from "Cavalleria Rusticana"	Mascagni
Aria, "Save me, O God"	Randegger
Symphonic Poem, "Orpheus"	Liszt
(Adapted for Piano and Organ by Mr. Farnham.)	
March	Gounod
Nocturne in G Major, Op. 38, No. 2	Chopin
Song, "Miserere"	Nevin
Andante, Fifth Symphony	Beethoven
(Adapted for Piano and Organ by Mr. Farnham.)	
Noël	Puck
Overture to "William Tell"	Rossini

ORGAN RECITAL at the factory of the Marklove Pipe Organ Co., Utica N.Y., on an organ constructed for the Baptist Church, Watertown, N.Y. (See list of new organs.)

March of the Magian Kings	
Cantilène Pastorale	Dubois
Toccata	
Mr. A. L. Barnes.	
Duett: "The King of Glory"	Lassen
Miss Alice M. Walrath and Miss Emily B. Greene.	
Andante from the Fifth Symphony	Beethoven
Mr. George S. Beechwood.	
Violin Solos, Serenata	Braga
Song without words	Thome
Mr. George McIntosh.	
Solo, with Violin Obligato, "O, Saviour, Hear Me,"	Gluck
Miss Walrath.	
Organ Sonata, No. 1 (Two movements.)	Mendelssohn
Miss Mystic Groff.	

We copy the following from the Utica *Morning Herald*:—

"Not only was the programme in itself interesting, but it served admirably to display the excellence of the new organ. The instrument is number 155, from the Marklove factory, and will be a great ornament to one of the prettiest church buildings in Watertown, now almost completed. The verdict of the audience as to its quality may be safely taken, for many of Utica's critical musical people were present. They regarded the organ as unusually successful, and found many points for particular commendation."

MIXTURES.

(FOUR RANKS.)

THE organ in St. Peter's Church, Montrouge (France), has been enlarged by Merklin & Co.

Prof. H. A. Lehmann has been engaged as organist of the First Baptist Church, Syracuse.

Mr. George W. Morgan has been giving organ recitals on the Hutchings organ in the First Congregational Church, San Francisco.

Mr. Abram Ray Tyler, organist of St. James' Church, New York, is to spend the summer months in Germany, France, and England.

Mr. George S. Hutchings, the organ manufacturer, is to build a residence in the colonial style, with all modern conveniences, near Clark's Observatory in Cambridge.

Miss Mabel Palmer, a pupil of Mrs. Isadora Smith Bassey of the East Greenwich Musical Institute, gave her graduating recital in the Academy Hall, June 6, performing, among other compositions, Prelude and Fugue in E minor of Bach, Offertoire in A flat Batiste, Sonata in B flat Mendelssohn, and a transcription of Weber's Overture to Euryanthe.

Mr. Frank Tait is to play a Grand Chœur for Organ and Orchestra which he has composed and dedicated to the Worcester County Musical Association, at the next Worcester Festival.

The Boston *Home Journal* announces the resignation of Mr. R. H. Chesson, Jr., who for twenty years has been organist and director of music of the Channing Church, Newton, Mass.

The $12,000 concert-organ, which was erected by J. W. Steere and Son, of Springfield, in the new Music Hall, Middletown, Conn., and dedicated May 26, was destroyed by fire on the evening of June 5.

Mlle. Pauline Guilmant, daughter of Mons. Alex. Guilmant, was married to Mons. Maurice Aliamet, of Douai, in La Trinité, Paris, on the seventeenth of May. At the ceremony, music was furnished by Mons. Eugène Gigout, organist, Mons. Marsick, violinist, and Mons. Frank, harpist.

Messrs. E. and J. Abbey have just placed a new organ in the Parochial Church of Notre Dame de Louviers, to be used for the choir accompaniments, which was publicly "opened" by Mons. Latouch, organist of St. Godard's Rouen.

Mr. William Rayment Kirby, Mus. Bac., having resigned his appointment of organist of the parish church, St. Mary, Newington, England, which he had held for a period of ten years, was presented with a handsome marble dining-room clock by the rector, church-wardens, and congregation. The members of the choir also presented him with a double inkstand fitted with a silver inscription plate.

The seventh anniversary of the inauguration of the St. Thomas Choir, Taunton, Mass., was observed by a special service on June 12, with Mr. Walter J. Clemson, M. A., organist and choir-master, and Mr. Edward G. Hall assistant organist.

"The Miracles of Christ," a cantata by Mr. T. Moe Pattison, was given with a chorus of about thirty voices.

The following is from *Le Monde Musicale*:—

(Translation.) Mr. Wm. Carl, the American organist, pupil of Mons. Alex. Guilmant, has just given, in New York, six grand organ recitals, which have had a certain éclat. The first was devoted to different composers, among whom we find J. S. Bach, F. Couperin, E. Silas, Händel, Salomé, Theo. Dubois, Mendelssohn, and Weber. In the second, besides the authors which we have designated, we see Alex. Guilmant, Gounod, Widor, Nicholas Clerambault, F. De la Tombelle, and G. MacMaster.

The fourth was composed of Massenet, César Frank, Jules Grison, Benjamin Godard, Ambrose Thomas, and Eugène Gigout.

The fifth contained only modern American composers; and lastly, the sixth was devoted entirely to the works of Mons. Guilmant. Mons. W. Carl and the artists who assisted have had a legitimate success in this musical enterprise.

At the Gethsemane Church, Minneapolis, an excellent organ recital was given May 30th by Mr. Felix Lamond, organist of Christ Church, Detroit. It is understood that Mr. Lamond has been offered the position of organist and choir-master at the church where the recital was given. If he accepts, he will doubtless prove a valuable acquisition to the musical circles of Minneapolis. The following programme was well rendered:—

Sonata in D minor No. 1	Guilmant
Barcarolle	Bennett
Andante cantabile (sixth symphony)	Widor
Fugue in G minor (the greater)	Bach
Adagio and Allegro from first organ Sonata	Mendelssohn
Andante and variations	Pierné
Marche Cortège	Gounod

The season for organ recitals is about over, but it is expected that after the vacation there will be a larger number than in any previous year. A. W. J.

QUESTIONS AND ANSWERS.

All questions must be accompanied by the full name and address of the writer and, if received by the tenth of the month, will usually be answered in the following number of THE ORGAN.

Only such questions as refer to the organ, to organists, organ builders, or to organ music, will be answered.

Correspondents are requested to write their questions in a clear and concise manner, writing on only one side of the paper.

BACH. Please give me the name of a good biography of J. S. Bach?

ANS. Johann Sebastian Bach, his work and influence on the music of Germany, by Philipp Spitta. (Novello Ewer & Co.)

M. Are organ pipes one-half the diameter an octave above any given note?

ANS. This principle could not be carried out; e. g., if the longest pipe of some 2 ft. stop were two inches in diameter, the shortest pipe (supposing the compass to be five octaves) would be but one-sixteenth of an inch in diameter. We think that more often the pipe a *tenth* above a given note will have one-half the diameter.

DULCIANA. Will you kindly settle a friendly dispute between two organ students, by informing us whether the Dulciana is string tone or organ tone?

ANS. Organ tone.

K. Does the quality of the material in organ pipes affect the *timbre*?

ANS. Other conditions being equal, it certainly does.

K. What objection is there, in the case of certain reed stops, to use half-length tubes in the basses?

ANS. The same objection for the bass that there is for the treble. It is a saving of material and space at the sacrifice of legitimate tone.

STUDENT. Did Schumann write any pieces for the organ?

ANS. For the Pedal-piano (or organ) six pieces in Canon form. Op. 56, 4 Sketches, Op. 58. 6 Fugues on the name Bach. Op. 60.

J. Should not mutation registers and the mutation ranks of mixtures be voiced with flute quality of tone?

ANS. The matter of quality has not received the consideration it merits, in this country at least. We think that the mixture family should combine in itself all the elements of quality to be found in the flue work, — Flute, Diapason, and String, — and to apportion these qualities in the different ranks properly would be to produce a perfect mixture.

H. In the old G organs, why was the lowest G-sharp omitted both in the manuals and the pedal?

ANS. In the days of unequal temperament tuning, the defects of the scale were thrown into this key, and it was therefore avoided in playing, hence the economy in stock, etc., in leaving out the lowest pipes.

B. A. Why do some builders place CC upon the right-hand side of the organ?

ANS. The fact that the majority follow the opposite plan is proof that it is not the best method. It may be regarded as a "notion," and perhaps descended from father to son.

BACH. Please inform me of an arrangement for organ of Mendelssohn's Wedding March.

ANS. Best's Arrangements No. 11. (Novello Ewer & Co.)

K. L. Where is the best location for the swell-pedal or swell-shoe?

ANS. If a balanced swell-pedal is used, about opposite upper C-sharp of pedal board, and so located as to allow the foot to have perfectly free access to the keys under it, whether the swell is open or shut.

MIXTURES.

THE following taken from the *Musical Courier* is from a "*Piano-sans-vive*":—

"A better 'organized' church than Grace does not exist in the city (N.Y.), — organs to the right of them, organs to the left of them, and into the very jaws of organs march the six hundred or more worshippers who weekly meet in the church.

"The great organ, dismembered by building and artifice, includes up and down-stairs organs, with attachments innumerable. An electric motor at the right foot, a small knob at the left, a forest of sleeping cork-like slippery stops, a hard bench, what looks like a small "melodeon," and a musical soul work in harmony. Now a thundering peal, again a rustle of angel's wings, now in this corner, again in that crevice; by and by through the ceiling frescoes sweet strains are whisked, switched, and rolled about after the manner of a swinging electric light, and scores of earth-lagged souls are wafted almost to the gates of heaven, out of the weird old building, nestled there in its gray cloak in the midst of the maelstrom of earthly selfishness in the hub of the hub of the universe."

Mons. Alex. Guilmant gave the last of his series of organ concerts in the Trocadéro, Paris, on May 26th, before a large and enthusiastic audience, an account of which, in *Le Monde Musicale*, is before us. The writer (who signs himself Guigue Talavernay) thus comments upon the various numbers:—

(Translation.) J. S. Bach and Händel naturally hold the place of honor in the programmes of the Trocadéro. The programme of last Thursday contained a prelude and fugue in B minor, and largo and allegro from the Concerto in F minor of Bach; also the Concerto in B flat of Händel. Nothing is more agreeable than to speak of these works, which have become consecrated by universal admiration. In praising them as they merit there is no fear of offending certain rivals. In taking exception one runs no risk of stirring up the susceptibilities of the authors. The prelude and fugue of Bach were well executed by a pupil of Mons. Guilmant, — Mons. C. L. Werner, organist in Baden-Baden.

Such a master, such a disciple!

Mons. Werner was also heard in a new composition of Mons. Guilmant, a soft reverie, entitled *Consolation*, which is, in reality, nature consoling us, and reassuring us of the future of music. Mons. Guilmant having abandoned the future of his pupil, charged him to show us the past, which he did with ordinary freedom.

I specially enjoyed the Concerto of Händel, and in the Concerto specially the first two parts. The introductory allegro, so decided, and the aria, full of a simple and imposing melancholy. A Serabande and a Musette of Couperin, and the choral in E of Kianberger, completed that part of the programme devoted to ancient composers.

The suite for organ, cello, and strings of Mons. Rheinberger (first hearing) is rather a duo for the two-string instruments, which is supported by an accompaniment on the organ.

The first movement (the programme announces *non moto*, which is a little vague) seems to me the best, the two last being less interesting. The second is a theme with variations, a little drawn out, but which, happily, permits the organ to leave the background and take a more important part.

REVIEW OF NEW ORGAN MUSIC.

FROM ARTHUR P. SCHMIDT, BOSTON.

Præludium grave,
Adoratio et Vox Angelica, } . . . . Theo. Dubois.
Hosanna,

Edited by Mr. Philip Hale.

THREE pieces composed by the organist of La Madeleine, Paris, who is well known here by his book of gems "House Pieces." These three pieces do not come up to the standard of his previous work, though they will find many admirers. The second piece, which is mostly a melody with accompaniment, pleases us the most, and is quite effective.

March des Rois Mages. . . . . Theo. Dubois.

An American edition of this well-known march of the Magian Kings, in which the original has been strictly followed. In the registration the use of the word "geigen" for the Geigen Principal will have a tendency to puzzle students, being somewhat uncommon.

10 Progressive Pedal Studies . . . . . G. W. Chadwick.

A series of rather difficult *Etud's*, ostensibly for the pedal, but in which the hands require no small amount of attention. They are melodious and intended for church use as well as for *études*, bearing such titles as Prelude, Offertory, Postlude, Response, and March.

FROM G. RICORDI & CO., LONDON.

Alla Marcia in C. . . . . W. T. Best.

A brilliant concert piece in the style of a march, opening with a short passage for the Tuba. The march theme (14 bars) is played partly on the reeds in the swell and partly on the great, with a *forte* combination. After a side-theme partly in E minor and partly in G, the march theme is repeated. The Trio in the key of the sub-dominant is complete in itself, having a first and second theme, ending with a repetition of the first theme. The original march theme follows, being slightly modified and embellished, working up to a climax, in which the Tuba plays an important part. The piece will be popular with organists who are able to cope with that style of concert music.

CIPHERINGS.

THE old organ-pipe factory, located for years past at Woonsocket, R.I., has been sold, and tobacco-pipes will hereafter be made in the building. — *Musical Courier.*

A change from speaking pipes to "dummies," as it were. Pity such an enterprise should end in smoke.

1st WAG. Perhaps they could not "raise the wind," organ pipes require it.

2d WAG. Maybe the treasurer was addicted to the flowing bowl, and, collections bad, he could not "stem the tide."

1st JOKER. The business being toney, perhaps there was not sufficient capital tobacker.

THE female organist of a Utica church has eloped and married a fourteen-year-old boy who pumped the organ. The affair has taken the wind out of the choir. — *Binghamton Republican.*

"PA, what are the stops of an organ for?"

"They are for varying the tone of the instrument. One causes a flute tone, another a deep tone, and so on."

"I see. Has the hand-organ stops?"

"No, my son. There is no stop to a hand-organ till you tell the man you will hit him with a brick if he doesn't move off." — *Musical Record.*

A CHURCH choir consists of one accomplished musician, and a lot of other folks who are densely ignorant of music. The accomplished one is the person you are talking with. — *The Magic Flute.*

NEW ORGANS.

NEW ORGAN IN THE FIRST BAPTIST CHURCH, ELMIRA, N.Y.

THE GIFT OF MRS. J. SLOAT FASSETT.

Built by Messrs. William King & Son of Elmira.

GREAT ORGAN.		SWELL ORGAN.	
Double Open Diapason	16 Ft.	Bourdon	16 Ft.
Open Diapason	8 "	Open Diapason	8 "
Dulciana	8 "	Salicional	8 "
Doppel Flöte	8 "	Æoline	8 "
Octave	4 "	St. Diapason	8 "
Harmonic Flute	4 "	Fugara	4 "
Twelfth	2⅔ "	Flauto Traverso	4 "
Fifteenth	2 "	Flautina	2 "
Mixture	3 Rks.	Oboe and Bassoon	8 "
Trumpet	8 Ft.		

CHOIR ORGAN.		PEDAL ORGAN.	
Violin Diapason	8 Ft.	Open Diapason	16 Ft.
Keraulophon	8 "	Bourdon	16 "
Melodia	8 "	Violoncello	8 "
Violin	4 "		
Flute d'Amour	4 "	PEDAL MOVEMENTS.	
Gemshorn	2 "	5 Combination Pedals for Great.	
Clarinet	8 "	" " " Swell.	
The usual Couplers.		Great to Pedal (reversible).	
		Water Motor.	

NEW ORGAN FOR THE RESIDENCE OF MR. H. H. VAIL, WOODSTOCK, VT.

Built by Mr. George S. Hutchings.

GREAT ORGAN.		SWELL ORGAN.	
Bourdon	16 Ft.	Bourdon Bass }	
Open Diapason	8 "	Bourdon Treble }	16 Ft.
Geigen Principal	8 "	Open Diapason	8 "
Melodia	8 "	Æoline	8 "
Dulciana	8 "	Quintadena	8 "
Doppel Flöte	8 "	Stopped Diapason Bass }	8 "
Flûte Harmonique	4 "	Stopped Diapason Treble }	
Clarinet	8 "	Flauto Traverso	4 "
		Violina	4 "
PEDAL ORGAN.		Flautina	2 "
Bourdon	16 Ft.	Oboe	8 "
Violoncello	8 "	Vox Humana	8 "

PEDAL MOVEMENTS.

Forte and Piano Combinations to Great.
" " " " " Swell.

Swell to Great Octave Coupler.
Reversible Great to Pedal Coupler.

Swell to Great }
Great to Pedal } Piston Knobs.
Swell to Pedal }

We had the pleasure of examining this organ before it left the factory. The case is finished in white enamel, and the front pipes are decorated in gold and silver. The Doppel Flöte and Melodia in the Great, and the Quintadena in the Swell, were specially pleasing.

THE first organ ever erected in the State of Wyoming has recently been built by Mr. Frank Roosevelt for St. Matthew's Cathedral, Laramie.

GREAT ORGAN.		SWELL ORGAN.	
Open Diapason	8 Ft.	Bourdon Treble }	16 Ft.
Salicional	8 "	Bourdon Bass }	
Doppel Flöte	8 "	Violin Diapason	8 "
Gemshorn	4 "	Dolce	8 "
		St. Diapason	8 "
PEDAL ORGAN.		Flûte Harmonique	4 "
Bourdon	16 Ft.	Cornet	3 Rks.
		Oboe	8 Ft.

PEDAL MOVEMENTS.

Two Combination Pedals for Great.
" " " " Swell.

Full Organ.
Great to Pedal (reversible).
Swell to Great (Octave) in addition to the usual Couplers.

NEW ORGAN FOR THE BAPTIST CHURCH, WATERTOWN, N.Y.

Built by the Machine Pipe Organ Co. of Utica, N.Y.

GREAT ORGAN.		SWELL ORGAN.	
Open Diapason	8 Ft.	Open Diapason	8 Ft.
Dulciana	8 "	Viol de Gamba	8 "
Melodia	8 "	Stopped Diapason	8 "
Principal	4 "	Keraulophon	8 "
Flute	4 "	Octave	4 "
Fifteenth	4 "		
		PEDAL ORGAN.	
PEDAL MOVEMENTS.		Bourdon	16 Ft.
Forte and Piano Great.		Sub-Bass	16 "

A NEW organ has been placed in the Congregational Church, Slatersville, R.I., having two manuals and nine speaking stops, by Mr. George S. Hutchings.

MIXTURES.

Mrs. Arthur H. Beverly (née Craft), for a long time organist of the Universalist Church, Waltham, Mass., committed suicide by saturating her clothes with kerosene, crawling into the furnace, shutting the door, and lighting the oil. Her mind had been turned from the effects of a long attack of "La Grippe."

A list of five hundred and twenty-five compositions which have been performed at the South Church, New York City, by Mr. Gerrit Smith, in his One Hundred and Fifty Free Organ Recitals, ending June 6, has been compiled (classified under their respective composers), for the benefit of students, by Mr. Gerrit Smith. The list, which is published by Nathan Bros., Art Press, New York, is in the form of an attractive little pamphlet, contains a specification of the organ in the South Church, and will be useful in many ways.

A RELIGIOUS CIPHER.

A CORRESPONDENT writes that, on every Sunday morning, middle C in the great organ ciphers during the service. From Monday morning till Saturday night the key refuses to stick down; hence, he has been unable to have it fixed. He is in despair, as his preludes and postludes on the swell and choir are unsatisfactory, and he is unable to support the congregation in the hymns. This being his first position, he is in daily fear of the committee finding him "incompetent."

There is something peculiar about a cipher. It is like the toothache, which vanishes when the dentist's chair is reached, mystifying one so much, that one is unable to tell which tooth has been aching. We frequently send to the factory for an "action man" to come and remedy a "cipher," only to find it impossible to make the key stick down after the man has arrived. It has been suggested that the rise of temperature on Sunday may have caused the cipher, but there are similar occurrences in summer when the church is warm through the week.

We know of but two remedies for a "religious cipher." One is, to take off your coat and cuffs Sunday A.M., and find the cause. The other is, to offer some time a bribe to give up half his day of rest, and come to your rescue, remaining inside the organ during the service.

BACH

YEARLY SUBSCRIPTION $2.00.

SINGLE COPIES 25 CTS.

THE ORGAN

DEVOTED TO

A MONTHLY JOURNAL

THE KING OF INSTRUMENTS

GUILMANT

BUXTEHUDE

BEST

EVERETT · E · TRUETTE ·

EDITOR & PUBLISHER

149 A. TREMONT ST. BOSTON.

HANDEL

THE ORGAN.

Vol. I. BOSTON, AUGUST, 1892. No. 4.

THE ORGAN.

A MONTHLY JOURNAL

DEVOTED TO THE KING OF INSTRUMENTS.

EVERETT E. TRUETTE, EDITOR AND PUBLISHER.

(Entered at the Boston, Mass., Post-office as second-class mail matter, June 1, 1892.)

CONTENTS:

George Washburne Morgan.

GEORGE WASHBURNE MORGAN.

GEORGE W. MORGAN, who was probably the first famous organist ever heard in this country, died at Tacoma, Wash., Sunday, July 10. He was born in Gloucester, England, in 1823, and at a very early age exhibited remarkable musical gifts. When only eight years old he played in church in his native city, performing the entire service in St. Nicholas Church. At an early age he was appointed assistant organist at the Gloucester Cathedral. In 1853 he came to this country, and created a great deal of enthusiasm by his remarkable playing. His pedaling was then considered phenomenal, and his performance of "concert music" — an unknown factor in organ music in this country previous to his arrival — placed him at that time at the head of the profession. In New York Mr. Morgan was, at different times, organist of St. Thomas's Church, St. Ann's Church, Grace Church, and Brooklyn Tabernacle, at the latter of which he remained for fourteen years. He has given a large number of concerts in New York, and has made a number of concert tours over the country with his daughter, a harpist. Just previous to the last trip he was taken ill, but recovered enough to start on the tour, nevertheless he failed rapidly, and died while in Tacoma, Wash.

REMINISCENCES OF ORGAN AND CHURCH MUSIC IN THIS COUNTRY.

BY AN ORGANIST.

BUT little justice has been done by the American critics and writers on music to one very important branch of the art, *i.e.*, organ and church music.

In England, Germany, and France, organists and church composers have always ranked as high as, if not higher than, musicians in other branches of the profession. In the "Memorial History of Boston" is an account of music in Boston during the past century, by J. S. Dwight, in which I think no mention is made of church music in any form, and organ music is only spoken of in connection with the Music Hall organ. I purpose to jot down a few recollections of church music and organists, hoping thereby to partly supply this want, and perhaps to influence other writers to do justice to this important department of the art of music in this country.

How well I remember the first really *good* organ-playing I ever heard! I was a boy of ten, and had come to the city from the country to visit an elder brother. The city was Boston, and the church was the *old* Trinity, on Summer Street. It was at Christmas time, and I had heard much of the wonderful music at this church. The organist was the late A. U. Hayter, formerly of England, and at that time probably the best church organist in this country.

That was long before the day of concert-playing. Such a thing as performing a piece *alone* on the organ had hardly been heard of. The organist of that day made all his reputation *as an accompanist* (no mean accomplishment). It is related of Mr. Hayter that he considerably astonished the natives by actually *playing with his feet* a figure *of two notes* (dominant and tonic) *allegro*, in a chorus by Regim. when accompanying the Handel and Haydn Society at one of their concerts.

He belonged to the old style of cathedral organists of the English school, the inventors of the "G manual"— said manual running down five notes *lower* than the German keyboards, the object of this extension in the bass being to save the vexation of having to spend two or three years in learning to play with the feet! The bass was almost entirely played "in octaves," and the five additional notes enabled the performer to produce, *with his left hand*, those low tones which are among the most impressive sounds emitted by the "king of instruments."

This method is all very well if the organist had nothing but the *feet* to play with his left hand. But of course "open position" (the only way of playing effectively on the organ) was quite out of the question. Nevertheless, some of the greatest church music ever written was composed and performed in this manner by the organists and composers of the old cathedral school, the best representatives of which, in this country, being the Musical Doctors Hodges and Tuckerman, the former of New York (dead long since), and the latter now resident in England, of whom more anon.

I have spoken of this peculiar style of playing, as the thing that impressed me most in that service was the low tones of the "trumpet" in the "great" manual. I shall never forget it! As the player held his hand on the lower part of the keyboard, and those low "mellow" tones came floating out into the great spaces of the solid granite walls of the old church, I felt that here was something beautiful, poetic, and a foretaste of what a musician might hope for in another world. I resolved to become an organist from that moment; and to this day the sound of the *bass* of a modern grand piano (a sound I can liken to nothing but striking on an iron stove with a poker) is excessively disagreeable to me.

Years after, in listening to the choral services in the English cathedrals, I heard the same beautiful sounds, and I then knew that I had heard in those boyish days one of the many charming effects of the grand cathedral service of England.

Mr. Hayter performed on an English organ, with a reversed keyboard. The pipes of the choir organ were placed so as to overhang the front of the organ gallery. I remember little about the singing, which I believe was done by a quartett. But one thing amused me greatly, and that was the queer way in which the organist made the vocalists wait between each verse of the Te Deum while he banged out and in the stop-handles for a moment or two, probably to give the listeners an idea of the "truly immense" character of the playing.

Mr. Hayter had but lately come to this country, and had the true "British" contempt for the musical knowledge of "the Yankees." It is told of him that he once laid a wager that it did not signify in the least *what* he played to the Trinity congregation, as long as they heard something in the way of a noise going on in the organ-loft. And to prove it he listened down three or four of the keys, drew a soft register, and instructed the "bellows blower" to work the handle "just three minutes by the clock" (the length of the ordinary "voluntary"), so that the cultivated and aristocratic congregation of Trinity were treated to a most original performance, consisting of *one chord three minutes long!*

Mr. Hayter continued to play at Trinity Church until, I think, about 1860, when he gave up his position, retired to his farm near Boston, and died there some years ago.

He was a man of considerable talent, and undoubtedly exercised much influence on the taste of the present Boston church organists. He was succeeded in his position by that excellent musician, Mr. J. C. D. Parker.

(*To be continued.*)

THE ART OF PRACTISING THE ORGAN.

BY THOMAS ELY, MUS. BAC., F.C.O.

"It is an art to know how to play — and an art to know how to practise," was the favorite maxim of my old professor of the clarinet, the famous Henry Lazarus. I heard it at least once every lesson, always spoken in the same impressive manner — so often that I confess I became rather tired of hearing it, and felt sometimes tempted to chime in with the second half of the maxim, during the dramatic pause which the worthy clarinetist always made between the sentences. This pause always reminded me of an incident that happened at a concert. In a certain recitation, just before the *low not* which was the point of the whole thing, the reciter was in the habit of making a long pause so as to make the audience more keen for the coming words, which were invariably followed by roars of laughter. On this occasion a small boy, who had evidently heard the piece before, during the pause called out from the gallery the words which the reciter was preparing to give out with such effect. Naturally his hearers were convulsed with laughter; and the poor fellow had to make an anti-climax of it by saying, "Just so." With a few more words as preface, I will at once to my subject. The following words are intended for earnest students, who wish really to *play* the organ, not merely to amuse themselves with light, fancy pieces, such as some of the compositions of Batiste, Wely, and others, more particularly of the French school. Most organists have very little time to spare, owing to their other studies, — pianoforte, harmony, composition, and often numerous private engagements, — so that it is very necessary that a plan of practice should be adopted which would enable one to do the greatest possible amount of work in the shortest time. I therefore recommend all who have not tried the method I propose to give a fair trial and note the results.

On getting a new piece, first of all play it through *once* on the organ, as an exercise in reading at sight. Then, do not practise it any more on the organ until you have mastered the manual part on the piano. Go through it carefully, picking out the passages difficult to finger, trying several modes and endeavoring to find the easiest and safest of them. A fault very common with beginners is to imagine that the notes written on the upper staff of five lines are all to be played with the right hand, and all those on the lower with the left. Get rid of this idea at once, and divide the work between the hands, so that it all lies conveniently under the fingers, sometimes taking even a single note of a passage with the left hand to help the right, when it would be impossible or difficult to play it *smoothly* with the right hand alone. By "fingering," I do not mean taking a pencil and scoring all over one's music. I once knew a student who, at every suggestion of his master with regard to fingering or registration, would take out his pencil and begin jotting down figures, directions as to quality of stops, etc.; and not satisfied with this, when practising afterwards would write on his music full directions, how a certain *crescendo* was to be obtained, or how composition pedals were to be worked during the playing of a difficult pedal passage. By the time he had prepared a piece, the hieroglyphics were enough to confuse the clearest sight. As much as possible trust to your memory. If you have been in the habit of using such artificial means as the above, give them up, and soon you will find them to be quite unnecessary and your memory improve considerably. After having thoroughly prepared a piece in this way, if I do not play it again for some months, at the end of that time I almost as unconsciously as an automaton adopt the same fingering and the same method of playing, without any written directions. For this I am indebted to my former master at the Royal College of Music, Prof. Walter Parratt, and it is by no means the least important point I learned from him. When the manual part can be played perfectly on the piano, with a smooth, even touch, difficult passages as well as the easier, then go to the organ and play the piece through once or twice, manuals and pedals.

Here let me add a word of caution : Do not practise quickly, play slowly, using soft stops, till you have every note correct, and then, and not till then, more quickly, with the proper expression. Now will be found the practical advantage of having prepared the manual work at the piano. More attention can be given to the pedalling, there is no abrupt stopping to find how to finger, or to practise difficult passages, consequently the blower's labor is not wasted. I always think it a waste of wind to practise finger passages on the organ, and a waste of money to those who have none too much to spend on organ-blowing. By this time the student ought to be able to give a fairly accurate rendering of the piece, but still, maybe, he will find certain passages very difficult — rapid pedalling in contrary motion to the left hand, or other intricacies. He should now practise these portions alone, very slowly at first, gradually quickening the pace as they become easier to him. Nothing makes a player more nervous in performing than the knowledge that, at some particular part of the composition, there are very difficult passages which he is afraid of, and more than surprised if he gets through without a breakdown ; so that he must persevere until they become easy to him and quite safe, if he wishes to satisfy himself and please his audience.

Many have perhaps wondered what is the reason of this great difference between the performances of two organists, the playing of one is so "drony," and that of the other so crisp and "fresh." They may both play without a single wrong note, and use exactly the same stops, yet there is the difference still felt. The solution of the problem, I think, will often be found in this, — the second of the two strikes the repeated notes, which are not tied, at every recurrence, the first takes every opportunity of holding them down, especially if they occur in the inner parts. Take Bach's well-known Prelude in E minor (Peters edition, vol. ii., p. 64). In the first bar, the last note of the top part is D sharp, *not* tied to the D sharp, the first note of the following bar, and numerous other instances will be found throughout the Prelude. Let the reader try for himself the difference in effect — first holding the notes down and afterwards striking each repeated note. Further, let him play the second page of the Prelude (Peters edition, p. 65), first holding down the repeated notes, many instances of which occur in both upper and inner parts, afterwards striking each afresh. I think then he will have little difficulty in understanding what I mean by "drony" and "fresh."

I have confined myself to accuracy and clearness of playing, and do not intend here to deal with the most important parts of phrasing and expression. Although these can be taught to a certain degree, yet if the student be not naturally gifted, if he cannot himself *feel* how the music should be rendered, and enter into the spirit of the composition, he will never become much more than a mechanical player, though he have the best of masters. Modern composers usually give full directions regarding change of manual, and the quality and loudness in stops, but in J. S. Bach's works scarcely any will be found, and each player must use his own judgment to a great extent, specially as many of the great master's works can be rendered in different ways, all of which are good. To take two very striking instances — how differently the Toccata and Fugue in D minor and the Passacaglia in C minor are interpreted by some of our greatest organists. However, I am wandering from my subject, which I intended to be on "practising" only.

I am confident that if the above instructions are carefully carried out there will be fewer of those poor, inaccurate, and dull performances one so frequently hears, most of which result, not from a want, but from a *bad method*, of practice. Above all, avoid the tolerably general method of playing through a piece without previous practice on the piano, with loud stops drawn, quite up to the proper pace, repeating *in toto* again and again, stumbling over difficult passages just in the same way on every repetition, and succeeding in little else than irritating one's self, and doing to distraction any one who has the misfortune to be within hearing distance.
London Musical Herald.

NOTABLE ORGANS.

I.

EXETER (ENGLAND) CATHEDRAL.

THE organ which is represented in the above cut was erected in 1665 by John Loosemore. At that time, and for some little time afterward, the reputation of this instrument centred on the large Double Diapason which it contained, its size being then considered enormous. (The longest pipe was twenty feet in length.) The organ has been remodelled at various times by Scheider, Jordan, Michan, Robson, Lincoln, and lastly by Henry Willis & Sons. Notwithstanding the

numerous alterations which this instrument has undergone, the case and front pipes remained intact for many years ; but they, too, were finally "remodelled," and the organ as it stands to-day bears almost no resemblance to the original instrument. The two towers were entirely removed several years ago, and the front pipes, which were of pure tin, were melted over to make new pipes. The instrument to-day is a full-sized concert organ, having four manuals and fifty-five speaking stops.

The above cut is copied from that admirable work on ancient organ-cases by Arthur G. Hill, B.A., F.S.A.

THE ORGAN.

BOSTON, AUGUST, 1892.

THE ORGAN is published the first of every month. Subscription price $2.00 per year (foreign countries $2.50), payable in advance. Single copies, 25 cents.

Subscribers will please state with which number they wish their subscription to begin.

The paper will be sent to all patrons till the editor is notified by letter to discontinue.

Subscribers wishing the address of their paper changed must give the old as well as the new address.

Remittances should be made by registered letter, post-office order, or by check payable to Everett E. Truette.

Programmes of organ concerts, with press notices of the same, specifications of new organs, and items of general interest to the subscribers, will be gratefully received.

Correspondence, to secure notice, must in all cases be accompanied by the name and address of the writer, not for publication, but as a guarantee of good faith.

Advertising rates sent on application.

Address all communications,

The Organ, 149 A Tremont Street, Boston, Mass.

☞ An active agent in every city is desired to whom a liberal cash commission will be allowed.

ANNOUNCEMENT.

IN response to the request of several organ builders and organists, a large photograph of the Boston Music Hall organ (built by Walker & Sons of Germany) has been prepared, copies of which we offer for sale. No respectable photograph of this organ was taken while the instrument was standing, owing to the fact that the case, with its abundance of detail, was mostly in shadow, while the burnished pipes were brilliantly illuminated from windows above. When the instrument was being removed several years ago, about twenty-five photographs were taken of various parts of the instrument,—the panels, key desk, one of the towers, etc. Having purchased these negatives, we placed five of the photographs, together with such photographs of the whole instrument as could be secured, in the hands of an artist, who made a large drawing, with all the detail of this grand organ-front. From this drawing the woodcut shown on the title-page of this journal was made, and a large photograph has been taken. We have had a number of these photographs printed and mounted on heavy card-board ready for framing. The size is 12 x 14 inches, and the price is $2.00.

THE continued discussion in many of the English musical papers between the advocates of the electrical action, particularly the Hope-Jones system, and those who claim all things for the tubular-pneumatic action, will surely lead to good results in the end. Such a discussion is one of the strongest incentives to the perfecting of each system.

A WESTERN paper in "noticing" a new organ speaks of "the cornet stop having *three banks of reeds*." Either the organ was a remarkable instrument or the reporter had a remarkable facility for writing up any subject which the editor requested. We should think the reporter could easily secure a prominent position in the office of some Boston daily. There is a demand for reporters who can write a column on a subject of which they know absolutely nothing.

THE *Echo*, a musical journal, published in Lafayette, Ind., now in its eighth year, contains the following comment on the ORGAN, which we gratefully acknowledge: "It presents a fine appearance and is ably edited. Of all the musical journals that have sprung into existence within the last year or two, this one appears the most healthy, and that there is

a field for it, no one can question. Our readers who are organists can be supplied monthly with some excellent voluntaries and interludes by subscribing to this paper."

THE annual banquets of the College of Organists and of the Guild of Organists which occurred in the famous Holborn Restaurant, London, were very successful affairs, and brought out not a small amount of encouragement for their respective organizations. We hope the day is not far distant when the disciples of the instrument in this country will organize themselves into a social body for mutual advancement and interchange of ideas and theories. A number of the petty barriers must decay and fall before any attempt to unite in one body will be successful.

THE "Specialist Committee on Church Music," which submitted its report at the annual convention of the New York State Music Teachers' Association, submitted two questions for discussion, the second of which is as follows: "What is the purpose of the organ 'postlude' in the service?" In many cases it is to show off the full power of the instrument and cover up the noise of social conversation on the topics of the day. We know of one church which positively refuses to allow the organist to play more than a half page of music after the service. They say "it interferes with the conversation of the members of the congregation who meet but this once a week and wish to have a half-hour of social intercourse without the noise of the organ." Fortunately there are some churches where the organist is encouraged to perform various pieces of the highest class of music as a "postlude," where half of the congregation wait after service to listen to this music, and where the instrument is considered worthy of its place and its object, instead of being like a boisterous youth who must be kept out of sight and hushed every time he opens his mouth to speak.

WE read in a Boston daily an announcement of the proposed innovations which were to take place at the festival of the graduates of the public schools in the Mechanics' Fair Building some time ago, among which is the following : "After these addresses another innovation is promised. The scholars and the audience will unite in singing 'America.' *If the organ is in good working order*, James M. McLaughlin, brother of Clerk McLaughlin, of the House, and one of the school music teachers, will officiate at the big instrument, otherwise the Cadet Band will furnish the music." This instrument was "in good working order" a short time previous to the festival, and we doubt if the services of the band were required to support the singers.

THE ORGAN IN RUSSIA.

THOUGH the Greek Church recognizes no instrumental music, the organ gets some small cultivation in Russia. Some little time ago the professor of the organ at one of the principal conservatories gave an organ recital. He had, it seems, six attendants — an organ-blower, a second ditto as assistant in case of need, a gentleman to turn over the music, two gentlemen, one on each side, to manipulate the stops, and lastly, an attendant to hold a lantern at his feet to throw light on the pedals. It is clear, organ recital playing is still in its infancy in the Czar's dominions, if this performance is to be taken as illustrative of high-class organ-playing, for it is reported that the performance in question was not thought to be a very brilliant one. However, it is satisfactory to learn that Russian musicians are taking some interest in the king of instruments. — *Musical Courier.*

WEDDING PROCESSIONAL.

(FROM "LOHENGRIN.")

Tempo di Marcia.

RICHARD WAGNER.

Gt. to Op. Diapason, with Trumpet.

Gt.

Sw.

Sw. 2 & 4 Ft. (P)

Ped 16 & 8 Ft.
Sw. to Ped.

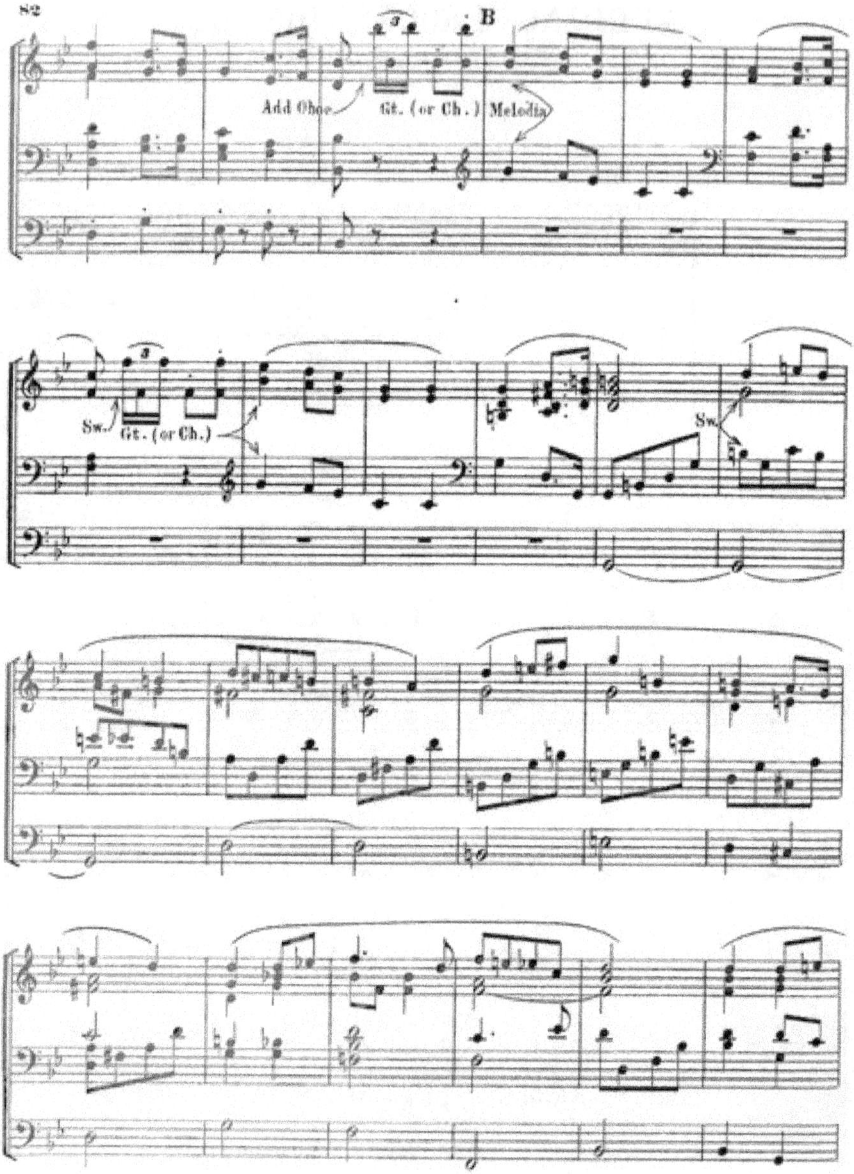
B
Add Oboe
Gt. (or Ch.)
Melodia
Sw.
Gt. (or Ch.)
Sw.

* If the Processional is not long enough, repeat from A or B.

ANDANTE.

W. SCHÜTZE.

Sw. St. Diap. &
Trem.

Ped. Bourdon.

MELODY.

Allegretto.

EVERETT E. TRUETTE.

Sw. Oboe & Flute
4 Ft. with Tremulant.

Ch.(or Gt.) Melodia
& Dulciana.

Ped. Bourdon 16 Ft.
Ch.(or Gt.) to Ped.

Copyright 1892, by Everett E. Truette.

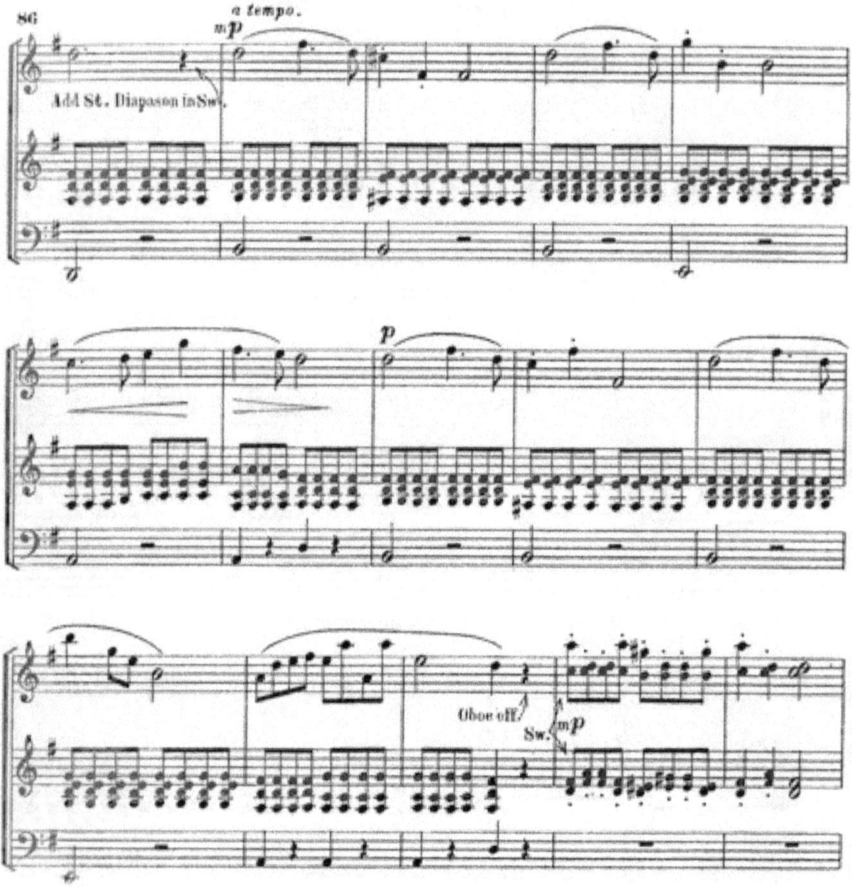
a tempo.
mp
Add St. Diapason in Sw.
p
Oboe off.
Sw.
mp
p
Add Oboe.
Sw.
Ch.

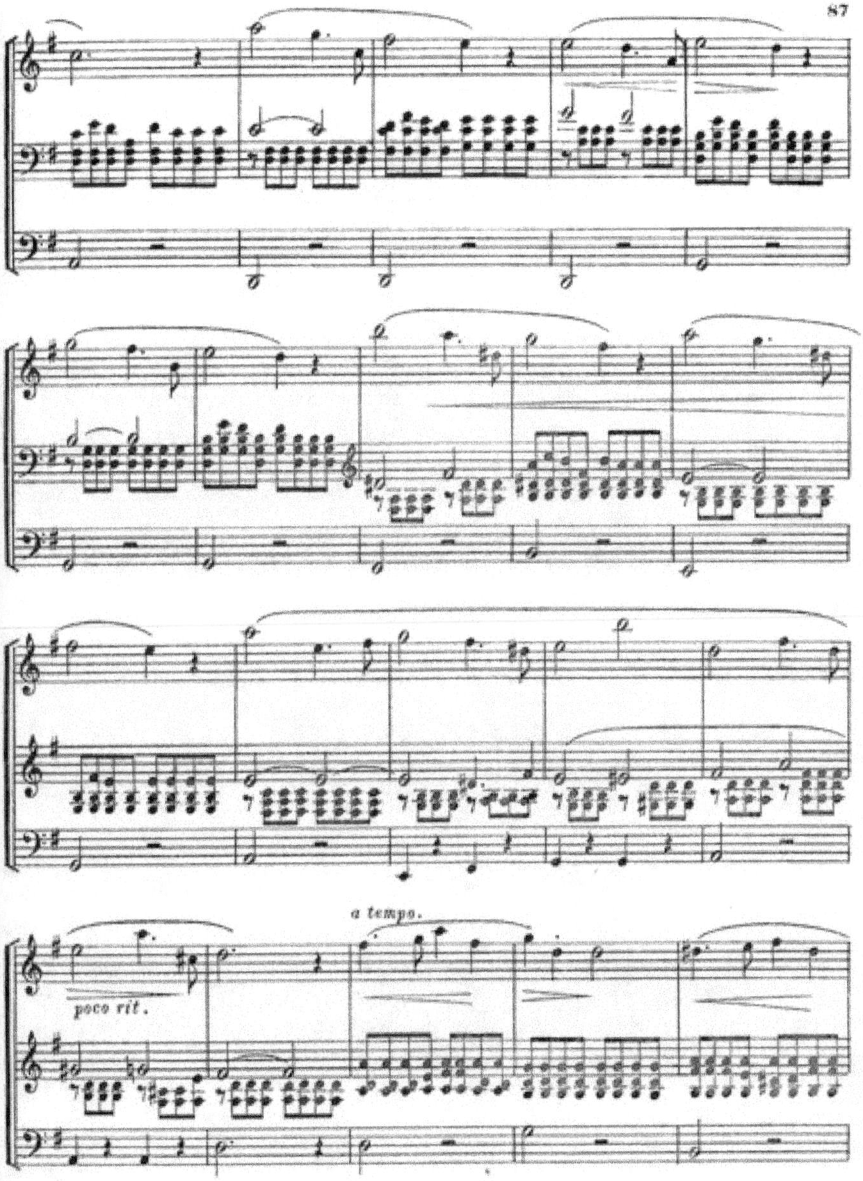
a tempo.
poco rit.

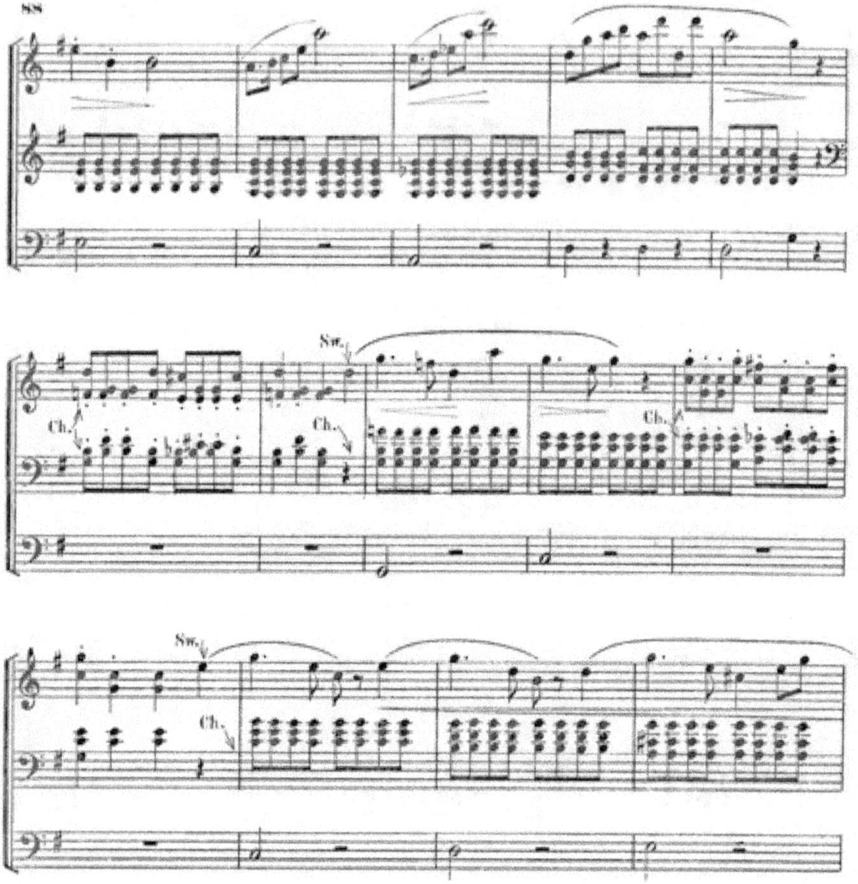
Sw.
Ch.
Ch.
Ch.
Sw.
Ch.
Sw.
Ch.
rall.

MIXTURES.

(FOUR RANKS.)

Mr. E. M. Bowman has gone to Europe for the summer.

Mr. Ben Sykes has been appointed organist of Trinity Church, Glasgow.

Mr. S. Round has been chosen organist of Portsmouth Parish Church, England.

Mr. W. S. Hoyte gave an organ recital in Royal Albert Hall, London (Sunday afternoon series), June 26.

Miss Charlotte Welles, organist of the Church of the Incarnation, New York, has gone to Paris to study with Widor.

Mr. Will C. Taylor, who has been studying with Guilmant in Paris for the past year and a half, has returned to New York.

An excellent half-tone portrait of Mr. E. M. Bowman may be found in the July number of *Music* published by Mr. W. S. B. Mathews, Chicago, Ill.

The fall examinations for those who wish to study the organ in the National Conservatory of Music, New York, are announced for Sept. 12 and 13.

The new organ in the Middletown, Conn., Opera House, which was destroyed by fire so soon after its completion, will be replaced by a new one in September.

It is rumored that the organ in Grace Church, New York, is to be somewhat altered before the fall, the present location of the console not giving entire satisfaction.

Mr. Clarence Eddy will remain in Chicago a large part of the summer, as he has a large class of pupils. A much needed vacation will be taken later in the season.

An organ recital was given in St. Saviour's Church, London, by Mr. J. Herbert Olding, on June 17. The programme included Concerto in B flat, Händel; Prelude and Fugue in F minor, Bach; and Fanfare, Lemmens.

Mr. E. H. Lemare has been chosen organist of Holy Trinity Church, London, where there is a large four-manual organ which was constructed by Walker & Son of Ludwigsburg, Würtemberg.

The organ recitals at the Royal Albert Hall, London, are attended by several thousand people every Sunday afternoon. Amongst the organists who have played with success have been : Messrs. H. L. Balfour, W. S. Hoyte, Sydney Naylor, and H. C. Tonking.

The *American Art Journal* for July 2 contains a history of the Music Teachers' National Association, illustrated with portraits of a number of the prominent members of the Association, among which are the familiar faces of Mr. E. M. Bowman of Vassar College and Mr. Arthur Foote of Boston.

A series of weekly organ recitals is being given in St. Michael's Church, Cornhill, London. The following organists were announced as engaged during the past two months : June 1, Dr. Peace ; June 15, Mr. W. De Manby Sergison ; June 22, Mr. W. J. Reynolds ; June 29, Mr. Fountain Meen ; July 6, Dr. W. J. Reynolds ; July 13, Dr. Westbrook ; July 20, Dr. W. J. Reynolds ; July 27, Dr. Pringuer.

Mr. Clarence Eddy suffered a serious loss by fire a few weeks ago. He was in New York City at the time, whither he had gone to wish his wife and her pupil, Mrs. Catherine L. Fisk, *bon voyage*, as they were departing for England, where they will remain till September. Mr. Eddy lost all his piano music, oratorios, cantatas, operas, and orchestral scores, besides a thousand dollars' worth of furniture. Most fortunately his organ library was nearly all saved.

On June 1 Dr. A. L. Peace, of Glasgow, opened a fine new organ of three manuals and fifty stops, built by Mr. J. J. Binns of Leeds for Baillie Street Chapel, Rochdale. Dr. Peace played an interesting programme of compositions ranging from Bach to Moranli, his own "Sonata da Camera" meeting with much acceptance. The organ occupies a novel position. The console is entirely separated from the instrument, and is fixed in the centre of the north gallery : around this console are seats for sixty singers, the organ divided on each side filling up the remaining area. The action is the builder's patent tubular-pneumatic system, and two of Mr. Binns's hydraulic engines are used to generate the wind ; the latter are in the vestry below. The cases are decorated, and there are 110 decorated front pipes. — *London Musical News.*

In 1756 an organ was built by Adrian Smith of London for King's Chapel of Boston. It is said to have been played upon and approved by Händel, and cost £500. It continued in use in the church until 1860, 104 years, when it was reconstructed and enlarged. In 1884 Hook & Hastings of Boston, in building a new organ for King's Chapel, retained some of the old stops and pipes, the new organ being built within the old oaken case, which with the gilded crown and mitre presents to the eye the same appearance as when originally put in the church. Additions and improvements are now being made in the organ by Mr. Hastings, which are to be completed for use when service is resumed in the fall.

Mr. A. E. Bizzey, A. C. O., was the recipient of a marble clock with an inscription on silver, and two volumes of "The Organist's Quarterly Journal," on Thursday, the 23d ult., on the occasion of his leaving Wood Green Congregational Church to take up his duties as organist and choirmaster at Putney Union Congregational Church. Mr. Bizzey has occupied the position of organist and choirmaster at the Wood Green Congregational Church during the past five years, and the presentation was made by the secretary of the church in behalf of the choir and congregation, the minister, Rev. W. G. Horder, adding two volumes of his own works as a personal testimony of esteem. — *London Musical News.*

Mr. Adam Wright of Birmingham (England) is a veteran organist. At the age of eighty-one he is hale and hearty, and full of reminiscences of his long life and work. An organist at the age of fifteen, he played for forty years at Carr's Lane Chapel, Birmingham, and recalls the conservatism of the older Congregationalists in the matter of music. "I have been called a pope," says Mr. Wright, "for advocating anthems, chanting, and sanctuses." At a Christmas-day service at Carr's Lane, about 1844, Psalm xlv. was chanted. The advocates of use and wont were horrified. They arranged a deputation to Rev. John Angell James on the subject of this shocking innovation. Mr. James refused to see the deputation, but announced next Sunday that, for the sake of the weaker brethren, there would be no more chanting. — *London Musical Herald.*

THE ANNUAL CONVENTIONS.

Nearly all the State music associations, as well as the National Association, held their annual conventions during the past month. While it is not within the province of this journal to record all the work of these useful organizations, a brief summary of that part of each convention which was devoted to the organ will, no doubt, prove of interest.

The fifteenth annual convention of the Music Teachers' National Association was held in Cleveland, Ohio, July 5 to 8. Among the thirteen officers of the association elected for the following year we find the names of the following organists : Mr. E. M. Bowman, President ; Mr. Gerrit Smith, one of the three constituting the executive committee ; and Messrs. Arthur Foote and A. A. Stanley on the examining committee for American compositions.

At the first evening concert, Mr. Geo. A. Parker of Syracuse performed a Toccata of Bach. At the second afternoon concert, Mr. W. B. Colson, Jr., of Cleveland, performed Meditation in B, by Aloys Clausmann, and Concert Piece of H. W. Parker. At the second evening concert. Mr. Wm. C. Carl of New York played Pastorale (new), Georges, McMasters ; Laus Deo (Messe de Mariage, Theo. Dubois) ; Allegro and Aria, from Concerto No. 10 of Händel; and "Marche de la Symphonie," "Ariane" of Guilmant. On the last afternoon and evening, Mr. H. G. Archer, of Pittsburgh, played a Fantasie in E-flat by Saint-Saëns; and Mr. N. J. Corey, of Detroit, gave Rheinberger's Sonata, No. 15. Among the other organists present were Messrs. H. C. Macdougal of Providence, J. H. Howe of Greencastle, Ind., and H. O. Fatmun, Springfield, O.

The New York State Music Teachers' Association held its fourth annual meeting in Syracuse, June 28-30. Prominent organists among the working staff were: Mr. S. N. Penfield of New York, Mr. John Hyatt Brewer of Brooklyn, and Mr. Gerrit Smith of New York. Mr. Wm. C. Carl performed the Toccata from the Fifth Organ Symphony, a Communion (MS.) of Guilmant, and Allegro from Concerto No. 10 of Händel; Mr. John Hyatt Brewer rendered "The Holy City" of Dudley Buck, Autumn Sketch, J. H. Brewer, and Andante, Homer N. Bartlett; and Mr. Geo. A. Parker performed Thiele's Theme and Variations in A flat and Wagner's Overture to "Tannhäuser," at the second session. At the opening of the third session Mr. Carl played "Marche de la Symphonie" from "Ariane" by Guilmant. In the afternoon Mr. Gerrit Smith read a paper on "Organ Playing," and Mr. Chas. H. Morse of Brooklyn performed the following selections:—

Concert Piece in A minor	. . . .	Whiting
Cantabile	. . . .	Lemaigre
Cantilena Pastorale	. . . .	Gibson
Fugue in E minor, Op. 48, No. 5	. . .	Salomé
Romanza, Op. 22, No. 2, for Organ and 'Cello	.	J. H. Brewer
Grand Fantasia, Op. 137, No. 3	. . . . .	H. N. Bartlett

Mr. S. N. Penfield received a vote of thanks and a gift of $200 for his valuable services as President, and Messrs. J. H. Brewer and Gerrit Smith were chosen on the programme committee for the coming year.

The Connecticut Music Teachers' Association held its third annual convention in Bridgeport, July 5, 6, and 7. Among the officers are the following organists: Mr. Alex. S. Gibson of Waterbury, President; Mr. F. A. Fowler, New Haven, Mr. A. L. Towne, Rockville, and Mr. Geo. A. Kies, Norwich, among the Vice-Presidents.

On the afternoon of the first day the following programme of organ music was given in the First Presbyterian Church:—

Prelude and Fugue in C minor (Mr. S. E. Ford) . Bach
Sonata, Op. 56 (Mr. A. L. Towne) . . . . Guilmant
Rhapsodie on Breton Melodies (Mr. W. R. Hedden) Saint-Saëns
Sonata No. 1 (Mr. Geo. A. Kies) . . . Mendelssohn
Allegro in F sharp minor (Mr. S. R. Ford) . . Guilmant
Andante from Symphony in D (Mr. A. L. Towne) Haydn
Toccata and Fugue in D minor (Mr. W. R. Hedden) Bach
Variations on "God save the Queen" (Mr. Geo. A. Kies) . . . . House

The following resolutions, in the direction of uniformity in the construction of church and concert organs, were adopted at a meeting of organists held in connection with the third Convention of the Connecticut Music Teachers' Association, July 7, 1892.

Resolved, — That in order to secure greater uniformity in organ construction, especially as regards those portions of the mechanism with which the player has directly to do, we earnestly recommend to all organ-builders, and to those engaged in preparing organ specifications, the observance of the following points, based upon resolutions and recommendations adopted some time ago by the English College of Organists, but modified so as to conform more nearly to modern requirements.

1. That the compass of the Pedal organ be from CCC to 1, — 30 keys, — whatever the size of the organ.

2. That the pedals be parallel with top facings, but without radiation or concavity; the long keys not less than seven inches in length; the short keys not less than six- and one-half inch long; the distance from centre to centre of two adjacent keys to be two and one-half inches.

3. That a plumb-line dropped from the middle e key of the manuals fall on the centre C of the pedal-board.

4. That a plumb-line dropped from the front of the Great organ keys fall two inches nearer the player than the front of the centre short key of the pedal-board.

5. That the height of the upper surface of the Great organ natural key, immediately over the centre of the pedal-board, be thirty-two inches above the upper surface of the centre natural key of the pedal-board.

6. That the relation between the manuals and pedals be subservient to the fixed relative position of the Great manual and the pedal-board, as already defined; it being understood that the position of the Great manual shall determine the position of the other manuals.

7. That it is undesirable to alter the relative positions of the several manual key-boards, as commonly found; viz., Swell above the Great, Choir (or Solo, if so named, in an instrument of but three manuals) below Great, and Solo above Swell.

8. That it is desirable that the name of the third manual, when there are but three, shall be Choir, not Solo, organ.

9. That the compass of the manuals shall be from CC to e in altissimo (e⁴); viz., sixty-one keys.

10. That the length of the manual natural keys be five and one-half inches, and that the amount of overlapping of the upper manuals be one and one-half inches.

11. That the height from the upper surface of one manual key to the upper surface of the corresponding key of the next manual shall not exceed two and one-half inches.

12. That the positions of the draw-stops belonging to the various manuals and to the pedals be as follows: those of the Great, Choir, and Solo organs, on the right of the player; those of the Swell and Pedal organs, on the left.

13. That the positions of all the mechanical draw-stops be over the upper manual; the Tremolo stops on the left; that the Pedal couplers, then the other mechanical draw-stops; all to be distinctly grouped by spacings. When, however, the couplers are operated by pneumatic pistons or electric buttons, there should be placed below the manuals to which they respectively belong.

14. That the several groups of draw-stops be placed in the following relative positions: left-hand side, from top to bottom, Swell organ, Pedal organ; right-hand side, from top to bottom, Solo organ (fourth manual), Great Organ, Choir organ (or Solo, when so named in an organ of but three manuals).

15. That the swell-shades shall be hung vertically, and operated by a suitable-shaped pedal placed in a properly prepared opening in the knee-board, over the space between the middle E and F of the pedal-board. If there be swell-pedals other than that affecting the Swell organ, they are to be placed in the same opening with it, and to the left of it, and so arranged that they may be operated together (by one foot) or separately.

16. That the order of the composition pedals be, from the centre outward, from f or ƒ to ƒƒ; and that the various sets be distinctly grouped, and that the order of combination thumb-pistons be, from left to right, from ƒ or ƒƒ to ƒ.

17. That the coupler of the Great organ to the Pedal organ be operated by a reversible pedal, located near the centre of the knee-board, in addition to the usual draw-stop.

18. That the several groups of composition and other mechanical pedals stand in the following order from left to right: Pedal organ, Swell organ, Pedal couplers, Great organ. It is recommended that all pedals which operate couplers be placed on a slightly higher level than the composition pedals; if composition pedals be applied to the Choir and Solo organs, that they project from the knee-board at the right of the player, at a different level from that of the adjoining sets.

RECOMMENDATIONS.

1. That the consideration of organ-builders be directed to the widely expressed desire for some means of operating the swell, in addition to the ordinary swell-pedal.

2. That all composition pedals affect proportionate combinations of the Pedal organ.

3. That a series of vents, one of which shall entirely silence the Pedal organ, be provided, to be operated by locking pedals, to reduce (or silence) the Pedal organ, without affecting its draw-stops.

4. That the draw-stops be arranged in terraces.

5. That all draw-stop knobs, placed on either side of the player, have oblique faces; but that, in case of large organs, the terraces be placed obliquely instead, at an angle of thirty degrees.

6. That all centre-pins be thoroughly secured.

7. That the attention of those engaged in the preparation of organ specifications be directed to the desirability of including in the Pedal organ, stops of sixteen, eight, and four feet, of characteristic qualities of tone, suitable for melodic use.

8. That the Choir (or Solo) organ, with the Fifteenth, reeds, and mutation-stops of the Great organ, be enclosed in a separate swell-box.

Signed,

F. A. FOWLER,
ALEX. S. GIBSON, } Committee.
GEO. A. KIES.

CORRESPONDENCE.

MONSTER ORGANS.

To the Editor of " The Organ " :

OBSERVING, at the close of an interesting article on " Monster Organs," in your July issue, a quotation from a letter of Mr. W. T. Best, stating, among other matters, that " No organ need have more than fifty stops," it occurred to me, — as doubtless it did to many of your organist-readers, that fifty is a small number of stops to distribute among four manuals and pedal, and I went to work to devise a specification of such an organ as would suit me, premising unlimited funds and a proper location. The result is given below ; with all deference to Mr. Best, one may venture to differ from him ; and I fail to find in this specification of eighty sounding stops any unnecessary repetitions of quality, or any stop which would be "a nuisance to the player." The only one as to which I have doubt is the Gt. Quint ; that may be needless.

As the report of the meeting of organists, which adopted the resolutions printed in another column, was made by me, let me say that due consideration was given to the question of " C under c," raised in your June issue, and that the meeting was unanimous that such relation between pedals and manuals is the correct one.

Ideal specification of an organ to have eighty sounding stops on four manuals and a pedal.

Manual Compass, CC to c⁴, 61 keys.
Pedal Compass, CCC to f, 30 keys.

GREAT.		SWELL.	
1 Open Diapason	16 Ft.	1 Bourdon	16 Ft.
2 Open Diapason	8 "	2 Open Diapason	8 "
3 Flute à Pavillon	8 "	3 Stopped Diapason	8 "
4 Gamba	8 "	4 Clarinet Flute	8 "
5 Gemshorn	8 "	5 Geigen Principal	8 "
6 Doppel Flocte	8 "	6 Salicional	8 "
7 Melodia	8 "	7 Dolce	8 "
8 Dulciana	8 "	8 Vox Celestia	8 "
9 Quint	5⅓ "	9 Wald Flocte	4 "
10 Flauto Traverso	4 "	10 Violina	4 "
11 Octave	4 "	11 Salicet	4 "
12 Geigen Octave	4 "	12 Flautino	2 "
13 Twelfth	2⅔ "	13 Cornett Dolce	3 Rks.
14 Fifteenth	2 "	14 Oboe	8 Ft.
15 Mixture	4 Rks.	15 Cornopean	8 "
16 Trumpet	16 Ft.	16 Vox Humana	8 "
17 Trumpet	8 "		
18 Clarion	4 "		

CHOIR.		SOLO.	
1 Dulciana	16 Ft.	1 Gamba	16 Ft.
2 Open Diapason	8 "	2 Open Diapason	8 "
3 Flauto Traverso	8 "	3 Stentorphone	8 "
4 Spitz Flocte	8 "	4 Orchestral Flute	8 "
5 Viola da Gamba	8 "	5 Viola Major	8 "
6 Quintadena	8 "	6 Zvoline	8 "
7 Dolcissimo	8 "	7 Concert Flute	4 "
8 Flute d'Amour	4 "	8 Violin	4 "
9 Gambette	4 "	9 Piccolo Harmonique	2 "
10 Octave	4 "	10 Euphone (free reed)	16 "
11 Flageolet	2 "	11 Orchestral Oboe	8 "
12 Mixture	3 Rks.	12 Tuba Mirabilis	16 "
13 Clarinet	8 Ft.	13 Tuba Mirabilis	8 "
14 Cor Anglais (free reed)	8 "		
15 Vox Angelica	4 "		

PEDAL.			
1 Open Diapason	32 Ft.	10 Traverse Flute	8 Ft.
2 Bourdon	32 "	11 Octave	4 "
3 Open Diapason	16 "	12 Violin	4 "
4 Violone	16 "	13 Flauto Traverso	4 "
5 Bourdon	16 "	14 Super Octave	2 "
6 Dulciana	16 "	15 Trombone	16 "
7 Quint	10⅔ "	16 Tromba	8 "
8 Doppel Flocte	8 "	17 Bassoon	8 "
9 Violoncello	8 "	18 Mixture	3 Rks.

The Choir organ, with the fifteenth, reeds and mutation stops of the Great organ, to be in a separate swell-box, the Solo organ in a third box, the swell pedals arranged to be operated together or separately. The usual unison couplers.

Yours cordially,

ALEX. S. GIBSON.

WATERBURY, CONN., July 16, 1892.

THE CHURCH GREEN ORGAN.

To the Editor of " The Organ " :

WILL you allow me to correct a statement made in the article written by Mr. Wm. Horatio Clarke (June number) regarding the organ formerly in the church called Church Green, which he writes was in use in a church at Providence, R. I., as late as 1872 ? Since that date, or a little earlier, the said organ has been in the church at the corner of Camden and Tremont Streets, Boston, called the " New South Church " — Unitarian. I have known the organ since 1860, and about six years ago it was partially rebuilt by our house. If I remember rightly, the plate bears the date of 1844, and to this day the organ is a very fine-toned instrument.

Yours, etc.,

GEORGE H. RYDER.

NEW ORGANS.

MESSRS. HOOK & HASTINGS have just shipped a two-manual organ to the First Congregational Church of Owosso, Mich. The scheme of the instrument is as follows : —

GREAT ORGAN.		SWELL ORGAN.	
Open Diapason	8 Ft.	Bourdon Bass	16 Ft.
Viola da Gamba	8 "	Bourdon Treble	16 Ft.
Dulciana	8 "	Open Diapason	8 "
Melodia	8 "	Salicional	8 "
Octave	4 "	Æoline	8 "
Flute d'Amour	4 "	Vox Celeste	8 "
Twelfth	3 "	Stopped Diapason	8 "
Fifteenth	2 "	Harmonic Flute	4 "
Trumpet	8 "	Violina	4 "
		Dolce Cornet	3 Rks.
		Oboe	8 ft.
		Bassoon	8 ft.

PEDAL MOVEMENTS.

Piano & Forte Combinations in Gt.
" " " " Sw.
Gt. to Ped. (reversible).

PEDAL.	
Double Open Diapason	16 Ft.
Bourdon	16 "

The usual Couplers.

New organ for Kimberley, S. Africa, to be erected by Sept. 1, by Messrs. Norman Bros. & Beard of Norwich, England.

GREAT ORGAN.		SWELL ORGAN.	
Open Diapason	16 Ft.	Bourdon	16 Ft.
Open Diapason (major)	8 "	Open Diapason	8 "
Open Diapason (minor)	8 "	Rohr Gedeckt	8 "
2d Diapason	8 "	Salicional	8 "
Wald Flote	8 "	Vox Angelica	8 "
Principal	4 "	Principal	4 "
Harmonic Flute	4 "	Lieblich Flote	4 "
Mixture	2 Rks.	Fifteenth	2 "
Mixture	3 "	Mixture	3 Rks.
Tuba	8 ft.	Contra Fagotto	16 Ft.
		Oboe	8 "
		Horn	8 "
		Clarion	4 "
		Vox Humana	8 "

CHOIR ORGAN.		PEDAL ORGAN.	
Gamba	8 Ft.	Open Diapason	16 Ft.
Dulciana	8 "	Open Diapason	16 "
Lieblich Gedacht	8 "	Bourdon	16 "
Dulcet	4 "	Quint	10⅔ "
Flauto Traverso	4 "	Violoncello	8 "
Clarinet	8 "	Trombone	16 "

3 Composition Pedals to Gt.
4 " " " Sw.
Gt. to Ped. (reversible).
Octave.

The usual Couplers and Sw. to Gt.

A small two-manual organ, having seven speaking stops, has been placed in Grace Presbyterian Church, Brooklyn, N.Y., by Messrs. Chapman & Simmes of New York.

Messrs. Hook & Hastings have just completed a two-manual organ in the Church of the Covenant, Washington, D.C., to replace the instrument which was recently destroyed by fire, and which was built by Mr. Hilborne L. Roosevelt.

A small two-manual organ is being erected in the First Baptist Church of Shelbyville, Ky., the builders being Messrs. Hook & Hastings.

QUESTIONS AND ANSWERS.

All questions must be accompanied by the full name and address of the writer and, if received by the 10th of the month, will usually be answered in the following number of THE ORGAN.

Only such questions as refer to the organ, to organists, organ-builders, or to organ music, will be answered.

Correspondents are requested to write their questions in a clear and concise manner, writing on only one side of the paper.

DUET. Please inform me the names of some duets for the organ.

ANS. Sonata in D minor, Op. 30, Merkel; Fantasia, Hesse.

BROOKLYN. Please tell me how to pronounce Rüfer and Reubke.

ANS. Approximately, Ree-fur (impossible to indicate the French *u*). Koyb-ker (the second *r* not sounded).

Y. Please name some interesting marches for the organ.

ANS. Festival March in D, Smart; Marche Solennelle, Lemaigre; War March of Priests, Mendelssohn (arranged by Best); Triumphal March, Dudley Buck.

ORGAN. I am endeavoring to induce the congregation for whom I play to get a new organ, but cannot give them any idea of how much it would cost. How can I estimate the expense of a new organ?

ANS. Submit your list of stops to the organ-builders whose advertisements are found in this journal, for an approximate cost.

TEACHER. In teaching the organ, should I require students to practise several lessons with the hands alone to become familiar with the organ touch, before taking up the pedal?

ANS. Most certainly not. The pedal should be taken up in the first lesson. A few lessons devoted to the pedal alone before touching the manuals would be advantageous.

A. G. M. Please name a few easy, melodious voluntaries suitable for a two-manual organ.

ANS. Three Andantes, Porter (Novello Ewer & Co.).
Andante Religioso
Communion } Deshayes (A. P. Schmidt).
Serenade, Schubert-Trueste (A. P. Schmidt).
"Two Preludes," Merkel (Novello Ewer & Co.).

STUDENT. Why do I get so fatigued by practising two hours on the organ when I can practise five hours on the piano with less effort?

ANS. Organ practice requires three times as much muscular effort as piano practice, and is correspondingly more fatiguing. Almost no one can endure more than a third as much of the former as of the latter.

G. B. D. I have a pupil who practises on a pedal piano, and I think that he practises faithfully, but after studying a year he will not hold down the notes which are tied through several measures. What course should I adopt to assist him?

ANS. This is the one argument against using a pedal piano for early organ practice. Nothing but practising all the time on an organ till the difficulty is overcome can be recommended.

SONATA. 1. In Guilmant's first sonata how can I play that measure of the pedal solo in which E flat above the staff occurs? My pedals run only to D.

ANS. Play that one note with the octave below it on the great (L. H.). The octave below gives somewhat the effect of the 16 Ft. tone in the pedal.

2. In the Introduction, there are several notes above the compass of my pedals. How can I play those notes?

ANS. The same way.

3. Is it necessary to repeat the first part of the first movement?

ANS. We have seldom heard it repeated.

4. On the last page of the first movement, the theme occurs in the pedal in octaves (key of D flat), which is impossible on my organ. What would you advise?

ANS. In the later French editions of this sonata, Mons. Guilmant has omitted the upper notes of these octaves.

CIPHERINGS.

Mr. Editor: WEST BILLERICA, MASS.

DEAR SIR,—The committee of our church, from motives of economy, have decided to make no appropriation for music, and have engaged me to play the organ for one year, beginning next month, for the practice it will afford me. I have only played the accordion and guitar, excepting a few gospel hymns on the piano. Hoping that you might aid myself and others through your columns, I would like some help from your valuable experience before beginning my engagement.

I have been to the organ once for practice, but could not make it go at all. The keys would make no sound whatever on striking them. There are twelve stopples on one side, and thirteen on the other, and not knowing which ones to pull, I did not dare to touch them. I tried to pump it by working with my right foot a large handle which was placed underneath, but it only made a slamming noise. I got a carpenter to bore some holes along the bottom of the front of the case to let the wind in, but even then it would not go.

There is one stopple marked "Bellows All-arm," which, when pulled out, flies right back again. Perhaps if we had a new stopple put in place of it, I should be able to make the keys sound. There are two rows of keys, and I suppose that the highest one is for the treble, and the lowest for the bass. There is one stopple marked "Pedal Checker," which may have something to do with the keys not sounding. All the other stopples have unfamiliar names which I could not understand, which I will send to you after I can find out how to make the keys sound.

The committee said that they could tell me nothing about the organ, but they thought some dust might have got into it and stopped it up and so put it out of tune that it would not go, or else perhaps the strings had got rusty or broken. They told me that they should want no involuntaries nor outvoluntaries played, so that people could hear each other talk before and after service, also that they should want no interludes nor excludes, but for me to play with all the noise I could beat on with when they were all singing, and to play lively music.

Hoping that you can give me some information, so that I can fill the position and do my duty as a humble church-member, I remain,

Respectfully yours,

SARAH L. BROWN.

ORGAN CONCERTS.

ORGAN CONCERT by Mr. Clarence Eddy, assisted by Mrs. Catherine L. Fisk, contralto. Independent Church, Jamestown, N.Y.

PROGRAMME.

Grand Festival March	George Carter
Overture to Oberon	Weber
Song, "Patria"	Mattei
Andantino	Chauvet
Funeral March of a Marionette	Gounod
"Am Meer"	Schubert
Spring Song	Mendelssohn
Songs, "Wait Thou Still"	Franck
"Calm as the Night"	Bohm
The Celebrated Largo	Händel-Whitney
Concert Fugue in G	Krebs
Nuptial Benediction	Dubois
Finale, Laus Deo	
Song, "What the Chimney Sang"	Gertrude Griswold
Saint Cecilia Offertory, No. 2	Batiste

ORGAN CONCERT in First Presbyterian Church, Batavia, N.Y., by Mr. Wm. C. Carl, July 1.

Toccata and Fugue in D minor	J. S. Bach
Pastorale	Geo. McMaster
Laus Deo	Th. Dubois
Organ Concerto in D minor, No. 10	G. F. Handel
Marche de la Symphonie "Ariane"	Alex. Guilmant
Marche Nuptiale	Ch. M. Widor
Romance (Durand)	Fr. Thomé
Minuetto	Filippo Capocci
Communion	Alex. Guilmant
Marche Gothique	Th. Salomé
Postlude Nuptiale	Alex. Guilmant

Songs were rendered by Mrs. Antonia Sawyer, contralto, and Mr. David G. Henderson, tenor.

Mr. WILLIAM CHURCHILL HAMMOND gave three organ recitals in the Second Congregational Church, Holyoke, Mass., during the month of June. The programme of the last recital contained only compositions of Josef Rheinberger, and is appended.

Prelude in C minor, Op. 27.	
Sonata-Pastorale No. 3, in G, Op. 88.	
Sonata No. 5, in F Sharp, Op. 111.	
Sonata No. 8, in E Minor, Op. 132.	
"Evening Quiet,"	From Characteristic Pieces, Op. 156.
"Vision,"	

ORGAN RECITAL by Mr. F. R. Adams in St. Paul's Church, Delaware, O., July 19.

Pastorale in F	Whiting
Fantasia in F	Best
Concert Etude in A minor (MS.)	Whiting
Fantasie on "O Sanctissima"	Lux
Offertoire in D minor	Batiste
Concert variations on "The Star Spangled Banner"	Paine

(Miss Mary N. Bing, alto, and Miss Nellie Brown, reader, assisted.)

A SERIES of Sunday afternoon organ recitals is being given in the Royal Albert Hall, London, which contains the largest organ in England (built by Messrs. Henry Willis & Son). The programme of the recital for the 19th of June is before us, in which Mr. H. C. Tonking performed the following selections:—

Fantasia on a Welsh March	Best
Intermezzo	A. Macbeth
Air du Dauphin	Roeckel
Funeral March and Hymn of Seraphs	Guilmant
Norwegian Bridal Procession	Grieg
Prayer from "Moses in Egypt"	Rossini

The programme was interspersed with songs by Miss Emily Horning and Mr. William Green.

Continued on page 95.

ORGAN CONCERTS

Continued from page 93.

ORGAN RECITAL in First Presbyterian Church, New York, by Mr. Wm. C. Carl, July 9.

Marche de la Symphonie " Ariane "	Alex. Guilmant
Aria and Allegro Tenth Organ Concerto	G. F. Handel
Gavotte	Neobarch
Toccata in E minor	F. de la Tombelle

Mr. Carl was assisted by the Gounod Quartette.

INAUGURAL RECITAL by Mr Clarence Eddy on the new organ in the Swedish Immanuel Church, Chicago. (Specification given in THE ORGAN for May.) In the miscellaneous programme Mr. Eddy performed the following compositions : —

Overture to Oberon	Weber
Largo	Handel
Concert Fugue in G	Kachs
Funeral March and Seraphic Song	Guilmant
Fantasie	Matthisen Hansen
Coronation March	Johann Svendsen
Nuptial March }	
Finale }	Dubois

AT the opening of the reconstructed organ in First German Baptist Church of Newark, N.J., Mr. Chas. F. Eichborn performed the following compositions : Vorspiel, Gleason (ar. by Eddy); Pleyel's Hymn with Variations, Burnap; Offertoire in G, Wely; Fugue in A minor, Bach; The Evening Star, Wagner; Communion in G, Batiste; and Overture to "Wm. Tell," Rossini-Back.
The organ was rebuilt by Messrs. Chapman & Symnes.

THE following selections were performed by Mr. Wm. C. Carl at the Commencement Exercises of the Bloomfield (N. J.) High School, June 24.

Marche de la Symphonie " Ariane "	Alex. Guilmant
Romance	Fr. Thomé
Allegro (10th Concerto)	G. F. Handel
Pastorale	Georges McMaster
Minuetto	Filippo Capocci
Variations on a National Air	Dudley Buck
Postlude Nuptiale	Alex. Guilmant

ORGAN RECITAL by Mr. F. R. Adams, in Delaware, O., under the auspices of the Epworth League.

Vorspiel to " Lohengrin "	Wagner
Prelude and Fugue in A minor	Bach
Sonata in A minor	Whiting
Offertoire in C minor	Batiste
Funeral march of a Marionette	Gounod
Fantasia on Irish airs (MS.)	Whiting
March and Chorus from " Tannhäuser "	Wagner-Adams

(Miss Flora Williams and Mr. W. B. Day, assisted.)

WE select the following paragraphs from a long account of the opening of a new organ, built by Mr. Frank Roosevelt, in the Presbyterian Church, Decatur, Ill. Mr. Clarence Eddy was the organist.

" In many respects perhaps the entertainment given at the new Presbyterian Church last night, possessed more interesting features than any ever given to the public of Decatur. First, there was the new church resplendent with its richness of architectural detail, probably the finest structure of its kind in Central Illinois, for the first time open to the public, which testified to its interest by crowding the building, both for inspection of the commodious and convenient arrangements, and to listen to the grand and inspiring strains of the king of instruments; then the organ, a noble work of mechanical and musical skill and the highest possible exponent of the organ builders' art; and lastly, the performer, the leading organist of the West — to the manor born — who has by the power of his art placed himself at the head of his profession, and whose masterly work has been heard and praised by the greatest artists and the severest critics, — and probably no man in the West is better fitted to interpret organ music than Clarence Eddy of Chicago.

Of the organ it is perhaps enough to say that it is one of the best of its kind, and the name of its maker, Frank Roosevelt, is a guaranty of its excellence.

All the fine points of the instrument were brought out by Mr. Eddy to the best advantage, and a rare treat was experienced by those who heard him last night. . . .

This, however, did not prevent a generous reception to all of Mr. Eddy's numbers. The softer and sweeter strains of the Andantino by Chauvet and the Funeral March by Guilmant were perhaps the best received by the audience, although the Schubert melody, "Ave Meer," was highly appreciated by those who had heard the moaning of the waves and the pounding of the surf upon the sea-shore.

ORGAN RECITAL in Plymouth Congregational Church, Minneapolis, Minn., by Mr. J. Warren Andrews, assisted by Miss Annie M. Sharell, Soprano, Miss Eva Lillian Merrill, Contralto, Mr. Fritz Schlacter, Cellist, Mr. Jessie Schuman, Violinist, July 28.

Solemn March in E flat	Smart
Songs, with Violin Obligato,	
"Dreams"	Strelzky
" Angel's Promise "	Ischrend
Violin Solo, " Romance "	Becker
Contralto Solo, " Wild Flowers "	Barri
(Second Organ Symphony.)	
Adagio and Finale	Widor
Offertoire in G	Shuey
Soprano Solo, " The Message "	Blumenthal
Duet, with Violin Obligato, Serenade	Schubert
Cello Solo, Andante Expressivo from 3d Concerto	Goltermann
Soprano Solo, " Canto di Lelia "	Nappé
Marche Cortège	Gounod

MR. SAMUEL A. BALDWIN has just completed a series of fifty Organ Recitals at the People's Church, St. Paul, Minn. The series covers a space between July 5, 1891, and July 9, 1892. The programmes have been most excellent. Appended is the last one : —

Fugue on Choral from " Le Prophète "	Liszt
Elegy, Op. 33	Tombelle
" On the Coast "	Buck
Minuet, Op. 40, No. 8	Salomé
Intermezzo from " Triumph of Love "	Baldwin
Fugue in D	Grison

Over three hundred compositions have been presented, representing seventy-three composers. The fifty recitals were given without repetition. Mr. Baldwin is a fine musician, and is doing a great deal musically for the Northwest.

J. W. A.

REVIEW OF NEW ORGAN MUSIC.

FROM RICHAULT & CO., PARIS.

Fantasia, in C minor, First Meditation, in B major, Andante, in D major. }	Aloys Claussmann.

Three extremely interesting pieces, composed by the organist of the cathedral at Clermont-Ferrand, which are written somewhat in the style of reveries, and contain many passages of striking originality. They are excellent works for the student who is somewhat advanced, to exercise his skill in registration, as their whole effect depends on a judicious selection of stops. With a fair-sized organ, a performer who has considerable skill in choosing suitable stops would find many beautiful passages.

VOL. I.　　　　SEPTEMBER, 1892.　　　　No. 5.

BACH

YEARLY SUBSCRIPTION $2.00.　　　　SINGLE COPIES 25 CTS.

THE ORGAN

DEVOTED TO

A MONTHLY JOURNAL

THE KING OF INSTRUMENTS

EINBERGER

GUILMANT

FRESCOBALDI

BUXTEHUDE

MERKEL

BEST

EVERETT · E · TRUETTE ·
EDITOR & PUBLISHER
149 A. TREMONT ST. BOSTON.

HANDEL

THE ORGAN.

Vol. I.   BOSTON, SEPTEMBER, 1892.   No. 5.

THE ORGAN.
A MONTHLY JOURNAL

DEVOTED TO THE KING OF INSTRUMENTS.

EVERETT E. TRUETTE, EDITOR AND PUBLISHER.

(Entered at the Boston, Mass., Post-office as second-class mail matter, June 1, 1892.)

CONTENTS:

FATHER SMITH.

STRANGE to say, there is no account extant of the early life of Bernard Schmidt, not even the date of his birth being known. Hamel's "*Traité Théorétique*" states that he was born about 1630. The sketch of his career after he settled in England, found in Hawkins's "History of Music," is here copied, being the most comprehensive to be found.

"Bernard Schmidt, or, as we pronounce the name, Smith, was a native of Germany, but of what city or province in particular is not known. Upon the invitations of foreign workmen to settle here, he came to England, and brought with him two nephews, the one named Gerard, the other Bernard; and, to distinguish him from these, the elder had the appellation of Father Smith. Immediately upon their arrival Smith was employed to build an organ for the royal chapel at Whitehall, but as it was built in great haste, it did not answer the expectations of those who were judges of his abilities. He had been but a few months here before Harris arrived from France, bringing with him a son named Renatus, who had been brought up in the business of organ-making under him; they met with little encouragement, for Dallans and Smith had all the business of the kingdom; but upon the decease of Dallans, in 1672, a competition arose between these two foreigners, which was attended with some remarkable circumstances. The elder Harris was in no degree a match for Smith, but his son Renatus was a young man of ingenuity and spirit, and succeeded so well in his endeavors to rival Smith, that at length he got the better of him.

"The contest between Smith and the younger Harris was carried on with great spirit; each had his friends and supporters, and the point of preference between them was hardly determined by that exquisite piece of workmanship of Smith, the organ now standing in the Temple Church; of the building thereof the following is the history, as related by a person who was living at the time, and intimately acquainted with both Smith and Harris.

"'Upon the decease of Mr. Dallans and the elder Harris,

Mr. Renatus Harris and Father Smith became great rivals in their employment, and several trials of skill there were betwixt them on several occasions; but the famous contest between these two artists was at the Temple Church, where a new organ was going to be erected towards the latter end of King Charles the Second's time; both made friends for that employment; but as the society could not agree about who should be the man, the Master of the Temple and the Benchers proposed that they both should set up an organ on each side of the church, which in about half a year or three-quarters of a year was done accordingly. Dr. Blow and Dr. Purcell, who was then in his prime, showed and played Father Smith's organ on appointed days to a numerous audience; and, till the other was heard, everybody believed that Father Smith certainly would carry it.

"'Mr. Harris brought Mr. Lully, organist to Queen Catherine, a very eminent master, to touch his organ, which brought Mr. Harris's organ into that vogue; they thus continued vying with one another near a twelvemonth.

"'Then Mr. Harris challenged Father Smith to make additional stops against a set time; these were the Vox-humane, the Cremona or Violin stop, the double Courtel or bass Flute, with some others I may have forgot.

"'These stops, as being newly invented, gave great delight and satisfaction to the numerous audience, and were so well imitated on both sides, that it was hard to judge the advantage to either. At last it was left to my Lord Chief Justice Jeffries, who was of that house, and he put an end to the controversy by pitching upon Father Smith's organ; so Mr. Harris's organ was taken away without loss of reputation, and Mr. Smith's remains to this day. . . . Now began the setting up of organs in the chiefest parishes in London, where for the most part Mr. Harris had the advantage of Father Smith, making, I believe, two to his one; among them some are reckoned very eminent; viz., the organ at Saint Bride's, Saint Lawrence near Guildhall, Saint Mary Ax, etc.'

"Notwithstanding the success of Harris, Smith was considered as an able and ingenious workman; and, in conse-

quence of this character, he was employed to build an organ
for the Cathedral of St. Paul; in which undertaking he
narrowly escaped being a great sufferer, for on the 27th day
of February, 1699, a fire broke out in a little room at the
west end of the North aisle of the church, enclosed for the
organ-builder's men, which, communicating itself towards
the organ, had probably consumed the same, and endangered
at least one side of the choir, but it was timely extinguished,
though not without damage to two of the pillars and some of
the fine carving by Gibbons. *Vide* "New View of London,"
457. The vulgar report was, that the plumbers, or some
others employed in soldering or repairing the metal pipes,
had been negligent of their fire; but the true cause of the
accident was never discovered. The organs made by Smith,
though in respect of the workmanship they are far short of
those of Harris, and even of Dallans, are justly admired, and
for the fineness of their tone have never yet been equalled.

"The name of Smith occurs in the lists of the chapel establishment from 1703 to 1709, inclusive, as organ-maker to
the chapel, and also to Queen Anne. He had a daughter
married to Christopher Schrider, a workman of his, who
about the year 1710 succeeded him in his places.

"The organ of St. Paul's, erected soon after the year
1700, had established the character of Smith as an artist;
whether Harris had been his competitor for building an instrument for that church, as he had been before at the Temple, does not now appear; but in the *Spectator*, No. 552, for
Dec. 3, 1712, is a recommendation of a proposal of Mr.
Renatus Harris, organ-builder, in these words, 'The am-

bition of this artificer is to erect an organ in St. Paul's Cathedral, over the west door, at the entrance into the body of
the church, which in art and magnificence shall transcend
any work of that kind ever before invented. The proposal
in perspicuous language sets forth the honor and advantage
such a performance would be to the British name, as well
that it would apply the power of sounds in a manner more
amazingly forcible than perhaps has yet been known, and I
am sure to an end much more worthy. Had the vast sums
which have been laid out upon operas without skill or conduct, and to no other purpose but to spend or vitiate our
understandings, been disposed this way, we should now perhaps have an engine so formed as to strike the minds of
half a people at once in a place of worship with a forgetful-
ness of present care and calamity, and a hope of endless
rapture, joy, and hallelujah hereafter.'"

Among the notable organs built by Father Smith, besides
those already named, may be mentioned an organ for Westminster Abbey, one for St. Giles-in-the-Fields, and one for
St. Margaret's, at which church Smith was elected organist,
with a salary of a hundred dollars a year. He was afterward appointed organ-maker in ordinary to the king, apartments in Whitehall being allotted to him, called in the old
plan "The Organ-builder's Workhouse." In 1683 he built
the organ in the Durham Cathedral. The organ in St. Paul's
was dedicated on Dec. 2, 1697. Father Smith died in 1708.

Organ for Processions

HISTORY OF THE ORGAN

IV.

THE above cut represents Paul Hoffaner, organist, in a
chariot, drawn by a camel, and is a fragment of one of Albert Dürer's paintings entitled "The Triumph of Maxi-
milian."

A few remarks concerning the general imperfections which
were prevalent in most organs in the middle of the seventeenth century will, perhaps, give a clearer idea of the value
of each invention and improvement. The swell-box was as
yet unknown, and while a few organs contained three manuals, the majority had but two, great and choir, with a
compass of GG to c³. Such mechanical accessories as combination pedals were unknown, and the pedal organ consisted almost entirely of stops borrowed from the great
(probably by means of the coupler). Considerable attention
was paid to the bellows, as the inequality of the wind was a
constant source of dissatisfaction. A German builder, named
Forner, of Wettin, invented the *anemometer*, for measuring the
pressure of the wind. By the aid of this little contrivance
the efforts to secure a steady supply of wind were more

fruitful, as it was possible to accurately test the effect of the
various experiments, the outcome of which was the placing
of weights upon the bellows, increasing the pressure of wind,
and producing a more steady supply.

Bernard Schmidt (see previous page), commonly called
Father Smith, to distinguish him from his son, who was also
named Bernard, was of German extraction. He
landed in England about the middle of the seventeenth century, in response to the advertised invitation for organ-builders to settle in that country.
His organs were of such excellence that his name
will ever remain foremost among the early masters
of the art. Such of his work as still remains,
notwithstanding all the inventions and improvements which have been made, can hardly be surpassed to-day; it is of such sterling quality. He was particularly careful in his choice of materials, — oak being a
favorite for wood-work, — and no flaw was ever patched, as
he preferred to put entirely new material and labor in the
place of anything which was imperfect. His voicing has
commanded the admiration of experts to the present day.

The famous contest between Father Smith and Renatus

Specie of
Mouth Organ

Harris about an organ for the Temple Church, which is one of the important events in the history of the organ, is fully described in the sketch of Father Smith. The contest ended in the acceptance of Smith's organ, which contained twenty-three stops. The case was hardly large enough, hence the pipes were crowded into a limited space. This organ contained the extraordinary addition of *quarter tones*, A-flat and D-sharp being distinct from G-sharp and E-flat. Smith also constructed organs for St. Paul's Cathedral, for the Durham Cathedral (also mentioned in the sketch of Father Smith), and two other very noteworthy instruments; viz., that of St. Catherine's, Leadenhall St., and the one in St. Peter's, Tiverton, all of which are still standing, though somewhat altered from their original specification. Smith was a performer as well as a builder, and held the position of organist at St. Margaret's, London, up to the time of his death, which probably occurred in 1708.

Bellows of the Organ in the Church of St. Ægidien in Sevenoaks, XVI. Century.

Thomas Harris and his son Renatus landed in England shortly after the Smiths, and became powerful rivals. Renatus, who succeeded his father, had some difficulty in establishing himself at the outset, but the contest with Smith gave him prestige in London, where he built some fine instruments, one of the finest of which is in the St. Sepulchre's Church, Snow Hill, and another in Christ's Church, Newgate Street, both of which have been rebuilt. He also placed organs in the cathedrals of Salisbury, Gloucester, and Worcester. Eventually he settled in Bristol, where he died in 1715.

(To be continued.)

NOTABLE ORGANS.

II.

HERTOGENBOSCH.

The splendid church of S. Jan Hertogenbosch, in North Brabant, contains an organ, the case of which is certainly the finest in Holland, and most probably the finest in Europe. The instrument dates from the year 1580, stands in a western gallery, and is of such vast proportions that the topmost portion of the woodwork rises to a height of 100 feet, and its depth from back to front is 10 feet. It would be difficult to conceive a more stately or magnificent design than is presented by this organ-case. The V-shaped towers are admirably contrived, and a splendid effect is obtained by the splaying backwards of the great side compartments of pipes. All the cornices and pilasters are richly carved, while carving is also lavishly used in the pipe-shades and great base-corbels of the case. The composition of the upper portion of the structure is extremely fine. The centre pipes of some of the compartments are elaborately chased and punched out, while the greater number are of burnished tin. The larger pipes in the side flats belong to the Great Organ Principal, which extends as far as thirty-two feet F, a rather remarkable compass. The instrument was built in the year 1580 by Cornellis Hoornbeck, but the case bears the date of 1602. The large amount of mixture work, and the original absence of pedal work, are striking features of this organ. The Pedal organ, which has been added in later times, is of very insufficient dimensions, and is remarkable as not possessing a sixteen feet Diapason. The effect of the large organ, with its bright pipes richly contrasting with the dark and sumptuously carved case, is really magnificent. The following is the list of the stops:—

GREAT ORGAN.
(*This manual extends to FFF.*)

Principal	24 Ft.
Octave	12 "
Super Octave	6 "
Quint	2 "
Mixture	8 to 14 kks.
Scharf	10 "
Trumpet	12 Ft.

UPPER WORK.

Bourdon	16 Ft.
Principal	8 "
Holflote	8 "
Quintadena	8 "
Octave	4 "
Octave	2 "
Tertian (Tierce & Larigot)	
Sesquialter	2 Rks.
Cymbal	3 "
Cornet discant	5 "
Trombone	16 Ft.

CHOIR ORGAN.
(*in front*)

Principal	8 Ft.
Quintaldena	8 "
Octave	4 "
Flote	4 "
Octave	2 "
Quint	1½ "
Mixture	5 to 8 Rks.
Scharf	½ "
Sesquialter	
Cornet discant	5 to 6 "
Trumpet	8 Ft.
Dulcian (Bassoon)	8 "

PEDAL ORGAN.
(*Added subsequently*)

Bourdon	8 Ft.
Trumpet	8 "
Bass Trumpet	16 "

ARTHUR G. HILL.

THE ORGAN.
BOSTON, SEPTEMBER, 1891.

THE ORGAN is published the first of every month. Subscription price $2.00 per year (foreign countries $2.50), payable in advance. Single copies, 25 cents.

Subscribers will please state with which number they wish their subscription to begin.

The paper will be sent to all patrons till the editor is notified by letter to discontinue.

Subscribers wishing the address of their paper changed must give the old as well as the new address.

Remittances should be made by registered letter, post-office order, or by check payable to Everett E. Truette.

Programmes of organ concerts, with press notices of the same, specifications of new organs, and items of general interest to the subscribers, will be gratefully received.

Correspondence, to secure notice, must in all cases be accompanied by the name and address of the writer, not for publication, but as a guarantee of good faith.

Advertising rates sent on application.

Address all communications,

The Organ, 149 A Tremont Street, Boston, Mass.

☞ An active agent in every city is desired to whom a liberal cash commission will be allowed.

ANNOUNCEMENT.

IN response to the request of several organ-builders and organists, a large photograph of the Boston Music Hall organ (built by Walker & Sons of Germany) has been prepared, copies of which we offer for sale. No respectable photograph of this organ was taken while the instrument was standing, owing to the fact that the case, with its abundance of detail, was mostly in shadow, while the burnished pipes were brilliantly illuminated from windows above. When the instrument was being removed several years ago, about twenty-five photographs were taken of various parts of the instrument, — the panels, key desk, one of the towers, etc. Having purchased these negatives, we placed five of the photographs, together with such photographs of the whole instrument as could be secured, in the hands of an artist, who made a large drawing, with all the detail of this grand organ-front. From this drawing the woodcut shown on the title-page of this journal was made, and a large photograph has been taken. We have had a number of these photographs printed and mounted on heavy card-board ready for framing. The size is 12 x 14 inches, and the price is $2.00.

THE following incident is related as happening to one of the prominent organ teachers of this country, who resides not more than five hundred miles from this office.

A fond parent called on Mr. X—— to inquire about organ lessons for his daughter, when the following conversation occurred :—

MR. X. How old is your daughter?

FOND PARENT. She is just fourteen.

MR. X. (impatiently). Why ! I am afraid she is too young. She could not reach the pedals.

FOND PARENT. Reach the pedals? Ugh ! You bet she could reach them if they were anywhere in the room.

THE following is from the Alumni Annual, a periodical published once a year by the Alumni Association of the New England Conservatory of Music.

"The Annual can tell a good story now and then, and the following has the merit of being true in every particular.

"A young lady organ student living outside the Home used to practise in a church near by, generally taking along for the sake of companionship a large mastiff named Rover. Rover was a dog of profound discernment, and the young lady came to look upon him as a critic of no mean order. Bach's Fugues, no matter how horribly performed, caused him to exhibit the blandest satisfaction; he rarely moved a muscle until the final note. Rink's "God Save the Queen," rushed through semi-occasionally, just to see how it seemed to play something jaunty, produced absolute indifference, and frequently a most disrespectful canine snore would smite the ear, proving that Rover didn't think it worth his while to keep awake.

"But Batiste's Dulciana offertory was too much for him. Those howls ! They ring in the ears yet. The walls echoed with them, and the rafters rang. With his head upraised, and his huge black jaws apart and pointing skyward, he poured forth his distracted wail until nothing but summarily turning him out would avail to quiet him.

"Some evolutionist may explain the phenomenon, — a keenly musical soul caught in its transition from the Anywhere to the Here, and imprisoned within that tawny coat. But who shall say ? "

THE Manchester (Eng.) Courier contains the following advertisement :—

Wanted, organist (male), good churchman ; stipend not exceeding £10. Address, with references.

Fifty dollars per year is a sample of the munificent (?) salary offered by many English churches for experienced organists.

ATTENTION is called to that part of the biography of Bernard Schmidt which states that plumbers did the soldering in the manufacture of metal pipe for the organ in St. Paul's Cathedral, London. Plumbers in those days must have been more skilful than now.

CIPHERINGS.

HARRY THUNDER, son of Prof. Thunder, succeeds his father as organist in St. Augustine Church. — Philadelphia Mirror. They must have a thundering time of it in that church, Sundays; and we don't see how the congregation can manage to keep asleep during the services. — Toledo American. We should think that the congregation would be constantly light'n'ing. — Musical Herald. We should think that by using the storage-battery system the organ could be blown by electricity; there must be plenty of it where there is so much thunder and light'n'ing.

* *

AN amateur organist, who broke down in playing the oratorio of the "Messiah," said, "I find the music is a little too hard for me to Händel." — Pretzel's Weekly. He was afterward found Haydn behind the organ. — Richmond Herald. He was obliged to give up his position and go to Chopin' wood.

* *

A CELEBRATED organist slipped off his bench recently, while playing a Bach Fugue as a postlude. He was immediately expelled from the church as a Bach-slider, and is now a fugue-ative. — Musical Herald. The next time he plays a "postlude," he had better hold on to the "post." — Richmond Paton. To which "post" do you a "lude," his post as organist, or the U. S. Mail ?

* *

THE immense organ in the cathedral at Riga, Russia, has one hundred and twenty-four stops. This is one hundred and twenty-three more than "Grandfather's Clock" has. — Lowell Courier.

GRAND CHOEUR.

THEO. DUBOIS.

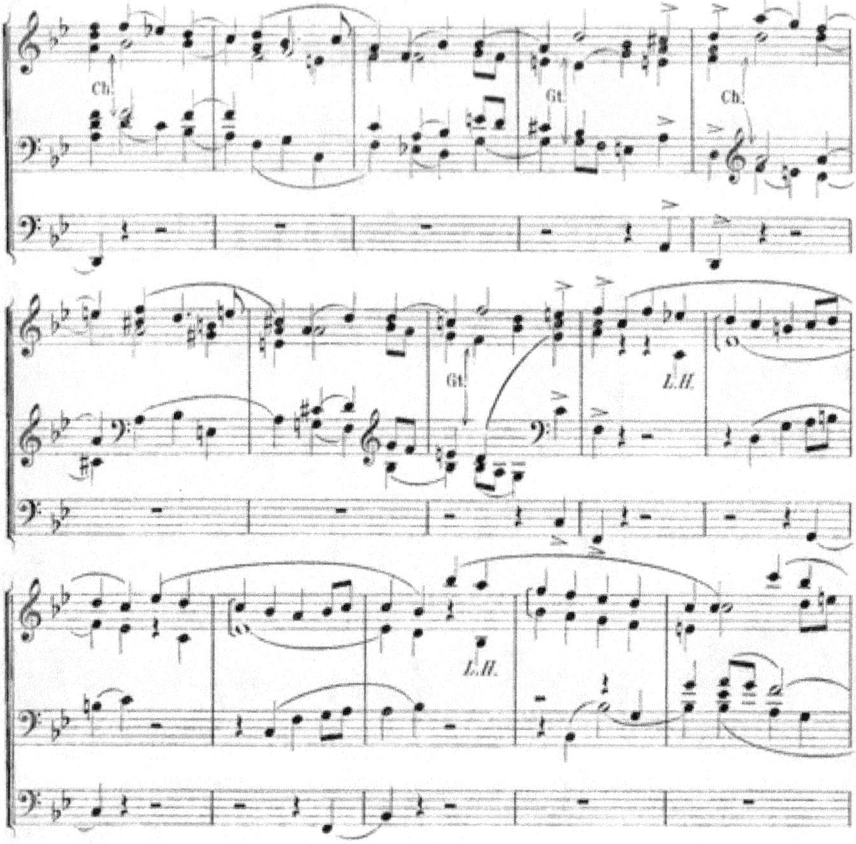
Ch.
Gt.
Ch.
Gt.
L.H.
L.H.
Full

Ch. 8, 4 & 2 Ft. (or Sw. 8 & 4 Ft.)

Gt.

a tempo, meno allegro.

allarg.

(Reduce Gt. to Op. Diapason.)

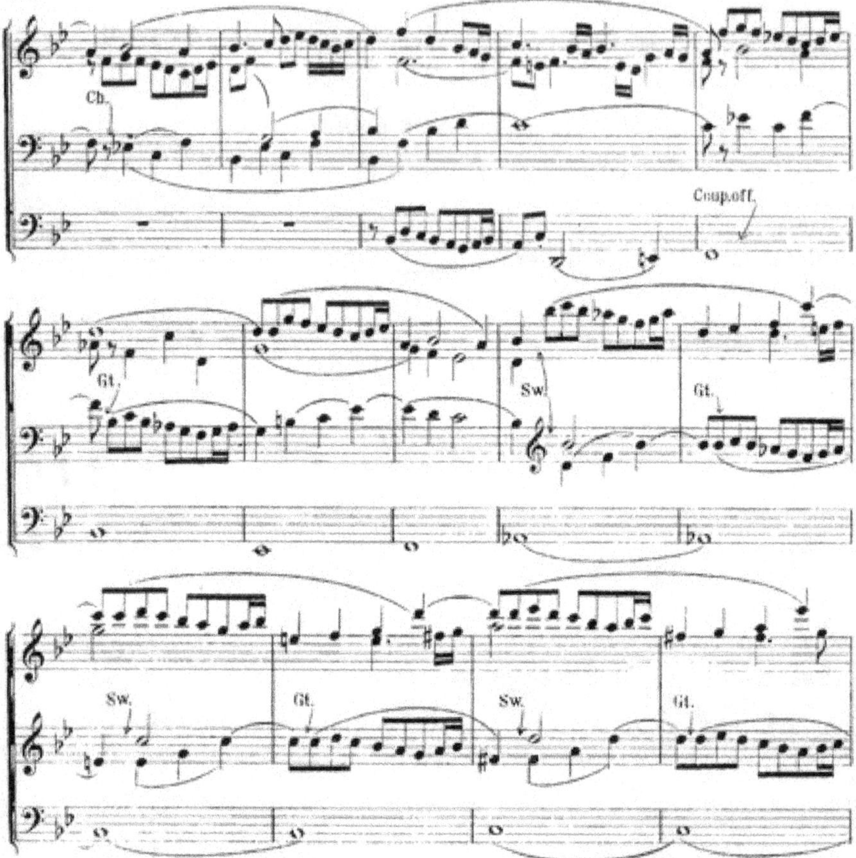
Ch.
Coup.off.
Gt.
Sw.
Gt.
Sw.
Gt.
Sw.
Gt.
Sw.
Gt.
Sw.

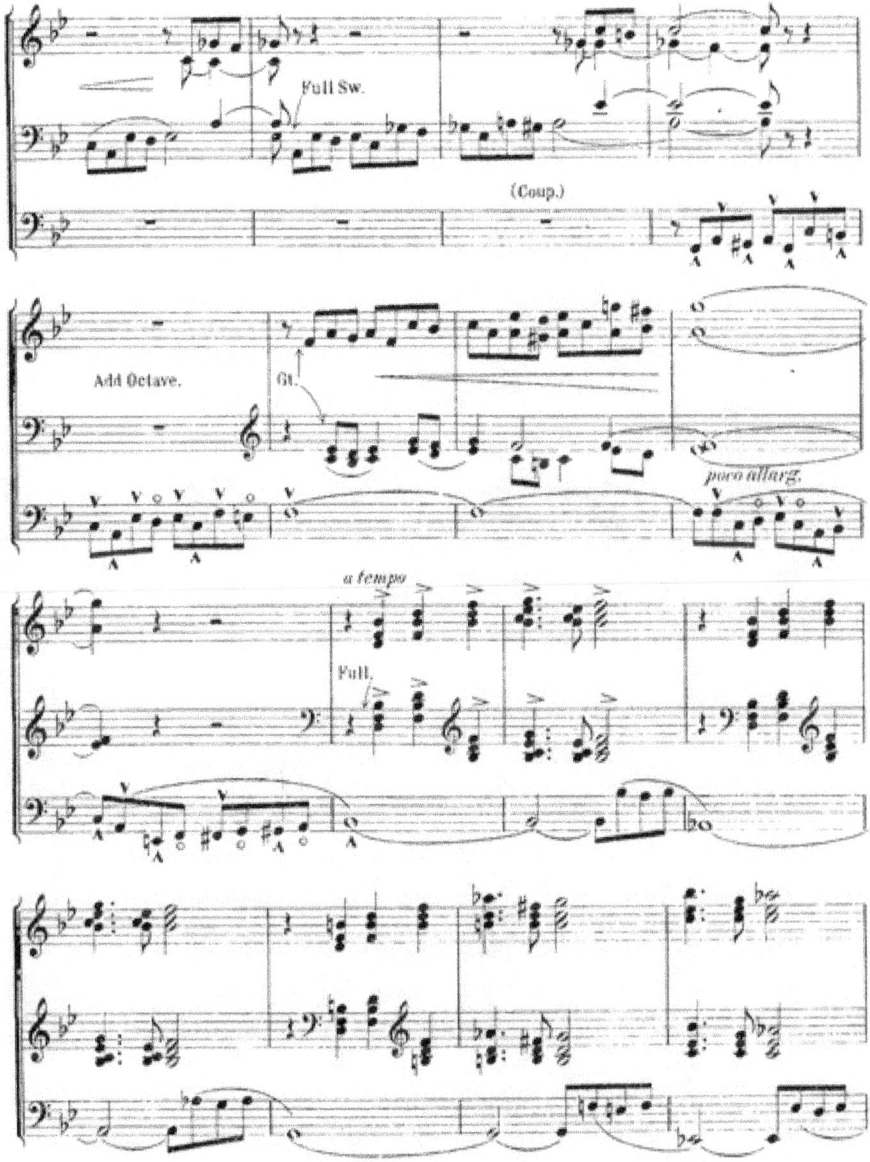
Full Sw.
(Coup.)
Add Octave.
Gt.
poco allarg.
a tempo
Full.

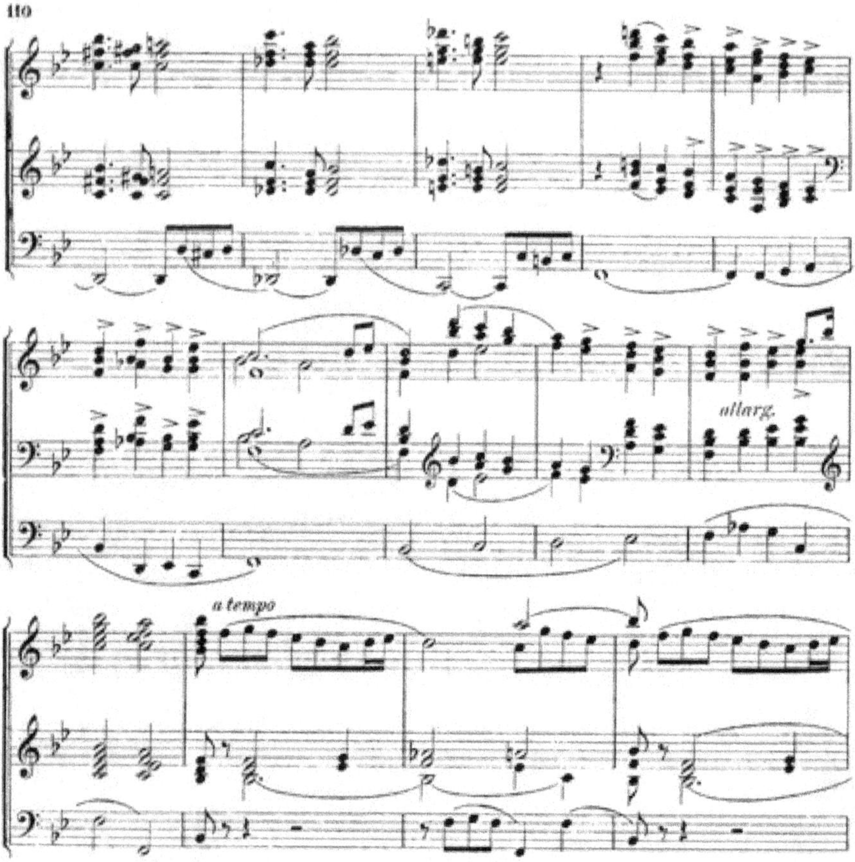
allarg.
a tempo
allarg.

ADAGIO.

Dr. FRANZ LISZT.

Cantabile con divozione.

Sw. St. Diap. & Fl. 4 Ft.
Gt. to Op. Diap.

Sw.

Ch. Flutes 8 & 4 Ft.

Ped Bourdon.

Add Oboe.

Ch.

Sw.

Ch.
Ch.
Sw.
Gt.
Sw.
Ch.
Gt.
Coup.
Sw.
Ch.
Prepare Ch. Dulciana only.
Oboe off Sw.
St. Disp. & Salicional.
St. Disp. off

REMINISCENCES OF ORGAN AND CHURCH MUSIC IN THIS COUNTRY.

BY AN ORGANIST.

II.

To digress from the subject of these pages, I am tempted here to give a short account of the development of what, for want of a better term, may be called the American style of organ and church music.

The term "American style," I am quite aware, will be likely to bring a smile on the reader's face. It is a term, by the way, first used by Dr. J. H. Wilcox, an organist who probably had more influence on the present generation of church players than almost any one else.

I remember very well the first time I heard the expression used; it was a year or two after the Boston Music Hall organ was opened. The firm of Walker & Co. had sent one of their best workmen over here to take charge of the repairs on the instrument, an old fellow by the name of Stürm; and it was in a conversation in very broken English (enlivened by a goodly number of fearful-sounding German oaths), between Stürm, Dr. Wilcox, and the writer, the main theme of which was the merits or demerits (mostly the latter on our part) of the Boston organ as a concert instrument, that the term was first used.

That there is a very distinct style of church playing in this country, I think no organist, after a moment's consideration of the situation, will deny. Mind, I do not defend it; in fact, I consider it a misfortune that there is such a style, but the fact remains. Now for a few words as to the reason of its existence :—

Our Protestant churches, as a rule, are small structures. Owing to the spread of "isms," and the want of any central authority of church government, it is the tendency of things religious to split into small factions, each section setting up a place of worship for itself, the consequence being that most of our churches are hardly worthy the name of "church," being in reality but little more than chapels ; although the name "chapel" will hardly express what one means by a small place of worship, as the writer happens to remember just here that the court "chapel" in Dresden (where probably the finest Catholic church-music in Europe is to be heard) is what would be called in this country a "cathedral," it being fully as large as the Cathedral of St. Patrick, in New York.

But now, supposing that a state of affairs could be brought about whereby the various Protestant denominations could be united in each large town to worship under one roof; as far as the impressive character of the services are concerned, there would be no comparison with the present poverty-stricken, small way of performing the service.

However, the "denominations" are here, with (from the necessity of the case) their small churches, small choirs, small organs, and the American church organist has to make the best of the situation.

But out of this state of things has arisen what may be termed the "American style" of church music. It would be difficult to explain exactly what I mean by this, but an approximate idea may be had by a glance at the music that forms the staple attraction of most of our choirs.

First, as to psalmody, or, as the American organist or choir-leader terms it, "hymn-tunes." They may be divided into four classes: I. The "old" tunes like "Duke Street," "Old Hundred," "St. Martyn's," etc.; these are mostly from German and English sources. II. The tunes used mostly in the Episcopal Churches. All the late hymn-books of this denomination are "made up" (stolen would be too harsh a term, I suppose?) mostly from a collection of hymns and tunes published in London a few years ago, under the title of "Hymns Ancient and Modern,"[1] of which collection it is said *more than twenty million copies have been sold !* It is

[1] It is reprinted in this country.

an excellent work, edited by Wm. Henry Monk, organist of New Cathedral, with the assistance of such modern church musicians as Arthur Sullivan, Barnby, McFarren, etc. These modern English tunes are of course intended for boy choirs, and are sung to a rather quick *alla breve tempo.* III. I class the tunes published by the firms of Ditson, of Boston, Root & Son, of Chicago, etc. Every little while one reads in the papers of "a new work on church music," the title of which is most likely to be, "The Sacred Harp," "The Lyre," (!) "The Musical Quiver," "The Sacred Banjo," etc. They are all very much alike ; the music consists almost entirely of the tonic, dominant, and sub-dominant triads repeated *ad nauseam* to (frequently) the most vulgar rhythms, suited only for dance music, and poor dance music at that. It is almost needless to say that such "music" should *never* find a place in any choir that aspires to an artistic and devotional rendering of the service. IV. *Arrangements* from oratorios, masses, and instrumental works; Mendelssohn's songs without words ; Schubert's songs ; the themes of slow movements of sonatas, quartets, symphonies, etc. I am inclined to rank these, in the absence of anything better, as among the most useful of any of the publications of the day. To be sure, arrangements from secular works are not church music, and cannot be defended as such ; but they are *good music,* and as such are a great improvement on the so-called "American tune."

The best works of this class are "The Grace Church Collection," by King, and "Wilson's Sacred Quartets," by the late Henry Wilson, for many years organist of Christ Church, Hartford, Conn., where, by the way, was maintained, while Mr. Wilson was at that church, a most excellent service.

(To be continued.)

A DINNER IN A SWELL-BOX.

WHEN the large organ in the Town Hall, Leeds, England, was being constructed at the factory of Messrs. Gray & Davison, the unusual size of the swell-box excited considerable attention. Henry Smart who, with Dr. Spark, drew the plans of the organ, and under whose direction the organ was constructed, conceived the idea of having a dinner in the swell-box, which was duly accomplished.

Dr. Spark, in his interesting biography of Henry Smart, gives the following account of that novel dinner :—

"One sent a fine salmon, another some choice *entrées* from Gunter's, somebody forwarded a splendid haunch of venison, this friend contributed a dozen of 'sparkling,' that one six bottles of '34 port, and so on. But, better than all these very nice comestibles and beverages was the intellectual feast — the feast of reason and the flow of soul. . . . We had jokes about the 'box' we had got into, the 'swells' that occupied it — greater than any swell that would ever come out of it, — our *crescendos* and *diminuendos,* the clearing of our pipes, and a hundred other *jeu d' esprits, bon mots,* etc., referring to the organ and the occasion.

"George Lake, who was then editor and proprietor of *The Musical Gazette,* wrote the following amusing account, which was published in his serial, Feb. 27, 1858 :—

A DINNER IN A SWELL-BOX.

"'We know not whether it is peculiar to Englishmen to seek their food in the most out-of-the-way places, but *certis* we have abundant examples of this odd propensity. In the summer time we call our friends and neighbors together, decide upon a place of *rendezvous,* pack up five times as much prog as can possibly be consumed in one day, and travel in a promiscuous manner to some sequestered spot where sandbugs, fieldmice, and water-wagtails abound. These folks do eat in the most astonishing manner, in spite of the disadvantages under which the edition of the meal is accomplished, *sans* table-cloth, to say nothing of *sans* table, *sans* sedentary anchorage, save that afforded by *terra firma — Anglicè*, Mother Earth — and *sans* many other comforts and conveniences; with a few such inadequacies as two forks between three people, one glass between four, or, on a hot day, when thirst is particularly prevalent, between six choking denizens of this enlightened hemisphere. There, and under these extraordinary circumstances, do they munch, and munch, and munch, like any sailor's wife at her chestnuts, and consider the prandial enjoyment far greater than when they are snugly ensconced at home, with their legs tucked under choice mahogany, and a proper complement of forks and glasses to each feeder. There certainly is a great mania for peculiarities of this order. We happened to find ourselves last summer at Ryde, and were not a little astonished to find that "quadrilles at 9" were perpetrated on board the Commodore's yacht, The Brilliant, riding at anchor in the calm waters of the Solent. Ryde has a pier of no inconsiderable length, and it puzzled us to know how ladies in full dress could be transported from their peaceful habitations to the aforesaid yacht, and we were curious to know the effect of the Terpsichorean exercise combined with the gentle heaving motion of a boat riding at anchor. A little observation revealed to us that the ladies proceeded to the pier-head in bath chairs, and were taken by instalments in small boats to the place of meeting. Now, a *soirée dansante* in a heaving house might be all very well with those accustomed to the rolling wave, but with fair ladies, whose health generally failed them on leaving the shore, it would naturally be very ill; and when we heard of some of the *belles* turning qualmish before the yacht was gained, wishing the Solent, the moonlight, the gondoliers, and all the romantic concomitants, at Halifax, New York, Jerico, Bath, Old Boots, or any other place of fashionable resort to which disagreeable people and things are often mentally (and verbally) consigned, and of their being in a downright state of indisposition when they got on board, we must say we were not at all surprised.

"'Such of our readers as are not acquainted with the internal economy of an organ will begin to think that a "swell box" is a sort of a slang term for a construction (such as a yacht) likely to be affected by the undulatory character of the ocean, and that we are about to report terrible cases and harrowing details of sea-sickness (*si sic omnes*). No such thing. The pipes belonging to the upper row of keys (in organs with two or three manuals) are enclosed in a box, and the pipes in the aggregate or even the manual, are called the "swell," because the box has Venetian shutters in front, which are opened by the pressure of a pedal spring, the most gradual crescendo being thereby produced. This box, in the magnificent organ now in the course of construction by Messrs. Gray & Davison for the Leeds Town Hall, is naturally of very large dimensions, and it was determined by the builders to hold a dinner therein. This novel entertainment, almost as eccentric in its way as the sandbuggy, fieldmousy watery-wagtailish recreation aforementioned, or the qualm-provoking festival subsequently commented upon, came off on the thirteenth inst., when a dozen hungry celeb-

rities assembled at 370 Euston Road, to discuss a genuine mahogany dinner. The table was not of mahogany, it is true, but we mean that the meal was of that complete and comfortable character to which we have already referred in contrast with the peculiar incompleteness and discomfort of picnic arrangements.

"'Success to the Leeds' Town Hall organ, and the healths of Messrs. Smart and Spark (the designers of the instrument), and the eminent builders, were, of course, drunk with enthusiasm. Messrs. Smart and Spark were present, and two or three gentlemen came from Leeds expressly to assist at the *solemnité*.

"'The "swell-box," by no means presented the bare appearance that such pipe-cages generally wear. It was gayly decorated with Union Jacks and other banners, with devices regal, patriotic, and eccentric. One little flag in particular caused cachinnation, and thereby promoted digestion. It bore the figure of a lion, and was the most fabulous depictment of the king of beasts that we ever gazed upon. The Leeds Corporate Arms occupied a conspicuous position, and they are funny enough. An owl *rampant*, surmounting the shield, an owl *rampant* on the dexter side, and a third owl likewise *rampant*, on the sinister (the latter twain looking most desperately knowing). The only remaining portion of the device we can call to mind was a sheep *defunct*, suspended; emblematic, we imagine, of hung mutton, which is a fine thing and in which every Corporation delighteth. Touching the decoration of the interior of this novel dining-hall, some one happened to remark that it resembled a ship's cabin, upon which Mr. George Cooper (of St. Sepulchre's, St. Paul's, and the Chapel Royal) said, "Of course. It's going to be a C organ." With this ready and legitimate joke we must close our "notice" of the "Dinner in a Swell-box."'"

CORRESPONDENCE.

ORGAN PEDALING.

To the Editor of THE ORGAN.

IN a paper read by Mr. Gerrit Smith at the New York State Music Teachers' Association, at Syracuse, June 30, 1892, he treats upon a subject of special interest to all organ players; namely, *Organ Pedaling*.
The paper is divided into three parts:—
1. The construction of the pedal board.
2. The proper system of marking pedaling.
3. The art of pedaling.
The first division, while interesting from an historical and scientific standpoint, does not claim our attention under the heading given. Mr. Smith cites sixteen different methods of pedal marking! This *is* interesting, and invites careful investigation. In reality there are ten different kinds of signs among the examples given: A, o, u, ⌂, ⌐, T, H, l, o, and the numerals 1, 2, 3, 4; and the application of these signs is indeed bewildering. That some method of pedal marking is desirable, few, if any, will deny; but a perfectly plain score, such as Guilmant and other eminent writers give to us, is more to be desired than the fantastic and unpractical editions frequently seen. Unless the method is simple, practical, and easily read, it would be better to have no markings whatever. Personally, I prefer to represent the toe and heel by the following signs: A, o. They are all we need, excepting a brace, ⌐⌐⌐⌐ when the toe is employed upon adjacent keys. These signs when placed above the

notes signify the *right* foot, and when placed below, the *left* foot.

Whether the toe signs point up or down is of little consequence, the principal thing being to have a sign which can be instantly distinguished from one representing the heel. I have used the round o for the heel because it is most easily made, and because it can never be mistaken for the toe sign. (Furthermore, it is always right side up!)

Dudley Buck merely inverts my toe sign. Frederic Archer, who, by the way, is not quoted in Mr. Smith's article, makes the toe like mine, but writes an inverted horse-shoe, ʊ, for the heel. This may be more suggestive of a real heel than the letter o, but on account of its being open it is somewhat similar to the inverted toe sign (ᴧ). S. P. Warren uses the same signs as Mr. Archer, but requires you to notice particularly *their position*; for by his system the signs when turned one way mean one thing, and when turned the other way they mean something else; for instance, ᴧ ∩ signify the right toe and right heel, while the same signs inverted, ʊ ᴗ, signify the left toe and left heel. Since these signs are all placed below the pedal notes, great care must be taken to distinguish their position. This is not alone trying to the eyes, but very confusing. It is moreover radically different from all the other systems in vogue, and must be pronounced most faulty.

W. T. Best employs the capital letters *R* and *L* for the right and left toe, which plan necessitates the addition of the small letter *h* when the heel is needed. His system is therefore complicated, and difficult to write, besides being one which can never become universal.

Mr. Smith naïvely tells us of a "True Method," as follows: 1. Right toe; 2. Right heel; 3. Left toe; 4. Left heel. This will certainly not require a patent! It is difficult to see wherein this "true method" is simple, concise, practical, or even reasonable. In the first place, it cannot be distinguished from marks of *fingering*. In the second place, the figure 1 does not any more suggest the right toe than the figure 2 does the right heel, while figures 3 and 4 are *left* only to the imagination! Mr. Smith argues that "odd numbers signify toes, and even numbers heels." At first this does seem very *odd*, but perhaps he was thinking only of his toes! Finally, since these numerals are all placed either below or above the pedal part, they are nearly, if not quite, as perplexing as the symbols employed by Mr. Warren; and although Mr. Smith affirms that "numbers are a universal language in civilized, or, what is the same thing, 'organized' nations," yet the art of pedaling will never be thoroughly understood or fully mastered until each one finds out a "true method" for himself.

In the third division of his paper Mr. Smith gives expression to some very sensible remarks, especially regarding the importance of knowing "How to sit," and the proper height of the bench. Instead of making the distance 21½ inches, however, from the top of the white pedal keys to the top of the bench, I would place the average at 20½ inches, as many players would be more comfortable at 20 inches, while others would prefer 21. Allow me to say that the latter distance is my own choice.

In regard to a free action of the ankle-joint, I quite agree with Mr. Smith. There can be no facility or grace of movement without this freedom and elasticity. Most players, however, raise the feet too high, as some pianists do the fingers. While freedom and elasticity should be acquired, yet the motion should be economized, like the breath in singing. Do not use more than is absolutely necessary, and let the action be quiet. A perfect *legato* should first be mastered, and then the *staccato* style may be easily acquired.

Mr. Smith says, "Two consecutive notes should not be played by the toe of one foot, except in cases of necessity, and *never* in scale playing." What would he do in the case of *octave* pedaling? Doubtless this is one of the "cases of necessity"! Cases of convenience might easily be found in which the toe of one foot would be most applicable for

two consecutive keys, for instance, in the scale of G flat major: —

D flat major: —

B flat minor (melodic form): —

Also in passages like the following: —

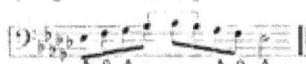

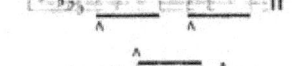

And even in the mooted scale of A flat major I see no objection to the following: —

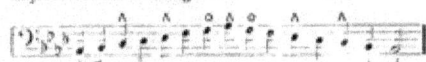

Although on general principles I prefer this way: —

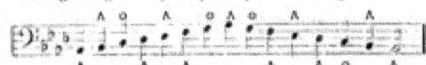

Other examples might be given, but the above will suffice and I will only add that the brace is not intended to indicate a "slide," but that the notes over which it is placed should be played legato, by attacking the first key with the side of the foot, and then turning the foot sidewise sufficiently to press down the next key, pains being taken to avoid any indistinctness or blurring. This can be accomplished by a little careful practice.

An absolutely free and independent use of the heel in pedal playing is seldom found, and yet it is as important as a skilful employment of the thumb upon the manuals.

The old school said, *avoid using the heels*; but the new school says, *use every means to obtain artistic results.*

Yours very truly,

CLARENCE EDDY.

THE EVOLUTION OF THE SWELL-BOX.

To the Editor of THE ORGAN : —

HAVING recently subscribed to THE ORGAN, I have been somewhat amused and considerably agitated over the effusion in the May number, concerning the duplication of the swell-box, which was signed "Gambette." It is apparent to almost any one that "Gambette" is not an organist ; at least, he has had little experience with legitimate organ music, though he may "play a little." One would surmise that he was a builder, for his argument (?) is not founded on the experience of a player. All this matter about the number of feet of "planed one and a half inch plank," cost of construction, inferior swell-boxes, position of the bellows, etc., has nothing to do with the subject, and would not be dragged into the argument by any one who was personally acquainted with the value of the limited means of expression which exist in an organ.

On one point I can agree with "Gambette" ; viz., a swell-box at its best is a poor medium of expression ; but why abandon the only known method of varying the tone of an organ stop, simply because it does not wholly meet the requirements ?

Every organist deplores the absence of expression in a solo played on the clarinet stop in the choir, when not enclosed in a swell-box. Expressionless and lifeless, it would not be less satisfactory if played by a machine. The same is true of other solo stops. Again, how aggravating it is to a singer, as well as to the audience, when an accompanist plays the whole accompaniment of the song without expression, *mezzo-piano* from beginning to end, regardless whether the soloist is singing *pianissimo* or *fortissimo*. Equally aggravating is it to accompany an Oboe solo with the choir Dulciana, when there is no choir swell-box. If the latter stop is voiced soft, not being too loud for the Oboe when the swell is closed, it cannot be heard when the swell is open, and if the Dulciana is loud enough for the Oboe when the swell is open, it covers up the solo when the box is closed.

Now, as to the great organ swell-box. Who has not experienced the thrill which passes through one's body when listening to the full organ, somewhat subdued by being enclosed in a swell-box, till the approach of the climax, when a gradual opening of the great organ swell-box permits the ponderous vibrations to escape and fill the building with tone, the equal of which cannot be found elsewhere, and which almost lifts one off one's feet with enthusiasm.

The argument that " smothering " the tone of an organ pipe is " detrimental to its delicacy " is false. Only the stops of large scales and great power are injured by being enclosed, and they are almost always left out of the box. Will " Gambette " have the audacity to state that an Oboe, Salicional, or Vox Humana, can be voiced so as to have more delicacy when placed outside a swell-box than when inclosed ? Will he attempt to prove that the tone of the " full swell," with the box closed, can be equalled without any box at all ?

Lastly, the statement that only "a few prominent organists " have indorsed the duplication of the swell-box is as false as most of the arguments offered by "Gambette," and the day is coming when every first-class organ will have two or more swell-boxes to vary the tone of the " king of instruments." EMILE LE BLANC.

To the Editor of THE ORGAN :—

ALLOW me to remark that the article on " The evolution of the swell-box," in your May number, by "Gambette," strikes the writer as true to the letter, and expresses the idea of many organists and builders of my acquaintance. The swell-box is to a certain extent very necessary ; but it may easily evolute into an evil, and then become an unnecessary evil. The great organ, the swell, choir, and solo, have or should have each its own sphere of action, as well as its own individuality, and the only way to accomplish this end is to

give them their own position and identity. Therefore, let the swell organ be the swell, and so on of each manual. The matter *in toto* has been so well handled by "Gambette," that anything further would be superfluous ; but I am joined by many a one in sending greeting to "Gambette," with a hearty Amen ! Yours truly,

OTTO SEVENHIRD.

RECOMMENDATIONS OF THE CONNECTICUT ASSOCIATION.

To the Editor of THE ORGAN : —

THE report and recommendations of the committee on " Organ Construction," presented at the Connecticut Music Teachers' Association Convention, and published in your August number, are judicious and timely.

I venture, however, to express my doubts as to the wisdom of the recommendations as to arranging draw-stops in terraces, and, to some extent, my disapproval of the oblique-faced knob.

In an organ of moderate size, much registration must be done by the hands, and often by the hand on the side opposite the draw-knob (or knobs) to be moved.

Now, to illustrate : on the organ which I play, the draw-knobs are arranged in terraces. The swell Bourdon is under the four-foot Violina ; if I wish to push them in, and perhaps also the Flautina and Mixture, which stand next on the upper row, I am sure that I could do it with much less exertion, more quickly, and more surely, if the knobs were nearer each other. My own preference is for this arrangement ; i. e., to have draw-knobs in all cases pull toward the player, set at an angle of thirty degrees, and not in terraces, but " flat." The oblique-faced knob is objectionable to me, personally, in that I find a constant tendency to pull toward myself, and so run the risk of breaking the rod.

I have written this note, hoping to hear from others, whose experience may be more valuable than mine ; and I confess that I am open to conviction and conversion. The report in question is most admirably and systematically drawn up.

Yours sincerely,

ALBERT J. BLAKESLEY.

WATERBURY, CONN., Aug. 11, 1892.

QUESTIONS AND ANSWERS.

All questions must be accompanied by the full name and address of the writer, and, if received by the 10th of the month, will usually be answered in the following number of THE ORGAN.

Only such questions as refer to the organ, to organists, organ-builders, or to organ music, will be answered.

Correspondents are requested to write their questions in a clear and concise manner, writing on only one side of the paper.

E. Please pronounce Lemaigre and Dubois.

ANS. Approximately, Ler-may-gr. Doo-bwar (*or* is sounded as in the word *arn*).

G. B. Who was Turley ?

ANS. Jean Tobie Turley was an organ-builder, born the 4th of August, 1778, in Treven-brietzen, near Potsdam, Germany, and died April 9, 1829. He constructed about twenty-five organs, the principal of which was in Jochimsthal.

E FLAT. I have a copy of Guilmant's Elevation in A-flat (A. P. Schmidt edition). On the second page, lower brace, third measure, the half-note E-flat, in the left hand, makes a discord. Is it correct ?

ANS. An error of the engraver, and also of the proof-reader. Instead of the half-note E-flat, there should be a quarter-note E-flat, followed by a quarter-note D-natural.

MIXTURES.

(FOUR RANKS.)

Miss Nellie McGowen, for years organist of the Mission Church, Roxbury, Mass., died August 13.

Mr. N. H. Arnold, organist of St. Stephen's Church, Providence, R.I., is abroad, combining pleasure and study.

John Labagh, of the firm of Labagh & Kemp, organ-builders of New York, died July 13. at the age of eighty-two.

An organ has just been built by Messrs. Hook & Hastings for the Emmanuel P. E. Church of Holmesburg, a suburb of Philadelphia.

It is expected that Mr. Clarence Eddy will visit Boston the middle of September, at which time he will take a much-needed rest after a busy summer.

Mr. Alfred Pennington, who has been abroad studying for nearly three years, during which time he has studied with Guilmant, and the late Prof. Haupt, has returned to Boston.

Mr. Frank Bradley, an organist of London, is going to Kimberley, South Africa, to exhibit the organ built by Messrs. Norman Bros. & Beard, a specification of which was given in The Organ for August.

During the past year Dr. William Spark has given forty-three recitals in the Leeds (England) Town Hall. The closing recital of this season was given July 23. Some of the recitals have been attended by over a thousand people.

Mr. Fred Redhead is substituting in St. Paul's Church, Des Moines, Iowa, during the absence of Mr. Gratian, the regular organist. Is Mr. Redhead a red head? Or is he a black head or white head who is Red head simply by name and not by hair? The spectacle of a black-headed Redhead reading black notes on white paper, and pressing black and white organ keys, as he red them, must have seemed like a living illustration of the Star Spangled Banner, red, white, and blue. Where's the blue? Why? The wind blew through the pipes. — *The Indicator, Chicago.*

The organist at a Cardiff (Wales) church found several of the notes soundless. An examination revealed the fact that no fewer than six birds, including a robin, had built their nests in the pipes. — *Musical Courier.*

The new pipe organ just placed in the Erie Pro-Cathedral was made by Master Charles Lejeal, the eighteen-year-old son of J. J. Lejeal, the Erie piano and organ dealer. — *Musical Courier.* We think this must be the "largest organ" out of (Le)jeal!

The great Plymouth Church organ of Brooklyn, built by Hook & Hastings in 1866, and which was characterized at the time by the Brooklyn *Eagle* as the "*New Long Island Sound*," is to be extensively remodelled by Mr. Hastings, carrying out plans of the organist, Mr. Chas. H. Morse. Specifications of the changes and improvements will be published later.

The following outburst of prose poetry, under the stimulus of an organ recital, has appeared in the *North Star :* "At times the quietness of the church was accentuated by what seemed like the gentle murmuring of the summer breeze amid the forest trees, and anon there arose birdlike notes, clear and sweet as the song of the thrush. Then the sacred edifice was filled with a sound as of thunder, and a shrill, sharp note as of the clarion call to battle went echoing down the aisles, to be succeeded in a moment or two by the cadence of the babbling brook, and the tinkling ripple of the wavelets on a summer sea against the side of the fairy craft skimming lightly o'er its surface." Music is not the food of love only. It nourishes the poetic feeling that lies underneath even a reporter's professional indifference, and sometimes, as in this case, there is a running over. — *London Musical Times.*

Continued on page 119.

MIXTURES.

Continued from page 117.

Messrs. Geo. Jardine & Son are erecting an organ for the Madison Avenue Baptist Church, New York, which is to have three manuals, pneumatic action, piston combination knobs, and an electric motor.

In 1703 Händel visited Lubeck, Germany, as a candidate for the position of organist in the ancient town. Finding, among the numerous requirements, that the new organist would be compelled to marry the daughter of the late organist, he withdrew his application, and left the town in disgust, journeying to Hamburg. How fortunate that the organists of the nineteenth century are not subjected to such senseless stipulations!

NEW ORGAN MUSIC.

Sonata (No. 3) Op. 70	P. Blumenthal
"Praise the Lord." Fantasie-Prelude . . .	N. W. Gade
Adagio, for Cello and Organ	Ph. Rufer
One Hundred and Seventy-eight Cadenzas .	J. Schildknecht
Meditation	E. T. Driffield
Pastorale	" "
Offertoire	" "
March	" "
Tempo de Minuetto	" "
Andante and Fugue	
Wedding March	William Faulkner
Festival Preludes	Jos. Steinhäuser

A series of organ concerts in the Payson Church, Easthampton, Mass., given by Mr. Fred L. Clark, ended with the following program: —

Sonata in C minor	Guilmant
Cantilèna in A minor	Grison
Grand March (Leonora)	Raff-Shelley
Theme and Variations (Violin and Organ) .	Rheinberger
"Vision"	Rheinberger
"Evening Quiet"	
Theme and Variations	Hesse.

ITEMS FOR LONDON.

Mr. H. C. Tonking gave an organ recital at the Royal Albert Hall, London, on Sunday afternoon, Aug. 21.

A Musical and Ecclesiastical Exhibition is about to be given at the Royal Aquarium, London, when, amongst other things, many of the leading organists will give organ recitals.

Two of the three latest English Musical Knights have been organists. Sir Walter Perratt is one of England's best organists. Sir Joseph Barnby has held many good appointments as organist, and is also conductor of the Royal Choral Society, perhaps the finest in the world. He is also Principal of the London Guildhall School of Music. Sir W. G. Cusins is better known as a pianist and conductor of a private band.   H.

REVIEW OF NEW MUSIC.

FROM THE LONDON MUSIC PUBLISHING CO.

The *Organists' Quarterly Journal* (part xcv.), edited by Dr. William Spark: —

Il Lago	Arranged by H. S. Trembach.
Two Favourite Airs of Händel. Transcribed by Dr. Wm. Spark.	

This number of the *Organists' Quarterly Journal* contains the customary liberal variety of selections. A Toccata and Fugue by Frank J. Sawyer is the most pretentious number, rather difficult, and containing some excellent pedal practice. Andante Impromptu in G, by Harry M. Gilholy, with a simple, melodious theme. Solemn march by Philip de Sayres; will be useful with students, as it contains good chord practice and octaves in the pedal part. Andante con moto by Walter P. Fairclough terminates the list of pieces contained in the current number of this successful periodical.

"Il Lago" is an arrangement of a romance originally written for violin and piano, which, with the Händel Arias, will prove useful additions to the list of arrangements for the organ.

NEW ORGANS.

NEW ORGAN IN HARVARD STREET M. E. CHURCH, CAMBRIDGEPORT, MASS.

Built by George S. Hutchings, Boston, Mass.

GREAT ORGAN.		SWELL ORGAN.	
Open Diapason . . .	8 Ft.	Bourdon Treble	16 Ft.
Dolcissimo	8 "	Bourdon Bass	
Melodia (Stopped Bass)	8 "	Violin Diapason . .	8 "
Octave	4 "	Salicional	8 "
Flute d'Amour . . .	4 "	Aeoline	8 "
Octave Quinte . . .	2⅔ "	Stopped Diapason . .	8 "
Super Octave . . .	2 "	Flute Harmonique . .	4 "
Mixture	3 Rks.	Violina	4 "
Trumpet	8 Ft.	Dolce Cornet . . .	3 Rks.
		Oboe	8 Ft.
		Bassoon	

PEDAL MOVEMENTS.	PEDAL ORGAN.	
Forte, Great Organ.		
Piano, Great Organ.		
Forte, Swell Organ.	Open Diapason . . .	16 Ft.
Piano, Swell Organ.	Bourdon	16 "
Reversible Gt. to Pedal Coupler.		
Swell Tremolo.	The usual Couplers.	

Messrs. George H. Ryder & Co. have placed a two-manual organ, with fourteen stops, in the Baptist Church, Andover, Mass.

Messrs. Merklin & Co. have placed a new organ, with electric action, in the Seminary of Bordeaux, France. The instrument has two manuals and seventeen stops.

Mrs. Ellen R. Eldridge has presented the Congregational Church of Yarmouthport, Mass., with a two-manual Hook & Hastings organ, which was opened on July 27.

Messrs. Hook & Hastings have just sent a two-manual organ to the parish of the Epiphany, Washington, D.C., which will be finished in a few weeks.

A new organ with two manuals, twenty stops, and three combination pedals, has been placed in the residence of Mr. I. B. Hosford, Haverhill, Mass., by Messrs. George H. Ryder & Co.

NEW ORGAN IN CONGREGATIONAL CHURCH, JACKSONVILLE, ILL.

Built by George S. Hutchings, Boston, Mass.

GREAT ORGAN.		SWELL ORGAN.	
Open Diapason . . .	8 Ft.	Bourdon Treble	16 Ft.
Dolcissimo	8 "	Bourdon Bass	
Melodia (Stopped Bass)	8 "	Violin Diapason . .	8 "
Octave	4 "	Salicional	8 "
Octave Quinte . . .	2⅔ "	Stopped Diapason . .	8 "
Super Octave . . .	2 "	Flute Harmonique . .	4 "
Trumpet	8 "	Violina	4 "
		Dolce Cornet . . .	2 Rks.
PEDAL ORGAN.		Oboe	8 Ft.
Open Diapason . . .	16 Ft.	Bassoon	
Bourdon	16 "	PEDAL MOVEMENTS.	
		Forte, Great Organ.	
		Piano, Great Organ.	
		Reversible Gt. to Pedal Coupler.	
The usual Couplers.		Swell Tremolo.	

Messrs. Hook & Hastings have just built an organ for the Temple K. K. B. Y. of Dayton, Ohio. The instrument shows four fronts, two on each side of the gallery, the keyboards being on the end of one of the divisions of the organ. The choir is located between the two parts in the organ gallery. The front pipes facing the auditorium rest upon the gallery rail, and conform to the line of the main arch of the building, making a design which is almost unique in its character.

Vol. I.   OCTOBER, 1892.   No. 6.

YEARLY SUBSCRIPTION $2.00.   SINGLE COPIES 25 CTS.

THE ORGAN

DEVOTED TO

A MONTHLY JOURNAL

THE KING OF INSTRUMENTS

RHEINBERGER
GUILMANT
FRESCOBALDI
BUXTEHUDE
MERKEL
BEST

·EVERETT·E·TRUETTE·

EDITOR & PUBLISHER

149 A. TREMONT ST. BOSTON.

HANDEL

The New England
Conservatory of Music.

CARL FAELTON, Director.

The Organ Department

offers unsurpassed facilities for acquiring a thorough and practical education in the art of Organ Playing. The course of study, which may be pursued, either in class or with private instruction, embraces work in Pedal Obligato Playing, Hymn Tunes and Chorales, with Interludes and Modulations. Afterwards Organ works of polyphonic character, Anthems and Improvisations, and for more advanced students works by all the great writers for the Organ, together with the study of Masses, Oratorios, etc.

There are in the Conservatory building for the exclusive use of this Department *fourteen* Pedal Organs, several of which possess three manuals each.

Those students who have acquired sufficient ability are aided in securing Church positions by the *Conservatory Bureau.* A large number of students have already been placed in lucrative positions by the Bureau.

TUITION: CLASSES OF FOUR, TERM OF TEN WEEKS, $20.00.

BOARD OF
INSTRUCTION.
{ GEORGE E. WHITING.
HENRY M. DUNHAM.
ALLEN W. SWAN.

{ Organ Practice, 10 cents per hour and upwards.
Pupils may enter at any time.
Fourth Term commences April 14.

Address, FRANK W. HALE,
General Manager,
Franklin Square, Boston, Mass.

United States Tubular Bell Co.
Incorporated under the Laws of Massachusetts.

OWNERS OF U. S. RIGHTS AND SOLE MANUFACTURERS OF

TUBULAR CHIME BELLS.

(HARRINGTON PATENTS).

For Churches, Turret Clocks, Public Buildings, Etc.

METHUEN, MASS.

These bells are established and in constant use in England, and over *one hundred* have been successfully placed in the United States in

DING-DONGS 2 bells,
PEALS   4 bells,
CHIMES 8, 13 and 15 bells,

They are in weight, LIGHTER
They are in tone, SWEETER
They are in price, CHEAPER
than the ordinary bell.

Descriptive catalogue sent on application.

Note. — A full set of Tubular Chimes is connected, electrically, with the keyboard of the

CHICAGO AUDITORIUM ORGAN.

THE ORGAN.

VOL. I.   BOSTON, OCTOBER, 1892.   No. 6.

THE ORGAN.
A MONTHLY JOURNAL
DEVOTED TO THE KING OF INSTRUMENTS.

EVERETT E. TRUETTE, EDITOR AND PUBLISHER.

(Entered at the Boston, Mass., Post-office as second-class mail matter, June 1, 1892.)

CONTENTS:

MR. CLARENCE EDDY.

No organist in this country is more widely known, from the Atlantic to the Pacific, than Mr. Clarence Eddy. Born in Greenfield, Mass., June 23, 1851, he showed a marked musical ability at the early age of five years. He received the best instruction the town afforded till he reached the age of sixteen, when he was sent to Hartford, Conn., to study with Mr. Dudley Buck. After a year of the most diligent study he was appointed organist of the Bethany Congregational Church, Montpelier Vt. In 1871 Mr. Eddy visited Germany, and studied with August Haupt in Berlin, the most prominent teacher of the organ in Germany for the past forty years. In later years Professor Haupt always spoke with intense enthusiasm of the remarkable progress which Mr. Eddy made, and of his phenomenal perseverance, which would have ruined the health of one possessing a less powerful physique.

Mr. Eddy won the admiration of Professor Haupt to such an extent that he was commissioned to represent the professor at a concert before the emperor.

At the end of his studies with Professor Haupt he received a letter containing the following : " In organ-playing the performances of Mr. Eddy are worthy to be designated as eminent ; and he is undoubtedly a peer of the greatest living organists."

Prior to returning to this country Mr. Eddy visited the principal cities of Germany, Austria, Switzerland, and Holland, giving recitals, in which he met with great success, and received marked expressions of praise from the leading critics.

On his return to this country he located in Chicago, where he has been the most prominent organist not only of the city, but of the West. Nor has his fame been confined to the West, for his recitals all over the country, from Boston to California, have established a reputation for him which is enviable.

He was appointed organist of the First Congregational

Clarence Eddy.

Church soon after his arrival in Chicago, and in 1875–76 gave his first series of twenty-five recitals. In 1876 he became general director of the Hershey School of Musical Art, in connection with which he gave his remarkable series of one hundred weekly recitals without repeating a number.

The one hundredth recital, June 23, 1879, was a gala occasion ; and most of the music was specially composed for that recital.

Undoubtedly Mr. Eddy has dedicated more organs in this country than any other organist, and great are the demands on his time for such occasions. The great Auditorium organ in Chicago, and the noted Denver organ, are among the large instruments which Mr. Eddy has opened.

At the Paris Exposition in 1889 Mr. Eddy was specially invited to give recitals in the Trocadéro ; thus increasing his glory abroad and at home. He gave recitals at the Centennial Exposition in Philadelphia, at the World's Fair in Vienna, and has made two concert tours to the Pacific coast with marked success.

Mr. Eddy is now organist of the First Presbyterian Church in Chicago, where he has officiated for fourteen years, and where his work is greatly admired.

The portrait which we present to our readers is an excellent likeness of one of our most honored organists.

REMINISCENCES OF ORGAN AND CHURCH MUSIC IN THIS COUNTRY.

BY AN ORGANIST.

III.

I PURPOSELY omit any mention at this time of church music in anthem form, chanting, as also of organ music proper, as I wish to speak of these important branches of the art in another connection.

It must have been about the year 1855 [1] that organists and musicians, generally, in Boston and New England, began to talk about a young man in Hartford, Conn. (he was then a student of Trinity College, but later, I think, organist of Yale College, New Haven, or, possibly, of some church in that city), as having a very unusual and unique talent for the organ.

I refer to the late "Dr." (his "Mus. Doc." was conferred by a Jesuit college in the vicinity of Baltimore, and was, of course, spurious) J. H. Wilcox, then, and for a good many years afterward, known as "John Wilcox."

Soon after the above date Mr. Wilcox, encouraged by the late Elias Hook (one of "nature's noblemen"), senior member of the firm of E. & G. G. Hook, — now Hook & Hastings, — removed to Boston. He was at first organist of Grace Church in Temple Street; but about that time Dr. (a real "Mus. Doc," by the way) S. P. Tuckerman happened to have one of his periodical "unpleasantnesses" with the "powers that be" of St. Paul's Church, and took himself off to England, when Mr. Wilcox was appointed his successor.

In the meantime, the young man had developed such a "passion" for everything connected with an organ, that he was given partial employment in the organ factory of the Messrs. Hook; first as an apprentice, and afterwards in the dual capacity of superintendent of the finishing of their organs when set up in the church, and as exhibitor of the completed instruments. It was in the latter capacity that Mr. Wilcox acquired the larger part of his fame.

He had been organist of St. Paul's only a year or two when he became a convert to the Roman Catholic faith, and was appointed organist and director of the music of the Church of the Immaculate Conception, then just finished, a position he held until a few years before his death, which occurred in 1873.

Much of his best reputation in Boston and vicinity was made at this church. He seemed to be peculiarly adapted to the music of the Catholic service, as usually performed in this country; that is, in the so-called "brilliant style."

When Mr. Wilcox first came to Boston, a young man of twenty-five or so, he was singularly attractive personally. He was of good height, very well built, with a distinguished-looking face, and with what is known as a "presence." He possessed also considerable personal magnetism, so that he made friends with great rapidity. To all this was added an unusually good classical education (for a musician), which, combined with his brilliant musical talents, quickly gave him a position in society, where he met Miss Chickering, daughter of Jonas Chickering, of the house of Chickering & Son, whom he afterwards married.

But, unfortunately, with all Mr. Wilcox's great gifts he was afflicted with a malady that finally ended his life; viz., softening of the brain. It was first noticed when he was in college, and grew upon him as he became older. This disease, no doubt, exercised a deteriorating influence on the development of his talents. He lacked the power of application. What knowledge he possessed of music was learned "off-hand." He was a pupil of Dr. Hodges, of Trinity Church, New York, for a short time; and this was about all the instruction he ever received.

Mr. Wilcox, with all his reputation, could not be considered a first-class performer on the organ. He never acquired a command of pedal obligato playing; consequently

[1] The writer makes no claim to exactness of dates.

he was utterly unable to perform even the easier pieces of the usual classical repertory, to say nothing of the great compositions of that school.

But now having told what Mr. Wilcox could not do, I will endeavor (a much more difficult task) to state what he could do, and that supremely well. First, it was really refreshing, for once, to meet a musical performer who was perfectly absorbed in his own instrument, and that instrument the organ. Among musical people one seldom hears anything but the everlasting talk about piano music, or, possibly, vocal music with piano accompaniment. The pianoforte is so come-at-a-ble; it is so easy to learn to play a little on; the piano-makers, piano-dealers, piano-players, and (especially) teachers, are so aggressive, and have, generally, such a sublime contempt for the other branches of the musical profession, that one wonders sometimes if there is any other kind of music worth listening to!

The writer used to amuse himself by occasionally sitting at the "receiving-clerk's" desk at the New England Conservatory, and noting the form of application of the swarms of pupils at the beginning of the term. The following was the usual conversation: Pupil: "I wish to take lessons." Clerk (from long experience, and to save a world of bother): "Vocal or Instrumental? Pupil (in almost every case): "Instrumental;" and instrumental it was, by which high-sounding term was meant that very poor instrument, the pianoforte! If they wished instruction in playing the organ, violin, or other orchestral instruments, they said so; but their idea of instrumental music was the piano? Consequently, I say again it was refreshing, for once to meet an artist like Mr. Wilcox, who was as far the other way, and could talk of nothing else but organ, organ, organ, from morning till night! Every bit of wood or metal that went into an organ was looked on by him with an artist's eye. He was full of contrivances for the better working of the various parts of the "action," shifting of the stops, composition pedals, etc. He also had a marvellous ear for "voicing," (one of the most difficult and important of this most difficult art of organ-building).

(To be continued.)

NOTABLE ORGANS.

III.

ST. PETER'S CHURCH, ST. PETERSBURG.

THE organ in the St. Peter's Church, St. Petersburg, was built by E. F. Walcker of Ludwigsburg in 1839-40, and, as

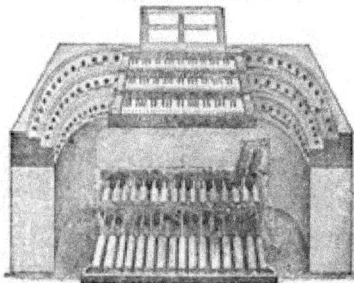

St. Petersburg Organ.

the accompanying cut of the console shows, has three manuals and two pedal claviers. There are sixty-five speaking stops, ten bellows, and thirty-seven hundred and eighty pipes. The special feature of this organ is its second pedal organ.

The first pedal organ has the usual variety of stops (thirteen in all), but the second pedal organ contains only five soft stops.

This firm have constructed several organs with two pedal claviers, but the extra pedal organ has proved impracticable, as the application of the modern combination movements enables a performer to change his combinations fully as quickly as he could change to another keyboard.

Appended is the specification : —

I. MANUAL.			II. MANUAL.		
Manual Untersatz	32	Ft.	Gedecht	16	Ft.
Principal	16	"	Gedecht	8	"
Tibia Major	16	"	Principal	8	"
Viola di Gamba	16	"	Flöte Douce	8	"
Octave	8	"	Viola d'Amour	8	"
Gemshorn	8	"	Dolce	8	"
Viola di Gamba	8	"	Octave	4	"
Flöte	8	"	Flauto Traverso	4	"
Octave	4	"	Rohr-flöte	4	"
Fugara	4	"	Quint	2⅔	"
Hohlpfeife	4	"	Octave	2	"
Terz	3⅕	"	Mixtures, V. bks	2	"
Quinte	3⅕	"	Posaune	8	"
Wald-flöte	2	"	Fagott (Bass)	8	"
Mixture, V. bks	2	"	Clarinet (Treble)	8	"
Cornet, V.	5⅓	"			
Scharf, III.	2	"	III. MANUAL.		
Tuba	16	"	Quintaton	16	Ft.
Trumpet Treble	8	"	Principal	8	"
" Bass			Salicional	8	"
			Bofen	8	"
			Gedecht	8	"
I. PEDAL.			Harmonica	8	"
Subbass	32	Ft.	Physharmonica	8	"
Untersatz	16	"	Spitz-flöte	4	"
Principal Bass	16	"	Flöte	4	"
Violin	16	"	Dolce	4	"
Hohlflöten "	8	"	Nasard	2⅔	"
Octave	8	"	Flautino	2	"
Octave	4	"			
Quinte	10⅔	"	II. PEDAL.		
Quinte	5⅓	"	Gedecht	16	Ft.
Posaune	16	"	Violoncello	8	"
Trumpet	8	"	Flöte	4	"
Clarine	4	"	Flautina	2	"
			Fagott	16	"

A FEW HINTS ON REGISTRATION.

THE selection of suitable stops with which to render any organ composition deserves more than passing notice, and many compositions which seem uninteresting would prove quite effective if more attention were given to the choice of stops. The following suggestions are intended for young organists who, from whatever circumstances may exist, are unable to obtain any instruction on this subject.

Before attempting to select any stops, the composition should be examined to determine its character. By determining whether the composition is polyphonic in character, or consists of a melody with accompaniment; whether there are long progressions of large chords, a march movement, or the harmony is open with few or no full chords; whether the general style is light, quiet, and subdued, or brilliant, heavy, and powerful; whether the prevailing feature is melody, harmony, rhythm, or coloring, and so on; the organist can immediately point out which combinations of stops are the most appropriate, and be is thereby better able to select a registration which will be suitable and effective.

To render these remarks more intelligible and instructive, examine the second composition in this number of THE ORGAN, — Adagio of Mendelssohn, for an example. No student, however stupid he may be, upon examining this movement could say that the general character was that of a melody with accompaniment, or a march. Neither would he call the harmony heavy and ponderous. The general character is seen at once to be quiet and subdued; therefore, such stops as the Trumpet, Open Diapason, 2 Ft. stops, and Mixtures, would be out of place.

Having determined the general character of the stops to be used, the next step is to point out the different phrases[1] showing where the registration may be changed without breaking up the construction of the composition by dividing the phrases into fragments. Upon a closer examination, it will be seen that the first eight measures of this movement are complete in themselves, and should not be separated. The second eight measures (omitting the last count of the last measure) are also complete, presenting the same melody, and partly the same harmony, an octave higher. These two phrases, then, can well be played with different stops (or combinations of stops), the second stop (or combination) forming a contrast to the first. The next four measures, beginning with the last count of the sixteenth measure, and ending with the second count of the twentieth measure, form a distinct phrase, and may be played on the first stop (or combination), or on some combination different from that used in the previous phrase. The following four measures can be separated and played on the same stop as the second phrase. Then follows a phrase of two measures and one count, which is repeated melodically a fifth higher. The next eight measures are distinct, though a division could be made in the middle. The following four measures constitute a return to the first theme (forty-first measure), which now appears as a melody with accompaniment, proceeding eight measures, when the same theme appears in the left hand. The following four measures, commencing with the fifty-sixth measure, contain repetitions of a single motive, and lead to the close (sixty-fourth measure), from which measure to the end could be considered a coda, in which effect we find fragments of the first theme, first in the upper part (sixty-fifth measure), and later in the left hand (sixty-ninth measure).

From this partial analysis of the composition the organist is enabled to determine at which points the registration may be changed, either by playing on a different manual, or by changing the combination of stops. The selection of suitable stops then becomes an easy matter.

The first phrase (or theme) of eight measures is in close harmony, and is of low pitch, being centred around middle C. Playing this theme on the Dulciana in the choir (or great), while this stop has the least character of any stop in an organ, the quiet, subdued effect which is desired is announced. The following phrase should then be played on a stop which presents a strong contrast to the preceding stop. The Salicional and Flute, 4 Ft., in the swell, would form a contrast, as would the Oboe, or the St. Diapason with Violin; but by using the St. Diapason alone the desired contrast is obtained, and the same quiet character of the movement continued. Reversing the order of these stops would give the same contrast, but the emphasis of a repetition would be lost, and the first phrase would not sound well on the St. Diapason, as the phrase is of such low pitch. The following four bars could be played on the Dulciana, but the Gamba is stronger. If the organ has but two manuals, it would be well to use the Melodia and Dulciana in the great. Returning to the St. Diapason on the last count of the twentieth measure is most natural. The last count of the twenty-fourth measure, with the twenty-fifth and twenty-sixth measures, should be played with the same stop or combination as measures sixteen to twenty. The following two measures can be played with the same combination, but a change is more satisfactory. The different combinations of stops should increase in power as the character of the movement grows stronger. Returning to the swell at the twenty-ninth measure, the Oboe can be added (adding the 4 Ft. Flute at the same time would brighten the combination). At the thirty-sixth measure (last count), by playing on the choir (or great), with Melodia and Dulciana, the return to the first theme is simple and satisfactory, the only change necessary being to put off the Melodia at the end of the fortieth measure. The following solo is effective with the combination already drawn in the swell (using the Tremulant is a matter of taste).

At the forty-ninth measure the theme in the left hand will

(Continued on page 137.)

[1] The term *phrase* is here used in its general sense, a short passage, and not in its technical sense, meaning four measures.

THE ORGAN.

BOSTON, OCTOBER, 1892.

THE ORGAN is published the first of every month. Subscription price $2.00 per year (foreign countries $2.50), payable in advance. Single copies, 25 cents.

Subscribers will please state with which number they wish their subscription to begin.

The paper will be sent to all patrons till the editor is notified by letter to discontinue.

Subscribers wishing the address of their paper changed must give the old as well as the new address.

Remittances should be made by registered letter, post-office order, or by check payable to Everett E. Truette.

Programmes of organ concerts, with press notices of the same, specifications of new organs, and items of general interest to the subscribers, will be gratefully received.

Correspondence, to secure notice, must in all cases be accompanied by the name and address of the writer, not for publication, but as a guarantee of good faith.

Advertising rates sent on application.

Address all communications,

The Organ, 149 A Tremont Street, Boston, Mass.

☞ An active agent in every city is desired to whom a liberal cash commission will be allowed.

ANNOUNCEMENT.

In response to the request of several organ-builders and organists, a large photograph of the Boston Music Hall organ (built by Walker & Sons of Germany) has been prepared, copies of which we offer for sale. No respectable photograph of this organ was taken while the instrument was standing, owing to the fact that the case, with its abundance of detail, was mostly in shadow, while the burnished pipes were brilliantly illuminated from windows above. When the instrument was being removed several years ago, about twenty-five photographs were taken of various parts of the instrument, — the panels, key desk, one of the towers, etc. Having purchased these negatives, we placed five of the photographs, together with such photographs of the whole instrument as could be secured, in the hands of an artist, who made a large drawing, with all the detail of this grand organ-front. From this drawing the woodcut shown on the title-page of this journal was made, and a large photograph has been taken. We have had a number of these photographs printed and mounted on heavy card-board ready for framing. The size is 12 x 14 inches, and the price is $2.00.

In clipping from other periodicals we always give credit to whatever paper from which we copy. We would thank a number of our exchanges if they would be equally courteous.

Among the visitors at this office during the past month were Mr. Clarence Eddy of Chicago, Mr. William C. Carl of New York, and Mr. J. Warren Andrews of Minneapolis.

Mr. Eddy is taking a short but much-needed rest after a very busy season, and is already booked for many concerts in the coming season. The Brooklyn Institute of Arts and Sciences are endeavoring to secure his services for some of the series of concerts which they are arranging for the coming season.

For years it has been customary to classify the different qualities of tone produced by the pipes of organ stops under four heads; viz., Organ, Flute, String, and Reed; but *The Indicator* (Chicago), in a description of the new organ in the Church of the Epiphany of that city, presumably copied from the programme announcement, informs us of a *fifth* quality of tone; viz., "Brass." Generally the "Reeds" include every stop in which the tone is produced by the vibrations of a reed, but in this organ such reed stops as the Trumpet, Cornopean, and Tuba are classified as "Brass." We have heard several poor Cornopeans, but have not yet heard one which was "brassy" enough to be called anything but a reed; however, the world is wide, and there is still much to learn.

Among the arrangements now being made for the musical part of the coming Columbian Exposition in Chicago, the organ will be well represented, if the present indications are correct. A large concert organ will be erected in the Music Hall (seating capacity of the hall two thousand), and an organ, specially constructed to support a large chorus, will be placed in the Festival Hall, where the seating capacity is expected to be about seven thousand, besides room for two thousand singers and two hundred musicians.

It is to be hoped that Messrs. Thomas, Tomlins, and Wilson, who have the whole charge of all affairs musical connected with the exposition, will see the wisdom of selecting a suitable person to take whole charge of the organ concerts. The onerous duties of these gentlemen will prevent their even thinking of the instrument, and with so many prominent organists present, as there undoubtedly will be, it would be a pity to neglect the opportunities for the most brilliant series of organ concerts ever known. If the selection of the performers is left to chance, taking only those who beg for the privilege, and there will be hundreds of them, the instruments will be degraded, and organ music in general will be voted a bore.

Mr. Johann Jones Wagner, who plays in the Nineteenth Congregational Church, declines to play any of the organ compositions of Mr. Ludwig Smith Bach, the organist of the Eleventh Presbyterian Church, situated in the next square, because they are rival (?) organists in the same city; and, notwithstanding the fact that the city has nine hundred thousand inhabitants, Johann seems to think that any encouraging recognition of the work of Ludwig would weaken his (Johann's) position by strengthening the position of his rival. The amount of this petty jealousy which exists in our cities is shameful, and not till we elevate our art above the effect of such contemptible feelings, can we hope for any number of representative American composers for the organ. "Organ publications do not pay," is the hackneyed but correct verdict of the publishers. We read among the advertisements of the electric cars, "If you would read this advertisement, others would read your advertisement." If you would play the compositions of your neighbors, your neighbors would play your compositions, and the financial failures which accompany your own publications would diminish at a gratifying rate. Most organists, when taking up a new composition, first look for the name of the composer. If he is a foreigner, the composition is at least worthy of a trial, but if he is so unfortunate as to be an American, and particularly if he is an acquaintance or a neighbor, there cannot be any merit in the work, and it is cast aside. Those who are willing to recognize what merit there is in the work of their professional brothers, are the ones whose own work shines with the fire of a broad and sound mind, and whose names will live the longest after they have departed.

COMMUNION IN E.

EDOUARD BATISTE.

Ch.
Gt.
Sw. to Gt. off
Ch.
(Add Cornopean in Sw.)
molto rit.
Add Tremulant.
a tempo
Ch.
Sw.
p
p
poco rit.
a tempo
p
p
a piacere rall.
Cornopian &
Tremolant off
Add Gt. & Sw. to Ped.

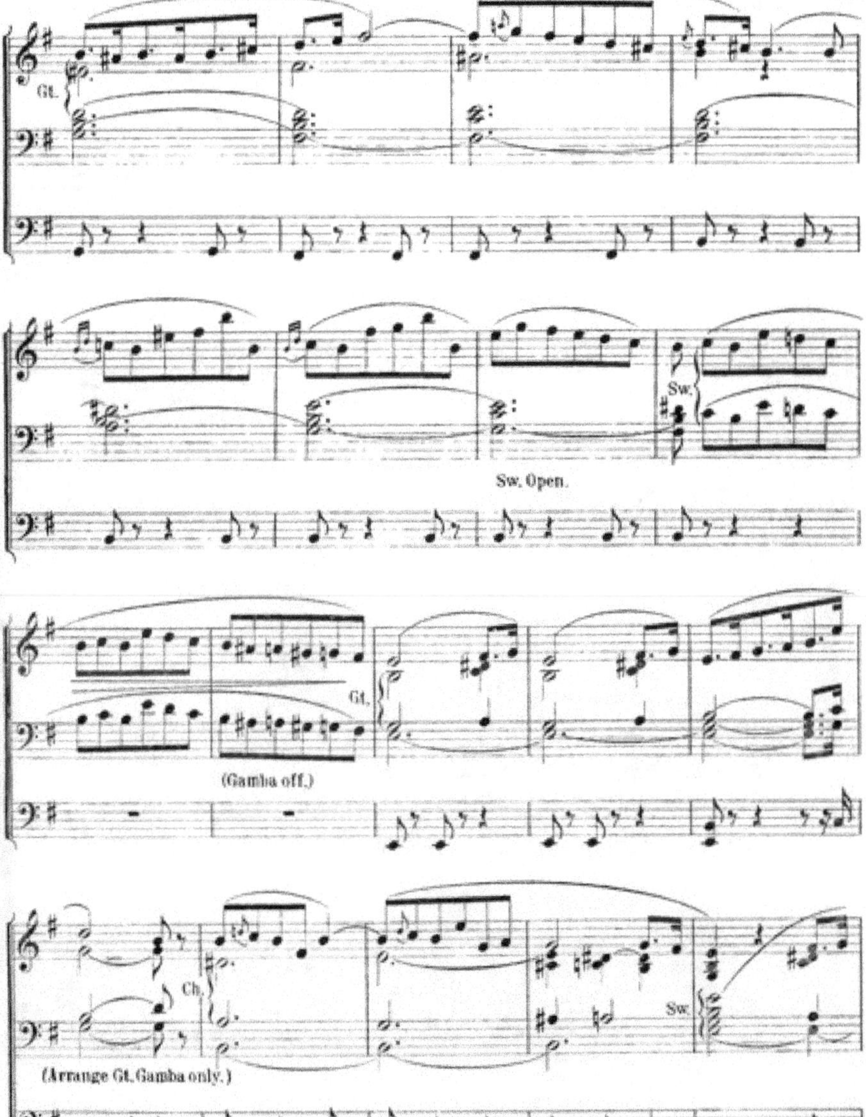

Gt.
Sw.
Sw. Open.
Gt.
(Gamba off.)
Ch.
Sw.
(Arrange Gt. Gamba only.)

Sw. to Ped off.

(Prepare Sw. Vox Humana (or Oboe) St. Diap.& Flute 4 Ft.)

molto rit.

Add Tremulant
Melodia in Ch. off.

a tempo

Ch.

Sw.

poco rit. a tempo

Expressivo a piacere

a tempo

Sw. Aeoline only.

Tremulant off

ADAGIO.

From The First Organ Sonata.

FELIX MENDELSSOHN – BARTHOLDY.

Gt.
Ch.
Sw. Add Oboe & Salicional.
Ch.
a tempo.
Sw. with Tremulant.
poco rit.
Melodia off.

Gt.
Sw.
Add Melodia in Ch.
Ch.
Ch.
Sw.
Gt.
Sw.
Oboe off.
Ch.
Ch.
St.Diap.only
(Prepare Sw. Aeoline.)
Sw.

A FEW HINTS ON REGISTRATION.

(*Continued from page 177.*)

be prominent, as desired, if played on the Gamba in the great. On a two-manual organ this prominence can be obtained by reversing the position of the hands from that of the preceding passage, and opening the swell. From the fifty-sixth to the sixtieth measures the repetitions of a motive should be played on different manuals, the last repetition, beginning with the third count of the fifty-ninth measure, being on the swell. At the sixty-fourth measure the swell should be reduced (putting off the Oboe), on the *second* count, as the preceding passage does not end till the first count.

At the sixty-ninth measure the theme appears in the left hand, and should be prominent, with Melodia and Dulciana (great or choir), for instance. The last five measures can be registered in several ways besides the one indicated. The upper part can be played on the St. Diapason in the swell, with the chords on the Dulciana in the choir (or great). Both parts can be played on the Salicional in the swell, though the crossing of the parts would be unsatisfactory. The registration indicated is effective, and if there is no St. Diapason in the choir, the Flute d'Amour 4 Ft., playing an octave lower, would sound well.

The registration which is indicated is but one of many effective registrations for this movement, but it will serve to illustrate the few ideas herein presented.

CIPHERINGS.

THE NEW CHURCH ORGAN.

BY

WILL M. CARLTON.

THEY'VE got a bran new organ, Sue,
  For all their fuss and search ;
They've done just as they said they'd do,
  And fetched it into church.
They're bound the critter shall be seen,
  And on the preacher's right
They've hoisted up their new machine
  In everybody's sight.
They've got a chorister and choir
  Agin MY voice and vote ;
For it was never MY desire
  To praise the Lord by note.

I've been a sister good and true
  For five and thirty year ;
I've done what seemed my part to do,
  An' prayed my duty clear ;
I've sung the hymns both slow and quick,
  Just as the preacher read,
And twice, when Deacon Tubbs was sick,
  I took the fork an' led !
And now their bold, new-fangled ways
  Is comin' all about ;
And I, right in my latter days,
  Am fairly crowded out.

To-day the preacher, good old dear,
  With tears all in his eyes,
Read — "I can read my title clear
  To mansions in the skies."
I al'ays liked that blessed hymn —
  I s'pose I al'ays will ;
It somehow gratifies MY whim,
  In good ole Ortonville ;

But when that choir got up to sing,
  I couldn't catch a word ;
They sung the most dog-gondest thing
  A body ever heard !

Some worldly chaps were standin' near,
  An' when I seed them grin,
I bid farewell to every fear,
  And boldly waded in.
I thought I'd chase their tune along,
  An' tried with all my might ;
But though my voice is good an' strong,
  I couldn't steer it right ;
When they was high, then I was low,
  An' also contrawise ;
An' I too fast, or they too slow,
  To "mansions in the skies."

An' after every verse, you know,
  They played a little tune ;
I didn't understand, an' so
  I started in too soon.
I pitched it pretty middlin' high,
  I fetched a lusty tone,
But oh, alas ! I found that I
  Was singin' there alone !
They laughed a little, I am told ;
  But I had done my best ;
And not a wave of trouble rolled
  Across my peaceful breast.

And Sister Brown — I could but look —
  She sits right front of me ;
She never was no singing-book,
  An' never went to be ;
But then she al'ays tried to do
  The best she could, she said ;
She understood the time, right through,
  An' kep' it, with her head ;
But when she tried this mornin', oh,
  I had to laugh or cough !
It kep' her head a bobbin' so,
  It e'en a'most came off !

An' Deacon Tubbs — he all broke down,
  As one might well suppose ;
He took one look at Sister Brown,
  An' meekly scratched his nose ;
He looked his hymn right thro' and thro',
  And laid it on the seat,
An' then a pensive sigh he drew
  An' looked completely beat.
An' when they took another bout,
  He didn't even rise,
But drawed his red bandanna out,
  An' wiped his weepin' eyes.

I've been a sister good an' true
  For five and thirty year ;
I've done what seemed my part to do,
  An' prayed my duty clear ;
But death will stop my voice, I know,
  For he is on my track ;
An' some day I to church will go,
  An' never more come back ;
An' when the folks get up to sing —
  Whene'er that time shall be —
I do not want no *patent* thing
  A squealin' over me !

The Equitable Gazette.

WATER-ORGANS.

In antiquity the adaptability of water to musical purposes early attracted the attention of inventors. Water-clocks were a useful and important discovery, which speedily assumed an artistic and musical form. The original idea of these pieces of mechanism was the dripping of water from one vase into another, which, proceeding at the rate of drop by drop, gave an exact indication of the time occupied in the exhaustion of the vase, and thus served for all the purposes of a clock. So thoroughly identified were the two things that the expression, "What is the water?" was a perfect equivalent for, "What is the time?" and the Greek orators spoke freely of the "water of their orations," meaning the space of time consumed in their delivery. Since water-clocks, though admirable indications of the time of day, would plainly be of no service at night, an inventor bethought himself of a plan by which the water, creating wind by the propulsion of a little wheel, should thus breath air through a tiny flute, which thereupon uttered a soft and melodious sound. This flute was so contrived, or, rather, the revolution of the wheel which formed it, that the hours of the night could be sounded in their order. From these beginnings a most extraordinary musical instrument was invented, more elaborate than any we have yet described, yet difficult to grasp in its complete mechanism, owing to no specimen or no drawing of it having been preserved to us. It was a box of flutes, wherein the instruments were set on end similarly to the method adopted with the pipes of an organ. This box was placed above a large vase containing water, the ends of the flutes being open and turned downwards towards the water. According to the commonly received account, the water was agitated by a boy, and the wind thus created in the interior of the instrument set the flutes playing. Such motion of the water, however, seems inadequate to producing the effect designed. More probably the wind was pumped through the water by means of pistons and levers, and the current of air thus admitted into the pipes caused them to sound.

In order to convert this mechanism of quaint and ill-regulated melody into a practicable and manageable instrument, nothing more was wanted but the addition of slides to the pipes, which could open and shut them at pleasure. By this simple means the sound could be directed and governed; and nothing more but the addition of keys, connected by strings with the slides, so as to command them at the will of the player, was required to turn this water-flute into an organ.

Water remained the concomitant of organs for almost a thousand years from that date onwards. The office fulfilled by the water was not that of a mere hydraulic appendage that can be dispensed with, as with us: the element was part and parcel of the organ, and the organist, wherever he went, was in company with vases full of water, funnels, pistons, and other apparatus which the water rendered necessary. This water-organ, clumsy as it may appear to be, was nevertheless not necessarily so; but certain parts of it could be carried from place to place with ease and convenience.

Into the history of the water-organ we do not propose to enter, having already treated it at length in a former contribution to this paper. It is interesting to remark, however,

for what a long time the water-organ endured in preference to that other form of the instrument which employed bellows. Even in the time of Louis the Pious, the son of Charlemagne, water-organs were still the popular form, and all organs made by George the Venetian, the celebrated builder of the age, were furnished by the hydraulic apparatus of which we propose to immediately give a description. Researches into the early history of the organ, it may be remarked, have remained a barren field for the investigators, owing to their confining their attention to the notices in Latin writers, which are few and far between. The real home of organ-building during the dark ages was not at Rome, in Italy, or even in Europe, but at Constantinople, where the organ, instead of being an obscure and neglected mechanism, was the fashionable instrument of the Greek world for centuries, being employed in the circuses, at banquets to usher in the guests, at state ceremonials, and on other public occasions as, for instance, at those ceremonies in the Golden Hippodrome on the first Monday after Easter, when the emperor received the acclamations of the people. Up till the downfall of the Western Empire the fortunes of the water-organ can be followed in Italy, and receive illumination from quarters and from writers whose professed aim in description is not a musical one. Gibbon speaks of the "enormous water-organs of the theatres," which in the later imperial times were employed in Rome; while delicacy of structure had attained a high degree of perfection, judging from the accounts of Ammianus of the portable water-organs which slaves were accustomed to carry about from house to house, in order to take part in the private concerts of their masters. At present we are not considering the subject of the water-organs, but merely the water mechanism connected with the instrument, which, in so far as it was auxiliary to the playing of the organ, may justly be considered as coming within the scope of "The Music of Water." This mechanism, in conclusion, we will now describe. There was, first, a large vase full of water, which had an inverted funnel in it, connected by a pipe with a flat box or wind-chest above, which contained the wind. On each side of this vase were cylinders with pistons inside them, which were worked with levers from below, like pumps. These cylinders had pipes running from them into the central vase, down through the water into the bell of the funnel. There were valves at the top, hanging by movable chains. When, therefore, it was necessary to fill these cylinders with air, the lever was raised, the valve immediately descended, and through the hole the air rushed into the cylinder. But directly the lever was pumped downwards and the air sent rushing up the cylinders of the piston, at the first puff the valve closed at the top, the air, therefore, rushing through the pipe into the central vase of water, and down into the bell of the funnel, whither the pipe reached. From thence with redoubled force, owing to the weight of the funnel, it was driven up the funnel's pipe and into the wind-chest.— *London Musical Times.*

Mons. C. M. Widor, the organist of St. Sulpice, Paris, has written a choral symphony which is to be produced this month in a new concert hall in Geneva.

ORGAN RECITALS.

INAUGURATION of the New Organ (Roosevelt) in Temple Keneseth Israel, Philadelphia : —

Baccarole . . . . Hofmann
  Mr. Maurits Leefson (Organist Temple Keneseth Israel).
a. Larghetto from Clarionet Quintet . . . . Mozart
A Chorus from Judas Maccabeus . . . . . Händel
  Mr. D. Wood (Organist St. Stephens, and Temple Baptist Church).
Offertoire . . . . Lefebure-Wely
  Mr. Carl Retter (Organist Temple Rodef Sholom and Calvary P. E. Church, Pittsburg, Pa.).
Jubilee Overture . . . . Weber
  Mr. Frederick Maxson (Organist Central Congregational Church).
Extemporization.
  Mr. Michael H. Cross, (Organist Holy Trinity Church).
a. Cantilène Pastorale . . . . Grison
b. Marche Nuptiale . . . . Guilmant
  Mr. S. Tudor Strong (Organist Oxford Presbyterian Church).
Toccata . . . . Dubois
  Mr. Maurits Leefson.

ORGAN RECITAL in the Centennial Hall, Sydney, Australia, by Mons. Auguste Wiegand : —

Marche du Roi d'Espagne . . . . Vilbac
Romanze in F . . . . Grison
Cavatina, "La Juive" . . . . Halévy-Vilbac
Fantasia, "Norma" . . . . Bellini
Festival March . . . . Haase
Une Plainte Mélodique . . . . Poussard
Nazereth . . . . Gosnod
Grand Chorus in F . . . . Grison

AT the fourteenth organ recital, given in Christ Church, Norfolk, Va., by Mr. J. J. Miller, the following programme was given : —

Toccata in D minor . . . . J. S. Bach
La Melancolie . . . . Fr. Prume
Lied an den Abendstern ("Tannhäuser") . . R. Wagner
  Mr. Wm. H. Turner.
Larghetto (from "The Water Music") . . . G. F. Händel
"Sunshine and Shadow." . . . . Dudley Buck
Fear not ye, O Israel. . . . . Dudley Buck
  Miss Myra Muse Southgate.
Marche Funèbre et Chant Seraphique. . . . Alex. Guilmant

SIXTH ORGAN RECITAL in St. James's Church, Batavia, N.Y., by Mr. Gilbert Caught, Sept. 8 : —

Sonata in C minor . . . . Mendelssohn
Fugue in G minor (the greater) . . . . . . Bach
Flute Concerto (two movements) . . . . . Rinck
Minuetto in B minor, Op. 93 . . . . . . Calkin
Evening Song } . . . . Van Eyken
Adagio in F. (Sonata No. 2) }
Serenade . . . . Jensen
The Harvest Home . . . . Spinny
Finale (Grand Chorus) . . . . Lemmens

ORGAN RECITAL in St. Paul's Cathedral, Melbourne, Australia, by Mr. Ernest Wood, June 8 : —

Sonata in D minor. . . . . Merkel
Andantino "La Cloche du Soir" . . . . . Chauvet
Offertoire in two Christmas Hymns . . . . Guilmant
Grand Solemn March . . . . Smart

INAUGURAL CONCERT in the Church of the Sacred Heart, Waterbury, Conn., September 14. New organ, built by Johnson & Son of Westfield, Mass. Mr. E. V. Canfield of Hartford played Overture, "A Night in Granada," by Kreutzer ; Allegretto, by Best ; A Descriptive Piece, and Tournament at Raab, by Loretz ; Overture, "Morning, Noon, and Night," Suppé ; and Mr. John L. Bonn, of Waterbury played Offertories of Urtz and Batiste.

A REVIEW of the concert in the *Waterbury Republican*, while praising the quality of the organ (i.e. what little was heard of it), criticises the performers for the monotony of their registration, though the reviewer charitably attributes it to a lack of familiarity with the instrument.

A CHAPTER OF DON'TS.

DON'T slide back and forth on the seat when playing a pedal passage. To easily reach the extreme notes of the pedal board, turn the body slightly toward those notes.

Don't go through any contortions of the body when about to remove the hands from the keys at the end of a composition which terminates with the full organ. The audience forget all about your playing in sympathizing with you in your apparent agony.

Don't sway back and forth when playing. An easy, graceful appearance at the organ requires but little motion of the body.

Don't improvise all the time on the Salicional and Violin with Tremulant. The combination is effective when properly used, but becomes tiresome with an overdose.

Don't think that because the Vox Humana (without Tremulant), combined with the Mixtures in the swell, sound "novel," they are pleasing. A dish-pan and poker would sound just as "novel" and about as agreeable.

Don't improvise every prelude and postlude which you play. You cannot stand Beethoven's music all the time. How can your congregation stand your music all the time ?

Don't use the Tremulant very often in accompanying singers.

Don't hold one chord or note a minute and a half while you change the stops and arrange your music. Remember that those who are listening to you have nerves.

Don't turn on the water for your motor too suddenly. It wrenches the motor and bellow's action.

Don't complain all the time that your present position is beneath you. He who looks up to himself must first lower himself to look up, and then only sees his former position, not the occupant.

Don't think that you know it all. Even the greatest organist can learn something new every week.

QUESTIONS AND ANSWERS.

All questions must be accompanied by the full name and address of the writer, and, if received by the 10th of the month, will usually be answered in the following number of THE ORGAN.

Only such questions as refer to the organ, its registers, organ builders, or to organ music, will be answered.

Correspondents are requested to write their questions in a clear and concise manner, writing on only one side of the paper.

J. J. K. Will you please tell me where I can procure a copy of Händel's B-flat Concerto for the organ? I have inquired at several music stores here, but have been unable to get it.

ANS. "Six Concertos of Händel," edited by Best (Novello Ewer & Co.), contains the concerto in B-flat.

FRANK K. L. Please suggest a good registration for the slow movement of Mendelssohn's second organ sonata.

ANS. Solo part played with Oboe and St. Diapason on swell, with accompaniment on the Dulciana (choir or great). If the organ has three manuals, the Gamba in the great should be used for the solo, commencing with the seventh bar, returning to the swell in the fifteenth bar. Great again in the seventeenth bar and swell in the nineteenth bar. This is simply one of a number of effective registrations for this movement.

PHILADELPHIA. Please inform me how to pronounce the following names: Guilmant, Gigout, Töpfer, and Stainer.

ANS. Approximately, Geel-marnt, Gee-goo (the first G is soft and the second hard), Turp'-fur, Stay'-ner.

H. F. C. I wish to give an organ recital in the church in which I play. Will you kindly give me the names of a few pieces of about the same grade as Religious March of Guilmant, and Communion in G of Batiste, which would make an interesting programme for a small three-manual organ.

ANS.

1. Marche Religieuse . . . . Guilmant
2. Fugue in G-minor (lesser) . . . . Bach
3. Adagio in A-flat . . . . Volckmar
4. Xmas Pastorale . . . . Merkel
5. Processional March . . . . Whitney
6. Andante in A-flat . . . . Dunham
7. Communion in G . . . . Batiste
8. Festival March in D . . . . Smart

NOTE. If the programme is too long, No. 4, No. 5, No. 6, or No. 7 can be omitted.

CORRESPONDENCE.

THE EVOLUTION OF THE SWELL-BOX.

To the Editor of The Organ.

DEAR SIR, — Emile Le Blanc's reply or remarks concerning Gambette's evolution of the swell-box leaves the writer in doubt as to whether the object in view is to belittle organ-players and organ-builders, or to display quite a deal of ignorance as to the tone qualities of various pipes or stops of a properly toned organ. I would like to say that the swell-box, if properly made and arranged, may be considered very good as a mode of expression, and is not so very detrimental to the large pipes; if so, why should we be "almost lifted off one's feet with enthusiasm" when applied to the great organ, where many of the largest pipes may be found?

Let your stories agree, Emile. A person who had listened to Rinck, once said to the writer that in his playing he made a grand swell effect in his performance on any manual without a swell, which, by the way, is accomplished by organists of our day. To properly perform on the organ should mean that many effects should be within the power of the performer besides the mere rendering of legitimate organ music. We have heard many first-class players use the Oboe as a solo, and accompany on the Dulciana, when the effect was anything but "aggravating." We have taken pains to inquire of a number of organists who play legitimate organ music, and have honorably graduated under some of our best teachers, and the majority agree with Gambette. Of course there may be points of minor difference. Will you allow me to say that I mistrust that Gambette can "play a little" better than many who have or may criticise his articles. It was our privilege to listen to a player of legitimate organ music on a large two-manual organ with both manuals incased in swell-boxes, with the exception of the Dulciana and Open Diapason in the great organ; and while many fine effects were produced, and we were "nearly lifted from our feet," still we agreed with the organist when he remarked that had he his way he would remove the swell-box entirely from the great organ. If we must have two swell-boxes, let it be the swell and choir manual; but leave, oh, leave us the effect of the great organ, pure and simple, also the pedal. I claim to know nothing, but give my opinion in hopes others who do know may give us —

           MORE LIGHT.

To the Editor of The Organ :

Is the almost universal practice of introducing the Violoncello as the third Pedal stop a good one, or is not the Flute better? The first object of the Pedal Organ being to furnish a foundation for the sounds of the manual department, the first stops must be of 16 Ft. — a Bourdon, usually, if alone, so that it may form a kind of compromise, and furnish a suitable bass to all stops, from Dulciana to full organ. (?) Then may come the Diapason of 16 Ft., the Bourdon being softened, or (better) replaced by a 16 Ft. Dulciana. Now, we may begin to make the Pedal really *independent*. Instead of coupling to obtain definition, let us have a stop of 8 Ft. My contention is that the Flute is much better than the Violoncello for this purpose. The nasal quality of the Violoncello stop causes it to be too prominent with soft organ, and not enough so with loud organ; while the Flute, with its round tone, is unobtrusively distinct under all circumstances; not being covered by loud organ, and rarely too strong for soft organ. In a place where four distinct qualities of tone are needed, on a three-manual organ, it is invaluable. Let me refer to Sonata Op. 19, of Ritter, p. 6, where the left hand plays the principal melody on the Gt. Gamba, the right alternating between Ch. Clarinet and Sw. Oboe. To couple any manual to the Pedal, at this point, is to destroy the needed contrast, and the Violoncello is too strong. Nothing but a Pedal Flute will meet the exigency. This is only one instance. There are many others which might be quoted. Taking the Flute for the third stop, let us put the Violoncello in as the fourth. The practice of many builders of using a Trombone as the fourth stop in the Pedal organ, is not to be defended on any ground of musical effect. But your space must not be occupied further to discuss this point. Let me suggest — Bourdon, or Dulciana of 16 Ft., Diapason, Flute, Violoncello, Gamba of 16 Ft., Quint, Trombone, Bassoon of 8 Ft., Dulciana (wood) of 16 Ft.   Yours cordially,

           ALEX S. GIBSON.

WATERBURY, CONN., Sept. 19, 1892.

Undoubtedly a Flute of 8 Ft. in the pedal organ is much more effective and more useful than a Violoncello of 8 Ft. The Flute requires more "standing-room," and costs more than the 'Cello, which is the reason many builders include only the latter in many of their organs. — ED.

MIXTURES.

(FOUR RANKS.)

MR. R. S. BURTON, a prominent organist of Leeds, died the 4th of August.

The French papers announce the death of Mons. Pickaert (former organist of Notre-Dame-des-Victoires), at the age of seventy-five years.

Mr. Arthur Whiting has been appointed organist of the Arlington-street Church, Boston.

The prize offered by the London *Musical News* for the best short introductory voluntary for the organ was won by Mr. W. G. Alcock, organist of Quebec Chapel.

Mr. M. E. H. Lemare, F. C. O., has been giving a series of organ recitals in the Concert Hall of the Exhibition in Genoa.

Dr. J. H. Gower, an organist of Denver, Col., is spending a couple months in Europe. He expects to return in October.

Mr. H. O. Farnum, formerly of Wittenberg College, has been appointed organist of Christ Church, Louisville, Ky.

Mr. J. Wallace Goodrich, organist of the Elliot Church, Newton, Mass., while driving recently, was thrown to the ground and somewhat injured. Mr. J. D. Buckingham, former organist of the Immanuel Church, Boston, substituted for Mr. Goodrich.

The "New Harmonic Organ," an instrument invented by Levi Orser, of London, Ontario, has made its appearance. The instrument is provided with twelve stops, by means of which twenty-four tones in each octave can be produced, there being a difference in intonation between C-sharp and D-flat, etc.

A new organ with electro-pneumatic action has been constructed in a church in Montivilliers, France, having thirty-six speaking-stops ("electric buttons"), six combination-stops, and seventeen combination-pedals. Mons. Alex Guilmant was the performer at the inauguration of the instrument.

"I am losing my taste for arrangements from orchestral works, overtures, etc., and prefer pure organ music from Bach to Rheinberger, Merkel, Smart, and Guilmant. Widor is good and clever, but I have not found myself able to sympathize with his music, though his playing of it at Newcastle was remarkably effective."— DR. WM. REA, *in London Musical Herald.*

The memorial organ to be presented to Grace Episcopal Church, San Francisco, by Mr. Edward F. Searles, will be built by Messrs. James E. Treat & Co., Methuen, Mass. (formerly Boston), and will be larger than that at Kellogg Terrace, Gt. Barrington, made by this firm. Mr. Treat says, "It will be constructed on common-sense lines, following the English standards. No effort will be made to boom the firm by the introduction of clap-trap appliances." As both these gentlemen know what constitutes a superior instrument, — the experience of the latter with pipe-organs dating from 1848, — it goes without saying that this will be one.

NEW ORGAN MUSIC.

Tempo di Minuetto	W. A. C. Cruickshank.
Toccata	G. Flügel.
Andante Serioso	G. Flügel.
Prelude Fugue and Variations	C. Franck.
Sonata in E-minor	C. F. Hendriks.
Prelude and Fuga, C-minor	C. F. Hendriks.
Three Pieces	A. Mailly.
Andante Religioso	Gabriel Marie.

NEW ORGANS.

NEW ORGAN IN TEMPLE KENESETH ISRAEL, PHILADELPHIA.

Constructed by Mr. Frank Roosevelt of New York.

GREAT ORGAN.		SWELL ORGAN.	
1 Double Open Diapason	16 Ft.	13 Bourdon (treble and bass, split knob)	16 Ft.
2 1st Open Diapason	8 "	14 Open Diapason	8 "
3 2d Open Diapason	8 "	15 Spitz-flöte	8 "
4 Gemshorn	8 "	16 Salicional	8 "
5 Viola di Gamba	8 "	17 Æoline	8 "
6 Stopped-flöte	8 "	18 Vox Celestis	8 "
7 Octave	4 "	19 Stopped Diapason	8 "
8 Hohl-flöte	4 "	20 Octave	4 "
9 Octave Quint	2⅔ "	21 Flûte Harmonique	4 "
10 Super Octave	2 "	22 Flageolet	2 "
11 Mixture	4 Rks.	23 Cornet	3, 4, and 5 Rks.
12 Trumpet	8 Ft.	24 Contra Fagotto	16 Ft.
		25 Cornopean	8 "
(Stops 4 to 12 included in the Choir Swell-box.)		26 Oboe	8 "
		27 Vox Humana	8 "

CHOIR ORGAN.
(Enclosed in a separate Swell-box.)

28 Contra Gamba (Stopped Bass)	16 Ft.	32 Quintadena	8 Ft.
29 Geigen Principal	8 "	33 Fugara	4 "
30 Dolce	8 "	34 Flûte d'Amour	4 "
31 Concert Flute	8 "	35 Piccolo Harmonique	2 "
		36 Clarinet	8 "

PEDAL ORGAN.

37 Open Diapason	16 Ft.	40 Violoncello	8 Ft.
38 Bourdon	16 "	41 Trombone	16 "
39 Quint	10⅔ "		

PEDAL MOVEMENTS.
(Roosevelt Patent Automatic Adjustable Combination Pedals.)

Three affecting Great and Pedal Stops.	Full Organ Pedal.
Three affecting Swell and Pedal Stops.	Pedal Organ Ventil.
Two affecting Choir and Pedal Stops.	Great to Pedal Reversing Pedal.
	Balanced Great and Choir Pedal.
Extended Action.	Balanced Swell Pedal.
Rotary Water Motor.	Sw. to Gt. Octaves in addition to the usual Couplers.

The pipes of the swell organ are placed below those of the great and choir, to give greater prominence to that part of the instrument.

MOUNT VERNON CONGREGATIONAL CHURCH, BOSTON, MASS.

New Organ, built by Geo. S. Hutchings, Boston.

GREAT ORGAN.		SWELL ORGAN.	
Open Diapason	16 Ft.	Bourdon Treble }	16 Ft.
Open Diapason	8 "	Bourdon Bass }	
Dulciana (blank slide)	8 "	Violin Diapason	8 "
Viola di Gamba	8 "	Salicional	8 "
Doppel-flöte	8 "	Æoline	8 "
Octave	4 "	Stopped Diapason	8 "
Flûte Harmonique	4 "	Quintadena	8 "
Octave Quinte	2⅔ "	Flauto Traverso	4 "
Super Octave	2 "	Fugara	4 "
Mixture	3 Rks.	Flautina (to draw with the next)	2 "
Trumpet	8 Ft.	Dolce Cornet	4 Rks.
		Cornopean	8 Ft.
		Vox Humana (blank slide)	8 "
		Oboe	8 "

CHOIR ORGAN.		PEDAL ORGAN.	
Lieblich Gedackt or Dulciana (blank)	16 Ft.	Open Diapason	16 Ft.
Geigen Principal	8 "	Bourdon	16 "
Dolcissimo	8 "	Violoncello	8 "
Melodia (stopped bass)	8 "	Bass Flute (blank slide)	8 "
Flûte d'Amour	4 "	Manual Couplers to be operated by Piston Knobs.	
Violina	4 "	Pneumatic Motors applied to the Great Organ and its Couplers.	
Piccolo Harmonique	2 "		
Clarinet (Bassoon Bass)	8 "		

PEDAL MOVEMENTS.

Forte, Great Organ.	Reversible Great to Pedal Coupler.
Mezzo, Great Organ.	All Couplers Double Acting on and off.
Piano, Great Organ.	Swell Tremolo.
Forte, Swell Organ.	Coupler Swell to Great at Octaves.
Mezzo, Swell Organ.	
Piano, Swell Organ.	

YOUNG WOMEN'S CHRISTIAN ASSOCIATION BUILDING, BROOKLYN, N. Y.

New Organ, built by Geo. S. Hutchings, Boston.

GREAT ORGAN.		SWELL ORGAN.	
Bourdon	16 Ft.	Stopped Diapason	8 Ft.
Open Diapason	8 "	Æoline	8 "
Salicional	8 "	Flûte Harmonique	4 "
Melodia	8 "	Oboe	8 "
Octave	4 "		
Dolce Cornet	3 Rks.	PEDAL ORGAN.	
Trumpet	8 Ft.	Open Diapason	16 Ft.
		Bourdon	16 "

PEDAL MOVEMENTS.

Forte, Great Organ.	Swell to Great at Octaves.
Piano, Great Organ.	The usual Couplers.
Swell Tremolo.	

A NEW organ, having electro-pneumatic action throughout, has been placed in the concert hall of the Columbian Exhibition in Genoa, by Messrs. W. G. Trice & Co. of Quarto al Mare, with the following specification:—

GREAT ORGAN.		SWELL ORGAN.	
Double Diapason	16 Ft.	Quintaton	16 Ft.
Open Diapason	8 "	Eulonism	8 "
Dulciana	8 "	Viola	8 "
St. Diapason	8 "	Celeste	8 "
Principal	4 "	Octave	4 "
Harmonic Flute	4 "	Mixture (Gamba)	3 Rks.
Fifteenth	2 "	Contra Fagotto	16 Ft.
Mixtures	4 Rks.	Cornopean	8 "
Trumpet	8 Ft.	Vox Humana	8 "

CHOIR ORGAN.		SOLO ORGAN (8 in. Wind).	
Lieblich Gedackt	16 Ft.	Horn	8 Ft.
Viola di Gamba	8 "	Orchestral Flute	4 "
Clarabella	8 "	Tuba Mirabilis	8 "
Flauto Traverso	4 "	Octave Oboe	4 "
Flautina	2 "		
Clarionet	8 "		

PEDAL ORGAN.

Pedal Open	16 Ft.	Octave	8 Ft.
Pedal Bourdon	16 "	Fifteenth	4 "
Pedal Violoncello	8 "	Trombone	16 "

NEW ORGAN IN THE CHURCH OF THE SACRED HEART, WATERBURY, CONN.

Built by Messrs. Johnson and Son, Westfield, Mass.

GREAT ORGAN.		SWELL ORGAN.	
Open Diapason	16 Ft.	Lieblich Gedackt	16 Ft.
Open Diapason	8 "	Open Diapason	8 "
Doppel-flöte	8 "	Salicional	8 "
Viola di Gamba	8 "	Dolcissimo	8 "
Octave	4 "	Stopped Diapason	8 "
Flûte Harmonique	4 "	Flûte Harmonique	4 "
Twelfth	2⅔ "	Violin	4 "
Fifteenth	2 "	Flautina	2 "
Mixture	4 Rks.	Cornet	3 Rks.
Trumpet	8 Ft.	Oboe	8 Ft.
		Cornopean	8 "

CHOIR ORGAN.		PEDAL ORGAN.	
Geigen Principal	8 Ft.	Open Diapason	16 Ft.
Melodia	8 "	Bourdon	16 "
Dulciana	8 "	Violoncello	8 "
Flûte d'Amour	4 "	Trombone	16 "
Clarinet and Bassoon	8 "		

PEDAL MOVEMENTS.

FF. and MF. combinations for Gt.	Sw. to Gt. in octaves, in addition to the usual Couplers.
FF. MF. and F. " Sw.	Pedal Couplers placed over swell manual.
Gt. to Ped. (reversible).	

VOL. I.   NOVEMBER, 1892.   No. 7.

BACH

YEARLY SUBSCRIPTION $2.00.   SINGLE COPIES 25 CTS.

THE ORGAN

DEVOTED TO

A MONTHLY JOURNAL

THE KING OF INSTRUMENTS

·EVERETT·E·TRUETTE·

EDITOR & PUBLISHER

149 A. TREMONT ST. BOSTON.

HANDEL

THE ORGAN.

VOL. I. BOSTON, NOVEMBER, 1892. No. 7.

THE ORGAN.

A MONTHLY JOURNAL

DEVOTED TO THE KING OF INSTRUMENTS.

EVERETT E. TRUETTE, EDITOR AND PUBLISHER.

(Entered at the Boston, Mass., Post-office as second-class mail matter, June 1, 1892.)

CONTENTS:

GUSTAV MERKEL.

GUSTAV MERKEL, who was one of the peers among the composers of organ music in Germany, was born at Oberoderwitz, Saxony, in 1827. His youthful days were not specially eventful, his musical studies being directed by Julius Otto and the celebrated organist, Dr. Johann Schneider, a resident of Dresden. Merkel pursued his favorite study of composition with Reissiger and Schumann, the influence of the latter being frequently apparent in his earlier writings. In 1858 he was chosen organist of the Waisenkirche, Dresden, but retained the position only for two years, becoming the organist of the Kreuzkirche in 1860, and Court Organist in 1864. In 1862 he accepted a professorship in the Dresden Conservatorium, and in 1867 he was elected director of the Singacademie, which position he held till 1873. He died in Dresden, Oct. 30, 1885, at the age of fifty-eight.

Merkel's printed compositions number nearly two hundred, most of which are for the organ. Foremost among these stand his nine Organ Sonatas: Op. 30, 42, 80, 115, 118, 137, 140, 178, and 183. The first sonata, for four hands and double pedal, is the most effective duet ever written for the organ. The second sonata, in G-minor, has been played a great deal in this country, and is probably the most popular one of the set. The fifth sonata, in D-minor, contains one of the best fugues which Merkel has written, and the slow movement is a gem. All the sonatas are characterized by their contrapuntal and fugal treatment rather than the stereotyped sonata form, particularly in the first movements. The counterpoint is always smooth and flowing, and specially adapted to the German organs.

Of his other compositions the most popular are the Weinachts Pastorale, Op. 56; Pastorale in G, Op. 103, and the Adagio in E, Op. 35; three compositions which, while they bear a striking resemblance, are overflowing with legitimate organ effects of rare beauty.

Of his less known compositions the following may be mentioned as specially adapted for concert purposes, and in many places would prove novelties: —

Variations, or a theme of Beethoven, Op. 45; Fantasia and Fugue, Op. 104; Introduction and Double Fugue, Op. 105; Concertsatz in E-flat minor, Op. 131.

REMINISCENCES OF ORGAN AND CHURCH MUSIC IN THIS COUNTRY.

BY AN ORGANIST.

IV.

But this was only one side of Mr. Wilcox's talent for the organ. To the public he was known as a brilliant extempore player. To my mind, however, he scarcely justified his reputation in this particular accomplishment. His knowledge of counterpoint and musical form was so very slight, that his performances were apt to be monotonous. He repeated himself too much; so that after hearing him once, you were apt to be disappointed in a second performance.

But now what was the secret of his great power over an audience? I answer: he was a born master of what is known to musicians as "instrumentation" and "tone color," in music. He always made the organ *sound* beautifully. The art that Berlioz and some other writers of orchestral music possessed, viz. of writing their musical thoughts *in such a manner for each instrument* in the orchestra, that the general effect was the best attainable, Mr. Wilcox was an undoubted master of, in performing extempore on the organ. In my opinion, had he been taught to write for the orchestra, and had he possessed the necessary power of application, he would have produced some good work in that direction.

But not only was he a master of "effects;" his ideas were frequently extremely "brilliant," perhaps not especially original, but they sounded excellently, when coming from under his fingers on a good organ. I said he was a master of "color," by which is meant the art of producing musical thoughts *that shall be appropriate to the sentiment of the moment;* for instance, military music, march rhythms, religious music, choral effects, music in the modern Italian and French style, of whom Rossini and Meyerbeer are good examples, etc. (the list is very long).

Now, Mr. Wilcox could produce these various sentiments in the hearer by his extemporaneous performances on the organ. I will endeavor to jot down a few recollections of his manner of playing. Remember they are only "recollections," and faint ones at that.

He frequently began his extempore performances by a series of linked chords in the plainest possible harmony, played on the 16 and 8 feet diapasons in the great manual, with the double open 16 feet pedal, coupled to great, as follows:—

It will be seen that there is nothing remarkable about this; but it sounds appropriate to the organ, and strikes the keynote of the moment, by putting the listener in a sympathetic

frame of mind for an organ performance. After this movement had gone on for perhaps twenty or thirty bars, he would introduce a more brilliant style of performance on the "full" organ, something like the following:—

The reader is begged to remember that these selections were played "extempore," and that, therefore, no great amount of finish in the connection of the phrases, or of the modulations, is to be looked for.

In exhibiting various "registers" or combinations of registers, some of Mr. Wilcox's happiest ideas were produced. Tone *quality* seemed to have the effect of forming interesting and frequently brilliant bits of melody in his mind. He was celebrated for his melodies on the stop called the "cornopean" or swell trumpet, of which the illustration is a tolerable example : —

The following was a favorite method with him of beginning his preludes for high mass, usually played on the great diapasons coupled to swell reeds : —

It will be seen at a glance that these selections are very "Frenchy;" that is, they sound a good deal like Batiste and Wely (although neither of these writers represents the old French school; but Mr. Wilcox played in this style for years before he ever saw a note of the organ music of these composers.

To my mind it is a great pity that Mr. Wilcox did not write down his extemporizations, and that no publisher stood ready to print them after they were written. Mr. Wilcox only published two works of any importance; one is his "Domine" and "Dixit Dominus," being the first two movements of a set of figured vespers (and a very effective work by the way), and a "Salve Regina." He also has a number of small pieces in a book of church music called the "Lyra Catholica."

As I said in another of these articles, he undoubtedly exercised a considerable influence on the present generation of church organists in this country; and that seems to be sufficient excuse for giving him a prominent place in these papers.

(To be Continued.)

HISTORY OF THE ORGAN.

V.

AMONG the other noted organ-builders of the eighteenth century are the names of John Byfield, who joined John Harris after the death of Renatus Harris, and Christopher Schrider, a German who became the son-in-law of Father Smith, and who succeeded him in the business of organ-building.

The Jordans, father and son, deserve special notice, as we are indebted to them for the invention of the swell-box (1712). Heretofore the pipes of the echo organ were enclosed in a wooden box, to render the tone softer; but the

An Organ of the IV. Century.

Jordans added a sliding shutter, which enabled the performer to produce a "swelling effect." The German builders were very slow in adopting this invention, the first example being in the organ of St. Michael's Church, Hamburg, built in 1762; and even today there are many organs in that country which are devoid of the only means of expression to be found in an organ. The organ in the Parochial Kirche, Berlin, where Professor Haupt played and taught for so many years, has no swell-box, and numerous other prominent German instruments are equally deficient. The Jordans are supposed to have been the first builders to introduce the reversed action.

John Snetzler, another famous builder, was born in Passau, Germany, about 1710. He constructed a few organs in his

(Continued on page 191.)

THE ORGAN.

BOSTON, NOVEMBER, 1892.

THE ORGAN is published the first of every month. Subscription price $1.00 per year, foreign countries $1.50, payable in advance. Single copies, 15 cents.

Subscribers will please state with which number they wish their subscription to begin.

The paper will be sent to all patrons till the editor is notified by letter to discontinue.

Subscribers wishing the address of their paper changed must give the old as well as the new address.

Remittances should be made by registered letter, post office order, or by check payable to Everett E. Truette.

Programmes of organ concerts, with press notices of the same, specifications of new organs, and items of general interest to the subscribers, will be gratefully received.

Correspondence, to secure notice, must in all cases be accompanied by the name and address of the writer, not for publication, but as a guarantee of good faith.

Advertising rates sent on application.

Address all communications,

The Organ, 191 A Tremont Street, Boston, Mass.

An active agent in every city is desired to whom a liberal cash commission will be allowed.

A NEW ENGLAND organist who is not altogether unknown in Boston, played on trial in a certain Catholic church one Sunday, when the sanctuary choir, being accompanied by the organ at the farther end of the church, sang badly off the pitch. After being severely criticised by the priest, the organist remonstrated by saying that the distance between the sanctuary choir and the organ was too great to enable a choir of comparatively young voices to sing exactly on the pitch. "My dear sir," replied the priest, "you must use more power and give them the key-note stronger: give them the *full organ on the pure flute.*" That organist has since become quite gray hunting through the treatises of Seidel, Töpfer, Hamel, Rimbault, Hopkins, Hill, Kuntze, and many others, endeavoring to find out how to give the key-note with "the full organ on the pure flute."

OH, consistency! We recently worshipped in a church where the organ was prohibited, but where spittoons were placed in every pew. The temple made with hands would be desecrated by the introduction of an organ, but God's temple was not polluted by taking into it the filthy weed that even the hog despised! Worship by a sweet-toned instrument is abominable, but worship by a foul-mouthed man is all right! *O tempora, O mores!*— *The Musical Messenger.*

THE weekly organ recitals at the Bow and Bromley Institute, London, were resumed October 1, Dr. A. L. Peace of Glasgow being the organist. These recitals have for years been the envy of American organists. A series of weekly organ recitals at which an admission fee is charged, and which are always well attended, frequently crowded, is something unknown this side of the water. We have attended several of the organ recitals of the Bow and Bromley Institute when we were compelled to wait outside in a crowd for a half-hour before the doors were opened. The admission was sixpence, and long before the concert began the hall was crowded. This is no uncommon occurrence, and testifies to the superior taste for organ music of the English public. In this country we go out into the highways and "request" the people to come in and occupy the empty benches.

AT the Eighteenth Triennial Exhibition and Fair of the Massachusetts Charitable Mechanic Association, now being held in their Exhibition Building (Boston), two organ recitals are given daily, and the organ is combined with the bands in

the other concerts. This organ (Roosevelt) was in a disgraceful condition at the last fair (1890), as the rain leaked through the roof, doing serious damage, and the association refused to appropriate money to repair the damage. The Solo organ reeds had to be disconnected, and several other stops were useless. This season, however, the chairman of the committee on music, Mr. Augustus Lothrop, has labored diligently to have the instrument repaired. The association were put to shame several times, and at last voted to repair the instrument, which task was undertaken and successfully executed by Mr. George S. Hutchings.

At the opening exercises, and during the first week, Mr. J. Frank Donahoe was the organist. At the opening exercises he performed March from Suite Op. 113, Lachner, and with the band, "Priest's War March," Mendelssohn. At his first recital he performed the following programme: Offertoire in D, Batiste; Waltzes, "To Thee," Waldteufel; Variations on an Original Theme, Hesse; Improvisation, and March from Damascus, Costa. At his other recitals the principal works were the overtures to "Fra Diavolo," "Bohemian Girl," and "Si J'étais Roi," several waltzes, and selections with the band. During the second week Mr. Arthur M. Raymond was the organist, and performed among other compositions, Grand Chorus, Guilmant; Overture to Stradella, Flotow; March from "Aida," Serenade, Schubert; Offertoire in D, Batiste; and several works with the band.

MR. FRANK ROOSEVELT having decided to go out of the business of organ-building, has sold to Messrs. Farrand & Votey of Detroit his patents, special stock, and special machinery. It will take till January to finish up the contracts already made, among which should be mentioned the large electro-pneumatic organs for the new concert hall of the Mendelssohn Glee Club, and for the All Saints Church, New York. These two instruments will be the crowning efforts of this enterprising house, and will illustrate what immense strides they have made in the application of electricity to organ actions.

ACCEPTING an invitation from Mr. E. F. Searles to inspect the elegant mansion erected by him at Great Barrington, and which the press of the country have many times endeavored to describe, without authority or an inside view, some twenty or more members of the Architects' Club of Boston took a special car on Monday, October 17, and after a pleasant ride of five hours were received by Private Secretary Bell. Proceeding at once to Kellogg Terrace, as it is called, the guests were allowed the freedom of the grounds and house, where they examined with critical eye the massive elegance, perfect detail, and princely furnishings of this unparalleled structure. Mr. Searles also kindly furnished for the occasion an organist, and the magnificent organ and hall in which it stands was a magnetic attraction. All enjoyed the informal programme of choice selections performed through the evening even to the midnight hour. This instrument, with its hall of perfect acoustics, is a revelation to the lovers of organ music, and the effect upon eye and ear cannot be forgotten. No better use of wealth can be made than that which tends to foster in the hearts of the people a love and interest in the organ and organ music, and an artistic production such as we find here is a fine example of such endeavor, which cannot fail to bear its fruits.

CHRISTMAS MARCH.

Tempo di Marcia.

EMILE Le BLANC.

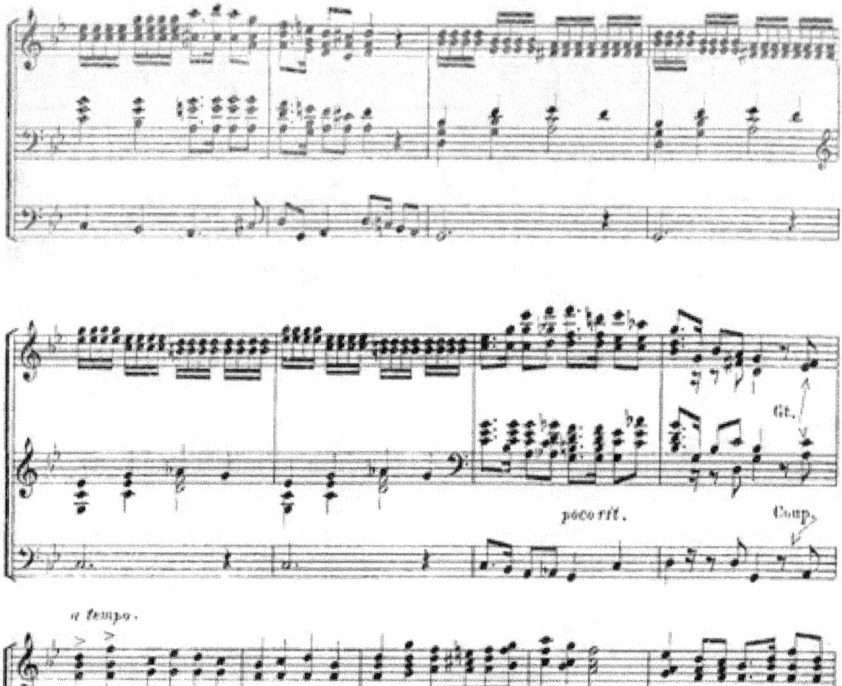
a tempo.
poco rit.
Gt.
Coup.
Coup off.

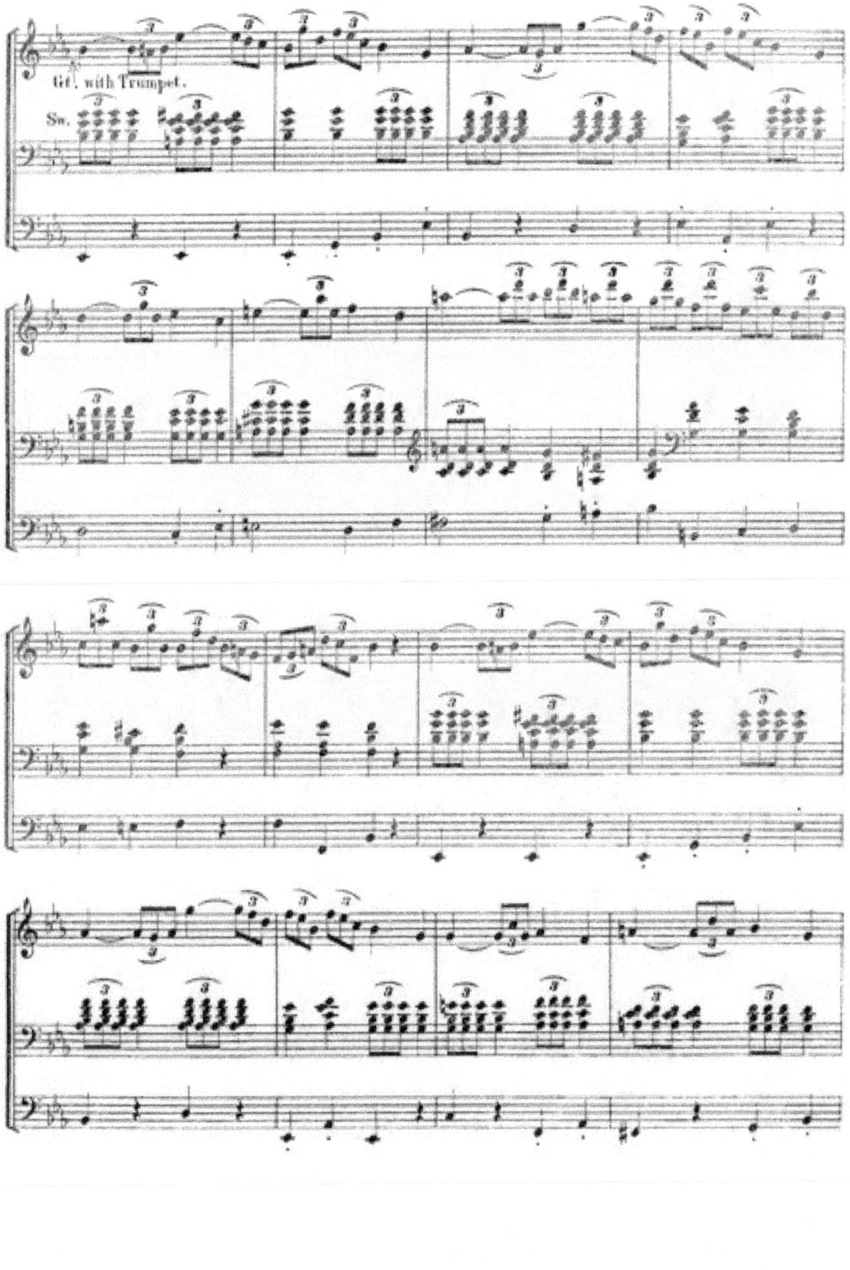
Gt. with Trumpet.
Sw.

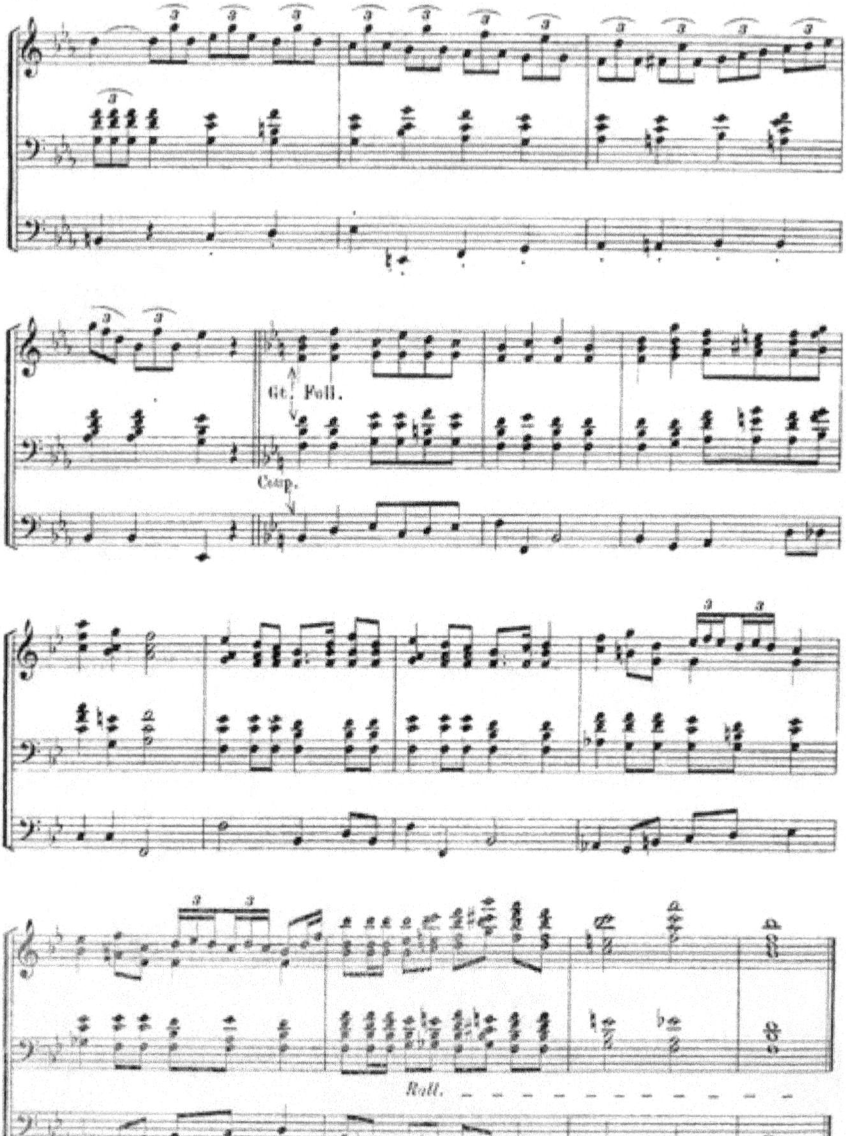
Gt. Full.
Coup.
Rall.

ANDANTINO.

ADOLPH HESSE.

Sw. St. Diap. & Violin.

Gt. Melodia &
Dulciana.

Ped 16. Sw to Gt. &
Sw to Ped.

Sw.

Add Flute 4 Ft.

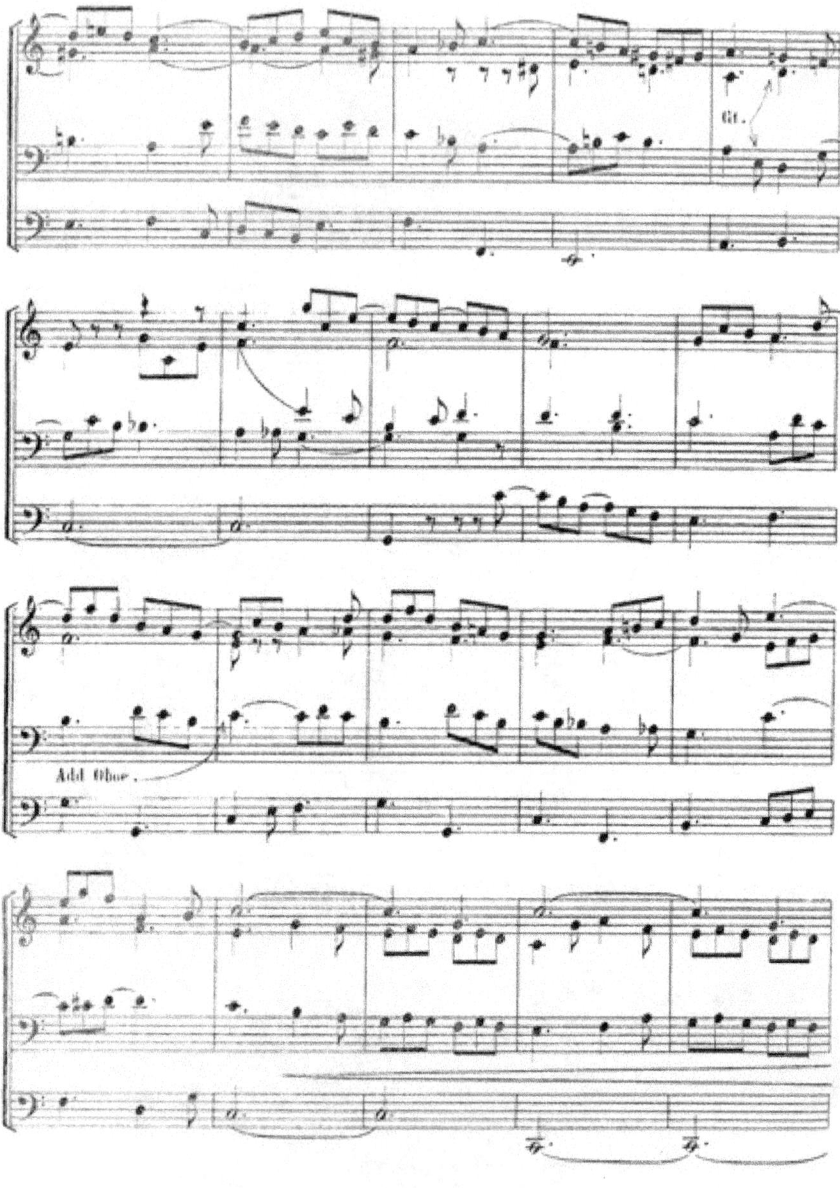
Gt.
Add Oboe.

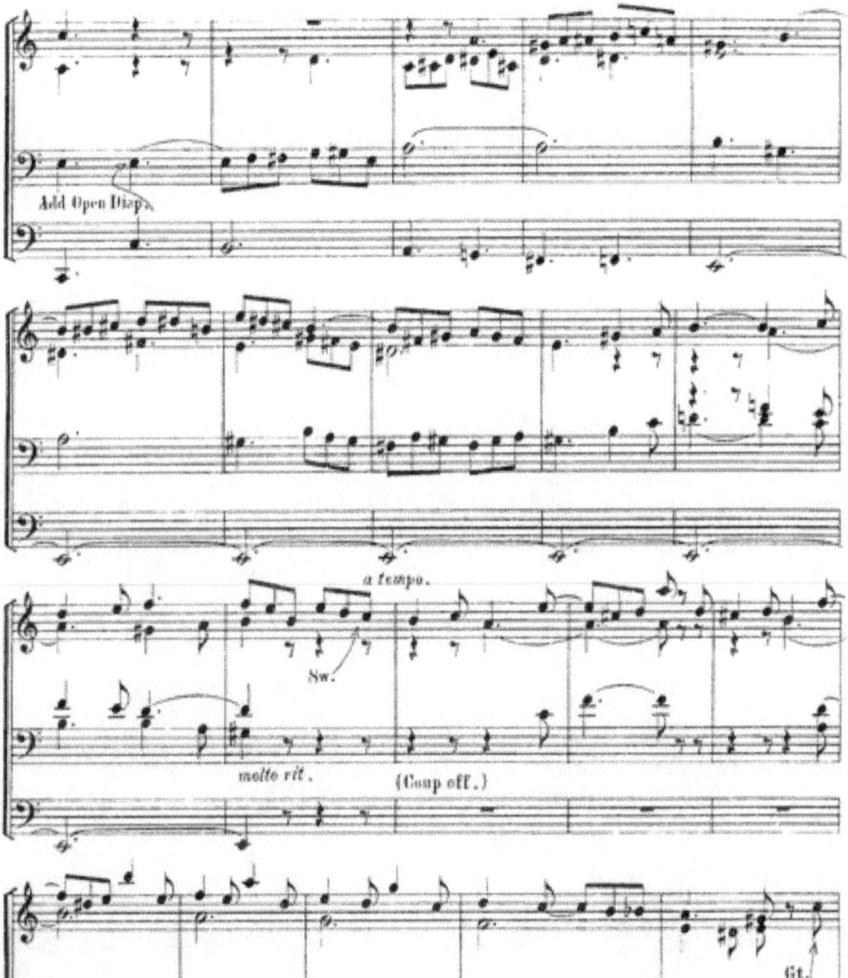
Add Open Diaps.
a tempo.
Sw.
molto rit.
(Coup off.)
Gt.
Coup.

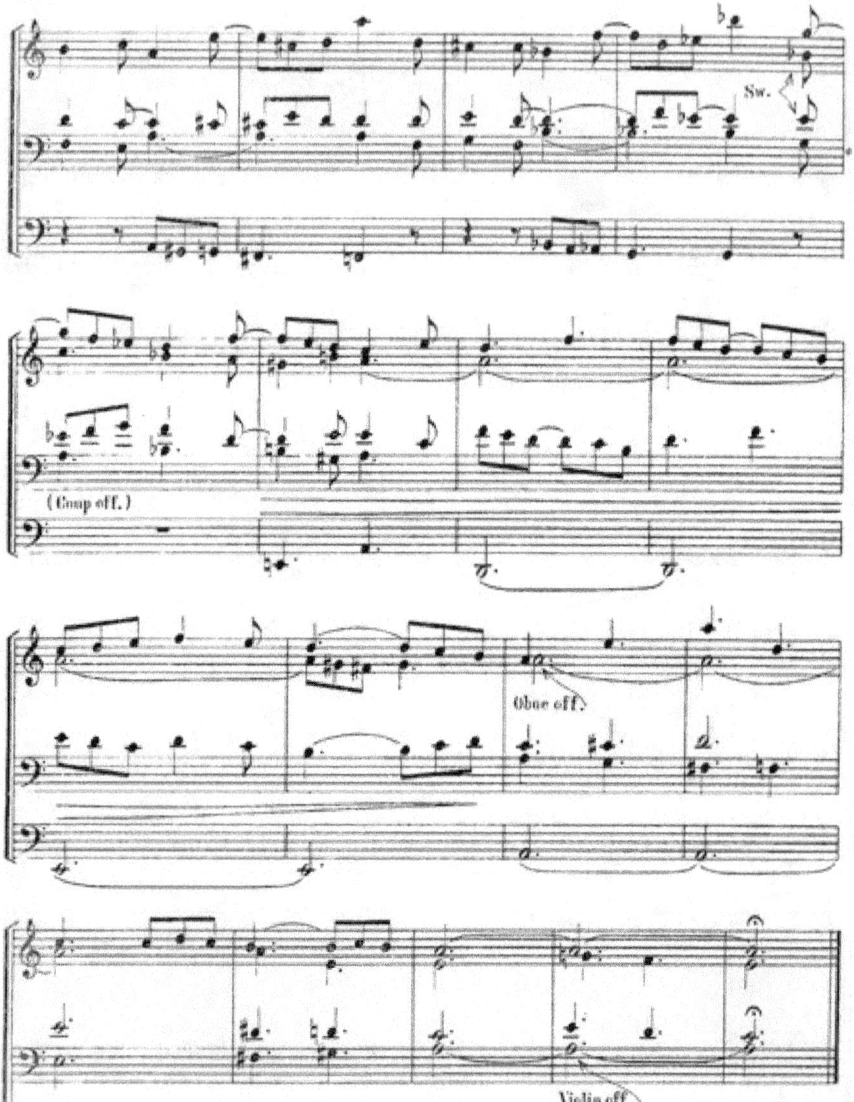
Sw.
(Coup off.)
Oboe off.
Violin off.

native country, and then settled in England, where he lived to an advanced age. The famous organ at Lynn Regis, in Norfolk, established his reputation. He invented that extremely useful stop, the Dulciana, which, with another novelty, the Double Diapason, was placed in this organ.

Snetzler had a poor knowledge of the English language, and created no little amusement by his original phrases whenever he became excited. At one time, when Dr. Wainright was playing on Snetzler's new organ at Halifax, his rapid playing caused Snetzler to shout, "He do run over de keys like one cat, and do not give my pipes time to speak." Another time, when asked if an old organ was worth repairing, he replied, " If they would lay out a hundred pounds on it, perhaps it would be worth fifty. Hopkins & Rimbault's Treatise gives a list of thirty-five organs built by Snetzler.

Samuel Green, born in 1740, was a builder of considerable repute, who devoted special attention to perfecting the action. His masterpiece was the organ in the Canterbury Cathedral. Green built in all about fifty organs.

The Englands, father and son, built some thirty or more organs between 1760 and 1812.

Paul Micheau was a native of Germany who went to England in 1580, settling in Exeter, where he had the care of Loosemore's famous instrument.

The Silberman family in Germany were among the most renowned organ-builders of the eighteenth century. Andreas Silberman, the founder of the race, was born in 1678, built twenty-nine organs, and died in 1733. Gottfried Silberman,

An Organ of the 8th. Century.

his brother, was born in 1684, built seven organs, and invented the "Claveris d'Amour." He died in 1754. Johann Andreas Silberman, eldest son of Johann Silberman, was born in 1712, and built fifty-four organs, the most noted of which are those in St. Thomas Church, Strasburg; St. Étienne, Basle; St. Theodore, Basle, and the Abbey of St. Blaise in the Black Forest.

Zacharias Thessner built, in 1702, the great organ in the Cathedral of Merseburg, which had sixty-eight registers, five manuals, and pedal. Adam Sterzing built, in 1703, an organ for the Church of St. Peter and St. Paul, at Görlitz, which had eighty-two registers. Heinrich Herbst and his son built, in 1718, an organ at Halberstadt with seventy-four registers, three manuals in front, and two manuals at the sides.

Two other famous builders were Johann Gabler, who built the noted organ in the Benedictine Abbey in Weingarten, and Christian Müller, who built the famous Haarlem organ.

This brings us down to the present era. To give an account of all the famous builders of to-day, or to chronicle all the inventions of this century, is beyond the province of this brief sketch, and would prove long and tedious to the average reader.

This series of articles on the "History of the Organ" will be supplemented (next month probably) by a short sketch of the progress of the instrument in this country, and will con-

tain a cut of the first organ (known as the Brattle organ) which was brought to this country. This cut was made from a photograph taken specially for THE ORGAN, and will be accompanied by an account of the instrument, specially written for this journal by Mr. Edwin A. Tilton.

MIXTURES.

(FOUR RANKS.)

THE keyboard of the organ in the Cathedral, Wells, Eng., is to be altered, so that the instrument may be available for both nave and choir services. A fund is being raised to defray the expenses.

The pipe-factory of Mr. Samuel Pierce, Reading, Mass., which, by the way, is one of the oldest in New England, has been recently enlarged by the addition of another building and an increase in the number of workmen. The business for a long time had been too large for the existing force of men, and now that the change has been made, all pipe organ materials, including pipes, action parts, keys, pedals, wires, pneumatic tubing, leather, etc., are supplied at short notice.

Organ recital in the Congregational Church, South Norwalk, Conn., by Mr. Alex S. Gibson, assisted by Mr. C. H. Mann, October 18. Programme : Overture, "A Night in Granada," Kreutzer ; Fugue in G-minor, Bach ; "March of the Magi Kings," Dubois ; "It is Enough" (Elijah), Mendelssohn ; "The Tournament at Raab," Op. 162, No. 12, Loretz ; Intermezzo Sinfonica, Mascagni ; "It was not so to be," Nessler ; Nuptial March, Guilmant.

Organ recital in Asylum Hill Congregational Church, Hartford, Conn., October 20, by Mr. S. Clarke Lord, assisted by Miss Mary H. Mansfield, Soprano. Programme : Sonata No. 3, Guilmant : Aria, "Hear ye, Israel," Mendelssohn ; Vision, Characteristic Piece, Rheinberger ; Intermezzo, from " Cavalleria Rusticana," Mascagni ; The Vesper Bell, Spinney ; Introduction and Bridal Chorus (" Lohengrin "), Wagner ; "There is a Blessed Home," Rotoli ; Coronation March, Svendsen.

Organ Concert in First Baptist Church, Franklin, Ind., by Mr. Clarence Eddy, October 13. Programme : Toccata and Fugue in D-minor, Bach ; Daybreak, Spinney ; Largo, Händel ; Overture to "Stradella," Flotow ; Andantino, Chauvet ; Spring Song, Mendelssohn ; Variations on "The Old Folks at Home," Flagler ; Fantasia " O Sanctissima," Lux ; Wedding Benediction, Dubois ; Finale, "Laus Deo," Dubois ; Offertoire in D, Batiste. Miss Electa Gifford contributed songs.

Organ concert in St. Paul's Church, Delaware, O., October 17, by Mr. Frank R. Adams. Programme : Fantasia, "O Sanctissima," Lux ; Toccata and Fugue in D-minor, Bach ; Sonata in A-minor, Whiting ; Offertoire in F-minor, Batiste ; Adagio (A-flat), Mendelssohn ; Finale from first act of "Lucrezia Borgia," Donizetti ; Coronation March, Meyerbeer ; Concert Variations and Fugue on "Star Spangled Banner," Paine.

Organ concert in Holy Family Church, Chicago, October 9, by Mr. Clarence Eddy. Programme : Toccata in F, Bach ; Pilgrim's Chorus, Wagner ; Hymn of Nuns, Wely ; Variations on "Home, Sweet Home," Flagler ; Overture to "Euryanthe," Weber ; Lamentation, Guilmant ; Nuptial Benediction and Finale, Dubois.

Inaugural Concert in Asbury Temple, Waltham, Mass., October 26. Programme : Second Sonata, Mendelssohn (Mr. Clarence F. Reed) ; Prelude, Dunham ; Funeral March and Song of Angels, Guilmant ; and Sortie in C, Whiting (Mr. H. M. Dunham) ; Offertoire in G, and Evening Hour, Ryder (Mr. Geo. H. Ryder) ; Fantasia in C (new), Reed (Mr. Reed) ; Schiller Festival March, Meyerbeer (Mr. Dunham) ; Tempest at Sea, Ryder (Mr. Ryder). The concert was interspersed with quartettes and songs.

CORRESPONDENCE

THE EVOLUTION OF THE SWELL-BOX.

To the Editor of The Organ:

An article in the September number of your journal, signed "Emile le Blanc," upon the above subject, in reply to one in a previous number (May), has come to my notice. Reference is made to the probable ignorance of "Gambette" upon the subject of "legitimate organ music," though "he may play a little." This may or may not be true in regard to the executive ability; but if "legitimate organ music" includes an element that instrumental effect which passes "thrills through one's body" by each movement of the swell-pedal, and, in addition to this ecstatic perforation of the system, alternates with another which "almost lifts one off one's feet with enthusiasm," perhaps the small attendance at the second service is accounted for, and he is well content to "play a little," out of regard to those who attend for something higher than massage treatment.

It may be in order to say here that "Emile" need not go out of the circle of his own acquaintances to find organists who play a great deal, and yet are lamentably ignorant of the construction and utility of the organ, even though it may be of "limited means of expression." Conversation with any builder of standing will bring out the statement that the mechanical attachments for "expression" of the modern organ are beyond the ability of most organists to manipulate.

A strange yearning seems to have broken out among the performers upon this beloved instrument. They have discovered that all stops not enclosed in a swell-box are "expressionless and lifeless," hence the necessity of placing the entire instrument, with slight exceptions, in such confinement; peradventure there may be some stray stop which may not be kicked into life by the heel and toe movement of the performer.

"How aggravating it is to a singer," says "Emile," "as well as to the audience, when the accompanist plays the whole accompaniment of the song without expression," etc. Yes, it must be; but, in American parlance, what is the matter with the swell? Why is it not used for this very purpose, as intended? Perhaps, however, he has had "little experience," etc. We have recently noticed a wail from a player of some note because he was unable to play an expressive solo on the great Gamba. This appeared to be a reason why the great organ should be enclosed in a box. In case he should wish to play an expressive solo on the front pipes, the situation would be simply discouraging. The same writer thinks "to have the reeds and mixtures under control a blessing." The loud reeds and mixtures are the life and brilliancy of the full organ; but although this is a portion of the great, which needs the most attention, the reeds may get an occasional tuning; but the mixtures — well, "hardly ever," (Pardon!) Under these conditions the more they are reduced the better; but we are not considering neglected organs.

The late Hilborne L. Roosevelt once said to the writer, when speaking of the organs of this country, "Why the people do not take care of their organs I do not understand." The reply would be, the people are apparently giving their money and attention to extra swell-boxes, adjustable combinations, push-knobs, and pedals.

In times past, and not so very long past, such musicians as Hayter, Hodges, Tuckerman, King, Wilcox, Thayer, Morgan, and others, were known to perform the music of divine service with satisfaction to their constituents upon instruments of "limited means of expression," i.e., one swell-box, half a dozen composition pedals, etc.; but we suddenly find ourselves in the midst of a generation of players who can do nothing except the keyboard resembles in appearance a central telephone station in its complication of "press the button" and foot appliances (and, as we have said, beyond the ability of the organist to manipulate with success), not called for in the score or necessary to the performer.

The keyboard of Guilmant's organ in *La Trinité*, Paris, is a marvel of simplicity compared with the American modern invention, and yet the master *manages* to execute music of the highest class to which the writer has been an eye-witness, and which, perhaps, "Emile" cannot play on any instrument. Cases without number can be cited where the composer had no such "helpers" (?) to performance. No mechanical device can take the place of brains, "Emile."

GAMBETTE.

DR. J. H. WILCOX.

To the Editor of The Organ:

Will you kindly use your influence with Mr. Organist to exhibit a little familiarity with his subject by allowing one more "l" to the name of the late Dr. J. H. Wilcox. When the Doctor was living he was quite resentful if his name was misspelled in this way. Also please say that Dr. Wilcox died in 1875, I think in July, and not 1873. And, again, who is authority for the statement as to "softening of the brain" having been so noticeable? The writer was for years quite intimate with him, and never heard of it in this way before.

MORE LIGHT.

PEDAL MARKING.

To the Editor of The Organ:

I note an article in a recent number of the London *Musical Opinion* credited to your journal, in regard to the nomenclature for pedals. It occurred to me that the arrangement I note here might be plain: $\begin{smallmatrix} R \\ L \end{smallmatrix}$ The upper marks evidently indicate the right and left toes, from their one-sided shape, while the letters R and L being left to designate the heel notes. Exclusively, there need be no confusion, and the worst tyro would instinctively follow the toe marks.

C. F. O.

A SECOND CHAPTER OF DON'TS.

Don't make so much noise in using the combination pedals. Such a racket does not add to the beauty of the music, even if it seems to indicate its "immense difficulty."

Don't keep the right foot on the swell-pedal all the time. It is not fair to make one foot do all the pedaling, besides, you unconsciously make a *crescendo* when not desired.

Don't change the combination which you are using just before the end of a phrase. Wait till the end.

Don't be afraid to use the Oboe (if you have a good one). It combines well with any foundation stop.

Don't take the hands off the keys at the end of a composition which ends with the full organ or any loud combination *à la arpeggio*, commencing with the upper note and ending with the pedal. It may be inoffensive with a soft combination, but it sounds slovenly with a loud combination.

Don't forget to turn the water off the motor Sunday. It is expensive.

Don't grumble because the pastor announces different hymns on Sunday from the ones selected and sent to you on Saturday. Even the weather clerk has to change his mind.

Don't commence every soft piece with the St. Diapason and Salicional (or Viola). The St. Diapason alone, with Violin, or with Flute 4 Ft., the Salicional and Violin are but a few of the combinations which sound well.

MIXTURES.

(FOUR RANKS.)

PROGRAMME of Organ Music performed by Mr. Wm. Huber, Jr., at the Baptist church, Hamilton, O., October 9. Prelude in G, Mendelssohn; Romance sans paroles, "Simple Aveu," Thome; Intermezzo, Op. 156, No. 4, Rheinberger; Offertoire in D, Bassal; Gavotte-Pastorale in G-minor, Durand; Sketch in C-minor, Schumann.

Mr. Geo. S. Hutchings has placed a two manual organ of sixteen stops in the Church of the Ascension, Waltham, Mass., and one of twelve stops in the Congregational church, Berkshire, N.Y.

Mr. J. Nelson Yolland, A. C. O., has received the appointment of organist of Seaford Church, Sussex.

Mr. Charles P. Scott, who has been staying in Germany for the past two years, has returned to Boston, where it is expected that he will locate permanently.

An organist for St. Michael's, Coventry, England, is to be selected by competition.

Mr. Clarence Eddy dedicated a large Vocalion organ in the Pilgrim Congregational church, Milwaukee, soon after his return from Boston and the East.

The weekly organ recitals at St. Michael's, Cornhill, London, were resumed September 28.

Mr. J. Alfred Pennington has received an appointment as organist in Quincy, Ill., at a salary of $1,000 a year.

Mr. H. J. B. Dart gives weekly organ recitals on Monday evenings at St. John's Church, Waterloo Road, London.

Mr. J. D. Buckingham, for several years organist of the Immanuel Church, Boston Highlands, has been engaged as organist and choir director of the Channing Church, Newton.

The Hope-Jones Electric Action is being applied by Messrs. Norman Bros. & Beard to the following organs: Hastings, All Souls' Church; London, St. Frideswide's Church; Liverpool, Pres. Church, Sefton Park; Blackheath, Christ Church.

Dr. Henry G. Hanchett, organist of the Marble Collegiate Church, New York, will deliver a series of four lectures on church music, in New York, during the present season.

The Worcester (Mass.) Festival of this year opened with an organ and song recital. Mr. Frank Taft of New York was the organist, and Miss Annabelle Clark and Mr. Arthur Beresford were the singers. Mr. Taft's numbers were Toccata and Fugue in D-minor, Bach; Benediction Nuptiale, Saint-Saëns; Wedding Hymn, Salomé; Adagio in F, Merkel; and a "Marche Symphonique" for organ and orchestra, written by Mr. Taft for the occasion. Mr. Taft was seriously handicapped at the outset by the "rheumatic condition" of the organ, and undoubtedly failed to do himself justice. The mucilage tendency of the action of some instruments has nearly ruined the reputation of many an organist.

An inaugural concert was given in St. Patrick's Church, Boston (the organ recently enlarged by Mr. George S. Hutchings of Boston), by Mr. Edward MacGoldrick, assisted by Mrs. Minnie Stevens-Coffin, Mrs. Ada May Benzing, Mr. George J. Parker. Mr. Peter Richardson, and the choir of the church, Sunday evening, October 2. Rossini's "Stabat Mater" was the work performed, preceded by two organ pieces played by Mr. MacGoldrick. — Chromatic Fantasia by Thiele, and Offertoire in A by Batiste, both of which were well rendered. Mr. MacGoldrick deserves special commendation for the success of the concert. We have never before heard the difficult accompaniments of this work so well played on an organ. The solo parts were exceedingly well rendered, and the chorus showed careful drilling, singing with much vigor and precision.

Among the organists who will probably be heard at the Columbian Exposition is Mons. Saint-Saëns, who will also conduct several concerts of his own compositions.

Mr. H. C. Macdougall, organist of Providence, R.I., is issuing a second volume of his "Melody Playing," the first volume of which was so successful. Theodore Presser is the publisher.

The Sunday organ recitals at the People's Palace, London, were resumed on September 11, by Mr. R. Jackson. There are two recitals given each Sunday in the year, except during August. The recitals are entirely free to the public, and the attendances are very large.

The new organ in the Park Avenue M. E. Church, Chicago, was dedicated Sunday, October 9, by Mr. Chas. F. Watt, organist of the church. He played Largo, by Händel; Batiste's Elevation in G, and Andante in G; "Songs without Words" of Mendelssohn, and Schubert's Serenade.

Mr. Harrison M. Wild gave an organ recital (first of this season) in the Unity Church, Chicago, October 2, with the following programme: Overture to "St. Paul," Mendelssohn-Best; Quartette, "Night Song" (arranged by C. A. Knorr), Abt; Sonata, Op. 77, Buck; Song, "Lend me your Aid" (Mr. Chas. A. Knorr, Gounod; Melody in F, Rubinstein-Brown; Allegretto, Capocci; Wedding March, Mendelssohn; Quartette, "Dedication Ode," Op. 15, Chadwick; "Montezuma," March and Chorus, Gleason.

The one hundred and eighth Organ Recital in Unity Church, Chicago, October 16, by Mr. Harrison M. Wild. Programme: Toccata, Hesse; Fantasia in C, Claussmann; Barcarolle, Bennett-Steggall; Choral March, Buck; Offertoire in F-minor, Salome; Overture to "Martha," Flotow.

First of a series of Four Organ Recitals at Christ Church, Louisville, Ky., October 4, by H. O. Farnham, A. C. M. Programme: Prelude and Fugue in C, Bach; Nocturne in G, Chopin; Sonata, No. 1, Guilmant; Elsa's Brautzug (Lohengrin), Wagner; Offertoire in F-minor, Batiste. The second recital will be given November 1.

Inaugural Recital, Highland Congregational church, Lowell, Mass., by Mr. Geo. E. Whiting, Oct. 5, 1892. Prelude and Fugue in C-minor, Mendelssohn; Fanfare, Cantabile, and Finale, Lemmens; Fantasie, "Registration," Whiting; Schiller Festival March, Meyerbeer; Pastorale, Whiting; Selections from "The Flying Dutchman," Wagner. Mr. F. M. Fessenden, organist of the church, performed Overture to "Oberon," Weber; Variations on "Home, Sweet Home," and "Loin du Bal," by Buck.

Organ recital in First Baptist Church, Auburn, N.Y., by Mrs. Mary C. Fisher, October 3. Programme: Prelude and Fugue in B-minor, J. S. Bach; Consolation, Op. 74, Guilmant; Third Choral, César Franck; Andante, Clous Claussmann; Bridal Song, Op. 26, Goldmark; Concert Variations on "Home, Sweet Home," Flagler; Symphony, No. 8 (two movements), Widor.

Mr. W. J. D. Leavitt, writing of his experiences in playing the great organ formerly in Music Hall, Boston, tells a pretty story of his most regular listener — a spider which had taken up its abode in the organ case over the performer's head. It remained there for about a year, Mr. Leavitt says. It was a musical little fellow, and when I began to play it would spin down almost to a level with my left shoulder and gently swing to and fro and listen. When I had finished a piece it would draw itself up to its nest, and when I began another, down it would come and resume its position as an interested listener. It had six legs. Two it would put out in the air as a balance pole; two it handled the web with, and the third it used in pulling itself up, hand over hand, as sailors climb a rope. I came at last to watch for the little fellow, and it was always faithful, so that I was sure of at least one attentive and appreciative listener. — *The Indicator.*

QUESTIONS AND ANSWERS.

All questions must be accompanied by the full name and address of the writer, and, if received by the 10th of the month, will usually be answered in the following number of THE ORGAN.

Only such questions as refer to the organ, to organists, organ builders, or to organ music, will be answered.

Correspondents are requested to write their questions in a clear and concise manner, writing on only one side of the paper.

CHURCH ORGANIST. In accompanying a chorus choir should the pedal be used all the time?

ANS. Not by any means. If the accompaniment consists of the voice parts only, the pedal should not be used when the basses are not singing, and not all the time that they are singing. If the accompaniment is independent, much discretion is necessary. Nothing detracts from the effect of chorus music more than the everlasting, ear-piercing rumble of a heavy Bourdon (such as is found in small organs with only one pedal stop) when used constantly from the beginning to the end, without regard to the character of the music. It is far better to use the pedal too little than too much.

H. M. T. 1. Is it injurious to an organ to leave the stops drawn through the week?

ANS. If the stops are left drawn through the week, dust is liable to get on the pallets and do more or less damage.

2. Should the swell be left open or closed?

ANS. When the church is to be closed during the summer, it is a good plan to leave the swell closed to keep dust out of the pipes; but the swell should be left open from Sunday to Sunday, that the temperature in the swell-box may be the same as that of the other parts of the organ, else the swell organ will not be in tune with the great and choir.

E. A. B. In my copy of the fifth book of Rink's Organ-School, (published by Oliver Ditson & Co.), I find the following passage, in the Flute Concerto, page 159, second brace, fourth measure:—

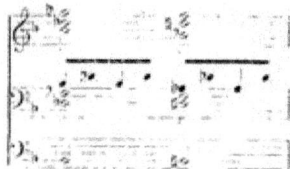

The second half of the measure does not sound right. Please explain what the trouble is.

ANS. The D-flat in the left hand, on the second half of the third count, should be D-natural; and in the best foreign editions B-natural will be found instead of the two notes of A-flat.

E. J. The stop marked Open Diapason 8 Ft. on the left hand side of my organ does not work properly. When I pull it out it comes out a foot, and no sound responds when playing on the swell keys. The officers of the church will

not pay for a man to come from New York to fix it. Can I fix it myself?

ANS. In all probability, the pin which joins the draw-stop rod to the stop action has slipped out of place. By following up the rod (inside the organ) till you come to that point, you can replace the pin.

A PNEUMATIC SWELL-PEDAL.

ORGAN-BUILDERS for years have been endeavoring to produce a pneumatic swell-pedal which should be both simple and efficient, but heretofore their efforts have been fruitless. In large organs the length of the swell-pedal action is often so great that the pedal is cumbersome and of little or no service for delicate expression. Organists without number have complained that the swell-pedal was centuries behind the other mechanical parts in degree of perfection. In the various attempts to produce a perfect pneumatic swell-pedal action, the difficulty has been to have the shutters start or stop at the same time that the motion was applied or discontinued at the "shoe" by means of the foot. In nearly every case the shutters would continue to open or close a fraction of a second after the foot had been removed from the "shoe."

Mr. Earnest M. Skinner, in the employ of Mr. Geo. S. Hutchings, organ-builder of Boston, has invented and patented a pneumatic swell-pedal action, which thus far has proved to be thoroughly practical, simple, and efficient. The pneumatic bellows are applied to the swell-pedal action (near the shoe) in such a manner that when the bellows are empty the action is mechanical, and when the bellows are filled with wind, the action is pneumatic. This is a valuable point, as the shutters are thus always under the control of the organist, while the action is so simple that it is nearly impossible for it to become deranged. We gave this pneumatic swell-pedal a thorough examination on a recent visit to the factory, and found that it responded instantly to any motion of the foot, no matter how slight. In sitting at the desk and looking up at the swell-shutters, it was impossible to see any lapse of time between the motion of the foot and the opening or closing of the shutters, while the shutters stopped immediately when the motion applied to the shoe was stopped. This invention will prove valuable in all large organs, where the length of the swell-pedal action has heretofore rendered the swell-pedal of little service, and organists will long remember the name of the inventor, Mr. Earnest M. Skinner.

CIPHERINGS.

WHY are organists sometimes called tramps?
ANS. Because they are pedlars.

JOHN. "Can you play that organ?"
JIMMIE. "No? but I ken lick the blower; that will make jest as much noise."

THE man who really wins a victory over himself, and over the world, the flesh, and the other fellow, is the hero who attends an organ recital celebrating the birth of J. S. Bach in which six of his Preludes and Fugues are performed, and who looks pleased, interested, and intellectual. — *Minneapolis Journal.*

SERVANT. "This room will be rented only to an organist."
ROOM HUNTER. "And why not to any other man?"
SERVANT. "Because organists are less troublesome — they never want their room put in order." — *Fliegende Blätter.*

NEW ORGANS.

SPECIFICATION OF THE ORGAN IN ST. PATRICK'S CHURCH, BOSTON.

Constructed by Messrs. Hook & Hastings, and recently enlarged by Mr. Geo. S. Hutchings.

GREAT ORGAN.

Double Open Diapason	16	Ft.
Open Diapason	8	"
Gamba	8	"
Doppel-flöte	8	"
Dulciana	8	"
Octave	4	"
Flauto Traverso	4	"
Twelfth	2⅔	"
Fifteenth	2	"
Mixture	5	Rks.
Scharf	3	"
Trumpet	8	Ft.
Clarion	4	"

SWELL ORGAN.

Bourdon	16	Ft.
Open Diapason	8	"
St. Diapason	8	"
Salicional	8	"
Quintadena	8	"
Octave	4	"
Flûte Harmonique	4	"
Violina	4	"
Flageolet	2	"
Mixtures	5	Rks.
Fag-tto	16	Ft.
Cornopean	8	"
Oboe	8	"
Vox Humana	8	"
Clarion	4	"

CHOIR ORGAN.

Geigen Principal	8	Ft.
Melodia	8	"
Gedacht	8	"
Dulciana	8	"
Fugara	4	"
Flûte d'Amour	4	"
Flûte Harmonique	3	"
Clarinet	8	"

The usual Couplers.
Compass of Manuals 61 notes.
" " Pedal 30 notes.

PEDAL ORGAN.

Double Open Diapason	16	Ft.
Bourdon	16	"
Quinte	10⅔	"
Octave	8	"
Trombone	16	"

COMBINATION PEDALS.

Full
Full to 5 Rks. Mixture } Great.
Full to Fifteenth
Full } Swell.
Mezzo
Full } Choir.
Mezzo

This organ is a typical instrument for a Catholic church, one which responds readily to the demands made upon it in such music as one hears in the Catholic church, and fulfils its mission perfectly. The full organ is very powerful, but not harsh, all forte combinations are smooth, and blend well with voices. The solo stops were not heard much at the inaugural recital. The instrument originally had but two manuals, the third manual having been just added, with other minor additions. The action is extended and reversed. There is no case above the level of the windchests, the pipes being decorated and exposed, with the longest pipes at the sides and the shortest in the centre. The pedal movements are rather stiff, as the stops are not pneumatic, and the swell pedal is poorly located; but we understand that pneumatics will be applied to the draw stops another season, and the swell pedal could be easily altered. The general effect of the organ is very satisfactory.

Messrs. Hook & Hastings have just finished three organs in Norfolk, Va. The instruments are being placed in St. Peter's Episcopal Church, the Central M.E. Church, and St. Luke's Episcopal Church. Each organ contains two manuals. We append the specifications of the instrument in St. Luke's Church : —

GREAT ORGAN.

Bourdon Bass)	16	Ft.
Bourdon Treble)		
Open Diapason	8	"
Dulciana	8	"
Melodia	8	"
Octave	4	"
Twelfth	2⅔	"
Fifteenth	2	"
Mixture	3	Rks.
Trumpet	8	Ft.

SWELL ORGAN.

Open Diapason	8	Ft.
Viola	8	"
Stopped Diapason	8	"
Flauto Traverso	4	"
Violina	4	"
Flautino	2	"
Cornopean	8	"
Oboe)	8	"
Bassoon)		

PEDAL ORGAN.

Open Diapason	16	Ft.
Bourdon	16	"
Violoncello	8	Ft.

The usual mechanical registers and pedal movements. Pneumatic action is used, and the organ is blown by a water motor.

(Continued on page 167.)

NEW ORGANS.

(Continued from page 165.)

NEW ORGAN IN ST. MARY'S ROMAN CATHOLIC CHURCH, SYRACUSE, N.Y.

Built by Mr. Frank Roosevelt.

GREAT ORGAN.

Double Open Diapason	16 Ft.	Octave	4 Ft.
First " "	8 "	Hohl-flöte	4 "
Second " "	8 "	Octave Quint	2½ "
Viola di Gamba	8 "	Super Octave	2 "
Principal-flote	8 "	Mixture	4 Rks.
Doppel-flöte	8 "	Trumpet	8 Ft.

All but the first three stops included in choir swell-box.

SWELL ORGAN.

Bourdon	16 Ft.	Flute Harmonique	4 Ft.
Open Diapason	8 "	Flageolet	2 "
Spitz-flöte	8 "	Cornet	3, 4, and 5 Rks.
Salicional	8 "	Cornopean	8 Ft.
Vox Celestis	8 "	Oboe	8 "
St. Diapason	8 "	Vox Humana	8 "
Octave	4 "		

CHOIR ORGAN.

(Enclosed in a separate swell-box.)

Contra Gamba	16 Ft.	Fugara	4 Ft.
Geigen Principal	8 "	Flute d'Amour	4 "
Dolce	8 "	Piccolo Har.	2 "
Concert Flute	8 "	Clarinet	8 "
Quintadena	8 "		

PEDAL ORGAN.

Open Diapason	16 Ft.	Violoncello	8 Ft.
Violone	16 "	Flute	8 "
Bourdon	16 "	Trombone	16 "
Quint	10⅔ "		

Swell to Great Octaves in addition to the Usual Couplers.

PEDAL MOVEMENTS.

Three Combination Pedals for Gt.		Full Organ.	
" " " Sw.		Pedal Ventil.	
Two " " Choir.		Gt. to Ped. (reversible).	
" " " Pedal.			

New organ in the Asbury (M.E.) Temple, Waltham, Mass., built by Mr. Geo. H. Ryder, under the immediate direction of the organist, Mr. C. E. Reed.

GREAT ORGAN.

Open Diapason	16 Ft.
Open Diapason	8 "
Viola di Gamba	8 "
Doppel-flöte	8 "
Gemshorn	8 "
Octave	4 "
Flauto Traverso	4 "
Twelfth	2⅔ "
Fifteenth	2 "
Mixture	3 Rks.
Trumpet	8 Ft.

SWELL ORGAN.

Bourdon Treble }	16 Ft.
Bourdon Bass }	
Open Diapason	8 "
Stopped Diapason	8 "
Salicional	8 "
Æoline	8 "
Flûte Harmonique	4 "
Violin	4 "
Flautina	2 "
Dolce Cornet	3 Rks.
Oboe	8 Ft.
Cornopean	8 "
Vox Humana	8 "

CHOIR ORGAN.

Contra Dolce	16 Ft.
Geigen Principal	8 "
Dulciana	8 "
Fugara	4 "
Flûte d'Amour	4 "
Piccolo	2 "
Clarinet	8 "

The usual couplers (operated by thumb knobs).

PEDAL ORGAN.

Open Diapason	16 Ft.
Bourdon	16 "
Violone	16 "
Violoncello	8 "
Flute	8 "

PEDAL MOVEMENTS.

FF., F. and P. combinations in Gt. F. and P. combinations in Choir.
FF., F. and P. " Sw. F. " " Pedal.

The action is extended, so that the console is located out on the platform beside the pastor's chair. The pedal couplers are operated by thumb knobs placed over the respective manuals. Through the efforts of Mr. Reed nearly twice the customary amount of space was allowed for the organ, hence the pipes have abundant speaking-room, and no part of the action is crowded, every part of the organ being accessible.

NEW ORGAN IN CENTRAL CONGREGATIONAL CHURCH, LYNN, MASS.

Built by Geo. S. Hutchings, Boston.

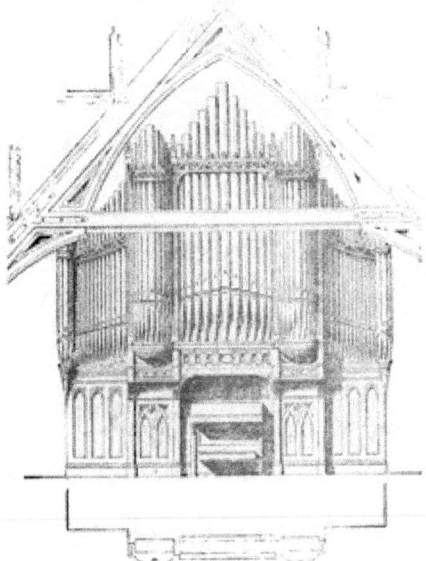

GREAT ORGAN.

Open Diapason	16 Ft.
Open Diapason	8 "
Viola di Gamba	8 "
Doppel-flöte	8 "
Octave	4 "
Flûte Harmonique	4 "
Octave Quinte	2⅔ "
Super Octave	2 "
Mixture	3 Rks.
Trumpet	8 Ft.

SWELL ORGAN.

Lieblich Gedacht Treble }	16 Ft.
Lieblich Gedacht Bass }	
Open Diapason	8 "
Salicional	8 "
Æoline	8 "
Stopped Diapason	8 "
Flauto Traverso	4 "
Fugara	4 "
Flautina	2 "
Dolce Cornet	2 Rks.
Cornopean	8 Ft.
Oboe	8 "
Bassoon }	8 "
Vox Celestis	8 "

CHOIR ORGAN.

Geigen Principal	8 Ft.
Dulcissimo	8 "
Melodia (stopped bass)	8 "
Flute d'Amour	4 "
Piccolo Harmonique	2 "
Clarinet (Fagotto)	8 "

PEDAL ORGAN.

Open Diapason	16 Ft.
Bourdon	16 "
Violoncello	8 "

PEDAL MOVEMENTS.

Forte, Mezzo and Piano Combinations in Gt. Gt. to Ped. Coupler (reversible).
Forte and Piano Combinations in Sw. Tremolo.
The usual Couplers.

NEW ORGAN IN PRESBYTERIAN CHURCH, EAU CLAIRE, WISCONSIN.

Built by George S. Hutchings, Boston.

GREAT ORGAN.

Open Diapason	8 Ft.
Dulciana	8 "
Melodia (stopped bass)	8 "
Octave	4 "
Octave Quinte	2 "
Super Octave	2 "
Trumpet	8 "

SWELL ORGAN.

Bourdon Treble	16 Ft.
Violin Diapason	8 "
Salicional	8 "
Stopped Diapason	8 "
Flûte Harmonique	4 "
Violina	4 "
Oboe	8 "

PEDAL MOVEMENTS.

Forte and Piano, Gt. Combinations.
Great to Pedal (reversible).
Tremolo.
The usual Couplers.

PEDAL ORGAN.

Bourdon	16 Ft.
Flute	8 "

Vol. I.   DECEMBER, 1892.   No. 8.

BACH

YEARLY SUBSCRIPTION $2.00.   SINGLE COPIES 25 CTS.

RHEINBERGER.   GUILMANT

The ORGAN

DEVOTED TO

A MONTHLY JOURNAL

THE KING OF INSTRUMENTS

FRESCOBALDI   BUXTEHUDE

MERKEL   BEST

· EVERETT · E · TRUETTE ·

EDITOR & PUBLISHER

149 A. TREMONT ST. BOSTON.

HANDEL

In 1756, when the Brattle organ was removed from King's Chapel, an organ constructed by Adrian Smith of London, said to have been approved by Händel, was erected in its place. This organ was in use one hundred and four years. In 1860 it was enlarged by Simmons & Wilcox. In 1889 Messrs. Hook & Hastings placed a new organ in the original case, retaining a few of the old pipes. Recently the same firm enlarged the instrument a second time.

Christ Church, Cambridge, contained an organ built by Snetzler as late as 1761, but the pipes were converted into bullets during the Revolution. In 1762 Geo. Harrison built an organ for Trinity Church, New York, which was destroyed by fire in 1777.

The "Independent Church" in this country, during the eighteenth century, opposed the use of organs for divine service so strenuously, that only Episcopal Churches contained organs, till in 1790 the old Brattle-street Church, Boston, abandoned its prejudice and consented to have an organ in its church. This organ was built by Samuel Green, and cost £400. Even after the organ had been ordered the opposition was so great that an effort was made to prevent the landing of the instrument. One wealthy member of the parish offered to pay the whole cost of the instrument into the treasury of the church for the benefit of the poor if the instrument should be thrown overboard in the harbor. The minister of the church refused to be bribed, and the organ was set up, remaining in use till 1872. It contained two manuals and sixteen stops. Another organ built by Snetzler was erected in St. Paul's Chapel, New York, in 1802, most of which still remains, though it was rebuilt by Odell in 1850.

Other early builders in this country were Josiah Leavitt and Thomas Pratt.

William Goodrich is considered by some to have been the father of organ-building in New England. He established so great a reputation that but three foreign organs were imported during his career.

Thomas Appleton, another noted New England builder, began his career in the factory of William Goodrich. His first organ was placed in Church Green, Boston, and is still in use in the "New South Church," Boston. He built another organ for St. Paul's Church, which was afterward sent to New Orleans, and constructed in all thirty-five organs for Boston, and about a hundred outside of Boston. He died in 1872. (See the June number of THE ORGAN for a sketch of his career and a portrait.)

In 1795 a builder named Loewe, an apprentice of Robert Gray of London, established himself in Philadelphia, and received the contract to build an organ for St. John's Chapel, New York. This organ was captured in its passage to New York by an English frigate, but was afterward redeemed on the payment of $2,000. Loewe died, and a builder named Thomas Hall set up the instrument. Christ Church, Philadelphia, contained an organ from 1766 to 1833 which was built by Phillip Seyring (?) St. Peter's Church possessed another organ built by the same builder. This organ had three manuals, twenty-seven stops, and sixteen hundred and seven pipes.

Towards the end of the eighteenth century a Moravian named Taneberger built an organ for the German Lutheran Church, Philadelphia. Another builder, John Rowe, was in business from 1795 to 1812. An organ was in use in the North Church, Salem, from 1808 to 1847. It was probably built by John E. Geib, who succeeded his father, Adam Geib. This instrument was replaced by another constructed by Simmons & McIntyre of Boston.

In 1820 Elias and George Hook, who had studied with the Goodriches, opened an organ factory of their own, little realizing what an important factor in the evolution of the instrument in this country they were establishing. They remained in business for fifty years or more, till removed by death.

As this article treats of the past and not of the present, no mention is made of the score of builders who are now flourishing and supplying the country with hundreds of instruments each year.

NOTABLE ORGANS.

V.

MARIEN-KIRCHE, DORTMUND.

A MAGNIFICENT mediæval organ-case still remains in the Marien-kirche at Dortmund, situated in a gallery placed high up over the nave arcade. This fine work dates from about the year 1480, and is exceedingly elaborate, as can be seen by the drawing. The organ itself is chiefly modern, so will not require notice here. The case presents the somewhat unusual Gothic feature of semi-circular towers, which are here treated in a beautiful manner. The way in which these latter are corbelled out in groined brackets is strikingly good.

As is usual in all old cases up to a certain date, the sides hang over considerably beyond the base, and are here supported by brackets, richly ornamented with intersecting cusps, in the true German fashion. All the carving, bratticing, panelling, etc., is splendidly cut and designed. The gallery is also a fine piece of work, thoroughly suited to the organ. It belongs to about the same period, although at first sight it appears to be somewhat later in style. All its details are exceedingly good. ARTHUR G. HILL, B.A.

REMINISCENCES OF ORGAN AND CHURCH MUSIC IN THIS COUNTRY.

(Concluded.)

THE year 1853 or '54 was signalized by the completion of the first instrument that could, by any stretch of the imagination, be called a *concert organ* on this continent; viz., the (old) organ in the Tremont Temple, Boston, built by E. & G. G. Hook (now Hastings).

Tremont Temple (observe the truly Oriental and religious sound of the word "temple") has always been a peculiarly "Boston notion." It is a sort of hybrid between a church

(Continued on page 185.)

THE ORGAN.

BOSTON, DECEMBER, 1892.

THE ORGAN is published the first of every month. Subscription price $1.00 per year (foreign countries $1.50), payable in advance. Single copies, 15 cents.

Subscribers will please state with which number they wish their subscription to begin.

The paper will be sent to all patrons till the editor is notified by letter to discontinue.

Subscribers wishing the address of their paper changed must give the old as well as the new address.

Remittances should be made by registered letter, post-office order, or by check payable to Everett E. Truette.

Programmes of organ concerts, with press notices of the same, specifications of new organs, and items of general interest to the subscribers, will be gratefully received.

Correspondence, to secure notice, must in all cases be accompanied by the name and address of the writer, not for publication, but as a guarantee of good faith.

Advertising rates sent on application.

Address all communications,

The Organ, 149 A Tremont Street, Boston, Mass.

☞ An active agent in every city is desired to whom a liberal cash commission will be allowed.

How did you like the half-tone of Gustav Merkel in our last issue? Pretty poor, wasn't it? If the electro-plater does that again he will wish his name was Isaac.

THOSE who purchased copies of THE ORGAN at the music stores last month, and found blank advertising bill-heads, instead of subscription blanks, tucked away between the pages, need not be alarmed. We are not in the habit of "dunning" in advance. It was simply a piece of stupidity which is liable to occur to any paper. The mailing girl said that she had such a headache, that she could not have told whether they were subscription blanks or government bonds. (Poor creature!)

WE read in an exchange that Mr. A., *one of the most talented pupils of Mr. B.*, has achieved a well-deserved success in a recent organ recital. Now, as a matter of fact, this Mr. A. studied for about three years with Mr. X., with whom he learned nearly all that he knows about organ-playing. After supplementing this study with a short term with Mr. B., he launches out as *one of the most talented pupils of Mr. B.* If such students would learn by heart the simple phrase, "Honor to whom honor is due," it is barely possible that in years to come they might escape the disappointment of similar cases of ingratitude.

THE rapid strides which have been made in electric action (even for small organs) during the past few years, are but the beginning of the "electric era" for the organ. But a few years ago electricity in an organ was considered an expensive and unreliable luxury, applied only when the funds were unlimited. But to-day the results of the simplifying process are most promising, and electric action is becoming fully as reliable, and not much more expensive, than direct action.

THE final shots which Roosevelt's factory will fire into the world before bowing their *adieu*, will be models of the perfection of electric action. The organ for the Mendelssohn Glee Club of New York will have electro-pneumatic action throughout. The console will be connected with the organ only by an inch-and-a-half cable, and will be movable. For organ concerts the console can be placed in the centre of the stage, facing the instrument. For concerts when the organ is used with chorus and orchestra, the console can be placed wherever desired, facing the conductor. For miscellaneous concerts the console can be wheeled into the anteroom, and used for a lunch-table if necessary.

MESSRS J. MERKLIN & CO., organ-builders of Paris, have kept up with the progress of the times, and have in the past year constructed several organs with electric action, all of which, according to the French journals, were highly satisfactory.

IT is a common thing to see the names of composers (as well as performers) mutilated by the hard-hearted compositors. One of the worst mutilations which has been seen lately appeared in the *Mechanics' Fair News* (Boston), in which Guilmant's name was transformed into *Gushmant*.

Le Menestrel informs us that Mons. Cavaillé-Coll, the veteran French organ-builder, who is now eighty-two years of age, has transferred his factory to his son Gabriel, who will continue the business with M. Kastner-Boursault as special partner; but *Le Monde Musical* contradicts this report, and states that Mons. Cavaillé-Coll, in spite of his advanced age, will continue to manage the business.

THE following letter, signed P. H. Chignell, appeared in the last number of the *Musical Opinion and Music Trade Review*, anent the letter on Pedal Marking, written by Mr. Clarence Eddy, which we printed in the September issue: —

"In Mr. Eddy's article under the above heading, he does not even mention the method which I find by far the most useful. I refer to the method used in the Litolff edition of Rinck's *Organ School*. The characters used are 1 and 2 for the right foot, and *a* and *b* for the left foot. These save all confusion, and can be used with two-lined music as well as the ordinary three-lined."

REVIEW OF NEW ORGAN MUSIC.

FROM RICHAULT & Co., PARIS.

Grand Offertory for a Festival Day,	
Meditation in B,	Jules Grison.
Fantasia on the Portuguese Hymn,	
Prelude	Georges Mac-Master.
Fantasia on Russian National Hymn	J. Planel.

The three compositions of Grison constitute the sixth book of his second collection of organ pieces, and are even more interesting than their predecessors. The offertory is in the style of a fantasia, and is effective. The second theme, in triplets, is specially pleasing, and evidently pleased the composer, for he has made extended use of it. The Meditation is the gem of this book, and is really beautiful. The introduction does not command one's admiration, but the theme on the third page is charming, and the second theme or trio — *a quasi* choral, alternating with reminiscences of the first theme — admits of the choicest registration. The ending is quite ingenious. The Fantasia on the Portuguese Hymn does not please us so much on first examination; though if well played on a brilliant concert organ, we doubt not that it would be effective. The fughetta in the middle of the Fantasia seems studied, but the latter part of the composition, wherein the theme is played in harmony on the Vox Humana, with a rapid Flute obligato, and the ending with full organ, are full of interest. The Prelude of Mac-Master is a simple and pleasing voluntary which would sound well on any organ. Planel's Fantasia has some interesting moments, but as a whole did not please us; however, it might improve on further acquaintance.

CANON.

GUSTAV MERKEL.

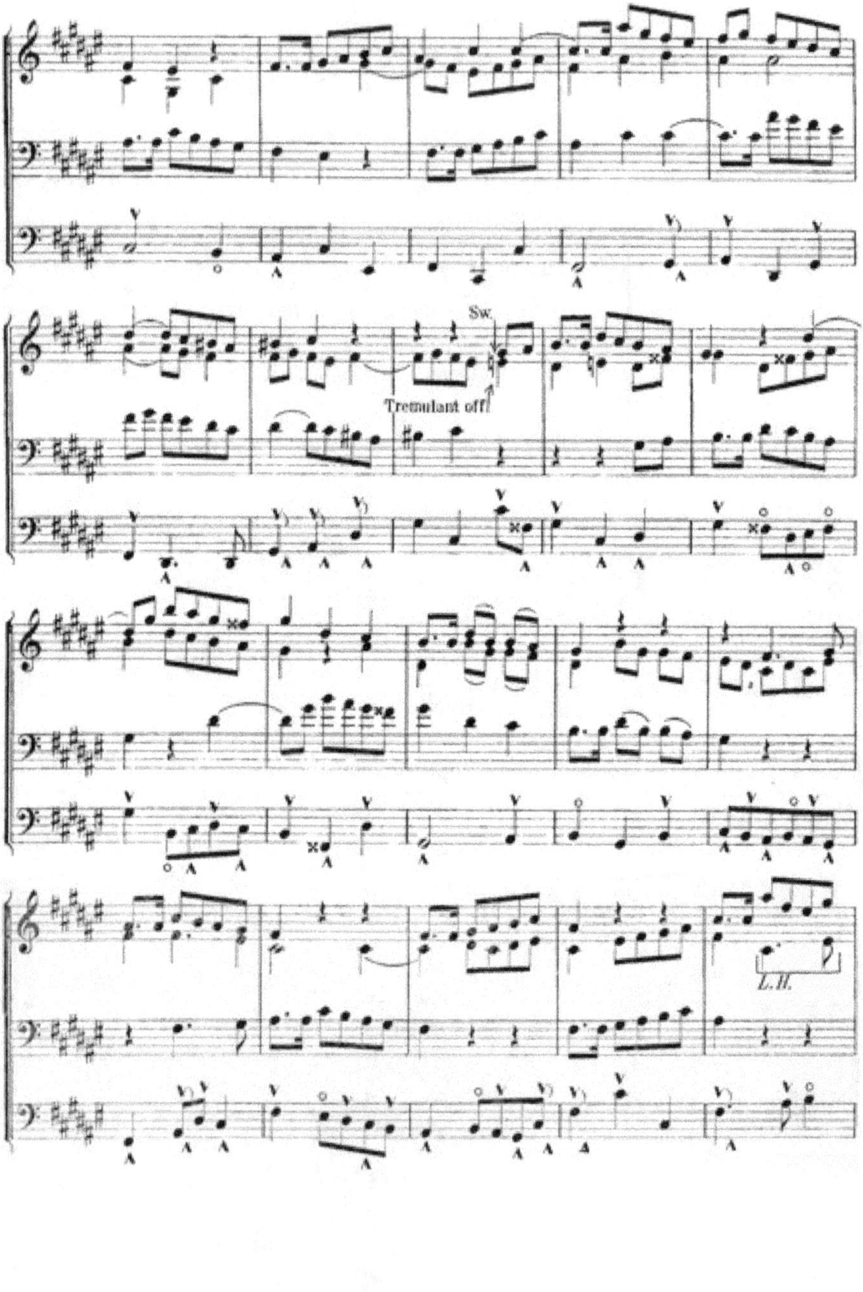
Sw.
Tremulant off
L.H.

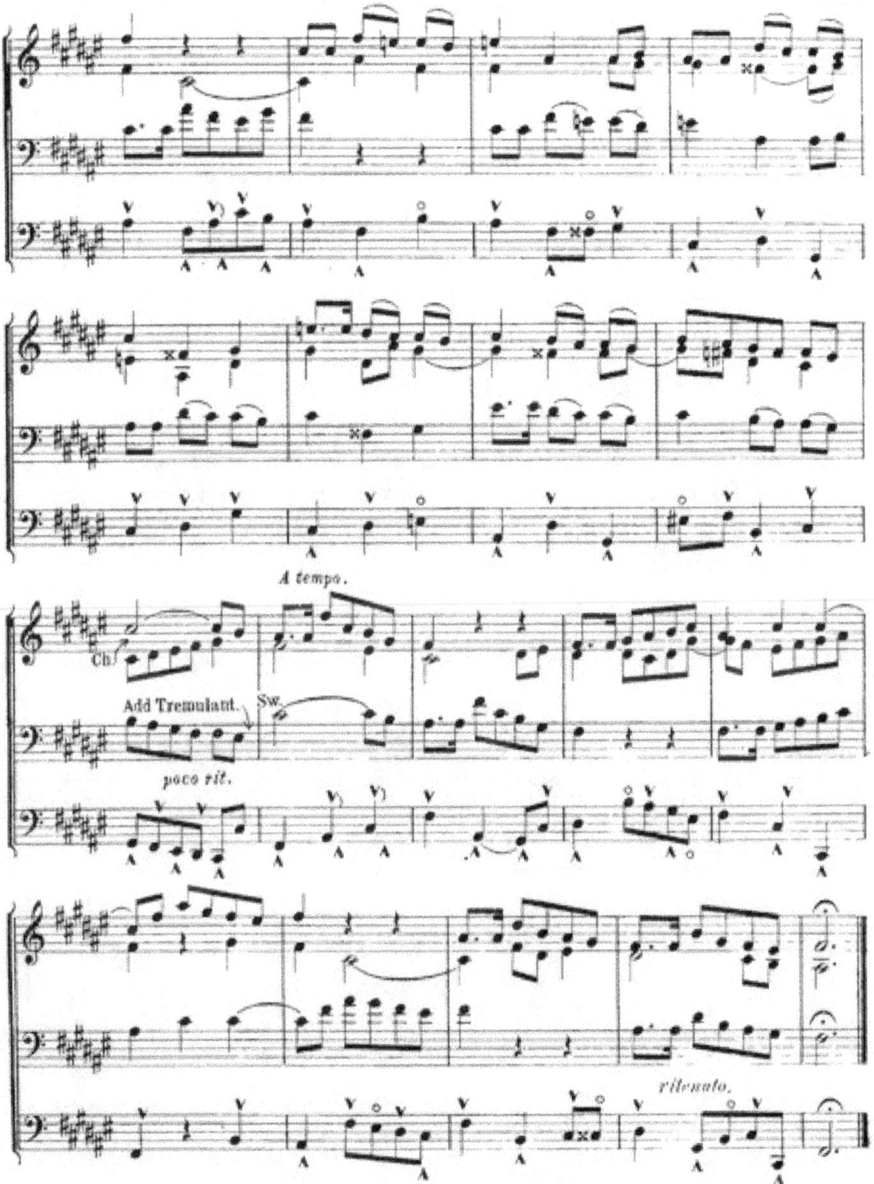
A tempo.
Ch.
Add Tremulant.
Sw.
poco rit.
ritenuto.

PRELUDE IN A MINOR.

GUSTAV MERKEL.

Allegro.

Gt. to Op. Diap.

Sw. 8 & 4 Ft.
Ped. 16 & 8 Ft.

Sw. to Gt. & Gt. to
Ped.

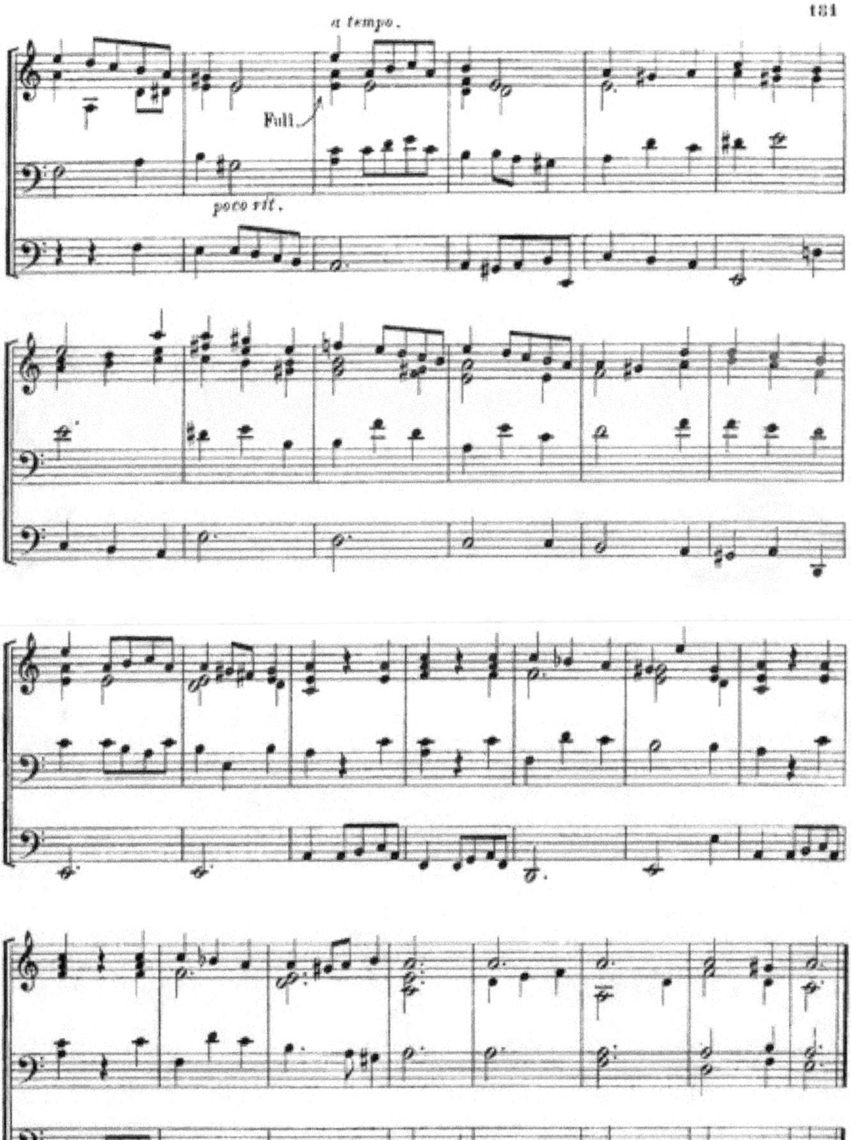
a tempo.
Full
poco rit.

ANDANTE.

EDOUARD BATISTE.

Gt. Doppel Flöte.
Sw. Oboe & Flute 4 Ft.

Ch. Dulciana.

Ped. Bourdon.

a piacere

Oboe off.
add St. Diap.

Add Clarinet in Ch.

A. On a two-manual organ, the Swell should be opened here & Melodia added to the Dulciana (Gt.) keeping the solo & accompaniment as at first, but playing the passages marked Gt. as indicated. At B. return to the first combinations.

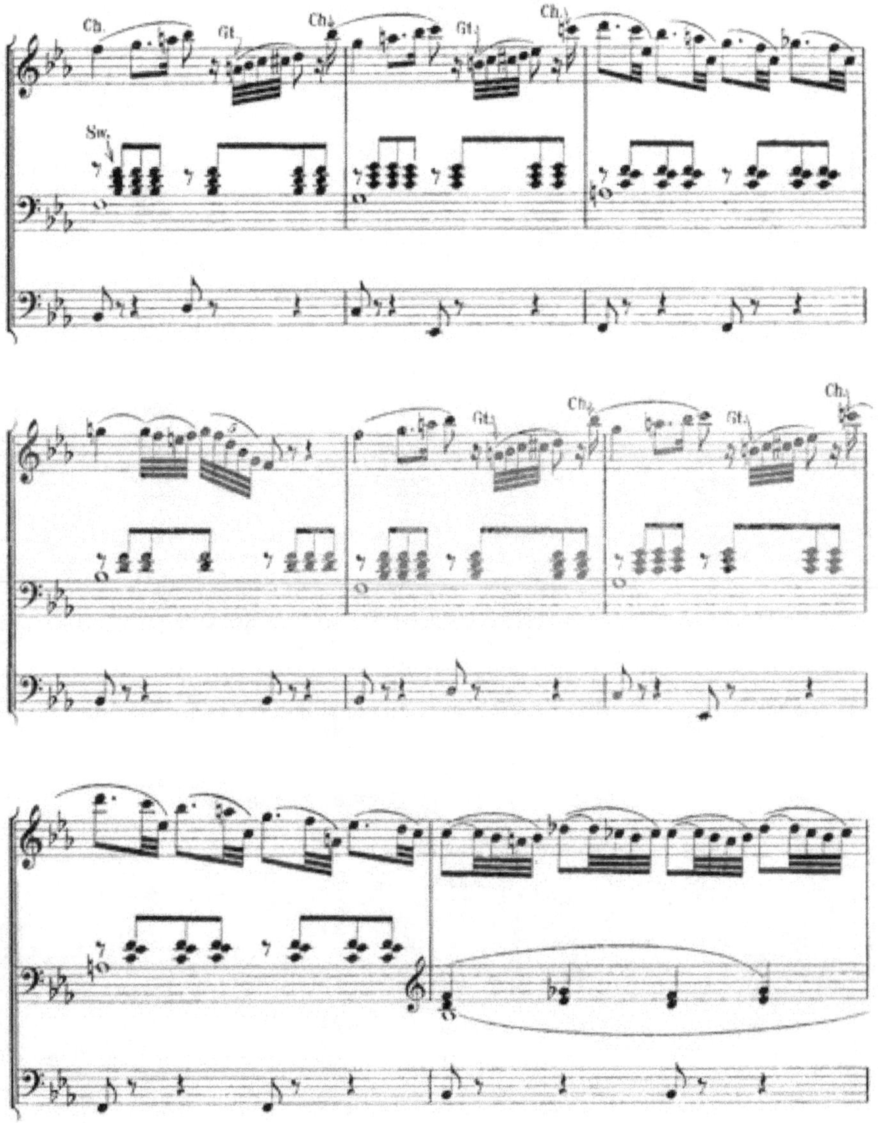
Ch.
Gt.
Ch.
Gt.
Ch.
Sw.
Gt.
Ch.
Gt.
Ch.

B
a tempo
rallentando
Sw. Add Oboe & Tremolant (Swell closed.)
Ch. Clarinet off.
16
ritardando
a piacere.

REMINISCENCES OF ORGAN AND CHURCH MUSIC IN THIS COUNTRY.

(Continued from page 175.)

and a hall for secular purposes. It can be hired for almost any kind of an entertainment, that is respectable, during week-days. I remember to have attended an exhibition (by "the great Blondin") of tight-and-slack-rope walking, when he closed the performance by walking to and fro with his head in a sack, on a rope suspended just below the ceiling, some sixty feet above the floor of the hall.

But some time between Saturday and Sunday a mysterious transformation takes place. That which during the rest of the week has been given up to worldly and secular purposes, assumes suddenly the air of a place of worship. The minister's desk is rolled to the front of the stage, the choir and organist take their places behind him, and everything is in readiness for "the performance of divine worship."

Previous to this organ being built for Tremont Temple, the only performances on the organ that could be called concert playing were heard at the opening of some new church organ, or before the beginning of the oratorios by the Händel and Haydn Society, in the Music Hall, which *then* possessed a rather poor three-manual organ.

The society for a long time kept up this most absurd custom of having the organist begin the evening's entertainment with "a piece on the organ." I remember to have heard Mr. C. C. Müller, formerly organist of the society, perform the concerto in F of Rink, as a prelude to the "Messiah"! That is, Händel's overture was not good enough, they must improve on him by the importation of Master Rink!

But to return to Tremont Temple. The (then) new organ, as I said before, was the first attempt on this side of the Atlantic to erect, in a public hall, a large instrument for concert purposes. It contained (if I remember rightly) about eighty registers, four manuals, and numerous combination pedal movements. At the time of its construction it was a very creditable piece of work, and did much to establish the fame of the firm that built it, a fame that has, however, been much extended since. It was considered of importance enough to be described at length by Hopkins and Rimbault, in their "History and Construction of the Organ," an honor paid, I think, to but few other instruments on this continent.

But the most important event connected with the first years of the Tremont Temple organ, was the *début* (to all intents and purposes), in this country, of the distinguished English organist, George Washburn Morgan. He had arrived from England a year or two previous to his appearing in Boston, and had been organist of Grace Church, in New York City. But as he was more of a concert player than a church organist, and as no other place but Boston contained a concert organ, his first appearance may be credited to the latter city. Mr. Morgan had a first-class reputation in England previous to his coming to this country, and as he was the first real concert organist heard here, and was a really fine performer, his playing made a great "sensation." I use the word *sensation* advisedly, as there were some things connected with his appearances at that time that were decidedly "sensational," to say the least.

The organist's bench, in the *old* Tremont Temple (the hall or church, or whatever it may be called, was burned a few years ago, and now presents a somewhat different appearance), was in a very prominent position, in full view of the audience; the consequence being that the performer's feet and lower limbs could be seen with great distinctness, as he sat at the instrument. Mr. Morgan also heightened the scenic effect of this part of his appearance by always wearing either white or very light-colored trousers. Not only this, but on his seating himself at the key-board to begin his performances, the audience were treated to the following unheard of proceeding :—

The performer was seen to take in his hand a large piece of chalk, and, elevating one foot, he proceeded to cover the bottom of the boot with the substance, afterwards proceeding

in the same manner with the other member. This took some time, and at the end of this extraordinary operation the feelings of the audience were worked up to the highest pitch of awe and expectancy.

However, Mr. Morgan had an excuse for this bit of sensational business, in the fact that the old Tremont Temple organ *pedal* action was exceedingly *stiff*, and required almost the whole weight of the player's body in order to put the keys down, and the use of the chalk was to prevent the feet slipping.

But it was decidedly a new revelation to hear the *bass* (and frequently pretty rapid basses too) played by the *feet!* Not only was this a great novelty, but Mr. Morgan's selections were something entirely new to his hearers. Previous to his coming, hardly anything had been heard at organ recitals but overtures, marches, and extempore playing, with perhaps an occasional selection from a mass by Haydn, or an oratorio played without *pedal obligato*. But the new performer treated us to a large number of *real organ compositions*. Bach and Händel's organ works, Mendelssohn's sonatas, etc. Besides, his manner of performing *orchestral* works, as overtures, slow movements from symphonies, selections from oratorios, etc., was entirely new to us. His *tempi* were taken faster in overtures and other rapid movements than we had been accustomed to.

He was exceedingly quick in changing his "combinations," and his selection of stops was generally in excellent taste. He has always had a great reputation as a "pedal player," but I think his pedal work, although excellent, was no better than that given us by other organists since that time.

As I remember his programmes, he did not perform many of the great works of the masters for the organ, but whatever he did play was done exceedingly well, and with great neatness of execution, both with hands and feet. The American organists are under very great obligations to Mr. Morgan for having shown them (at a time when they needed it) what could be accomplished on a large organ by the hands (and feet) of a master.
GEORGE E. WHITING.

CIPHERINGS.

MISS JONES. "What a lazy fellow that John White is!"

MISS SMITH. "Is that so? Why?"

MISS JONES. "I saw him at dancing-school last night, and to-day he was sitting down at the organ up in the town hall, resting his hands on the keys, and practising the various steps with his feet. I call that a downright lazy way to learn how to dance. I shall never dare to dance with him for fear he will sit down right in the middle of the dance."

* * *

WORSHIPPER. "There was no soprano in the choir to-day. What was the matter?"

ORGANIST. "The soprano had a dream last night, in which an angel told her the Lord wanted her to sing Anthem No. 95 to-day."

WORSHIPPER. "Well?"

ORGANIST. "Well, the soprano got mad, and said she wouldn't be bossed by anybody."— *The Musical Messenger.*

* * *

ACCORDING to an exchange a German professor of the art instrumental in St. Louis has a method of instruction, the virtue of which lies in its appalling brevity. It is thus illustrated in dialogue :—

TEACHER. "You wants do learn do blay ze organ?"

PUPIL. "Yes."

TEACHER. "Dot's right. Zit py me, right glose py me. Now zee — dis vas A, unt dis vas B, unt dis vas C, unt dis vas D, unt dis vas E, unt dis vas F, unt dis vas G."

PUPIL. "Yes."

TEACHER. "Now ve blays de Fuga in G-moll of Bach." — *Ex.*

ORGAN NEWS IN NEW YORK.

(From our own Correspondent.)

NEW YORK, Nov. 21, 1892.

I INTENDED in this letter to dwell upon a certain subject, but although I have waited almost until the last moment, I find that it is not sufficiently ripe, and therefore I must postpone it until my next.

I had occasion to visit, a few weeks ago, the New York Avenue M. E. Church in Brooklyn, and was more than agreeably disappointed in the superb instrument by Hutchings, which was placed there a little over a year ago. The instrument is imposing in its aspect, the cabinet work being of the finest selected oak, exquisitely finished, and the displayed pipes artistically grouped on two sides of the organ chamber, and finely gilded. Through the courtesy of the organist, Mr. Carl G. Schmidt, I was able to look at the key-board, and I found it strikingly handsome, and most compact and accessible, in spite of the quantity of mechanical stops and pedal combinations. The full-organ tone is very smooth, deep, and impressive, and the character of the solo stops, especially in the string department, is very striking. I understand that a critical review of this instrument is to appear in a new musical paper which will be published for the first time in January next. I shall look forward with much interest to that article. As in a majority of instances the effectiveness of the organ is considerably impaired by its rather cramped position in a recess on one side of the pulpit, I would like to see such an instrument placed in the position of the one at Plymouth Church, Brooklyn, of which I shall speak presently. The organist, Mr. Schmidt, told me that he was more and more pleased with it, and that all professionals and amateurs who had heard it or played it were also delighted with both its rich voicing and its excellent action.

Yesterday I attended the dedication of the new Collegiate Reformed Church, corner of West End Avenue and 77th Street, a perfect gem of architecture and decoration. I was greatly disappointed in the organ (although a brand-new Roosevelt), which reflects no credit whatever on the builder, except perhaps in the decoration of the displayed pipes. The general effect of the instrument is unbalanced, coarse, glaring, and decidedly unsympathetic. Although a small two-manual instrument of perhaps some twenty or thirty stops (I had no opportunity of examining it closely), if I were to judge from the efforts of the organist, the action must be hard and unwieldy. A choir of sixteen picked voices from the three collegiate churches of the city did some capital work in spite of its being handicapped by most execrable accompaniments. The organist seemed to take special delight in marking *tempo* with the swell pedal, and you can imagine the effect. There was nothing particular in the way of solo playing to call for any special mention.

Last evening I wended my way to Plymouth Church, Brooklyn, attracted by the announcement that the organ, recently overhauled, would be re-dedicated. This instrument,[1] as you are probably aware, was built by the old firm of Messrs. E. & G. G. Hook of Boston, in 1866, and at the time was considered a masterpiece in this country, on account of its size and its mechanical appliances. I do not think that the *voicing* was ever equal to some specimens of Erben, of which there are still two or three doing good service in this city, — a monument to his good work, and a pattern for modern organ-builders.

The late Mrs. Emma Abbott Wetherell, a faithful member of Plymouth Church, left in her will certain amounts for various objects in Plymouth Church; amongst them, as stated last night, $5,000 to be expended on the organ. I was about trimming my quill to chronicle the disastrous failure that the committee had made in the expenditure of that money, when a timely apology on the part of the chief speaker informed us that the organ had unfortunately not yet been completed, and, in fact, not yet put in perfect tune. Therefore I shall leave

[1] See our mention of New Organs this month for specification. — ED.

my criticisms on that score until it is entirely finished. The musical portion of the service was very effectively rendered by a combination of two of the best choirs in Brooklyn, numbering altogether some seventy voices, with two quartets of soloists; and they did some magnificent work in spite of some very poor accompaniments, especially to the solos. It was a question in my mind as to whether the trouble lay with the ability of the organists, or with the nature of the instrument. At the close of the service I came to the conclusion that there was a little of both; for one of the organists certainly played much better than the other, and brought out several of the good points in the instrument.

As far as solos were concerned, the following were rendered: As a prelude the slow movement from the Merkel Sonata for two performers was somewhat indifferently rendered. In this case I think that the trouble was due to the rather unwieldy nature of the organ. This movement was followed by Händel's Largo, which was not at all well played. In fact, the organist seemed to have no conception whatever of the spirit of the composition. It was played in very questionable *tempo*, and with the loud Diapasons of the great organ. It was also, I think, a rather unhappy selection to play after the Merkel movement. At the offertory one of the organists played the Allegro Cantabile from Widor's Fourth Symphony. It had considerable of the *allegro* and very little of the *cantabile*. Its rendition was careless and thoroughly colorless. In fact, I think that the organist has no conception whatever of the character of the composition, and I must say that the unwieldy nature of the organ does not lend itself to that class of compositions which requires most artistic and smooth stops, such as Widor has in his organ in St. Sulpice. For the postlude they played the Allegro movement of the Merkel Sonata for two performers, which of course, being played with full organ and in a brisk *tempo*, was more adapted to the characteristics of the organ, and was consequently more effective than the previous solos.

The position of that organ in Plymouth Church is certainly an ideal one. The building is a regular four-square meeting-house with absolutely nothing in the way of pillars, arches, rafters, beams, or anything else to support the immense plastered ceiling. A gallery runs around the building, and on it, at the back of the church and over the platform, stands the instrument, with absolutely nothing to impair its effectiveness. I wonder how long it will be before architects or building committees will realize the importance of the *position* for the organ.

Mr. Gerrit Smith has already begun his series of organ recitals on Monday afternoons, and Mr. Horatio W. Parker has begun his series on Saturday afternoons. I have not yet had an opportunity of attending either, but hope to do so shortly.

The alterations in the organs at Grace Church not having yet been fully completed, I hardly think that Mr. Warren will begin his recitals much before January.

Yours fraternally,

JUXTUS FRANKUS.

THE following letter arrived too late for insertion last month: —

NEW YORK, Oct. 25, 1892.

The all-absorbing topic of interest in organ circles, i.e. among builders, organists, — professional and amateurs, — and others interested, is the announcement which was made public several days ago, of Mr. Frank Roosevelt having fully and definitely decided to abandon the organ-building business, which he has so successfully carried on for many years as successor to his lamented brother, Mr. Hilborne L. Roosevelt. This announcement came as a very great surprise, especially as Mr. Roosevelt had but recently given up his rather limited quarters in West 18th Street, where the works had been located ever since they were founded in

1872, and removed to the very handsome and spacious building at Park Avenue and 131st Street, which he occupies in almost all its entirety, and where his facilities for doing business have been greatly enhanced.

A somewhat brief history of this concern may perhaps not be amiss here. Mr. Hilborne L. Roosevelt, quite a young man, very well off in this world's goods, and with the very best of social connections, was a most enthusiastic musician, one of the founders and most active members of the famous "Mendelssohn Glee Club," and had a particular leaning towards the king of instruments. As a matter of amusement, I believe, he learned all the details of its construction, at the works of the now extinct firm of Hall, Labagh & Kemp, in Bedford Street, this city. In 1872 he made, I believe, his first organ, which was placed in the Church of the Holy Communion in this city. He afterwards rapidly built other instruments, such as those in the Church of the Holy Trinity, the Dominican Church, and Grace Church, this city, which at once placed him at the very head of the organ-building fraternity in this country, at the time when Erben, Odell and Jardine of this city, and Hook & Hastings of Boston, vied with each other for the honors of first place. Mr. Roosevelt created a decided revolution in organ-building by his close attention to the finish of many minor details which had been up to that time neglected. He used to make periodical visits to Europe, and, being possessed of ample means, he could secure there all the latest improvements of the best English, French, and German builders, which are not a few, and promptly applied them in his productions. As a result, we have to-day very many specimens of remarkable workmanship, which will last for many years to come as monuments to his industry and love of his work.

Mr. Hilborne Roosevelt was prematurely called to his fathers in 1886, I believe, at the yet unripe age of thirty-five or thirty-six years. His brother Frank immediately succeeded him in the business, and to this day has carried it on with great credit to himself and to the name that his brother had so earnestly and successfully labored to establish. I have not seen the work that his factory has turned out in the last few years, but I am told by connoisseurs that it has been, if anything, superior to the old, and that in his new factory Mr. Roosevelt has spared no expense to make everything as perfect as money and brains could make it. It seems, however, that his efforts have not met with a desirable response from those who should have encouraged him in his ever-improving work; and, being a man of independent means, and not desirous perhaps of worrying himself into an early grave through disappointment, has very wisely decided to withdraw from the field. I understand that it is his firm intention not to sell the business out, and much less to allow any one to continue the business under his name. I feel that this decision of Mr. Roosevelt is undoubtedly a great loss, and will be in a measure a severe blow to organ work in this country. However, I am confident in the belief that there are one or two makers who will probably take up the work that he lays down, and carry it on in the future.

Whilst it is undeniable that the Roosevelt work as far as action and finish, from the key-board to the last pallet and screw, has been almost beyond criticism, still I cannot say that I have ever been very enthusiastic over their peculiar style of voicing. There are a great many organists who like it, and again others who do not. It has always seemed to me as if their voicing has been characteristic of the French; that is, with the string and reed qualities predominating, which makes them more of a colossal harmonium, and lacks the full, round, and pervading organ tone.

I understand that the last pieces of work that will probably be turned out by Mr. Roosevelt before he closes his business, will be a large three-manual organ for the new hall of the Mendelssohn Glee Club. Another very large three-manual organ for the Church of All Saints, in Harlem, and the very difficult alterations, which he is now carrying on, to the organs in Grace Church, all of this city. I hope I may be able to inspect these instruments, and if so, I shall be only too glad to give you a full account of them in my next.

It does seem somewhat of a coincidence that one of the first pieces of work of any magnitude and importance made by Mr. Hilborne Roosevelt when he started, should have been the chancel organ at Grace Church, and that one of the last that Mr. Frank Roosevelt is about to make, should be the alterations to that same organ after the lapse of so many years.

There is, I am sorry to say, not much else to chronicle in the organ line in this city at present, as the season for recitals has not yet begun, but I trust that my next may have much of interest in this connection.

JUXTUS FRANKUS.

MIXTURES.

(FOUR RANKS.)

Mr. GEORGE E. WHITING gave an organ recital at the New England Conservatory, Nov. 17.

Robert Franz, who was at one time organist at the Ulrichskirche, Halle, died Oct. 24, at the age of seventy-seven.

The house in Weimar in which J. S. Bach was born has been marked with a memorial tablet.

Mr. Moses Carpenter, formerly organist of St. Mary's Church, Boston, died early in November.

Mr. I. V. Flagler will continue his lectures on the organ in New York this season.

An hydraulic engine has been attached to the bellows of the new organ of the College of Organists in London.

Mr. Jas. A. Pennington recently gave an organ recital in the Cathedral, Illinois.

Mr. Herve D. Wilkins is giving his thirteenth series of organ recitals in Rochester, N.Y.

Mr. Jas. E. Bagley, organist of Christ Church, Rochester, N.Y., will give a series of organ concerts in Rochester this winter.

The organ in the Emanuel Episcopal Church, Rockford, Ill., is being rebuilt by the Lancashire-Marshall Pipe Organ Co.

Mr. J. L. Browne, of Minneapolis, has been appointed to the position of organist of Christ Church, St. Paul, Minn.

Mr. James F. Slater, F. C. O., has been appointed organist of the parish church of Middleton, England.

Sir John Stainer, M.A., Mus. Doc., who was at one time organist of Magdalen College, Oxford, England, has been elected to an honorary fellowship in the college.

Mr. C. E. Miller is giving a series of weekly organ recitals at St. Augustine and St. Faith's Church, London. The recitals commence at 5.10 P.M.

A new organ at All Hallows Church, London, was opened the 29th of October by Dr. E. H. Turpin, honorary secretary of the College of Organists.

Gustavus Baylies, who has been organist of several fashionable churches in numerous Western cities, has been arrested in St. Louis, charged with several cases of embezzlement.

Mr. Geo. S. Hutchings has just completed a two-manual organ of eleven registers for St. Philip's Church, Cambridge, Mass., and another of the same size for Asbury Memorial Church, Providence, R.I.

Mr. Gerard Taillandier has resigned his position as organist and director at St. Vincent de Paul's Church, Boston, to accept a similar position at St. Mary's Church.

Messrs. Farrand and Votey are making extensive alterations in their factory, preparatory to the reception of the machinery from Mr. Frank Roosevelt's factory, which will probably be transferred about Jan. 1st.

At Mr. Harrison M. Wild's 117th concert, in Unity Church, Chicago, the principal numbers were: Prelude and Fugue, Op. 37, No. 3, Mendelssohn; Pontifical Sonata, Lemmens, and three pieces by Lemaigre.

The Peterborough (England) Cathedral is to have a new organ, $26,000 has been donated to the cathedral for this purpose, with the stipulation that the instrument must be built by Messrs. Hill & Son of London.

One of our exchanges, the monthly magazine entitled Music, edited by Mr. W. S. B. Mathews, and published in Chicago, has just ended its first year, and commences its third volume under the most favorable circumstances.

At the Inaugural Ceremonies of the Columbian Exposition, held in the Auditorium, Chicago, the latter part of last month, Mr. Clarence Eddy played a festival overture on "A Strong Castle is our Lord," Nicolai-Liszt, and Triumphal March of Dudley Buck.

Mr. Harrison M. Wild gave his 114th recital in Unity Church, Chicago, Nov. 6, assisted by Mr. Clarence Dickinson (organist of the Church of the Messiah), a quartette, and a violinist, in which the following compositions were given:—

Festival Prelude (four hands), Jansen; Sonata, No. 1, Mailly (Mr. Dickinson); Andantino, Op. 48, No. 9, Salomé; Esquisse in G-minor, Hervey; Gothic March, Salomé; and Overture to "Euryanthe," Weber-Warren (Mr. Dickinson).

The re-opening of the organ improvisation and plain chant courses in the school founded by M. Gigout (organist of St. Augustine), took place last month. The exhibition exercises of the end of the year, which could not be given as usual last July, will take place during the month of December.

Organ recital in the Unity Church, Chicago, Oct. 30, by Mr. Harrison M. Wild. Programme: Introduction and Fugue, Op. 70, Guilmant; First Organ Concerto, Händel; March in E-flat, Salomé; Chorus of Angels, Scotson Clark; Offertoire in A-flat, Read; Rienzi March, Wagner. The programme was varied by quartettes and a song.

Mr. Taft performed among other works, Toccata in F, Bach; Concert Variations on "Last Rose of Summer," Bach; Overture to "Masaniello," Auber; Marche Symphonique, Taft; Wedding Music, Lohengrin, Wagner; Toccata and Fugue in D-minor, Bach; St. Cecilia Offertory, Batiste; and Sonata in C-minor, Mendelssohn.

Organ concert in the Church of the Messiah, Chicago, Oct. 25, by Mr. Clarence Dickinson. Programme: Chromatic Fantasia and Fugue, Thiele; Pastorale Sonata, Rheinberger; Berceuse and Vesper Bells, Spinney; Overture to "Stradella," Flotow-Buck; Communion, Batiste; Variation on "The Last Rose of Summer," Buck; March in E-flat, Wély.

Mr. J. Warren Andrews played the following selections at the benefit concert of the Young Ladies' Club of Plymouth Church, Minneapolis, Minn., the last of October: Offertoire in G, Capocci; Second Movement of Sonata in C, Dethier; Overture to "Poet and Peasant," Suppé; Berceuse in D, Spinney; and Variations on "Auld Lang Syne," for four hands, by Thayer, Mrs. Andrews assisting.

The organ proved well adapted for the church, and gave general satisfaction. The solo stops were naturally not heard to any extent in such a programme, but those which were used were very pleasing. Such a miscellaneous programme, while extremely interesting as a concert, never seems appropriate for an inauguration of an organ, as one hears so little of the organ at the time of all times when it should be predominant.

A "Complimentary Benefit" Concert, tendered to Mr. Theodore Spinney, was given in the First Presbyterian Church, Bridgeport, Conn., the last of October. The following organ numbers were performed by Mr. Spinney: Overture "Die Stumme Von Portici," Auber; Concert Fantasia on themes from "The Huguenots" Meyerbeer-Spinney; Paraphrase on Pleyel's Hymn, Spinney; "Representation of a Thunder-storm."

Organ recital in first Presbyterian Church, Greensburg, Pa., Oct. 28, by Mr. Clarence Eddy. Programme: Overture to "William Tell," Rossini-Buck; Harvest Home, Spinney; Peasant's March, Fumagalli; Variations on "Old Folks at Home," Flagler; Prayer and Cradle Song, Guilmant; "March of the Magi Kings," Dubois; Fantasia, "O Sanctissima," Lux; "At Evening," Buck; Fugue in G-minor, Bach; "Hymn of Nuns," Wély and Offertoire in D, Batiste. Miss Christine Nichon contributed songs.

Mr. Eddy gave the above programme at the First Presbyterian Church, Wellsville, O., Oct. 27, in opening a new Wirsching Organ.

A new organ, built by Casavant Brothers, has been placed in the Basilica, at Ottawa, Canada, the main part of the instrument consisting of thirteen stops in the great, eleven in the swell, eight in the choir, and nine in the pedal, is divided into two parts and placed in chambers on the north and south of the gallery at the west end of the church. Connected with this is an electric organ, also divided into two parts, located on either side of the Sanctuary at the other end of the church, and consisting of a choir organ of five stops, a swell organ of six stops, and a pedal organ of one stop.

Mr. J. Warren Andrews proposes to give up his present studio in Century building, Minneapolis, and establish a new studio in rooms connected with the Plymouth Church, of which he is organist. The rooms will be specially fitted up for those who wish to study organ and church music. A two-manual organ, with four stops in the great, eight in the swell, and one in the pedal, to be blown by an electric motor, is now being built by Mr. Geo. S. Hutchings of Boston for this studio. Mr. Andrews proposes to organize special classes in the various branches of church music, and hopes to receive sufficient encouragement to establish a summer school.

The daily organ recitals at the Mechanics' Fair, Boston, were continued during the past month. Among the organists were Mr. E. Harrington Woodman, and Mr. Frank A. Taft of New York. The principal works performed by Mr. Woodman were: Overture to Samson, Händel; Prelude and Fugue in G, Bach; Sonata, No. 4, Mendelssohn; Sonata in C-minor, Salomé; Toccata from Fifth Organ Symphony, Widor; Toccata in E-minor, Tombelle; Marche Gothique, Salomé; Pilgrim's March, Wagner; Fantasia in E-flat, Saint-Saens; March of the Three Kings, Dubois; and Wedding Hymn, Woodman.

An inaugural concert was given in the Church of Our Lady of Victories, Boston, Nov. 6, with the following programme: Organ Prelude (Mr. Walter J. Kegler); Kyrie and Gloria Cherubini (by the choir under the direction of Mr. Alfred de Sève); Veni Sancte Spiritus, Neukom (Mr. John J. McCluskey); Prelude, Whiting, and March from Suite, Lacelace (Mr. John C. Kelley); Largo (with violin obligato), Händel (Miss Mary Howe and Mr. de Sève); Trio, "Hear My Prayer," Abbot; Regina Coeli, Cherubini; Cavatina, Raff (Mr. de Sève); Alma Virgo, Hummel; Sonata, Whiting (Miss Roche); Ave Maria (with violin obligato), Gounod (Miss McLaughlin and Mr. De Sève); "The Heavens are Telling," Haydn (the Cathedral choir).

The following from a Norfolk (Va.) daily: "Christ P. E. Church was well filled yesterday afternoon, when the first organ recital of the season was given by the organist, Mr. J. J. Miller, assisted by Miss Lizzie A. Taylor, soprano, and Mr. William H. Turner, violinist. These recitals are musical treats, and that they are appreciated is evidenced by the large audiences which attend. The following is the programme which was most excellently rendered yesterday: Concerto in F, 'The Cuckoo and the Nightingale' (two movements), G. F. Händel; Reverie (for violin), B. C. Fasconico; Impromptu, Op. 142, No. 2, Franz Schubert; 'At Evening' (Idyl), Dudley Buck; Intermezzo from 'Cavalleria Rusticana,' P. Mascagni (soprano solo with violin obligato); Coronation March (Prophète), G. Meyerbeer."

During the past month Mr. Frank Taft has been in Ohio giving numerous concerts. In the Cincinnati Music Hall, during the Floral Fair, he gave six organ recitals, including such works as Toccata and Fugue in D-minor, Bach; St. Cecelia Offertory, Batiste; Serenade, Taft; "Dream after the Ball," Broustet; Sonata in C-minor, Mendelssohn; Vorspiel, and Introduction to Third Act, "Lohengrin," Wagner; Storm Fantasia, Lemmens; Toccata in F, Bach; Variations on "Last Rose of Summer," Buck; Pontifical March, Tombelle; Variations on "Old Folks at Home," Taft; and Spinning Chorus from "The Flying Dutchman," Wagner.

Organ recital by Mr. Alex S. Gibson, in Disciples Church, Danbury, Conn., Nov. 16. Programme: Overture, "A Night in Granada," Kreutzer; Toccata and Fugue in D-minor, Bach; Offertory in C, No. 15, Wély; Allegretto in A, Op. 117, Merkel; Gavotte in F, Archer; Offertory in F, Op. 9, Batiste; Variations on an American Air, Flagler; Festival March in D, Smart. Mr. Gibson was assisted by a violinist and an elocutionist.

Mons. C. L. Werner, a pupil of Mons. Alex Guilmant, who met with such success in a concert with Mons. Guilmant in the Trocadero, Paris, has been appointed organist of the Stadt-Kirche of Baden-Baden.

Mr. H. W. Parker gave an organ recital in the Church of the Holy Trinity, New York, Nov. 12.

CORRESPONDENCE.

EVOLUTION OF THE SWELL-BOX.

To the Editor of THE ORGAN:

I HAVE read with much interest the article signed "Gambette" in your November number of THE ORGAN. He advises "Emile" to use his brains. The writer of this article plays a three-manual organ, which, until recently, has had no combination pedals whatever, and the writer has had to use his brains a good many times in order to get the effect desired. I have now the following combination pedals: Great Forte, Great Mezzo Forte, Swell Forte, Swell Piano, Great to Pedal reversible; and they are a great help. The action of the organ is also rather hard, not being pneumatic. I have heard a prominent pupil of Guilmant give an organ recital on a fine three-manual organ, with all of the combination pedals needed (and he played a fine programme), and he used them very sparingly, making most of his changes with the hands. The writer does not like the idea of enclosing most of the great organ in the swell-box; while some good effects may be obtained, the general effect of the great organ is lost. While talking with a prominent builder on the subject, he said, "When I want the full, great organ, I want to hear it, and not have it shut up in the swell-box, where it is out of place." I am sorry for the player who could not get any expression out of the Gamba on the great, and hope that he will use some other stop and let the Gamba remain where it should be, namely, with all the rest of the great organ, and out of the swell-box.   OCTAVE.

GEORGE S. HUTCHINGS,

Church Organ Manufacturer,

23 TO 27 IRVINGTON STREET,

BOSTON, MASS.

Builder of some of the most famous organs in the country, among which may be mentioned The New Old South, Emmanuel, Second Church, Park St. Church, St. Paul's, Spiritual Temple, and Church of the Advent, all of Boston ; also South Congregational Church, Middletown, Conn., New York Avenue M. E. Church, Brooklyn, N. Y., St. Paul's School, Concord, N. H., and All Saints Church, Worcester, Second Congregational Church, Holyoke, Mass., Grace Church, Providence, R.I., Plymouth Church, Minneapolis, First Congregational Church, Omaha, Neb., First Congregational Church, San Francisco, Cal., Independent Presbyterian Church, Savannah, Ga., and many others.

Send for catalogue.

NEW ORGANS.

Messrs. Hook & Hastings have been making extended renovations to the great Plymouth Church organ, a description of which is given below, showing the organ as it stands to-day, including the new stops that have been added or substituted.

This organ has always been a noted instrument. At the time it was built it was the largest in America, and now, after nearly thirty years of use, it still stands, a monument to its makers.

GREAT ORGAN.

Open Diapason	16	Ft.
Open Diapason	8	"
English Open Diapason	8	"
Clarabella	8	"
Stopped Diapason	8	"
Viol da Gamba	8	"
Octave	4	"
Flûte Harmonique	4	"
Twelfth	2⅔	"
Fifteenth	2	"
Mixture	3	Rks.
Scharff	3	"
Trumpet	16	Ft.
Trumpet	8	"
Clarion	4	"

CHOIR ORGAN.

Still Gedeckt	16	Ft.
Open Diapason	8	"
Dulciana	8	"
Melodia	8	"
Quintadena	8	"
Octave	4	"
Flauto Traverso	4	"
Piccolo	2	"
Clarinet	8	"

PEDAL ORGAN.

Open Diapason	32	Ft.
Open Diapason	16	"
Violone	16	"
Bourdon	16	"
Violoncello	8	"
Bell Gamba	8	"
Trombone	16	"

SWELL ORGAN.

Bourdon	16	Ft.
Open Diapason	8	"
Salicional	8	"
Stopped Diapason	8	"
Spitz-flöte	8	"
Flûte Harmonique	4	"
Vox Celeste	4	"
Viol d'Amour	4	"
Flautino	2	"
Mixture	5	Rks.
Euphone	16	Ft.
Cornopean	8	"
Oboe	8	"
Vox Humana	8	"
Clarion	4	"

SOLO ORGAN.

Tuba Mirabilis	8	Ft.
Stentrophon	8	"
Keraulophon	8	"
Philomela	8	"
Hohlpfeife	4	"
Cor Anglais	8	"

PEDAL MOVEMENTS.

Forte, Mezzo, and Piano Combinations for Gt.

Forte and Piano Combinations for Sw.

Forte and Piano Combinations for Ch.

Forte and Piano Pedal (double-acting).

Grand Sforzando Pedal.

Grand Crescendo Pedal.

Great to Pedal (reversible).

Pneumatic Action.

NEW ORGAN IN FIRST METHODIST CHURCH, DULUTH, MINN.

(Built by Geo. S. Hutchings of Boston, Mass.)

GREAT ORGAN.

Open Diapason	16	Ft.
Open Diapason	8	"
Dolcissimo (blank)	8	"
Viola da Gamba	8	"
Doppel-flöte	4	"
Flûte Harmonique	4	"
Octave	4	"
Octave Quinte	2⅔	"
Super Octave	2	"
Mixture	3	Rks.
Trumpet	8	Ft.

CHOIR ORGAN.

Lieblich Gedackt (blank)	16	Ft.
Geigen Principal	8	"
Dulciana	8	"
Melodia	8	"
Flûte d'Amour	4	"
Violina	4	"
Piccolo	2	"
Clarinet	8	"

PEDAL ORGAN.

Contra Bourdon (blank)	32	Ft.
Open Diapason	16	"
Dulciana (blank)	16	"
Bourdon	16	"
Violone (blank)	16	"
Violoncello	8	"
Flûte (blank)	8	"

SWELL ORGAN.

Bourdon Bass	16	Ft.
Bourdon Treble	16	"
Open Diapason	8	"
Salicional	8	"
Aeoline	8	"
Quintadena	8	"
Stopped Diapason	8	"
Octave (blank)	4	"
Flauto Traverso	4	"
Fugara	4	"
Flautino	2	"
Dolce Cornet	3	Rks.
Contra Fagotto (blank)	16	Ft.
Cornopean	8	"
Oboe	8	"
Vox Humana	8	"

PEDAL MOVEMENTS.

Forte
Mezzo } Great Organ.
Piano

Forte
Mezzo } Swell Organ.
Piano

Reversible Great to Pedal Coupler.

Swell to Great at Octaves.

Swell Tremolo.

The usual Couplers.

Pneumatic motors applied to Great Organ and its Couplers.

NEW ORGAN IN THE CHURCH OF OUR LADY OF VICTORIES, BOSTON.

(Built by Messrs. Hook and Hastings.)

GREAT ORGAN.

Open Diapason	16	Ft.
Open Diapason	8	"
Clarabella	8	"
Viola da Gamba	8	"
Octave	4	"
Twelfth	2⅔	"
Fifteenth	2	"
Mixture	3	Rks.
Trumpet	8	Ft.

CHOIR ORGAN.

Geigen Principal	8	Ft.
Dulciana	8	"
Melodia	8	"
Flauto Traverso	4	"
Piccolo	2	"
Clarinet	8	"

SWELL ORGAN.

Bourdon Treble	16	Ft.
Bourdon Bass	16	"
Open Diapason	8	"
Salicional	8	"
St. Diapason	8	"
Flûte Harmonique	4	"
Octave	4	"
Fifteenth	2	"
Cornopean	8	"
Oboe	8	"
Bassoon	8	"
Vox Humana	8	"

PEDAL ORGAN.

Open Diapason	16	Ft.
Bourdon	16	"
Violoncello	8	"

PEDAL MOVEMENTS.

Forte, Mezzo, and Piano Combinations for Gt.

Forte and Piano Combinations for Sw.

Gt. to Ped. (reversible).

The usual Couplers. Pneumatic action. Water motor.

BUTTRICK MEMORIAL ORGAN, HIGHLAND CONGREGATIONAL CHURCH, LOWELL, MASS.

(Built by Cole & Woodberry, from plans of Mr. W. B. Goodwin, of Lowell.)

GREAT ORGAN.

Principal Diapason	8	Ft.
Viola Dolce	8	"
Flauto Concerto	8	"
Flautiberto	8	"
Octava Acuta	4	"
Flauto Soave	4	"
Quinta Octava	2⅔	"
Octavina	2	"

SWELL ORGAN.

Contra Viola	16	Ft.
Viola Principal	8	"
Dolciano	8	"
Viola Ætheria	8	"
Doppel-flöte	8	"
Salicetto Dolce	4	"
Hohlpfeife	4	"
Violetina	2	"
Corno di Capella	8	"

PEDAL ORGAN.

Bourdon Principal	16	Ft.
Lieblich Gedackt	16	"
Flauto Basso	8	"

PEDAL MOVEMENTS.

F. and P., Gt.

F. and P., Sw.

Sw. to Gt. Octave and Sub-Octave in addition to usual Couplers.

Vol. I.   JANUARY, 1893.   No. 9.

BACH

YEARLY SUBSCRIPTION $2.00.   SINGLE COPIES 25 CTS.

THE ORGAN

DEVOTED TO

A MONTHLY JOURNAL

THE KING OF INSTRUMENTS

REINBERGER

GUILMANT

FRESCOBALDI

BUXTEHUDE

MERKEL

BEST

· EVERETT · E · TRUETTE ·
EDITOR & PUBLISHER
149 A. TREMONT ST. BOSTON.

HANDEL

THE ORGAN.

VOL. I.   BOSTON, JANUARY, 1893.   No. 9.

THE ORGAN.

A MONTHLY JOURNAL

DEVOTED TO THE KING OF INSTRUMENTS.

EVERETT E. TRUETTE, EDITOR AND PUBLISHER.

(Entered at the Boston, Mass., Post-office as second-class mail matter, June 1, 1892.)

CONTENTS:

GIROLAMO FRESCOBALDI.

GIROLAMO FRESCOBALDI, who was a skilful harpsichord-player, was born in Ferrara, a small Italian city about twenty-eight miles north of Bologna, in 1587. When but a boy he possessed a remarkable voice, and frequently wandered from town to town singing, on which occasions he was followed by crowds of admirers. History tells us very little of his life, but at the age of twenty he had acquired considerable notoriety as a talented organist. He studied with François Milleville till he journeyed to Belgium to become familiar with the Netherlandish doctrines, with which he was greatly in sympathy. In 1608 he returned to the sunny South and took up his residence in Milan. About this time his compositions were being published and were receiving very favorable notices. In 1614 or 1615 he went to Rome to fill the position of organist at St. Peter's. His reputation had become so great, and the love for organ music was so predominant with the Italian people of that age, that thirty thousand people flocked to the cathedral to hear his first recital.

His life in Rome, as far as can be learned, was uneventful, he devoting most of his time to composition. He was one of the inventors of the fugue, or rather the first to apply it to organ music in Italy, and revived the double counterpoint of the old French School which had fallen into disuse, except in the hands of Orlando di Lasso who still employed it in his writings. No other Italian organist exerted so much influence on organ music as did Frescobaldi, and undoubtedly he prepared the way for Lotti and Scarlatti, and later for Bach and Händel. Sir John Hawkins has this to say, in his History of the Science and Practice of Music, concerning the influence of Frescobaldi:—

"Of many musicians it has been said that they were the fathers of a particular style ; as that Palestrina was the father of the church style, Monteverde of the dramatic, and Carissimi of the chamber style ; of Frescobaldi it may as truly be said that he was the father of that organ style which has prevailed not less in England than in other countries for more than a hundred years past, and which consists in a prompt and ready discussion of some premeditated subject in a quicker succession of notes than is required in the accompaniment of chorale harmony. Exercises of this kind on the organ are usually called toccatas, from the Italian, to touch ; and, for want of a better word to express them, they are here in England called voluntaries. In the Romish service they occur at frequent intervals, particularly at the elevation, first communions, and during the offerings; and in that of our church in the morning prayer, after the psalms and after the benediction, or, in other words, between the first and second service ; and in the evening service after the psalms."

THE LOCATION OF THE BALANCED SWELL-PEDAL.

THE various organ-builders of this country place the swell-pedal shoe at various points in front of the pedal key-board, ranging from the centre to the extreme right. Some place it in an opening in the case of the organ; some allow it to project over the pedals, so that the short pedal-keys directly under the shoe are useless; while others locate it so high above the pedals that it is difficult to get the foot on it.

All organists will agree that a universally fixed location would be a great improvement over the present variable position. We have always claimed that the shoe should be placed opposite upper A (or A-sharp) of the pedal key-board, in an opening in the case, so that the heel part of the shoe does not project more than a half-inch over the short pedal keys. The shoe should be as low as possible, and still clear the cover board over the ends of the pedal keys. The angle of the shoe should correspond with a vertical plane passing through the shoe and the centre of the organ seat.

The location at the centre, or to the right of the centre, of the pedal key-board has one argument in its favor; but in our minds there are several arguments against it. When in or near the centre, either foot can be used to operate it, so that the upper octave of pedals can be used (with the right foot) when using the swell-pedal; but in compositions where the swell-pedal is used almost constantly, it is generally necessary to play in the upper and lower octaves of the pedal key-board so interchangeably that to be constantly changing the foot which is on the swell-shoe would be annoying. Then, again, all the space in the centre of the case in front of the pedal key-board is needed for combination pedals.

We have received so many letters from both organists and builders on this particular subject, that we have solicited the opinions of a number of organists, which we present to our readers, with the hope that in time our builders will adopt a fixed location, so that organists will always find the swell-pedal shoe in the same location. Quite a number of organists have not yet replied to our request, but we hope to be able to give our readers their opinions in our next issue.

MR. ARTHUR FOOTE'S REPLY.

"After an experience of fourteen years with an organ (the Walcker Organ of the First Church, Boston), in which the balanced swell-pedal is at the extreme right, I feel strongly that that is the most convenient place to have it, and most of all when I happen to play an organ in which the swell-pedal is placed in the middle."

MR. GEORGE E. WHITING OF BOSTON WRITES:

"The swell-pedal on an organ with pedals running up to F should be sunk into the case with an opening of at least eighteen inches square directly over the upper B or C of the pedal key-board."

MR. HARRISON M. WILD OF CHICAGO THINKS

that, "all things considered, the best position of the swell-pedal seems immediately in the centre, far enough in to be out of the way of the composition pedals and the pedal key-board. Either foot may then be used, and people short of stature reach it with ease. For many organists (?) the best position would be to the left of the pedal-board, just out of reach."

MR. HARRY ROWE SHELLEY OF NEW YORK WRITES:

"I think that the best position for the swell-pedal depends upon the length of the right leg of the performer. Experienced organists know how cramped they feel at some instruments, as though the knee was bent upon hitting the chin, while at others entire freedom of motion is experienced. For my part a vertical ratchet pedal at the extreme right of the pedals, controlled by the full strength of the lower body muscles, by means of which any gradation of tone, from the slightest movement of a *pp* long-drawn-out passage to the most savage attack of a modern organ transcription, may be obtained freely and easily, without the liability of straining the ankle muscles and chords, or of arriving at the desired climax just behind time. One feature that recommends the balanced swell-pedal is the impossibility of a vulgar interpretation as far as sudden swellings and *sff's* are concerned; but then, again, with the beautiful smooth increase and reduction of tone produced by the balanced swell-pedal disappears that piquancy and snap that is so charming and desirable in compositions requiring such an interpretation."

MR. ALLAN W. SWAN OF BOSTON AND NEW BEDFORD.

"If the pedal key-board has only twenty-seven keys I prefer the swell-pedal in the usual place, at the right of the entire key-board; but if there is a full compass of pedals (thirty keys), it is too great a reach in that place to be convenient, and the best location to my mind is in the space between A-sharp and C-sharp, as it interferes less with the pedalling of the left foot if the right foot is on the swell-pedal. Wherever it is placed, it should be far enough away from the pedals not to interfere with a free use of them. I have seen organs where it was almost impossible to use the two highest notes on account of the swell-pedal being in the way, especially when the heel part of the shoe was down."

MR. WILLIAM C. CARL OF NEW YORK.

"I prefer the balanced swell-pedal (when but one) to be placed midway between the extremes of the pedal-board, and always find it more convenient than at the side."

MR. J. WARREN ANDREWS OF MINNEAPOLIS.

"In my experience I have found the position in the centre of the pedal-board the most convenient. The pedal, being self-balancing, enables the player to leave it at any time when necessary to use the right foot in pedaling; and when either foot is used for an extended passage with heel and point, the other foot can operate the swell-pedal as required; then, too, the centre is more quickly and easily reached than the extreme right. Before using a pedal placed in the centre as described, I confess to a feeling of prejudice against it, but after using it in this location for a little over a year, I most strongly advocate its being placed in a central position.

It would be of great advantage to organists if organ-builders would adopt a uniform place (say a little to the *right* of the centre) and angle for the swell-pedal. It is a matter requiring considerable practice in playing strange organs, to locate exactly and *at once* the position of the swell-pedal. Its position, even in different organs built by the same builder, is seldom uniform. A pedal placed at the extreme right, at such an angle as to oblige an organist to "toe in" while using it, is a most excellent way of preventing its use, which in some cases is *extremely desirable*."

MR. HENRY M. DUNHAM OF BOSTON THINKS

"that the swell-pedal should, first of all, be uniform in all organs; that it should be at a convenient distance at the right of the centre for the average organist, and not above the composition pedals, but between them."

MR. S. B. WHITNEY OF BOSTON WRITES:

"With regard to the position of the swell-pedal, my preference is to have it a little to the right of the centre of the pedal key-board, and placed so as not to interfere with any pedal passage which might occur for the left foot, while the swell was being operated by the right foot. I think it a mistake to place the swell-pedal directly over the C-sharp key, especially when it is a balanced-swell-pedal; for it often happens that it is placed so near the pedal-keys, that when the swell is closed the heel of the swell-pedal completely covers the C-sharp, so that it is impossible to play it."

MR. ALEX S. GIBSON OF WATERBURY, CONN.

"When there is but one swell-pedal, my idea of the best location is over the E and F next above middle C of the pedal key-board. This puts the pedal within easy reach, keeps it out of the way of short keys, and allows a certain freedom to the left foot in places where all the pedal work is done by it, as in light accompaniments."

MR. FRANK TAFT OF NEW YORK.

"I find better results may be obtained when it is placed over the centre of the pedal keys. There are numerous cases in which the upper register of the pedals is employed, which demand the use of the swell-pedal, which, if placed in the centre, enables the organist to play with ease and retain a normal position. The same passages with the pedal placed at the side become difficult and awkward."

MR. WALTER J. CLEMSON OF TAUNTON, MASS.

"I should recommend its being placed a little to the *right* of the centre. It could then be worked by *either* foot, which would be a distinct advantage when a pedal passage is in the upper scale."

AN ANCIENT ENGRAVING.

A German musician executing a piece of music on a Portative Organ. Copied from an engraving of Israel van Meckan, XV. century.

OUR FIRST ORGAN-MUSIC COMPETITION.

A PRIZE of ten dollars ($10.) will be given for the best March for THE ORGAN. The composition must be written on three staves, must be from seventy-five to a hundred bars in length, and must bear a motto only. A sealed envelope, bearing the same motto and containing the form given below (which should be cut from this journal), filled out with the name and address of the competitor, must accompany each composition.

Compositions will be received till the 1st of March, when they will be submitted to the following judges, who have kindly consented to examine the compositions :—

> MR. CLARENCE EDDY of Chicago.
> MR. GEORGE E. WHITING of Boston.
> MR. S. B. WHITNEY of Boston.

The successful composition must become the property of THE ORGAN, and will be printed with the name of the composer in the journal issued the first of April.

The mottoes of the unsuccessful competitors will also be printed, and their compositions will be returned if the accompanying envelopes contain sufficient postage.

Compositions should be addressed: Editor THE ORGAN, 149 A Tremont St., Boston. (Prize Competition.)

Organ Music Competition.

Name

Address

Motto

CORRESPONDENCE.

THE EVOLUTION OF THE SWELL-BOX.

To the Editor of THE ORGAN :

SIR, — I am much interested in the correspondence initiated by "Gambetto."

As a means of obtaining expression one cannot be deaf to the fact that the swell-box is clumsy and insufficient. Its powers are purely dynamic and very feebly imitate true or acoustic expression. The latter, whether in the passion of the voice or the imitation of that passion by the orchestral instrument, invariably takes the form of a swelling out of overtones for *forte*, and a diminution of them for *piano*.

For instance, the tone of the orchestral horn played softly very closely resembles that of a good organ claribel (melodia), i.e., a strong ground-tone with feeble harmonics of open pipe sequence; more strongly blown it reaches to the stridence of the trumpet, but the ground-tone does not appear to increase, if indeed it does not decrease, a matter hard to judge.

Now, in the organ swell this is reversed. If a string-toned or reed stop be used with closed shutters the overtones are relatively conspicuous, while the ground-tone swells out as the shutters open.

We have thus a radical and insuperable defect, very much

(Continued on page 209.)

CIPHERINGS.

I USED to blow the organ in a good old country choir;
I kept the bellows crowded full and never used to tire;
I seemed to catch a vision of the promised happy land
When that old organ thundered underneath the player's hand.
Now here's the point I'm making, —please to notice " where I'm at," —
That wind was *raw material*, and mighty raw at that;
But when it came a-rushing that old organ's piping through,
It then was *finished product*, way up on its finish too.
I did the hard *raw labor* — pumping in the wind, you see.
The organist did better —a skilled worker, sir, was she.
A hundred boys could handle my pump job at any day;
The church was minus music when that woman stayed away.
And so in early childhood I pumped out this settled law,
To dodge old competition, just quit handling the *raw*
And learn to make *skilled product*, you will live to find your fill
Of good things will be greater as you cultivate your skill.
The folks who at the organ stay there ever pumping wind
Have hardly cause to grumble when they tag along behind
These folks who learn to handle every pedal, stop, and key
That lets the wind from prison in a flood of harmony.

Rural New Yorker.

* * *

WHY ought organ-pipes to talk and walk ?
Because they have lips and feet.

* * *

ORGANISTS must be careful. A man was recently fined in a police-court of Boston for pedaling without a license. — *Musical Herald.*

* * *

" WHAT is your son doing ? "
" He is a draughtsman."
" Ah ! Learning to be an architect ? "
" No. He pumps the organ in our church."

Washington Evening Star.

THE ORGAN.

BOSTON, JANUARY, 1893.

THE ORGAN is published the first of every month. Subscription price $1.00 per year (European countries 10s. 5d.), payable in advance. Single copies, 15 cents.

Subscribers will please state with which number they wish their subscription to begin.

Subscribers wishing the address of their paper changed must give the old as well as the new address.

Remittances should be made by registered letter, post-office order, or by check payable to Everett E. Truette.

Correspondence, to secure notice, must in all cases be accompanied by the name and address of the writer, not for publication, but as a guarantee of good faith.

Advertising rates sent on application.

Address all communications,

The Organ, 149 A Tremont Street, Boston, Mass.

☞ An active agent in every city is desired to whom a liberal cash commission will be allowed.

Single copies of THE ORGAN can be procured of

NOVELLO, EWER & CO.	New York.
G. SCHIRMER	New York.
OLIVER DITSON CO.	Boston.
L. H. ROSS & CO.	Boston.
N. E. CONSERVATORY	Boston.
H. B. STEVENS CO.	Boston.
LYON & HEALY	Chicago.
THEODORE PRESSER	Philadelphia.
WM. H. BONER & CO.	Philadelphia.
TAYLOR'S MUSIC HOUSE	Springfield, Mass.
GALLUP & METZGER	Hartford, Conn.
RICHAULT & CO.	Paris.
R. F. VINDER, (Virgo, Mahillon & Co.)	London.

ADJUSTABLE BINDERS FOR THE ORGAN.

FOR the benefit of those who wish to preserve THE ORGAN in a neat and convenient binder, forming an attractive book in which all the numbers of a volume can be well preserved, we have had a number of adjustable binders made, which we offer to subscribers for $1.50 apiece (postage ten cents extra). These binders are made of stiff boards (paper), covered with red cloth, with morocco back and corners. On the cover is stamped in large gilt letters : THE ORGAN, VOL. I, 1892-3. Each number of the journal as it arrives can be fastened in the binder by simply cutting, with a penknife, a slit near the back at the top and bottom, and passing through the slits little metallic strips which are bent over and held down by rings.

AN item of news concerning an organ which was placed in Mascagni's apartments is being tossed about among the different musical journals in this country, as well as in England and France ; and as each editor who copies it feels bound to go his exchange one better, the organ will soon be reported as the largest in the world.

THE Musical Record tells the world that " able lady organists are scarce." So are men who are able to crochet.

THE following anecdote of Bishop Brooks is worth relating. When Mr. J. C. D. Parker, who was at that time organist of Trinity Church, Boston, was consulting with the noted divine in regard to the selection of music for a certain passage in the Bible, the bishop selected a certain tune or chant (it matters not which) ; the organist suggested that it was inappropriate, as the words were joyous, and the music which had been selected was in the minor mode, and ought to be major. Bishop Brooks, who never concealed his lack of familiarity with music and its terms, asked what the difference was between major and minor. Mr. Parker illustrated

by playing a major chord, followed by a minor chord, repeating each several times, till Bishop Brooks broke out, " Oh, yes, I see the difference ; the minor chord sounds as if the major chord had been sat upon."

THE polyglot system of naming the stops has been adopted in an organ recently erected in Lowell, Mass. Looking over the specification we find : " Doppelflöte," " Contra Viola," " Flauto Soavo," " Quinta Octava," " Principal Diapason," " Viola Principale," " Dolciano," " Hohlpfeife," " Salicetto Dolce," " Octavino," " Bordone Principale," " Viola Ætheria," " Cosmo di Capella," " Lieblich Gedeckt," " Flauto Basso," " Octava Acuta," and so on ad nauseam. The accompanying description of the stops is equally unique. We read that the " Principal Diapason " is " powerful and rich " (good qualities for a politician) ; that the " Viola Ætheria " is " most distant and etherial string " ('tis but a dream) ; that the " Violetimo " is " soft, airy string " (like the voice of a dude) ; that the " Corno di Capella " is " sweet, mellow reed " (possibly flag-root). Where would this style end in a large organ ? There is the " Flauto Concerto " very fullo and roundo with a tone just righto for a solo, doncherknow ? We judge from the specification that " Flautileno " is Volapuk for Flute of 8 Ft. A Flute of 4 Ft. would be Octavo Flautileno, or possibly Flautilenatino. The 2 Ft. stop of this family would have to be Duodecimo Flautileno or Flautilenatimissimo. What could we call the 1 Ft. Flute which was in the old Boston Music Hall Organ ? Flautilenatimissitinavo ?

THE Musical Messenger has discovered that " the first pipe organ was made by Archimedes, B.C., 220." This is a valuable discovery (?) ; for, notwithstanding all the laborious researches of our music historians, no precise date has heretofore been given for the invention of the first principles of organ-building. All historians have agreed on the B.C., but they have been compelled to wait for the Musical Messenger to add not only 220, but the name of the inventor, — Archimedes. It now remains for some enterprising journal to inform the world of whom Archimedes learned his trade. This reminds us of the story of the colored preacher who informed his congregation that " when de Lord made de fust man he set him agin de fence to dry," whereupon one of his learned hearers asked, " Who made dat fence ? "

To return to Archimedes, various historians have mentioned that he invented, or more likely improved, the Hydraulic Organ (though they do not state that it was the first organ), but the date seems to be a flexible number. One historian puts it 30 B.C., another, 100 B.C., and one even places it 2000 B.C. The Musical Messenger has endeavored to strike a happy medium, and puts it 220 B.C. In the course of the next few months we may expect to read of this discovery of the name and date of the builder of " the first organ " in various papers, each with added information, till finally we shall know just how many miles of trackers the instrument contained.

THE Musical Messenger is nothing if not original. In another column it states that " the great organ in the old Mormon Church, Salt Lake City, has 2,704 pipes, each thirty-two feet long, and large enough to admit the body of a man of ordinary size." Whew ! That church must be enormous. We presume the organ does not occupy more than one quarter of the edifice, and 2,704 organ pipes, of thirty-two feet in length, if standing, as they usually are, would occupy a floor-space about two hundred feet by fifty feet. Each pipe would sound the lowest recognizable musical tone, CCC, and neither melody nor harmony would be possible on the instrument. The Messenger further adds that " these large pipes are for the bass notes." Yes, Messenger, thirty-two feet pipes are usually for bass notes ; but this organ has nothing but bass notes ; in short, it must be a notoriously bass instrument.

SERENADE.

Transcribed for the Organ by
Everett E. Truette.

Allegretto.

Ch. GOUNOD.

Gt. Doppel Flöte.

Sw. 8 & 4 Ft.
Ch. Clarinet, Melo-
dia & Dulciana.

Ped. Bourdon 16 Ft.
Sw. to Ped.

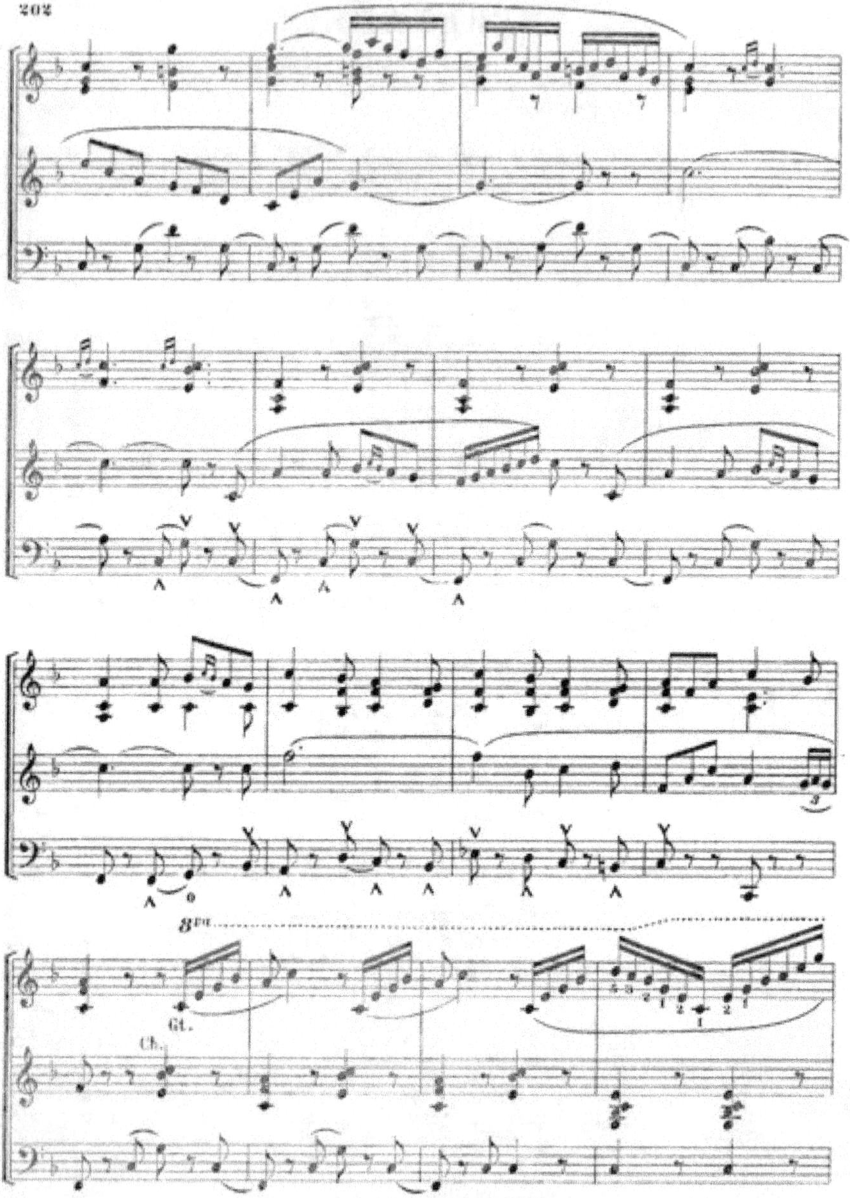
8va
Gt.
Ch.

Ch: Clarinet off.

Add Cornopean (or Oboe) & Trem. in Sw.

Sw.

(Sw. partly open.)

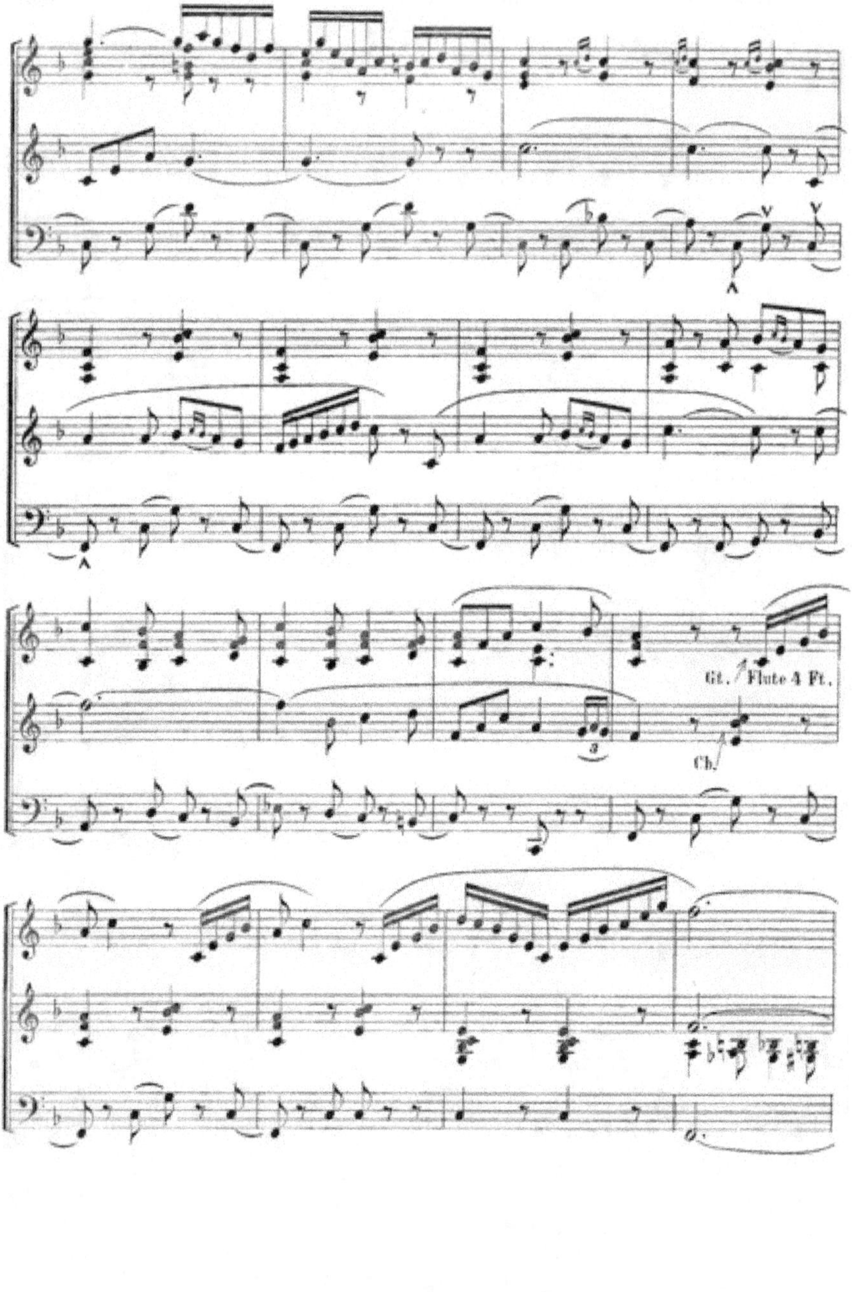
Gt. Flute 4 Ft.
Ch.

Ch. Dulciana only.

Sw.

(Arrange Sw. Vox Humana, Flute
4 Ft. & Trem.)

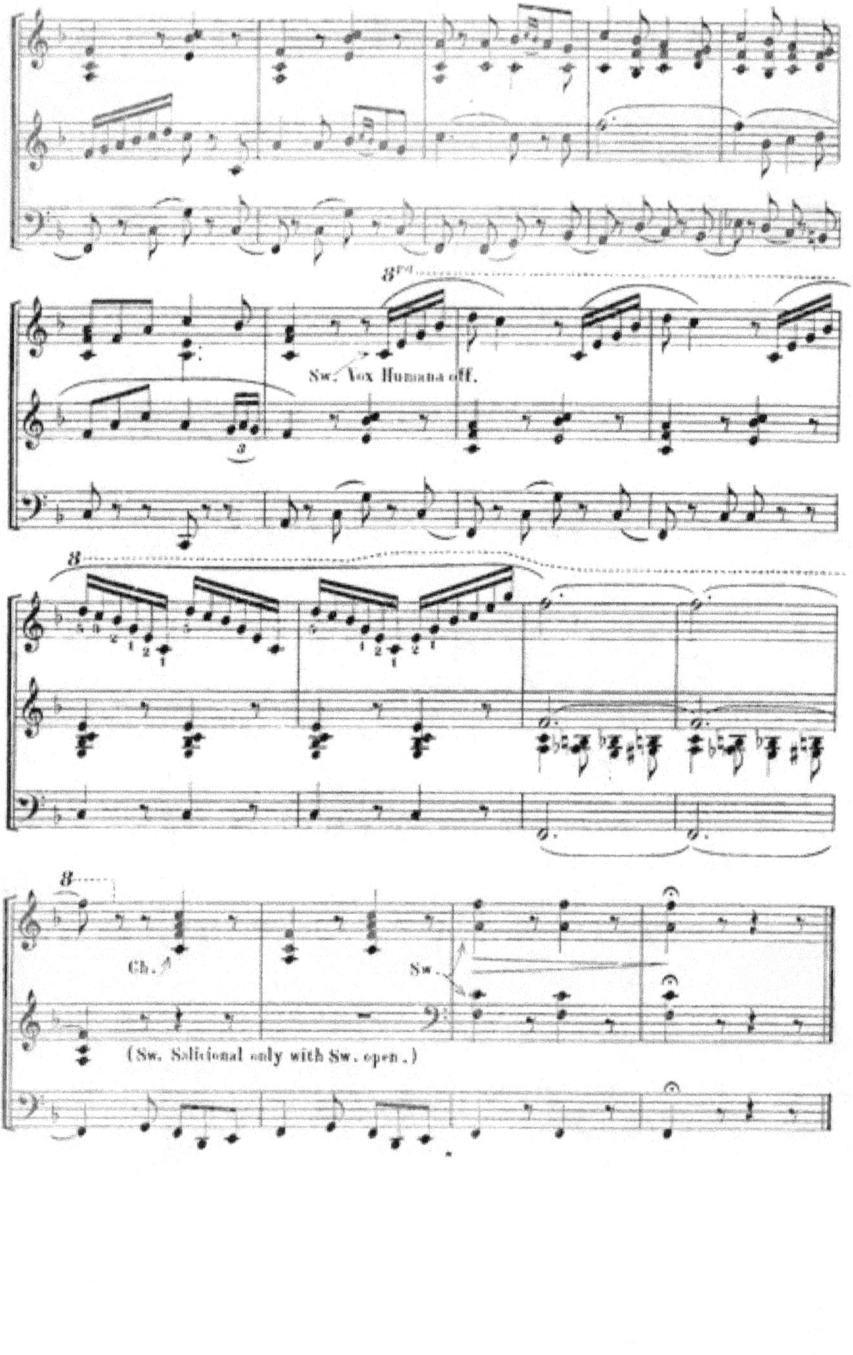
Sw. Vox Humana off.
Ch.
Sw.
(Sw. Salicional only with Sw. open.)

ANDÀNTE CON MOTO.

Dr. W. VOLKMAR.

Sw. 3 & 4 Ft.
without Oboe.

Ch. (or Gt.) Melo-
dia & Dulciana.

Ped. Bourdon 16
Ft. Ch.(or Gt) to
Ped.

(Add Oboe in Sw.)

Sw. with
Trem.

Ch.

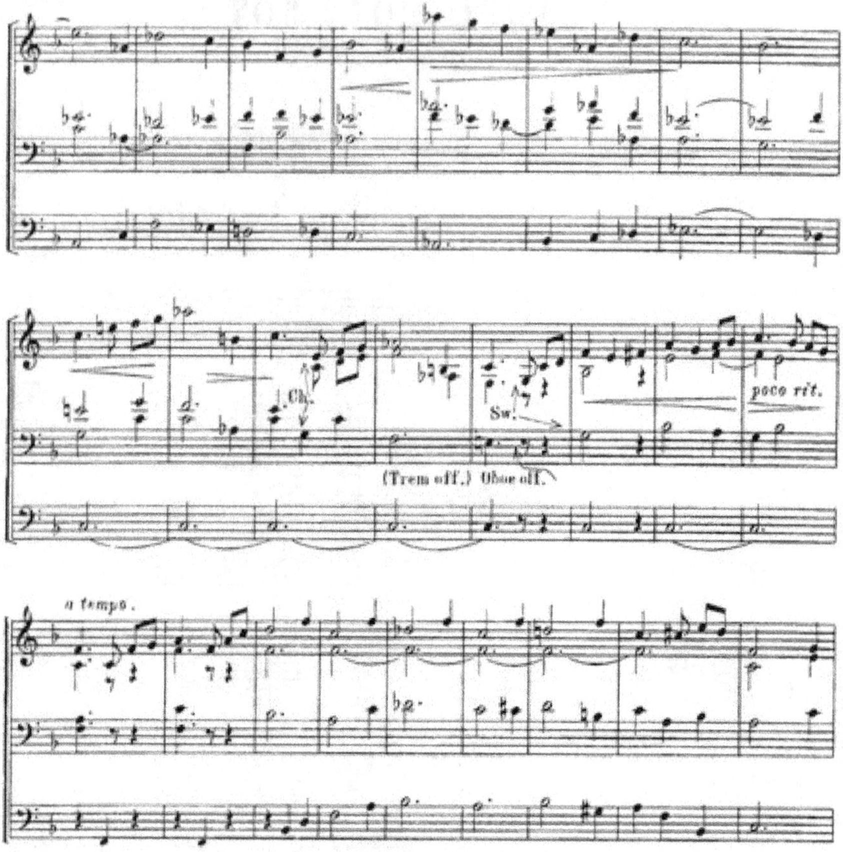
Ch.
Sw.
poco rit.
(Trem off.) Oboe off.
a tempo.

CORRESPONDENCE.

(Continued from page 199.)

limiting the expressive use of the swell. At the same time we must not forget that the dynamic expression is a fine effect on its own merits.

It would also appear that as it is the best imitation of acoustic expression its powers should be extended to all orchestral imitation stops.

Again, organ-builders have, quite empirically, discovered that the method of increasing the organ tone is not so much by adding unison stops, or purely dynamic arrangement, as by adding artificial overtones to imitate the acoustic *forte*.

It would thus appear reasonable to include much of the mutation and mixture work in the swell box or boxes, to impart to them the power of gradually swelling out over the fixed ground-tone.

Another interesting empiricism, illustrating the good effect of imitating the acoustic crescendo, is the organist's device of "Swell Reeds to Great Diapasons," thus using stops strong in overtones to swell out over fixed ground-tone. Unfortunately the usefulness and suggestiveness of this combination have led to its becoming hackneyed; but the idea suggests itself that the effect ought to be obtainable without hampering the registering by coupling.

It is obvious that for imitation of the acoustic crescendo much greater importance should be given to mixture and mutation work than the present race of builders appear inclined to do. The development of the acoustic crescendo fully accounts for the good effect of "breaks" in the mixtures.

There is one absurd oversight all but universal in the swell; that is, *it has no bass*. "Gambette" rightly quotes "Hopkins and Kimbault" as an authority; but no point is more rigidly insisted upon in that work than the theory that pedal stops are the basses of the manual stops. It thus follows that the swell should have a selection of appropriate pedal stops in its own box, an arrangement I always adopt when I have the power, and find extremely grand in results. If my memory serves me, Walcker's Boston Organ had some such stops, and in their prize instrument they formed a separate pedal department instantly available, as in my organs. The present general unenclosed basses are as ridiculous and inartistic as the "stopped bass" of the old fiddle g swell.

THOMAS CASSON.

COLL. OF ORGANISTS, LONDON, 30th Nov., 1892.

MONSTER ORGANS.

To the Editor of THE ORGAN:—

SIR,—As a very recent subscriber to your paper, I have only just seen the letter of Mr. Alex S. Gibson, which appeared in a back number of THE ORGAN, wherein he demurs to Mr. W. T. Best's statement that "*no organ need have more than fifty stops*," and gives as an amendment a specification of an ideal instrument of eighty registers.

If not too late I should like to reply to your correspondent that we are hardly in a position at present to estimate the soundness of Mr. Best's judgment on this question. He is speaking from an experience far beyond that which we can attain to in this country, in this year of grace, though we be ever so enthusiastic searchers; an experience, by the way, quite of recent date even to him.

The truth of Mr. Best's statement is, however, beyond question, but it is dependent upon principles of construction and of *tone-building* not as yet understood, certainly not practised, by any firm of organ-builders in the United States.

It is the building up of tones which are distinctly and strongly *individual*, and the absence of repetition in the instrument of such tones, which constitutes the necessary condition.

A large majority of the stops found in the organs of this country are perfectly colorless, or at best are compound in their character. In the organ referred to by Mr. Best he has an instrument before him which is capable, with its comparatively few stops, of tenfold more effect in combination, charming in detail, admirable in the variety of tints which are at command in blending, and grand beyond all comparison with the ordinary organ in the *tout ensemble*.

Mr. Gibson's ideal specification belongs to quite another school, perhaps hardly fair to compare. He duplicates not only in different manuals, but in the same manual, the result of which is not merely negation, but annihilation.

I would say, for instance, of his great organ foundation stops, that it would be impossible to place them on any soundboard in such a position that the one should not destroy the other.

In dealing with this subject it has to be understood that to make available to the utmost such an organ as Mr. Best presupposes when he speaks of fifty stops being sufficient, the reckless grouping of stops of like pitch has to be avoided, and it is a matter of experience as well as of art to know where to place them in an organ that they may serve their purpose to the utmost. The single soundboard, the one wind reservoir, the primitive belongings of early days, in fact, have to give place to more approved methods.

In most cases the principle of the "survival of the fittest" is admirably exemplified: the stops are feebly individual, and such little character as they possess is exercised in killing one another, so the more stops the player draws the less effect he produces.

I quite appreciate Mr. Gibson's needs, and I feel sure that when opportunity offers, and he sees the more scientific and infinitely more effective system exemplified to which Mr. Best refers, with the addition of control by the player rendered as easy and as sensitive to his hand as the finest concert piano, he will be the first to join the new standard and to sing its praises. CARLTON C. MICHELL.

BOSTON, Dec. 13, 1892.

THE CLOSING OF THE ROOSEVELT FACTORY.

NEW YORK, November 18, 1892.

To the Editor of THE ORGAN:

I HAVE the honor to announce my intention to close the Roosevelt Organ Works, and retire from the business of manufacturing organs. The work now on hand will be completed about January 1, 1893, and after that time no organs will be built under the name of Roosevelt.

It is my pleasure to further announce that I have completed negotiations with the Farrand & Votey Organ Company of Detroit, whereby the exclusive right to the use of all the patents and systems controlled by me passes to them. It is their intention to incorporate their various specialties with my own, and as they have also secured the services of a number of my department foremen, and other leading men, they should be now in a position to produce instruments of great perfection.

The Farrand & Votey Organ Company intend to establish offices in New York and Chicago. The New York office will be located in this building, and will be in the charge of Mr. John W. Heins, who has been connected with my office for many years. Mr. Heins has secured the services of some of my best tuners, and consequently will be equipped to properly care for our organs. The Chicago office will be located at No. 269 Dearborn St., and will be in charge of Mr. W. J. Davis, at present my Western representative.

I can recommend all interested to correspond with the Farrand & Votey Organ Company, as I am convinced that they will endeavor to maintain the present high standard of organ-building in the United States.

FRANK ROOSEVELT.

MIXTURES.

(FOUR RANKS.)

Mr. W. E. MULLIGAN gave an organ recital at St. Mark's Church, New York, Dec. 4.

Mr. F. Slade Olver of Chicago has moved to Holton, Kan.

Mr. Clarence Dickinson gave an organ concert in the Church of the Messiah, Chicago, Dec. 13.

Mr. Wm. H. Donley has been appointed organist of Plymouth Church, Indianapolis, O.

Organ recital in Unity Church, Chicago, Dec. 14, by Mr. Harrison M. Wild, in which the following organ compositions were given: Fantasia Sonata, Hesse; Prelude du Deluge, Saint Saens-Guilmant; Adagio, Op. 35, Merkel; Two Fantastic Sketches and Toccata, Spinney; Overture to the "Caliph of Bagdad," Boieldieu.

Messrs. Farrand & Votey of Chicago are to build an organ for the Columbian Exposition. The instrument, according to numerous reports, will have four manuals and sixty-one stops, costing ten thousand dollars.

Mr. Walter E. Hall gave an organ recital in the Church of the Epiphany, Chicago, Dec. 2.

Mons. Alex Guilmant gave an organ recital at the Bow & Bromley Institute, London, Dec. 3.

Mr. J. K. Strachan of Glasgow, a pupil of Mons. Alex Guilmant, gave an organ recital at the Bow & Bromley Institute, London, Nov. 26.

"At the opening of a small organ in the Forest of Dean, not so long ago, a report of the musical performances ended: 'Nor must we forget the organ-blowing by Mr. H——, whose efforts left nothing to be desired.'" — London Musical News.

Mr. Clarence Eddy during the past month has given concerts in Memphis, Tenn., Racine, Wis., and Kankakee, besides several recitals in Chicago.

Mr. H. Davan Wetton, formerly organist of St. Gabriel's Pimlico, London, has received the appointment of organist to the Foundling Hospital, London.

At the Faculty Recital of the Northwestern Conservatory of Music, Minneapolis, Minn., Mr. J. Warren Andrews performed the following organ compositions: Sonata, Op. 88, Rheinberger; and Toccata and Fugue in D-minor, Bach.

The choir of St. Thomas' Church, Taunton, Mass., Walter J. Clemson, M.A., organist, gave a festival service on Thanksgiving Day. Mr. Clemson played for prelude and postlude, Allegretto, Mace, and Thanksgiving March, Calkin.

Organ recital in Olivet Congregational Church, Bridgeport, Conn., by Mr. Alex. S. Gibson, Nov. 22. Programme: Overture, "A Night in Granada," Kreutzer; Fugue in G-minor, Bach; Sonata, Op. 183, Merkel; Pastorale, Op. 33, No. 4, Toonbelle; The Holy Night, Buck; Variations on an American Air, Flagler; Overture to "Poet and Peasant" (requested), Suppé. Mr. Gibson was assisted by Miss Ada C. Sterling and Master Frank Fosdick.

Organ recital in the Unitarian Church, New Bedford, Mass., Nov. 30, by Mr. Allen W. Swan. Programme: Overture to Samson, Handel; Larghetto from Second Symphony, Beethoven; Gothic March, Prayer, Scottish Eclogue, and Melody in C, by Salomé; St. Ann's Fugue, Bach; Elevation, Dunham; Allegro in A-minor, Whiting.

Organ recital at First M. E. Church, Kenton, O., Nov. 22, by Mr. F. R. Adams, assisted by Miss M. Josephine Baskey, soprano. Programme: Sonata in A-minor, Whiting; "My Redeemer," Buck; Toccata and Fugue in D-minor, Bach; Funeral March of a Marionette, Gounod; Offertoire in C-minor, Batiste; "Dost Thou Know That Sweet Land?" Thomas; Finale from "Lucrezia Borgia," Donizetti-Adams; Communion in G, Batiste; March and Chorus from "Tannhäuser," Wagner.

Organ concert in Unity Church, Chicago, by Mr. Harrison M. Wild, Nov. 27. Programme: Concert Piece in C, Thiele; Sonata No. 2, Guilmant; Marche Rustique, Lied and Marche de Fete, Gigout; Overture to "Masaniello," Auber. At these weekly organ recitals Mr. Wild is assisted by Mrs. Theodore Brentano, soprano, Mrs. F. S. Bagg, contralto, Mr. Charles A. Knorr, tenor, and Mr. John Morley, bass.

A couple of men stood in front of Mason & Hamlin's window on Fifth Avenue the other day, and looked at the three-manual organ displayed there. "What's them three keyboards for?" said one. "Oh! that's so three folks can play organs together," was the reply, to which the other answered, "Oh, yes; that's why the bench is so long, so the three can sit there at once." — Musical Courier.

Mr. H. O. Farnam gave the third of the present series of organ recitals, in Christ Church, Louisville, Ky., Dec. 6, with the following programme: Concerto in B-flat, Handel; Melody and Intermezzo, Parker; Pastorale Sonata, Rheinberger; "At Evening," Buck; Polonaise Militaire, Chopin.

Programme of organ music rendered by Mr. Wm. Huber, Jr., at the Baptist Church, Hamilton, O., Dec. 4: Pastorale in F, Op. 42, Kretschmer; Romanza in B-flat, from Concerto in D-minor, Mozart; Adagio in D, Op. 20, Dienel; Sanctus, Gounod; Le Desir, Op. 23, Hauser; Scherzo, Op. 9, No. 17, Kinross.

Organ recital at the Congregational Church, Westport, Conn., Dec. 5, by Mr. Alex S. Gibson, who performed the following organ compositions: Overture, "The Pearl of Bagdad," Loretz, Jr.; Toccata in D-minor (Bach); Bach; Air and Gavotte from Suite, Bach; Sonata No. 4, Guilmant; Pastorale in E, Op. 33, No. 4, Toonbelle; Prelude and Fugue in G, Mendelssohn; March in E-flat, Wely.

A new organ for the Railroad Chapel, Chicago, was dedicated last month by Mr. Clarence Eddy. The organ has twenty-six speaking-stops, seven combination pedals, six combination pistons, and was built by the Wording Organ Co. of Salem, O.

One hundred and fifteenth organ recital of Mr. Harrison M. Wild, Unity Church, Chicago, Dec. 4. Programme: Passacaglia, Bach; Quartet; Sonata, Op. 14, Ritter (Mr. E. Howard Wells); Song; Nuptial Song, Dubois; March in E-flat, Wely (Mr. Wells); Quartet; Festival March in D, Grison.

Mr. C. E. Miller has been giving weekly organ recitals at the Church of St. Augustine and St. Faith, London, on Monday afternoons for the past two months, with programmes confined principally to legitimate organ music. Four of Rheinberger's sonatas were given during November.

At a concert in the First Free Baptist Church, Minneapolis, Mr. J. Warren Andrews performed the following compositions: Offertoire in G, Wely; Gavotte, Thomas; Fantasia (The Storm), Lemmens; and Finale of First Organ Sonata, Buck.

Westminster Church, Minneapolis, Dec. 6, organ music played by Mr. J. Warren Andrews: Vesper Bells, Spinney; Gavotte, Thomas; Largo, Handel; Fanfare, Lemmens; Floyd's Hymn (four hands), Thayer, Miss Ottilie Messenger assisting.

Organ Concert in the Carleton Music Course, Northfield, Minn., by Mr. J. Warren Andrews, Dec. 5. Fourth Organ Sonata, Mendelssohn; Communion in G, Batiste; Fugue in G-minor, Bach; Meditation in E-flat, Dubois; Marche Militaire, Schubert; March of the Magi Kings, Dubois; Vesper Bells, Spinney; Gavotte, Thomas; Fantasia (The Storm), Lemmens.

Messrs. Merklin & Co., of Paris have just erected a two-manual organ of thirteen stops in the residence of Mons. Bisson, the well-known dramatic author.

The diploma of the fellowship has been conferred on Dr. Armes, M.A., of the University of Durham, England, by the Council of the College of Organists.

Dr. E. J. Speck has resigned his post as organist of Holy Trinity, Worcester, England, a position which he held for nearly twenty years.

The death is announced of Mr. A. J. Smith, F. C. C. G., late organist of Norwich (England), parish church.

Inaugural recital on a new organ (built by Emmons Howard of Westfield, Mass.), by Mr. John J. Bishop, assisted by a quartette, in the North M. E. Church, Manchester, Conn., Nov. 16. Organ numbers: Grand Chorus, Guilmant; "Peasant Wedding," Soderman; Bridal Song, Jensen; A Russian Romance, Hoffmann; Serenade, Gounod; "Tros du Cavalière," Rubinstein; Overture to "William Tell," Rossini.

Organ recital by Mr. Harrison M. Wild, in Unity Church, Chicago, Nov. 20. Programme: Fugue in D-minor, Scarlatti; Fantasia and Fugue, Op. 109, Merkel; Cantilène, Salomé; Allegretto Grazioso, Tours; Polonaise Militaire, Chopin; Overture to "Zampa," Herold. The programme was interspersed with two songs and a duet.

Second organ recital of Mr. S. Clarke Lord, Asylum Hill Congregational Church, Hartford, Conn., Nov. 17. Programme: Sonata in E-flat, Op. 6, Fink; Evening Quiet, Op. 156, Rheinberger; Prize Song from "The Meistersinger," Wagner; Bridal Song from "Wedding Symphony," Goldmark; Offertoire in C-minor, Grison; Marche Cortège, Gounod. Songs by Mr. Clinton H. Newton.

Inaugural recital in the First Presbyterian Church, Eau Claire, Wis., by Mr. J. Warren Andrews, assisted by Miss E. Belle Farr, organist, a contralto and a violinist, Nov. 21. Organ Numbers: Fantasia, Op. 87, Hesse; Communion in G, Batiste; Grand Chorus, Guilmant; Minuet Romantique, Smith-Patterson; Variations on "Old Folks at Home," Flagler; Ave Maria, Liszt-Meulen; Gavotte, Thomas; Improvisation; Nuremberg Variations, Thayer.

Several organ-builders in this country have been "invited" to build the large organ for the World's Fair Exposition. In each case there seems to be a desire to get a first-class instrument for about one-half the actual cost. The managers and committees of the several departments of the Exposition demand and probably receive good salaries for their services, and yet they will turn to organ-builders and argue that the cost (?) of building the organ ought to reduce the cost of the instrument about one-half. If some of the officers of the Exposition were compensated on the same basis, i.e., one-half their value, it is an extremely small sum which they would receive.

Programme of a recital in the Centennial Hall, Sydney, Australia, by M. Wiegand: Hosannah, Chorus, Mag. Dubois; Elevation B-flat, Wely; Andante in B-flat, Widor; Bridal March and Chorus, Wagner; Air Varié, Hiles; Toccata in F-minor, Gigout; Fugue in G-minor, Bach; Minuetto in B-flat, Capocci; March from "Athena," Guilmant; Improvisation.

The following programme was performed by Mr. W. T. Best in the Birmingham Town Hall the latter part of October: Toccata in F-sharp-minor, Hatton; Traumerei, Schumann; Prelude and Fugue in B-minor, Bach; Capriccio, Capocci; March in A-minor, Best; Concerto in G, Handel; Andante in E-minor, Smart; Rhapsodie sur Cantiques Bretons, Saint Saëns; Marche Hongroise, Liszt.

At the anniversary concert in the Auditorium, Chicago, commemorating the opening of the hall, which was given Dec. 9, Mr. Clarence Eddy performed Toccata in A, Best; Nuptial Benediction, Dubois; Finale, Loux Deo, Dubois; Am Meer, Schubert; The Last Sleep of the Virgin, Massenet; Variations on the Austrian Hymn, Attrup; Prelude and Fugue on B. A. C. H., Liszt; Storm Fantasia, Lemmens, and Torchlight March, Guilmant. "Mr. Eddy was the organist upon the occasion of the opening of the structure, and has very appropriately presided at each anniversary, and it is hoped will for years be the recognised organist whenever the date recurs. Chicago is to be congratulated that it is not obliged to go beyond her own gates for such a distinguished artist." — *The Indicator.*

In these days of hydraulic blowers and gas-engines, the organist is apt to forget that the human blower regards himself as being quite as important, if not a more important, factor in the musical portion of the church service than the organist himself. The following true story may serve to recall to the organ-player this fact. Amid the manifold distracting cares of a harvest thanksgiving-service, the vicar's wife, who was presiding at the organ, forgot for a few moments that the time had come for the "Venite." During the short and uncomfortable pause which ensued, the old blind blower crept round the side of the organ, and in a whisper which could have been readily heard at the west door, thus delivered himself, "Missus, there's somethin' agone wrong with the orghin. I'm a-blowin' at it, but I can't git no sound out." — *Musical News.*

A festival service and organ recital was given in St. Stephen's Church, Boston, exhibiting the new organ (built by Mr. C. C. Michell), Nov. 27, in which Mr. Walter J. Kugler played: Organ Hymn and Postlude in F, Whiting; Night Song, Vogt; Grand Chœur, Salomé; "Hark, Hark, My Soul," Choral with variations, and Benedictus from Mass in C, Silas. Mr. R. B. Gillette played Offertoire de St. Cecilia, Batiste; Marche Religieuse, Guilmant; Elegy, Lemaigre; Toccata from Fifth Organ Symphony, Widor. Mr. Michell played Fantasia and Fugue in G-minor, Bach.

During the months of November and December Mr. William Churchill Hammond gave his annual series of organ recitals in the Second Congregational Church, Holyoke, Mass. Each programme opened with two or three works of ancient composers of the German, Italian, or French schools, and ended with several works of the modern composers. Each programme but the last contained a sonata, beside several other works in the larger forms. The following sonatas were performed: No. 1, in E-flat, Dudley Buck; No. 4, in D-minor, Guilmant; No. 10, in B-minor, Rheinberger; No. 5, in F-sharp minor, Rheinberger. Of the other important numbers we mention, Christmas Offertorium, Lemmens; March of the Magi Kings, Dubois; Symphonic Poem, "A Nativité," Tombelle; Grand Chœur Triomphale, Guilmant; Toccata, Widor; Chromatic Fantasia in A-minor, Thiele. The remaining selections were from such composers as Gabriel, Frescobaldi, Bassi, Clerambault, Titelouse, Speth, Wagner, Givey, Haydn, Händel, Fischer, and Kittel.

An inaugural recital was given in St. Stephen's Church, Boston, Dec. 5, by Mr. George E. Whiting, with the following programme: Overture in C, Mendelssohn; Fantasia in E-minor, Whiting; Sonata in C-minor, Mendelssohn; Organ March, Wély; Pastorale and Concert Finale Whiting; Overture to "Wm. Tell," Rossini. Miss Jessie Ringen sang a couple of new songs composed by Sig. A. Rotoli, being accompanied by the composer at the piano, and Mr. Walter J. Kugler at the organ.

Mr. Whiting is always an interesting player, and while he was not at his ease during the first part of the programme, owing to a lack of familiarity with the organ, and an annoying cipher in the Mendelssohn Sonata, his performance of this characteristic programme was no exception. His own Fantasia in E-minor, which we had never heard before, we should like to hear again, as there are many interesting passages wherein Mr. Whiting produced some pleasing orchestral effects of more than ordinary interest. In the Rossini Overture Mr. Whiting was at his best, his naturally brilliant execution, together with the excellent repeating qualities of the pneumatic action, combining to give us a brilliant performance. The Pastorale and Finale were also extremely well played. It is a great pity that the latter has never been published, as many organists who have heard Mr. Whiting play it would like to have the composition on some of their own programmes.

Mr. S. B. Whitney's Communion Service is to be given with full orchestral accompaniment at the Church of the Advent, San Francisco, Cal., on Christmas Day.

Mr. B. J. Lang, organist of King's Chapel, Boston, gave a dinner-party in honour of Dr. Dvořák, on his visit to "the Hub" the first part of December.

It is announced that the Italian organist, Sig. Capocci, whose compositions are well known in this country, will be heard in London, in April. A concert is announced at the Bow and Bromley Institute the 25th of this month.

Mr. J. V. Flagler gave a lecture recital at St. John's Church, Ithaca, N.Y., Dec. 15. Beethoven was the subject, and selections from the first, second, and fifth symphonies were performed.

Mr. F. J. Stevens has been engaged as organist at St. Vincent de Paul's, So. Boston.

Mr. Harrison M. Wild's programme for his weekly recital on Dec. 18 was in the nature of a Christmas programme, and contained Christmas Postlude, Garrett; Offertory on Xmas Hymn, Guilmant; Xmas Pastorale and Xmas March, Merkel; Variations on Xmas Hymn, Oakeley; and Sonata Op. 25, Van Eyken.

Mr. S. B. Whitney inaugurated a large three-manual Hutchings organ at the Central Cong. Church, Lynn, Mass., Dec. 3, and a two-manual organ of the same make at the Church of the Ascension, Waltham, Mass., Dec. 8.

Messrs. Hook and Hastings of Boston have finished, during the past month, organs for Gorham, N.H.; Kingston, N.Y.; Malden, Mass.; Bellefonte, Pa.; and Durham, Conn. The last-named instrument is a large two-manual organ. They are also building an organ for New York City, having tubular pneumatic action throughout, with console detached and located underneath the instrument.

The following programme was rendered by Mr. Clarence Eddy on a Vocalion organ in the Belle City Opera House, Racine, Wis., Nov. 30, and repeated in the New German Catholic Church, Menominee, Mich., Dec. 17. Overture to "Serabelle," Flotow-Buck; "Daybreak," Spinney; Largo, Händel; Variations on "Old Folks at Home," Flagler; Andantino, Chauvet; Spring Song, Mendelssohn; Fantaisie, "O Sanctissima," Lux; St. Cecilia Offertory in D, Batiste; Wedding Benediction and Finale, Dubois.

The Lancashire-Marshall Organ Company of Moline, Ill., have been pressed to the full capacity of the works of late. They have just placed organs in the Methodist Church, Oshkosh; St. Mary's and the Presbyterian Church, Appleton, Wis; Missouri Valley College, Marshall, Mo.; and M. E. Church, Kirkville, Mo. They are now building for the Baptist Church, Moline, Ill.; Methodist Church, Omaha, Neb.; U. B. Church, Johnstown, Pa. Also they are building a large organ with tubular pneumatic action for St. John's Cathedral in Milwaukee — an instrument that will be one of the largest and most complete in the West.

The Lancashire-Marshall Company are getting their full share of the work, and their execution of it always gives complete satisfaction. — *Exchange.*

Mr. Clarence Eddy opened a new organ built by J. W. Steere & Son of Springfield) in the Second Pres. Church, Memphis, Tenn., Dec. 2. We quote the *Appeal-Avalanche* on Mr. Eddy's performance:—

"Mr. Clarence Eddy, the organist who dedicated the grand instrument, is one of the most celebrated performers in America. He is a native of Chicago, having presided over the organ in the Second Presbyterian Church of that city for thirty years. His programme of last evening was carefully arranged, and was carried out in the most masterly and artistic style. The most difficult subjects were brought out clearly and distinctly, while the intricate part of his work was interpreted with a sweet and sympathetic touch. There is an individuality about Mr. Eddy's playing that distinguishes him from the less skilful performer. With him the organ is not the noisy instrument it often appears when in the hands of unskilful players, but under his touch the great pipes breathe forth the most eloquent notes, and those to whom were strangers to the wonderful melody that can be obtained from so large an instrument were astonished at the ease with which he was able to control its wonderful resources. The hearers manifested the warmth of their appreciation by long and frequent applause. The programme was chosen with great care and embraced masterful compositions from Händel, Wagner, Flotow, Gounod, etc., were selected with the view of testing the instrument. From introductory notes of Best's Toccata in A-major, there was no doubt about the superiority in the rich, deep tone, and its perfect mechanical construction. The Storm Fantasie of Lemmens, a descriptive piece, was superbly rendered. The first weird notes were of the finest shading, then rising, the depth of power exhibited the wonderful resources of the organ. The Pilgrims' Chorus was also a most effective bit of work, as was the St. Cecilia Offertory of Batiste, 'The Old Folks at Home,' with variations, went to the hearts of the hearers, and elicited prolonged applause."

REVIEW OF ORGAN MUSIC.

FROM RICHAULT & CO., PARIS.

Preludes and Prayers (2 books) . . . . C. V. Alkan.
(Selected and arranged by César Franck)

Méditation Religieuse . . . . A. Deeq.

The preludes and prayers of Alkan, with one or two exceptions, are written in the style of rhapsodies, and require special treatment in the hands of the organist. A stereotyped registration on a small organ would render the compositions uninteresting in the extreme, but with a fair-sized instrument which has a goodly number of combination pedals, a skilful performer could bring out the emotional side of the composition, and they would prove interesting. No. 11 of the Prayers (Bk. 1) pleases us the most, and No. 7 of the Preludes (same book) seems the least interesting. No. 2 of the Prayers (Bk. 2) (one of the exceptions mentioned above) is a simple but pleasing melody, written in the style of Mozart.

The Meditation of Deeq has two attractive themes which are ingeniously combined in a strong climax near the end of the composition.

QUESTIONS AND ANSWERS.

All questions must be accompanied by the full name and address of the writer, and, if received by the 10th of the month, will usually be answered in the following number of THE ORGAN.

Only such questions as refer to the organ, to organists, organ-builders, or to organ music, will be answered.

Correspondents are requested to write their questions in a clear and concise manner, writing on only one side of the paper.

OCTAVE. In playing the cadenza in Merkel's G-minor Sonata, should the registration remain the same as in the previous passage?

ANS. The great should be reduced to octave after the chord which precedes the cadenza, and the first nine bars of the cadenza played on the full swell (closed). The great to pedal coupler being on, the theme in the pedal stands out prominently. At the tenth bar of the cadenza change to the great organ, and with a gradual opening of the swell, lead up to full organ at the return of the Introduction.

ORGAN. How is the size of an organ determined?
ANS. Usually by the number of speaking stops.

PEDAL. 1. What course of study can I use with advantage with a pupil who has great difficulty in acquiring pedal *technique*?

ANS. Try "Exercises for the Pedal," by H. M. Dunham.
2. Should students be taught to play without looking at the pedals?

ANS. There are many first-class organists who never look at the pedals when playing, and fully as many more who look at the pedals constantly; however, beginners will learn to pedal by *feeling* for the notes fully as rapidly as by *looking* for them, and their eyes can thus be kept on the music, which will facilitate their reading at sight.

GUILD. Do you know of any organization similar in purpose to the American Church Choir Guild of 830 Warren Ave., Chicago, Ill.? The work of this guild is confined to those of the Protestant Episcopal Church. I would like to learn of some similar organization dealing with people of other creeds.

ANS. We have not heard of any guild, or association, of choirs outside of the Episcopal denomination, though there seems to be a demand for such an association, as the field is large and fruitful.

NEW ORGANS.

LAST month Messrs. Hook and Hastings exceeded their usual record — "an organ a week " — by finishing complete six two-manual instruments in the following places: —

Westport, Conn., Congregational Church; Ionia, Mich., First Baptist Church; Norwalk, O., First Congregational Church; Kankakee, Ill., First Presbyterian Church; Ypsilanti, Mich., First Baptist Church; Williamsport, Pa., Second Presbyterian Church.

The specification of the last-named organ is given below: —

GREAT ORGAN.		SWELL ORGAN.		
Open Diapason	8 Ft.	Bourdon Bass)		
Viola da Gamba	8 "	Bourdon Treble)	16 Ft.	
Dulciana	8 "	Open Diapason	8 "	
Melodia	8 "	Viola	8 "	
Octave	4 "	Æoline	8 "	
Flûte d'Amour	4 "	Voix Celeste	8 "	
Twelfth	2½ "	Stopped Diapason	8 "	
Fifteenth	2 "	Quintadena	8 "	
Trumpet	8 "	Violina	4 "	
		Flûte Harmonique	4 "	
PEDAL ORGAN.		Dolce Cornet	3 Rks.	
Double Open Diapason	16 Ft.	Cornopean	8 Ft.	
Bourdon	16 "	Oboe	8 "	
Violoncello	8 "			

The usual Mechanical Registers and Pedal Movements. The organ is blown by a water motor.

NEW ORGAN IN ST. MARY'S CHURCH, CHARLESTOWN. MASS.

Built by Messrs. Woodberry & Harris of Boston.

GREAT ORGAN.		SWELL ORGAN.		
Open Diapason	16 Ft.	Bourdon (Treble and Bass)	16 Ft.	
Open Diapason	8 "	Open Diapason	8 "	
Doppel-flöte	8 "	Salicional	8 "	
Viola da Gamba	8 "	Stopped Diapason	8 "	
Octave	4 "	Quintadena	8 "	
Flûte Harmonique	4 "	Octave	4 "	
Twelfth	2⅔ "	Violina	4 "	
Fifteenth	2 "	Flautino	2 "	
Mixture	3 Rks.	Cornopean	8 "	
Trumpet	8 Ft.	Oboe	8 "	
Clarion	4 "	Vox Humana	8 "	

CHOIR ORGAN.				
Lieblich Gedeckt	16 Ft.			
Geigen Principal	8 "			
Dulciana	8 "	PEDAL ORGAN.		
Melodia	8 "	Double Open Diapason	16 Ft.	
Flûte d'Amour	4 "	Dulciana	16 "	
Piccolo Harmonique	2 "	Quinte	10⅔ "	
Clarinet	8 "	Violoncello	8 "	
		Trombone	16 "	

COMBINATION PEDALS.

Full Organ.
F., MF., and P., Great.
F., MF., and P., Swell.
F. Choir.
Gt. to Ped.

The Usual Couplers.
Four Piston-knobs for Great Organ Couplers.
Three piston-knobs for Pedal Organ Combinations.

Reversed Action. Organ in two parts. Wind pressure, 3½ inches.

NEW ORGAN IN ST. STEPHEN'S CHURCH, BOSTON.

Built by Mr. C. C. Michell.

GREAT ORGAN.		SWELL ORGAN.		
Hohl-flöte	16 Ft.	Geigen Principal	8 Ft.	
Principal Diapason	8 "	Viole d'Orchestre	8 "	
Small Diapason	8 "	Viole Celeste	8 "	
Octave	4 "	Rohr-flöte	8 "	
Octave Quinte	3 "	Octave	4 "	
Super Octave	2 "	Mixture	3 Rks.	
Mixture	4 Rks.	Contra Fossaune	16 Ft.	
		Cornopean	8 "	
		Oboe	8 "	
		Vox Humana	8 "	

CHOIR ORGAN.				
Viola	8 Ft.	PEDAL ORGAN.		
Viole Sourdine	8 "	Great Bass	16 Ft.	
Gedeckt	8 "	Violone	16 "	
Salicet	4 "	Quinte Flute	10⅔ "	
Flauto Traverso	4 "	Great Flûte	8 "	
Clarinet	8 " †	Dolce	8 "	

† On heavy wind.

Besides the usual couplers there are octave couplers in swell and choir, Ch. to Gt. Sub-octave, and Sw. to Gt. Octave, all of which have no visible effect on the keys. Four combination pistons for great, four for swell, and one for full pedal. The pedal couplers are operated both by pedal and piston-knobs, all of which are double-acting. The Tremulants of the choir and swell are operated by a pedal, either collectively or singly. The wind is supplied from seven separate reservoirs.

This instrument has the first pneumatic action which we have ever seen which would *repeat* perfectly. The voicing of many of the stops is as unique as it is novel. The Viole Celeste reminds one of the work of French builders, and is very acceptable. The Diapasons seem hardly rich enough for the amount of four and two feet stops (with octave couplers). The key-board of the great organ is the lower key-board. This is advocated by some organists, but to our mind the key-board on which the most difficult execution is performed should be at the same height as the piano forte key-board. The lower keyboard of a three-manual organ cramps the wrists and often prevents a perfect freedom of execution in such music as is generally played on the great organ. The pedal key-board is concave. If all our organs had concave pedals the advantages of such could be realized; but if an organist plays on a horizontal pedal-board this week, and meets with concave pedals unexpectedly the week after, he is for a time "all at sea," and wishes that either he or the concave pedals were on shore.

At the inaugural recital (see Mixtures) such of the solo-stops as were used as such displayed an individuality of voicing which is not always met with in this country.

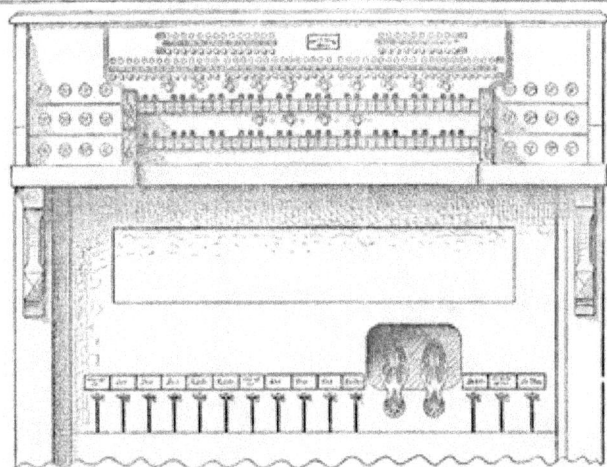

NEW TUBULAR PNEUMATIC ORGAN.

(ON EXHIBITION AT THE MECHANICS' FAIR, BOSTON.)

(Awarded a Gold Medal.)

Built by Mr. George S. Hutchings of Boston.

The above cut is a representation of the console (without the pedal key-board) of the organ which was exhibited at the Mechanics' Fair, Boston, during the month of November, a specification of which appears below. This organ was constructed to exhibit the tubular pneumatic action and changeable combination pistons which this firm have just perfected and which are being patented. The particular advantages which are claimed are, simplicity, adaptibility to any organ, and the extreme lightness of the touch.

The system of changeable combination pistons and pedals is unique, being simple, and having the combination not only visible, but also under the immediate control of the performer. For example, at the left of the builder's name-plate (see cut) is a set of double push-knobs (two rows), each vertical pair representing one stop, with small plates containing the names of the stops between the rows. This set of push-knobs represents all the stops of the swell-organ, and is connected with No. 2 of the swell-organ combination piston-knobs. The upper row of this set of push-knobs is marked "on," and the lower row "off." To "set" a combination for this combination piston-knob, the small push-knobs of the upper row, representing such stops as are desired, are pushed in. This particular combination can then be drawn at any time by means of the combination piston-knob No. 2, without affecting any draw-stop combination which may be "on." If it is desired to change this combination, such stops as are wanted in addition are secured by pushing in the small push-knobs representing those stops; while to put "off" any stops already "on," the small push-knobs corresponding to those stops in the *lower* of the two rows are pushed in. It is not necessary to put "off" a combination to change it, as the change can be made while the combination is "on." There are six sets of these small push-knobs controlling the combinations of the six combination piston-knobs (three for each manual). Two other combination piston-knobs draw full great and full swell. All the combination piston-knobs of a manual are so connected that when one is depressed, any other one which happens to be "on" is thrown "off."

The ten adjustable combination pedals are identical with the combination piston-knobs, so that the combinations may be controlled by either hand or foot.

The "Prolongment Harmonique" (!!!) is for the purpose of *sustaining* one or more notes on the great after the hands are removed from the keys. The idea (a useful one, by the way) is not new, as Cavaillé-Coll for ten years or so has made a sustaining pedal (controlled by a *pedal* which is more serviceable). This organ contains the Pneumatic Swell-Pedal, a description of which appeared in this journal a couple of months ago.

A word concerning the "light action." We have never been in favor of "feathery actions," and, particularly for the pedal key-board, we think a little resistance is desirable. When we hear an organist play the pedal solo part in Bach's Toccata in F on one of these "feathery actions" without blurring any of the phrases, we will be convinced that they are desirable. In justice to the builder we would say that this action can be stiffened, with but little trouble, to suit any one's taste.

Of all the *adjustable* combination systems which we have examined this one is the most practical, and requires the least study to comprehend. Every combination is always visible to the eye, and it is not necessary to "lock" or "unlock" them. There is no possible danger of throwing the combination "off" by a slip of the hand or foot, and it is not necessary to put a combination "off" in order to change it.

Appended is the specification:—

GREAT ORGAN.			SWELL ORGAN.		
Open Diapason	8	Ft.	Lieblich Gedackt	16	Ft.
Dulciana	8	"	Violin Diapason	8	"
Viola da Gamba	8	"	Salicional	8	"
Melodia	8	"	Æoline	8	"
Flûte d'Amour	4	"	Stopped Diapason	8	"
Octave	4	"	Quintadena	8	"
Trumpet	8	"	Flauto Traverso	4	"
			Violina	4	"
PEDAL ORGAN.			Flautino	2	"
Bourdon	16	Ft.	Oboe	8	"
Violone	8	"			

MECHANICAL REGISTERS.

Great to Pedal.	Swell to Great.
Swell to Pedal.	Great Organ Separation } Piston-knobs.
Pedal at Octaves.	Full Organ }
Pedal Unison Separation.	Prolongment Harmonique }

COMBINATION PISTONS.

1, 2, 3, and 4 Adjustable Combination piston-knobs to Great.
1, 2, 3, and 4 Adjustable Combination piston-knobs to Swell.
Full Great Adjustable piston.   Full Swell Adjustable piston.

PEDAL MOVEMENTS.

1, 2, 3, and 4 Adjustable Pedal Combinations to Great.
1, 2, 3, and 4 Adjustable Pedal Combinations to Swell.
Full Great Adjustable pedal.   Full Swell Adjustable pedal.
Reversible Great to Pedal.   Full Organ.
Swell Tremolo.   Swell to Great at Octaves.

VOL. I.　　　　　　FEBRUARY, 1893.　　　　　　No. 10.

BACH

YEARLY SUBSCRIPTION $2.00.　　　　　　SINGLE COPIES 25 CTS.

THE ORGAN

DEVOTED TO

A MONTHLY JOURNAL

THE KING OF INSTRUMENTS

·EVERETT·E·TRUETTE·

EDITOR & PUBLISHER

149 A. TREMONT ST. BOSTON.

RHEINBERGER

GUILMANT

FRESCOBALDI

BUXTEHUDE

MERKEL

BEST

HANDEL

The New England
Conservatory of Music.

CARL FAELTON, Director.

The Organ Department

offers unsurpassed facilities for acquiring a thorough and practical education in the art of Organ Playing. The course of study, which may be pursued, either in class or with private instruction, embraces work in Pedal Obligato Playing, Hymn Tunes and Chorales, with Interludes and Modulations. Afterwards Organ works of polyphonic character, Anthems and Improvisations, and for more advanced students works by all the great writers for the Organ, together with the study of Masses, Oratorios, etc.

There are in the Conservatory building for the exclusive use of this Department *fourteen* Pedal Organs, several of which possess three manuals each.

Those students who have acquired sufficient ability are aided in securing Church positions by the *Conservatory Bureau.* A large number of students have already been placed in lucrative positions by the Bureau.

TUITION: CLASSES OF FOUR, TERM OF TEN WEEKS, $20.00.

BOARD OF INSTRUCTION.
{ GEORGE E. WHITING.
HENRY M. DUNHAM.
ALLEN W. SWAN.

{ Organ Practice, 10 cents per hour and upwards.
Pupils may enter at any time.
Fourth Term commences April 14.

Address, FRANK W. HALE,
General Manager,
Franklin Square, Boston, Mass.

THE ORGAN.

Vol. I.   BOSTON, FEBRUARY, 1893.   No. 10.

THE ORGAN.

A MONTHLY JOURNAL

DEVOTED TO THE KING OF INSTRUMENTS.

EVERETT E. TRUETTE, EDITOR AND PUBLISHER.

(Entered at the Boston, Mass., Post-office as second-class mail matter, June 1, 1892.)

CONTENTS:

ORGAN MUSIC IN PARIS.

(From our own Correspondent.)

JUST before Christmas a very interesting concert was given at the Court Chapel at Versailles by M. Alex. Guilmant, assisted by M. Warmbrodt of the National Opera; Brun, solo violin at the opera; Louis Dérwis, baritone, and other less noted soloists, and a female chorus. It could hardly be called an organ recital in our restricted sense of the term; for though there were a few organ solos, and though the organ furnished the ground-tone, so to speak, of the whole concert, yet almost all the works given abounded in delightful effects in *ensemble* music. It was this blending of the *timbre* of different tone-producers which gave the great novelty and charm to the concert, and this is the particular point I wish to dwell upon. In some of the pieces, organ, piano, violin, vocal soloists, and chorus were all sounding together. It is a truism to say that the French are a clever people; but they are nowhere more clever, it seems to me, than in the beautiful effects they produce in concerted music. We shall do well to follow their example in America, for some of our organ recitals stand sorely in need of being made more interesting, and thus more instructive. The popular taste in this way will be elevated at a much faster rate. I believe the Mason organ-builders in Boston have set a good example by giving concerts of concerted music at their store on Tremont Street. There is no reason why organ, piano, violins, and voices should not be heard together. Are their qualities a whit more different than those of the instruments in a modern orchestra which blend so well together?

But to speak of the most important features of the concert, Guilmant began by playing a transcription of one of Bach's Cantatas; this was rendered in a most finished style. Then M. Brun played a romance for violin by Svendsen, with organ accompaniment. How beautiful the violin sounds with the organ if it is properly accompanied? Why are they not heard more often together in America? I suppose most readers of THE ORGAN are familiar with Rheinberger's six charming pieces for violin and organ. If not, they ought to be. Then followed Gounod's sacred song, "Je te rends Grâce, Ô Dieu d'Amour," which in America is generally sung to the words "Glory to Thee, my God, this night." In this the effects were beautiful; the sustained parts of the accompaniment were taken by the organ, the middle portion with running passages by the piano, and in the climax, organ, piano, and solo voice all joined most effectively. Another beautiful concerted piece was a chorus, "Angelus," by Paul Deschamps. In this there were solo voices, a female chorus, a violin, which played an obligato part, a piano, and the organ; sometimes heard separately, and sometimes together. The rest of the programme was made up of selections from Berlioz, Saint-Saëns, and Massenet, almost all giving some novel and pleasing effect in tone-color. I mustn't forget to speak of the rendering of the Aria from Bach's Orchestral Suite in D, by MM. Brun and Guilmant, which was one of the most lovely things of the occasion. During the concert Guilmant played the following organ solos: Prelude in G-major, Mendelssohn, and two pieces of his own, "Marche sur Tête Confesseur" and "Postlude Nuptiale."

The organ in the chapel is not large, but a very good one. I wish I could transport the readers of THE ORGAN to the glorious chapel itself, with its high airy ceiling and gorgeous frescos. It was an ideal place for an organ recital.

All American admirers of Guilmant (and what organist is not his admirer?) will be pleased to know that on New Year's Day he was decorated by President Carnot with the order of *Chevalier de la Légion d'Honneur*.

In my next letter I shall hope to say something of the music on Sundays at La Trinité, St. Sulpice, and La Madeleine, and of the wonderful improvising of Guilmant.

         "OUTRE MER."

ORGAN MUSIC IN LONDON.

(Special correspondence to THE ORGAN.)

       LONDON, Dec. 30, 1892.

DEAR ORGAN, — I have lately been attending some recitals given Sunday afternoons on the great organ at Albert Hall. It is in this vast auditorium, in the form of an amphitheatre, that the Royal Choral Society gives its oratorios, under the leadership of Sir Joseph Barnby; and very grandly do the choruses sound in so great a space. The organ, which occupies the same position at the back of the stage as did our Music Hall organ, and somewhat resembles it in outward appearance, is a magnificent instrument, built by Willis, and its full power fills — yes, more than fills — the great hall. With the addition of numerous octaves, twelfths, fifteenths, mixtures, and similiar stops of a penetrating character which such large organs receive, the tone with full organ becomes most unpleasantly loud; and one is reminded of the description of the organ in Winchester Cathedral in the tenth century : "To such an amount does it reverberate, echoing in every direction, that every one stops with his hand his gaping ears, being in nowise able to draw near and bear the sound which so many combinations produce."

Each recital has usually been given by a different organist. The programmes, one of which I enclose you, have been interesting and well played. But unless the organist is thoroughly familiar with the mechanical construction of so large an instrument, and the tone-color of its various stops and combinations, and knows just where to put his hand for whatever he wants, there is sure to be a too long holding of final chords, than which nothing is more distressing, and a certain hesitancy in the playing which destroys the listener's pleasure in the performance.

Of course one hears some excellent music at St. Paul's, where Dr. Martin is organist, and also at Westminster Abbey, where Dr. Bridge is at the organ. It is in such places, and especially in connection with the service, that the organ becomes that grand, impressive, noble instrument — the king, in truth, of all others. In St. Paul's, as also at the Abbey, the organ is divided, part being on one side, part on the other, of the choir, the long trackers running under the floor. The tone is full and rich, and is echoed and re-echoed in that lofty dome which is the glory of St. Paul's Cathedral. Dr. Martin's playing is always in thorough keeping with the service he is accompanying ; voices and organ combine to lift one for a time away from one's self to better and higher thoughts. This is a subject on which the organist cannot exercise too much care ; for it is in his power to make more beautiful, or almost utterly to destroy, all pleasure and rest in the service. Certainly too much cannot be said concerning the responsibility of his position, nor can it be too strongly urged that he give this most important point of his organ-work earnest and thoughtful study. With a fine organ the temptation to display its solo stops and its volume of tone is such that its true office, that of adding dignity and impressiveness to the worship of God, is oftentimes forgotten. In this connection I call to mind a very beautiful instance of its employment during a part of the communion service at St. Paul's. Several stanzas of one of the grand old German chorals were sung by the choir, unaccompanied. Between each stanza the organ supplied an interlude, similar in character to the hymn just sung, keeping up the thread of the thought, and seeming almost like an answering choir. The effect was most beautiful and impressive.

London offers many advantages to the organ student. He has opportunities to study the character of playing best suited to the services of the church, as well as to hear much good solo work. Most of the churches, also, so far as I have been able to observe, possess excellent instruments. But one difficulty always besets him wherever he goes, unless he enters a school, — the opportunity for practice. Even in the schools this difficulty is not always overcome, and the organs used by the students are not such as to give them much pleasure or encouragement in their work. In truth, the organ student's path in the beginning is a rather thorny one, and it takes considerable perseverance to overcome the many difficulties which rise up before him. But when the first hard struggle is past, the delight and satisfaction in his work more than compensates for the trials of the beginning.

With best wishes I am,

　　　　Faithfully yours,

　　　　　　　　WILLIS.

NOTABLE ORGANS.

VI.

CENTENNIAL HALL, SYDNEY, AUSTRALIA.

THE organ in the Centennial Hall, Sydney, Australia, the largest organ in the world, was built by Messrs. Hill & Son of London, was completed in 1890, and is said to have cost about $60,000. Appended is the specification : —

GREAT ORGAN.

Contra Bourdon	32 Ft.		Harmonic Flute	4	Ft.
Bourdon	16 "		Principal	4	"
Double Open Diapason	16 "		Octave	4	"
Open Diapason (1)	8 "		Gemshorn	4	"
Open Diapason (2)	8 "		Twelfth	2⅔	"
Open Diapason (3)	8 "		Fifteenth	2	"
Open Diapason (4)	8 "		Mixtures	III. Bks.
Harmonic Flute	8 "		Cymbal	IV. "
Viola	8 "		Sharp Mixture	IV. "
Spitz-flöte	8 "		Furniture	V. "
Gamba	8 "		Contra Posaune	16 Ft.
Hohl-flöte	8 "		Posaune	8 "
Rohr-flöte	8 "		Trumpet	8 "
Quinte	5⅓ "		Clarion	4 "

SWELL ORGAN.

Double Open Diapason	16 Ft.		Twelfth	2⅔ Ft.
Bourdon	16 "		Fifteenth	2 "
Open Diapason	8 "		Harmonic Piccolo	2 "
Viol di Gamba	8 "		Mixture	IV. Bks.
Salicional	8 "		Furniture	V. "
Dulciana	8 "		Trombone	16 Ft.
Vox Angelica	8 "		Bassoon	16 "
Hohl-flöte	8 "		Horn	8 "
Octave	4 "		Trumpet	8 "
Gemshorn	4 "		Cornopean	8 "
Harmonic Flute	4 "		Oboe	8 "
Rohr-flöte	4 "		Clarion	4 "

CHOIR ORGAN.

Contra Dulciana	16 Ft.		Lieblich-flöte	4 Ft.
Open Diapason	8 "		Twelfth	2⅔ "
Gamba	8 "		Fifteenth	2 "
Dulciana	8 "		Dulcet	2 "
Flauto Traverso	8 "		Dulciana Mixture	III. Bks.
Hohl-flöte	8 "		Bassoon	16 Ft.
Lieblich Gedeckt	8 "		Vox Humana	8 "
Octave	4 "		Clarinet	8 "
Violina	4 "		Oboe	8 "
Celestina	4 "		Octave Oboe	4 "

SOLO ORGAN.

Quintaton	16 Ft.		Flauto Traverso		2 Ft.
Open Diapason	8 "		Contra Fagotto		16 "
Violin Diapason	8 "		Cor. Anglais		8 "
Flauto Traverso	8 "		Corno di Bassetto		8 "
Doppel-Böte	8 "		Orchestral Oboe		8 "
Stopped Diapason	8 "		Harmonic Trumpet		8 "
Viola	8 "		Octave Oboe		4 "
Octave	4 "		Contra Tuba		16 "
Flauto Traverso	4 "		Tuba		8 "
Harmonic Flute	4 "		Tuba Clarion		4 "

ECHO ORGAN.

Viol d'Amour	8 Ft.		Flageolet		2 Ft.
Unda Maris (II. Rks.)	8 "		Glockenspie l.		IV. Rks.
Lieblich Gedeckt	8 "		Echo Dulciana Cornet		IV. "
Viol d'Amour	4 "		Basset Horn		8 Ft.

PEDAL ORGAN.

Double Op. Diapason, wood	32 Ft.		Bass Flute		8 Ft.
Double Op. Diapason, metal	32 "		Twelfth		5⅓ "
Contra Bourdon	32 "		Fifteenth		4 "
Open Diapason, wood	16 "		Mixture		II. Rks.
Open Diapason, metal	16 "		Mixture		III. "
Violone	16 "		Mixture		IV. "
Gamba	16 "		Contra Trombone, wood		64 Ft.
Dulciana	16 "		Contra Posaune, metal		32 "
Bourdon	16 "		Posaune		16 "
Quint	10⅔ "		Trombone		16 "
Octave	8 "		Bassoon		16 "
Principal	8 "		Trumpet		8 "
Violoncello	8 "		Clarion		4 "

8 Pneumatic Comb. Pistons to Gt.		6 Combination Pedals to Ped.	
8 " " " Sw.		4 " " " Gt.	
7 " " " Ch.		Choir Tremulant	
7 " " " Solo.		3 Pedals for Pedal Couplers.	
3 " " " Echo.			

The combination piston-knobs are placed *below* their respective manuals (organ-builders in this country still persist in placing them *above* the manual). Tubular Pneumatics are used throughout the organ, and the bellows are worked by a gas-engine. The organ occupies a floor space eighty feet by twenty-six feet. The instrument was inaugurated by Mr. W. T. Best, who afterwards gave a cycle of twelve recitals. (See THE ORGAN for July for programmes of the whole cycle.)

CORRESPONDENCE.

AN IDEAL ORGAN.

To the Editor of THE ORGAN:

SIR,—"*An Ideal Organ!*" Will any one define this term? Supposing, for instance, that we could induce the organists of New England to give in brief form, each one, his conception of such an instrument, and we were to classify replies under two headings,—say, "present" and "future;" those dealing with the organ as they know it, and those writing as they conceive it might become. I wonder how many replies could be classified under the latter heading?

Mr. Best's definition of an organist as a good "*up-to-the-twelfth-and-fifteenth*" player is a witty and all-embracing title. He plays Händel and Bach with fair loyalty to the text; he approaches the instrument like a trained boxer, and there is clearly no "darned nonsense" about him! He has only to look, or at most to speak, to put to utter discomfiture the nervous but aspiring young student round the corner with his "new-fangled" notions.

Nor is the day past, now in 1893, when Mr. Best's long-ago-given definition is inapplicable. There is a certain raising of the head, broadening of the chest, and generally defiant attitude still fashionable.

We still have our "*up-to-the-twelfth-and-fifteenth*" players, and I fear me, if the truth be spoken, that they are largely in the majority,—let me add, by way of qualification, "*helplessly*" so.

How are they to be approached? Not after the manner of the Toréador, for most of them are good fellows, trying to make the best of a position where no encouragement is offered; nor do they need the back-to-back "shoving-up" process commonly necessary to progress on the other side of the Herring Pond.

If in true conservative spirit we propose to hold for them all that they rely upon in the organ which is worth retaining in our "Ideal Organ," and offer the inducement of immensely increased resources of effect, and with this gain simplified control besides, we then surely appeal to them on grounds which every American recognizes.

But besides the artistic there is the overwhelming interest of the commercial element to be considered.

(Continued on page 233.)

THE ORGAN.

BOSTON, FEBRUARY, 1893.

THE ORGAN is published the first of every month. Subscription price $2.00 per year (European countries 10s. 5d.), payable in advance. Single copies, 15 cents.

Subscribers will please state with which number they wish their subscription to begin.

Subscribers wishing the address of their paper changed must give the old as well as the new address.

Remittances should be made by registered letter, post-office order, or by check payable to EVERET E. TRUETTE.

Correspondence, to secure notice, must in all cases be accompanied by the name and address of the writer, not for publication, but as a guarantee of good faith.

Advertising rates sent on application.

Address all communications.

The Organ, 149 A Tremont Street, Boston, Mass.

☞ An active agent in every city is desired to whom a liberal cash commission will be allowed.

Single copies of THE ORGAN can be procured of

NOVELLO, EWER & CO.,	New York.
G. SCHIRMER,	New York.
OLIVER DITSON CO.,	Boston.
L. H. ROSS & CO.,	Boston.
N. E. CONSERVATORY,	Boston.
H. B. STEVENS CO.,	Boston.
LYON & HEALY,	Chicago.
THEODORE PRESSER,	Philadelphia.
WM. H. BONER & CO.,	Philadelphia.
TAYLOR'S MUSIC HOUSE,	Springfield, Mass.
GALLUP & METZGER,	Hartford, Conn.
RICHAULT & CO.,	Paris.
R. F. VIRGOE, (Sole Agent for Gt. Britain)	London.

IT is greatly to be regretted that the expected series of organ concerts in this country which were to be given by Mr. W. T. Best and Mons. Alex Guilmant, will probably be delayed till another season. Mr. Theo C. Knauff, who had the matter in charge, writes us that, while many subscriptions were received, the necessary funds to inaugurate the series, which were guaranteed by private parties, have not as yet been forthcoming.

A CORRESPONDENT writes us from Queensland, Australia, under the date of Nov. 22. "There is little or no organ playing or news just now; as our summer is coming on, and as the temperature seldom drops below 85°, no more playing than is absolutely necessary is done here. In February the rainy season sets in, and the heat is enervating in the extreme, and ciphering, sticking, etc., are the order of the day with the organ, while the rainfall is so excessive that it acts on the atmosphere, making the keys of the organ dripping with moisture. *A fact.*"

Outside this office window the thermometer registers *four degrees below zero,* and down on Summer Street, where the firemen have been pouring streams of water all night in a burning building, the ice is *twelve feet thick.*

PROFESSOR WILLHARTITZ of Los Angeles, Cal., has been making a study of the average longevity of musicians. From his somewhat lengthy table we find that the average life of organists is fifty-seven years and six days. Great Scott! have we got to die so soon? We will be courageous, for, Professor Willhartitz to the contrary, many organists draw a capital prize in the lottery of existence, and win thirty or forty years additional life.

By looking back to our June issue we read of several organists who have been in active duty at church for fifty, sixty, and sixty-five years. There is hope in our hearts, even if we haven't "got fifteen dollars in our inside pocket."

FROM a Western paper we quote the following extract from a criticism of an organ concert: " 'The Storm' was played in a masterly manner, but was marred in the attempt to introduce scenic effect into the concert-room, — a thing of questionable taste. The attempt was especially unfortunate this time, for when the lights were turned down the young man who was pumping the bellows stopped work. When the lights were turned up the young man appeared at the south door, declaring that it had been 'too dark to pump.' The amusement now created perhaps compensated for the disappointment."

THE following (from the Brisbane [Australia] *Telegraph*) is rich. The italics are ours.

"The Saturday night organ recital at the Wesleyan Church was well attended, and seems in a fair way to become a popular institution. Mr. Benson presided at the organ, and received the assistance of Mrs. Menser and Mrs. Buzacott as vocalists, and of Mrs. Buzacott and Mr. H. W. Burge on harp and violin respectively. *The general tone of the organ numbers was brilliant and lively,* and displayed the organist's masterly skill on the instrument. Mr. Benson opened the recital with 'Let the Bright Seraphim,' from Händel's oratorio, 'Samson;' and strangely bracketed with it was Gounod's 'Funeral March of a Marionette,' a well-known morceau that does not gain by transference from piano to organ. A lively gavotte by Scotson Clarke, and a barcarole with a stormy interlude, taken from Sterndale Bennett's 'Fourth Concerto,' were the next bracketed numbers. During 'The Evening Prayer,' by Smart, two lusty brass bands in the immediate neighborhood completely obliterated the *piano effects of the organ.* A showy orchestral overture by Volkmann won exceeding applause, and as a finale Mr. Benson played a 'Triumphal March,' by Lemmens. Mrs. Buzacott's harp solo, 'A Hymn of Nuns,' was admired for its graceful melody, and the *lingering subtones of the organ* were effective. Mrs. Menser chose Gounod's 'Ave Maria,' Mr. Burgh playing the violin obligato, accompanied by harp and organ. It was not altogether an artistic success. *'The Angel's Serenade'* (Braga) was sung by *Mrs. Buzacott to her harp,* Mr. Burge accompanying on the violin. Mrs. Menser was much applauded for her singing of Tours's 'The Gate of Heaven.' "

REVIEW OF ORGAN MUSIC.

FROM RICHAULT & CO., PARIS.

Prayer	A. Deeq.
Preludes and Prayers (Third Book)	C. V. Alkan.
Arranged by César Franck.	
Pastorale,	
Marche Nuptiale }	F. de la Tombelle.

The first composition is a somewhat simple piece, suitable for an opening voluntary.

The third book of Preludes and Prayers arranged by César Franck completes the series. The first two books were reviewed by us last month.

Both compositions by Tombelle are pleasing, and will find places on our concert programmes.

FROM S. BRAINARD'S SONS CO., CHICAGO.

THE ORGANIST'S COLLECTION.

A collection of high-grade organ music and arrangements for organ, selected from well-known composers, containing such names as Händel, Schubert, Mendelssohn, Wagner, Chopin, Gounod, Best, Smart, Tours, Hesse, Calkin, Dienel, Clark, and Batiste. The selection of pieces has been well made, and organists who are looking for a collection of standard compositions will find this a desirable work. Fifty-six compositions and one hundred and eighty-one pages. Price not given.

ALLEGRETTO.

GUSTAV MERKEL.

Sw. Oboe, Viola &
Flute 4 Ft.

Gt. Doppel Flöte & Flute
Har. 4 Ft. Ch. Melodia
Dulciana & Flute 4 Ft.

Ped. Bourdon. Sw. to
Gt. & Sw. to Ped.

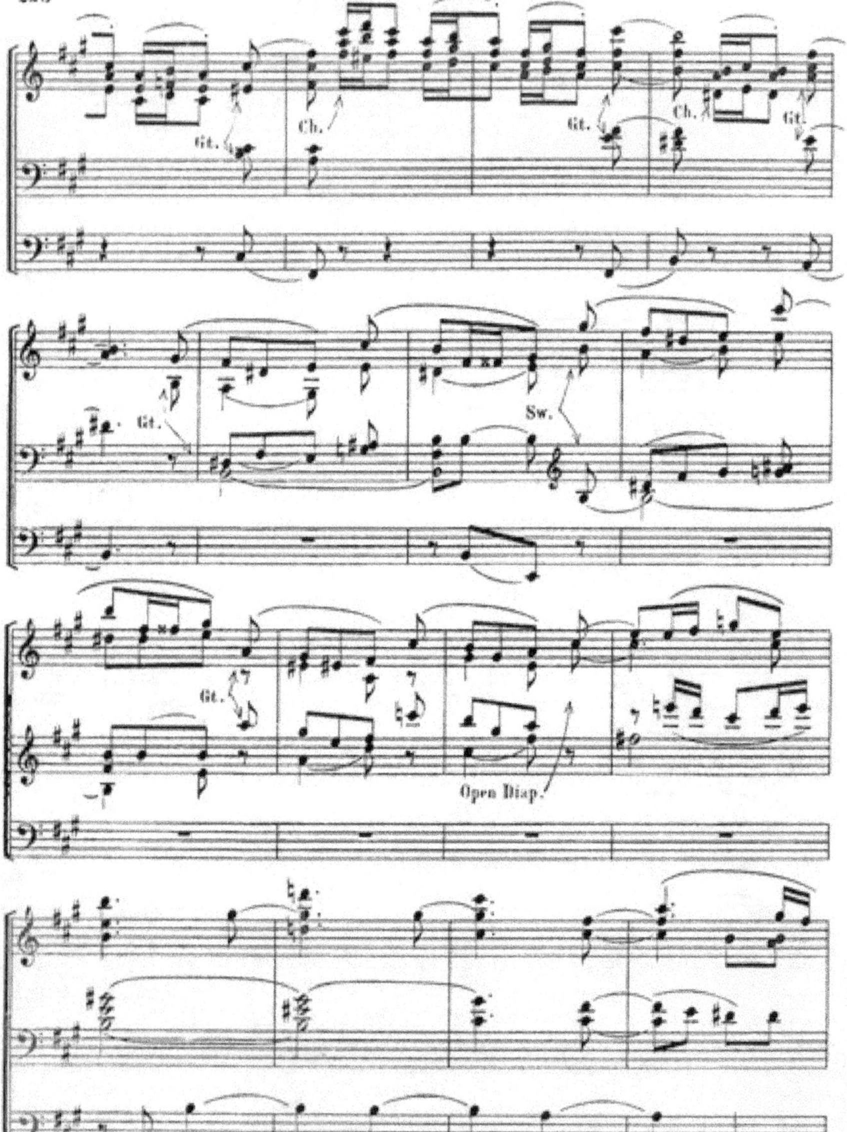
Gt.
Ch.
Gt.
Ch.
Gt.
Gt.
Sw.
Gt.
Open Diap.

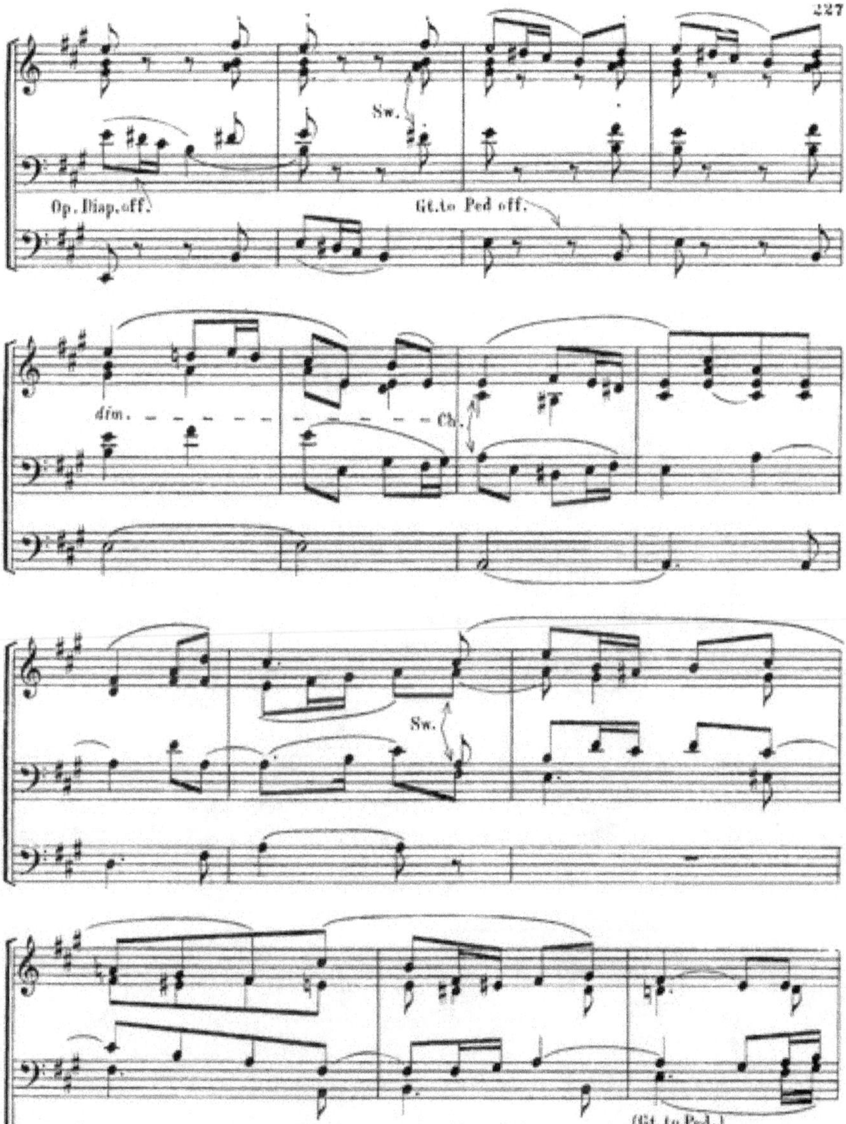
Sw.
Op. Diap. off.
Gt. to Ped off.
dim.
Ch.
Sw.
(Gt. to Ped.)

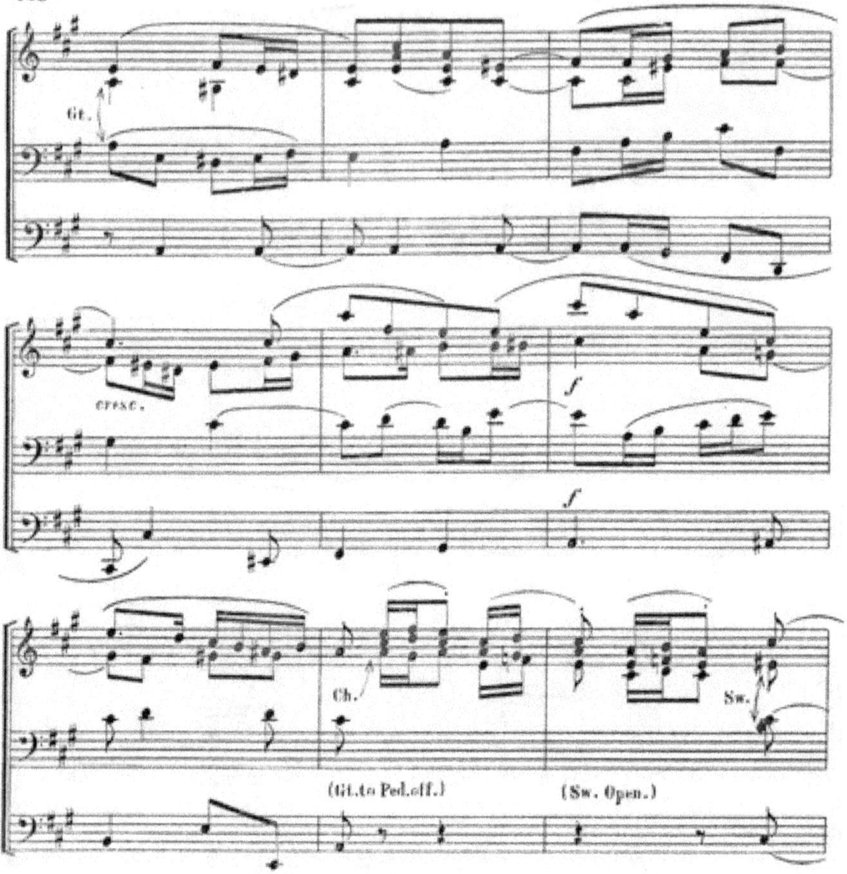
Gt.
cresc.
f
f
Ch.
Sw.
(Gt. to Ped. off.)
(Sw. Open.)
Ch.
Sw.
Ch.

(Sw. closed.)

Sw.

(Melodia in Ch. off.)

Gt.

cresc.

cresc.

Gt.to Ped.

f

f

dim.

Ch.

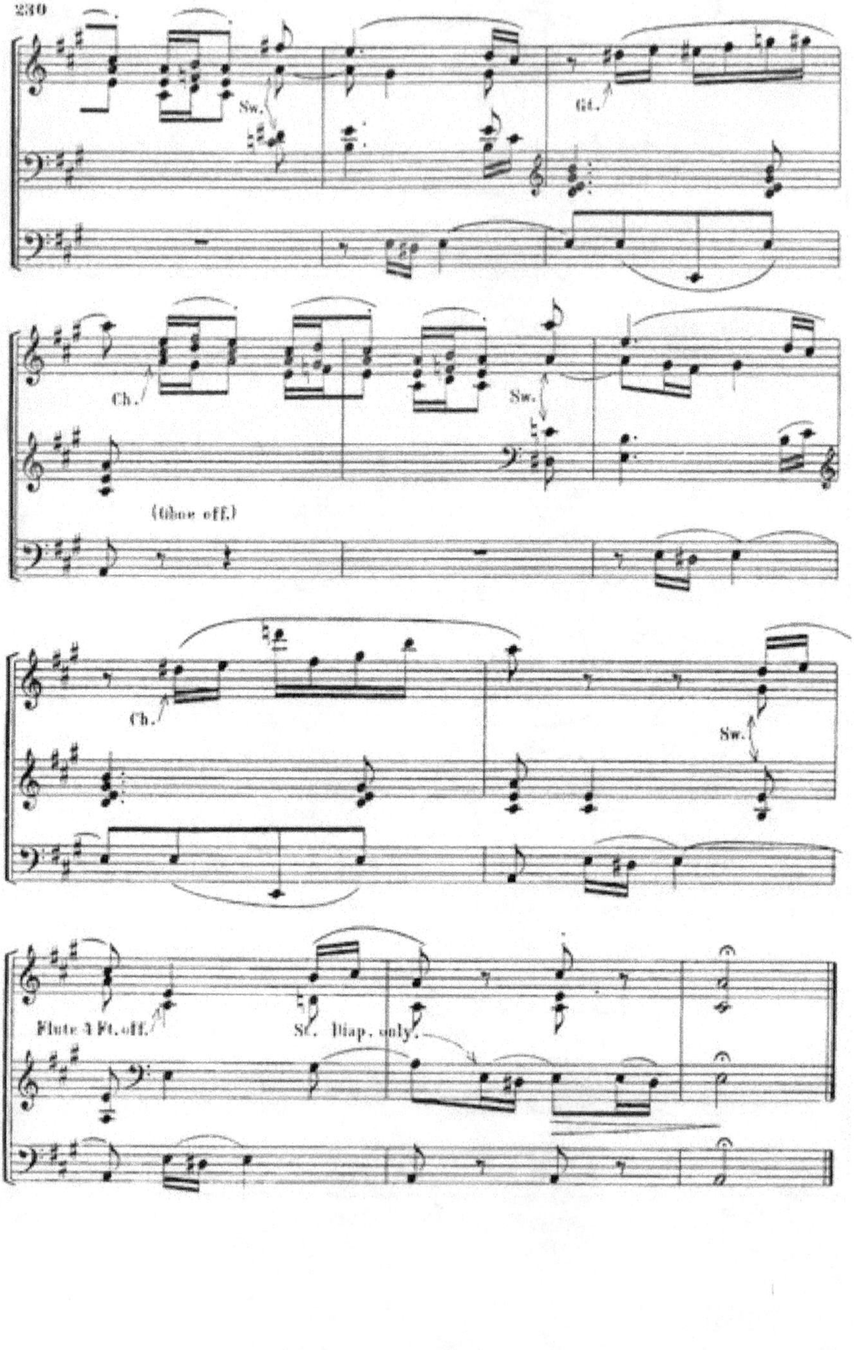
Sw.
Gt.
Ch.
Sw.
(Oboe off.)
Ch.
Sw.
Flute 4 Ft. off.
St. Diap. only.

ADAGIO.

Dr. W. VOLKMAR.

Sw. St. Diap. &
Flute 4 Ft.

Ch. (or Gt.)
Melodia & Dulciana.

Ped. Bourdon 16 Ft.
Ch. to Ped.

Ch. or Gt.

Sw. with Oboe.

Ch.

Sw.

Ch.

(Add Viola in Sw.)

Sw.
Ch.
Sw.
Oboe off.
(Ch. to Ped. off. Sw. to Ped. on.)
Ch.
Sw.
Flute 4 Ft. off.
Viola only.

CORRESPONDENCE.

(Continued from page 232.)

Suppose we say, then, in addition to the advantages offered to the artist, that we can offer to the purchaser such an instrument, in mechanical construction more durable, and less costly to provide as well as to maintain, than be can find in the present market, and we come pretty close to the definition of "An Ideal Organ."

We have arrived, then, at this conclusion as a step toward the realization of the "ideal." Simplicity of construction is indispensable, — all interests point to it as essential.

When, therefore, we hear of clever devices for adjustable combination movements, contrivances for making an organ of forty registers appear as one of seventy, — as I could point out in England, — and other strange and extraordinary organic excrescences, we know that we are adding complication to complication, and are piling straw on the already overweighted camel.

With simplicity of construction will follow very closely facility of control. I suppose it will not be questioned that an organ of fifty speaking-registers under easy command of the player is preferable to one of seventy which is practically unmanageable. And if that be granted, then the next aim is to render your fifty-register organ effective to the utmost ; and now we come upon ground absolutely untrodden in this country.

Here for the time we are at a "standstill" with our "ideal," for we cannot define what it *should* be, with no experience to aid us as to what it *might* be ; except to say, as some of the more imaginative may do, "I want to feel that I can express any kind of music on the organ, and I need, to do this, some different tonal treatment, or the addition of such." A good step, — make the demand, and it will readily create the supply.

Here we are in 1893 not doing half as good work as they did in Germany in 1593. Construction is identically the same, while design is infinitely inferior.

Demand governs supply, and the almighty dollar rules both ! The man who can bring all three under control carries the day, — and long life to him if he be a true artist !

BROOKLINE, Jan., 1893.
M. C.

LOOKING AT THE FEET WHILE PEDALING.

To the Editor of THE ORGAN :

In the last number of THE ORGAN there is an "answer" in the department of Questions and Answers with which I desire to take square issue. Under the second question of the general inquiry, "Pedal," the answer states : "There are many first-class organists who never look at the pedals when playing, and fully as many more who look at the pedals constantly." This is a reply to the question, "Should students be taught to play without looking at the pedals?" It may be true that the number of *first-class* organists who constantly look at their feet equals the number of first-class players who do not, but I very much doubt it. In fact, I wish to say that I have never seen *one first-class* player who looked constantly at his feet, and should be pleased to have a list of *five* named, or even *two*. To teach a pupil that he is to look constantly at his feet is to tie him in leading-strings, and I should hope that no teacher of to-day would instruct a pupil in that way. Of course there are times when one looks at his feet, and a beginner must of course do a good deal of "looking," but it should be *temporary*, and understood as *only* temporary, and not to be tolerated when he becomes a *first-class* player. I can name a list of *first-class* players, no one of whom ever thinks of looking at his feet, *except at certain times and places* which every organist knows about, and which it is not necessary to discuss. I should say to the inquirer under this head, "Students should most decidedly *not* be taught to watch their feet when playing the pedals."

HARTFORD, CONN.
JOHN S. CAMP.

If the writer of the above will take the trouble to read the whole of the answer to the question, as given in the January

number of THE ORGAN, he will find that teachers are not advised to teach their pupils to look at their feet in pedaling. In addition to what he has quoted may be found the following. "However, beginners will learn to pedal by *feeling* for the notes fully as rapidly as by *looking* for them, and their eyes can thus be kept on the music, which will facilitate their reading at sight." With regard to "first-class organists who look at the pedals when pedaling," take the three most prominent concert organists in Boston, — Messrs. George E. Whiting, Henry M. Dunham, and S. B. Whitney. Mr. Whiting almost never looks at the pedals. Mr. Dunham very frequently looks at them, and Mr. Whitney watches the pedals almost constantly. The playing of the latter two gentlemen is not in the slightest degree impaired by the habit of looking at the pedals. It is with them purely a habit, and could be easily overcome if it were necessary. It seems to us that "first-class players, no one of whom *ever* thinks of looking at his feet, *except at certain times and places*," will cover about all first-class players. There may be a few who look at their feet at *uncertain* times and places, but how are they "first-class"? Now, pupils, you must *never* look at your feet in playing. What *never!* Well — hardly — pardon the Pinaforical reminiscence, we should say, "except at certain times and places."

ED.

ORGAN ARRANGEMENTS.

To the Editor of THE ORGAN :

YOUR articles in early issues from English organists regarding organ arrangements, transcriptions, orchestral and operatic, etc., may be surely excused on the plea that it raises the taste of the humbler classes; but, dear Editor, is it not evading the point? May I ask a few questions? Are such arrangements compatible with the prescribed, conventional, arbitrary constitution of the organ? We might give a general effect of imitation in the color, but in the main thing can we give the expression? Do not these transcriptions demand of the organ the saying of things which on account of its make-up it cannot say? Take the German School, and the plea is that people cannot feed on "Roast Beef" or "Straight Mutton" without its proper attendants. I am not an orthodox, but have we no standard that we can present to our students? Will some learned doctor enlighten us, through your columns, where the line is to be drawn? The line should not be drawn so tight for popular concerts as for the church ; but let some honest, profound gentleman give us the standard. Yours respectfully,

DETROIT, MICH.
O. S. RICHARDS.

THE LOCATION OF THE SWELL-PEDAL.

THE following letters on this subject were received too late for our last issue.

Mr. E. M. Bowman of New York writes : —

"Referring to your favor received some time ago, I would say that I consider the best position for a balanced swell-pedal in an organ of three manuals which has but one swell, is over the F pedal, therefore a little to the right of the centre of the pedal keyboard."

Mr. W. T. Best of Liverpool replies : —

"I have always urged that this piece of mechanism should be in the centre, even if there be two or three, as in the largest organs. The position on the right is absurd, and has caused legions of one-legged organ-players, always busy with the abysses of sound and the punishment of the left foot. I may add, as regards the pedal-board, that its middle D (not C) should always be under the middle C of the manuals."

PERFECT PNEUMATIC ACTION.

To the Editor of THE ORGAN :

IN the last issue of THE ORGAN appears a notice of a new organ constructed by Mr. Michell, in which the statement is made "that the pneumatic action is the only one seen by the writer which will repeat perfectly." There are three other pneumatic actions which I have seen that will do this.

(1) Roosevelt's tubular pneumatic action. (2) Basset's patent pneumatic action (used by Steere & Turner, and recommended by Roosevelt when their tubular action is not used). (3) Hutchings newly patented tubular pneumatic action recently exhibited in connection with a small two-manual organ at the Mechanics' Fair in Boston. Hutching's action has the feature also; viz., that the resistance can be made much or little by a regulating screw, which is a boom for organists.

Yours truly,

HARTFORD, Jan. 16, '93. JOHN S. CAMP.

THE DECLINE OF CHURCH ORGAN-BUILD-ING IN THE UNITED STATES.

SEVERAL articles which have appeared in the musical journals of London upon the Pipe Organ Trade in America, and copied by the trade journals here, contain enough truth to irritate some of the craft, who seem inclined to the opinion that the work of American builders is beyond the criticism of our English brethren. To any one conversant with the history of organ-building here for the past forty years, it must be patent that the blighting touch of unhealthy competition, and the ecclesiastic cry for quantity, has drawn the attention of the makers of this unequalled instrument from the legitimate and substantial characteristics of appearance, tone, and action, to the study of a minimum of cost, a maximum of claptrap mechanism, overblown stops, and cheap construction.

One looks in vain for the mahogany table and slides, veneered topboards, wrought-iron register action parts, hard wood "backfalls," and generally perfect stock and permanent construction, with case architectural and ornamental which characterized the works of Erben and Appleton. It is a delight to one who may have the true appreciation of organ tone, to visit old Trinity (N.Y.), and listen to that marvel of sweetness and solidity, a legacy from builder Erben and his accomplished colleague and voicer, Mr. Berry, which the latterday saints have not been allowed to despoil by "revoicing."

It is a significant fact that almost without exception the few financially successful builders of to-day are those who have no love or respect for the organ as a musical instrument, who are shrewd enough to see that, placed above the commercial level of a cook-stove, there is no profit in manufacturing; and for an incentive to the purchase of such, an elaborate description of the commonest features and mechanical devices of the "touch-the-button" order is given, which would almost convey the idea that the works of the masters could be performed without the least exertion by the amateur.

The ordinary parts of the organ, such as a "wind trunk," are dilated upon as having an "extraordinary sectional area," a feature which the foreman of the factory should be able at a glance to order of sufficient size. We should think it strange if in the description of a house attention was called to the extraordinary sectional area of the chimney — items equally commonplace.

To build the average church organ of to-day no reputation is necessary, and the "hurry-up" methods employed by many, such as the substitution of a glued-up board for a panel, screws and dowels for dovetails and tenons, one set of swell-shutters where there should be two, pine or other soft-wood pieces containing a working pin, the shoddiest of felt, cheap varnish for gum shellac, not to mention low-grade and green lumber, etc., makes the way easy for the common wood-worker of limited experience to enter the arena of competition with the weapon of low prices which no conscientious builder can withstand. Added to this is the fact that the "committee" are ever ready to improve or "rebuild" at a figure which, if included at the outset, would render rebuilding unnecessary, thus putting a premium upon cheap construction.

In the matter of cases the best examples can be found in private hands, where the professional architect is allowed proper latitude for correct outline and detail, but usually the demand for extra stops, etc., precludes the possibility for such an allowance, and the design (?) is furnished by the builder upon the "skeleton" plan, suggestive of a ship under bare poles. Seventy-five dollars' worth of "tomato-can" decorations are introduced to take the place of cornices, arches, and bays. In short, organ cases, as pieces of church furniture, and proper receptacles for the pipes of this noble instrument, have become nearly obsolete. If such liberty is allowed with the exterior, what can be inferred of the interior and concealed parts?

For the voicing of the instrument no special education is demanded. A knowledge of the "slitting" principle, as applied to a metal pipe, — for which we thank our German friends, and musically of great value when used with judgment, — is the chief accomplishment. This is allowed to run riot, and its effect is heard in all the metal work to the exclusion of purity, which is the wished-for and advertised quality.

With the ebb of the swell-box flood, which has engulfed more than two-thirds, and threatens the inundation of the entire instrument, — a state deplored by many intelligent players, — and a return to the form in which the distinctive character of each manual is preserved, will come a greater necessity for fine voicing.

Did any one ever hear of a young man studying to be an organ-builder? Yet here is an instrument which has retained its sacred character against all structural and tonal assaults, upon which is performed through studied education the sublime compositions of master minds, and the music of divine service. The inconsistency of the situation is clear as day-light. For this service the highest order of education is called into play, but the speaking factor in such service is to-day in America verging on a condition of musical and mechanical degradation to which the church is unwittingly a party.

The closing of the leading and high-class manufactory of this country for lack of profitable return upon the capital invested instead of sinking to the level of "trade" organ-building, which with the ample capital at hand might have been carried on to the discomfiture of the horde of cheap builders which are springing up in all parts of the country, is a heroic and noble treatment of the matter which is in perfect harmony with the standard established by the founder of the house of Roosevelt. GAMBETTE.

MIXTURES.

(FOUR RANKS.)

THE semi-annual entrance examination for organ students in the National Conservatory took place Jan. 10.

Mr. Harry Lindley gave an organ recital in the Second Presbyterian Church, Newark, N.J., the last of December.

The First Baptist Church of Kingston, N.Y., has just opened a new organ built by Hook & Hastings, containing two manuals and twenty registers, and blown by a water motor.

Mr. John D. White has given a series of five organ recitals in Chickering Hall, New York.

Mr. Clarence Eddy dedicated a new organ in Muscatine, Ia., Jan. 2.

Mr. Frank G. Rohner, after an absence of four years, has returned to Chicago. He gave an organ concert in the First Methodist Church, Dec. 30.

Christmas music at Unity Church, Chicago, by Mr. Harrison M. Wild, Offertoire in F, Grison; Offertoire on Christmas Hymns, Guilmant; Hallelujah Chorus, Handel.

Two organs in the Cathedral of Guadalajara, Mexico, built by Merklin & Co. of Paris, were inaugurated on Christmas.

Mons. Widor, organist of St. Sulpice, Paris, has gone to Buda-Pesth to conduct the performance of his ballet "La Korrigane."

Mr. Walter E. Hall gave an organ recital in the Church of the Epiphany, Chicago, Jan. 12.

A new organ, constructed by Messrs. Woodberry & Harris, having two manuals and twenty-one speaking stops, was inaugurated in Trinity Church, Gloucester, Jan. 12, by Messrs. Charles Allton Clark of Boston, and John S. Camp of Hartford, Conn.

Mr. G. B. Polleri, an Italian organist, has written an opera, "Colombo Fanciullo," which has proved successful in Italy.

Messrs. Hook & Hastings are now building a two-manual organ in the Church of the Holy Nativity, New York City, where the keyboards are a long distance from the organ, the connections being about fifty feet long. Owing to the peculiar conditions existing in the church, tubular-pneumatic action has been used throughout on keys, pedals, and draw-stops.

Mr. G. Riseley, organist of the Bristol (Eng.) Cathedral, has recently been appointed a professor of the organ in the Royal Academy of Music.

Dr. Wm. Spark, the noted organist of Leeds, England, gave a performance of his cantata "Immanuel" in the Leeds Town Hall, Christmas Eve. Dr. Spark conducted, and Mr. J. Herbert England was the organist.

Joseph Hanisch, for sixty-three years organist of the Cathedral in Riegensberg, Southern Germany, died in October.

New organ music by E. Bossi: Fantasia, Prelude, Musette Choral, Scherzo, Cantabile, Alleluia Final.

Mr. Chas. L. Capen, organist of the Roman Catholic Church, "The Gate of Heaven," South Boston, was presented with a gold watch and chain and a roll-top desk by his pupils on Christmas.

Mr. E. O. Flagler has been organist of a church in Poughkeepsie, N.Y., for forty years.

An organ in the Cathedral of Sévrous, France, built by Merklin & Co., of Paris, was opened Jan. 19 by Mons. Dallier, organist of St. Eustach (Paris), and Mons. Ogé, organist of the cathedral.

A new organ has been placed in the Chapel of the Sacred Heart, Troyes, France, which was opened last month by MM. Clolu & Léonché.

Sidney Town Hall, Organ Concert, Nov. 18, by Mr. A. Wiegand. Programme: Symphony in D-minor, Haydn; Romance in A-flat, Mozart; La Molinara, Beethoven; Dance Macabre, Saint-Saëns; Le Soir, Gounod; Sixth Symphony, Widor.

Messrs. Hook & Hastings have just completed an organ in the Congregational Church of Gorham, N.H., having two manuals.

A two-manual organ of nineteen registers has been placed in Mr. S. B. Whitney's choir-room, Church of the Advent, Boston, by Mr. Geo. S. Hutchings.

Organ recital in St. Paul's Cathedral, Melbourne, Australia, by Mr. Ernest Wood, Nov. 17. Programme: Third Sonata, Mendelssohn; Sketch, Op. 58, No. 4, Schumann; Offertoire in D-flat, Salomé; Fanfare, Lemmens.

The weekly organ recitals at the Bow and Bromley Institute, London, have been suspended from Christmas till early in February.

Inaugural recital by Dr. E. H. Turpin on the new organ built by Mr. James J. Binns, Temperance Hall, Derby, England. Toccata and Fugue in C, Bach; Vorspiel, to 3d act of "Die Meistersinger," Fugue, Reubke; Con Moto Moderato, Smart; Fantasia Concertante, Guison; and pieces for organ and violin.

Opening of new organ (built by Mr. Emmons Howard) in the Swedish Church, Bridgeport, Conn. Mr. Thos. A. Spinning performed the following: Offertoire de St. Cécilia, Batiste; Swedish Wedding March, Söderman; Chorus of Pilgrims, "Tannhäuser," Wagner; Fantasia, Spinning.

Mr. Gerrit Smith, organist of the South Church, New York, conducted a performance of Sullivan's "The Light of the World," given in the church Christmas afternoon; Mr. F. K. Gilbert was the assistant organist.

One hundred and nineteenth organ concert in Unity Church, Chicago, by Mr. Harrison M. Wild, Jan 15. Programme: First Movement of Sixth Organ Symphony, Widor; Sonata, Op. 119, Rheinberger; Chorus from "Oberon," Weber-Batiste; "The Death of Ase," from "Peer Gynt," Grieg-Merse; Swedish Wedding March, Söderman-Gleason; Processional March, Guilmant.

Seventeenth organ recital by Mr. J. J. Miller, at Christ Church, Norfolk, Va., Jan. 9. Programme: Allegro (Sixth Organ Concerto), Handel; Adagio (Sixth Organ Symphony), Widor; Fantasia ("The Storm"), Lemmens; March of Israelites ("Eli"?), Costa.

Mr. Fred L. Clark gave an organ concert in Payson Church, Easthampton, Mass., Jan. 17, with the following programme: Canon Fiore in D-minor, Dienel; Invocation in B-flat, Guilmant; Pastorale in G (Second Organ Symphony), Widor; Scherzo Symphonique, Renaud; Largo Cantabile, Haydn-Best; Tannhäuser March, Wagner-Westbrook; Variations on the Russian Hymn, Freyer; Songs by Mr. Birge, baritone.

Mr. Henry M. Dunham gave an organ recital in Brockton, Mass., Jan. 4, with the following programme: Sonata in C-minor, Guilmant; Elsa's Wedding Music, Wagner; Festival March, Dunham; Lamentation, Guilmant; Fuga in C, Mendelssohn; Benediction Nuptiale, Dubois; and Finale from Variations in C, Rink. Sig. Augusto Rotoli and Mr. Wm. H. Dunham assisted.

During the past month Mr. Geo. S. Hutchings has completed organs for the following places: St. Mark's Church, Fall River, Mass.; Studio Organ for Mr. J. Warren Andrews, Minneapolis; Elizabethtown, N.Y.; Waterbury, Vt., and Masonic Temple, Dover, N.H. Each has two manuals and from fourteen to sixteen registers.

Christmas music at the First Church, Waterbury, Conn., by Mr. Alex S. Gibson. Holy Night, Buck; Prelude in G, Whitney; Alla Marcia, Op. 51, No. 2, Guilmant; Pastorale in G, Salomé; Intermezzo, Sonata, Op. 119, Rheinberger; Grand Chorus, Guilmant.

Mr. H. G. Hanson gives the list of his present series of organ concerts in Christ Church, Louisville, Ky., Feb. 7, with the following programme: Sonata, No. 6, Mendelssohn; Fugue in A, Guilmant; Weinachts Pastorale, Merkel; Toccata, Mailly; Entr' acte ("Manfred"), Reinecke; and Processional March, Whitney.

Third organ concert of Mr. S. Clarke Lord, Asylum Hill Congregational Church, Hartford, Conn., Dec. 23. Programme: Pastorale from "Noële Concerto," Corelli; The Holy Night, Buck; March of the Magi Kings, Dubois; Christmas Offertorium, Lemmens; Christmas Fantasy, Best.

Opening of a new organ in the Methodist Church, Portsmouth, N.H. Dec. 25, by Mr. H. A. Reed of Nashua, N.H. Programme: Christmas Prelude, Guilmant; Priest's March, Mendelssohn; Communion in E-minor, Batiste; Fanfare, Lemmens; Vorspiel, Wagner; Andante in G, Batiste; Christmas March, Le Blanc.

The organ in Notre-Dame, Andelys, France, built in 1572 by Nicholas Dabenoise, and enlarged in 1644, 1641, and 1761 has been entirely rebuilt by Mons. Cavaillé-Coll. At the inaugural concert Mons. Deslandres of Batignolles and Mons. Mansou of Haut-Pas were the performers.

The organ built for the Church of the Redeemer, Providence, R.I., by Hook & Hastings in 1870 has just undergone extensive alterations by the builders, a new manual being added, together with couplers and pedal-movements to make its scheme like those of organs built at the present time.

It is announced in Arcadia (Montreal), that the proprietors of Windsor Hall have some thoughts of placing an organ in the hall. The original plan of the building called for a concert organ, but it was omitted, it is understood, on the score of expense.

A new organ in the Baptist Chapel, Nottingham, England, was destroyed by fire Jan. 1.

Mons. Alex Guilmant has been created a Chevalier de la Légion d'Honneur by the President of the French Republic.

Mons. Alex Guilmant gave an organ recital at the Wesleyan Chapel, Hampstead, England, the last of December.

Messrs. Jardine & Co. of Manchester, England, are to build a four-manual organ for the Liverpool School for the Blind, which will be built on the Hope-Jones system.

The January issue of our contemporary, the Presto, is out in the form of a year-book, consisting of one hundred and fifty pages, a large part of which is devoted to several chronological tables of events for the past year.

Mr. W. H. Donley has been giving a series of weekly organ concerts in Plymouth Church, Indianapolis. The following programme was rendered at the fourth concert, Jan. 21: Theme and Variations, Op. 47, Hesse; Offertoire in E-flat, Op. 39, No. 2, Batiste; Adagio, Sonata, Op. 13, Beethoven; Allegretto, Op. 62, Dorand; Vorspiel, Third Act of "Lohengrin," Wagner; Marche Cortège, Gounod; Gavotte, Leo; Vesper Bells, Spinney; Overture, "La Bonduc," Auber.

Mr. F. P. Trench of Lawrenceville, N.J., has all his organ music, operas, oratorio, masses, etc., in a fire which visited his studio while he was out of town the first of the month. Only a few manuscripts which were in another building remained when he returned to town.

Mr. F. Slade Olver gave an organ concert in the First Baptist Church, Moline, Ill., Jan. 5, with the following programme: Sonata in D-minor, Van Eyken; Andante (First Symphony), Mendelssohn; Storm Fantasia, Lemmens; Danse des Prêtresses des Dagons, Saint-Saëns; March in C, Welty; Overture, "Merry Wives of Windsor," Nicolai; Fantasia in C-minor, Hoyte; Gavotte, Clark; Variations on "A Scotch Air," Buck; Overture to "Zampa," Herold.

Mr. Olver repeated the same programme in the Presbyterian Church, Monmouth, Ill., Jan. 7.

The daily papers announce that the late Mr. Elvin D. Hall of Boston had purchased an organ valued at $18,000, which was delivered the day after his death. No further information can be obtained.

At Mr. Gerrit Smith's one-hundred and sixtieth organ concert in the South Church, New York, Jan. 23, the principal works performed were Concert Fugue in C, Hampt; Fantasia, on Ancient Christmas Carols, Best; and March of the Three Kings, Dubois. These recitals will be continued throughout the season on Mondays at 4.30 o'clock.

Musical Notes, a new monthly musical periodical was born Jan. 1. Its chief object, as announced in the Salutatory, is "the encouragement of musical talent and taste in this vast country."

The journal presents an unusually attractive appearance, containing twenty-four pages of reading matter and eight pages of music. The essays found in the initial number are of great value to all musicians, and undoubtedly Musical Notes will become a favorite with all lovers of the art side of musical journalism. Annual subscription, $2.50. Single copies, 25c. Musical Notes Pub. Co., 35 Broadway, N.Y.

Mr. William Edward Mulligan is giving a series of monthly organ recitals on the first Sunday of each month in St. Mark's Church, New York. At the January recital he performed the following compositions: Fantaisie de Concert, Tombelle; Prologue and "Darkness" from "The Redemption," Gounod; "Daybreak," Spinney; Offertoire in G, Wely; Marche Funèbre, Chopin; and Offertory on Christmas Hymn, Guilmant. At the next recital the principal numbers will be Trios (for violin, 'cello, and organ) Rheinberger; Scherzo (Seventh Symphony), Beethoven-Best; and Tannhäuser March, Wagner-Bartlett.

Christmas Programme of Mr. Wm. Huber, Jr., at the Baptist Church, Hamilton, O. Grand Offertoire de Noel, Op. 8, Thayer; Weinachtslied, Matthison-Hansen; "For unto us a child is born" ("The Messiah"), Handel; Christmas Prelude in G, Whiting; Pastorale from the "Nativity Concerto," Op. 6, No. 8, Corelli; Marche des Rois Mages, Dubois.

The organ in the Church of the Immaculate Conception, Malden, Mass., was played for the first time on Christmas Day. It is from the manufactory of Hook and Hastings, and has two manuals and twenty-two registers. It is blown by a water motor, and the action is extended and reversed.

Opening of the enlarged organ in Madison Ave. Baptist Church, New York (see New Organs), last month. Overture to "Martha," Flotow (Mr. Homer N. Bartlett); Fantasia, Op. 116, No. 3, Bartlett, and Allegretto, Guilmant (Mr. Gerrit Smith); Andantino, Franck, and Offertoire in D, Batiste (Mr. William Edward Mulligan); Introduction to third act, "Lohengrin," Wagner (Mr. Bartlett).

A new organ has just been finished by Hook & Hastings for the Church of the Epiphany, Durham, Conn. The instrument shows two fronts, and has two manuals.

At Mr. Gerrit Smith's one hundred and fifty-eighth recital in South Church, Madison Ave., New York, the following organ compositions were performed: "Hark, the Herald Angels Sing," Frost; Andantino, Franck; Pastorale in F, Tombelle; The Holy Night, Buck; Adoratio et Vox Angelica, Dubois; Fantasia (written for Mr. Smith's one hundred and fiftieth recital), Bartlett.

Shakespeare knew everything, even something about organs. He says (2 Henry IV., Induction): —

> "Rumor is a pipe
> Blown by surmises, jealousies, conjectures;
> And of so easy and so plain a stop,
> That the blunt monster with uncounted heads,
> The still-discordant wavering multitude
> Can play upon it."

London Musical News.

One hundred and eighteenth organ concert by Mr. Harrison M. Wild, in Unity Church, Chicago, Jan. 8. Overture to "Samson," Handel; Elegy—Fugue, Op. 44, No. 2, Guilmant; Adagio, from Symphony in F, Haydn; Melody in C, Silas; Pastorale, Wachs; March, from "Egmont," Beethoven; Prelude in G, Whiting.

The Song Friend, a useful monthly music journal published by S. W. Straub, 243 State St., Chicago, contains some sound advice to teachers and students. Organists are not forgotten, and many a plea for their advancement appears in its columns. One dollar per year.

Mr. F. G. Ogbourne gave a series of three organ concerts at St. Matthew's, Bayswater, London, during the month of December. The programme of the last concert is appended. Toccata in C, Bach; Cantilene in A-minor, Guilmant; Concerto in B-flat, Handel; Theme and Variations in G, Lemmens; Sonata, No. 6, Mendelssohn; Fantasia ("The Storm"), Lemmens; Improvisation on a Christmas Carol; Overture in C, Mendelssohn.

At Mr. Allen W. Swan's second organ recital, in Unitarian Church, New Bedford, Mass., Sunday, Jan. 4, the following programme was rendered: Minuetto in F, Salome; Pastorale in E, Tombelle; Sonata, No. 2, Merkel; Canzonet in G, Chipp; Adagio Cantabile (from Quartet in D), Haydn; Cantilene in A, Guilmant; March from "Aida," Verdi.

Mr. J. V. Flagler, organist of the First Presbyterian Church, Auburn, N.Y., has organized two choruses for the purpose of supplying the music in the church. A female chorus of two hundred render the music in the morning, and a male chorus of the same size sing in the evening. The scheme has proved satisfactory thus far, and the members of the church are well pleased.

The Etude, edited and published by Theodore Presser, 1704 Chestnut St., Philadelphia, a very valuable musical monthly devoted specially to the interests of teachers and students, has proved to be a necessity with thousands of teachers throughout the country. Its tone is always liberal, and never offensive; and those who subscribe for it can feel sure that they will receive more than their money's worth of sound, healthy reading and advice. It has a circulation of 18,000, and the subscription is $1.00 per year.

Organ Concert in Pilgrim Congregational Church, Cambridge, Mass., Jan. 18, by Miss Georgiana M. Frye, assisted by Miss Grace E. Taylor and Mr. E. L. Hay, organists, Miss Helen B. Wright, soprano, and Miss Jeannette Wilson, Contralto. Programme: Toccata in C, Bach, and Vesper Bells, Spinney (Miss Frye); Ritornelle, Chaminade (Miss Wilson); Fantasia, "The Storm," Lemmens (Miss Frye); Cantilene Nuptiale, Dubois (Mr. Hay); "The Old and the Young Music," Concone (Miss Wright); Offertoire de Noel, and La Contemplation, Thayer (Miss Taylor); "If I but Knew," Smith, and "There is your Music," Maxson (Miss Wilson); Chromatic Fantasie, Thiele, and Last Chord, Sullivan (Miss Frye); "Violet, come rejoice with Me," Rice, A Leaf, Neidlinger, and Solveigs Lied, Grieg (Miss Wright); Marche Cortège, Gounod (Miss Frye).

Mr. Henry M. Dunham, professor of the organ at the New England Conservatory of Music, Boston, and a member of the Advisory Board of that institution, gave an organ recital at the Shawmut Church, Jan. 19, with the following programme: Processional (Carillon), Rosher; Sonata in E-minor, Tombelle; Adagio in F (violin and organ), Merkel; In Memoriam, Dunham; Pastorale in G, Best; Scherzoso (Sonata in E-minor), Rheinberger; Intermezzo (with organ, piano, and violin accompaniment), from "Cavalleria Rusticana," Mascagni; "Glory to God" (with piano and organ accompaniment), Rotoli; Overture to Athalie, Mendelssohn-Best. Mr. Dunham was assisted by Mr. William H. Dunham, tenor, Mr. Willis Nowell, violinist, and Sig. Augusto Rotoli, accompanist.

The church was crowded to its greatest capacity, many people finding only standing-room. Mr. Dunham is always an interesting performer on the organ, and at this concert he was at his best. His choice of registration is generally excellent, and, while one might take exception to the liberty which he takes with the tempo when changing his combinations, the changes themselves are always pleasing, the contrasts being in excellent taste. This freedom of tempo certainly has the merit of always avoiding a "scrambling for the stops," and is by far the fewer of the two evils. "In Memoriam" was written in memory of the late Mrs. E. F. Searles, and introduces the favorite hymn ("Abide with Me"?) of Mrs. Searles. It is effective, and the latter part is very beautiful. Best's Pastorale and Rheinberger's Scherzoso were particularly well played, and gave great satisfaction. The tempo of Rosher's Carillon was too rapid to give the effect of the Carillon which was intended by the composer. The Sonata—the principal work on the programme—was exceedingly well played, the second movement in particular showing the skill of the performer in selecting the most effective combinations.

No organ concert which we have attended for the past year has given so much genuine enjoyment as this one, and our only regret is that the demands on the organist's time prevent his giving a series of concerts each season, as he was in the habit of doing several years ago.

OUR FIRST ORGAN-MUSIC COMPETITION.

A PRIZE of ten dollars ($10.) will be given for the best March for THE ORGAN. The composition must be written on three staves, must be from seventy-five to a hundred bars in length, and must bear a motto only. A sealed envelope, bearing the same motto and containing the form given below (which should be cut from this journal), filled out with the name and address of the competitor, must accompany each composition.

Compositions will be received till the 1st of March, when they will be submitted to the following judges, who have kindly consented to examine the compositions: —

> MR. CLARENCE EDDY of Chicago.
> MR. GEORGE E. WHITING of Boston.
> MR. S. B. WHITNEY of Boston.

The successful composition must become the property of THE ORGAN, and will be printed with the name of the composer in the journal issued the first of April.

The mottoes of the unsuccessful competitors will also be printed, and their compositions will be returned if the accompanying envelopes contain sufficient postage.

Compositions should be addressed: Editor THE ORGAN, 149 A Tremont St., Boston. (Prize Competition.)

Organ Music Competition.

Name ....

Address ....

Motto ....

NEW ORGANS.

PROPOSED SPECIFICATION OF AN ORGAN FOR ONE OF THE MUSIC HALLS OF THE COLUMBIAN EXPOSITION.

To be built by Messrs. Farrand & Votey.

GREAT ORGAN.

Double Open Diapason	16	Ft.
First Open Diapason	8	"
Second Open Diapason	8	"
Gemshorn	8	"
Viola da Gamba	8	"
Principal Flute	8	"
Doppel-flöte	8	"
Octave	4	"
Hohl-flöte	4	Ft.
Octave Quinte	2⅔	"
Super Octave	2	"
Mixture	III.	Rks.
Scharf	III. and IV.	"
Trumpet	8	Ft.
Clarion	4	"

SWELL ORGAN.

Bourdon Treble }	16	Ft.
Bourdon Bass }		
Open Diapason	8	"
Violin Diapason	8	"
Salicional	8	"
Vox Celestis	8	"
Stopped Diapason	8	"
Quintadena	8	"
Octave	4	"
Salicet	4	"
Flûte Harmonique	4	"
Flageolet	2	"
Cornet	III., IV., and V.	Rks.
Contra Fagotto	16	Ft.
Cornopean	8	"
Oboe	8	"
Vox Humana	8	"

CHOIR ORGAN.
(In Swell-box.)

Contra Gamba	16	Ft.
Geigen Principal	8	"
Dolce	8	"
Concert Flute	8	"
Fugara	4	"
Flûte d'Amour	4	"
Piccolo Harmonique	2	"
Cor. Anglais	8	"
Clarinet	8	"

SOLO ORGAN.
(In a Separate Swell-box.)

Stentorphone	8	Ft.
Philomela	8	"
Hohl Pfeife	4	"
Tuba Major	16	"
Tuba Mirabilis	8	"
Tuba Clarion	4	"

PEDAL ORGAN.

Double Open Diapason	32	Ft.
Open Diapason	16	"
Violone	16	"
Bourdon	16	"
Quint	10⅔	"
Violoncello	8	"
Flute	8	"
Super Octave	4	"
Trombone	16	"
Trumpet	8	"

ECHO ORGAN.
(Operated from Solo Keyboard.)

Claribella	8	Ft.
Dolcissimo	8	"
Dulcet	4	"
Vox Humana	8	"

COMBINATION PISTONS.

F., MF., and P., Great.
F., MF., and P., Swell.
F. and P., Choir.
F. and P., Solo.

ADJUSTABLE PISTONS.
(Reversible.)

Two affecting Great and Pedal.
Three affecting Swell and Pedal.
Two affecting Choir and Pedal.
Two affecting Solo and Pedal.

PEDAL MOVEMENTS.

Full Organ (also Crescendo).
Pedal Organ Ventil.
Gt. to Ped. (reversible).
Sw. to Gt. (reversible).
Three Swell Pedals.
Pedal to open all boxes.
Pedal to close all boxes.
Pedal for Solo off, Echo on.
Sw. to Gt. Superoctave, Ch. to Gt. sub-octave, and Solo Super-octave on itself, in addition to the usual couplers.

THE ORGAN IN MADISON AVE. BAPTIST CHURCH, N.Y.

Built by Henry Erben in 1859. Enlarged by Geo. Jardine & Son.

GREAT ORGAN.

Open Diapason	16	Ft.
Open Diapason	8	"
Viola da Gamba	8	"
Wald Flute	8	"
Dulciana	8	"
Stopped Diapason	8	"
Night Horn	4	"
Principal	4	"
Quintena [1]	2⅔	"
Fife [1]	2	"
Mixture	III.	Rks.
Trumpet	8	Ft.
Clarinet	8	"

SWELL ORGAN.

Bourdon Treble }	16	Ft.
Bourdon Bass }		
Open Diapason	8	"
Viol d'Amour	8	"
Stopped Diapason	8	"
Principal	4	"
Flageolet	2	"
Cornet	III.	Rks.
Cornopean	8	Ft.
Oboe	8	"

CHOIR ORGAN. [1]
(In Separate Swell-box.)

Salicional	8	Ft.
Æoline	8	"
Melodia	8	"
Flûte Harmonique	4	"
Salicet	4	"
Piccolo	2	"
Vox Humana	8	"

PEDAL ORGAN.

Open Diapason	16	Ft.
Violin Gamba	16	"
Violoncello	8	"
Trombone	8	"

Six Piston Knobs to Swell. Three Combination Pedals to Great. Reversible Great to Pedal. Electric Motor.

[1] Entirely new.

NEW ORGAN IN ST. JAMES'S CHURCH, MILWAUKEE.

Built by Lancashire-Marshall Organ Company, Moline, Ill.

GREAT ORGAN.

Open Diapason	16	Ft.
Open Diapason	8	"
Open Diapason	8	"
Viola da Gamba	8	"
Doppel-flöte	8	"
Flûte Harmonique	4	"
Octave	4	"
Twelfth	2⅔	"
Fifteenth	2	"
Mixture	IV.	Rks.
Trumpet	8	Ft.
Clarion	4	"

SWELL ORGAN.

Bourdon	16	Ft.
Lieblich Gedeckt	16	"
Open Diapason	8	"
Salicional	8	"
Stopped Diapason	8	"
Flauto Traverso	8	"
Violin	4	"
Flautino	2	"
Dolce Cornet	III.	Rks.
Contra Fagotto	16	Ft.
Cornopean	8	"
Oboe	8	"
Vox Humana	8	"

CHOIR ORGAN.

Contra Dulciana	16	Ft.
Geigen Principal	8	"
Dulciana	8	"
Melodia	8	"
Unda Maris	8	"
Flûte d'Amour	4	"
Fugara	4	"
Piccolo	2	"
Clarinet	8	"

PEDAL MOVEMENTS.

Forte }
Mezzo } Great Organ.
Piano }
Forte }
Mezzo } Swell Organ.
Piano }
Forte }
Mezzo } Choir Organ.

Reversible Great to Pedal Coupler.
Sw. to Gt., sub-octave and super-octave, in addition to the usual couplers.

PEDAL ORGAN.

Open Diapason	16	Ft.
Violon	16	"
Bourdon	16	"
Quinte	10⅔	"
Violoncello	8	"
Flute	8	"
Trombone	8	"

Pneumatic motors applied to Great Organ. Tubular pneumatic applied to Pedal Organ and all couplers. Choir, and part of Great, enclosed in the Swell-box. Electric motor.

ORGAN FOR THE EMMANUEL LUTHERAN CHURCH, FORT WAYNE, IND.

Built by William King & Son.

GREAT ORGAN.

Open Diapason	16	Ft.
Open Diapason	8	"
Dulciana	8	"
Viola da Gamba	8	"
Doppel-flöte	8	"
Octave	4	"
Flûte d'Amour	4	"
Twelfth	2⅔	"
Fifteenth	2	"
Mixture	IV.	Rks.
Trumpet	8	Ft.

SWELL ORGAN.

Bourdon	16	Ft.
Violin Diapason	8	"
Keraulophon	8	"
Stopped Diapason	8	"
Æoline	8	"
Harmonic Flute	4	"
Violin	4	"
Flautino	2	"
Cornet	III.	Rks.
Oboe and Bassoon	8	Ft.
Cornopean	8	"

PEDAL ORGAN.

Open Diapason	16	Ft.
Grand Bourdon	16	"
Dulciana	16	"

The usual couplers.

PEDAL MOVEMENTS.

Forte }
Mezzo } Great Organ.
Piano }
Great to Pedal (reversible).

NEW ORGAN IN PRESBYTERIAN CHURCH, BELLEFONTE, PA.

Built by Messrs. Hook & Hastings.

GREAT ORGAN.

Open Diapason	16	Ft.
Open Diapason	8	"
Dulciana	8	"
Salicional	8	"
Melodia	8	"
Octave	4	"
Flûte d'Amour	4	"
Twelfth	2⅔	"
Fifteenth	2	"
Mixture	III.	Rks.
Trumpet	8	Ft.

SWELL ORGAN.

Bourdon (divided)	16	Ft.
Open Diapason	8	"
Viola	8	"
Stopped Diapason	8	"
Quintadena	8	"
Flauto Traverso	4	"
Violina	4	"
Flautino	2	"
Dolce Cornet	III.	Rks.
Cornopean	8	Ft.
Oboe }		
Bassoon }		

PEDAL ORGAN.

Open Diapason	16	Ft.
Bourdon	16	"
Violoncello	8	"

Pneumatic action and water motor.

PEDAL MOVEMENTS.

Forte and Piano Combinations for Gt.
Forte and Piano Combinations for Sw.
Gt. to Ped. (reversible).

VOL. I.　　　　　MARCH, 1893.　　　　　No. II.

BACH

YEARLY SUBSCRIPTION $2.00.　　　　SINGLE COPIES 25 CTS.

THE ORGAN

DEVOTED TO

A MONTHLY JOURNAL

THE KING OF INSTRUMENTS

EVERETT·E·TRUETTE·
EDITOR & PUBLISHER
149 A. TREMONT ST. BOSTON.

HANDEL

THE ORGAN.

Vol. I.　　　　　　　　BOSTON, MARCH, 1893.　　　　　　　　No. 11.

THE ORGAN.

A MONTHLY JOURNAL

DEVOTED TO THE KING OF INSTRUMENTS.

EVERETT E. TRUETTE, EDITOR AND PUBLISHER.

(Entered at the Boston, Mass., Post-office as second-class mail matter, June 1, 1892.)

CONTENTS:

FRIEDRICH KUHMSTEDT.

BY HORATIO CLARKE.

THE spirits of departed men live in the writings which they leave. As the leaf of the geranium plant gives forth a more abundant fragrance when it is bruised, so from the afflicted lives of some talented men, their sufferings and disappointments bring forth higher and more refined ideas, which take form in their literary and musical utterances.

Among many compilations for the organ may be found short extracts from the writings of Friedrich Kühmstedt, which never fail to find a lodgement in the hearts of players who love those tender and serene sentiments which are expressed in his compositions. His thoughts are more than usually melodious, with harmonies of great depth and variety.

He was born in Oldisleben, Saxe-Weimar, Dec. 20, 1809. His rare musical talent was manifested at an early age, but his parents opposed its development, and strove to dissuade him from following a professional life. But their resistance was in vain, as he could not live without using the means at his command in cultivating that art in which his spirit lived.

With the resistance which surrounded him in his home, he struggled through his years of boyhood and youth, in cultivating himself in the fundamental principles of musical theory, and in the practice of technical work, to fit himself to become a master of the organ. In his ardent studies he so over-

tasked the delicate nerves and muscles, of his hands, — not an unusual mistake with young enthusiasts, — that insidiously the seeds of much future trial were sown.

He became a diligent student at the University of Weimar, from which he was graduated in 1828. At this time, at the age of nineteen, he was so poor that he went on foot one hundred and fifty miles to Darmstadt to obtain the advice of the great organist, C. H. Rinck, who was then at the height of his fame as a teacher, player, and composer. The good organist so appreciated the gifted young man, that he kept him as his choicest pupil for three years in the theoretical and practical department of organ music, with such results as his future compositions exhibit, some of them excelling those of his eminent master.

He then returned home to his parents, and devoted himself to his musical writing. But he had so overworked his muscles by his unremitting practice, that the clouds began to gather around his aspirations for future fame and prosperity. There were indications of a paralysis in his right hand, which gradually became so positive, that he could foresee the demolishing of all his ideals and hopes as an organist.

It was a deadly blow to his enthusiasm and future prospects, as he did not regain the use of his hand as a player. Notwithstanding this great misfortune, with its depressing results, he did not give up in despair, but put his energy and patience into that form which would best utilize the knowledge he had gained, by fitting himself to be a professor of the art, and as a composer.

He was now twenty-two years of age, and for five weary years he suffered the privations of poverty to such an extent that he could with difficulty obtain the means for daily subsistence. Yet he struggled on with perseverance, until a glimmering of light began to dawn, for in 1836 he was called to the position of director and professor of music in the Seminary at Eisenach, the ancestral home of the great Bach family. Although the salary amounted to but $150 per year, it was a fortune to him after such indigence.

But a more severe blow was about to befall him. Having obtained a permanent position, he was now ready to marry the one of his choice, and looked forward to a happy home-life. They were married in the church, and as they left its portal his joyous bride, overcome with emotion, fell dead from a heart-stroke, and he was left to mourn in the deepest grief. After months of sorrowing distress he began to seek consolation in musical composition, and his thoughts were expressed in oratorios, operas, orchestral symphonies, and many pieces for the organ.

His oratorio, "The Transfiguration," with German text, was published with full orchestral score in Leipzig. His operas and symphonies are not to be obtained, but his voluminous organ sonatas, preludes, postludes, fugues, and fantasies are accessible to all organists. His "Fantasia Eroica," Op. 29, for the organ, is one of the grandest compositions ever published for the instrument. It is in F minor, and in its variety, contrasts, fugal form, and harmonic progressions, may well take its place as one of the most classical of organ compositions, requiring talents of the highest order for its rendition. It seems to hold in its environs a noble spirit struggling to assert itself in the stately form of organ music.

In his later years Kühmstedt became famous as a teacher, and published excellent treatises on musical science. But when the circumstances became such that the burden of his life was made easier, and the fruits of his incessant efforts through unusual difficulties began to give the encouragement of prosperity, the time had come for him to go the inevitable way of all humanity, and at the age of 50, while industriously engaged in the full activity of his profession, he died at Eisenach, Jan. 10, 1858.

A study of his organ works will fill the mind of the player with gems of exquisite beauty, in which the suffering spirit of the modest but noble Kühmstedt will be felt. Let the talented students who meet with discouragements in their musical progress, and who by pain and sickness are held back in their attainments, learn that others before them have suffered; for the motto, "Through Difficulties to Triumph," is one of the laws of success in all the departments of life.

THE LAW OF STRAINS.

MUSICAL people and concert-givers are complaining of great difficulties in obtaining a pianist to accompany them, and say that a good, reliable player is as hard to find as that rara avis,—an accomplished general housework girl. This is a sad condition of affairs, indeed; especially so when conservatories of music, not to mention numberless local piano teachers, turn out "players" by the hundreds every year. Something must be rotten in Denmark. A "good accompanist" is invaluable; but it seems the average pianolin despises this art of playing accompaniments, and consequently the field is occupied by a very few, who are always in demand. In their wild desire to rush to the top people sometimes miss a pretty fair thing at the bottom.—"*Entre Nous*" *in Boston Herald.*

PLAYERS of this sort are, by virtue of the turning-out process, made to their own order, and, unfortunately, in compliance with a growing and imperative demand. Accompanists are born, and grow in grace in harmony with their opportunities: they supply a demand no less imperative, but exceedingly rare. Between the two classes there may be — indeed, there often is — a gulf as wide as the world, as deep as the sea. To properly fulfil his mission the accompanist must be of the stuff of which poets are made; the ordinary player may be neither, and yet afford a certain charm to a much ruder sense; and as such indifferent sense is that which prevails almost universally, the necessity for the existence of somebody or something which can gratify it is readily manifest. For the skilled accompanist neither apology nor explanation is necessary.

The turned-out player is unconscious of the subtile instinct which inspires the fingers of the true accompanist, regarding his efforts as so much wasted energy which might be utilized in solo effects, and the position he occupies before the public as a sacrifice; but many an artist will cheerfully concede divided honors with the modest individual who sits at the keyboard, anticipating, supporting, encouraging, the singer at the footlights; constant to every emotion, every inspiration, as is a shadow to its substance.

The accompanist is not a contestant for footlight laurels; his work is a reward unto itself, for it is the one duty in which the true musician may be conscious of artistic merit without paying the penalty of egotism.

In a less secular way the organist who may be fortunate enough in his professional surroundings to be screened from view, if he be of gentle mould and subject to inspiration such as the mere player never knows, illustrates more fully the self-negation which real music makes possible in a real musician; and his instrument, the place and the occasion, may lift him into the realm where waking dreams are made, his only connection with earthly things being through the command of the rubric, "Here shall be said, or sung," etc.

Happy mortal, if he possesses a little of the player's practicality, and gets back to earth in time to take up the interrupted thread of the service! but the memory of that flight is, perhaps, an inspiration worth a decade of hand-worship over the footlights, and his reward is always with him.

But there are players and players *toujours*. If they have not by heredity the true poetical inspiration that lifts music above commonplace considerations, it cannot be acquired by Jenner's method. Musical instinct exists by first intention, or not at all; and the result in so many, many cases is just what is lamented, *entre nous*, in the *Herald*.

The "pianokin," however, is blissfully unconscious of his incompleteness, and in most cases will so continue, his cousin, the organokin, his most opportune re-enforcement. Together they will sweetly play, and perhaps as sweetly sing; for all things are possible to the naturally obtuse, believing that they are bound for the land of (the musical) Canaan.

Unto the end will they so remain; and the end will never come.

There is a written law, declaring a limit to strain upon all animate and inanimate things. Does the mission of the "pianokin" indicate a limit to the law, or that his victims have conquered even Death?   EDWIN A. TILTON.

THE HOPE-JONES SYSTEM OF ELECTRICAL ORGAN CONTROL.

CONSIDERABLE stir has been made in the English organ world by the introduction of what is known as the "Hope-Jones System" of electrical organ control; and as arrangements have been made by the inventor and Mr. W. J. Clemson of Taunton, Mass., to patent and introduce the system in the United States, we propose to place before our readers a series of short illustrated articles on this plan of organ control. The matter will be treated more from the organist's than the organ builder's point of view, yet care will be taken that the reader has the opportunity of becoming acquainted with the leading features of the mechanism employed.

In this country applications of electricity to the control of organs have been more numerous than in England, yet all the world over it seems that electricity is generally only applied to very large organs, and to such instruments as are awkwardly situated and consequently difficult to control by other means.

The Hope-Jones System was designed in the interest of the organist, not of the organ-builder. Its primary object is to give the performer better and more ready control of his instrument, whether great or small, but it is at the same time evident, from the large number of English firms that have taken out licenses to manufacture under the patents, that it befriends the organ-builder also. Before proceeding to details it may be well to give a few general remarks upon the main features of the system.

The "action" of the organ is pneumatic; but as this pneumatic is of a small and improved form, and is placed right up against the work it has to perform, its movement is more rapid than that of the human finger. The only part which electricity has to play is to control the pneumatic action, and this is accomplished by means of the movement, through a space scarcely greater than the thousandth part of an inch, of an armature valve which weighs but the sixtieth part of an ounce. In other electric systems dynamos or large batteries have been used, but in that we are treating of the current consumed is so small that a single Lechlanche cell will furnish sufficient current for a large organ.

The various registers are governed, not by the usual drawknobs, but by an additional set of tumbler keys, called "stopkeys." The pneumatics for controlling the sliders or vents are like those for controlling the pallets, of an unusual form, and insure a rapidity of action which is startling. The keys and pedals are fitted with a "double touch," and the power of drawing stops on either the first or second touch is conferred upon the performer. An electric switch transposes the music played into any desired key. Automatic electrical resistance balances control the pedal stops at will, and confer upon the performer the power of instantly obtaining a bass which automatically suits itself to the power and tone of the manual stops in use. The console (which in the largest instrument does not measure more than 3'8" x 3'0" x 3'6") is placed on casters and is movable, being connected with the organ by means of a flexible cable of wires about an inch in diameter. Beyond the electro-pneumatic levers, the keys, and the composition touches, nothing that can be called "mechanism" is made use of. Coupling and all other combinational effects are obtained electrically at small cost.

(To be continued.)

NOTABLE ORGANS.
VII.
KING'S COLLEGE, CAMBRIDGE, ENGLAND.

THE old organ in King's College, Cambridge, England, only the front of which remains to-day, was built by one of the Dallams in the early part of the seventeenth century. The instrument was built on the spot, the whole of the materials being brought in the rough. Its construction occupied more than a year; meanwhile the builder and his men boarded at the College Hall. The instrument was rebuilt in 1804 by Avery, and later it was again reconstructed by Hill.

CORRESPONDENCE.
AN IDEAL ORGAN.

To the Editor of THE ORGAN :

SIR, — By a curious coincidence the answer to M. C.'s invitation to define the above term seems to be implied by two independent writers in the same issue of your paper. First, in the able letter of Gambette, which I entirely indorse; and secondly, by Mr. O. S. Richards, under the heading of "Organ Arrangements."

Let me deal with the latter first, as needing the briefer comment.

Mr. Richards argues against the general adoption of organ arrangements, orchestral and operatic, on the ground that they are incompatible "*with the prescribed, conventional, arbitrary constitution of the organ ; for these transcriptions demand of the organ the saying of things which, on account of its make-up, it cannot say.*"

Quite so, and the argument is sound, — as far as it goes. But why not break up this "*prescribed, conventional, arbitrary constitution*"? Why be any longer tied down to the lines of an organ of 1593, as adopted here, not nearly so fine as the really grand organ of Lubeck of that date, when the splendid European achievements of 1893 and their outcome are within reach, if the demand be made? Why be satisfied with an instrument wholly unfitted for the expression of the largest portion of music written, the most exquisite portion being excluded, when the remedy is at hand?

And here "Gambette" exactly probes the sore. His letter is a plain statement of facts, to be read, marked, and learned.

Organ-building here is simply a trade, with the absence of the recommendation of many other trades which young men enter and learn. It is entirely embraced in the knowledge of how to make a bellows, a soundboard, and perhaps I ought to add a bellows' handle ; and in the voicing-room by the universal use of that most baneful but useful of all instruments to imbeciles, — the proportional dividers! As "Gambette" says, with no exaggeration, "*For the voicing of the instrument no special education is demanded.*" If to this we add the mechanical acquirement of an old-fashioned bell-hanger, with his wires and square, we have the entire qualification needed by the organ-builder of to-day, so far as trade is concerned ; for, to quote Gambette once more, "Did any one ever hear of a young man studying to be an organ-builder?"

"The ideal organ," very much in the future, must be one to meet Mr. Richards's needs as a player, — and the requirement of art, from Gambette's view. We get a glimpse of it, and hope for a nearer inspection. I am with both these men ; but I must go a little farther, and say that it is possible to regard all the conditions to which they refer, and yet meet the requirement of trade produce in remunerative return. Competition is healthful and favorable to produce, quite as much in lines of art as otherwise ; and there is such an abundant field open to men who possess the necessary qualification for such competition in organ construction, that there need be no doubt of results in the contest, even on the same platform of prices which are generally recognized. Indeed, more than this, I believe the return would be handsome, and a monopoly of the best work which the trade could seek certain. Where are the competitors which could touch, at double the prices now at command, such an ideal organ as "Gambette" and Mr. Richards and hosts of other men would welcome? And the whole reason is, that professional men all find the study of the organ unremunerative ; they must needs be content with the best which the trade can supply. The trade itself, unlike the piano-trade, can very seldom boast a player who can do more than play a hymn tune! There is therefore no conception of anything better, and so the old and worn-out model is repeated here, there, and everywhere. Even the players rebel, for it means a new study, if some slight innovation is introduced by the organ-builder, which implies extraordinary use!

(Continued on page 257.)

THE ORGAN.

BOSTON, MARCH, 1893.

THE ORGAN is published the first of every month. Subscription price $1.00 per year (European countries 10s. 5d.), payable in advance. Single copies, 25 cents.

Subscribers will please state with which number they wish their subscription to begin.

Subscribers wishing the address of their paper changed must give the old as well as the new address.

Remittances should be made by registered letter, post-office order, or by check payable to Everett E. Truette.

Correspondence, to secure notice, must in all cases be accompanied by the name and address of the writer, not for publication, but as a guarantee of good faith.

Advertising rates sent on application.

Address all communications,

The Organ, 149 A Tremont Street, Boston, Mass.

☞ An active agent in every city is desired to whom a liberal cash commission will be allowed.

ON a recent visit to the Church of the Advent, while examining the new organ, one of the "wee small" choir-boys, who was *perhaps* fond of organ music, but evidently more attracted by pedal gymnastics, ran up to the organist with, "O Mr. Whitney, do play that piece which you play mostly with your feet."

NOW comes a Western paper containing a "notice" of an organ concert which might have been written by a professor of Greek, or by a bootblack, but by a musician conversant with his subject — NEVER! We quote just one sentence. The organ "is furnished with the pneumatic knobs, a device by which the full power of the instrument is brought out without the use of stops." He might have added, warranted not to whine, whistle, or whittle in public.

IT becomes necessary for us to remind some of our readers that THE ORGAN is devoted exclusively to "the king of instruments." We have neither the space nor the inclination to notice the numerous compositions and programmes which have not the remotest connection with our department, and which are sent to us by the dozen. It is obvious that programmes of piano recitals, vocal recitals, dog-shows, and prize-fights are out of place in our columns; and while we find just as much enjoyment in a good piano recital as in an organ concert, we are compelled to "pass them by with never a word."

WHILE sitting in the editorial sanctum, scratching our pate for something funny for a cipher, the door slowly opened and a maiden of uncertain age (she might have been fifteen, and, alas! might have been fifty) timidly walked in. The editor looked at her and she looked at the editor, and after she had cast a careful glance around the room, taking in the cuts and pictures of numerous organs, the odd pipes, etc., she responded to an inquiring look of the editor with, "Can I obtain vocal lessons here?" After the first shock we took pity on her apparent lack of a proper amount of perceptive protoplasm, and remarked gently that we treated pipe organs, not vocal organs. To her gentle "Oh!" we ventured the inquiry, "What vocal teacher are you seeking?" We were floored when she replied, "I do not know." We mildly suggested that possibly Signor Lucinowkowsky, two doors south, could attend to her case. With a smile and, "Oh, yes!" she departed. We breathed a sigh of relief and went out to lunch.

IT is a great pity that the resident organists of this city — the once-upon-a-time reputed Hub of the Universe, and even to-day boasting as one of the most musical cities in the country — evince so little interest in the growth of organ concerts in their midst. There was a time, not long ago, when the leading organists of the city vied with one another in giving one or more organ concerts each season. While the free concerts were well attended, and those which required a paid admission received but a little support, the interest in organ music was steadily rising, and in the horizon could be seen the future popularity of this class of music; but, alas! "in the twinkling of an eye" every one of the organists discontinued his series of concerts, and we have only a stray organ concert now and then, when some organist rises from his lethargy to show his friends that he still plays the organ. In New York this state of things is unknown, for, during "the season," that metropolis can boast of more organ concerts in any one week than we have in fifty-two weeks.

We hope that Mr. Horatio Parker, who leaves New York for "the Hub" the first of May, will bring with him a little of his reputed enthusiasm for organ concerts, and help to start the ball rolling again in this city. There is no reason why, with such organists as Whiting, Dunham, Whitney, Swan, Hale, and a half-dozen others, we should not have a "season of organ concerts" comparing favorably with New York, Chicago, and other cities.

CIPHERINGS.

THE rector of a country parish in Texas, who was revising his sermon on Sunday morning, was waited upon in his study by his organist, who asked what he should play. "I don't know," said the rector absent-mindedly; "what kind of a hand have you got?" — *The Indicator.*

* * *

It is the organist's fault that the church-goers are often played out. Don't lay everything to the preacher. — *The Magic Flute.*

* * *

A dead frog was found in a church organ in Georgia. It is supposed that the creature was frightened to death by a choir rehearsal. — *Musical Record.*

* * *

—"So Jack is married, eh? Do you think he'll get along well with his wife?"

"I am quite sure he will. They sang in the same choir for two years without quarrelling." —*Chatter.*

* * *

The new Pipe Organ Factory of Messrs. Smith & Kinsley of Reading, Mass., was badly damaged by fire a short time since. A kerosene lamp was accidentally knocked down. It exploded, setting fire to a large amount of combustible material which was near by. The building was badly gutted. We understand that the loss is fully covered by insurance.

OFFERTOIRE.

Andantino Moderato.

TH. DUBOIS.

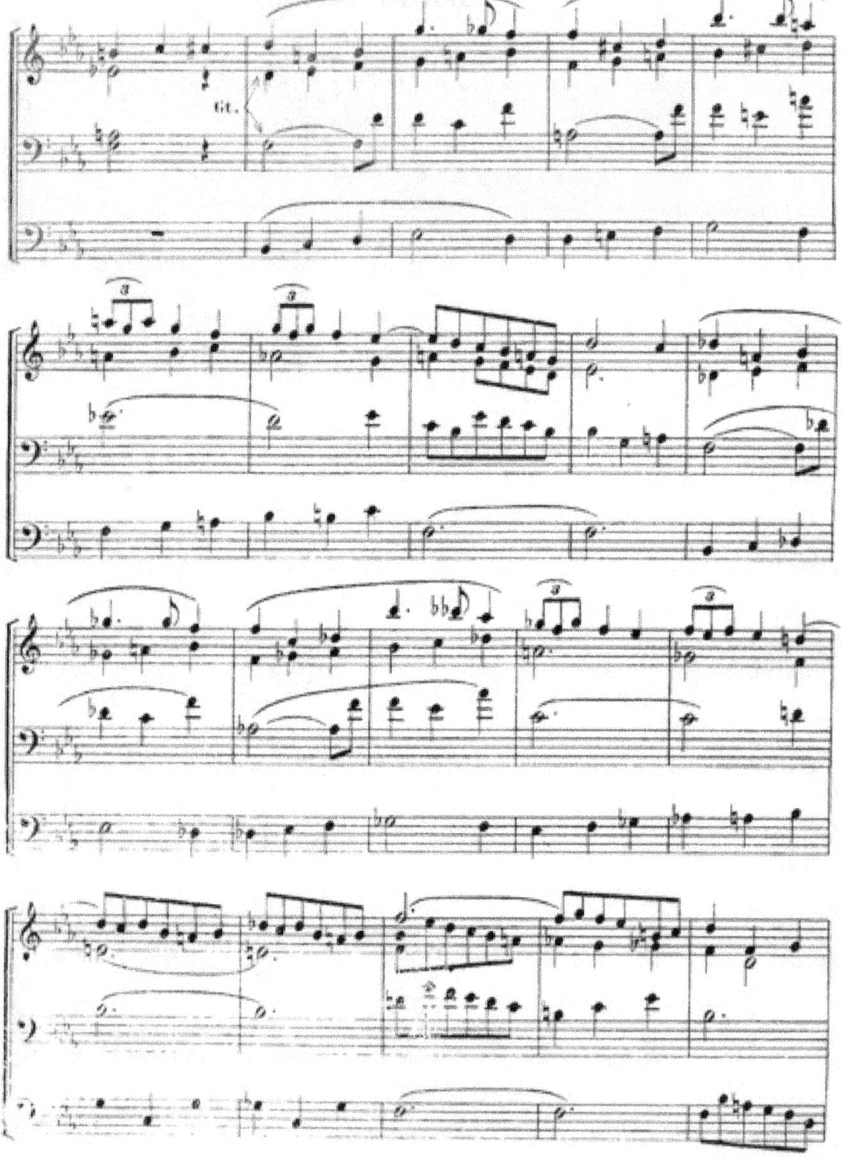
Gt.

Gt.
Op. Diap. in Gt.
Sw. with Oboe.
Gt.
Add Octave.
Ch.
Sw. Oboe off.
(Op. Diap. off.)

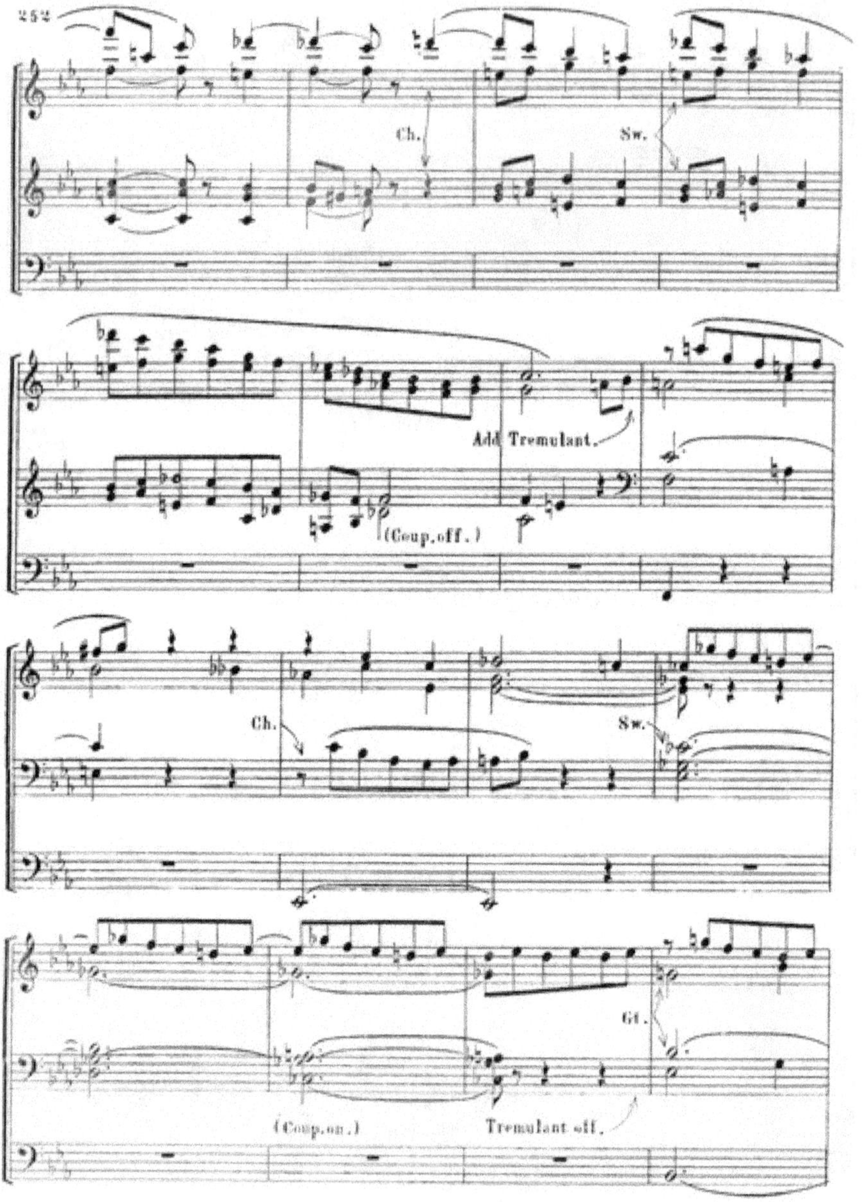
Ch.
Sw.
Add Tremulant.
(Coup.off.)
Ch.
Sw.
Gt.
(Coup.on.)
Tremulant off.

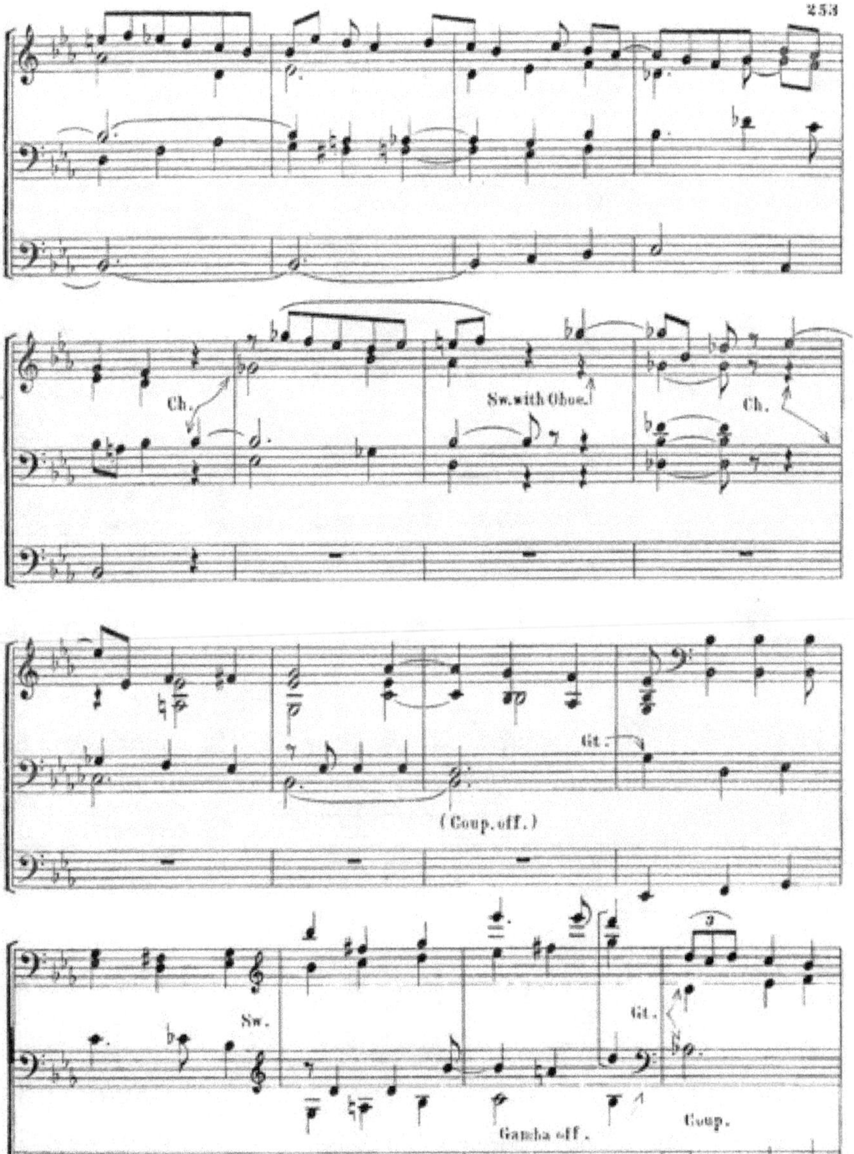
Ch.
Sw. with Oboe.
Ch.
Gt.
(Coup. off.)
Sw.
Gt.
Gamba off.
Coup.

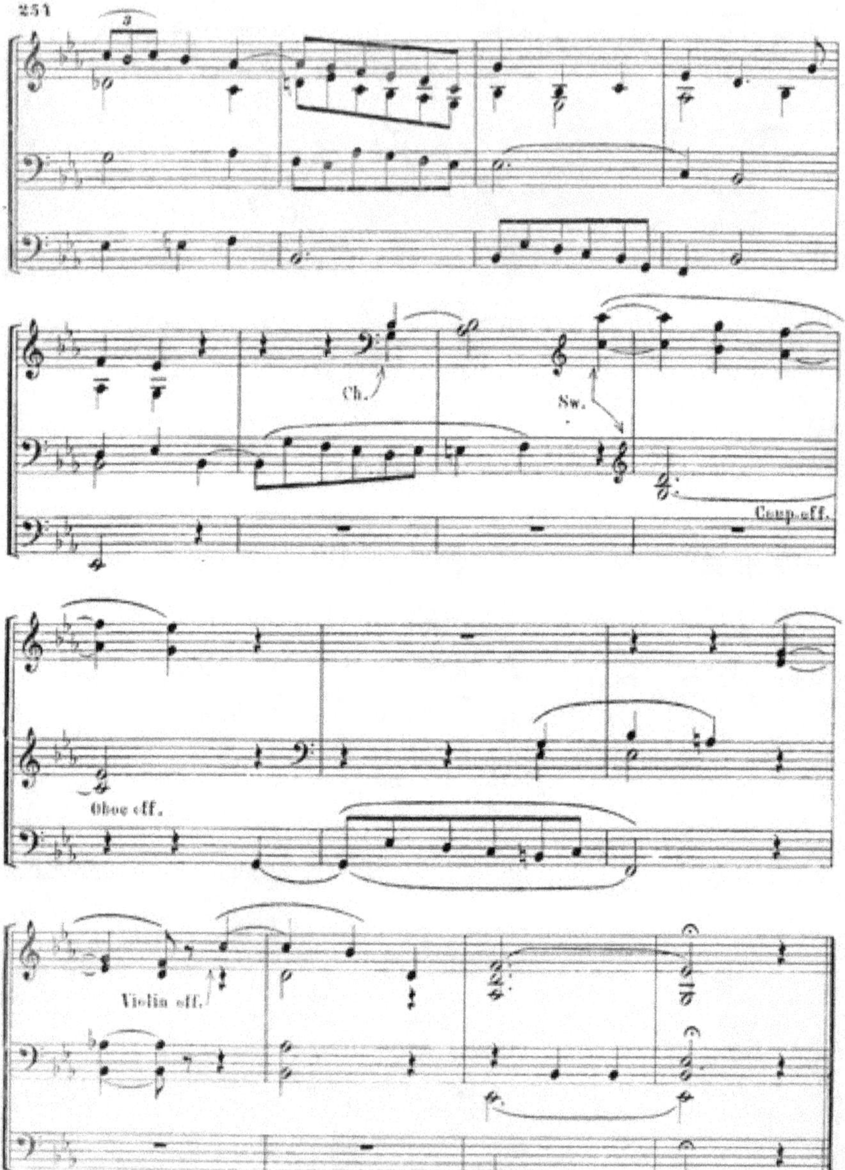
Ch.
Sw.
Coup. off.
Oboe off.
Violin off.

ADORATION.

Andante Sostenuto.   *J. LEMMENS.*

Gt. Doppel Flöte or
Melodia.

Sw. Oboe, St. Diap.
& Salicional.

Ped Bourdon, Sw. to
Gt., Gt.& Sw. to Ped.

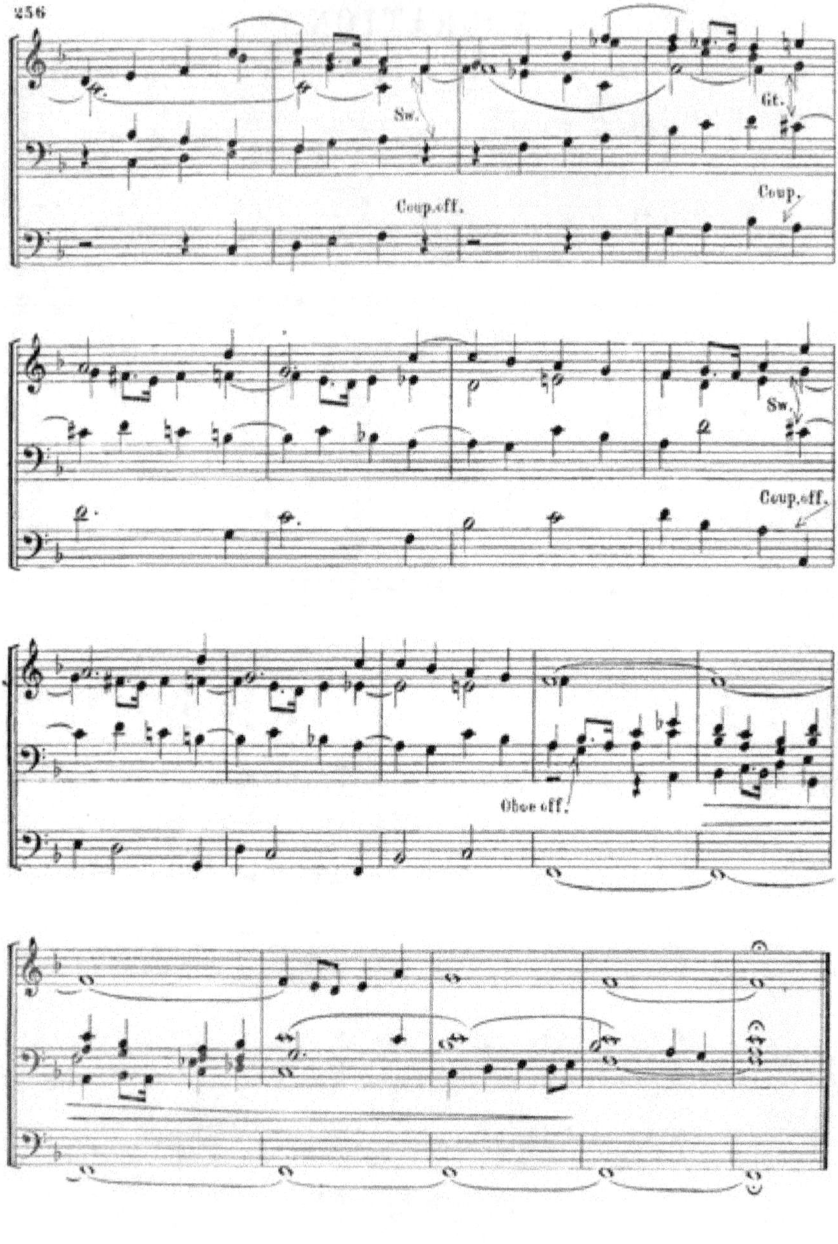
Sw.
Gt.
Coup.off.
Coup.
Sw.
Coup.off.
Oboe off.

CORRESPONDENCE.

(Continued from page 241.)

It is impossible to hold long to an unaltering course, — no matter what the line may be, for we see it in nature and in everything, — without ultimate deterioration; and "Gambette's" complaint of this deterioration in organ-building is quite consistent with the following : —

Some eighteen months ago I was called upon to remove to another position and to revoice an organ in South Boston. The instrument was forty years old. To my surprise I found this organ in correct scaling, throughout, in all the super-work, differing in this respect entirely from the modern organs of the same builder.

A foreman in a metal-shop (to the uninitiated I may say the "metal-pipe shop") finds it easier to get his trebles made neatly if they are large ; so he alters his scale in all his small work to suit the exigencies of the case, and his boss is none the wiser. This probably takes place either in trade supply, or in some large organ factory where the trade demands and can pay its own metal-men.

This one starts in business with such knowledge as Gambette and I have defined ; he gets his metal pipes from the same source. Another leaves the big firm to set up on his own account, and, worldly wise, he takes away with him all data likely to serve him ; in fact, he runs on lines professed to be identical with the great firm which employed him : he has absolutely no other idea ; he has no conception of anything beyond the income of so many more dollars. He too perpetuates the error, and in time he starts his own metal-shop, and then he introduces further monstrosities and further deterioration, to be again followed by some one who leaves him to take a similar course. That is the history of the trade all over the States. It is therefore this trodden, worn-out path which needs to be left, before any healthful results can accrue.

I wonder how many professional men and amateurs of influence will stand by and support such an enterprise, supposing they can bring the thing done on thoroughly artistic lines and sound commercial basis — in fact, put theory into practice. Yours,

CARLTON MICHELL.

1 BATAVIA STREET, BOSTON, Feb. 9, 1893.

P. S. By the way, "Willis" in his letter in your last issue is in error in speaking of the "longtrackers running under the floor" in the divided organs of Westminster Abbey and St Paul's Cathedral, Eng. There is not a tracker or square in either instrument.

PROPORTIONATE SCALES OF ORGAN PIPES.

To the Editor of THE ORGAN :

ONE of your former numbers contained an account of articles adopted at a meeting of Connecticut organists, concerning the establishing of certain principles of detail as a standard in organ construction ; such as the relative positions of manuals and pedals, register-knobs, etc.

When such a standard shall be adopted by organists and builders, it may not be out of place to suggest that a Standard of Proportionate Scales of Pipes shall also be adopted. This is a subject upon which many organists are not well informed, which is of vital importance in the tone-quality of the organ.

The selection of scales is usually left to the builder, and the builders do not agree with each other on this point. Yet an organist should be so thoroughly educated in the structure and voicing of pipes, that when an organ is to be built for his use, he should have a dominating voice in the matter, and, by judicious conference with the builder, have heed given to his suggestions. To this end an organist should study the scales as a necessary part of his theoretical education, so that his opinion may have weight with the builder, who frequently is not a practical musician himself.

All things considered in regard to wind pressure and power, in the voicing of organ pipes, the peculiar character-istic of each set of organ pipes used depends upon the scale ; for in the voicing of a pipe no desired quality of tone can be produced beyond its scale limitations.

Having decided upon the scale of the Open Diapason as a standard as to whether the middle C pipe shall have a diameter of 2 1-2 or 2 1-4 inches, according to the scale lines, then every other metal stop should have a proportionate relation to the scale of the Open Diapason. Instead of any further suggestion in this article, I would like to have an expression through your columns from other organists and builders concerning this important subject, in order that a standard may be attained. OPEN DIAPASON.

MIXTURES.

(FOUR RANKS.)

Dr. J. Albert Jeffery has resigned his position as organist of All Saints' Cathedral, Albany, and will be succeeded by Mr. J. Benton Tipton.

The organ in the Hereford (England) Cathedral, originally built by Renatus Harris in 1686, has been remodelled and is now quite a modern organ.

The death is announced of Mr. Charles Wilberforce, who was organist of St. Anthony's Chapel, Liverpool, for thirty years. He was seventy-six years of age.

Carl August Fischer, a noted organist and composer of Dresden, died Dec. 25, at the age of sixty-four.

Messrs. Hinners & Albertsen have placed a two-manual organ of thirteen speaking-stops in Grace Church, Peoria, Ill.

Mons. Dubois, father of Mons. Th. Dubois the organist, died the last of January, at the age of ninety.

Mr. J. K. Strachan has been giving weekly organ concerts in St. Andrew's Hall, Glasgow.

The P. E. Hospital Chapel, Philadelphia, have had their organ of twenty-two registers reconstructed by Mr. Geo. S. Hutchings.

An effort is being made by the London College of Organists to obtain a Royal Charter of Incorporation.

Dr. W. H. Longhurst entered the Canterbury (England) cathedral as a chorister ninety-two years ago, and is still the organist of that Cathedral.

Messrs. Hook & Hastings have just finished an organ for the Baptist Church of Selma, Ala., which has two manuals and twenty-six registers. The organ is blown by a water-motor.

The organ in the Manchester (England) Town Hall is undergoing extensive alterations.

NEW ORGAN MUSIC.

Fantasia Triomphale (for organ and orchestra)	Th. Dubois.
Toccata and Fugue, Op. 104	G. Flügel.
Five Chorales, Op. 19	C. Piutti.
Fest Hymnus	C. Piutti.
In Memoriam (Pastorale and Fugue on G-A-D-E)	C. Piutti.

Mr. Edward Sims, who was for fifty-seven years organist of St. Michael's Church, Coventry, England, died recently at the age of ninety-three.

Mr. Walter C. Gale gave an organ recital Feb. 8, on the new Roosevelt organ in the hall of the Mendelssohn Glee Club, New York.

An organ having two manuals and twenty-four registers has just been shipped from the factory of Messrs. Hook & Hastings to Zion P. E. Church of Rome, N.Y. The instrument will be blown by a water-motor.

The vicar of Christ Church, Bath, England, in trying to bring about a better observance of Sunday, has a monthly organ recital, given by the organist, Mr. H. J. Davis.

A new organ erected by Mons. Cavaillé-Coll, for Cardinal Langénieux, Archduke of Reims, France, was inaugurated by Mons. Jules Gilson, organist of the Reims Cathedral, Mons. Dubout, and Mons. Floquet, organist of Rouen, who performed works of Guilmant, Dubois, Dietsch, Keene, and Prison.

A Memorial Organ is to be placed in Christ Church, Brooklyn, Mrs. Margaret B. Elson having given $6,000 for that purpose.

Mr. Sebastian Sommer will celebrate the twenty-fifth anniversary of his connection with the Evangelical Lutheran Church, New York, on Easter next.

The following officers have been elected by the stockholders of the Farrand & Votey Organ Company of Detroit : E. H. Flinn, President; A. E. F. White, Vice-President; E. S. Votey, Secretary ; W. R. Farrand, Treasurer. All the above, with F. A. Robinson, constitute the Board of Directors.

While in Glasgow this winter Mons. Guilmant performed, with orchestra, his Symphony in D-minor, for organ and orchestra, also a transcription of the Symphony in Bach's 29th Cantata.

The Liverpool City Council have at last permitted fortnightly orchestral concerts in St. George's Hall to be given on Sunday afternoons, alternating with Mr. Best's organ recitals.

Mons. Eugene Gigout, the French organist, will give a series of recitals in London next April.

Mr. Geo. S. Hutchings has recently rebuilt the organ in the Church of St. John the Baptist, New Bedford, Mass.

Mr. Frederick W. Bridgman, for some years organist of the United Presbyterian Church, Edinburgh, died Dec. 28, at the age of fifty-nine.

Mr. J. J. Miller gave his eighteenth organ concert at Christ Church, Norfolk, Va., Feb. 6, with the following programme: Toccata in D-minor, Bach; Benediction Nuptiale, Saint-Saens; Storm Fantasia, Lemmens; March and Chorus ("Tannhäuser"), Wagner. The Norfolk papers speak of the growing interest in these recitals, which draw a larger audience at each recital.

Mrs. Laura Beck, for fourteen years organist of the First Baptist Church, Medford, Mass., died of pneumonia Feb. 12, at the age of forty-five.

Mr. Fred L. Clark gave his fourteenth organ concert at Payson Church, Easthampton, Mass., Feb. 28, with the following programme: Prelude and Fugue in C, Bach; Pastorale, Op. 103, Merkel; Wedding Hymn, Selson; Sanctus, from Messe Solennelle, Gounod; Adagio in D, Drexel; Scherzo, Capocci; Marche Cortège, Gounod.

Mr. Harrison M. Wild gave his one hundred and twenty-third concert in Unity Church, Chicago, Feb. 12, performing the following organ works: "Wer nur den lieben Gott lasst walten," Hesse; Sonata, Op. 23, Tombelle; Consolation, Funeral March and Folk Song, Mendelssohn; and Overture, "La Dame Blanche," Boieldieu.

Mr. George A. Kies gave an organ concert in Park Church, Norwich, Conn., Jan. 28, with the following programme: Fugue in D, Bach; Allegro, Op. 18, No. 2, and Invocation, Guilmant; Sonata Pontificale, Lemmens; Variations on Russian National Air, Freyer; The Lake, Spark; and Overture to Athalie, Mendelssohn.

Mr. Will C. Macfarlane gave two organ concerts on Feb. 6 and 13 in All Soul's Church, New York. The programme of the second concert was as follows: Concert Satz in C-minor, Thiele; Meditation, Grison; Allegro in C, Wood; Symphony, No. 2, Widor; Overture, Nocturne, Scherzo, and March, "Midsummer Night's Dream," Mendelssohn.

Mr. W. H. Donley gave an organ recital in Christian Church, Franklin, Ind., Jan. 26, playing among other things Overture to "The Merry Wives of Windsor," Nicolai; "Jerusalem the Golden," with Variations, Spark; Selections from "Rienzi," Wagner; and Variations on a Scotch Air, Buck.

The programme of Mr. Harrison M. Wild's one hundred and twenty-fourth concert in Unity Church, Chicago, contained the following numbers: Prelude and Fugue in C, Bach; Second Concerto, Handel; Andante in F, Wely; A Twilight Picture, Shelley; Variations on "God Save the King," Hesse; and Slavonic Dance, Op. 152, No. 2, Vilhar.

Mr. Allen W. Swan gave his third organ concert in the Unitarian Church, New Bedford, Mass., Feb. 12, with the following programme: War March of Priests, Mendelssohn; Cujus Animam, Rossini; Prelude and Fugue in G, Bach; Bridal Song, Goldmark; Gavotte, Lacc; Andante Con Moto, Chauvet; Serenade in G, Widor; Funeral March, Best; Concert Piece in G, Guilmant.

Mr. W. H. Donley gave his fifth organ concert in Plymouth Church, Indianapolis, Feb. 11, performing the following: Sonata in D-minor, Van Eyken; Adagio from Symphony No. 2, Haydn; Scherzo Pastorale, Grieg; Reverie du Soir, Saint-Saens; Marche Funèbre, Guilmant; Gavotte, Popper; Pièce Symphonique, Grieg; Berceuse, Kullerath; and Overture to "Pique Dame," Suppé.

At a Presbyterian Church in North Britain the younger members, desiring to move with the times, started a movement for an organ.

After much opposition from their seniors they carried their point, and an organ was duly installed in the church. Soon after the formal opening of the instrument, one of the young men who initiated the movement overtook a neotiltzznat "elder" on the street, and asked, "Well, elder, what do you think of the organ?"

The elder replied cautiously, "Man, I'm afeared I'm given to like it."

Mr. Henry A. Reed inaugurated a new Hutchings organ (gift of Mrs. S. A. Hall) in the Methodist Church, Greenland, N.H., Feb. 5, with the following programme: Offertoire de St. Cecilia, Batiste; Lullaby, Vogt; Grand March, Wagner; Processional, Batiste; Prayer and Cradle Song, Guilmant; Gavotte, Mignon, Thomas; and Fantare, Lemmens.

Diplomas of fellowship have been awarded by the London College of Organists to Messrs. Edwin A. Crndin, Ernest Dale, Herbert Hodge, Percy D. Hodwell, John Holgate, Frederick W. Holloway, Arthur E. Jones, Thomas Keighley, Mus. Bac., Charles J. May, Miss Edith Jane Parker, Messrs. Charles Seel, Mus. Bac., Cardinal Taylor, H. William Tupper, and Thomas J. Wondill.

Mr. Harrison M. Wild inaugurated a new organ in Grace Church, Peoria, Ill., Feb. 14, performing the following compositions: Sonata, Op. 42, (two movements), Guilmant; Hallelujah Chorus, Handel; Wedding March, Mendelssohn; Nocturne, Op. 6, No. 2, Chopin; Concert Variation on "Old Folks at Home," Flagler; Funeral March, Chopin; Offertoire de St. Cecilia, Batiste; "Home Sweet Home," Buck; Mignon, Gavotte, Thomas; Overture to "Poet and Peasant," Suppé; Overture to "Wm. Tell," Rossini.

Mr. W. T. Best has been confined in the house for a month or more with a painful attack of the gout, which disease, it will be remembered, deprived us of a visit from the celebrated organist on his return from Australia a couple of years ago. It was then his intention to return to England by the way of the States, visiting several of the larger cities. We still have hope that he will be heard in this country before long. There is a rumor that he will perform in the Columbian Exposition during the coming summer.

Mr. W. J. D. Leavitt, at one time a prominent concert organist in Boston, died after a brief illness Jan. 29. He was born June 28, 1841; studied at home and abroad, and from 1865 to 1870 was principal of a conservatory in Oneida, N.Y. He returned to Boston, and was closely connected with the fame of the then noted Boston Music Hall organ. He composed an oratorio, several cantatas and operettas, as well as an opera and one or two pieces for orchestra. His writings for the organ included a sonata, several marches and fantasies.

A musical enthusiast who excels in playing the violin once undertook to play the organ at a large parish church at a service. After going on smoothly for a while, he began to think there was something short, and that it was perhaps the pedals. A friend who was with him undertook to try the pedals, and, marking the notes of a hymn down in a small diary, knelt down on the floor, and, putting his head under the seat, played the pedals with his hands. History does not relate how it sounded, but both gentlemen are quite proud of the way each played the organ, and relate the story with great glee. — *London Musical News.*

A new organ (see NEW ORGANS for specification) in St. Michael's P. E. Church, Amsterdam Ave., New York, was inaugurated Jan. 30, by Messrs. Wm. C. Carl, Ed D. Jardine, Edward G. Jardine, and Walter O. Wilkinson, with the following programme: Air in E-flat, Mozart; and Offertoire in C-minor, Hainworth (Mr. Wilkinson); Prelude and Fugue in D, Bach (Mr. Carl); First Movement of Fourth Concerto, Handel (Mr. E. D. Jardine); Air from "Jerusalem," Pierson; and Russian Hymn varied, Thayer (Mr. Wilkinson); Allegro and Aria from Tenth Organ Concerto, Handel; and Toccata, Widor (Mrs. Carl); Representation of a Thunder Storm (E. G. Jardin); La Cinquantaine, Gabriel Marie; and Marche de la Symphonie (Ariane), Guilmant (Mr. Carl).

The programme of the opening recital, inaugurating the organ in "Exhibition Concert Hall," Brisbane, Australia, has just reached us, though the recital was given Dec. 20, 1892. The programme is as follows: "God Save the Queen," Best (Mr. W. G. Willmore); Overture to "Wm. Tell," Rossini (Mr. W. G. Willmore); Barcarole (Fourth Concerto), Bennett; and Gavotte (Mignon), Thomas (Mr. S. G. Benson, R.A.M.); Concert Variations on Russian National Hymn, Freyer (Mr. Willmore); Selection from "Ivanhoe," Sullivan (Mr. Seymour Dicker); Fantasia on two English Airs, Guilmant (Mrs. Willmore); Marche Cortège, Delibes (Mr. Dicker); "La Dove," Mozart (Mr. Willmore); Toccata (V. Symphony), Widor (Mrs. Willmore); Idyl, Buck (Mr. Dicker); Orchestral Overture (?) Herman (Mr. Benson).

The new Hutchings organ in the First Methodist Church, Duluth, Minn. (see THE ORGAN for December for specification) was inaugurated February 7, 8, and 9, by three organ concerts given by Mr. J. Warren Andrews and Mr. Sidney Brown. Mr. Andrews gave the first and last concerts, his programmes containing the following works in particular: St. Ann's Fugue, Bach; Storm Fantasia, Lemmens; The Village Harvest Home, Spinney; "Old Folks at Home," with Variations, Flagler; Fifth Concerto, Handel; Grand Chœur in D, and Pastorale in A, Guilmant; Largo, Handel; and Marche Funèbre, Guilmant. Mr. Brown's principal numbers were, Inauguration March, Clark; Prelude and Fugue, Rinck; "Nearer My God to Thee," Hagen; Offertoire, Batiste; and "On the Coast," Buck.

Mr. Charles Albion Clark gave an organ concert at Tremont Temple, Boston, Jan. 31. He was assisted by Miss Sophy C. McClearn, Contralto, and Mr. W. Archibald Willis, Bass, in the following programme: Finale in E flat, Pastorale in A, and Caprice in B-flat, Guilmant; "Pro Peccatis" ("Stabat Mater"), Rossini; Toccata and Fugue in D-minor, Pastorale in F, and Aria in D, Bach; "Could I," Tosti; "An Old Song," Nevin; Communion in G, Batiste; Allegro in E-flat, Whiting; Serenade, Raff; "Fair is My Love," Horton; "Allah," Chadwick; and Postludium in C, Whiting. Mr. Clark deserves credit for his bravery in continuing to give organ concerts in the only public hall containing an organ of which "Musical Boston" (?) can boast. That his friends are always ready to assist him was proven by the generous applause which greeted every number.

The Incorporated Society of Musicians of England held its Eighth Annual Conference[1] in London, Jan. 2-6. The objects of the society are briefly: to unite in one body as many professional musicians as possible; to elevate the status of the members, and aid the musical education of the people; to promote the culture of music; to provide opportunities for friendly intercourse between the members of the society; to provide against the exigencies of age, sickness, misfortune, and death, and to publish a list of the members and accounts of the proceedings of the society. There are enrolled on its list of membership over a thousand names, including over three hundred organists, and from all reports the society is doing a great and noble work for the cause of all professional musicians in England.

---

[1] This account of this Conference was unavoidably omitted in the last issue of THE ORGAN. — Ed.

Sir Joseph Savory, M.P. (representing the mayor), delivered the address of welcome, at the Egyptian Hall, Mansion House. The annual report was read by Mr. E. Clodfield (hon. general secretary), and addresses were delivered by Sir John Stainer, Dr. A. C. Mackenzie, Principal of the Royal Academy of Music, Mr. W. H. Cummings, R.A.M. and F.S.A., Dr. Henry Hiles, F.C.O., Dr. Campbell, Dr. Merrick, Mr. E. Prout, Mr. H. W. Carte, Mr. W. S. McNaught, Mr. J. L. Roeckel, and others.

A visit was paid to several of the churches, specially to the Temple Church, where Dr. E. J. Hopkins gave a description of the organ. Sir Joseph Barnby, Dr. Chas. Vincent, and Wm. Rootham were elected chairmen for the next conference, which will be held in Bradford in Jan., 1894. We are pleased to note that THE ORGAN was among the representatives at the Conference.

Mr. William Churchill Hammond gave two organ concerts (Jan. 25 and Feb. 1) in the Second Congregational Church, Holyoke, Mass., with the following programmes: Overture to "Samson," Händel; Andante from E minor Symphony, Schubert; A Christmas Fantasia, Best; Melody, Grieg; Minuetto from Suite Arlésienne, Bizet; Marcia Villereccia Famagalli. Second Concert: Overture "Occasional," Händel; Larghetto, Op. 130, Spohr; Suite in E ("Messe de Mariage"), Dubois; Bridal Song, Goldmark; Introduction and Bridal Chorus, "Lohengrin," Wagner.

It is rumored that Mr. B. B. Gillette has resigned his position as organist of Trinity Church, Boston, and that Mr. Horatio W. Parker of Holy Trinity Church, N.Y., will be his successor.

Inaugural Concert in the Church of St. Simeon, Philadelphia, Pa., (new organ built by Messrs. Wm. King & Son) Jan. 25, by Mr. D. D. Wood, assisted by Mr. Chas. F. Lawson and the vested choir of the church, consisting of fifty men and boys, and twenty-five ladies. Andante from Symphony in A-flat, Mozart; Minuet, Mozart; Händel; "Sing Unto God," Händel; Improvisation, Wood; St. Cecilia Offertory, Batiste; Andante, Lila; Offertory, No. 6, Wely; Gloria, Mozart.

Mr. Wm. Otis Brewster inaugurated a new organ in South Park Ave. M. E. Church, Chicago, Feb. 23, playing the following compositions: Sixth Concerto, Händel; Toccata in D-minor, Bach; Chorus and March, "Tannhäuser," Wagner; Variations on a familiar Air, Brewster; Prayer in F, Guilmant; March Rakoczy, Berlioz; Improvisation; Postlude, B-flat, Wely; Overture to "Stradella," Flotow. The specification of the organ (built by Messrs. Geo. Kilger & Son, St. Louis) is as follows: Great organ: Double Open Diapason, 16 Ft.; Open Diapason, Viol di Gamba, Spitz-flöte, and Doppel-flöte, 8 Ft.; Octave and Flute Harmonique, 4 Ft.; Twelfth, Fifteenth, III. Rank Mixture, and Trumpet. Swell organ: Bourdon, 16 Ft.; Open Diapason, Salicional, Dolce, St. Diapason, and Quintadena, 8 Ft.; Violin and Flauto Traverso, 4 Ft.; Flagaolet, 2 Ft.; III. Rank Mixtures, Cornopean, Oboe, and Vox Humana. Choir organ: Geigen Principal, Dulciana, and Melodia, 8 Ft.; Flute d'Amour, 4 Ft.; and Clarinet. Pedal organ: Double Open Diapason and Bourdon, 16 Ft.; Violoncello, 8 Ft.; and Trombone, 16 Ft. Combination Pedals: Forte, Mezzo, and Piano, Great organ: Forte and Piano, Choir organ: Gt. to Ped. reversible.

Sir John Goss was conducting a rehearsal of one of his compositions, when suddenly he heard one of the tenors singing a B-flat when the rest of the choir were singing B-natural. Instantly checking the choir, he exclaimed:—

"How dare you sing that note flat? If you can actually sing a semi-tone below the choir, and not perceive it, you are the worst man I have ever had in my choir."

The tenor listened to the rebuke, and quietly remarked that in his copy the note was printed B-flat.

"Impossible!" returned Sir John.

"But it is," said the tenor.

"Bring the copy here," said the conductor.

On looking at the score he found that the tenor was right, and that a misprint had occurred. More excitement still. Sir John thus addressed the trembling tenor:—

"If you, sir, can sing B-flat against all the choir singing B-natural, simply because you have B-flat marked in your book, you are the most correct and the most wonderful singer I have ever conducted."— *The Musical Record.*

St. Paul's Church, the grandest house of worship in Milwaukee, is inhabited by ghosts; at least such is the theory of police officials, based on developments for which they say there can be no other explanation. Several times during the last two weeks the people living in the vicinity of Marshall and Knapp Streets have been awakened about midnight by the grand strains of the church organ, while the church at the same hour was in darkness. Shortly before midnight last night the people were awakened by the playing of the organ. United States Court Commissioner Bloodgood, who lives opposite the church, telephoned to Rev. Chas. Stanley of the strange occurrence then going on, and the latter summoned the police. A detail of ten policemen, with the minister and a number of the neighbors, surrounded the church at one o'clock this morning, determined on capturing the man who thus play the church organ at midnight. The organ had stopped playing just before the arrival of the police. A guard was placed at every window and door, while a detail of police entered the

church, led by the Rev. Mr. Lester. The gas was lighted, and then began the search. It was thorough; but, strange to say, from cellar to attic no one was found. Stranger still, not a door nor window was found open through which any one could have entered or escaped. While the search was being made Mr. Roberts, an organ-maker and an expert, was sent for. He arrived just as the search was finished. He made an examination of the organ, and said there was no doubt that the organ had been played on within two hours. This he knew from the sweaty condition in which he found the pipes. It was but corroboration of what the neighbors knew was a fact. Everybody was dumbfounded, and no one had a theory except the police, who are confident that the church is haunted, and that the ghosts play the organ at midnight. — *Milwaukee Dispatch.*

JUDGING A JUD(G)E.

I was reading somewhere the other day (says "Cleis," in the Otago *Witness*) about a certain Abbé Vogler, an eccentric organist of the last century, who used to travel about Europe astonishing the natives by the odd things he could do on the organ. Having an enormous hand, he was able to stretch two octaves with ease; but the chief use to which he put this unnatural advantage, when staring before the unInstructed multitude, was to play such things as "Chow-Tew, a Chinese song," "A Hottentot melody in three notes," "The Fall of the Walls of Jericho," "Thunderstorms," and a "Representation of the Last Judgment according to Reubens." In short, Mr. Jude's programme at Knox Church the other night would have suited him exactly. The Abbé Vogler, it should be said, was for all that a genuine musician. He was well enough able to play good music when he liked, and in the elevated fugal style, it is said, could distance all rivals; but for money-hunting purposes he preferred claptrap, finding claptrap more to the public taste. Whether this description would also fit Mr. Jude it is impossible to say. We may assume that Mr. Jude could play a Bach fugue if he liked, and on that assumption his performances on the Knox Church organ must be taken as a condescension to the ignorance and bad taste of his audience. He knew, or thought he knew, his public, and played down to their level. Let us hope in all charity that so it was. Spite of the atmosphere of puffery which Mr. Jude seems to carry about with him, we must believe that he is capable of better things at the organ than the imitating of harps and hurdy-gurdies, the rattle of rain on a tin roof, and the rumbling of stage thunder among the lower pedals. "Descriptive organ music," forsooth! A single overture of Händel's were worth the whole of it.— *Brisbane Telegraph.*

A CRYSTAL JUBILEE.

A musical service was recently held in the Peddie Memorial Baptist Church, Newark, N.J., called a Crystal Jubilee, commemorating fifteen years of the alliance of Rev. Dr. Boyd and Mr. E. M. Bowman, in the relation of pastor and organist. The Sunday evening address was interspersed with appropriate organ and choir selections, closing with a high tribute to the organist.

A WORD PERSONAL.

"And now," said Pastor Boyd, once more resuming, "a personal word. Mr. Bowman, born in Vermont of good Yankee stock, began the study of music at the age of twelve, and I am safe in saying that, during his studies in this and other lands, he has devoted from fourteen to sixteen hours out of every twenty-four to his chosen profession. His record of hard work, unwearied application, and patient mastery of details, I am sure is not surpassed in the career of any other great artist. During the fifteen years of our joined labors I have never known him to be once late at a service, nor can I recall a single service omitted by him on account of illness. These two facts speak volumes. His work in St. Louis brought our church musical service to the highest standard, and made the quartet, over which he presided, the finest musical organization in that music-loving city. His work in Newark speaks for itself to-night. No eulogy from me can exhibit its thoroughness and sincerity better than has already been displayed, not only by his masterly command of the king of instruments, the organ, but also in the magnificent achievements this evening of the Cecilian Choir, an organization which is the child of his brain and heart.

"During all these busy years, crowded with labors, there has never been one solitary misapprehension between us, nor a single unkind word, thought, or look. It speaks much for the almost infinite patience of my friend and co-worker, that he could bear so successfully with one whose duties without the least friction, joined as he has been to such a passionate and combustible man as I am. Church quarrels frequently arise from antagonisms between the organ loft and the pulpit; and even music has not always charms to soothe the savage breast. But our union has actually been uninterrupted in spirit as well as in form. Neither has ever been for one moment jealous of the other, or afraid to freely suggest and criticise each other's ideas and performances lest the silver cord of friendship be sundered. Both of us have realized that our common work was to serve Christ and His church,—he to preach the Gospel in song as I in the mother tongue.

"And as we gratefully review together the past to-night, and see how goodness and mercy have followed us all through these years of mutual effort, there seems to both of us to be but one strain that may adequately express the gratitude of our hearts to Almighty God, and that is the sublime chorus of Händel's Messiah; 'Hallelujah! Hallelujah! For the Lord God Omnipotent Reigneth!'"

OUR PARIS LETTER.

(From our own Correspondent.)

Paris, 9 February, 1893.

As the series of organ recitals so numerous during the spring in Paris have not yet commenced, all I can offer to the readers of the organ this month is an account of the playing of some of the famous French organists, and a few remarks on the organs themselves. In April, Guilmant gives a series of organ recitals with orchestra at the "Trocadero," which is the public place of amusement and of instruction for *tout Paris*. They are said to be very fine, and I shall hope to send complete accounts to The Organ. But *allons*, — hoping that this letter won't seem too dry and prosy.

Every Sunday morning I go to the mass at La Trinité, where, as every one knows, Guilmant plays the grand organ, and Salomé the chancel organ, which is used to accompany the choir. It is quite as good as a lesson to hear Guilmant render the great organ works of Bach, Händel, Rheinberger, Merkel, and others, and to follow (or rather to attempt to follow) his wonderful improvising. And this word "improvising" leads me to what is perhaps the most interesting and useful point I can touch upon for my musical friends in America. Nothing has impressed me more in listening to Guilmant, Widor, Dubois, and other organists here, than their wonderful facility in improvising, and at the same time the comparative rarity with which they make use of this power. I have now been in Paris three months, and during that time Guilmant has played, I should say, about six fugues of Bach as *sorties*, and several works of Händel, Mendelssohn, Lemmens, etc. His other pieces, such as elevations and prayers, he has improvised. In connection with this fact, let it be known that Guilmant can improvise with the most wonderful originality, and also in perfect form, in any style, from a simple prelude on ; and that he thinks nothing of improvising a grand fugue on two subjects. In fact, it quite makes your head ache to see him as he performs this last marvel. The comparison between this style of organ playing and that of many of our American organists (and that, too, often of so-called famous ones) is too obvious to need development. Of course we cannot all be "Guilmants," for his improvisations are practically organ compositions. No one can extemporize, in the higher sense of the word, unless he has genuine creative ability such as Guilmant has. But how a man who cannot create on paper can originate musical ideas on the spur of the moment, is something I fail to see. The plain truth is, that our American organists are too often lazy, and the musical taste of the people who hear them is not yet sufficiently cultivated, to insist upon their doing their duty. For it is much easier to dribble out a solo on the clarinet, with a rambling, incoherent accompaniment, and an occasional kick at the pedals, than it is to waste the organ music of Bach, Mendelssohn and Händel, and the effective music, written expressly for the church service, of more modern composers. I speak thus strongly on this point because the more familiar I become with the French organists, the more I see how inferior to them we are in America. No improvement can be made in our national school, till musical opinion insists that an organist shall not extemporize except in form; let it be free, if you will, but in some form. And first of all (and this is Guilmant's own advice), let every young organist devote himself to the great works of the great masters, and then, using these as models, in time and with study he will be able to extemporize all that is necessary for church use.

The organ at La Trinité, which has forty-six speaking stops, is very fine. It needs, however, no especial mention, save in regard to the effect of the full organ. In this respect it is better I think than most of our American organs, too many of which in their full-organ tone sound like poorly blended combinations of solo stops, and miss that rich and yet penetrating tone which one finds in the organs of Cavaillé-Coll. In regard to the organ at the Madeleine, to which I go often Sunday afternoons, to visit M. Dubois, I am surprised to notice that the pedal organ extends only to C. This, of course, would prevent the execution of many important organ works — the G-minor fugue, for instance. Too many of our pedal organs stop at D, instead of going to F; but we may congratulate ourselves that we have few, if any, which extend only to C.

Through the kindness of M. Richault, the well-known editor of music, I am able to announce the publication of three pieces for organ by Aloys Claussmann, a young composer of some prominence here. I understand they will soon be on sale in America. This next week I am to meet the organist and composer, F. de la Tombelle, and in my next letter I may be able to tell my readers some of his views on organ music and organ playing.   Outre Mer.

QUESTIONS AND ANSWERS.

All questions must be accompanied by the full name and address of the writer, and, if received by the 10th of the month, will usually be answered in the following number of The Organ.

Only such questions as refer to the organ, to organists, organ builders, or to organ music, will be answered.

Correspondents are requested to write their questions in a clear and concise manner, writing on only one side of the paper.

E. T. S. Will you tell me, please, through the columns of your journal (1), if there is any list of Best's Arrangements for the organ, and where procured, and also (2) the best method for teaching the Reed Organ.

Ans. (1) Messrs. Novello, Ewer, & Co., the publishers of Best's Arrangements, issue a catalogue of organ music which contains the required list. If this cannot be secured we would recommend ordering No. 5 of the series, which contains a complete list of the arrangements. Nos. 34 and 78 also contain the list. (2) Of the Reed Organ Methods mentioned in your letter we prefer Landon's.

K. L. B. Who is the greatest organist in this country?

Ans. Opinions differ. There are several great organists in the United States, each of whom is considered by his particular friends to be the greatest.

Country Organist. Please name some easy voluntaries for a small two-manual organ.

Ans. Prayer in E, Lemmens; Adagio in A-flat, Volkmar; Invocation in B-flat, Guilmant; Three Andantes, Foster.

C. J. B. Will you kindly name a few theoretical works on the organ which would be interesting and instructive to a student.

Ans. "Organ Building for Amateurs" (illustrated), by Wicks; published by Ward, Lock, & Co. of London (sold in this country for $2.00). "An Outline of the Structure of the Pipe Organ," by Clark; published by O. Ditson Co., Boston, $1.50. The Organ, Its History and Construction," by Hopkins and Rimbault; published by Robert Cocks & Co., London, sold by Novello, Ewer, & Co., New York, $10.00.

Sticker. Are the terms "Sticker" and "Tracker" synonymous?

Ans. No. See this department of the June number.

W. R. K. Why was the Great Boston Organ removed from the Music Hall? Where is it now?

Ans. An extended article on this very subject is awaiting publication in these columns, and until it appears, suffice it to say that this instrument, a gift of public subscription, was sold for about one-twentieth its original cost, to enable the heartless corporation to place a dozen or more extra seats in the hall and have a few more square feet of stage-room. The instrument is now "lying in state" in a "shanty" erected in the South Burial Ground. More anon.

GEORGE S. HUTCHINGS,
Church Organ Manufacturer,

23 TO 27 IRVINGTON STREET,

BOSTON, MASS.

Builder of some of the most famous organs in the country, among which may be mentioned The New Old South, Emmanuel, Second Church, Park St. Church, St. Paul's, Spiritual Temple, and Church of the Advent, all of Boston ; also South Congregational Church, Middletown, Conn., New York Avenue M. E. Church, Brooklyn, N. Y., St. Paul's School, Concord, N. H., and All Saints Church. Worcester, Second Congregational Church, Holyoke. Mass., Grace Church, Providence, R.I., Plymouth Church, Minneapolis, First Congregational Church, Omaha, Neb., First Congregational Church, San Francisco, Cal., Independent Presbyterian Church, Savannah, Ga., and many others.

Send for catalogue.

NEW ORGANS.

NEW ORGAN IN ST. MICHAEL'S P. E. CHURCH, NEW YORK.

Built by Messrs. Geo. Jardine & Son.

GREAT ORGAN.			SWELL ORGAN.		
Double Open Diapason	16	Ft.	Bourdon	16	Ft.
Open Diapason	8	"	Violin Diapason	8	"
Doppel-flöte	8	"	Salicional	8	"
Gamba	8	"	Stopped Diapason	8	"
Stopped Diapason	8	"	Quintadena	8	"
Octave	4	"	Violin Principal	4	"
Clarinet Flute	4	"	Flageolet	2	"
Twelfth	2⅔	"	Cornet	III. Rks.	
Fifteenth	2	"	Cornopean	8	Ft.
Mixture III. and IV.	Rks.		Oboe and Bassoon	8	"
Double Trumpet	16	Ft.	Vox Humana	8	"
Trumpet	8	"	CHOIR ORGAN.		
Clarion	4	"	Geigen Principal	8	Ft.

PEDAL ORGAN.			German Gamba	8	"
			Melodia	8	"
Contra Diapason	32	Ft.	Dolcissimo	8	"
Double Open Diapason	16	"	Vox Celestis	II. Rks.	
Violon	16	"	Principal	4	Ft.
Bourdon	16	"	Flauto Traverso	4	"
Violoncello	8	"	Harmonic Flute	4	"
Principal	4	"	Gemshorn	4	"
Octave	2	"	Solo Piccolo	2	"
Cimbale	III. Rks.		Harmonic Reed	16	"
Euphone	16	Ft.	Clarinet	8	"

PEDAL MOVEMENTS.

F., MF., and P., Combinations in Great.
F. and P., Combinations in Swell.
F. and P., Combinations in Choir.
Reversible Pedal (on or off) on Gt. Reeds.

The blowing apparatus is located in the crypt, and is worked by a gas-engine.

NEW ORGAN IN ST. JOHN'S EPISCOPAL CHURCH, NORTHAMPTON, MASS.

Built by Mr. Geo. S. Hutchings of Boston.

GREAT ORGAN.			SWELL ORGAN.		
Open Diapason	8	Ft.	Bourdon Treble }	16	Ft.
Dolcissimo	8	"	Bourdon Bass }		
Melodia	8	"	Violin Diapason	8	"
Octave	4	"	Salicional	8	"
Flöte d'Amour	4	"	Æoline	8	"
Octave Quint	2⅔	"	Stopped Diapason	8	"
Super Octave	2	"	Flöte Harmonique	4	"
Mixture	III. Rks.		Violina	4	"
Trumpet	8	Ft.	Flautino	2	"
			Dolce Cornet	III. Rks.	
PEDAL ORGAN.			Oboe and Bassoon	8	Ft.
Open Diapason	16	Ft.			
Bourdon	16	"	The usual couplers and pedal movements.		
Violoncello	8	"			

ST. PATRICK'S CHURCH of Brockton, Mass., will have its new organ finished in a few days. It is the intention to have the instrument opened by several prominent organists. Definite arrangements for the concert have not yet been made. The organ is from the factory of Messrs. Hook & Hastings.

GREAT ORGAN.			SWELL ORGAN.		
Open Diapason	16	Ft.	Bourdon Bass }	16	Ft.
Open Diapason	8	"	Bourdon Treble }		
Viola da Gamba	8	"	Open Diapason	8	"
Doppel-flöte	8	"	Salicional	8	"
Flûte Harmonique	4	"	Gedackt	8	"
Octave	4	"	Flauto Traverso	4	"
Octave Quint	2⅔	"	Violina	4	"
Super Octave	2	"	Dolce Cornet	III. Rks.	
Mixture	III. Rks.		Cornopean	8	Ft.
Trumpet	8	Ft.	Oboe (with Bassoon)	8	"
CHOIR ORGAN.			PEDAL ORGAN.		
Geigen Principal	8	Ft.	Open Diapason	16	Ft.
Dulciana	8	"	Bourdon	16	"
Melodia	8	"	Violoncello	8	"
Flöte d'Amour	4	"	PEDAL MOVEMENTS.		
Piccolo Harmonique	2	"	F., MF., and P. combinations to Gt.		
Clarinet	8	"	F., MF., and P. " " Sw.		
			Gt. to Ped. (reversible).		

The usual couplers. Pneumatic action applied to the Great and its couplers. The action is extended and reversed.

NEW ORGAN IN CHRIST CHAPEL, NEW YORK.

Built by Mr. Geo. S. Hutchings of Boston.

GREAT ORGAN.			SWELL ORGAN.		
Open Diapason	8	Ft.	Bourdon Treble }	16	Ft.
Dulcissimo	8	"	Bourdon Bass }		
Melodia (Stopped Bass)	8	"	Violin Diapason	8	"
Octave	4	"	Salicional	8	"
Octave Quint	2⅔	"	Stopped Diapason	8	"
Super Octave	2	"	Flöte Harmonique	4	"
Trumpet	8	"	Violina	4	"
			Oboe and Bassoon	8	"
PEDAL ORGAN.					
Bourdon	16	Ft.	The usual couplers and pedal movements.		
Flöte	8	"			

NEW ORGAN FOR THE CHURCH OF THE LIVERPOOL SCHOOL FOR THE BLIND.

Built by the Hope-Jones Electric Organ Co. (Ltd.).

GREAT ORGAN.			SWELL ORGAN.		
Double Dulciana	16	Ft.	Bourdon	16	Ft.
Open Flute	8	"	Geigen Principal	8	"
Open Diapason	8	"	Kuba-flöte	8	"
Harmonic Claribel	8	"	Salicional	8	"
Dulciana	8	"	Vox Angelica	8	"
Principal	4	"	Gemshorn	4	"
Harmonic Flute	4	"	Harmonic Piccolo	2	"
			Dulciana Mixture	III. Rks.	
MECHANICAL.			Trumpet	16	Ft.
Sw. to Gt. (1st and 2d touch).			Oboe	8	"
Sw. to Gt. Super. Sw. to Gt. Sub.			Clarion	4	"
Sw. to Gt. Unison. Sw. to Gt. Super.			MECHANICAL.		
Ch. to Gt. 3 Composition Pedals.			Sub Octave, Super Octave, and Sw. to Sw. 2d touch.		
CHOIR ORGAN.			Tremulant. 3 Composition Pedals. Expression Lever.		
Open Diapason	8	Ft.			
Keraulophon	8	"	SOLO ORGAN.		
Lieblich Gedackt	8	"	Tuba Mirabilis	8	Ft.
Viol d'Orchestre	8	"			
Vox Celestis	8	"	PEDAL ORGAN.		
Salicet	4	"	Open Diapason (1st and 2d touch)	16	Ft.
Lieblich-flöte	4	"	Bourdon	16	"
Orchestral Oboe	8	"	"Great" Double Dulciana	16	"
Corno di Bassetto	8	"	"Swell" Bourdon	16	"
Vox Humana	8	"	Principal	8	"
			Open Flute	8	"
MECHANICAL.			Ophicleide (1st and 2d touch)	16	"
Sub Octave. Super Octave.					
Sw. to Ch. (1st and 2d touch).			MECHANICAL.		
Tremulant. 2 Composition Pedals and Expression Lever.			4 Couplers and 2 Comp. Pedals.		

Stop Switch and Six Pedal. (First touch F., Second touch FF.)

The tables, sliders, and bearers of the soundboards are of mahogany. Split pallets below treble C. Bellows double leathered throughout. Pedal-board of oak, with oiled birch keys. Distance between the manuals, 2½ inches.

NEW ORGAN IN THE CHURCH OF ST. SIMEON, PHILADELPHIA, PA.

Built by Messrs. Wm. King & Son of Elmira, N.Y.

GREAT ORGAN.			SWELL ORGAN.		
Contra Gamba	16	Ft.	Bourdon	16	Ft.
Open Diapason	8	"	Violin Diapason	8	"
Dulciana	8	"	Salicional	8	"
Doppel-flöte	8	"	Stopped Diapason	8	"
Octave	4	"	Fugara	4	"
Harmonic Flute	4	"	Flauto Traverso	4	"
Twelfth	2⅔	"	Flautino	2	"
Fifteenth	2	"	Mixture	II. Rks.	
Trumpet	8	"	Oboe and Bassoon	8	Ft.
PEDAL ORGAN.			CHOIR ORGAN.		
Open Diapason	16	Ft.	Keraulophon	8	Ft.
Bourdon	16	"	Æoline	8	"
Violoncello	8	"	Melodia	8	"
PEDAL MOVEMENTS.			Flöte d'Amour	4	"
Forte, Mezzo, and Piano Great.			Piccolo	2	"
Forte and Piano Swell.			Clarinet	8	"
Gt. to Ped. (reversible).					
Two Adjustable Pedals (Great).					

VOL. I. APRIL, 1893. No. 12.

BACH

YEARLY SUBSCRIPTION $2.00. SINGLE COPIES 25 CTS.

THE ORGAN

DEVOTED TO

A MONTHLY JOURNAL

THE KING OF INSTRUMENTS

RHEINBERGER

GUILMANT

FRESCOBALDI

BUXTEHUDE

MERKEL

BEST

EVERETT · E · TRUETTE ·
EDITOR & PUBLISHER
149 A. TREMONT ST. BOSTON.

HANDEL

THE ORGAN.

VOL. I. BOSTON, APRIL, 1893. No. 12.

THE ORGAN.

A MONTHLY JOURNAL

DEVOTED TO THE KING OF INSTRUMENTS.

EVERETT E. TRUETTE, EDITOR AND PUBLISHER.

(Entered at the Boston, Mass., Post-office as second-class mail matter, June 1, 1892.)

CONTENTS:

ALEXANDRE GUILMANT.

FELIX ALEXANDRE GUILMANT, undoubtedly the most noted organist and composer of organ music which France can claim as her own, was born March 12, 1837, at Boulogne-sur-Mer, where his father was, for nearly fifty years, organist at the Church of St. Nicholas. The people of the whole town worshipped the venerable form of the old man who for so long a time had been in their midst, and who had officiated so many Sundays at the old organ. He lived to the advanced age of ninety-seven, dying at Meudon in 1887.

When but a small boy, Mons. Guilmant commenced the study of music with his father, making such marvellous progress that, at the early age of twelve, he frequently took his father's post. He studied harmony diligently with Gustavo Carulli (son of a somewhat noted guitarist), who resided in the same town. His hunger for musical knowledge was so ravenous that he mentally devoured every theoretical work to which he could gain access, and acquainted himself with the compositions of classical writers. He went to the church daily, where in solitude he labored for hours, — sometimes for ten hours, tiring out several blowers, — perfecting himself in organ playing, with such gratifying results that he was appointed organist of St. Joseph's at the youthful age of sixteen.

At the age of eighteen he brought out his first Festival Mass in F, other similar works following in close proximity. In 1857, at the age of twenty, he was appointed *maître de*

chapelle at St. Nicholas, and soon afterward teacher of singing in the Music School. He organized the Orphean Singing Society, which became celebrated in that vicinity, soon after which he was elected a member of the Philharmonic Society.

On a trip to Paris he heard Mons. Jacques Lemmens, the celebrated Belgian organist, who was a professor in the Brussels Conservatory. Mons. Guilmant then went to Brussels, and became the favorite pupil of Mons. Lemmens. Being called upon frequently to inaugurate new organs, Mons. Guilmant acquired a reputation which was far-reaching, and which preceded him to Paris, to which city he journeyed in 1862; when, on April 2, he assisted in the inauguration of the now famous organ in the Church of St. Sulpice. His performance of several organ numbers was thus described by Professor Elwart : —

"The able Boulogne organist, Guilmant, played in immediate succession a Toccata and Fugue of Bach, Pastorale of Kullak, and several pieces of his own composition, among them a Communion, which was pre-eminently distinguished by deep feeling. Finally, the young artist, a pupil of his father and of the celebrated Lemmens, played a Grand March, on a theme by Händel. This Cavaillé-Coll organ is so complicated in its combinations, that usually about one month is necessary to become acquainted with it thoroughly. A Guilmant took but two hours to prepare himself. All admired the spirit and intellect of the organist of St. Nicholas, and after the concert he received the heartiest congratulations of those artists whom he had invited to attend. It is indeed a notable thing for a youthful artist to leave left his predilections and his allotted work resolutely behind him and gone forth to seek the baptism of a Parisian verdict upon his rising fame."

In 1865 Mons. Guilmant inaugurated an organ in the Carmelite Church, Kensington, London, which was built by Cavaillé-Coll. In this concert he was assisted by Mons. Widor, at that time of Lyons, but now of Paris.

Soon after this he inaugurated the great organ in Nôtre Dame, Paris, at which time he gave the initial performance of that masterpiece, which was specially composed for this occasion; namely, his *Marche Funèbre et Chant Séraphique.* This composition opened the eyes of the French organists to the resources of a modern organ for producing varied tone-colors, and created a sensation. Mons. Guilmant thus achieved a complete triumph in Paris before establishing himself in that city; and in 1871, when he was called to take the post of organist at La Trinité, at the death of Chauvet, he had an enviable reputation. This reputation rapidly spread in foreign countries, particularly in England, whither he journeyed frequently for various concert engagements.

He went to Rome, and opened the new organ built by Merklin, in the Church of St. Louis des Français, giving daily concerts for two weeks, during which time many of the organ works of Bach and Handel were heard for the first time in Italy. During this visit Pope Leo XIII. decorated him a Commander of the Order of St. Gregory the Great. He went to Riga, Russia, and gave a series of concerts on Walcker's great organ, at that time the largest organ in the world.

During the Paris Exposition of 1878 Mons. Guilmant inaugurated his famous series of organ recitals in the hall of the Trocadéro, in which many of the organ works of Bach and Händel have been performed for the first time in Paris. Some years afterward he secured the co-operation of Mons. Colonne's orchestra, giving the concertos of Bach and Händel, with orchestral accompaniment. For nearly twenty years he has made annual, and oftentimes semi-annual, trips to England for concerts. In 1890 he played at St. George's Chapel, Windsor, at the request of the Queen, who was charmed with his marvellous skill in improvising. He is still organist at La Trinité, having retained the position for twenty-two years. A few months ago the President of the French Republic nominated him a *Chevalier de la Légion d'Honneur.*

Mons. Guilmant has been one of the most prolific composers for the organ since the time of Bach; his works being not only numerous, but of widely varying character. His first sonata in D-minor stands pre-eminent among his compositions. This work, though first appearing for organ alone, was conceived for organ and orchestra; but the opportunities for its performance as such being rare at that time, he wisely published the work first as a sonata for organ alone, and some years afterward as a symphony for organ and orchestra. This sonata has been extensively praised, and occasionally condemned. Some have called it "too emotional" for a sonata. Others, while acknowledging its melodic beauties, have shaken their would-be-learned pates in unexpressed doubt. The composition is the work of a Frenchman, and a Frenchman is nothing if not emotional. Must the work be in the style of Bach or Beethoven to win the approval of such critics? Let us have Bach's trio sonatas for Bach, Rheinberger's sonatas for Rheinberger, and, above all, let us have this sonata, without a suggestion of an alteration, for Guilmant. It reflects in every phrase the gifts of the artist-composer. It displays the geniality of the man, and, above all, it is perfectly adapted to the organ, containing no impossibilities, but utilizing the best resources of the instrument.

Lack of space forbids extended notice of the other compositions of Mons. Guilmant; but what better proof of the versatility of this composer do we need than a glance at his Air and Variations in G, Grand Chœur in D, Marche Funèbre et Chant Séraphique, Marche Religieuse, Fugue in D, First Meditation, Lamentation, and Scherzo Symphonique?

NOTABLE ORGANS.

VIII.

STRALSUND.

ONE of the finest specimens of a late renaissance organ-case is to be seen at the west end of the church of St. Nicholas, at Stralsund, a quaint old town situated on a neck

of land jutting into the Baltic, and which in earlier times connected the island of Rügen with the main coast. Stralsund is in many respects a remarkable town, and is said to be one of the few that have never during their history been destroyed or pillaged by a victorious army. It consequently contains many objects of interest both to the artist and the antiquary. The church of St. Nicholas is an imposing structure of brick, having a solemn and dignified interior, chiefly due to the simplicity and fine proportions of its architecture. The nave arcade is very lofty, and is supported on piers of octagonal section, surmounted by plain moulded caps. The great organ stands in a stone gallery at the western end of the church, and presents a front which is broken up into a multitude of compartments containing pipes of all sizes. The two great towers contain 16ft. pipes, and are apparently supported from below by two large figures representing a man and woman. The central portion of the case is recessed back, and relieved in the centre by a continuous series of V-shaped towers, separated one from the other by bold cornices. On the summit of each large tower is an angelic figure playing upon a musical instrument. The top of the case terminates in a curved pediment. Each of the compartments is provided with a carved shade, in most cases shaped so as to fit over the extremity of each individual pipe. The whole of the woodwork has been painted in a light tone. The date of this case is *circa* 1660, a time at which many great organs were built in this part of Europe. The design is strongly Dutch in many respects, and is certainly very magnificent.

ARTHUR G. HILL, B.A., F.S.A.

THE LATEST.

THERE is now building in Detroit, Mich., a $6,000 organ for the new Second Baptist Church in Atlanta, which will be the only one of the kind ever brought to the South. It will be a genuine novelty in these parts, and will astonish the natives when the new church is ready. This remarkable instrument is in the nature of two organs in one. The tubular pneumatic organ, played strictly on the principle of compressed air, and without any of the classical contrivances of the ordinary organ of the day, will start at one side of the pulpit, and what is called the echo organ will be across the church in the opposite corner, veiled from view. The two organs will be connected by an invisible electric wire, and when the organist strikes up "Old Hundred," for instance, on the pneumatic instrument, by simply touching a button the music on the instrument at hand comes, but an electrical current speeds through the wire and opens up the valves in the echo organ, which at once carries on the same tune. This it can do in four separate and distinct ways; to wit, by the vox humana, or a sound in beautiful imitation of a human voice singing in the distance; second, the vox æteria, or ethereal reed, representing a most sacred, spiritual, and mysterious musical effect; third, by the vox mæris, or a softened sound, representing the rising and falling and swish of the waves of the sea in the distance, or lost by the dulcimer, or sounds of the greatest softness and sweetness imaginable. By touching the buttons, for instance, "Old Hundred" would be taken up in either of the above ways by the echo organ at the will of the organist, but it would be impossible for the congregation to tell where the mysterious music came from. In addition, the tubular pneumatic organ will contain all of the usual of mechanism necessary to produce the effects of a full orchestra, the flute, clarionet, trumpet, violoncello. — *Savannah News.*

My notice has been called to the above clipping, with the query, "Are not the organ-builders of the West outstripping those of the East in the modern equipment of this instrument?" I have given some special attention to the subject, and in my investigations, among others, consulted the proprietor of one of our largest manufactories of church organs in this city, who said that whatever the comparative output of instruments, or the improvements upon them might be, it was certain that in regard to descriptions of new organs the Western vocabulary of technicalities far outweighs that of the East.

Continuing the conversation, and warming up with the subject, he said, "We have been constructing an instrument which is nearly completed, the particulars of which would soon have been given to the public, but as our fathers were old and tried friends I have no objection to giving you the exclusive news, for the usual compensation." He therefore arranged with his office man to prevaricate about his absence should any one call, and, leading the way, opened a concealed door, and we were ushered into a second "setting-up" room, the existence of which would never be suspected. The room was ample in floor space and height, and of admirable acoustic proportions, and evidently planned with a correct knowledge of tonal effects, and imitating in some respects the auditorium of a church; the usual central chandelier and open-work above, and at one end the suggestion of a chancel, at the other a key-desk containing four manuals and a pedal key-board of full scale, in the usual position, with C under the seat. In addition to the usual terraces of register-knobs at the sides, were arranged over and about the sides of the desk various recesses covered with glass doors of strangely beautiful prismatic appearance, the purpose of which will appear later on. At an expression of surprise at not seeing a case, or the usual display of front pipes, the builder said, "There is no longer an interest in organ cases or decorative pipework; simple perforations through the walls to allow the sound to pass out is all. As you will see later, the tone is utilized in a different manner, and the expense of the case is devoted to more sensational features. The key-desk is now made the attractive point; upon this no expense is spared."

As some changes were being made in the wind system, the organ could not be played, but a verbal description, the builder assured me, was all I could stand at one interview. The scheme of the organ proper was about fifty stops, and apportioned in the usual way, with nothing to call for comment; but accepting an invitation to sit upon the bench, a strange feeling of ecstasy took possession of me. I then remembered that the builder had opened one of the glass doors covering a small group of push-knobs, and pressed one. I am not

the equal of Guilmant, but, unconsciously placing my fingers upon the keys, it seemed that I could have made music fit for the Old World. I felt that my playing would suit even Philip Hale. My informant pressed another button, and the reaction came. I was myself again, and turned to him for explanation. "That," he said, "is the effect of the electric current combined with the prismatic rays of the open glass door. I cannot give you the inside facts, as the papers are still in the Patent Office; but you can see that if the organist has a single volt of inspiration, this will augment it. We do not claim more." Looking closely at the knob, I saw engraved upon it the word "Inspiration." I had scarcely expressed my surprise when he pressed another button labelled "Offertory." "I am sorry," he said, "we have no wind to-day to illustrate the next improvement, but if you turn and look to the right of the chancel you will observe the cowl of a nickel-plated urn projecting from the wall a few inches. By playing on the fourth manual the harmony of the softer stops will issue from the end of the wire and mingle with the reading of this portion of the service, even moving the closer-fisted of the congregation to give a bill in place of the usual Canada quarter. If you will step over and look closely at the end of the wire, a series of longitudinal nicks will be seen. We find this gives a delightful Nikisch character to the tones, and do not expect any adverse criticism, except possibly from Warren Davenport. This novel, or rather Scriptural effect, is produced by the electric current combined, etc." Still wondering, my attention was called to the upper four corners of the room, near the ceiling. Projecting out were the flaring ends of four trumpet-shaped tubes respectively. They impressed me with being extraordinary in the details of shape and finish. Remarking upon this, the builder said, "Those trumps were obtained from Gabriel. We learned that the dead had quietly formed an Amalgamated Association, and would refuse to rise. They were, in fact, 'dead set' against it, and we bought out the entire stock of trumps."

Smiling and raising his hand he continued, "We cornered the trump market." (I was conscious of a nervous strain in the absence of a musical one.) "By pressing either of these five buttons, any stop of either manual can be directed to one or all of the corner trumps. The effect is weird, novel, and aggravating, as the organist can push the back trump-knobs just when you think you will decide on the front trumps; in fact, he practically holds the trumps, and can sway the audience ad lib." Looking at the knobs, I saw they were marked "North," "South," "East," "West," "Full." My wonder grew apace as he continued: "This remarkable effect is produced, at very little expense above the cost of the trumps, by a combination of the electric fluid and tubular pneumatics in the proper proportion. Papers at the Patent Office. But here," continued this Ajax of art, "is the most wonderful of all our undertakings. You will see here" (touching a black glass door which had upon its face in small gilt letters, "Funeral") "the masterpiece of organ mechanisms. If you will kindly step down from the seat the funeral effect will not interfere with the examination of this great invention." Opening the door, there appeared another group of push-knobs. The centre one was marked "Yawn." I noticed the builder was careful to stand one side. He said, "When the glass door is opened a singular prismatic effect is produced in combination with the tubular electric current and the other crystals. It gives the organist the 'blues;' at such a time it would cost him $10, net, to smile. You can see that he is in a proper mood to officiate on a solemn occasion. But this is not all. By pressing the central knob a blast of damp air is forced through the ventilator, which extinguishes a fixed number of the chandelier lights (the services are held at evening), and a 'churchyard yawn' of such a grave character is heard as would move the bones of Shakespeare, if they were in American soil. Push-knobs around the central one are marked *pp*, *p*, *f*, and *ff*. We have disconnected the last, as the effect was disastrous upon the workmen; but it is hardly fair, as their nervous

(Continued on page 281.)

THE ORGAN.

BOSTON, APRIL, 1893.

THE ORGAN is published the first of every month. Subscription price $1.00 per year (European countries 60s. 9d.), payable in advance. Single copies, 15 cents.

Subscribers will please state with which number they wish their subscription to begin.

Subscribers wishing the address of their paper changed must give the old as well as the new address.

Remittances should be made by registered letter, post-office order, or by check payable to Everett E. Truette.

Correspondence, to secure notice, must in all cases be accompanied by the name and address of the writer, not for publication, but as a guarantee of good faith.

Advertising rates sent on application.

Address all communications.

The Organ, 199 A Tremont Street, Boston, Mass.

☞ An active agent in every city is desired to whom a liberal cash commission will be allowed.

Single copies of THE ORGAN can be procured of

Novello, Ewer & Co.	. . . .	New York.
G. Schirmer	. . . .	New York.
Oliver Ditson Co.	. . . .	Boston.
L. H. Ross & Co.	. . . .	Boston.
N. E. Conservatory	. . . .	Boston.
H. B. Stevens Co.	. . . .	Boston.
Lyon & Healy	. . . .	Chicago.
Theodore Presser	. . . .	Philadelphia.
Wm. H. Boner & Co.	. . . .	Philadelphia.
Taylor's Music House	. . . .	Springfield, Mass.
Gallup & Metzger	. . . .	Hartford, Conn.
Richault & Co.	. . . .	Paris.
R. F. Vibert, (Sole Agent for Gt. Britain)		London.

OUR FIRST ORGAN MUSIC COMPETITION.

MESSRS. CLARENCE EDDY, George E. Whiting, and S. B. Whitney have unanimously awarded the prize of ten dollars for the best march for the organ to Mr. John S. Camp of Hartford, Conn., whose composition bore the motto, "Hofmann." This composition will be found in this number of THE ORGAN.

Only three compositions for the competition ("Hofmann," "Zero," and "Wagner") arrived in time to be examined by the judges. Another competition will be announced next month.

"A joke is a joke, but when a man ties his horse to me, taking me for a lamp-post, it is no joke." In all probability Messrs. Smith and Kinsley, in reading an announcement of the burning of their factory among "Cipherings," last month, would fail to see the joke.

This item was sent by mail to the printer at the last moment. Naturally the foreman, not knowing the difference between a "cipher" and a wind-trunk, inserted the item in the first corner where he found sufficient space.

RETROSPECTIVE AND PROSPECTIVE.

WITH the present number, the first year of THE ORGAN is concluded. Contrary to the prophecies of many who scanned the pages of the initial number of this journal, and contrary to the expectations of many friends, THE ORGAN has survived the trials and vicissitudes of its infant epoch. Bumps, mumps, and measles have come and gone, the doctor's bills are all paid, and we are about to enter the period of early youth, healthier, stronger, and more ready than ever to battle with the exigencies of the future.

We trust that our readers will pardon our vanity when we claim that we have done all (and possibly a little more) that

was promised in our salutatory. This same vanity does not, however, prevent our acknowledging that there have been many shortcomings in each issue; but we claim that there has been a steady improvement, and that many of these shortcomings will disappear in the coming volume.

There was an endless list of obstacles in the way to prevent such a periodical as THE ORGAN existing even a half-year. Our exclusiveness in catering entirely to one branch of music, and that branch numerically one of the least popular; the lack of unlimited capital at the start, not having any "backers," nor even the pledged support of "the trade," which would demand periodical puffs in return; the inability of the uneducated to appreciate the utility of our intended work, and the unwillingness of those who "know it all" to even acknowledge that there could possibly be any merit in a periodical devoted to their branch of music; the unwillingness of many writers and composers to contribute (even when well paid) essays and compositions to a "new and unknown" journal; and, by no means the least of all, our inexperience, are but a few of the rough roads over which we have been compelled to travel.

To those who have not only subscribed for the journal, but have contributed numerous articles, items, and compositions, as well as tendering many graceful and encouraging compliments, we are extremely grateful, and hope that we have earned a continuation of their confidence and support.

To those who have placed advertisements in our columns, and have thereby contributed an appreciable financial support, and specially to those who, at the outset, when only a "dummy" served to show the proposed form of the journal, willingly trusted their orders for "ads" in our care, we owe special gratitude. Their confidence, as well as financial assistance, gave us courage, and invited the confidence of others. We hope that each one has received, or will receive, a sufficient return to repay the outlay many times over. We invite their continued patronage and the patronage of others, while we call the attention of our readers to every advertisement in the journal. A better or more appropriate class of advertisers cannot be found. Not a single advertisement is out of its sphere; toilet soaps, baking-powders, and wash-wringers being conspicuous by their absence.

The influence of THE ORGAN in devoting so much more space to this branch of music than is possible in general music journals, in encouraging interchange of thought on mooted subjects, and in specially treating of organ music and organ news, will naturally be more widespread in each succeeding volume. We by no means claim that we have pleased all our subscribers. Not at all. We have received a number of letters complaining that the tone of the journal was too lofty, requesting us to give the readers more of the A B C's. On the other hand, many have elevated their nasal protuberances and mildly suggested "chestnuts." However, for every letter of complaint we have received a hundred complimentary letters, which indicates that a majority of our readers indorse our course; and yet it is always our intention to consider the demands of all our readers, and each request is carefully examined before being placed on file.

Our policy has been to contract no large debts, to be paid for out of future prosperity. While this policy may have prevented one or two elaborate undertakings which would have attracted patrons, it has the advantage of insuring a solid financial position; and if we were compelled to assign to-morrow, the only liabilities would be the unexpired subscriptions and advertisements, for each one of which a check for the exact amount due would be ready. Our circulation, while not as yet astonishing in its size, has become more widespread than many think possible. We have subscribers in twenty-nine States of this country; in various localities in England, Ireland, Scotland, and France; in Ontario, New Brunswick, and Prince Edward Island; in Victoria, Queensland, and New South Wales, Australia, as well as in Honolulu, Hawaii.

The value of the journal is well attested by the fact that, even at this late date, nine out of every ten subscribers ask

(Continued on page 281.)

MARCH.

Tempo di Marcia Risoluto.

JOHN S. CAMP.

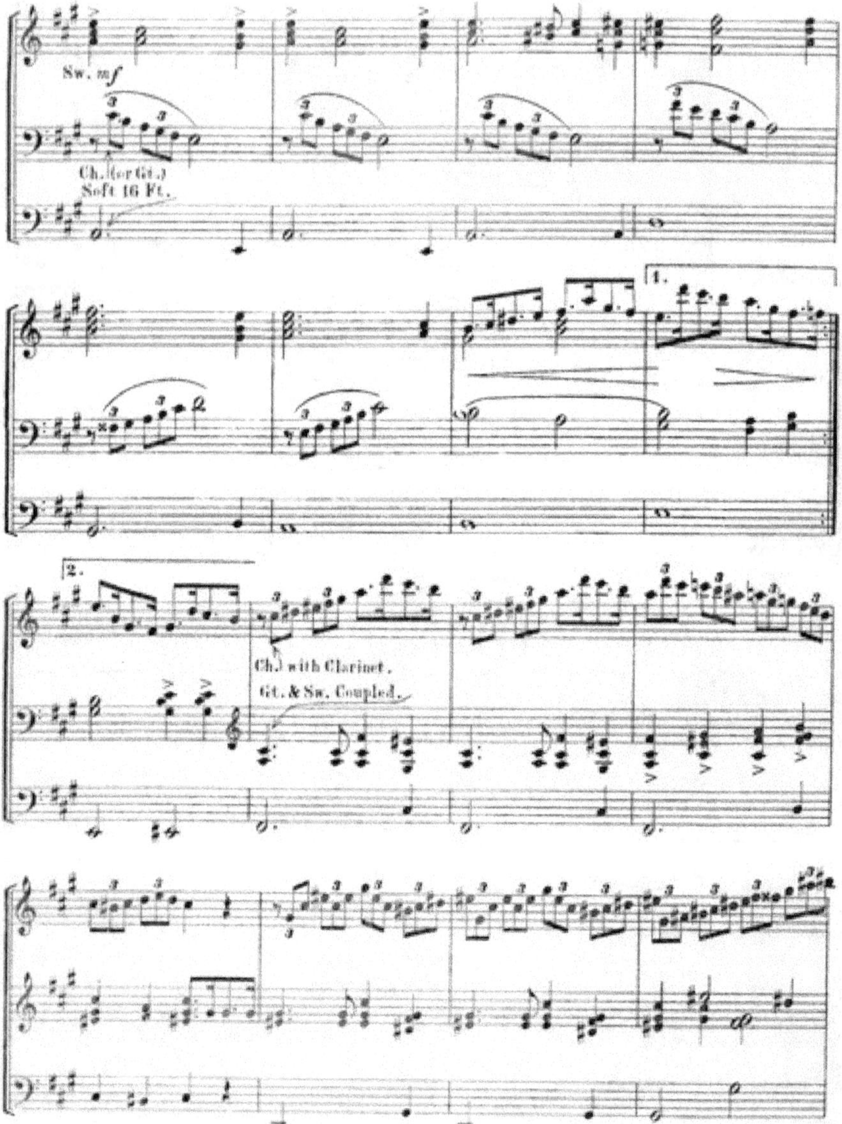
Sw. mf
Ch. (or Gt.)
Soft 16 Ft.
1.
2.
Ch. with Clarinet.
Gt. & Sw. Coupled.

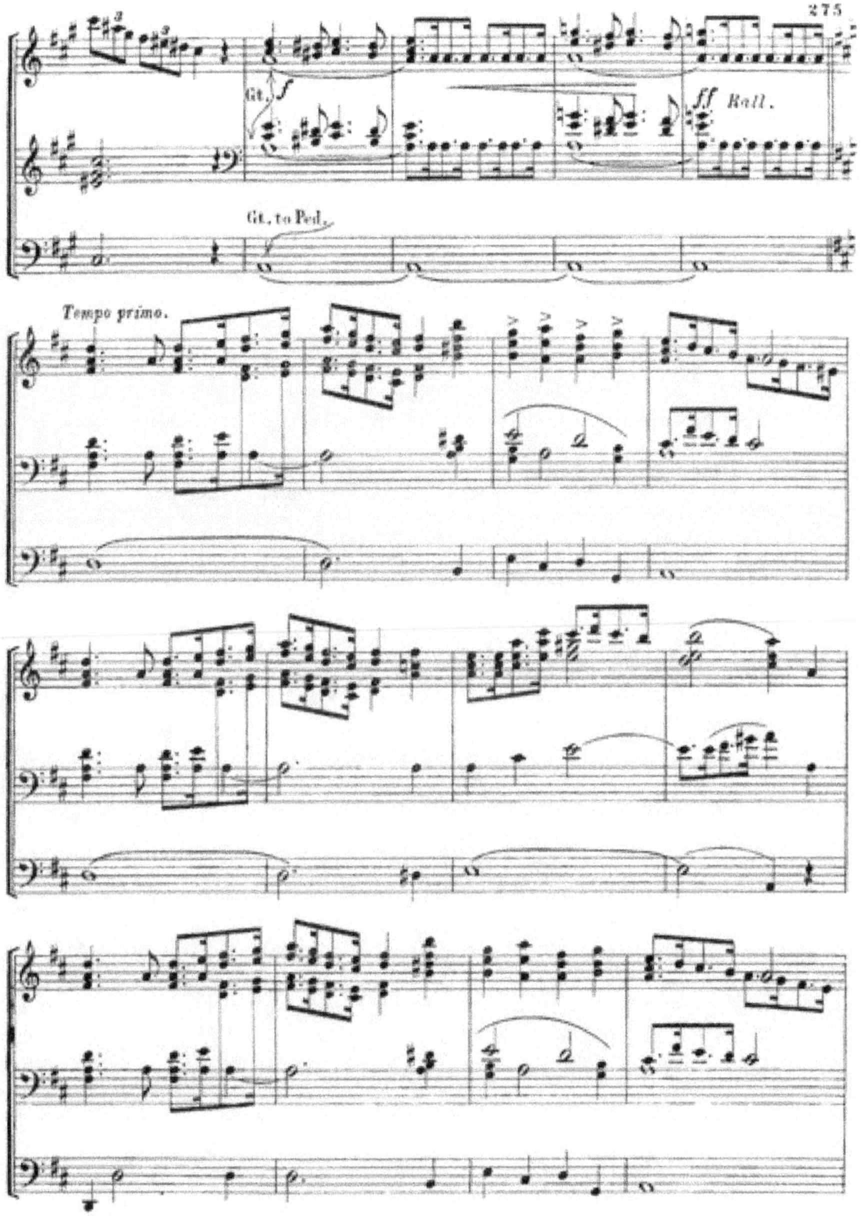
Gt.
ff Rall.
Gt. to Ped.
Tempo primo.

Coup. off.

mf. Ch. & Sw. Coupled. Sw. Ch.

Sw. Ch.

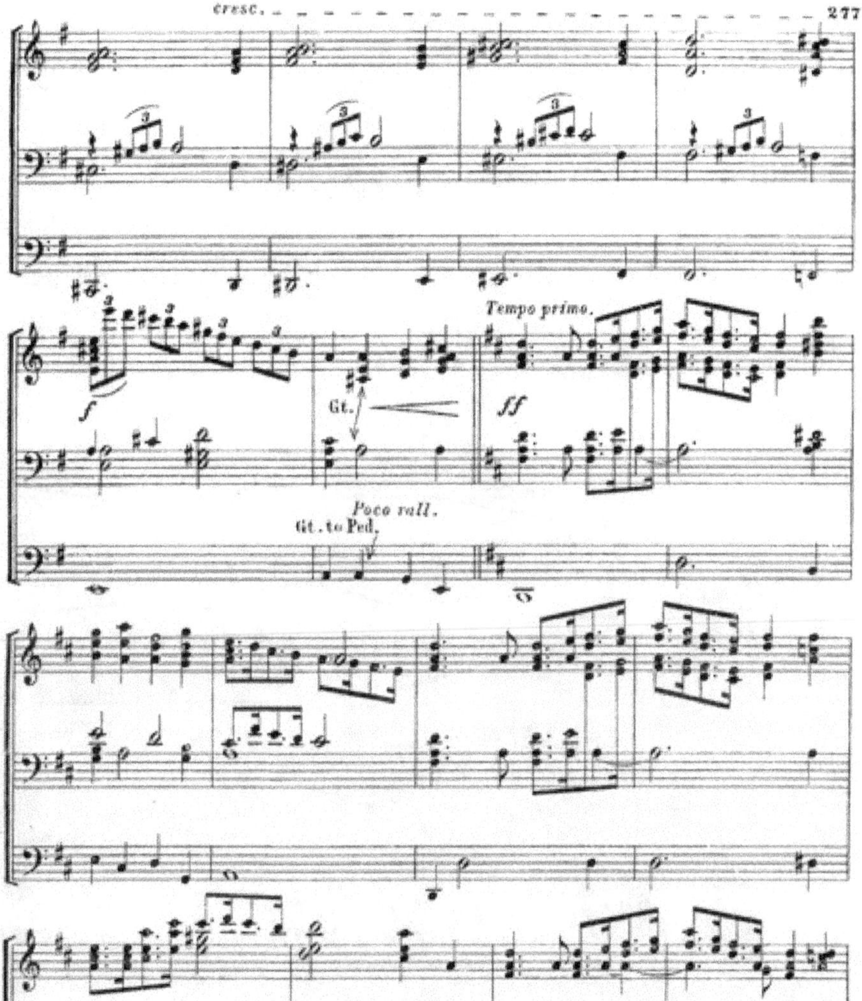
cresc.
f
Gt.
Poco rall.
Gt. to Ped.
Tempo primo.
ff

Piu Mosso.

FIVE INTERLUDES.

(OR SHORT AND EASY VOLUNTARIES.)

I.

EVERETT E. TRUETTE.

Sw.
Gt. to Ped. off.
Sw.
Gt. Melodia & Dulciana.
Melodia off
Gt.
Sw. St. Diap. only.
rall.
Sw. Viola.

THE LATEST.

(Continued from page 271.)

systems are under an abnormal strain keeping these secrets. They are single men. If it is found that the elderly females succumb to the yawn, a full line of stretchers will be furnished, and the sexton connected with the electric current by tubular pneumatics. We have left a blank knob for that purpose. The use of discarded gravestones for bellows-weights we find adds greatly to the sepulchral effect. (As such have been used by Erben and Appleton, we make no claims for this brand of stone *per se*.) If the funeral services are over a simple case of mother-in-law *ff* will suffice; but for an aged wealthy member of the parish *ff* will not only cause the people to mourn the departed, but they will wish themselves dead. This funeral department is expensive; it costs about that of a good case and decorated front pipes, but it is new. We think if it had been done in the days of Bach he would have stepped down from the bench and gone 'to sea.'"

While overwhelmed with thought at what I had been shown, I noticed we had been giving our attention to one side of the key-desk only. Could there yet be anything "later" than what I had already seen? The mysteries of the left side had not been unveiled. But no time for retrospection, for this wizard of the organ opened upon this side a crystal marked "Marriage." The usual group of push-knobs, surrounded by a series of holes, one of which contained a peg, and was labelled "Sarah." The builder explained: "At the close of the marriage service, and in place of the usual wedding-march (for which we shall always owe Mendelssohn), the organist, who has been duly electrified, and is in a joyous mood, presses the aforesaid button. At once, by a combination of hypo-tubular and electric pneumatic force, the tower chimes are caused to ring a joyous peal. At the same time the tones of the full organ are heard, through an opening above the Porte-Cochère, formed like a 'gargoyle,' the classic strains of 'The bells go ringing for Sarah.' The entire organ can be played at this critical moment automatically by simply pushing a button, giving the organist an opportunity to mingle with the crowd and see the fun. By inserting the peg into other holes in the cribbage-board section, the bells, etc., can 'go ringing,' for any other named bride in the parish. You will see two other push-knobs marked respectively 'Rice' and 'Shoes.' Simultaneously with the organ tones can be fired through this opening with great force the above commodities. It is sufficiently large to accommodate the Chicago slipper, and the necessary force to project it is obtained by the use of a bellows of rhinoceros hide and sheet steel, combined with the tubular pneumatic electroids. We have other improvements," he continued, "in course of construction which are not ready to exhibit to-day. We hope to produce an appliance which can be used to kiss the bride electrically. We have already produced the kiss, but the sensation of the mustache is the great difficulty. The ladies are very discriminating." My brain was weary with wonder; and as we passed out I asked, "Is this wonderful instrument intended for a Boston church?"—"Yes: it is for the Church of the Incarnation, Jerusalem Avenue, Back Bay." GAMBETTA.

REVIEW OF NEW MUSIC.

FROM NEW ENGLAND CONSERVATORY.

ORGAN ACCOMPANIMENT AND EXTEMPORE PLAYING.

BY GEORGE E. WHITING.

A valuable work treating of Psalmody, Extempore Interludes, Chanting, Transposition, Organ Accompaniment, The Use of the Organ, Instrumentation, Playing from Full Score, etc. A work which every organ student should possess, one for which there is a great demand, and one which will be valuable to many experienced organists.

RETROSPECTIVE AND PROSPECTIVE.

(Continued from page 272.)

for all the back numbers when subscribing, and a half of the remaining subscribers order all the back numbers inside of a month after they have subscribed. We still have a few copies of each issue left to supply such subscribers, though the number for two or three months will soon be exhausted.

We have invariably been conservative in foretelling our plans for the future, as "there is many a slip," etc.; but we can safely announce the following list of writers and composers who, with many others, will contribute to the columns of THE ORGAN during the coming year:—

Messrs. Charles A. Capen, Horatio Clarke, Henry M. Dunham, Clarence Eddy, Philip Hale, J. W. Hinton, B.A., E. A. Tilton, George E. Whiting, Arthur Whiting, and S. B. Whitney. The first chapter of a serial entitled, "The Organist's Retrospect," a posthumous narrative by Horatio Clarke, will appear in the May number, continuing in the following numbers, after which it will appear in book form. Our Paris correspondent will continue to contribute monthly letters, and we are negotiating for similar letters from New York and London. (Our former correspondent in London was compelled to discontinue his letters, owing to a contemplated change of residence to Germany.) The organ music at the World's Fair will be carefully treated, and every effort will be made to keep our readers informed on all the events transpiring in the "organ world."

If all our present subscribers who have found the journal satisfactory will renew their subscriptions, and each one send in one new subscriber, we will be able to carry out several cherished improvements for the coming year, which will render THE ORGAN much more valuable than at present.

TREMONT TEMPLE (Boston) ORGAN DESTROYED BY FIRE.

ABOUT 7.35 A.M., Sunday, March 19, fire broke out behind the organ in Tremont Temple, completely gutting the hall and ruining the organ. This instrument was constructed by Messrs. Hook & Hastings in 1880, and was opened by Messrs. S. B. Whitney and B. J. Lang, October 8. The organ contained four manuals, fifty-two speaking-stops, and ten combination pedals, including a grand crescendo having a vertical movement. The case was painted a delicate cream color, with gilt trimmings (in keeping with the decoration of the hall), and the displayed pipes were burnished.

The loss of this instrument removes the only organ available for concert purposes in Boston, and, for the present, will be sadly missed. While there were many commendable points about the instrument, the extremely narrow policy to which the builders adhered with this particular organ, they having the sole care of the instrument year after year, has prevented its use for organ concerts to any extent of late. Many of our leading organists agreed that it was hardly available for high-class concert work.

To be more particular. The absence of any stop softer than the Salicional in the swell; the Dulciana in the choir being too soft to accompany almost every solo stop or combination in the swell; the ponderous weight necessary to depress the swell-pedal; the unheard of locations of the two reversible pedals which worked the Gt. to Ped. coupler; the extreme power necessary to depress some of the combination pedals, and the comparative uselessness of a full-organ pedal which always draws the over-powering Tuba.

Some of these defects may seem trifling; but they are trifles which every organist who gave a concert on the organ had to encounter, and, furthermore, with one or two exceptions, each one of these defects could have been easily obviated at any time if the builders had consented. Take one case in particular. A full-organ pedal which draws all couplers and all stops (pneumatically, without affecting the draw-stops), except such stops as the Vox Humana, Clarinet, and Tuba (specially when the latter is voiced so very loud), is one of the most useful combination pedals which can be placed in a large organ. If the Tuba is added to the pedal its utility is reduced at least seventy-five per cent; for it is easy to draw the Tuba with the hand, in conjunction with the full-organ pedal, whenever it is required, but in the countless instances where the full-organ *without* the Tuba is required, the pedal is useless if the Tuba is attached to it. During the years in which the greatest number of organ concerts were given on this organ, a strong effort was made to have this Tuba disconnected from the full-organ pedal. The organist of the society who worshipped in the Temple Sundays acknowledged that the change would be very acceptable to him. Nearly every one of the organists who were using the instrument for concert purposes acknowledged that it was a desirable and necessary alteration. The superintendent of the Temple sent an order to the builders to make the alteration, but they flatly and positively refused to comply, their only excuse being that "it would seriously disarrange the internal construction of the instrument." No less than a half-dozen of the workmen who have taken care of this instrument, and who are probably as familiar with its "internal construction" as the builders themselves, acknowledged that a pocket-knife in the hands of any one of ordinary sense, who was familiar with organ construction, would make the change in a short space of time, without "disarranging the internal construction" of the instrument. From that very date the decline in popularity of this organ for concert purposes began, till they could be counted each year on the sore fingers of a small boy's left hand. In former years there were more *series* of concerts than *individual* concerts of late.

Now let us look at the other side of the case. As we said before, there were many commendable points about this instrument. The action of the great, with or without couplers, was excellent. The four manuals were placed in the most compact manner possible, the distance between the manuals being a half-inch (if we are not mistaken) less than is customary. The apparent distance (in playing) from the choir up to the solo was the shortest we have ever experienced between these two manuals. The voicing of many of the stops was extremely satisfactory, notably the Stentorphone in the solo organ, the Gemshorn, Doppelflöte, and Flute Harmonique in the great organ, the English Diapason, Flute d'Amour, and Vox Angelica in the choir. Two couplers of more than ordinary utility were the great to solo, and choir to great sub-octave. The Grand Crescendo and Diminuendo Pedals working vertically and not by means of a "power bellows," enabled the performer to control the crescendo and diminuendo better than in any other form of Grand Crescendo Pedal.

For six or eight years this organ was an important factor in the growth of organ music in Boston. Its commendable features were praised and its defects were commented upon. It is now an unrecognizable mass of charred wood and melted metal. Let us hope that the instrument which will probably take its place will have all the commendable features, with many more, in place of the defects of the destroyed organ.

MIXTURES.

FOUR RANKS.

MR. WALTER C. GALE has been engaged as organist of Holy Trinity Church, Harlem, N.Y.

Mr. W. F. Mac Tysson gave an organ concert in the First Baptist Church, Plainfield, N.J., Feb. 28.

Mr. George S. Hutchings has erected a two-manual organ, having sixteen registers, in Middlebury, Vt.

Mr. Harrison M. Wild's weekly organ recitals in Unity Church, Chicago, have been discontinued till further notice.

Mr. Minor C. Baldwin is giving a series of Lenten Organ Recitals in Chickering Hall, New York.

Mr. William E. Clayton, organist of Dr. Paxton's church, New York, has been taking a short vacation at his home in Maine.

Mr. W. H. Woodcock, Mus. Doc., will succeed Mr. Horatio W. Parker as organist of Holy Trinity, New York.

The Hook & Hastings organ now being erected in the Presbyterian Church of Pottstown, Pa., contains two manuals and twenty-one registers, and will be blown by a water motor. It stands against the wall at the side of the church, and is made twenty-six feet in width and only six feet in depth.

Dr. Bridge gave an organ concert at Westminster Abbey, Feb. 27.

It is said that at the inaugural recital given by Mr. Clarence Eddy, in the Campbell Park Presbyterian Church, March 3, the sum of $3,000 was realized by the sale of tickets.

Richard W. Crowe, Mus. Doc., has resigned his position as organist of St. Ann's Church, Brooklyn.

Messrs. Hook & Hastings have just shipped an organ for the Central Union Church of Honolulu, H.I. The instrument has two manuals and twenty-five registers, and will be erected by their Pacific Coast representative.

The death is announced of Mr. George Ferrey, who was for forty-two years organist of Christ Church, Priory, London.

An excellent half-tone portrait, with a brief sketch of the career of Mr. N. H. Allen, a prominent organist of Hartford, Conn., appeared in the last issue of the *Violist*, New York.

A new organ has just been placed in the new Epworth M. E. Church of New Haven, Conn., which will be opened within a few weeks. It is built by Hook & Hastings, and contains two manuals and twenty-four registers.

MM. Jaquot & Didier of Rambervillers, France, have placed an organ in the Church of Euville, Meuse.

At the last examination of the London College of Organists, fourteen candidates received diplomas of fellowship; and out of a hundred and five candidates, twenty-seven received diplomas of associateship.

Mr. George H. Ryder has closed up his business of organ manufacturing, and has identified himself with Mr. George S. Hutchings as agent, still retaining his office at Music Hall Building, Boston.

Mr. Geo. A. Kies gave an organ concert at Park Church, Norwich, Conn., Feb. 25, with the following programme: Third Sonata, Mendelssohn; Choral Prelude, Bach; Variations in A-flat, Thiele; Offertoire in F, Petrali; Barcarolle in G, Hofmann; Choral March, Buck.

A new organ constructed by Messrs. E. & J. Abbey was inaugurated in Notre Dame, Versailles, in February, by MM. Fauchey & Fauchet. The organ has two manuals, eighteen stops, and eleven combination pedals with pneumatic action.

On March 5 Mr. Harrison M. Wild gave his one hundred and twentieth concert in Unity Church, Chicago, playing the following organ pieces: Finale (VI. Symphony), Widor; Ninth Sonata, Merkel; Funeral March of a Marionette, Gounod-Best; Cantilène Pastorale, Guilmant; Fanfare, Lemmens; Overture to "Peter Schmoll," Weber.

Mr. Fred L. Clark gave his fifteenth recital in Payson Church, Easthampton, Mass., March 28, with the following programme: Fantasia in E-minor, Merkel; Serenade, Widor-Loret; Nuptial March, Guilmant; Andante from a String Quartet, Tschaikowski; Melody and Intermezzo, Parker; Minuetto, Salomé; St. Cecilia Offertory, Grison.

At the Lutheran Church of St. Trinitatis, in Jersey City, on Feb. 20, Mr. Alex S. Gibson of Waterbury, Conn., played these numbers: I. Fugue, etc.

Paris has at last been favored with a new concert hall containing an organ. The Count of Harcourt has founded this concert hall (in rue Rochechouart), which contains an organ built by MM. Merklin & Co., and several concerts will be given by Mons. Dallier, at an early date.

At Mr. Harrison M. Wild's recital in Unity Church, Chicago, March 12, the following compositions were given: Toccata and Fugue in C, Bach; Sonata Funèbre, Lemmens; War March, Mendelssohn; Funeral March ("Saul"), Handel; Nuptial March, Guilmant; Danses Croates, Op. 152, No. 1, Vilbac.

Mr. Loraine Holloway, F. C. O., formerly of London, came to this country in December, and is now organist of the church of St. John the Evangelist, Boston. We understand that this church advertised in England for an organist, to be selected by competition, and that Mr. Holloway was selected for that post.

A new organ built by Mr. Samuel Bohler of Reading, Pa., has been placed in St. Luke's Lutheran Church of that city. The organ has two manuals and twenty-one speaking-stops, the bellows being worked by an electric motor. Messrs. C. Wornberger & Branner, with other organists, performed at the opening recital.

Mr. Clarence Eddy, assisted by Mrs. Genevra Johnstone Bishop, gave a concert in the Presbyterian Church, Beaver, Pa., the last of February. Mr. Eddy performed the following selections: Toccata in A, Bach; "Am Meer," Schubert-Eddy; Fugue in G-minor, Bach; Overture to "Wm. Tell," Rossini-Buck; Hymn of Nuns, Wely; Variations on Austrian Hymn, Adrup; Concert Piece, Op. 33, Lux; Toccata in G, Dubois.

NEW ORGAN MUSIC.

Prelude	Horatio W. Parker.
Vision	Horatio W. Parker.
Pastorale Interlude	Horatio W. Parker.
Nocturne	Horatio W. Parker.
Fourth Sonata	Otto Dienel.
Fantasia (Op. 118)	E. Silas.
Twelve Pieces	J. G. Herzog.
Intermezzo	Josef Rheinberger.
Alla Marcia	Josef Rheinberger.
Thema Variato	Josef Rheinberger.
Passacaglia	Josef Rheinberger.
Fugato	Josef Rheinberger.
Finale	Josef Rheinberger.
("Meditations" Nos. 7–12.)	
Pastorale	O. Thomas.
Pastorale	P. Wachs.

Programme of the first opening recital of the late exhibition at the Exhibition Concert Hall, Brisbane, Australia: "God Save the Queen," Best; Overture to "Wm. Tell," Rossini; Barcarolle (Fourth Concerto), Bennett; Gavotte ("Mignon"), Thomas; Concert Variations on "Russian National Air," Freyer; Selections from "Ivanhoe," Sullivan; Fantasia on Two English Airs, Guilmant; Marche Cortège, Delibes; "La Dove," Mozart; Toccata, Widor; Idyll, Buck; Orchestral Overture, Hesman. Mr. and Mrs. W. G. Willmore, Mr. S. G. Benson, R.A.M., and Mr. Seymour Dicker were the organists.

A new argument for the organ in church. At Dufftown. During a dispute, the clerk was asked what authority there was in the New Testament for the organ. He replied by asking another question: What authority was there in the New Testament for clergymen wearing trousers ?—*London Musical Herald.*

Mr. Wm. Churchill Hammond gave his twentieth recital in the Second Congregational Church, Holyoke, Mass., March 1, with the following programme: Prelude in E-minor, Bach; Idylle ("Solitude"), Godard; Sonata No. 4, Guilmant; Isolde's Lament and Death, "Tristan und Isolde," Wagner. A string quartet assisted. At the preceding recital the following compositions were given: Prelude in D, Bach; Andante Cantabile, Tschaikowski; Sonata No. 10, Rheinberger; Symphonie Poem, "Orpheus," Liszt.

Mr. Clarence Eddy inaugurated a new organ (built by Mr. Carl Barckhoff) of Salem, O.) in Campbell Park, Presbyterian Church, Chicago, March 3, playing the following compositions in a miscellaneous programme: Toccata in A, Best; Prayer and Cradle Song, Guilmant; Schiller March, Meyerbeer; Variations on Austrian Hymn, Attrup; Concert Fugue in G, Krebs; Pastorale, from a Suite, King; "The Holy Night," Buck; Concert Piece, Lux; and Overture to "Wm. Tell," Rossini-Buck.

A new Wirsching organ in Memorial Presbyterian Church, Dayton, O., was opened in February by Mr. Clarence Eddy, who played the following pieces: Toccata in A, Best; "Au Matin," Schubert; Fugue in G-minor, Bach; Overture to "Wm. Tell," Rossini-Buck; Hymn of Nuns, Wély; Variation on the Austrian Hymn, Attrup; March of the Magi Kings, Dubois; Prayer and Cradle Song, Guilmant; Pastorale, from a Suite, King; "The Holy Night," Buck; Concert Piece, Lux; Toccata in G, Dubois.

Organ Concert in the Baptist Church, Arlington, Mass., by Mr. J. Frank Donahoe, March 7, in which the following pieces were performed: Overture to "Occasional Oratorio," Handel; Berceuse and Funeral March of a Marionette, Gounod; Overture to "Zanetta," Auber; Pastorale, Kullak; Offertoire, Op. 31, Batiste; Schiller March, Meyerbeer. The organ, which was built in 1879, has been recently enlarged by Mr. George S. Hutchings, and now contains twenty-eight speaking-stops (two manuals) and eight combination pedals. A large and enthusiastic audience enjoyed the popular programme, and demanded numerous encores. The performance of the various numbers has received many favorable comments.

The organ recently placed in Mr. J. Warren Andrews' Studio, at Plymouth Church, Minneapolis, by Mr. George S. Hutchings, contains the following stops: Great Organ: Op. Diapason, Melodia, and Dolcissimo, 8 Ft., and Octave, 4 Ft. Swell Organ: Bourdon, 16 Ft.; Violin Diapason, Salicional, Æoline, and St. Diapason, 8 Ft.; Flute Harmonique and Violina, 4 Ft.; and Oboe, 8 Ft. Pedal Organ: Bourdon, 16 Ft. Five composition pedals, reversed action, and electric motor. At its opening Mr. Andrews performed the following pieces, selected entirely from the works of J. S. Bach: Passacaglia and Fugue in C, First Movement of Sonata, No. 1, Toccata and Fugue in D-minor, Pastorale in F, Vorspiel, "Wir glaub All," and St. Ann's Fugue. Mr. Andrews was assisted by a soprano, a contralto, and two violinists.

A new organ in the Cathedral of Soissons, France, built by MM. Merklin and Co., was inaugurated with great pomp the last of January. The French custom of having every new organ tested, as it were, by a specially appointed board of examiners, consisting of a number of prominent organists, would be beneficial if adopted in this country. The organists who were prominent in this particular board of examiners were, MM. Dallier of St. Eustache, Paris; Ogé of the Cathedral, Maltin of St. Remi, Robin; Jacquemin of Mère Dame, Ilasse; Supret of St. Martin, Chauny; and Verneuil of the Basilica of St. Quentin. The organ has three manuals, thirty-six stops, and fourteen combination pedals.

Mons. Dupuis of Rouen, France, has recently constructed a new organ in the church of Sanvic. MM. Madeleine, Tessot, Santreuil, and Raugheolee of Havre, performed at the opening.

The organ in the Congregational Church, Middleborough, Mass., was destroyed March 14. The church was struck by lightning and totally destroyed.

The programme of Mr. Harrison M. Wild's one hundred and twenty-eighth organ concert in Unity Church, Chicago, contained the following numbers: Hallelujah Chorus, Beethoven-Best; Sonata, O. Fffti, Lenten to; Funeral March, Guyon; Berceuse, Smith; "God save the Queen," Op. 39, Best; and Romeo Cromes, Op. 152, No. 4, Villar.

Mr. Walter J. Clemson, M. A., organist of St. Thomas Church, Taunton, Mass., conducts a performance of King Arthur, a dramatic cantata by John More Smith, April 10.

Organ recitals were given at the Bow and Bromley Institute, London, during last month, by the following organists: Mr. Herbert F. Ellingford (on the 4th), Mr. Frank N. Abernethy (on the 11th), and Mr. F. Cunningham Woods (on the 18th).

Mr. Benjamin Edson Hallett gave an organ concert in the Baptist Church, Hyannis, Mass., a short time ago, in which he was assisted by Mrs. W. E. Crowell, soprano, Mr. Edmund Eldridge, tenor, Mr. Clinton F. Hallett, violinist, and the Hyannis Orchestra.

Mr. Geo. E. Whiting gave an organ concert at the N. E. Conservatory March 23.

Mr. Harrison M. Wild's last concert of this season, at the Unity Church, Chicago, was given March 26, with the following programme: Introduction and Fugue, Op. 17, Krueger; Adoratio et Vox Angelus, and Fantasia Triomphale, Dubois; Fantasia on the Russian Hymn, Planté; Nocturne, Op. 48, No. 1, Chopin-Forgas; Prelude, MacMorster; Toccata (Fifth Symphony), Widor; and Easter Offertoire, Op. 20, No. 1, Grison.

Mr. Frank Treat Southwick has been appointed organist of St. Andrew's M.E. Church, New York.

The Church of our Saviour, Longwood, Boston, changes organists after Easter; Mr. Goodrich taking Mr. Atwood's place.

J. C. Warren has been engaged at Rev. Dr. Hale's church, Newbury Street, Boston, to succeed Mr. George W. Chadwick.

Mr. William Shelmerdine, who was for forty years a prominent organist in Nottingham, England, died Feb. 20 at Pwllheli, Wales.

Mr. Wm. S. Chester is giving a series of Lenten recitals on Wednesday afternoons at St. George's Church, New York, where he has a large three-manual Jardine organ, which has seventy-five speaking-stops. On the 15th his selections were the following: Nuptial March, Guilmant; Largo, Handel; Coronation March, Meyerbeer; Entr'acte, "Rosamunde," Schubert; Marche Funèbre et Chant Séraphique, Guilmant; and six movements from "Die Meistersinger," Wagner.

Just before going to press we received from Australia the following items, which will interest our readers: A new organ with twelve stops in the gospel, eleven in the swell, seven in the choir, and four in the pedal, was opened in St. Joseph's Church, Warrnambool, Victoria, Jan. 29. The instrument was constructed by Fincham of Melbourne. Mons. A. Wiegand performed the following compositions at his organ recital, Jan. 26, in the Town Hall, Sydney: Grand Chœur, Batiste; Chanson d'une Jeune Fille, Dupont; Duck, "Credo' perche Scorso," Mozart; Fantasia on "Il Trovatore," Verdi; Fantasia, "The Storm," Batiste; Fugues Fleuries, Maitly; "Pio Peccatis," "Stabat Mater," Rossini; March, "Truny is Steel," Pinsuti.

Mr. G. B. Fenton, organist of St. Stephen's Church, Richmond, played the following compositions at the Melbourne Town Hall, Jan. 24: First Sonata, Mendelssohn; Prelude and Fugue in G, Bach; Christmas Offertoire, Lemmens; A Dream of Mozart, Shaw; Air and Variation, Best; Dramatic Fantasia, Neukomm. Mr. Neville Barnett, F. C. O., gave the following programme in St. Mary's Cathedral, Jan. 31: First Sonata, Mendelssohn; Larghetto (Clarinet Quintette), Mozart; Concerto in F, Handel; Aria, "Mein glaübiges Herze," Bach; Allegretto in E-minor, Guilmant; Allegretto and Andante, "Peer Gynt," Grieg; "Träumerei," Schumann; Andante in F, Wély; Toccata in B-minor, Batiste.

OUR PARIS LETTER.

PARIS, 10 March, 1893.

To the Editor of THE ORGAN:

THIS letter will have to be rather fragmentary, as none of the spring recitals have been given as yet, though the weather here is already quite warm and balmy. Last Saturday a new building in the Jardin d'Acclimatation, called the Palais d'Hiver was completed. It is a kind of indoor concert garden; the hall itself is about as large as our Music

Hall, and is designed for popular concerts and various light entertainments. Eventually it is to have a fine organ, but Cavaillé-Coll has set up a small two-manual organ temporarily. At the opening ceremonies last week a concert was given with full orchestra, soloists, and organ. President Carnot was present, and by his special invitation Guilmant played several of his own pieces. Among others the "Grand Chœur," in mi bémol, and the well-known "Élévation," in la bémol, and also played the accompaniment in Gounod's Meditation upon Bach's Prelude in C major. Of course the effect was not very striking, as the organ was far too small for the hall; but it could be seen that the acoustics of the building were well adapted for a large organ. Guilmant has just gone to London for two weeks, by invitation of the Prince of Wales, to preside at the examinations of the Royal College of Music.

Last week I had the pleasure of calling upon Monsieur F. de la Tombelle, the well-known composer, who, by the way, is a "real live" French baron. I don't know as this fact is generally known in America. He has a charming hôtel on the Rue Newton, very near the Arc de Triomphe. He is a rather young man, with dark brown hair brushed back from his brow in true artistic fashion, and with a bright interesting face. He was formerly a pupil of Guilmant. I had an interesting chat with him on French music. He is a great admirer of the German school, or appeared to be, and yet he seemed to think that the German composers were often very prolix, and that the greatest French composers, Saint-Saëns and Massenet, for example, had succeeded in getting from them about all that was worthy of imitation. This remark seemed to me rather ultra-patriotic, to say the least; especially in the case of Massenet, who is a pronounced imitator of Wagner (as who can help being?), but who often imitates him so badly that he falls between two stools, neither being true to his French nationality nor copying well the German school.

The readers of THE ORGAN, especially those who are studying to become organists themselves, may like to know of some of Guilmant's most important principles in organ teaching. Perhaps the two principles upon which he insists the most, and which will be most useful to cite, are the necessity of phrasing in all the voices with both hands and feet, and the equal necessity of cultivating a good organ touch in full chords. In playing full chords it is necessary to strike them with the utmost precision and vigor, and not to let them up too soon, but when the hands are raised that they should be raised with the same precision as in the attack. A good example of organ phrasing is found in Bach's second organ fugue, which Guilmant plays as follows: —

Fuga No. 2.

When one comes to the stretto in this fugue it will be seen how necessary the phrasing is to bring out the full meaning of Bach. Any one who will master the phrasing in this fugue may feel sure he has conquered one of the most important principles of true organ playing.

To-night Widor, the famous composer, as well as organist, takes part in a chamber concert in which some of his own compositions are to be played, — a sonata for violin and piano, and a quartet for strings. By the time of my next letter the large organs which are silent during Lent will be sounding again, and I trust that Guilmant's recitals at the Trocadéro will also have begun. OUTRE MER.

CORRESPONDENCE.

AN IDEAL ORGAN.

To the Editor of THE ORGAN :

IN your issue of this month Mr. Carleton Michel has answered my question that you kindly inserted in your February issue. As I stated in my question of that date, "Why evade the question?" Mr. Michel has evaded it! He did not draw the line that I so much desired! Is the problem to be solved by laying the blame on the organ-builders? I herald all improvements in organ-building. But there is no "Ideal" in the shape of a pipe organ that I can dream of, or delude my mind into believing, that will ever possibly fulfil the expression of works that is now demanded of it! It may be in the range of possibilities; I would not discourage it. Twenty years ago the telephone was not dreamed of. But why theorize? Let us put the organ where it belongs! Since the introduction of mammoth organs throughout our country, the sole effort has seemed to be, to make it suitable for concert purposes! I have yet to learn of one that has not been a signal failure.

Let us first take the great and magnificent Music Hall Organ at Cincinnati. How perplexing, and perhaps discouraging, has been the utter indifference that has been shown to this great organ. It is scarcely heard half a dozen times in a year. And then chiefly employed on some political or religious occasion to play a few simple hymns or national airs. George Whiting's audiences in the immense auditorium were limited frequently to twelve or thirteen listeners, while Cincinnati sends five to eight thousand to listen to the Thomas Orchestra. The return for this $50,000 for a grand concert organ, as an investment, is practically an unproductive gold mine. Then again in your issue of this month some one asks the question, Why was the great Boston Organ removed from Music Hall? Where is it now? This great organ, erected at an expense of about $60,000, sold at about one-twentieth its original cost to enable the heartless corporation (you say) to place a dozen more extra seats in the hall, and have a few more square feet of stage-room. The same experience!

The magnificent Roosevelt organ ($32,000) in the Chicago Auditorium bids fair to experience a like result. But to our subject. We have instrumentation sufficient to properly fulfil all our realizations in the expression of the spiritual in music. The pipes cannot take the place of the strings, and although we are overwhelmed by the massiveness of the diapasons, we feel the spark divine that comes from the mobile character of a group of little brown instruments. The organ cannot be king in this respect, only king as it is counterpoint compelling. A chromo lithograph might interest us, please us by its beauty of coloring; but to the educated the finely worked tracery of lines showing pathos and passion are needed to fulfil their realization of the expression of things divine.

Is the organ any other but God's chosen instrument? Can we by any means break down the barriers that hedge it in? I think we are only deluding ourselves when we are giving it music to say and do that, as I said before, is incompatible with her construction! Is there not some learned doctor that has the courage to draw the line for us?

Perhaps if compositions for the organ were *restricted*, and only compositions of a strictly polished counterpoint character, there would be less of this slapdash transcription of operas, overtures, etc. (that are a libel on the instrument), as only then would composers of value and merit compose for the instrument!

Mr. C. Michel says, "But why not break up this arbitrary constitution? . . . Why be satisfied with an instrument wholly unfitted for the expression of the largest portion of music written, the most exquisite portion being excluded, when the remedy is at hand?"

Would it not have been better to have put it this way: "Keep the organ inviolate in its arbitrary constitution, giving

(Continued on page 287.)

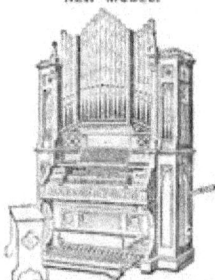

CORRESPONDENCE.

(Continued from page 264.)

it such music as is adapted to its demands; and be satisfied that it is created for sanctuary purposes, which, in the majority of our denominational usages, is *conventional* and *arbitrary*, conceding and allowing that it is not suited to a large portion of exquisite music written."

If it is a failure in the representation of concert music of the romantic school, we are obliged to find use for it in the church. And, if this is the case, transcriptions of operas, overtures, etc., would not be in keeping with the place where everything of a *secular* suggestion ought to be excluded. With all the proposed appliances of swell and electrical apparatus, touch, and mechanical contrivances, I fail to see that the remedy is feasible. The only remedy at hand is a more thorough education of musicians into a knowledge of a true school of organ music. A classical school that is replete in fulness and depth of thought, combining beauty, polish, elegance, and grace suited to the grandeur and sublimity of its thunder tones, and which is adapted to the divine service.

And just here I must repeat my question. Will some Doctor of Music give us a standard that we may present to our pupils and live up to ourselves? A standard in the exercise of which we will not lose respect for ourselves, and not have to cater to a popular taste that loves those delicious sweets that are not best suited to the needs of their systems. But give us a *standard*, the same as we would expect in literature, painting, etc., letting the line be drawn tight if need be, only that we get the truth!

The words of Scaneder define the mission of the organ about as clearly as any I have met. He defines as follows: "An organ consecrated to the sanctuary and to sacred music is intended to be subservient to the edification of a congregation assembled together for divine worship, to support, to accompany in a proper manner the singing, and the instrumental in promoting a devotional frame of mind, and the edification of the soul, and its elevation of everything earthly to the contemplation of things invisible and divine." A Noble Object!

Yours most respectfully,
O. S. RICHARDS.

DETROIT, MICH., March 8, 1893.

CIPHERINGS.

GIRL. "Do you play the organ by note?"
DUDE. "Oh, no! I play by ear."
GIRL. "I don't see how you reach the upper keys."
—*Ex.*

* * *

THE master of ceremonies at a recent fashionable wedding in church was quite tight in telling the organist, who had forgotten his music, to "improvise anything he pleased." Improvising generally means "impoverishing."—*Musical Herald.*

* * *

ORGANIST. "Certainly we can tell you all about organ swells. An organ swell is a young man who comes in ten minutes late to service, takes off his gloves, dusts the organ seat with a scented handkerchief, and then plays fantasias from Italian operas." — *Musical Herald.*

* * *

THEY put up an organ at a county fair and invited all their local talents to exhibit it. The first played the Hallelujah Chorus, the second the Dead March in *Saul*; the next day a new-comer played the Dead March in *Saul*, and another the Hallelujah Chorus; and thus it went on. Finally, a member of the committee hit on an expedient which should do away with the monotony without offending the artists. He put a sign on the instrument, "Visitors, please not Händel." — *Ex.*

At a late Cincinnati wedding the organist entertained the audience awaiting the bridal part by a series of voluntaries, the last of which was, "Trust her not, she is fooling thee," at which he was hard at work as the bridal procession walked up the aisle. — *Detroit Free Press.*

* * *

MORE POWER NEEDED.

MINISTER. "I think we should have congregational singing."
ORGANIST. "Then we must have a new organ."
"Why so?"
"This instrument isn't powerful enough to drown 'em out." — *Topeka Capital.*

* * *

SYMPATHY.

CAPTAIN (*to* STOWAWAY). "So, you young rascal, you ran away from home, did you? You ought to be thrashed for leaving home, and thrashed again for getting aboard ship without permission."

STOWAWAY. "Please, sir, my sister commenced takin' organ lessons an' practisin' scales on the organ, an' — and I thought there would be no organs on ship" —

CAPTAIN. "Come to my arms, my son, I had a musical sister once myself." — *Ex.*

NEW ORGANS.

NEW ORGAN IN EUCLID-AVE. BAPTIST CHURCH, CLEVELAND, O.

Built by Mr. Geo. S. Hutchings, Boston.

GREAT ORGAN.		SWELL ORGAN.	
Open Diapason	16 Ft.	Bourdon Treble }	16 Ft.
Open Diapason	8 "	Bourdon Bass }	
Viola da Gamba	8 "	Violin Diapason	8 "
Doppelflöte	8 "	Salicional	8 "
Octave	4 "	Æoline	8 "
Flûte Harmonique	4 "	Stopped Diapason	8 "
Octave Quint	2⅔ "	Quintadena	8 "
Super Octave	2 "	Flauto Traverso	4 "
Mixture	III. Rks.	Fugara	4 "
Trumpet	8 Ft.	Flautino	2 "
		Dolce Cornet	III. Rks.
		Cornopean	8 Ft.
CHOIR ORGAN.		Oboe	8 "
(The entire Choir Organ enclosed		Vox Humana	8 "
in a separate Swell-Box, and operated by a Balanced Swell Pedal.)		PEDAL ORGAN.	
Geigen Principal	8 Ft.	Open Diapason	16 Ft.
Dolcissimo	8 "	Bourdon	16 "
Melodia (Stopped Bass)	8 "	Violoncello	8 "
Flûte d'Amour	4 "	The usual Mechanical Registers and	
Violina	4 "	Couplers.	
Piccolo Harmonique	2 "	Pneumatic Motors applied to the	
Clarinet (Reed in Bass)	8 "	Great Organ, and all its Couplers.	

A LARGE two-manual organ is now being erected in the First M. E. Church of Tacoma, Wash., by Hook & Hastings. We append herewith a description of its stops.

GREAT ORGAN.		SWELL ORGAN.	
Open Diapason	16 Ft.	Bourdon	16 Ft.
Open Diapason	8 "	Open Diapason	8 "
Dulciana	8 "	Viola	8 "
Salicional	8 "	Stopped Diapason	8 "
Melodia	8 "	Quintadena	8 "
Octave	4 "	Flauto Traverso	4 "
Flute d'Amour	4 "	Violina	4 "
Twelfth	2⅔ "	Flautino	2 "
Fifteenth	2 "	Dolce Cornet	III. Rks.
Mixture	III. Rks.	Cornopean	8 Ft.
Trumpet	8 Ft.	Oboe }	8 "
		Bassoon }	
PEDAL ORGAN.		PEDAL MOVEMENTS.	
Open Diapason	16 Ft.	Forte, Combination, Great Organ.	
Bourdon	16 "	Piano, Combination, Great Organ.	
Violoncello	8 Ft.	Forte, Combination, Swell Organ.	
Pneumatic Action to both Gt. and		Piano, Combination, Swell Organ.	
Sw.		Reversible Gt. to Ped.	

ANNOUNCEMENT.

VOLUME II. OF THE ORGAN

COMMENCES

❊ MAY 1, 1893. ❊

Among the Contributors will be

MR. CHARLES A. CAPEN.

MR. HORATIO CLARKE.

MR. HENRY M. DUNHAM.

MR. CLARENCE EDDY.

MR. PHILIP HALE.

MR. J. A. HINTON, B.A.

MR. EDWIN A. TILTON.

MR. GEORGE E. WHITING.

MR. ARTHUR WHITING.

MR. S. B. WHITNEY,

AND OTHERS.

A serial entitled **THE ORGANIST'S RETROSPECT**, *a posthumous narrative by Horatio Clarke, will commence with the May number and continue through following numbers, after which it will appear in book form.*

The monthly letters from Paris will be continued, and similar letters from London and New York will be presented to the readers. All the organ arts of the World's Fair will be chronicled.

Each number will be illustrated with cuts of notable organs and portraits of noted organists, besides representations of organ mechanism.

The following premiums are offered to those of the present subscribers who care to solicit other subscribers:

PREMIUM LIST.

	PRICE
Batiste, Four Elevations. (For 3 Subscribers.)	$1 50
Batiste, Offertoire in G, and Elevation in E flat. (For 3 Subscribers.)	1.50
Parisot, Elevation (For 2 Subscribers.)	.90
Grison, Communion. (For 2 Subscribers.).	.80
Grison, St. Cecilia Offertoire. (For 2 Subscribers.)	.90
Tombelle, Pastorale and Marche Nuptiale. (For 3 Subscribers.)	1.60
Tombelle, Sonata. Op. 23. (For 4 Subscribers.)	2.25
Tombelle Sonata. Op. 33. (For 4 Subscribers.)	2.00
Truette, A Graded List of Studies and Pieces for the Organ. (For 1 Subscriber.)	.60
Whiting, Organ Accompaniment and Extempo Playing. (For 5 Subscribers.)	2.50
Clarke, An Outline of the Structure of the Pipe Organ. (For 4 Subscribers.)	2.00
Locher, An Explanation of Organ Stops. (For 4 Subscribers.)	2.00
Wicks, Amateur Organ Building. (For 4 Subscribers.)	2.00
Whitney's Organ Book. (For 4 Subscribers.)	2.00
Eddy, Church and Concert Organist. (For 6 Subscribers.)	3.00
Eddy, Church and Concert Organist (Bk. 2). (For 6 Subscribers.)	3.00
Eddy, The Organ in Church. (For 6 Subscribers.)	3.00

Any of the above works sent (postage prepaid) on receipt of the price.

Subscription (in advance), $2.00 ; European Countries, 10s. 5d. Single Copies, 25 Cents.

EVERETT E. TRUETTE, Editor and Publisher,

149A Tremont Street, Boston, Mass.

THE ORGAN

VOLUME II.

MAY, 1893—APRIL, 1894.

INDEX.

INDEX

VOL. II. No. I.   MAY, 1893.   WHOLE No. 13.

BACH

YEARLY SUBSCRIPTION $2.00.   SINGLE COPIES 25 CTS

THE ORGAN

DEVOTED TO

A MONTHLY JOURNAL

THE KING OF INSTRUMENTS

EVERETT · E · TRUETTE ·
EDITOR & PUBLISHER
149 A. TREMONT ST. BOSTON.

HANDEL

The New England Conservatory of Music.

CARL FAELTEN, Director.

The Organ Department

offers unsurpassed facilities for acquiring a thorough and practical education in the art of Organ Playing. The course of study, which may be pursued, either in class or with private instruction, embraces work in Pedal Obligato Playing, Hymn Tunes and Chorales, with Interludes and Modulations. Afterwards Organ works of polyphonic character, Anthems and Improvisations, and for more advanced students works by all the great writers for the Organ, together with the study of Masses, Oratorios, etc.

There are in the Conservatory building for the exclusive use of this Department *fourteen* Pedal Organs, several of which possess three manuals each.

Those students who have acquired sufficient ability are aided in securing Church positions by the *Conservatory Bureau.* A large number of students have already been placed in lucrative positions by the Bureau.

TUITION: CLASSES OF FOUR, TERM OF TEN WEEKS, $20.00.

BOARD OF INSTRUCTION.
GEORGE E. WHITING.
HENRY M. DUNHAM.
ALLEN W. SWAN.

Organ Practice, 10 cents per hour and upwards.
Pupils may enter at any time.
School Year from Sept. 7, '93 to June 21, '94.

Address, FRANK W. HALE, General Manager, Franklin Square, Boston, Mass.

THE ORGAN.

Vol. II. BOSTON, MAY, 1893. No. 1.

THE ORGAN.

A MONTHLY JOURNAL

DEVOTED TO THE KING OF INSTRUMENTS.

EVERETT E. TRUETTE, EDITOR AND PUBLISHER.

(Entered at the Boston, Mass., Post-office as second-class mail matter, June 1, 1892)

CONTENTS:

ADOLPH FRIEDRICH HESSE.

ADOLPH FRIEDRICH HESSE, great organ-player and composer, son of an organ-builder, was born Aug. 30, 1809, at Breslau. His masters in the pianoforte, composition, and the organ, were Berner and E. Köhler. His talent was sufficiently remarkable to induce the authorities of Breslau to grant him an allowance, which enabled him to visit Leipzig, Cassel, Hamburg, Berlin, and Weimar, in each of which he played his own and other compositions, and enjoyed the instruction and acquaintance of Hummel, Rinck, and Spohr. In 1831 he obtained the post which he kept till his death, — that of organist to the church of the Bernhardins, Breslau. In 1844 he opened the organ at S. Eustache in Paris, and astonished the Parisians by his pedal playing. In 1851 he was in London, and played on several of the organs in the Crystal Palace in Hyde Park — protesting much against the unequal temperament in some of them. But his home was Breslau, where he was visited by a constant stream of admirers from far and near up to his death, Aug. 5, 1863. Hesse was director of the Symphony-Concerts at Breslau, and left behind him a mass of compositions of all classes. But it is by his organ works that he will be remembered. His "Practical Organist," containing twenty-nine pieces, — amongst them the well-known variations on "God save the King," — has been edited by Lincoln and published by Novello. A complete collection of his organ works was edited by Steggall and published by Bousey. SIR GEORGE GROVE, D.C.L.

THE ORGANIST'S RETROSPECT.[1]

BY HORATIO CLARKE.

CHAPTER I.

THE organ was draped in mourning.

During the service the desk was closed and the Spirit of Music hushed her grief in silence; for the hands which had pressed the keys and made those pipes speak eloquent tones of comfort, and which had moved the hearts of many with emotion, were crossed upon the breast of the form now passive before the altar.

The sanctuary was filled with those who had gathered to testify their respect for the life and character of one who, although not intimately known to many, had made a deep impression upon all.

At the close of his remarks the minister said, —

"I am not prone to indulge in eulogy, but I cannot forbear referring to my personal acquaintance with our gifted friend. His gentle and retiring spirit will continue to live in our memories. He was my helper in my labor of religious instruction here, and to-day I feel my great loss. He had the rare power of carrying out my thoughts in musical language, so that good impressions would be fixed in the mind.

"He knew what melodies and harmonies would best mingle in consonance to express deeper sentiments than words could frame, and many of your hearts have been touched during this short year in which he has ministered these heavenly strains to us.

"He had learned to *serve* with his chosen art without expecting laudation, and he made it holy for the good of others. He was filled with the spirit of charitable judgment for the opinions of those from whom he differed in thought, and he did not speak disparagingly of the efforts of others, nor did he wound by egoistically thrusting his own cherished and confirmed ideas among them.

"With a refined and well-balanced mind, his profession did not render him effeminate. It is hard to part from such a friend, but his living influence will ever remain with us when we bear him thoughtfully in remembrance."

Then an old white-haired man arose and came forward. Clasping his hand on the rigid fingers of the organist, he said with deep feeling, —

"I am too late to say what I wished to whisper in his living ear; but, my friends, a few weeks ago, when my dear old wife was dying, she looked up into my face and whispered that she wished that she might hear these cold fingers touch the harmonies of yonder silent organ again, for when she last worshipped here his music thrilled some inner chord of her heart, — and as she breathed these words she passed away. If I could only have told him of this, it would have comforted him, to know how much good his music had been doing."

This touching incident found response throughout the audience, for there had been a mysterious power in the influence of the music which found utterance through this talented organist.

As the venerable speaker removed the pressure of his hand, what caused him to start with violent emotion? Had a state of catalepsy been mistaken for death? Was this a condition of suspended animation? Was there any effect in the touch of the old man's hand which could have started the latent pulse of that cold form into the beginning of a higher earthly existence, wherein his life would be quickened into a more powerful influence for blessing his fellow-creatures?

Turning to the congregation with uplifted hands, he passionately exclaimed, —

"He is *living! He* BREATHES!"

As with the force of an electric shock, the entire audience rose with excitement; but immediately, by imperative request, all left the edifice, as the organist was carried to the pastor's study in his funeral casket, where the application of restoratives caused his eyes to slowly open, to behold the face of his friend bending over him.

One year before this eventful day a grand organ had been placed in the church as the gift of a wealthy benefactor of the society, and the generous donor had also sent this cultivated musician as its appropriate organist. It was in a thriving city of the Empire State, and the minister was a man of broad charity, who made no sectarian discrimination between men, recognizing all as belonging to the brotherhood of humanity; and he devoted his life to ministering unto those whom he could assist in improving their spiritual and social condition.

Ernest Osborne, the organist, had not sought to make himself known, and did not speak of himself. From the time of his introduction, he had made a powerful impression upon the worshippers through his musical talents. His name had not been heralded as a famous player, nor had he been published abroad as a celebrated composer, although critics who had examined his manuscripts pronounced them to be of high classical structure. When importuned to give them to the public, he always replied that since the works of the great masters could be easily obtained, he would not distract attention from them by attempting to thrust his fancies and studies upon the musical world.

"Strongest minds
Are often those of whom the noisy world
Hears least."

As an interpreter of classical organ music few could excel him when he was untrammelled; but his organization was so sensitive that he could not endure playing before the general public, and he confined his work to the requirements of religious services. His unusual gift at improvisation in this field gave him a power over his listeners which brought them into sympathy with his musical thoughts, lifting them above material things; and many came to listen to his music who had no interest in the forms of religious worship.

Four days before these funeral services Mr. Osborne had requested the minister to call upon him, as he was unable to leave his room. He told his friend that he felt that he might not live many days; that for a number of weeks he had perceived the encroachment of nervous prostration, which was settling into a pressure around the heart. Up to this time it had not interfered with his professional duties, but, should this be the end, he should reverently accept the solemn event to which all past generations have bowed in submission as the common lot of man.

He seemed so imbued with a true spiritual philosophy, that there were neither forebodings nor complaints. He had just received information that a large inheritance from his mother's family in England simply awaited the proper identification, with his legal credentials, and he desired to have his will made at once. Without deploring the delay in the good fortune which was about to come, he expressed the hope that, if his life should be spared, he could use the remainder of his existence in being more useful to the world with his competency.

After the documents had been signed and the notary had departed, he took from his desk a sealed package, and told the minister that during the past few weeks he had recorded an outline of his musical experiences and thoughts as he had looked back upon the history of his life, which was the only external memorial which he could leave by which he might be held in remembrance, should it be wise for any other eyes to read.

Alone in the dreary night which followed, the deadly strife between the vital force and its enemy was so severe that the rays of the morning sun shining on that weary face awakened no expression of life, — and thus the struggling spirit closed its artistic labor in the service of the King of Instruments.

Under the extraordinary circumstances of the revivification of the life of Ernest Osborne for a nobler work, to which all former experiences were but preparatory, the retrospect of his life as an organist was recorded with the intention of its being a posthumous publication. It was written in a simple and unaffected style characteristic of the organist; and his friend, the minister, felt that other kindred natures might find sympathy, encouragement, and strength, could they gain an insight into the motives of one who sought high ideals in sincerity of purpose, while following a professional career which was now ended.

(To be continued.)

THE HOPE-JONES SYSTEM OF ELECTRICAL ORGAN CONTROL.

II.

In continuation of our former article on this subject, we will now proceed to describe in greater detail some of the leading features of the system. First we must deal with one form of the electro-pneumatic lever employed, — a form which will serve more or less to show the principle always adopted by Mr. Hope-Jones.

In our illustration, Fig. 1, we give a rough section of part of an ordinary pallet and slider soundboard. Below this, and slightly to the left hand, we show a section through one of the electro-pneumatic levers used for opening the pallet P through the medium of the pull-down N.

The following enumeration of the various parts of the

apparatus and description of its working will doubtless give
the reader a grasp of the action : —

A. Wind-chest under pressure from bellows.
B. Horse-shoe electro-magnet to attract armature disk.
C. Small soft iron armature disk with a movement of about one-hundredth of an inch in a vertical direction.
D. Adjustable metal valve-seat having boxes at base perforated with minute holes, Q.
E. Hard-wood cap to hold valve-seat and fit on over magnet plate, forming small air-chamber.
F. Small motor or bellows.
G. Channel connecting motor and air-chamber in cap.
H. Pallet opening or closing inlet to large motor of bellows.
J. Wire coupling pallet and small motor.
K. Pallet opening or closing exhaust on large motor.
L. Wire coupling both pallets.
M. Large motor coupled to pull down working pallet in soundboard.
N. Pull-down wire.
O. Magnet plate.
P. Soundboard pallet.
Q. Small holes in valve-seat.

DESCRIPTION OF WORKING.

Normally,
The soundboard pallet P is closed.
The large motor M is closed.
The exhaust pallet K is open.
The inlet pallet H is closed.
The small motor F is inflated.
The disk C is blown up against the valve-seat, closing the exit to atmosphere.
The small air-chamber O is opened to the wind-chest A, and so is under pressure.

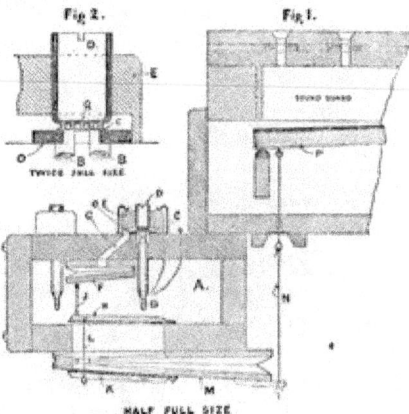

Fig. 2.   Fig. 1.

TWICE FULL SIZE

SOUND BOARD

HALF FULL SIZE

When the key is depressed,
An electrical contact is made at the key.
A current of electricity circulates round the magnet B.
The magnet B immediately grips down the disk C, closing communication with the wind-chest A, and allowing the air under pressure in the cap-chamber O to exhaust to atmosphere.
The small motor F collapses, opening inlet H to large motor M, and closing exhaust K.
The large motor is inflated and the soundboard pallet P opened, thus permitting the pipes to speak.

In Fig. 2 we give an enlarged view of the armature valve, with its valve-seat and disk. These pieces of apparatus are the result of a great amount of careful thought and patient experiment. The weight of the valve, the pressure of the air, the size of the small holes in the valve-seat, the diameter of the small bosses through which these holes are pierced, etc., bear definite and peculiar proportions to each other. The result of this is that the valve becomes extremely sensitive to faint electric impulses, and moves through its minute space of travel with a rapidity and certainty that are truly aston-

ishing. The electro-magnet B is not constructed in the ordinary manner, but is wound so as to cover all traces of self-induction, and so avoid the minute sparking at the key-contact which has rendered other electric actions uncertain through consequent oxidization. The Hope-Jones electro-pneumatic lever does not require one-hundredth part of the current necessary to operate any of the forms previously introduced ; and on this account a single Leclanché Cell is found to be sufficient to control a large cathedral organ through a cable several hundred feet in length. Not only does this cell operate the organ, but it supplies so much more electrical current than is necessary, that ample margin is provided for the irregularities of adjustment certain to be met with in practical work. On this account it is reported that the action never fails.

The rapidity of attack and repetition of electro-pneumatic action constructed in accord with this system is most remarkable, and has a peculiar influence on the tonal effect of an organ. When a tracker or ordinary pneumatic action is used, the full speech of the pipes is not obtained unless the keys be held for an appreciable time. If we consider the tracker action, for instance, we shall see that upon striking a staccato note the pallet is opening (and so impeding the wind travelling in the reverse direction to the pipes) during the whole downward travel of the key. The pallet is also coming upwards and closing the orifice during the whole of the upward travel of the key. When the Hope-Jones electro-pneumatic action is used, the pallet flies open to its full limit the moment the key begins to descend ; and it lies open during the whole downward and upward travel of the key, until the contact is broken. This matter of attack, which we should have deemed of little practical advantage, exercises, we are informed, a remarkable effect upon the tone. It allows of thicker tongues being used for the reeds, while it imparts to an old and otherwise poor instrument, such as that at St. John's Church, Birkenhead, England, a dignity and apparent power of tone which such authorities as Dr. Haydn Keeton, organist of Peterboro Cathedral, and Dr. Roberts, organist of Magdalen College, Oxford, England, speak of as " startling " and " astounding."

(*To be continued.*)

PLAYING THE ORGAN FROM MEMORY.

THE following letter to the Chicago *Tribune* on the above subject, written by Mr. Clarence Eddy, has created quite a sensation in some sections of the organ world : —

CHICAGO, March 22
EDITOR OF THE *Tribune,* — Your issue of to-day contains a report of an organ concert which took place in this city last evening. After mentioning some of the selections contained in the programme, your reporter makes the following assertions : —

" All of these were played from memory ; and the freedom in expression and increased animation revealed in the player's work by reason of his being unhampered by notes, lent unusual worth to the performance, and demonstrated than organists, like pianists, are heard at their best only when they have memorized the compositions they play."

As an organist of considerable experience, and a personal friend of many distinguished players of the organ whose views on this subject coincide with mine, I take exception to the import of the above statement. In only one particular is the organ like the piano : namely, that the key-boards are similar. The structure of the organ is vastly more complicated than that of the piano, while its scope and tonal resources are incomparable. In order to completely master a large organ, one must not only have a perfect command of the manual keyboards, but of the pedals and the vast array of mechanical accessories. He must not only comprehend the instrument as a whole, but thoroughly understand the workings of every detail. It is often necessary to prepare certain combinations of stops long before they are brought into action, and the mind is constantly forced to act far in advance of the fingers and feet.

Now, to burden the mind with memorizing the notes, in addition to these requirements, is as harmful as it is useless ; and I maintain that organists are heard at their best when they are unhampered by the mental strain attendant upon committing to memory the compositions they play. The "increased animation" which your reporter discovered last evening, I observed to be rather a frequent hurrying and unsteadiness of the tempo, caused by nervousness, which rendered the work of the player indistinct and inaccurate.

(*Continued on page 17.*)

THE ORGAN.

BOSTON, MAY, 1893.

THE ORGAN is published the first of every month. Subscription price $1.00 per year (European countries 1os. 56.), payable in advance. Single copies, 05 cents.

Subscribers will please state with which number they wish their subscription to begin.

Subscribers wishing the address of their paper changed must give the old as well as the new address.

Remittances should be made by registered letter, post-office order, or by check payable to Everett E. Truette.

Correspondence, to secure notice, must in all cases be accompanied by the name and address of the writer, not for publication, but as a guarantee of good faith.

Advertising rates sent on application.

Address all communications.

The Organ, 149 A Tremont Street, Boston, Mass.

☞ An active agent in every city is desired to whom a liberal cash commission will be allowed.

Single copies of THE ORGAN can be procured of

NOVELLO, EWER & Co.	New York.
G. SCHIRMER	New York.
OLIVER DITSON Co.	Boston.
L. H. Ross & Co.	Boston.
N. E. CONSERVATORY	Boston.
H. B. STEVENS Co.	Boston.
LYON & HEALY	Chicago.
THEODORE PRESSER	Philadelphia.
Wm. H. BONER & Co.	Philadelphia.
TAYLOR'S MUSIC HOUSE	Springfield, Mass.
GALLUP & METZGER	Hartford, Conn.
RICHAULT & Co.	Paris.
K. F. VIRGOE, (Sole Agent for Gt. Britain)	London.

ONE of the most convincing arguments of the value of THE ORGAN as an advertising medium may be found in the fact that every firm whose contract for advertising expired with the end of the first volume has renewed the contract for volume two.

A CORRESPONDENT writes that Boston will want to secure the large organ which is to be used at the World's Fair. We are afraid not. Boston is busy removing its large organs to the cemeteries, or burning them up. In all probability only a small organ will be placed in the reconstructed Tremont Temple, and that will be put in some corner as much out of the way as possible. We are having an epidemic of putting organs out of the way.

WE read in the *Musical Visitor* that "Tremont Temple, Boston, is again in ruins," and that the editor of THE ORGAN "not only loses his fine organ, but his office and belongings, as they were in the same building. He has our heartfelt sympathy."

We thank the *Musical Visitor* for its expression of sympathy, but our office is five blocks south of Tremont Temple, and our only personal loss was a box of toilet articles, which was in the anteroom of the Temple.

Musical Notes, a monthly musical journal published in New York, after a brief existence of three months has expired. When the managers of any proposed publication, in soliciting patronage ("ads" for instance), resort to the argument that some other existing periodical, which is in the same field of patronage, is worthless and patronized by no one, their argument may prove a boomerang. Daisies will grow beside a bed of the finest roses, fulfilling their mission regularly, and oftentimes continuing to grow and bloom long after the rose-bushes have decayed and ceased to exist. Better a bed of blooming daisies than a bed of decayed rose-bushes! However, we bear no ill-will towards *Musical Notes.* It was an attractive and useful monthly, and we regret its premature demise.

A CERTAIN priest who had ordered a new organ for his church, devised several original methods of moving his parishioners to be generous toward the organ fund, one of which was to read to his congregation the descriptive letters which he had received from the builder. Now, this priest was none too familiar with the technical terms of an organ, though he knew that pipes and bellows were essential parts of the instrument; but here are his remarks to his congregation : "I have received a letter from Mr. Jardine, who is building our new organ, and I suppose you all would like to know what he says. Well, Mr. Jardine writes that he will put an Open Die-ap-i-son and a Stopped Die-ap-i-son in the great organ. These are fine stops; but he further writes that in the *swell-box* he will put a *bourdon.*"

WE still have hopes of hearing Mr. W. T. Best and Mons. Alex Guilmant in this country during the coming fall. Every effort is being made to bring them to the World's Fair, and if they once cross the water they will be heard in many cities of the country. In Boston we are without any concert organ (New York is not much better off), and the recitals would have to be given in some church. This fact would necessitate a large guaranty fund to defray the expenses. THE ORGAN has undertaken to raise that fund, to insure two and possibly four recitals by these artists. Further particulars will be announced when more definite arrangements have been made. Mr. Clarence Eddy of Chicago writes us that interested parties in about twenty cities have guaranteed the expenses of concerts by these artists. Mr. Best is still in poor health, and unable to be at his regular post in Liverpool, therefore no positive announcement can be made at present.

WE have before us a descriptive circular issued by a firm of reed organ manufacturers which is extremely characteristic of the tendency of modern advertising. We quote a few lines : —

"Thirty-four Grand Stops condensed into seventeen (double-named) stops." We select a few, with the accompanying explanation (!) "(1) Celeste (2) Voix Celeste ; a very sweet stop. . . . It produces the sweetest tones ever heard. . . . On this patent alone $100,000 have been spent in various ways." "(7) Sub Bass (8) Manual Sub Bass ; new and original. Two *full* sets of Golden Tongue Reeds, of *one-half octave each.*" "(9) Piano (10) Grand Expression ; a very soft pedal stop, as often used in the *foot* pedals of a $1,000 upright pianoforte." (Who ever saw a *hand* pedal?) "(23) Vox Humana (24) Tremolent. A Fan Wheel. Not a cheap box with a cheap flap that cost five cents, but a revolving fan. *It fans the music* as you play. This music, when the stop is on, imitates an opera singer, *bringing out orchestral effects that cannot be produced without it.*" (Oh, give us a fan quick !) "(27) French Horn Piccolo Stop" "(33) Automatic Valve Bellows Stop (34) Percussion Pedal Valve Stop. This useful stop is placed on back, inside of organ, and prevents bellows from bursting. It is indispensable," etc. This "grand organ" contains "five (5) full octaves ; eighteen sets of *Golden Tongue Reeds* of *one-half octave each.*"

Three of the prizes offered by the National Conservatory of Music for composition have been awarded to Boston organists. A prize of $300 for a suite for string orchestra was awarded to Mr. Frederick Bullard, who studied with Rheinberger, and returned to Boston not long ago. A prize of $200 for a piano concerto was awarded to Mr. Joshua Phippen, formerly organist of the Arlington-street Church. A prize of $500 for a cantata was awarded to Mr. Horatio W. Parker, the organist of Trinity Church.

FESTAL MARCH.

SCOTSON CLARK.

(Gt. to Ped. off.)

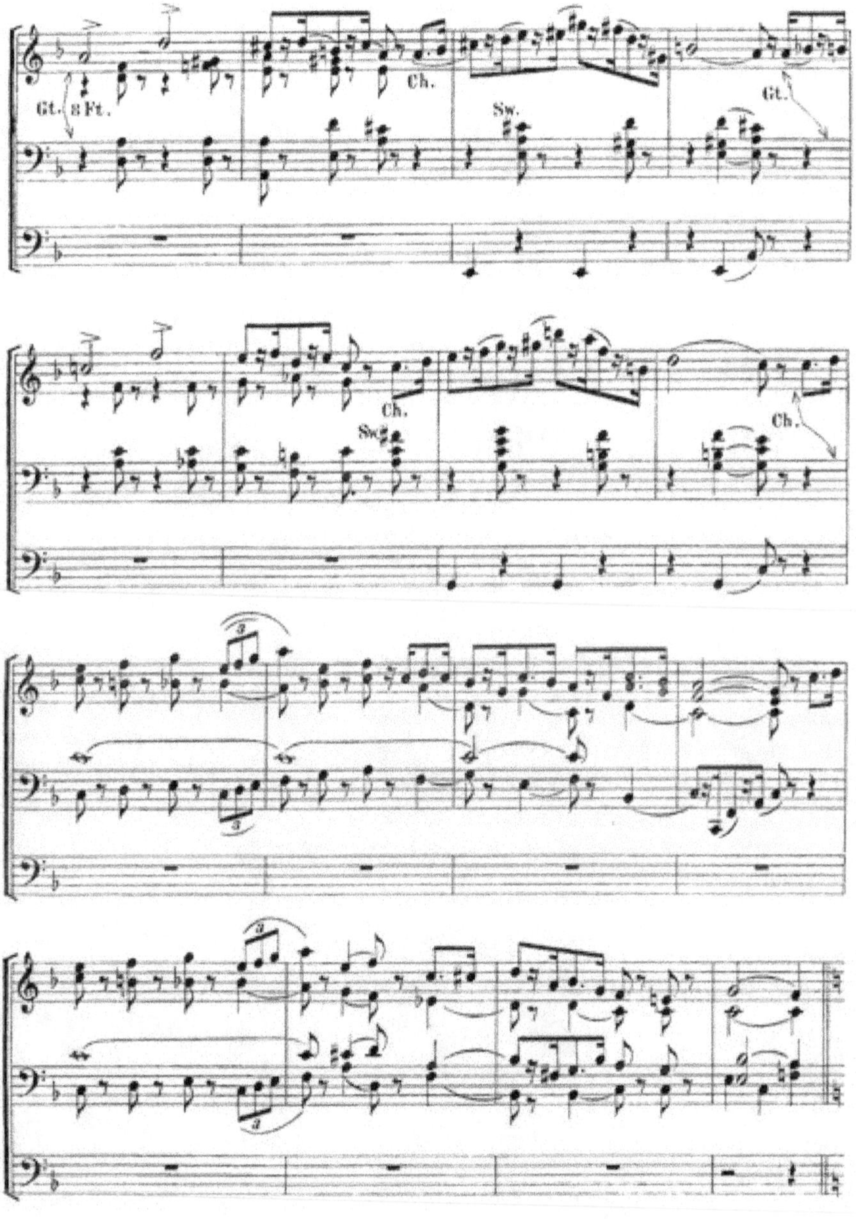

Gt. 8 Ft.
Ch.
Sw.
Gt.
Ch.
Sw.
Ch.
3
3
3
3

12

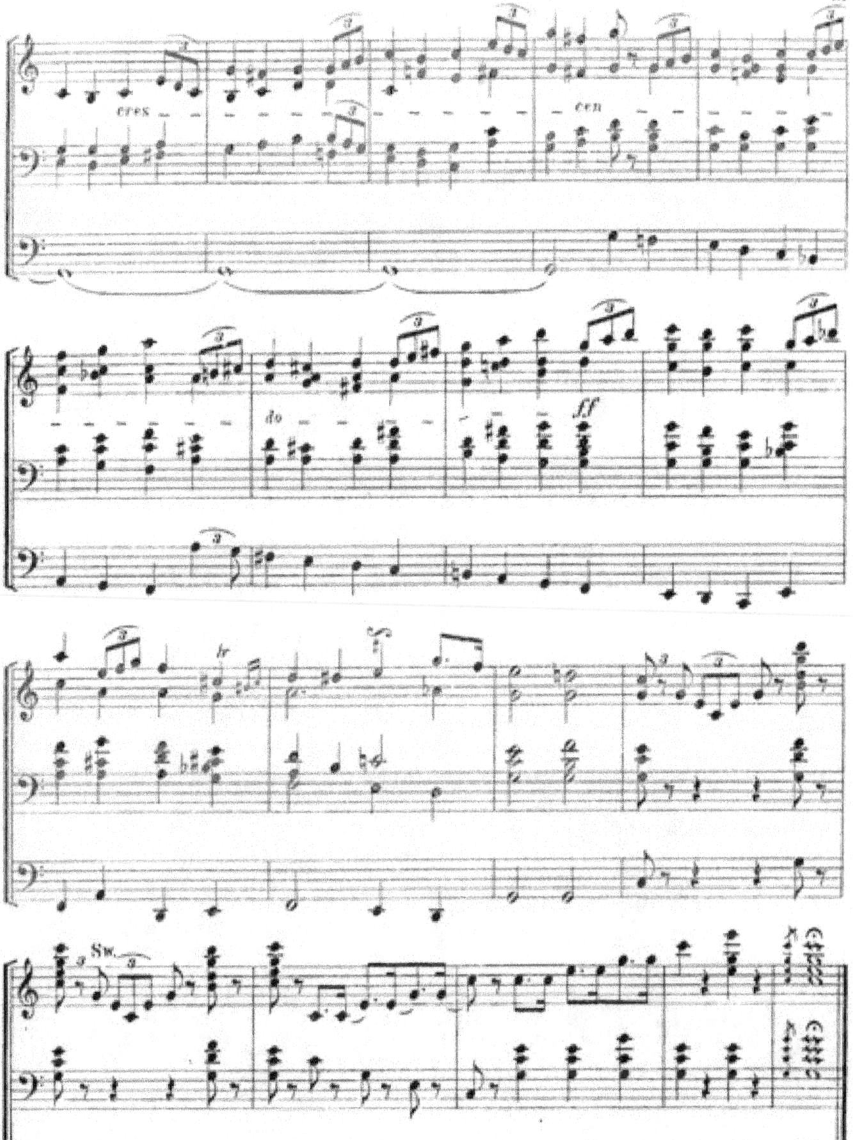
cres
cen
do
ff
tr
Sw.

FIVE INTERLUDES.
(or Short and Easy Voluntaries.)
II.

EVERETT E. TRUETTE.

a tempo.
Sw. Add Oboe.
rit.
Oboe off.
Flute & Violin off.
Sw. St. Diap. & Trem.

Add Flute 4 Ft.

Flute off. Add Violin.

St. Diap. & Salicional only.

Clarinet in Ch. off. Trem. off.

Ch.

Sw. Salicional only.

rit.

PLAYING THE ORGAN FROM MEMORY.

(Continued from page 7.)

In my opinion greater "freedom of expression" might have been attained if the player had referred occasionally to his notes, while the value of his performance from an artistic standpoint would not have suffered in the least. Among the most noted organists of my time whom I have known personally and with whose playing I am quite familiar, are, August Haupt, Gustav Merkel, A. G. Ritter, W. T. Best, Alexandre Guilmant, Theodore Dubois, Eugene Gigout, Charles M. Widor, Dudley Buck, Samuel P. Warren, John K. Paine, Eugene Thayer, Frederic Archer, George E. Whiting, and George W. Morgan.

As a rule, all of these artists have been in the habit of playing from notes in public, and even their own compositions. Who can say they were at such times not "heard at their best"?

It would be better for critics to confine themselves to a plain statement of facts, than to express an opinion at variance with sound judgment based upon a practical knowledge of the subjects they write upon.

Yours very truly,

CLARENCE EDDY.

This letter has called forth replies from Mr. Harrison M. Wild and Mr. Louis Falk. Lack of space and the length of the letters prevent our reproducing them entirely, but the following excerpts will give a fair idea of these replies. Mr. Wild writes:—

"As to the young artist's concert, I know it as his first attempt at public playing by memory, and, barring his pardonable nervousness, which resulted in a lack of clearness at times, more than compensating sounds were made by results obtained in other parts of the works, by lightning-like changes of registration, and, greatest of all, by the effect produced upon the audience, as evidenced by its attention and applause, and the verbal encomiums afterwards by onlookers not in any way interested in the welfare of the young musician.

"As to memorizing, we can but look at that from two standpoints: first, the doing away entirely with the music. The mere mechanical portion of an organ performance is so trifling that the mind that can memorize the Bach G-minor Fantasia and Fugue, or the Thiele Variations, or the Rienkle Sonatas, can in a few moments so fix the registration for a strange organ as to leave fantasy free. I make bold to assert that Mr. Eddy could write out within five minutes the registration of the foregoing three numbers, for any specification submitted, and, having done it, would not have to think one iota should, when at any particular point a change could be thought of and made, where necessary for the effect in that point or farther along. If Mr. Eddy will grant the possession of this ability, the remainder of the organ-memorizing is placed upon the plane of pianoforte-memorizing, and who shall say that the piano performance, simple or otherwise, is not more artistic without notes than with? That such memorizing is physically harmful, none but the expert physician or personal experience can determine. That it is for the best artistic results Mr. Eddy will not deny, when he remembers the performances of artists such as Archer, Crennold, Middelschulte, and the like, who were, or are, tried in the fire of public appearance. I know St. Saëns plays by memory. A pupil of mine, who has studied with Guilmant, says Guilmant has a wonderful memory, and plays at a moment's notice any one of a host of pieces. Best told a pupil of mine, when the rumor went the rounds of his failing eyesight, that granting that, he could get along without the notes now, since he knew by memory most of the music he would need. Mr. Middelschulte told me that Haupt knew by memory all of Bach's works, and repeatedly played them without the notes."

Mr. Falk writes:—

.... "In regard to memorizing, I question whether playing or singing from memory is under all circumstances the proper way of rendering music in public, for it very frequently leads the performer into faults, such as inaccuracies, interpolations, and mannerisms entirely foreign to the sense of the composition. Witness the contortions of many pianists, violinists, and singers as living examples of my assertion. Again: Why does not Theodore Thomas conduct his matchless concerts from memory? Does not the score, which he is constantly following, detract from his ability to properly direct his orchestra? Has he more work to perform than an organist sitting before the great Auditorium organ? Let us see. The conductor uses his brains and hands with which to guide those fifty to a hundred players; the organist uses his brains, hands, and feet to master five keyboards, a hundred and twenty registers, and innumerable combinations; he is required to represent every instrument of a large orchestra, either individually or collectively, in the performance of some pieces. What would become of the player's wits and his accumulative memory in case of the not infrequent mishaps to some parts of the organ during his playing? The chances are that he would wish to have his music before him. We shall probably have the pleasure of listening to many organists of world-wide fame during the coming summer, and I dare say they will, one and all, play with their music before them. Does it follow that masters like Guilmant and Best are incapable of memorizing what they propose to play? Indeed, it seems to me that, if anything, the efficient organist is better equipped and qualified to commit music to memory than any other specialist in music. He is, or ought to be, thoroughly familiar with the theory of music from the simple chord to the intricacies of the double counterpoint, in order to properly assume the duties of his profession."

especially in Catholic and Protestant Episcopal churches, where impersonation in accompanying plain song is almost imperative. It may therefore be understood that the reason why an organist plays with the music before him, is because he considers it to his advantage, and not because of any defect in his musical training."

It seems to us that playing from memory is a overscience, and one which almost any organist can adopt if he wishes. There are but few organists who cannot repeat at least a part of their yesterday's programme from memory, and yet the rendering would not be enhanced by so doing. Performing long programmes from memory no longer excites the awe and wonder that it did years ago, as it is now so common, and "the effect produced upon the audience" — as Mr. Wild writes — is apt to be confined to the artist's friends from the country. We doubt if this "effect" would be noticeable at all if the organist were entirely out of sight. If an organist is able to play a programme from memory, it will be very convenient some time when he is called upon to give a recital with but five minutes' notice, or when some one has stolen his music, which was left at the organ a few hours before. If he plays from memory from choice, and happens to forget some passage, it will prove a "convenient nuisance," — "a delusion and a snare." Nearly all the great organists, the world over, can play from memory whenever they desire; but it is convincing, that hardly one of them ever gives an organ concert entirely from memory.

PARIS LETTER.

(From our own Correspondent.)

PARIS, 11 April, 1899.

At last some organ recitals to chronicle for your delectation, although via England! I only trust that some English correspondents of THE ORGAN have not stolen my thunder by sending an account of them before mine. Guilmant, during his recent visit to England and Scotland, gave two organ recitals, one at Glasgow and one at Falkirk. At the former his organ solos were:—

Fantasia and Fugue in G-minor	Bach.
Prière et Berceuse, Tempo di Minuetto in C-major, and Lamentation	Guilmant.
Scherzo Symphonique Concertant, and Pastorale in F-major	Lemmens.
Canon in E-major (Fanfare)	Salomé.
Grand Chorus in D-major	Guilmant.

At the latter, among numerous pieces, vocal, etc., he played the following solos:—

Toccata and Fugue in D-minor	Bach.
Offertoire in D-flat	Salomé.
Canon in B-minor	Schumann.
Legende and Symphonique Finale	Guilmant.
Toccata in G-major	Dubois.
Andantino in D-flat	Chauvet.
Funeral March and Hymn of Seraphs	Guilmant.
Allegro from Tenth Organ Concerto (with Cadenzas by Guilmant)	Händel.
Nuptial March in E-major	Guilmant.

Some of the annotations of the latter programme, written by a local organist, though not as bad as some of the Western criticism recently quoted in THE ORGAN, yet seemed to me rather amusing. The Toccata in D-minor, for example, is described as "a piece of striking effects, introduced by Instrumental Recitatives consisting of passages assigned to different keyboards, and intersected by masses of florid harmony." This criticism is certainly both "massive" and "florid," whether the Toccata is or not. Our Scottish friend also evidently believes in the organ as the "King of Instruments;" for in a note to the Funeral March he tells us that "a concert organ by its crushing effects (!) can easily represent even so great a theme as the passing of this world into the eternal."

To return to Paris: organ recitals are gradually beginning

to be given. Yesterday quite a good concert was given at the Jardin d'Acclimatation, devoted entirely to the works of Widor, the famous organist at St. Sulpice. Widor himself led the orchestra, and the programme included a "Suite pittoresque" for organ and orchestra, and the Second Organ Symphony, besides other works for orchestra alone. Widor is certainly a most talented and versatile composer, although I do not consider his organ playing as fine as that of Guilmant: he composes in rather higher forms.

The music at La Trinité on Easter Day was very fine. The choir, under the direction of Salomé, sang Beethoven's First Mass in glorious style, and Guilmant played the following organ pieces: at Communion, portions of Lemmens' Second Sonata, "O Filii," followed by a magnificent transcription on one of Bach's Cantatas. For a "sortie" he improvised a fugue in the most wonderful style. The fugue had a quick, flowing subject, ending with a trill, and when he came to the stretto it was impossible to conceive how he kept the subject straight in the different voices, to say nothing of the execution. Long life to Guilmant! for I don't see who is to succeed him when he is dead.

OUTRE MER.

MIXTURES.

(FOUR RANKS.)

THE London College of organists received over $3,250 for examination fees during the past year.

Mr. George Ernest Lake, organist of All Saints', London, is dead.

Mr. Sydney Naylor, at one time organist of St. George's, Bloomsbury, London, died the last of March, at the age of fifty-one.

Messrs. Geo. Jardine & Son are building a large three-manual organ for St. Patrick's Church, Jersey City.

A new organ for the Congregational Church, Mystic, Conn., has been built by Mr. Geo. S. Hutchings. The instrument has sixteen stops.

Mr. Geo. S. Hutchings has placed a new organ having two manuals and fifteen registers in the Concord Chapel, Oakland, Cal.

Messrs. Hook & Hastings have just finished a two-manual organ in the Congregational Church of Griggsville, Ill. It has eighteen registers.

Mr. Frank G. Rohner gave an organ concert at the Park Ave. M. E. Church, Chicago, April 4.

Mr. Wm. C. Carl, organist of the First Presbyterian Church, New York, was tendered a benefit at the First Baptist Church, Bloomfield, N.J. March 29.

Mr. J. F. Kitchen gave a series of organ concerts in the First Presbyterian Church, Newark, N.J., during the month of March.

The First Baptist Church of Georgetown, Ky., has just received a new Hook & Hastings organ. It has two manuals and seventeen registers, and is blown by a water motor.

Mr. M. P. Möller has just received an order from Pearl-street Baptist Church, N.J., for a $2,000 organ, and another from St. Paul's Church, Savannah, Ga., for a $1,200 two-manual organ.

Mr. James Kendrick Pyne, one of the oldest of the English organists, recently died at the age of eighty-two. He was organist of Bath Abbey for nearly fifty years.

The new organ just erected in the First M. E. Church of Lincoln, Ill., is from the factory of Hook & Hastings, and has two manuals and twenty-two registers, a water motor furnishing the wind.

The opera "Puritania," by Edgar Stillman Kelly, has been dedicated to Mr. Clarence Eddy.

Mons. Eugene Gigout, the celebrated French organist, is to give a series of concerts in Hartford, England, inaugurating a new organ.

Messrs. Hook & Hastings have just completed a two-manual organ of twenty-seven registers in the Central Christian Church of Indianapolis, Ind. They are also building an organ of about the same size for the College Avenue Baptist Church of the same place. The organ in the Central Christian Church is blown by a water motor.

Mr. Wm. C. Carl gave four organ recitals in the First Presbyterian Church, N.Y., during the past month. One programme was devoted to German composers, and one to Italian composers. Quite a number of works were performed for the first time in New York, and the programmes contained many novelties.

The last organ built by Mr. Frank Roosevelt is now being set up in the Church of All Saints, Harlem, N.Y.

The alterations on the organ in Grace Church, New York, are still unfinished. It has been decided to put the old console back down-stairs. This combination will be unique, as there will be two consoles, — the old one down by the chancel, and the new one up in the gallery. They can be played mutually or individually at either end of the church.

Mr. F. H. Hastings, of Hook & Hastings, is experimenting with an entirely new system of electric action, whereby all the intermediate valves and small bellows between the key and pallet are done away with, and the electric current is connected with the pallet itself. Thus far the experiments have been very successful. A small test organ is to be built on this principle, for exhibition.

Organ recital April 15 at the Unitarian Church, Littleton, N.H., by Mr. Geo. H. Ryder: Fantasie, Lemmens; Largo, Händel; Priest's March, Mendelssohn; Tempest at Sea, Ryder.

Mr. Geo. W. Chadwick has been engaged as organist at Dr. Miner's Church, Columbus Ave., Boston.

Mr. B. L. Whelpley has been engaged as organist of the Church of the Unity, Boston.

The last organ built by Messrs. Geo. H. Ryder & Co., before closing their factory, was placed in the Wesley M. E. Church, Haverhill, Mass., and contained twelve speaking-stops and five pedal movements.

The Chicago Post for April 9 paid homage to the work of Mr. Clarence Eddy in the First Presbyterian Church, Chicago, by giving a sketch of his work in connection with that church. The article is illustrated with a cut of Mr. Eddy and cuts of the two ladies of his choir.

To any one who has examined the little leather buttons which are used in connecting trackers and squares, as well as in other parts of an organ, it may be a surprise to know that Mr. S. Elliott of Winchester supplied one organ firm with a quarter of a million of these buttons in one year.

Organ recital at St. Patrick's Church, Buffalo, N.Y., April 2. Improvisation (Mr. Chas. S. Jardine); Improvisation in B-flat, Clark, and Introduction and Fugue, Rink (Miss Ella Kemp); Marche des Girondins, Clark (Mr. N. Kiefer); Flute Concerto, Rink (Mr. Wendelin Weber); Selection from Mendelssohn (Mr. Kiefer), and "Farewell" Mr. Jardine.

Mr. E. J. McGoldrick performed the following selections at St. Patrick's Church, Boston, April 2. Allegro Vivace (Fifth Symphony), Widor; Finale from Fantasia in C, Volckmar; March from Fifth Symphony, Beethoven; Parade Sonata, Lemmens, and Schiller March, Meyerbeer.

Mr. Wm. Churchill Hammond gave his seventy-second recital at the Second Congregational Church, Holyoke, Mass., March 3, with the following programme: Prelude in C-minor (Second Sonata), Mendelssohn; Lamentation in D-minor, Guilmant; Sonata No. 1, Wolfram; Themes from "Parsifal," Wagner.

Messrs. Henry Pilcher & Sons of Louisville will exhibit a three-manual organ in the Liberal Arts Building at the World's Columbian Exposition. The instrument will contain twelve stops in the great, a part of which will be in the choir swell-box; twelve in the swell; seven in the choir, enclosed in a swell-box, and six in the pedal. There will be eight pedal movements, six adjustable piston combinations, and five extra piston movements.

The following-named American organists have been invited to perform at the coming exposition in Chicago: Messrs. Clarence Eddy, Harrison M. Wild, Louis Falk, Walter E. Hall, and Wilhelm Middelschulte of Chicago; George E. Whiting and S. B. Whitney of Boston; S. P. Warren, William C. Carl, and Frank Taft of New York; R. Huntington Woodman of Brooklyn; David D. Wood, Philadelphia. Among the lady performers is the name of Mrs. Mary A. Dodrick of Georgetown, D.C.

Mr. J. Warren Andrews gave the second of the series of inaugural recitals on his new studio organ at the Plymouth Church, Minneapolis, April 12, with a programme selected entirely from the works of Händel, in which he was assisted by Miss Eva M. Alcott, soprano; Mr. W. R. Heath, tenor; Mr. Fritz Schleicher, violinist, and a number of pupils of Mr. Schleicher. The following works were given: Fourth Concerto, "I know that My Redeemer Liveth" from "Messiah;" "Air Varie" (violin); Selection from "Joshua;" "Oh! had I Jubal's Lyre " ("Joshua"); Fifth Concerto; Largo (ten first violins, string quartet, and organ).

A funny incident once interfered with a performance of "Redemption" in St. Louis. The two negroes who were engaged to blow the organ were responsible for it. Some one, with equal generosity and indiscretion, had furnished the darkies with a jug of beer, to which they took turns when the full organ was not in use. When the heavy tax was gone it so happened that the organ had a short red, and one negro ran down to replenish, the other engaging to supply the wind is called upon during his absence. The messenger had not reached the street before Prof. Epstein began the introduction to a grand chorus. The full organ required the two pumps at once, and the one darky struggled in vain to supply the requisite power. It was no go. The musicians and people had to await the coming of the second darky and the jug.

The Hope-Jones Electric Organ Co., are to build a four-manual electric organ for Sir Clereus Glynn, Bart., for his new music-room at Ewell, Surrey, England.

Mr. E. M. Bowman gave an organ concert at Vassar College, April 14.

Signor Filippo Capocci, the Italian organist and composer, gave a recital in the Row & Romiley Institute, London, April 15.

Mr. George A. Kies gave an organ recital in Park Church, Norwich, Conn., April 22, playing: Torchlight March, Guilmant; Cantilène Nuptiale, Dubois; Pompes Funèbres, Mailly; Minuet, Salomé; Variations on "Jerusalem the Golden," Spark; Gavotte ("Mignon"), Thomas; Concert Satz, No. 1, Thiele.

Mr. Henry Carter has been elected to succeed Mr. W. Ward Stephens as organist of the Church of the Redeemer, Morristown, N.J.

Mr. Henry Eyre Brown will succeed Dr. Hanchett as organist of the Marsh Collegiate Church, N.Y.

Dr. Jeffreys will succeed Mr. E. J. A. Zeiner as organist of the First Presbyterian Church, Yonkers, N.Y.

Mr. Walter E. Hall has resigned his position as organist at the Church of the Epiphany, Chicago, and accepted a similar position in Pittsburg.

Mr. Clarence Eddy gave organ concerts in Duluth April 18, in La Porte April 21, and in St. Louis April 25 and 26.

Mr. E. Minshall, who has been organist of the City Temple, London, for a period of seventeen years, during which time his service was voluntary, has severed his connection with that church. It is understood that Mr. Minshall was treated rather shabbily by the church authorities, and that Dr. Parker apologized to him, but to no avail.

At a concert given for the benefit of the Free Scholarship Fund of the Dunbury School of Music, April 19, Mr. Alex S. Gibson of Waterbury played the March in D, by Mr. John S. Camp, which appeared in our issue for April: Sonata, Op. 183, Merkel; Eclogue Ecossaise, Salome; Cantilène Nuptiale, Dubois.

Mr. Thomas Wingham, a well-known English organist, died March 24, at the age of forty-seven.

At a miscellaneous concert in the Central Congregational Church, Philadelphia, Mr. Frederic Maxson played March from "Leonora" Symphony, Raff; Prière and Capriccio of Lemaigre, and, with Miss Mabel Phipps at the piano, Guilmant's Pastorale for piano and organ.

NEW ORGAN MUSIC.

Sonata in F-minor, Op. 292 . . . . Fumagalli.
Eight Preludes, Op. 46 . . . . Schuig.
Concert Fantasia in Scottish Melodies . . . . . Peace.

A new organ has just been put in the Unitarian Church, Littleton, N.H. by Mr. George S. Hutchings. The instrument has sixteen registers.

A two-manual organ, with seven stops in the great and eleven in the swell (the gift of Mr. Richard C. Sno-), built by Mr. John Brown of Wilmington, Del., was erected in the First M. E. Church, Vineland, N.J. in February.

Mr. Arthur M. Raymond has been engaged as organist of Mount Vernon Church, Boston. Mr. Raymond has been the organist of the First Parish Church, Hingham, for nine years, and the society of that church presented him with a purse as a token of their esteem.

Dr. Hanchett gave his final organ concert in the Marble Collegiate Church, New York, April 24. He goes to a church in Brooklyn for the coming year.

Mr. John S. Camp gave an organ recital at the Congregational Church, Hartford, Conn., April 12, performing the following compositions: Fanfare, Ascher-Westbrook; Prayer and Bridal Chorus, Guilmant; Overture to "Wm. Tell," Rossini-Buck; Swiss Song, Hoarville-Camp; Pastorale, Hite-Camp; Gavotte, Thomas-Camp; St. Cecilia Offertory, No. 2, Batiste; Chorus of Angels, Clark; Spring Song, Shelley; Melody, Salome; Offertoire in E-flat, Wely.

Mr. F. R. Adams gave an organ concert at St. Paul's Church, Delaware, Ohio, with the following programme: Marche Religieuse, Guilmant; Pastorale in F, Whiting; Prelude and Fugue in A-minor, Bach; Marche Triomphale (piano and organ), Guilmant; Sonata in E-minor, Ritter; Fantasia in F, Best; Air in Dauphin, Brocchd-Best; Offertoire in D, Op. 8, No. 2, Batiste; Pastorale (piano and organ), Guilmant; Theme and Variations from Serenade, Op. 8, Beethoven, and Overture to "Stradella," Flotow.

Mr. G. A. Kles gave an organ recital at Park Church, Norwich, Conn., April 8, with the following programme: Fugue in E-minor, Bach; Meditation, No. 1, Guilmant; Aria, "Jerusalem, thou that killest," from "St. Paul," Mendelssohn (Mrs. Kles); Variations on an American Air, Flagler; "Fear not ye, O Israel," Buck; Scottish Eclogue, Salome; and Overture to "Euryanthe," Weber. The closing recital of the series was given April 22.

An organ concert was given in the Railroad Chapel, Chicago, Ill., in March, by Mr. R. Huntington Woodman, with the following programme: Overture, "Zampa," Harold; Offertoire in D, Salome; Bridal Song, Jensen; March of Magi Kings, Dubois; Offertoire in D-minor, Batiste; Gavotte from "Mignon," Thomas; Funeral March of a Marionette, Gounod; Minuet from "Samson," Handel; Pilgrim's Chorus, Wagner.

A new organ (twelve speaking-stops) built by Mr. John Brown of Wilmington, Del., was opened March 23 by Messrs. S. Tudor Strong and Chas. F. Blandner, with the following selections: Pilgrim's Song of Hope, Batiste; Offertoire de S. Cecile, Grison; Offertoire in F, Wely; Romanza in G, Beethoven; Andante Cantabile, Widor; Fantasia ("O Sanctissima"), Lux; Gran Coro Trionfale, and Capriccio, Capocci.

A correspondent asks for information concerning the publication of the following compositions: Ten Religious Meditations, Op. 122, by Wely, and Fourth Suite of pieces for organ by Chauvet. If any one of our readers has a copy of these works, he will confer a favor by sending us the names of the publishers.

OUR SECOND ORGAN-MUSIC COMPETITION.

A PRIZE of ten dollars ($10.00) will be given for the best Pastorale for the organ. The composition should be written on three staves, must be from seventy-five to a hundred bars in length, and must bear a motto only. A sealed envelope, bearing the same motto and containing the form given below (which should be cut from this journal), filled out with the name and address of the competitor, should accompany each composition.

Compositions will be received till the 1st of August, when they will be submitted to the following judges, who have kindly consented to examine the composition: —

Mr. CLARENCE EDDY of Chicago,
Mr. GEORGE E. WHITING of Boston.
Mr. S. B. WHITNEY of Boston.

The successful composition must become the property of THE ORGAN, and will be printed with the name of the composer in the journal issued the first of October.

Compositions should be addressed: Editor THE ORGAN, 149 A Tremont St., Boston. (Prize Competition.)

Organ Music Competition.

Name

Address

Motto

REVIEW OF NEW ORGAN MUSIC.

FROM NEW ENGLAND CONSERVATORY OF MUSIC.

Organ School . . . . H. M. Dunham.

A TEXT-BOOK for acquiring the fundamental principles of pipe organ playing, consisting of four parts, the first part being devoted to organ mechanics, stops, and registration; the second part containing exercises and studies for manuals only; the third part devoted entirely to pedal studies; and the fourth part containing twenty studies for manuals and pedals. Part I. is intended to give the student a general idea of the contents of an organ, and contains such useful illustrations as a wind-chest, key-action, pneumatic action, tremulant, and several illustrations of organ pipes as well as an outline plan of the interior of a three-manual organ. This is all condensed into twenty-two pages, and can be easily digested by the most obtuse student without any struggling with long technical descriptions which confuse instead of enlightening the young mind. Parts II. and IV. were published separately some time ago, but have been slightly altered and incorporated in this work.

This "Organ School" is the best work of its kind we have ever seen. It fulfils its mission completely. It is intended as an elementary method and not a treatise. Hence it is adapted to the needs of every beginner in studying the organ, and will be adopted at once by many teachers; while Part I. which is published separately ($1.00), will be useful to all students and many teachers. Price of the complete work $2.50.

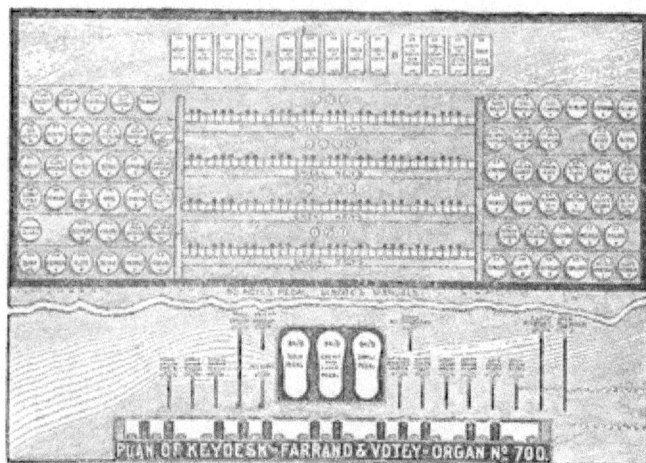

PLAN OF KEYDESK—FARRAND & VOTEY ORGAN N° 700.

CORRESPONDENCE.

POSITION OF THE PEDAL-BOARD.

To the Editor of THE ORGAN:

I PLAY upon a three-manual organ. A plumb-line dropped from the front of great organ keys falls two inches back of the front of pedal short or sharp keys. Dr. E. J. Hopkins of London, and other English authorities, tell me that a plumb-line should drop four inches in *front* of short pedal keys, Roosevelt organs are built so. My pedals are *six inches* too near me by this rule. Messrs. Jardine, Hook & Hastings, etc., only differ two inches from this scale, as they say a plumb-line dropped from front of great organ keys should fall two inches in *front* of pedal sharp key. I have found so much difficulty in practising such music as Bach's G-minor Fugue, or Toccata in F, that I have given up the attempt in despair. I have written to the builder, and in reply he says, " Regardless of the weight of authority named in your letter, I must deny correctness of your contention. For many years I have built organs with the pedal keys placed according to the scale used in St. Luke's organ, which have been, and are being, used by organists of repute, who apparently do not find the slightest difficulty in rendering concert music of the highest grade, and who never have made mention of any trouble in pedaling." Now if all the gentleman "organists of repute" have made no complaints, it is because of their shortness of stature; for I contend that a man of say five feet, eight inches, the average height, must experience considerable difficulty in playing such pedals — a man under medium height would not; but organs should not be constructed for men of short stature, but of average height. I have no doubt this builder does his best to persuade the music committee of my church that I am an ignoramus, a crank, and a fool; therefore, if you will lay this subject before several organists "*of repute,*" and print their replies, so that I may lay it before my music committee, you will confer a very great favor on

Yours respectfully,

F. C. C. G

NOTABLE ORGANS.

IX.

FESTIVAL HALL, WORLD'S FAIR.

THIS instrument, a specification of which was printed in the February issue of THE ORGAN, is being built by the Farrand & Votey Organ Co., of Detroit. It will contain sixty-three speaking-stops and four thousand and fourteen pipes. The instrument, though not as large as many other organs, will be very powerful, as many stops will be constructed on large scales, and the wind pressure will be high. The echo organ will be placed three hundred feet from the main organ, and will be connected by an electric cable. The bellows will be operated by electric motors.

NEW ORGANS.

NEW ORGAN IN CHRIST CHURCH, RYE, N.Y.

Built by Mr. Geo. S. Hutchings, Boston.

GREAT ORGAN.		SWELL ORGAN.	
Open Diapason	16 Ft.	Bourdon Bass }	16 Ft.
Open Diapason	8 "	Bourdon Treble }	
Viola da Gamba	8 "	Open Diapason	8 "
Doppel-flote	8 "	Salicional	8 "
Octave	4 "	Æoline	8 "
Octave Quinte	2⅔ "	Quintadena	8 "
Super Octave	2 "	Stopped Diapason	8 "
Mixture	III. and IV. Rks.	Flauto Traverso	4 "
Trumpet	8 Ft.	Fugara	4 "
		Flageolet	2 "
CHOIR ORGAN.		Dolce Cornet	III. Rks.
		Cornopean	8 Ft.
Geigen Principal	8 Ft.	Oboe	8 "
Dulciana	8 "		
Concert Flute	8 "	PEDAL ORGAN.	
Flûte d'Amour	4 "		
Piccolo Harmonique	2 "	Open Diapason	16 Ft.
Clarinet	8 "	Bourdon	16 "
		Violone	16 "
		Violoncello	8 "

The usual pedal movements and couplers.
This organ is tubular pneumatic, with slide wind-chests.

(*Continued on page 29.*)

(Continued from page 20.)

NEW ORGAN IN THIRD PRESBYTERIAN CHURCH, ROCHESTER, N.Y.

Built by Messrs. Johnson & Son, Westfield, Mass.

GREAT ORGAN.

Double Open Diapason	16 Ft.	Flauto Traverso	4 Ft.
Open Diapason	8 "	Twelfth	2⅔ "
Spitz-flöte	8 "	Super Octave	2 "
Viola da Gamba	8 "	Mixture	IV. Rks.
Dolce	8 "	Trumpet	8 Ft.
Doppel-flöte	8 "	Clarion	4 "
Octave	4 "		

SWELL ORGAN.

Bourdon Treble }	16 Ft.	Flûte Harmonique	4 Ft.
Bourdon Bass }		Gemshorn	4 "
Open Diapason	8 "	Flautino	2 "
Salicional	8 "	Dolce Cornet	III. Rks.
Æoline	8 "	Contra Fagotto	16 Ft.
Vox Celeste	8 "	Cornopean	8 "
Stopped Diapason	8 "	Oboe and Bassoon	8 "
Quintadena	8 "	Vox Humana	8 "
Violin	4 "		

CHOIR ORGAN. *(In a Swell-box).*

Geigen Principal	8 Ft.	Flûte d'Amour	4 Ft.
Dulciana	8 "	Piccolo	2 "
Melodia	8 "	Clarinet	8 "
Fugara	4 "		

PEDAL ORGAN.

Quinttaten	32 Ft.	Violoncello	8 Ft.
Double Open Diapason	16 "	Flöte	8 "
Dulciana	16 "	Trombone	16 "
Bourdon	16 "		

PEDAL MOVEMENTS.

F., MF., and F. Combinations, Gt.
F., MF., and P. " Sw.
F. Combination, Ch.
F. and P. Combinations, Ped.
Gt. to Ped.
(All double acting but the F. Peds.)

All the pipes of the Great, except the Diapasons, are in the Choir swell-box.
Pneumatic action for Great and its Couplers.
Swell Pedals in the centre.

MUSIC HALL, WORLD'S COLUMBIAN EXPOSITION.

New Organ to be built by the Carl Barckhoff Church Organ Co.

GREAT ORGAN.

Open Diapason	16 Ft.	Bourdon	16 Ft.
Open Diapason	8 "	Open Diapason	8 "
Viola da Gamba	8 "	Violin Diapason	8 "
Gemshorn	8 "	Stopped Diapason	8 "
Doppel-flöte	8 "	Salicional	8 "
Quinte	5⅓ "	Quintadena	8 "
Octave	4 "	Principal	4 "
Hohl-flöte	4 "	Flûte Harmonique	4 "
Twelfth	2⅔ "	Flageolet	2 "
Fifteenth	2 "	Cornet	III. Rks.
Mixture	IV. Rks.	Cornopean	8 Ft.
Trumpet	8 Ft.	Oboe	8 "
		Vox Humana	8 "

SWELL ORGAN.

(see above)

CHOIR ORGAN.

Diapason d'Amour (?)	8 Ft.
Melodia	8 "
Dulciana	8 "
Violina	4 "
Flûte d'Amour	4 "
Piccolo Harmonique	2 "
Clarinet	8 "

SOLO ORGAN.

Stentorphone	8 Ft.
Concert Flute	8 "
Viola Pomposa	8 "
Hohl Pfeife	4 "
Tuba Major	16 "
Tuba Mirabilis	8 "

PEDAL ORGAN.

Grand Open Diapason	16 Ft.
Violon	16 "
Bourdon	16 "
Resultant	32 "
Cello	8 "
Flute	8 "

COMBINATION PISTON-KNOBS.

6 for Great Organ.
7 " Swell "
6 " Choir "
6 " Solo "

COMBINATION PEDALS.
(Double-acting.)

Full Organ and all Couplers.
Forte Pedal Organ.
Piano Pedal Organ.
Bourdon in Pedal Organ (Couplers "off ").
Piano Great and Pedal.
Choir, Melodia and Clarinet.
Swell, Salicional.
Solo, Concert Flute.

COUPLERS *(Piston-knobs).*

Octave Coupler, Great.
Octave Coupler, Pedal.
Super-Octave Coupler, Sw. to Gt.
Sub-Octave Coupler, Ch. to Gt.
In addition to the usual Couplers.

The bellows will be operated by two independent electric motors, with a pressure of four and six inches.

Each stop in the pedal is supplied with forty-two pipes (instead of thirty) to carry the Octave Coupler throughout. The combination piston-knobs are placed *below* their respective manuals, as they should always be placed. (Eastern builders please copy.—ED.)

NEW ORGAN IN THE CHURCH OF THE FIRST PARISH SOCIETY, BROOKLINE, MASS.

Built by Messrs. Hook & Hastings, Boston.

GREAT ORGAN.

Open Diapason	16 Ft.	Swell Organ	
Open Diapason	8 "	Bourdon	16 Ft.
Viola da Gamba	8 "	Open Diapason	8 "
Doppel-flöte	8 "	Salicional	8 "
Octave	4 "	Stopped Diapason	8 "
Twelfth	2⅔ "	Æoline	8 "
Fifteenth	2 "	Flauto Traverso	4 "
Mixture	III. Rks.	Violin	4 "
Trumpet	8 Ft.	Mixture	III. Rks.
		Oboe	8 Ft.

CHOIR ORGAN.

Lieblich Gedeckt	16 Ft.	Open Diapason	16 Ft.
Dulciana	8 "	Bourdon	16 "
Melodia	8 "	Quint	10⅔ "
Flûte d'Amour	4 "	Cello	8 "

PEDAL MOVEMENTS.

Great, F. and P.
Swell, F. and P.
Great to Pedal.
Pedal Full and Reduce to Bourdon.

Sub-Octave Coupler in Choir, in addition to usual Couplers.
Water motor.

ST. GEORGE'S CHURCH, NEW YORK.

Organ enlarged by Messrs. Geo. Jardine & Son.

GREAT ORGAN.
Gallery Division.

Double Open Diapason	16 Ft.	Bourdon	16 Ft.
Grand Open Diapason	8 "	Open Diapason	8 "
Open Diapason	8 "	Stopped Diapason	8 "
Gamba	8 "	Dulce	8 "
Stopped Diapason	8 "	Clarina	8 "
Gross Quinte	5⅓ "	Echo Flute	4 "
Grand Principal	4 "	Principal	4 "
Geigen Principal	4 "	Piccolo	2 "
Twelfth	2⅔ "	Cornet	III. Rks.
Fifteenth	2 "	Cymbale	IV. "
Mixture	III. Rks.	Cornopean	8 Ft.
Sesquialtera	IV. "	Vox Humana	8 "
Trumpet	8 Ft.		
Clarion	4 "		

SWELL ORGAN.
Gallery Division.

(see above)

Chancel Division.

Double Open Diapason	16 Ft.	Bourdon	16 Ft.
Open Diapason	8 "	Open Diapason	8 "
Bell Gamba	8 "	Dulciana	8 "
Doppel-flöte	8 "	Salicional	8 "
Melodia	8 "	Stopped Diapason	8 "
Harmonic Flute	4 "	Principal	4 "
Principal	4 "	Flageolet	2 "
Mixture	II. Rks.	Cornet	II. Rks.
Sesquialtera	III. "	Oboe	8 Ft.
Trumpet	8 Ft.		

PEDAL ORGAN.
Gallery Division.

Open Diapason	32 Ft.	Choir Organ.	
Open Diapason	16 "	*Gallery Division.*	
Violon	16 "	Bourdon	16 Ft.
Contra Bass	16 "	Dulciana	8 "
Grand Quinte	10⅔ "	Viola da Gamba	8 "
Violoncello	8 "	Lieblich Gedeckt	8 "
Octave	8 "	Violina	4 "
Sesquialtera	III. Rks.	Vienna Flute	4 "
Trombone	16 Ft.	Piccolo	2 "
		Clarinet	8 "
		Bassoon	8 "
		Vox Celestis	4 "
		Campanella	4 "

Chancel Division.

Open Diapason	16 Ft.
Bourdon	16 "
Violoncello	8 "

INTERCHANGEABLE COUPLERS.
Gallery Great to Chancel Great.

" Swell " " "	
" Choir " " "	
" Solo " " "	
" Great " " Swell.	
" Swell " " "	
" Choir " " "	
" Solo " " "	
" Organ to Chancel Organ.	
" Organ Separation.	

SOLO ORGAN.
Gallery Division.

Doppel-flöte	8 Ft.
French Horn	8 "
Harmonic Flute	4 "
Quintaton	4 "
Gemshorn	4 "
Tuba Mirabilis	8 "
Vox Angelica (Free Reed)	8 "

The usual couplers and pedal movements.

The two parts of the organ are connected by two hundred feet of electric cable.

ANNOUNCEMENT.

VOLUME II. OF THE ORGAN

COMMENCES

❋ MAY 1, 1893. ❋

Among the Contributors will be

MR. CHARLES A. CAPEN.

MR. HORATIO CLARKE.

MR. HENRY M. DUNHAM.

MR. CLARENCE EDDY.

MR. PHILIP HALE.

MR. J. A. HINTON, B.A.

MR. EDWIN A. TILTON.

MR. GEORGE E. WHITING.

MR. ARTHUR WHITING.

MR. S. B. WHITNEY,

AND OTHERS.

Subscription (in advance) $2.00. European Countries, 10s. 5d.

Single copies, 25 cents.

EVERETT E. TRUETTE, Editor and Publisher,

149a Tremont Street, Boston.

VOL. II. No. 2.   JUNE, 1893.   WHOLE No. 14.

BACH

YEARLY SUBSCRIPTION $2.00.   SINGLE COPIES 25 CTS.

THE ORGAN

DEVOTED TO

A MONTHLY JOURNAL

THE KING OF INSTRUMENTS

REINBERGER

GUILMANT

FRESCOBALDI

BUXTEHUDE

MERKEL

BEST

EVERETT · E · TRUETTE ·
EDITOR & PUBLISHER
149 A. TREMONT ST. BOSTON.

HANDEL

The New England
Conservatory of Music.

CARL FAELTEN, Director.

The Organ Department

offers unsurpassed facilities for acquiring a thorough and practical education in the art of Organ Playing. The course of study, which may be pursued either in class or by private instruction, is very complete and comprehensive. The early grades embrace work in Pedal Obligato Playing, Hymn Tunes, and Chorales, with Interludes and Modulations. In the medium grades are studied Organ works of polyphonic character, Anthems and Improvisations, and by the more advanced students the works of all the great writers for the Organ, together with the study of Masses, Oratorios, etc.

The Department is provided with fourteen Pedal Organs for practice, several of which possess three manuals each.

Those students who have acquired sufficient ability are aided in securing Church positions by the *Conservatory Bureau.* A large number of students have already been placed in lucrative positions by the Bureau.

TUITION: CLASSES OF FOUR, TERM OF TEN WEEKS, $20.00.

BOARD OF INSTRUCTION.
{ GEORGE E. WHITING.
HENRY M. DUNHAM.
ALLEN W. SWAN. }

{ Organ Practice, 10 cents per hour and upwards.
Pupils may enter at any time.
School Year from Sept. 7, '93 to June 21, '94. }

Address, FRANK W. HALE, General Manager, Franklin Square, Boston, Mass.

THE ORGAN.

VOL. II. BOSTO No. 2

THE ORGAN.

BOSTON, JUNE, 1893.

Published the first of every month. Subscription price $1.00 per ye
pean countries 10s. 3d.), payable in advance. Single copies, 15 cent

Subscribers will please state with which number they wish
scription to begin.

Remittances should be made by registered letter, post-office
by check payable to Everett E. Truette.

Correspondence, to secure notice, must in all cases be accompa
the name and address of the writer, not for publication, but as
tee of good faith.

Advertising rates sent on application.

Address all communications,

THE ORGAN, 149 A Tremont Street, Boston, Mass.

Single copies of THE ORGAN can be procured of

NOVELLO, EWER & CO.	New York.
G. SCHIRMER	New York.
OLIVER DITSON CO.	Boston.
L. H. ROSS & CO.	Boston.
N. E. CONSERVATORY	Boston.
H. R. STEVENS CO.	Boston.
LYON & HEALY	Chicago.
THEODORE PRESSER	Philadelphia.
WM. H. BONER & CO.	Philadelphia.
TAYLOR'S MUSIC HOUSE	Springfield, Mass.
GALLUP & METZGER	Hartford, Conn.
RICHAULT & CO.	Paris.
R. F. VIRGOE, (Sole Agent for Gt. Britain)	London.

CONTENTS:

IN our last issue the reproduction of a drawing in the article on the Hope-Jones System was a little deceptive. Fig. 2 is marked as "twice full size," while Fig. 1 is marked "half full size." These words correctly describe the original drawing, but do not apply to the reduced block. Fig. 1 should be considered as *one-fourth full size*, and Fig. 2 as *full size*.

MR. J. W. CHUTER, organist of Andover (England) Parish Church, is Mayor of the town. This is almost equal to a case in a small manufacturing town in the State of New Hampshire. The pastor of the church is also organist and sexton: shovels the paths in winter, and does farming in summer, all on a salary of $900.

al Organ at the World's Fair will not be com-
the middle of June, there will be no organ
ronicle till our next issue. Mons. Alex
fons. Camille Saint-Saëns have accepted the
managers, and will be heard at the fair prob-
month of September. Mr. Best is in such
he has been granted a three months' leave
he finance committee of St. George's Hall
verpool, to enable him to regain his health.
improbable that he will be able to visit this

ALL the nonsense going the rounds of several papers about the "haunted organ" in St. Paul's Church, Milwaukee, is positively ridiculous. Just at midnight the organ was heard by a number of people. The police surrounded the church, and no one was found within the walls. The sexton *thought* he found moisture of human hands on the organ-keys (how he must have been perspiring himself!) The music is described as "soft and sweet," and yet people in the next block were awakened by the sounds. Anything for a journalistic sensation! This is on a par with the recent sea-serpent episode.

The Indicator, Chicago, has done itself up proud in its special number issued the middle of the past month. Many of our dailies and weeklies have astonished their readers of late with special numbers commemorating the World's Fair; but *The Indicator* has surpassed them all in point of style and elegance. This enterprising and spicy weekly has issued a special made up of eighty pages of superior calender paper, supplemented with seven large plates of colored views (fourteen in all) of the buildings at the World's Fair. The supplement makes a portfolio in itself, and will be a valuable souvenir for any one. An enormous edition of the special has been issued, and non-subscribers can secure copies by sending twenty-five cents to *The Indicator*, Chicago. Among the articles is one on the history of the Fair — its conception, execution, the results and cost of construction. Bravo! *Indicator!* Here's to a continuation of your success!

THE *Musical Courier*, in reviewing an organ composition by a certain modern French composer, thus raps the knuckles of some of the best composers of organ music of the present day:—

"Among the French writers for this noble instrument, Wély and Batiste hold an honored place; but the majority of their successors offer few melodies that are attractive, few harmonic combinations and successions that are new and beautiful, and little counterpoint that is strong, noble, dignified, and in all respects worthy a grand organ or a vast edifice."

The compositions of Wély and Batiste are all right as examples of "sweet tunes which one can whistle;" but the writer of the above, who seems to have found "strong, noble, and dignified counterpoint" in their writings, must have been under the influence of the recent Paderewski mania, and unaccountable for what he (or she) has written.

FESTIVAL HALL ORGAN, WORLD'S FAIR.

THE case of the great organ built by Messrs. Farrand and Votey for Festival Hall, World's Fair, as shown in above cut, is composed of staff, a composition chiefly of plaster-of-paris, and moulded into panels. The show pipes will be most elaborately decorated. These run the extreme height of the building, making the height of the instrument thirty-eight feet; showing twenty-five feet above the chorus seats. The depth is twenty-five feet, and width thirty-four feet. Most of the instrument is now at the Fair, and it will be completed about the middle of June. This instrument, when having fulfilled its mission at the Fair, will not go to Boston, but to the University of Michigan. (Boston has already one concert organ stored in a shed.) The University of Michigan gets the instrument partly as a gift, only paying the small sum of $15,000 for its purchase. The Columbian Exposition pay $10,000 for its use during the Fair season. Word has been just received by Mr. Eddy from Saint-Saëns and Guilmant, that they will be at the Fair for concerts. But we feel grieved to state that, on account of illness, Best will be unable to leave home.   W. G. PEARCE.

CORRESPONDENCE.

To the Editor of THE ORGAN :

IF we accepted the Pythagorean philosophy, we might take one of your correspondents to be a reincarnation of the original "Mrs. Partington," who took her broom to sweep back the flood-tide from her doorstep. The "multiple swell" finds almost universal approval. The many devices for facilitating organ-control will be weeded out until the best become standard; "conservative" builders will be driven to adopt the improvements, or to leave the business, and it will take more than the thin voice of a four-foot "string-tone" to drown the noise of the waves, and more than its power — nay, though it became even sixteen or thirty-two feet — to keep back the rising flood. "Come with us, 'Gambette,' and we will do thee good."   ALEX S. GIBSON.

WATERBURY, CONN., April 24, 1893.

THE HOPE-JONES SYSTEM OF ELECTRICAL ORGAN CONTROL.

III.

THE electro-pneumatic lever, of which an illustration was given in our former issue, is the one most commonly used by Mr. Hope-Jones when a pallet and slider soundboard is to be operated; but several other varieties are employed for operating the valves of Roosevelt and other styles of soundboard, as also for the various forms of drawstop mechanism. Of these we do not think it necessary to treat, as the variations in design refer more to details than to principles. It may be mentioned, however, that in the electro-pneumatic lever for operating stop sliders a peculiar form of balanced valve is used, which suddenly admits sufficient wind to throw the slider fully on, or fully off, as the case may be, instantaneously. There is also a self-acting arrangement known as a "pneumatic buffer," which prevents the unpleasant noise which would otherwise result from such rapid action.

If the few electrical switches for coupling which are sometimes placed within the organ be excepted, the set of electro-pneumatic levers, as described above, is *the only mechanism which the organ contains.* From the organ a flexible cable of twisted wires about an inch in diameter is carried to the little portable console. This cable, though outwardly appearing to differ little from an ordinary rope, has required considerable thought and care in construction. The electric current is conveyed through this cable not by a single wire, but by several hundred of very fine copper threads, twisted together in such a manner as to reduce "self-induction" to a minimum. These fine threads of copper if taken singly would readily be broken, but when twisted and woven into a compact cable may be handled with as little thought and care as an ordinary rope, without fear of damage. The movable console consists of a light, open carved-wood case, designed to support in their proper positions above the pedal-board the manual-keys and stop-keys. The only mechanism in this console is the set of springs or arms for making electrical contacts when the keys are depressed or the stop-keys operated, and the set of small rollers behind the stop-keys for throwing over certain of the stops when the composition pedals or combination pistons are operated.

We will in our next article reproduce a photograph of one of these consoles.

(*To be continued.*)

PARIS LETTER.

ARISTIDE CAVAILLÉ-COLL.

PARIS, MAY 10, 1893.

THE celebrated firm of church-organ builders of which Aristide Cavaillé-Coll is now the head, has been in existence for two centuries. For many years the father, of the same name, was in business with the present owner; but it is the latter who has invented most of the improvements in organ mechanism which have made the name of Cavaillé-Coll so famous. Many of the large organs in Paris are the work of this builder; namely, those in St. Sulpice, La Madeleine, La Trinité, Nôtre Dame, and St. Clotilde. He has also sent organs to England, Belgium, Spain, Holland, and America. The factory, which employs about a hundred workmen, is situated on the left bank of the Seine, not far from St. Sulpice. Seen from without, it is a rather unattractive set of buildings,

THE ORGAN FACTORY OF ARISTIDE CAVAILLÉ-COLL.

but within it is full of interest. Especially interesting is the sanctum of Cavaillé-Coll himself, with its many pictures of organs of all countries and centuries, and its numerous machines for testing the quality of pipes, and for determining harmonic effects. One contrivance, designed to exemplify the relation existing between a groundtone and the resultant natural scale, was very novel. It consisted of a large pipe, low C, I believe, and a number of small pipes comprising the harmonic series; i. e., c, g', c', b-flat', etc., and of bellows below. When all the small pipes were made to speak, one could plainly hear the large pipe give the fundamental, by means of sympathetic resonance.

Cavaillé-Coll's most important improvements have to do with the voicing of reeds and mixtures. He is also celebrated for preserving the characteristic differences between the various flutes; such as Flûte Harmonique, Flûte Traversière and Flûte Octavin. In my opinion, his reeds are voiced far better than those of any other country. His organs are also renowned for the utmost perfection of mechanism. Some of the encomiums of the great organists are noteworthy. Lemmens, the master of many of the French organists, Guilmant, Widor, etc., said of Cavaillé-Coll: "Organbuilders of all countries are forced to borrow his wonderful inventions, which, true artist that he is, he has given over to the trade." Widor speaks in the highest terms of praise of the beautiful character of his solo stops, and of the remarkable sonority of his *plein jeu*. Guilmant, my master, tells me that his organ at La Trinité, which is very large and complicated, has not been inspected for twenty years; and although, as he himself acknowledges, this is far too long for an organ to be left to itself, I can bear witness to the fact that to this day it speaks with the utmost precision and regularity. Cavaillé-Coll as yet has not entered largely into the building of organs with electric actions, though I am told he looks with favor upon the improvements of the English inventor, Hope-Jones. He has received thirteen medals for successful competition at expositions in all parts of the world. He has also been made Chevalier de la Légion d'Honneur.

Some of the latest organs built by the firm are the following: An organ *de salon*, of two manuals, for the Princesse de Scey, *née* Singer (of sewing-machine fame); a church organ of two manuals for St. Just; and a grand organ *de tribune* for the parish church at Andelys.   OUTRE MER.

THE ORGANIST'S RETROSPECT.[1]

BY HORATIO CLARKE.

CHAPTER II.

IN the west of England, where the river Dee separates Cheshire from Wales, the venerable Episcopal city of Chester presents a rich field for the researches of the antiquary and archæologist. Within the boundary of the old Roman walls stands the ancient Gothic Cathedral, dating back to the year 1095, it having originally been the Abbey of St. Werburgh.

At the time of the coronation of Queen Victoria, my reverred father was the organist of this old Cathedral of Chester, two years after which time I was born, an only child. I can remember going with him into the organ gallery over the choir screen in my earliest years, and hearing the grand tones resound through nave and transept. As the voice of the white-robed choristers below rose and blended with the solemn organ tones, a sensation of rapture filled my little heart with feelings unutterable, and laid the foundation for a reverence for what is termed sacred music, which has surrounded my past life with the spirit of holiness.

Standing by the side of my talented father, I could look over the railing between the oak-carved pinnacles and see those reverent boy-singers in the antique stalls of the choir below; and during the musical service the grotesque sculptures in stone which stared from cornice and arch seemed like restless spirits brought to life from beneath the old tombstones which formed the pavement upon which the feet of the worshippers rested. The influence of this noble music caused my mind to be permeated with a sense of refinement and a longing for glorious ideals which no adverse influences have been able to subdue.

My father had received the degree of Doctor of Music, and was a thorough cathedral organist, possessing a love and enthusiasm for every part of the service of the Church of England. He was a man of high moral and intellectual character, and respected his position. On account of the gradual failure of his health he obtained a leave of absence for two years, in order to try the effect of the climate of America, and placed a deputy organist in charge of the music.

This decision was made just after the great Birmingham Musical Festival, when Mendelssohn conducted his oratorio of "Elijah." My father was a warm friend of the noted composer, and always met him on his visits to England. At the time of their last meeting I was about seven years old, and I have never forgotten that when he was talking with my father, who had taken me with him, how he gently stroked my head and said that the little son looked as though he had a musical nature. Then he took both my hands and pressed them between his own, as if imparting the spirit of his genius through that tender touch. I felt thrilled with that passing mark of notice, which was given for my dear father's sake, and that honor has always inspired me.

My mother belonged to one of the prominent aristocratic families of the county, and had incurred the displeasure of the nobility in having married a worthy musician whom she loved, rather than accepting the hand of a wealthy baronet. She had a gentle and highly cultivated nature, united to an unselfish disposition.

> "She was a woman of a steady mind,
> Tender and deep in her excess of love;
> Not speaking much, pleased rather with the joy
> Of her own thoughts: by some especial care
> Her temper had been framed, as if to make
> A being — who, by adding love to peace,
> Might live on earth a life of happiness."

It was a sacrifice for my father to rend asunder his connection with past associations and make the attempt to settle in a comparatively new country, where, at that time, musical science had not made rapid progress; but to him it was a question of life or death. My mother cheerfully consented to give up our artistic home and accompany him, that she might minister to his recovery, and in the spring we took passage for the United States.

Our destination was the metropolis of New England, where my father had letters of introduction. On his arrival he was chosen conductor of a long-established choral organization, and was offered the position of organist at the old King's Chapel. In order that he might have an incentive to keep active, he accepted both positions, and took a residence in a pleasant suburb of the city where the neighborhood was refined and the air pure.

He frequently took me with him to the service on Sundays; but the limitations of the place seemed to deaden or stifle the resonance, so that the effect of the music was dull and spiritless. In place of the rich voices of boy-choristers, there was simply a cultivated quartet of mixed voices in hymns and anthems which could not be rendered with the grandeur and solemnity of the full English Cathedral service, which I had been accustomed to hear from my infancy.

Real organ music had not then been developed in this city. The organ had three manuals, with an incomplete set of pedals, and it was said to be nearly a hundred years old. From the oaken case above the head of the organist the faces of the two smiling cherubs looked out as serenely as in the preceding century. The keys were set within the case, and the stops were arranged up and down on each side, the knobs being round, of solid ebony or rosewood, without inscription, the names being affixed to the wood at the side of the stop. Incomplete as were the capabilities of this instrument, my father patiently bore with its imperfections, and made the best of its better qualities.

In our new home life began afresh, and my father's health at first seemed to improve. On pleasant days he would take me on long walks out into the country, and made a practical use of his education in applying his knowledge to everything in nature. He had many friends among artists; and, as he delighted in sketching, he often choose them for companions in search of fine vistas and bits of landscape.

His old disease seemed to be baffled; but in the autumn days his weak lungs began to trouble him. On his return from conducting an oratorio in December, he was prostrated, and after a week's illness his life ended. The shock of bereavement was more than my mother's nature could bear. Suffering from an affection of the heart, she did not recover from this blow, and at the end of another week I was an orphan, and among strangers.

I was too young to know how my father's affairs were settled, and I was sent to live in another town with a Mr. Rodman, who, having no children, agreed to bring me up through the years of my minority. His wife, a thoroughly domestic woman, had no love for children, and received me with marked coldness, seeming to resent my presence as an intrusion.

I did not know what arrangements had been made for my support, but was given to understand that I was dependent upon the family into which I had been introduced as a member, and that whatever work I was capable of doing would be required of me, and that I should be obedient to them in all things.

For a while the great change in my circumstances seemed to benumb me during the day; but when each night I was sent alone to bed in darkness, not being allowed to have a light, I would give way to my grief at the loss of my dear parents, until sleep became my comforter.

Each morning I was called before daylight, and was required to bring in all the wood to be used during the day, as there was no coal burned; and when the ground was covered with snow, I had the paths to make to the street and to the barn. Besides this, I had the poultry to feed, and a certain number of large sticks of wood to saw each week-day.

In due time I was sent to the public school. Hitherto I had not mingled with children at large, excepting with the choir-boys of the old cathedral in Chester; for my parents had taken charge of my education at home, and I was naturally timid, and shrank from contact with the rough ways of boys.

On the first day of my appearance in the school yard, as soon as I was espied as a new-comer, the ruder boys set upon me, calling me names, pushing me about, and even tripping me to the ground, when a kind-faced boy at the other side of the yard ran in among the crowd, and, taking me by the hand, became my protector.

But at the end of the week he was seized with a prevailing fever, and died; and again I was left alone in my little world. Such an impression was made upon me by this gentle boy, whose grave is marked by a simple white stone bearing only the inscription, "Charles, Aged 8 years," that in all subsequent years, in visiting that locality, I have been to the old cemetery, and have sought out the resting-place of that early friend, and could never forget such kindness from the innocent heart of one whom none excepting myself now remember.

Many times in my childish years, when burdened with my little troubles and griefs, have I secretly gone to his grave, and, stretching myself beside its short mound, have wished to be buried beneath that turf, where I also might be at rest, and if there were a life beyond feel the grasp of his welcoming hand as I should enter its bright portal.

Often in later years, while meditating in this old churchyard among the ancient moss-covered headstones, when the deep resonance of the organ in the adjacent church would seem like sounds from another sphere vibrating over long-forgotten graves, my thoughts would take the elegaic form of a stately funeral march, which would wail with the mystery of existence and suffering; with earnest longings for immortality, followed by resignation to inevitable destiny; with the endless procession of dying humanity enshrouded in the darkness of despair, with successive generations, each in turn being borne to the silence of the grave, to rest from strife and anxiety — some hoping for the light of a better world, and others content to be forever free from pain and fear. Thus would these organ tones awaken reveries in harmony with reflections on the sleeping dead, and die away like the rumble of a storm that had passed with the distant thunder-clouds.

(To be continued.)

TRIUMPHAL MARCH.

A. M. SHUEY.

Tempo di Marcia.

Gt. Full.

Sw. 8 & 4 Ft. with Oboe
Ch. Flutes 8 & 4 Ft.

Gt.

Reduce to Oct.

Ped. 16 & 8 Ft.
Sw. to Gt., Gt. & Sw.
to Ped.

Reduce Gt. to
Open Diap.
Coup. off.
Sw.
Gt.
Sw.
cresc.
p
poco a cresc.
Gt.
Gt.
Coup.
Coup. off.
Sw.
Gt.
Sw.
cresc.

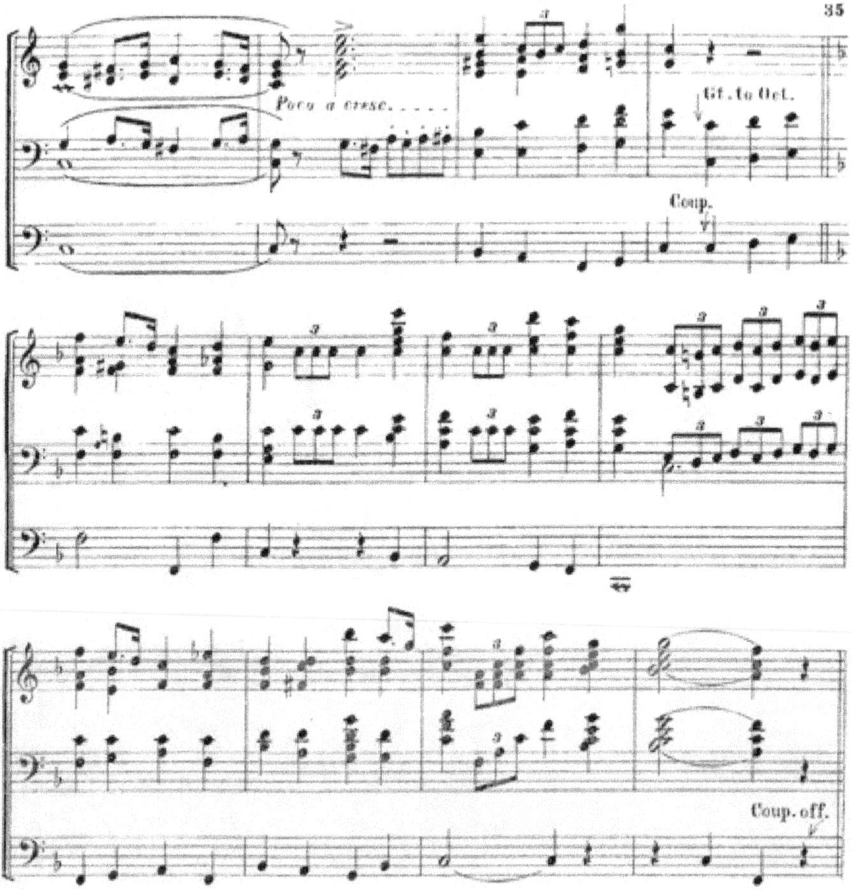
Poco a cresc. . . . .
Gt. to Oct.
Coup.
Coup. off.
Ch.
Sw. with Cornopean.

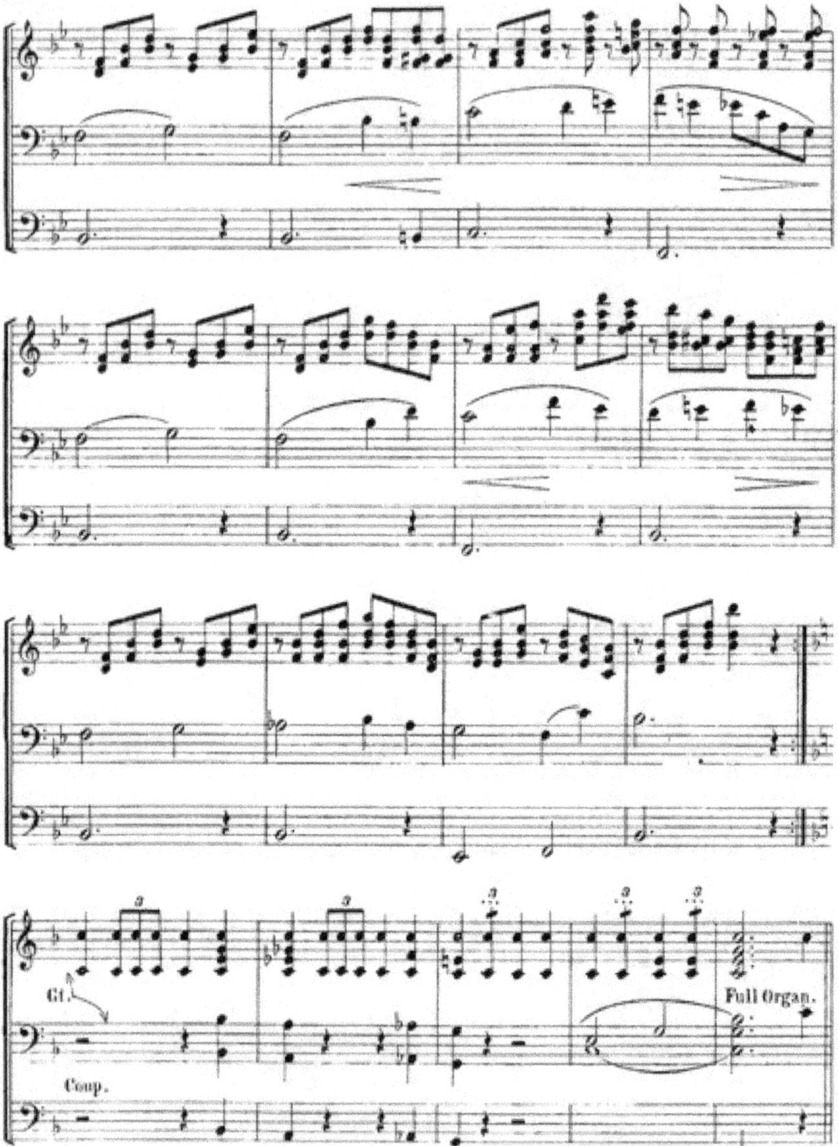
Gt.
Coup.
Full Organ.

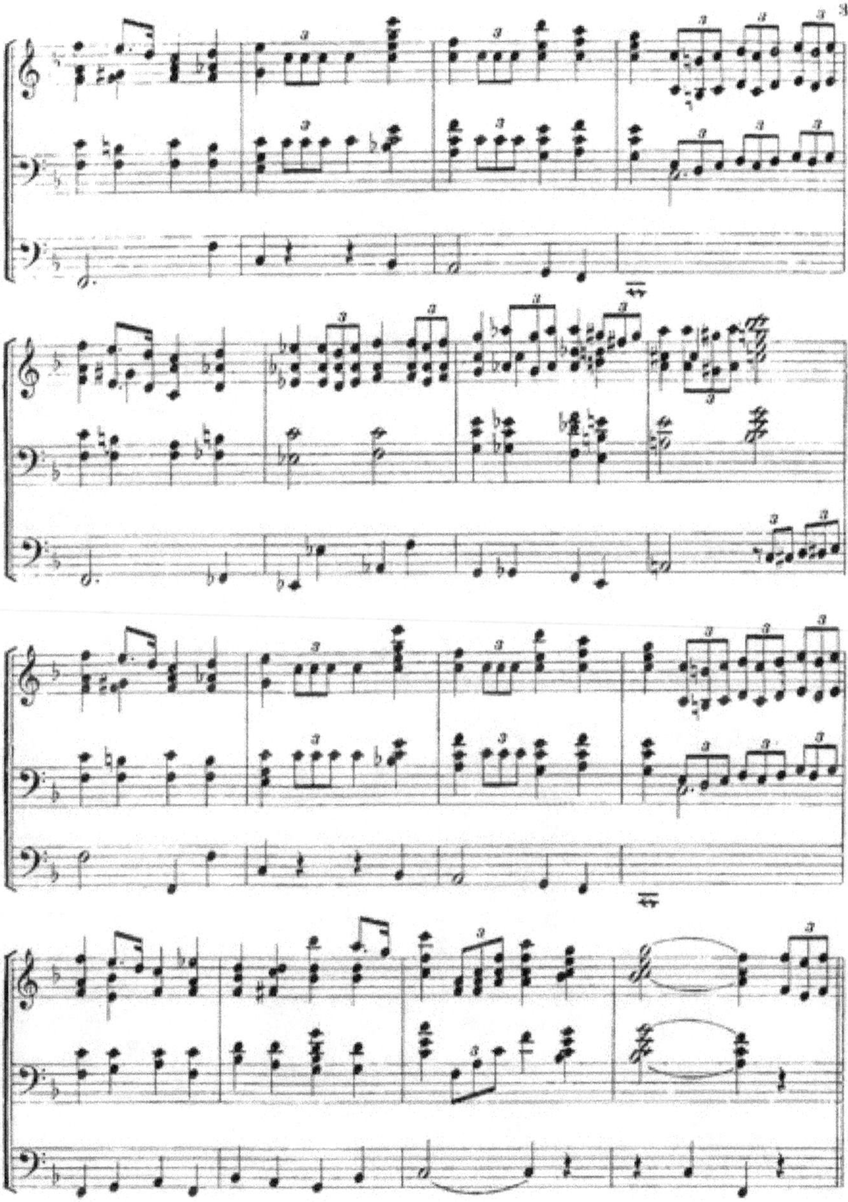

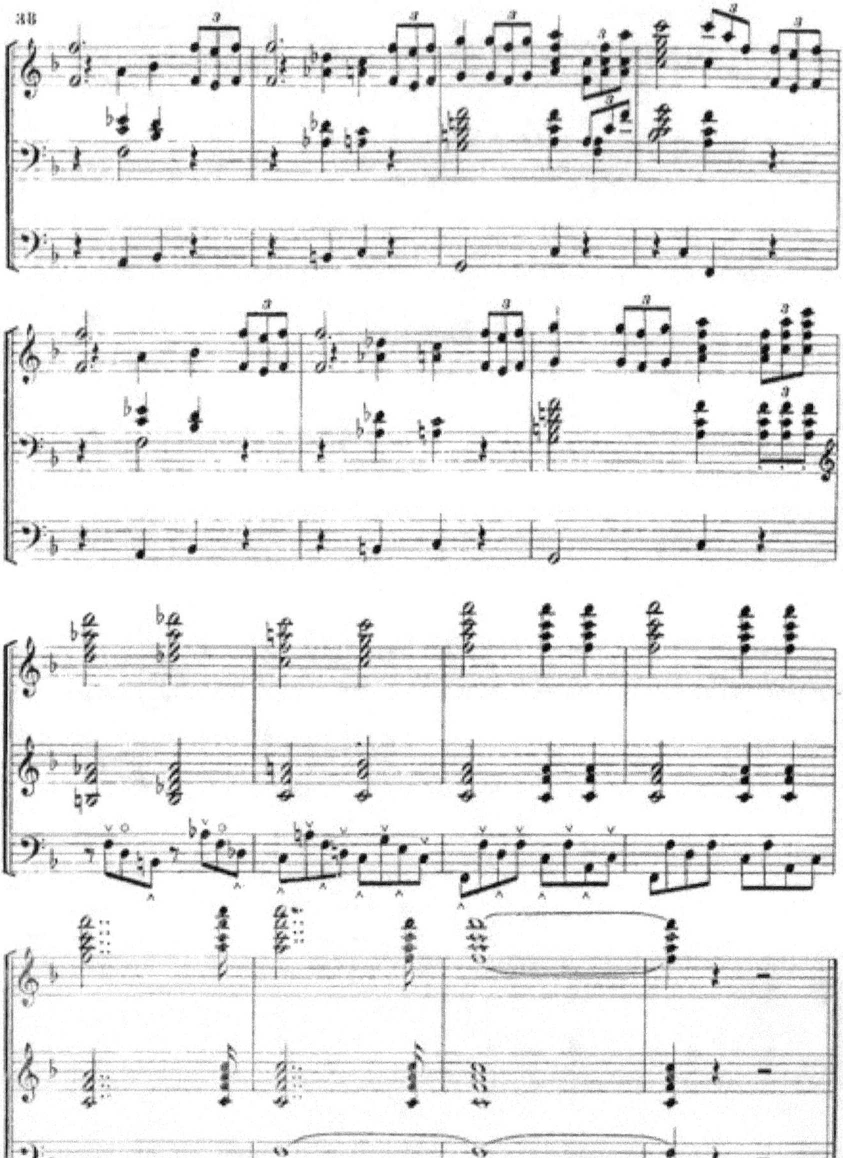

ADAGIO.

D. W. VOLCKMAR.

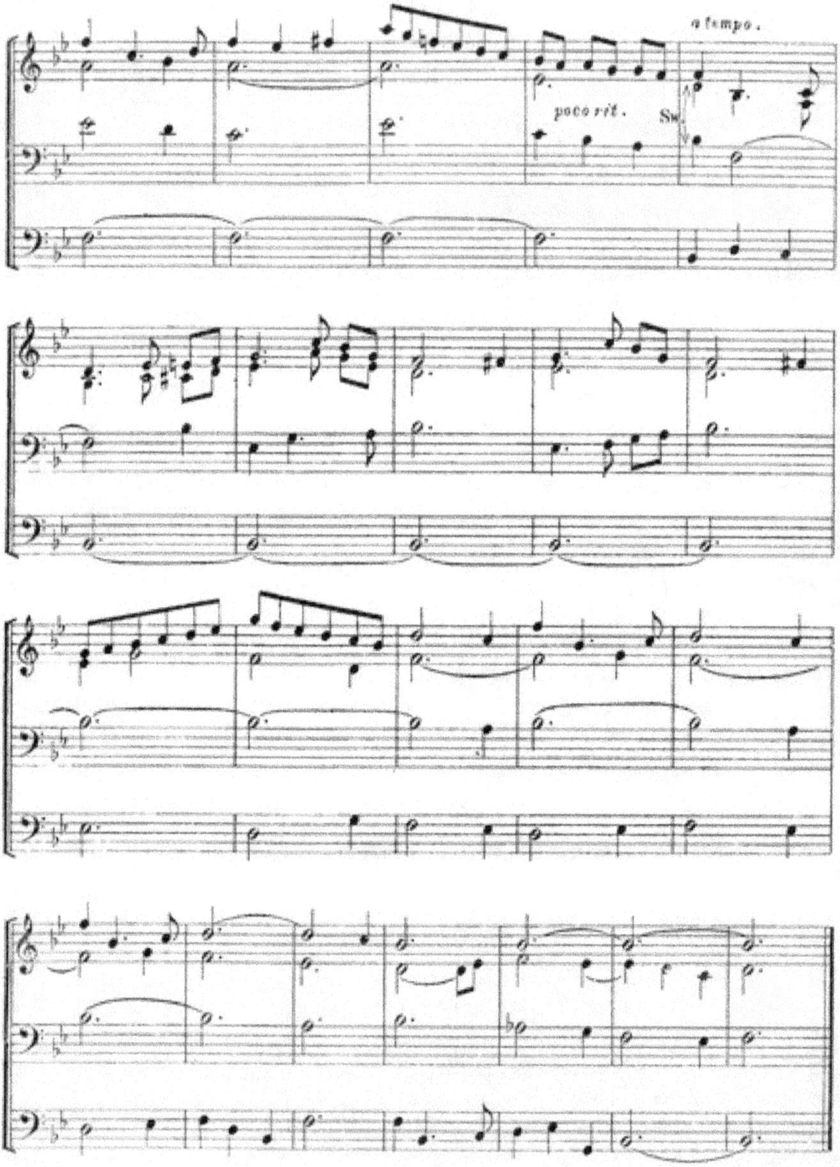
a tempo.
poco rit.
Sw.

CIPHERINGS.

OUR ORGANIST.[1] (FROM "OUR CHOIR," BY C. G. BUSH.)

COPYRIGHT, 1883, BY G. P. PUTNAM'S SONS.

THE MULTIPLE SWELL.

THERE have recently appeared in several successive numbers of THE ORGAN various articles upon the *swell*. The discussion was first started, I believe, by a writer signing himself "Gambette," and it has been continued by several contributors, all anonymous, by the way. Gambette is squarely opposed to the *multiple swell*. He apparently, too, views with disfavor the *single swell*. It is difficult to understand how any practical organist of to-day, who plays the modern school of organ compositions and transcriptions, or who is desirous of doing the best quality of work as a choir accompanist, can take such a position. Gambette & Co.'s objections, however, do not cease with the swell or swells. They are opposed to the modern system of combination pistons (or pedals), the undue number of which excites their disapproval, so that they compare the appearance of some modern consoles to that of a telephone desk. They urge that because certain organists (whose names are not given) can play effectively various standard compositions without the use of artificial aids, and have expressed a distaste for the swell, therefore such aids and accessories are unnecessary. Guilmant is brought into the discussion, and the comparatively simple appearance of his organ keyboard as regards knobs, etc., adduced as a "clincher" against them. And one of his

[1] By kind permission of Messrs. G. P. Putnam's Sons.

pupils (name omitted) is cited who plays well certain compositions, unaided by combination pedals or multiple swell. The further claim is made that the effect of the pipes is impaired by their confinement in a swell-box, and that it is impossible to secure the best tonal results in the construction of pipes if they are to be so enclosed and muffled. Now, as to the fact that certain standard compositions can be performed without the use of multiple swell and combination pedals (or knobs), no organist will dispute. But what has that fact to do with the question? There is, on the other hand, a school of organ literature already large, and constantly increasing, which CANNOT be *adequately* performed without the use of both the above appliances. To give one very simple example: I recently used Westbrook's transcription of Schubert's Ave Maria for a voluntary. The registration calls for the melody to be given out *first* by the clarinet on the choir organ *uncoupled*. How would this sound if played upon a choir organ unenclosed in a swell-box? To my mind it would be cold and immeasurably expressionless; at all events, I did not try it, but, by coupling the choir to the swell, secured light and shade. Some one may ask, Why not always do this? My reply is, that the melody will not unfrequently be of such range as to interfere with the left-hand part, which is being played at the same time upon the swell organ; and, still further, it is (to my mind) desirable that extended phrases requiring both hands be played upon the choir organ alone; and, when so played, be under the control of a swell-pedal, to avoid monotony and colorlessness. To revert to the example already mentioned, Dr. Westbrook's registration would have been very effective had the clarinet been under the control of a swell-pedal: and will any sound player argue that the use of the flute (4'), clarinet, or *any* solo stop found on the choir or solo organs, would not be greatly improved if placed under the control of a swell-pedal?

Because in the past, *good* effects have been produced upon organs lacking modern appliances, is that any reason why better effects should not be produced by new appliances serving to bring the various resources of the instrument more fully under the performer's control, and enabling him to have much more expression in his *cantabile* playing and choir accompaniments? Let us apply this principle to the orchestra. Suppose that the small orchestra for which Bach and Händel wrote had never been enlarged, we should have had much beautiful and charming music, doubtless; *neither*, *however*, for a small orchestra. But the orchestra kept pace with demands made upon it by the compositions of men of genius, until, under the influence of Richard Wagner, we have orchestral effects which for fulness and sonority far excel any produced by his early predecessors. Not that a small orchestra was or *is* bad, but the orchestra of to-day far exceeds it. Again, conceive of organ recitals where, as some would prefer, no swell at all were used. Would not the effect be one of intolerable monotony, colorlessness, and lack of expression? How would we like to hear a singer who never varied from one fixed volume of tone, or varied only by sudden changes, like adding or withdrawing a stop? It seems to me that to-day upon all sides the demand is for *increased* expression, rather than the opposite.

Orchestral playing is more severely criticised in this particular than ever before. Volume, sonority, fine tone, are all very well; but finely graduated expression in its various departments is now more strongly insisted upon than ever before, owing to the constant advance in musical education and intelligence.

This general desire for increased expression is felt in connection with the organ, and progressive builders have been, and are now, striving to render the organ more expressive and more controllable.

The players who inveigh against the present improvements cannot surely be of the progressive school. They are either hidebound with conservatism, or too lazy to adapt themselves to a changed condition of affairs.

As to the construction of the pipes in connection with the multiple swell, an absolute decision is not easy. It may be, as is claimed by some organists and organ-builders, that the tone of the pipe is unfavorably affected by being enclosed in a swell-box; but, admitting this to be true, our contention is that the advantages gained more than compensate for this disadvantage. As a matter of fact, it has been my privilege to see several organs, both large and small, equipped with the multiple swell, and in no instance was the tone perceptibly injured so far as I could perceive; nor did I hear from organists present, with whom I conversed, any unfavorable expressions upon this point.

Unfortunately, the average organ-builder is averse to new ideas; and right here is where we may look for one source of opposition to this and other improvements. Extra labor, and the planning and trouble necessary to produce a modern instrument, are distasteful, and will not be entered upon unless strong pressure is brought to bear. It is so easy to make the same good old-fashioned instruments which their fathers made before them, and it is a much simpler instrument to play upon, provided it is in order.

Organists in this country owe a great debt of gratitude to the Roosevelts, who forced other builders to follow them, even if unwillingly, in their efforts to improve the state of organ-building in this country.

I find that the progressive players like Dudley Buck, Samuel P. Warren, Harry Rowe Shelley, R. H. Woodman, and others, favor decidedly the multiple swell and all other improvements which serve to give the organ greater expression and bring it more fully under the control of the performer. Indeed, how can any good player do otherwise?

In closing, I wish to appeal to the younger organists throughout the country, who are studying seriously and striving to advance the cause of good organ music. Why not *combine*, as far as possible, and leave no worthy effort untried to *compel* builders to conform to the best modern ideas in the construction of organs? *Insist* upon this point, and whenever the decision rests with you, refuse to indorse a specification or an instrument unless both, so far as circumstances will allow, are in touch with the best ideas of to-day.

Here in Connecticut we met last July and formulated our recommendations, which have been printed and circulated all over the State. Doubtless these recommendations are not perfect, but they represent the fruit of much discussion and a strong desire on our part to advance the cause of organ-building.

Why cannot the same step be taken in every State? If it should be, it would not be long before the combined opinions of organists all over the country would make itself felt, and better and more uniform and controllable organs would be built. May this desirable result be brought to pass at no very distant day!   JOHN S. CAMP.

HARTFORD, CONN., March, 1893.

MIXTURES.

(FOUR RANKS.)

MR. WALLACE P. DAY conducted a performance of "Ruth," by Gaul, and "The Tale of the Viking," by Whiting, in Grace Church, Jacksonville, Ill., April 28.

Mr. Geo. S. Hutchings is building a two-manual organ of twenty-six registers for Epworth Memorial Church, Cambridge, Mass.

Dr. Geo. F. Brooks gave an organ recital at the West Church, Boston, a short time ago, on the organ which has several times been offered for sale.

Mr. Geo. S. Hutchings has built a two-manual organ, with twenty registers, for the Baptist Church, Weston, Mass.

Mr. Clarence Eddy gave an organ concert in the Presb. Church, La Porte, Ind., April 21, with the following programme: Sonata, Wiemann; Andantino, Chauvet; Gavotte, Martini; Offertory in C Minor, Batiste; "Ave Meer," Schubert; Concert Fugue, Kuehn; Nuptial Benediction and "Largo Dvo," Dubois; Variation on "Home, Sweet Home," Flagler; Overture to "Stradella," Flotow.

Mr. Geo. S. Hutchings is building an organ for the M. E. Church, Everett, Mass., which will contain two manuals and twenty-two registers.

The large two-manual organ now being erected in the Second Presbyterian Church of Pittsburg, Pa., by Hook & Hastings, will be opened in a short time. It contains twenty-five registers.

Mr. Robt. F. Virgoe, member of the College of Organists, London, won, on the 19th of November, 1892, elected an Assoc. Philharmonic Society of London. W. H. Cummings, Esq., F. S. A., Hon. R. A. M.; G. H. Robinson, Esq., Mus. Bac., Camb. (organist and choir-master Charter House); E. H. Turpin, Esq., Mus. Doc., Canterbury, F. C. O., L. I. C. L. (Election).

Messrs. Hook & Hastings finished complete and shipped during the past month five two-manual church organs. They are now erecting another one-hundred-foot building, which will make their floor space aggregate fifty-one thousand square feet.

The Hope-Jones Electric Organ Company, Limited, of Birkenhead, has received instructions to rebuild the three-manual Casson Organ belonging to J. Martin White, Esq., of Balruddery, Dundee. The work is to be put in hand at once.

Mons. Alex Guilmant gave a concert on a new electric organ at St. Clement's, Nantes, May 1. The organ was built by Mons. Debierre.

Dr. E. J. Hopkins celebrated his fiftieth anniversary as organist at the Temple Church, London, May 7.

The pupils of Mons. Eugene Gigout gave a recital in April, among whom were MM. Denaut, Rousse, Vivet, Verdeau, and Guilmant.

Mr. W. E. Snyder gave an organ recital at the Woodland Ave. Cong. Church, Detroit, Mich., April 15.

Mr. Thomas Bemick Richardson, for thirty years organist of St. Mary's, London, died the last of April at the age of sixty-two.

Sig. Enrico Bossi recently gave a concert at the Royal Conservatoire, Milan.

Mr. H. P. Chelius has resigned his position as organist to the Tremont Temple Baptist Society, Boston.

Mons. Eugene Gigout inaugurated the new Merklin organ in Salle d'Harcourt, Paris, in April, with the following programme: Sonata in F, Mendelssohn; Cantabile, Franck; Third Rhapsody, Saint-Saens; Toccata in F, Bach.

Mr. York gave an organ recital at the Cass Ave., M.E. Church, Detroit, Mich., in April.

On May 1st the Maxklove Pipe Organ Co. of Utica, N.Y., was succeeded by Messrs. Morey & Barnes, who will continue the manufacture of pipe organs at the factory, 60 John St.

Mons. Albert Mahaud, the blind organist, has been making a tour of France, giving concerts in various cities. He recently gave a concert on the electric organ in Notre-Dame-de-Bon-Port, Nantes.

The organ in the Town Hall, Manchester, England, which has been recently enlarged, will probably be formally reopened soon.

Let poor struggling church organists take courage. Mr. Rufus Hatch, the well-known New York financier, who recently died, was, in early life, organist of a Chicago church. — *Musical Messenger.*

There will be a competition for the R. Huntington Woodman free scholarship for the organ at the Metropolitan College of Music, New York, July 15. The scholarship will last for a year. For particulars, apply to the Secretary, 21 E. Fourteenth St., N.Y.

Sir John Stainer, Dr. J. F. Bridge, and Dr. E. H. Turpin, three distinguished organists of London, have been invited to represent England at the Congress of Musicians, to be held by the American College of Musicians, under the auspices of the World's Fair Auxiliary, at Chicago, July 3.

Mr. S. B. Whitney, for the first time in twenty years, has been obliged to be absent from his post at the Church of the Advent, Boston, on account of illness. After a short sojourn in Atlantic City he has returned to Boston, and is quite himself again.

Mr. Samuel Bakler has recently placed a three-manual organ in St. John's Reformed Church, Philadelphia, Pa., which was opened by Mr. H. A. Clarke, Mus. Doc., May 9, who writes to the builder that he considers this organ "a very superior instrument. The stops are finely voiced, well balanced, and the variety of tone is large for the size of the instrument."

In the last issue of THE ORGAN an organ concert at the Bow & Bromley Institute, London, was announced as given April 15, by Sig. Capocci. The item was taken from a London weekly, which was issued on that day. At the last moment Sig. Capocci was so ill that he could not appear, and the concert was indefinitely postponed.

The organ and gallery in the Church of our Lady of Succor, at Naples, fell to the floor of the church during a recent service. There were forty-five musicians in the gallery at the time, all of whom were more or less injured, the leader fatally.

A monument has been erected to the memory of Friedrich Schneider, in Dessau, Germany. It was to be unveiled on Whit-Sunday.

Recipe for a chaste organ effect, to illustrate "Satan in confusion, terror-struck departs," from Hymns Ancient and Modern, 107: play on swell eight and four feet. Pedal coupled to great with Posaune, sixteen feet. Pedals to be played staccatissimo. The result is very realistic, and was lately heard at a well-known extreme church. — *London Musical News.*

The Sunday afternoon organ recitals in Albert Hall, London, proved very popular, a large audience attending nearly every recital. The organists were Messrs. H. L. Balfour, W. S. Hoyte, and H. C. Tonking.

The first organ ever built in the United States is said to be still in existence, and located in Brattleboro, Vt. This instrument, which is for sale, is about the size of an upright piano, and does not look unlike one. There are two draw-stops on either side of the key-board, and the pipes are inside the box or case. A long iron pedal, similar to that in the fluidic organ, works the bellows. The owner claims that he can prove its authenticity, and that every pipe in the instrument is perfect. A photograph may be seen at this office.

Mr. Wm. C. Carl opened a new organ (built by Mr. S. S. Hamill of E. Cambridge, Mass.,) in the First Presb. Church, Mansfield, Ohio, May 9, playing the following selections: Sonatina, Bach; Preludes, Corelli; Festival March, Nevin; Concerto in D-minor, Handel; Pastorale, MacMaster; Scherzo and March from "Ariane," Guilmand; Noel, Dubois; Andantino, Salome; Fantare, Deshayes; Vorspiel, "Lohengrin;" and March from "Tannhäuser," Wagner.

Mr. I. V. Flagler inaugurated a new organ, built by Messrs. J. W. Steere & Son of Springfield, in the Epworth M. E. Church, Cleveland, Ohio, May 15, with the following programme: Improvisation; Sonata No. 4, Flagler; Scene in the Alps, Flagler; Idylle, Guilmand; Minuet, Salome; Vesper Chimes, Smith; Concert Variations on "America," Flagler; Gavotte "Mignon," Thomas; Paraphrase on "Robin Adair," Flagler; Transcription, "Tannhäuser," Wagner. Mr. Flagler also gave the above programme at the inauguration of a new organ in the Third Presbyterian Church, Rochester, N.Y., May 11. The organ was built by Messrs. Johnson & Son of Westfield, Mass. Specification in THE ORGAN for May.

Not long since a pastor of a Western church was preaching a few Sundays in a Boston church, with the intention of accepting a call from the latter church. In making suggestions to the standing committee with regard to several alterations in the organ which he should request the committee to make, he recommended that the organ should be moved from the east end of the church to the gallery at the west end, saying that "*it could be placed on rollers, rolled to the other end of the church, and raised to the gallery by means of a derrick.*" The organ was thirty feet high and twenty feet deep.

On April 18 an orchestral concert was given at the Salle d'Harcourt with one number for organ and orchestra, — Guilmand's first Sonata, the author himself taking the organ part. When one is accustomed to the arrangement for organ alone of this noble work, it is a great revelation to hear it given as it was conceived. The effects of the wind instruments in the Pastorale were most delicate and beautiful, and the brass is used at the end of the Finale in a masterly fashion; all of which is entirely lost without the orchestra.   OUTRE MER.

Mr. Henry M. Dunham gave an organ recital at the Shawmut Church, Boston, May 4, with the following programme: Toccata and Fugue in D-minor, Bach; Musette, from Concerto for stringed instruments, Handel-Best; Fugue, from Overture to "Samson," Handel-Best; Lament, from "Peer Gynt" Suite, Grieg-Morse; Sonata in G-minor, Dunham; Prayer and Cradle Song, Guilmand; and Overture in D-minor, Smart. The organ was in better tune than at the last recital; and, while the programme was perhaps a little less interesting, the various combinations had a more agreeable effect on the ear. The interpretation and rendering of the various numbers were characterized by the same individuality, clearness, and good taste in the selection of combinations which we noted at the previous recital.

Mr. M. P. Möller of Hagerstown, Md., has just sold five organs, among which is one for Dubois, Penn., which will be twenty feet high and fourteen feet wide, and one for Shelbyville, Ind., costing $2,600.

Mr. Joseph Gratian, organ-builder of Alton, Ill., has invented a combination swell-pedal and grand crescendo which is controlled by one pedal. It draws the stops and opens the swell at the same time, or vice versa, without affecting the draw-stops.

Mr. William Churchill Hammond gave his seventy-fifth recital in Holyoke, Mass., May 1, with a Children's Programme: March in D-minor, and Andante (Rossmande), Schubert; March of the Magi Kings, Dubois; Scenes of Childhood, Schumann; and Offertoire "St. Cecilia," Batiste.

Mr. J. J. Miller gave an organ concert in Christ Church, Norfolk, Va., April 24, with the following programme: Finale from First Sonata, Guilmand; "Sunshine and Shadow," Bach; Funeral March and Spring Song, Mendelssohn; Fanfare (by request), Lemmens.

They tell quite a good story of George Chadwick, the composer, up in the New Hampshire town that claims to be his birthplace. He was young when he played the organ in a large Congregational church up there, and though his response were played with delicacy and taste, one of the prominent members of the church sent him a letter one day, saying that he should thereafter make his response "short and impressive." He did. As soon as the minister got to the end of his prayer, Chadwick pulled out

all the stops, leaned with both arms on the keyboard, and tangled up his feet exclusively on the pedal bass. Then he quietly took his hat and walked out. He was not re-engaged. — *Boston Record.*

Mr. Clarence Eddy inaugurated a new Farrand & Votey organ at the Visitation Convent, St. Louis, Mo., April 26, playing Prelude and Fugue in D, Bach; Andantino, Chauvet; Gavotte Moderne; "O Sanctissima," Lux; "Prayer," Lemaigre; Spring Song, Mendelssohn; March of the Magi Kings, Dubois; "The Holy Night," Buck; Variations on "Old Folks at Home," Flagler; Overture to "Stradella," Flotow.

Mr. William Churchill Hammond gave his seventy-third and seventy-fourth recitals in the Second Congregational Church, Holyoke, Mass., April 19 and 28, performing the following compositions: Theme and Variations, Hesse; Allegretto from Twelfth Symphony, Haydn; Fourth Sonata, Mendelssohn; Andante, Wedding Song, Parker; Toccata in F, Widor; Largo Cantabile, from Fifth Quartet, Haydn-Best; First Sonata, Mendelssohn; Andante Pastorale, Parker; Allegro in D, Widor.

Mr. Clarence Eddy gave an organ concert in the First M. E. Church, Duluth, Minn., April 28, with the following programme: Sonata in C-minor, Wermann; Marche of the Magi Kings, Dubois; "The Holy Night," Buck; St. Cecilia Offertory, Batiste; "Ave Maria," Schubert; Fugue in G-minor, Bach; Variations on "Home, Sweet Home," Flagler; Concert Piece, Lux; Gavotte in F, Martini; Pilgrims' Chorus, Wagner; Overture to "Wm. Tell," Rossini.

Mr. Wm. C. Carl gave his twelfth and thirteenth recitals at the First Presb. Church, New York, May 5 and 13, with the following programmes: Sinfonia de la Cantate, Bach; Andante Con Moto and Andante Cantabile, from Suite No. 2 (MS.), Deshayes; Cazedon and Moonet Antique, Neustedt-Carl; Nuptial March, Guilmand; and Fanfare (new), Loret. On the thirteenth: Sarabande et Fugue the, Couperin; Prelude, Chrombach; Danse des Sylphes, Berlioz; Hosannah, Lemmens; Adantino, Salome; Marche de la Symphonie, "Ariane," Guilmand; and Finale, Sixth Symphony, Widor.

Mr. Chas. Bigelow Ford gave an organ concert in St. Peter's P. E. Church, New York, May 11, with the following programme: Fugue (St. Ann's, Bach; Intermezzo from Pastorale Sonata, Rheinberger; Marche Religieuse, Guilmand; Grand Choeur, Dubois; Adagio (First Sonata), Mendelssohn; Chromatic Fantasia, Thiele; Pilgrim Chorus, Wagner; Overture to "Oberon," Weber. The Pilgrim Chorus was performed on the two organs, that in the gallery being played by Mr. L. Carroll Beckel.

The new Roosevelt organ in Christ Church Cathedral, St. Louis, Mo., was inaugurated April 25, by Mr. Clarence Eddy, who gave two recitals, playing the following: Sonata, Wermann; Nuptial Benediction and "Lost Deo," Dubois; Xmas Pastorale, Whitings; Toccata in A, Best; "Last Sleep of the Virgin," Massenet; Offertoire in C-Minor, Batiste; Pastorale in G, Widor; Scherzo-Symphonique, Guilmand; Adagio from Sonata No. 2, Buck; Festival March, Carter; Toccata in F, Bach; Vorspiel, "Lohengrin," Wagner; "A Royal Procession," Spinney; Variations on the Austrian Hymn, Hoop; Lamentation, Guilmand; Fantasia in E (MS.), Merkel; Fugue in G, Krebs; "In Paradise," and "Alleluia," Dubois; Schiller March, Meyerbeer; Theme, Variations, and Finale, Thiele.

In the last issue of THE ORGAN there appeared the specification of the instrument which was being constructed for the Music Hall, World's Fair, by the Carl Barckhoff Organ Company of Salem, Ohio. At the last moment it became necessary to make some alterations in the hall, which rendered it impossible for the organ to be set up as planned. According to the arrangement made by the authorities of the exposition with the organ company, the former were to forfeit $10,000 if for any reason the organ was not accepted. Accordingly, that sum has been paid to the Carl Barckhoff Organ Company, and the company has further received a certificate stating that the refusal to accept the organ was due solely to the alterations in the hall, which prevented the installation of any organ.

The annual series of organ concerts, which Mons. Guilmand inaugurated fifteen years ago, were to begin in the Trocadéro, Paris, the 29th of May.

Mr. Frank Taft has just ended a concert tour through Iowa, Nebraska, Missouri, Wyoming, Kansas, Texas, and Colorado.

The U. S. Circuit Court has ordered the sale at auction of the real and personal estate of the Kimball Organ Company to meet the judgments of the creditors.

"It's curious," said Wilkins, "how coming events cast their shadows before them. I'll wager a fiver none of you gentlemen can guess what was the last thing played on the Tremont Temple organ at the time of the fire."

"'The Lost Chord'?" suggested Dumbley.

Wilkins shook his head. "' 'Die-No'?" said the classical gentleman.

Wilkins shook his head again.

"What was it then?" asked a practical member.

Wilkins got up, reached for his hat, and went to the door, then he replied, "The hose!" — *Boston Budget.*

Mr. George S. Hutchings, the popular organ-builder, entertained about sixty of his employees at a house-warming and reception, in his new residence, Brookline and Henry Streets, Cambridge, May 17. The house, which has just been completed, is extremely attractive inside and out, and the guests, one and all, were charmed with the comfortable surroundings. There are about eighty men employed at the factory on Irvington Street, and it is doubtful if any organ factory in the country possesses a better class of employees. Two-thirds of the men are performers of more than ordinary ability on some musical instrument, showing that their capabilities are not confined to adjusting roller-boards, winding trackers, gluing up bosses, pipes, or voicing reeds. The musical programme of the evening, rendered entirely by the employees, consisted of several male quartets, sung effectively, tenor, bass, and baritone solos, eliciting generous applause, as well as interesting cornet, violin, and piano solos. Early in the evening a closely covered wagon arrived at the door, when immediately Mr. and Mrs. Hutchings were escorted to a remote corner of the house, and detained with several prolonged "yarns," while the contents of the wagon were smuggled into the parlor. These were surrounded by the guests, and completely hidden from view as the host and hostess were permitted to return to the parlor. Mr. Bowen, superintendent of the factory, addressed Mr. Hutchings with a well-chosen and witty speech, and in behalf of the employees presented him with a mahogany table, an elegant silver service, and a beautiful bouquet lamp. A more surprised organ-builder never breathed; in fact, for seventeen seconds he did not breathe. After prolonged applause Mr. Hutchings responded, and thanked the donors heartily. After a sumptuous collation and extended good wishes to the host and hostess, the guests departed to their homes, more than glad that they were among those who constructed organs at 23 Irvington Streets.

Mr. R. Huntington Woodman gave an organ recital at the New York Ave. M. E. Church, Brooklyn, May 18, with the following programme: Marche Religieuse, Guilmant; Prière, Lemaigre; St. Cecilia Offertory, Batiste; Funeral March, Chopin; Night Song, Vogt; Minuet, Händel; Largo, Händel; Wedding Procession, Rubinstein; Overture in D, Smart; Adagio in D-flat, Merkel; Toccata (First Sonata), Tombelle.

LET US AVOID THE CONFUSION.

Not long since an order came to a certain organ-builder to "send some one over at once to fix our organ." Accordingly a man was despatched to the church, and "fixed" the organ. The bill was sent and paid at once. The following Monday morning the authorities of the church appeared at the office of the organ-builder, and demanded that the money be refunded at once. Explanations followed; and it turned out that the order to "fix the organ" referred to the reed-organ in the vestry; and the organ-builder had "fixed" the pipe organ in the church.

"Mr. John Smith has bought an organ." A simple sentence like this ought to be perfectly intelligible. But is it? There is no possible doubt about who bought an organ, neither can one fail to understand what Mr. Smith did, though it is none of our affair whether or not he paid for the instrument; but what did he buy? Why, an organ, to be sure!

What is an organ?

1. A one-legged instrument strapped to the neck of a man who turns a crank and thereby makes music (?).

2. An instrument which our ancestors, who could not afford a piano, generally placed in the "setting-room" for Jane to play on, the tone of which was a cross between that of a jew's-harp and a toy trumpet.

3. A machine in which you press a button and blow ("we do the rest"), producing music which combines the technique of Joseffy, the force of Rubinstein, and the iciness of Von Bülow; which would not play a wrong note for a hundred-dollar bill, and which saves hours and days of labor wasted in practice. The tone is — is — well — is simply indescribable.

4. The noblest and grandest, the largest and most powerful, the "king of instruments," which combines nearly all the tone-colors of the orchestra, to which is added the rich diapason tone — the envy of the composers for the orchestra.

Which kind of an organ did Mr. Smith purchase?

Now, the confusion arising from this multiplicity in the use of the word organ is increasing every year, and ought to be checked, by universally adopting a distinctive name for

each of these four instruments which lay claim to the term organ. Surely the instrument which has the greatest claim on the simple word organ, both by priority and superiority, is the pipe organ, known as the church organ, — the "king of instruments."

The portable instruments of the organ genus, which are always accompanied by a man, and often by a monkey (some say by two monkeys), are often, and should always be, called hand-organs, or, better still, barrel-organs, for are not all organs played by hand?

The instruments variously known as cabinet-organs, American organs (poor America!), and harmoniums, are all reed-organs, and should always be called reed-organs.

The machines which discourse sweet sounds by means of holes in a band of paper are, to a certain extent, automatic, and if always called automatic organs would escape a large part of the ridicule which is hurled at them.

Supposing this Mr. Smith had gone to New York to secure an estimate for a church organ, and had written down the addresses of the "organ factories" found in the directory, the disappointment, leading to disgust, which he would experience as he arrived at each "factory," to find that only one out of every seven was a pipe-organ factory, would be impossible if each instrument was always spoken of by a distinctive name.

There is nothing new about these distinctive names; but let them be universally adopted when speaking or writing of these instruments, and the confusion will be at an end.

EMILE LE BLANC.

ANECDOTES.

The architect of a certain church happened to be at the door of the church when the organ was being unloaded. The sight of the thirty-two-feet open pedal pipes filled him with dismay. He hastened off to the priest, and told him that he had not planned the walls and roof strong enough to withstand such tremendous sounds as must come from those monster pipes. The priest then became alarmed, and sought an interview with the organ-builder.

The builder tried every means at his command to reassure the priest, without any effect. Finally he suggested that the priest interview some expert. This he consented to do, and wrote to the late Eugene Thayer, who replied that "the only case on record when musical sounds had destroyed the walls of any building or city, was when the blowing of the rams' horns destroyed the walls of Jericho, and this was undoubtedly due to the fact that the rams' horns were so deucedly out of tune."

It was a little church on the corner. The organist had gone through the agony of a series of contortions and gyrations commonly known by the term Voluntary. The congregation had sung the Doxology, and the choir progressed well into an anthem in which the words oft occurred, "Oh, what bliss awaits us when we soar to heaven's heights!" The soprano had given out the theme in high, sweet notes, to which the bass had responded in deep, rich tones, and now the alto and tenor were singing in duet, "Oh what bliss," etc., when a couple, who had unfortunately arrived late, walked up the broad aisle to about the fourth row front. A faint smile seemed to lurk in the corners of tenor's mouth, while the choir seemed likely to have some difficulty in coming in on the chorus; but during a brief interlude on the organ, after the duet, the choir rallied and came in on the chorus, "Oh what bliss, what bliss awaits us!" etc., while Mr. and Mrs. Bliss marched solemnly to their pew, the unconscious cause of inward merriment to the choir, who, by the way, were facing the congregation, and under the necessity of preserving a proper decorum.

GEORGE S. HUTCHINGS,

Church Organ Manufacturer,

23 TO 27 IRVINGTON STREET,

BOSTON, MASS.

Builder of some of the most famous organs in the country, among which may be mentioned The New Old South, Emmanuel, Second Church, Park St. Church, St. Paul's, Spiritual Temple, and Church of the Advent, all of Boston; also South Congregational Church, Middletown, Conn., New York Avenue M. E. Church, Brooklyn, N. Y., St. Paul's School, Concord, N. H., and All Saints Church, Worcester, Second Congregational Church, Holyoke, Mass., Grace Church, Providence, R.I., Plymouth Church, Minneapolis, First Congregational Church, Omaha, Neb., First Congregational Church, San Francisco, Cal., Independent Presbyterian Church, Savannah, Ga., and many others.

Send for catalogue.

S. ELLIOTT,

MANUFACTURER OF ACTIONS FOR

PIPE ORGANS.

WINCHESTER, - - MASS.

WOODBERRY & HARRIS,

399 ALBANY STREET,

BOSTON, MASS.

(Next building to West End Power Station.)

Builders of the following noted organs,
Plymouth Church, Syracuse, N. Y.
Fourth Church, Somerville, Ill.
...

Church, Chamber, and Chapel Organs,

Old Organs rebuilt, enlarged and revoiced: also, organs tuned and repaired by competent workmen.

Motors for blowing organs furnished and applied.

Organists and
Church Committees

ARE CORDIALLY INVITED TO EXAMINE THIS NEW MODEL.

LISZT ORGAN. Style 804.

This new and improved model is attracting wide attention among church committees and organists. It is decidedly superb, is small Pipe Organs, and is unquestionably the most perfect instrument of its class. Send for specification. Sent free to any address.

ORGANS ALSO RENTED.

MASON AND HAMLIN ORGAN AND PIANO CO.

154 & 155 TREMONT STREET, BOSTON, U.S.A.

Branches: { 158 Fifth Avenue, New York.
{ 185 Wabash Avenue, Chicago.

OUR SECOND ORGAN-MUSIC COMPETITION.

A prize of ten dollars ($10.00) will be given for the best Pastorale for the organ. The composition should be written on three staves, must be from seventy-five to a hundred bars in length, and must bear a motto only. A sealed envelope, bearing the same motto and containing the form given below (which should be cut from this journal), filled out with the name and address of the competitor, should accompany each composition.

Compositions will be received till the 1st of August, when they will be submitted to the following judges, who have kindly consented to examine the composition :—

MR. CLARENCE EDDY of Chicago.
MR. GEORGE E. WHITING of Boston.
MR. S. B. WHITNEY of Boston.

The successful composition must become the property of THE ORGAN, and will be printed with the name of the composer in the journal issued the first of October.

Compositions should be addressed : Editor THE ORGAN, 149 A Tremont St., Boston.   (Prize Competition.)

Organ Music Competition.

Name ....

Address ....

Motto ....

REVIEW OF NEW ORGAN MUSIC.

FROM RICHAULT & CO., PARIS.

Scherzo in B-minor
Élevation in D-flat
Cantilène in E-minor
Offertoire in E   } Aloÿs Claussmann.
Élevation in A
Communion in D
Pastorale in D

Seven pieces from the "First Collection" of this composer. They vary in length from five to ten pages, and in price from sixty cents to a dollar. Notwithstanding the great variety in the character of the different pieces, we do not find them as interesting as the last works of this composer which we reviewed. Each one of the pieces is almost dependent on an effective registration; and while this registration is carefully indicated, there are many organs with which an entirely different registration would have to be used, and we doubt if the pieces would prove as effective in each case. The Communion in D is the most pleasing. It has a bold theme, played on the great Diapasons, repeated on the swell (flute and string tone). This is followed by an imitative passage between the hands, on great and choir. The two themes are then combined, and the piece closes with several reminiscences of the first bar of the second theme.

FROM AUGENER & CO., LONDON.

Fantasia on a Chorale . . . . W. T. Best.
Andante in C . . . . W. T. Best.
Fugue in F . . . . Samuel Wesley.
No. 47 of Cæcilia Collection.

Another Fantasia in the inimitable style of this composer, brilliant, effective, and somewhat difficult. After a short introduction the Chorale is given out as a pedal solo, with florid interludes between the lines of the Chorale. After a repetition of the introduction, in the key of the dominant, the first line of the Chorale is taken as the subject of a short fughetta, after which the elements of a fantasia again assert themselves, bringing the piece to a brilliant ending.

NEW ORGANS.

NEW ORGAN IN MT. VERNON M. E. CHURCH, WASHINGTON, D.C.

Built by M. P. Möler, Hagerstown, Md.

GREAT ORGAN.		SWELL ORGAN.	
Double Open Diapason	16 Ft.	Lieblich Gedeckt	16 Ft.
Open Diapason	8 "	Viola Diapason	8 "
Cone Gamba	8 "	St. Diapason	8 "
Doppel-flöte	8 "	Aeoline	8 "
Principal	4 "	Harmonic Flute	4 "
Flûte d'Amour	4 "	Violina	4 "
Twelfth	2⅔ "	Flautina	2 "
Fifteenth	2 "	Dolce Cornet	III. Rks.
Mixture	III. Rks.	Oboe and Bassoon	8 Ft.
Trumpet	8 Ft.	Vox Humana	8 "

PEDAL ORGAN.		CHOIR ORGAN.	
Double Open Diapason	16 Ft.	Open Diapason	8 Ft.
Bourdon	16 "	Dulciana	8 "
Violoncello	8 "	Melodia	8 "
		Flauto Traverso	4 "
PEDAL MOVEMENTS.		Clarina	4 "
F. and P. Combinations in Gt.		Clarinet	8 "
F. and P. " " Sw.			
F. and P. " " Ch.		Pneumatic Action.	
Full Organ.		The usual couplers operated by	
Gt. to Ped. (reversible)		piston-knobs.	

The organ is twenty-eight feet high, twenty-three feet wide, and twelve feet deep. It was opened by Dr. Bischoff.

UNIVERSALIST CHURCH, GLOUCESTER, MASS.

New organ built by Mr. George S. Hutchings.

GREAT ORGAN.		SWELL ORGAN.	
Open Diapason	16 Ft.	Bourdon (Treble and Bass)	16 Ft.
Open Diapason	8 "	Violin Diapason	8 "
Dulcissimo	8 "	Salicional	8 "
Melodia (Stopped Bass)	8 "	Aeoline	8 "
Octave	4 "	Stopped Diapason	8 "
Flûte d'Amour	4 "	Quintadena	8 "
Octave Quinte	2⅔ "	Flûte Harmonique	4 "
Super Octave	2 "	Violina	4 "
Mixture	III. Rks.	Flautino	2 "
Trumpet	8 Ft.	Dolce Cornet	III. Rks.
		Oboe and Bassoon	8 Ft.
PEDAL ORGAN.			
Open Diapason	16 Ft.	The usual couplers and pedal move-	
Bourdon	16 "	ments.	
Violoncello (Blank)	8 "		

NEW ORGAN IN ST. JOSEPH'S CHURCH, WARRNAMBOOL, VICTORIA, AUSTRALIA.

Built by Fincham & Hobday, Melbourne. Opened January 29.

GREAT ORGAN.		SWELL ORGAN.	
Double Diapason	16 Ft.	Bourdon	16 Ft.
Open Diapason	8 "	Open Diapason	8 "
Gamba	8 "	Claribel	8 "
Dulciana	8 "	Gamba	8 "
Claribel	8 "	Vox Celeste	8 "
Principal	4 "	Octave	4 "
Harmonic Flute	4 "	Rohr-flöte	4 "
Octave Quinte	2⅔ "	Super Octave	2 "
Fifteenth	2 "	Mixture	III. Rks.
Mixture	III. Rks.	Cornopean	8 "
Trumpet	8 Ft.	Oboe	8 "
		Vox Humana	8 "

CHOIR ORGAN.		PEDAL ORGAN.	
Harmonic Flute	8 Ft.	Open Diapason	16 Ft.
Keraulophon	8 "	Bourdon	16 "
Vox Angelica	8 "	Viola	8 "
Geigen	8 "	Violoncello	8 "
Suave Flute	4 "	4 Piston Comb. to Gt.	
Har. Piccolo	2 "	4 " " Sw.	
Clarinet	8 "		

ANNOUNCEMENT.

VOLUME II. OF THE ORGAN

COMMENCES

❊ MAY 1, 1893. ❊

Among the Contributors will be

MR. CHARLES A. CAPEN.

MR. HORATIO CLARKE.

MR. HENRY M. DUNHAM.

MR. CLARENCE EDDY.

MR. PHILIP HALE.

MR. J. A. HINTON, B.A.

MR. EDWIN A. TILTON.

MR. GEORGE E. WHITING.

MR. ARTHUR WHITING.

MR. S. B. WHITNEY,

AND OTHERS.

Subscription (in advance) $2.00. European Countries, 10s. 5d.
Single copies, 25 cents.

EVERETT E. TRUETTE, Editor and Publisher,

149a, Tremont Street, Boston.

VOL. II. No. 4.   AUGUST, 1893.   WHOLE No. 16.

BACH

YEARLY SUBSCRIPTION $2.00.   SINGLE COPIES 25 CTS.

THE ORGAN

DEVOTED TO

A MONTHLY JOURNAL

THE KING OF INSTRUMENTS

RHEINBERGER

GUILMANT

FRESCOBALDI

BUXTEHUDE

MERKEL

BEST

EVERETT · E · TRUETTE ·
EDITOR & PUBLISHER
149 A. TREMONT ST. BOSTON.

HANDEL

THE ORGAN.

Vol. II.   BOSTON, AUGUST, 1893.   No. 4

THE ORGAN.

BOSTON, AUGUST, 1893.

Published the first of every month. Subscription price $1.00 per year (European countries 100. 5d.), payable in advance. Single copies, 25 cents.

Subscribers will please state with which number they wish their subscription to begin.
Remittances should be made by registered letter, post-office order, or by check payable to Everett E. Truette.
Correspondence, to secure notice, must in all cases be accompanied by the name and address of the writer, not for publication, but as a guarantee of good faith.
Advertising rates sent on application.
Address all communications,
THE ORGAN, 149 A Tremont Street, Boston, Mass.

Single copies of THE ORGAN can be procured of

NOVELLO, EWER, & Co.	New York.
G. SCHIRMER	New York.
OLIVER DITSON CO.	Boston.
L. H. ROSS & Co.	Boston.
N. E. CONSERVATORY	Boston.
H. B. STEVENS Co.	Boston.
LYON & HEALY	Chicago.
THEODORE PRESSER	Philadelphia.
WM. H. BONER & Co.	Philadelphia.
TAYLOR'S MUSIC HOUSE	Springfield, Mass.
GALLUP & METZGER	Hartford, Conn.
RICHAULT & Co.	Paris.
R. F. VINSON (Sole Agent for Gt. Britian)	London.

CONTENTS:

AN unusually large number of organs have been built in this country during the past year, and, until the present financial depression throttled all branches of business, nearly every organ-builder was overrun with contracts.

WHILE the large number of new organs which have been "opened" has given the country a goodly number of inaugural concerts, the lovers of organ music have not been very well fed. In most of the musical centres the total number of organ concerts during the past season has been below that of the season of '91–'92.

GIVING organ concerts (in this country) is generally so much a labor of love and reputation that, unless the ambition runs high, and the purse is full, organists will fall into the general opinion that the time can better be applied in other directions. "'Tis a pity, but 'tis true;" and all those who look forward to the time when the organ will be as high in public favor as its "wee sister," the piano, should exert every possible influence to keep up the interest in organ music.

VACATIONS are in order; many churches are closed, and a large number of organs which have been used weekly, and frequently daily, will remain silent for the next month, or longer. Most organists are careful to leave the swell *open* during the winter, to allow the changes of temperature, which are frequent, to affect the pipes of the swell to the same extent that they do those of the great, keeping the instrument in better tune; but nine out of ten will go away on their vacation with "never a thought" of this same swell-box, which, being open, is made a receptacle for the clouds of dust which float over the organ during the summer cleaning. On their return they find that the Oboe is in bad condition, several pipes do not speak, and others are croaky, the Salicional is slow of speech, while the Vox Humana, "a thing of beauty," is not "a joy forever." You cannot protect the pipes of the great, choir, and pedal; but the swell, which contains the most delicate stops, can easily be left closed, and in September will be found in a better condition than you expect.

REFERRING to the question of a new Music Hall for the city of Boston, the following paragraph, copied from a letter to the *Boston Herald* (printed July 14), over the signature of James E. Treat, is *apropos:*—

"Especially a question to be settled for this city — the home of the finest choral society — is the facility for oratorio performances, which an opera house does not furnish. I beg to suggest a plan: Place new internal works behind the architecturally beautiful case (if not already spoiled by neglect), not generally known to be of American design and manufacture, really a fine work, and which so long screened some of the wisdom and more of the folly of the old "great organ;" give it a central and elevated position, where its grandeur, graceful curves, and free tonal effect would be appreciated, with fixed seats in amphitheatre form for chorus at one end of a hall of maximum size, and a perfectly appointed stage for symphony or opera use at least sixty feet wide at the other, the entrances, etc., being on each side as stated. We have only to invent, if there is not one already invented, a comfortable chair (not merely a seat), with reversible back, and nothing will prevent an oratorio performance in the afternoon, and an opera in the evening. By means well known, the "console," or key-desk, of the organ may be located any place near the conductor. The organ could be screened by curtains, if desired, on opera night, and the chorus seats would be quite desirable for that performance. The level floor would serve the purpose of balls, etc., by removal of seats. The question of location and purchase of land should be deferred until the plans are selected. The designer should not be handicapped by land limit. It should occupy an entire block or centre of a square accessible on all sides."

We heartily indorse Mr. Treat's suggestion of placing the large organ with chorus seats at one end of the Music Hall, and a well-appointed stage for opera, etc., at the other end. It would require but a small amount of planning to arrange such chorus seats so as to be available for gallery seats when opera or symphony was being given at the other end of the hall, and the complaint that an organ would be in the way in an opera house would thus disappear.

JOHANN CHRISTIAN HEINRICH RINK.

JOHANN CHRISTIAN HEINRICH RINK was born at Elgersburg, in Saxe-Gotha, Feb. 18, 1770. He studied under Kittel at Erfurt, and thus received excellent training, as Kittel was one of the best pupils of J. S. Bach. At the age of nineteen Rink was appointed to the organistship of Giessen, where he held several other appointments. In 1806 he was elected "professor" at the Darmstadt college; in 1813 was ap-

Cr. H. Rinck
geb. den 18 Febr. 1770.

pointed court organist, and in 1817 chamber musician to the Grand Duke, Ludwig I. He made several tours through Germany, and was everywhere received with favor. At Treves he was specially honored, and in 1831 was elected a member of the Dutch Society for Encouragement of Music. In 1838 he received a cross of the first class from his Grand Duke, and in 1840 was made "Doctor of Philosophy and Arts" at the University of Giessen. He died at Darmstadt, Aug. 17, 1846, at the age of seventy-six. His compositions number about one hundred and twenty-five, including sonatas for the pianoforte, violin, and violoncello; a "Pater Noster" for four

voices, with organ accompaniment, and two motets. His principal work was the celebrated "Practical Organ School," in six parts, with which every organ student is familiar. This set of études is deservedly popular with most organ teachers, and forms a part of the early training of nearly every prominent organist.

NOTABLE ORGANS.

XI.

ST. SULPICE, PARIS.

ONE of the largest and most notable organs in the world is that in the church of St. Sulpice, Paris. The original organ, built by the celebrated Clicquot, was completed and inaugurated on May 17, 1781. Several changes were made and some parts of the instrument were reconstructed in the following years. In 1857 Cavaillé-Coll began a thorough remodelling and enlarging of this organ; and when it was reopened on the 29th of April, 1862, by Lefébure Wély, the organist of the church, it was one of the largest and most celebrated organs in the world. To-day it is still pre-eminently at the head of all French organs.

Owing to the limited space which was available, Mons. Cavaillé-Coll was obliged to construct the organ in seven distinct stories, the third, fifth, and seventh containing the wind-chests and pipes, while all the mechanism and reservoirs were located in the intervening stories.

Six large reservoirs, fed by five huge feeders, capable of supplying over a thousand cubic feet of wind per minute, distribute the wind to the numerous wind-chests by means of thirty regulating reservoirs, having numerous degrees of pres-

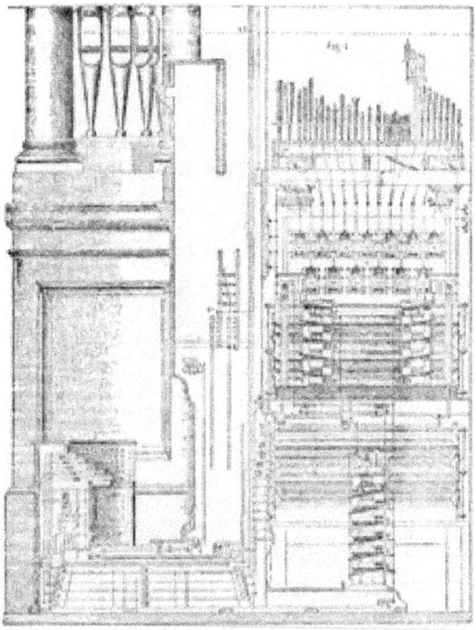

VERTICAL SECTION OF REVERSED CONSOLE AND PART OF THE FIRST TWO STOPS.

sure. This organ is composed of five manuals and a pedal clavier, one hundred speaking-stops and eighteen mechanical registers, twenty combination pedals, ten adjustable combination stops, and six thousand, seven hundred and six pipes.

CONSOLE OF THE ORGAN IN ST. SULPICE, PARIS.

The action is reversed, and the tiers of draw-stops are arranged to form a semicircle with the manuals, thus bringing all the knobs within easy access of the performer. A liberal use of the pneumatic lever is made throughout the organ. The effect of the crescendo on the swell organ is remarkable, and has never been surpassed. The organ is blown by five men, as motors are seldom if ever used in Parisian churches. Appended is the specification: —

I. GRAND CHŒUR. 13 Stops.

1 Salicional	8 Ft.	8 Basson . . . . . 16 Ft.
2 Octave	4 "	9 Première Trompette . 8 "
3 Gross Fourniture	IV. Rks.	10 Seconde Trompette . 8 "
4 Gross Cymbale	VI. "	11 Basson . . . . . 8 "
5 Plein Jeu	IV. "	12 Clairon . . . . . 4 "
6 Cornet	V. "	13 Clairon Doublette . 2 "
7 Bombarde	16 Ft.	

II. GREAT ORGAN. 13 Stops.

14 Prin. Harmonique	32, 16 Ft.	21 Bourdon . . . . 8 Ft.
15 Montre	16 "	22 Bourdon . . . . 8 "
16 Bourdon	16 "	23 Flûte à Pavillon . 8 "
17 Flûte Conique	16 "	24 Prestant . . . . 4 "
18 Flûte Harmonique	8 "	25 Grosse Quinte . . 5⅓ "
19 Flûte Traversière	8 "	26 Doublette . . . 2 "
20 Montre	8 "	

III. BOMBARDE. 20 Stops.

27 Soubasse	16 Ft.	37 Grosse Quinte . . 5⅓ Ft.
28 Flûte Conique	16 "	38 Grosse Tierce . . 3⅕ "
29 Principal	8 "	39 Quinte . . . . 2⅔ "
30 Flûte Harmonique	8 "	40 Octave . . . . 4 "
31 Bourdon	8 "	41 Octavin . . . . 2 "
32 Gambe	8 "	42 Cornet . . . . V. Rks.
33 Violoncelle	8 "	43 Bombarde . . . 16 Ft.
34 Keraulophone	8 "	44 Baryton . . . . 8 "
35 Flûte Octaviante	4 "	45 Trompette . . . 8 "
36 Prestant	4 "	46 Clairon . . . . 4 "

IV. CHOIR ORGAN. 20 Stops.

47 Violon Basse	16 Ft.	57 Quinte . . . . 2⅔ Ft.
48 Quintaton	16 "	58 Doublette . . . 2 "
49 Quintaton	8 "	59 Plein Jeu Harmonique
50 Flûte Traversière	8 "	60 Tierce . . . . 1⅗ "
51 Salicional	8 "	61 Larigot . . . . 1⅓ "
52 Viole de Gambe	8 "	62 Piccolo . . . . 1 "
53 Unda Maris	8 "	63 Euphone . . . . 16 "
54 Flûte Douce	4 "	64 Trompette . . . 8 "
55 Flûte Octaviante	4 "	65 Clarinette . . . 8 "
56 Dulciana	4 "	66 Clairon . . . . 4 "

V. SWELL ORGAN. 22 Stops.

67 Quintaton	16 Ft.	78 Fourniture . . . IV. Rks.
68 Bourdon	8 "	79 Cymbale . . . . V. "
69 Flûte Harmonique	8 "	80 Cornet . . . . V. "
70 Viole d'Orchestre	8 "	81 Bombarde . . . 16 Ft.
71 Voix Céleste	8 "	82 Clar. Anglais . . 16 "
72 Prestant	4 "	83 Trompette . . . 8 "
73 Flûte Octaviante	4 "	84 Trompette Har. . 8 "
74 Dulciana	4 "	85 Basson et Hautbois . 8 "
75 Nasard	2⅔ "	86 Cromorne . . . 8 "
76 Doublette	2 "	87 Voix Humaine . . 16 "
77 Octavin	2 "	88 Clairon . . . . 4 "

PEDAL ORGAN. 12 Stops.

89 Principal Basse	32 Ft.	95 Contre Bombarde . 32 Ft.
90 Contre Basse	16 "	96 Bombarde . . . 16 "
91 Soubasse	16 "	97 Basson . . . . 16 "
92 Flûte	8 "	98 Trompette . . . 8 Ft.
93 Violoncelle	8 "	99 Ophicléide . . . 8 "
94 Flûte	4 "	100 Clairon . . . . 4 "

PEDAL MOVEMENTS.

1 Orage (Storm Pedal).	11 Choir Ventil (Reeds).
2 Coupler, Gt. Ch. to Ped.	12 Great Ventil (Reeds).
3 " Gt. to Ped.	13 Swell Ventil (Reeds).
4 Ventil Pedal (Reeds).	14 Coupler, Gt. Ch. to F. Manual.
5 Sub. Octave Gt. Ch.	15 Coupler, Gt. to I.
6 Sub. Octave, Gt.	16 Coupler, Bombarde to I.
7 Sub. Octave, Bombarde.	17 Coupler, Ch. to I.
8 Sub. Octave, Ch.	18 Coupler, Sw. to I.
9 Sub. Octave, Sw.	19 Tremolo.
10 Bombarde Ventil (Reeds).	20 Swell Pedal.

A large three-manual Roosevelt organ was inaugurated in the Ohio Wesleyan University the 1st of June, at which time Mr. Clarence Eddy performed Fantasia and Fugue in G minor, Bach; "Am Meer," Schubert; Pilgrim's Chorus, Wagner; Allegretto, Foote; A Royal Procession, Spinney; and Overture to "Oberon," Weber. Mr. Frank R. Adams performed Sonata in A minor, Whiting; Fantasia on Irish Airs, Whiting; Prayer in E, Grison; March and Chorus from "Tannhäuser," Wagner.

Mr. R. Huntington Woodman inaugurated a two-manual organ (built by Messrs. Morey & Barnes) in the Baptist Church, Whitesboro, N.Y., playing the following selections: Fugue in G minor, Bach; Canticle Nuptiale, Dubois; Bridal Song and Wedding March, Jensen; "At Evening," Buck; Prière, Lemaigre; Marche Religieuse, Guilmant; Toccata, Tombelle; Improvisation; Pilgrim's Chorus, Wagner; Pastorale, Kullak; Melody, Widor; Allegretto, Guilmant; Offertoire in D minor, Batiste.

THE ORGANIST'S RETROSPECT.[1]

BY HORATIO CLARKE.

CHAPTER IV.

On my seventh birthday my father gave me a very sweet-toned flageolet made of polished boxwood, which I had learned to play quite well. My sleeping-room was in a remote part of the house, in an attic chamber; and, knowing that Mrs. Rodman could not be disturbed, when the weather became warm I would sit on my little trunk in the dark, before retiring, and for an hour at a time would play the many melodies which had been fixed in my memory.

These airs and themes would bring before me such clear visions of the past, with their soothing influences, that my slumber would be peaceful. It is this characteristic of music in presenting to the mind associations of the past by means of familiar melodies which gives it such a power among the people at large, moving their emotional natures with tender memories of the departed loved ones.

> "Such songs have power to quiet
> The restless pulse of care,
> And come like the benediction
> That follows after prayer."

This is a province peculiar to melody, rather than of harmony. The melodic form is a natural expression of sentiment, while the harmonic form is a result of musical culture.

On the way to my chamber I had to pass through a garret which was stored with the disused things of other days. Among these was a square black box, which contained an old violin which Mr. Rodman had used in his earlier years. I asked him if he would be willing to have it strung up and let me use it. He readily gave his consent, took it to his shop to be cleaned and fitted up, and purchased a new bow. I found that I could finger it in tune, and with some practice could draw a steady tone with the bow.

This gave me a new impulse, and took my mind from my trials; for I was soon able to play all the melodies which I had mastered on the flageolet. Mr. Rodman became much interested in my progress on the violin, and for his own enjoyment would take me evenings to his office at the factory, and with his ophicleide play the bass part to simple church music, while I played the air on the violin. This led him to determine to give me all the advantages in his power toward my musical improvement.

At that time the leading musician of the village was a printer by trade. He led the choir in the Orthodox church as violinist, and taught a few pupils on the pianoforte and violin. He was a man of much natural ability, of high aspirations, and possessed a genial nature. I was placed in his charge for instruction; and after playing through the time-honoured "Duos" of Pleyel, I began a systematic course in Spohr's "School for the Violin."

My progress was so satisfactory to my teacher, that after a few lessons he had me enter the church choir and play the tenor part on the violin, transposing the notes an octave lower than they would naturally be played, until I was furnished with a viola. I was proud of such an honor, and it was a delight for the welcome hour of the Sunday service to arrive.

Our church orchestra contained two first violins, one second, a viola, flute, clarinet, post-horn, violoncello, ophicleide, and a double-bass. Before the singing we first played through the tune, and repeated the last line of the hymn for an interlude. The singing of the chorus choir was excellent; and the instruments and voices blended so well that all who participated enjoyed the music, although to me it was extremely plain, compared with the noble Anglican service of my early remembrance.

We were located in an arch in the rear of the singers, in a high gallery back of the congregation. During the lengthy address the players generally leaned back in their chairs

against the wall, and either slept with handkerchiefs drawn over their heads, or whispered the town gossip of the week; for they attended church to make music, and not as worshippers. I doubt if any of those old players, of whom I alone survive, ever retained a single sentence of the years of sermons which were delivered to more interested hearers.

Dear old players! Your hearts were filled with music, and your fingers touched no discordant combinations. How earnestly you played those simple notes which charmed the ears of those sedate worshippers, as they rose and faced the choir in each hymn! And when the stately organ drove you from your accustomed places after years of faithful attendance, and all appreciation of your unremunerated offerings was forgotten, how cold and formal seemed the service, if perchance you ever felt inclined to enter the old meeting-house again and mingle with the occupants of the pews below!

As in many towns in that section of New England, there was a church of the Unitarian denomination near by, which contained an organ, where a quartet choir was hired. But our singers had no fellowship with these select musicians, nor did the congregations of either society have any common sympathies in either family or town matters; for in those days there was a distinct boundary line between any prospective affiliation of the predestinated Trinitarian with the self-elected Unitarian.

There was also an Episcopal church adjoining the old cemetery, which had its organ and established service of chants and Te Deums, year in and out. Its aristocratic element attended to its own affairs, satisfied with its ancient historical record, and held to its dignified forms inherited from royal associations.

Members of these three choirs were never associated together musically, and were quite unconscious of the existence of each other. A singing-school was held each winter in the Orthodox chapel. During the last half of the term the church players would assist in the preparation for a final concert, which was given in the church with free admission.

On one of these occasions I heard for the first time a portable melodeon, or seraphine, as they were then called, on which harmony could be played; and for many months it was the dream of my waking hours to become the possessor of one of these instruments. I spent much time in trying to design one on paper which I might construct for myself, but I could not devise how to produce the musical part, and was obliged to relinquish the plan. Then it became my chief study to find a way in which I could earn money enough to attain my object.

Since the general introduction of music in the public schools, the church choirs and the singing-schools have ceased to be the rallying points of musical interest. The latter were then popular institutions in New England, and were the principal means of general musical education, as those who owned pianos were comparatively few in number.

The voices of the singers were then as pure, and they sang in tune and with as much expression, as in more modern times. The ability to read vocal music at sight was fully equal, if not superior, to the attainments in these later years; for they then depended upon themselves in their judgment of the relation of intervals, when there were not many musical instruments in the home.

In organizing a chorus choir at the present time, it is doubtful if the members who would be gathered together, even with the advantages afforded by the instruction in the public schools, would be able to sing as readily at sight as the singers of forty or fifty years ago. I record this as a fact from my own experience in recent years of choir work.

(To be continued.)

Mons. Auguste Wiegand, the "city organist" of the Town Hall, Sydney, N.S.W., performed the following programme at his recital, May 10: Concerto, No. 10, Handel; Elevation in A, No. 2, Vilboa; Ave Maria in B flat minor, Doss; Sonr Mosique, Couperin-Guilmant; Offertoire in G, Wely; Fugue in G minor, Schumann; Majestic Chorus in D, Lacey; Cantabile in A, Wely; Andante, Widor.

TEMPO DI MINUETTO.

JOHN S. CAMP, Op. 3, No. 4.

Gt. 8 & 4 Ft. *f*

Sw. 8 Ft. with
Reeds. (Box open.)
Ch. Op. Diap. St.
Diap. & Flute 4 Ft.

Ped. Bourdon.
Sw. to Gt.
Ch. to Ped.

Ch.

Gt.

Add. Op. Diap.
16 Ft. & Gt. to Ped.

Poco dim. . . . .

l. H.

f

Ch.
Op. Diap. 16 Ft. &
Gt. to Ped. off.
Cello 8 Ft. only.
Sw.
Ch. with Clarinet.

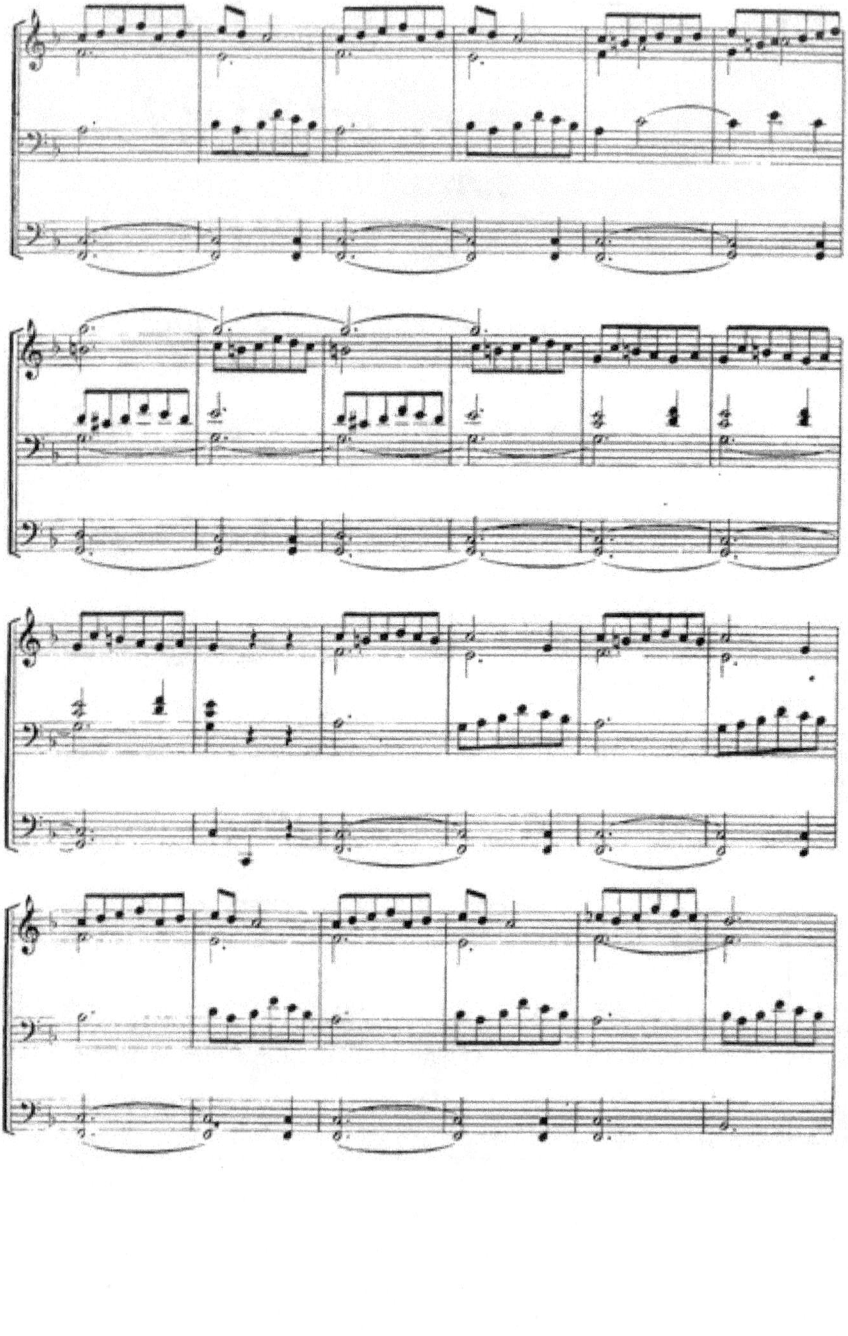

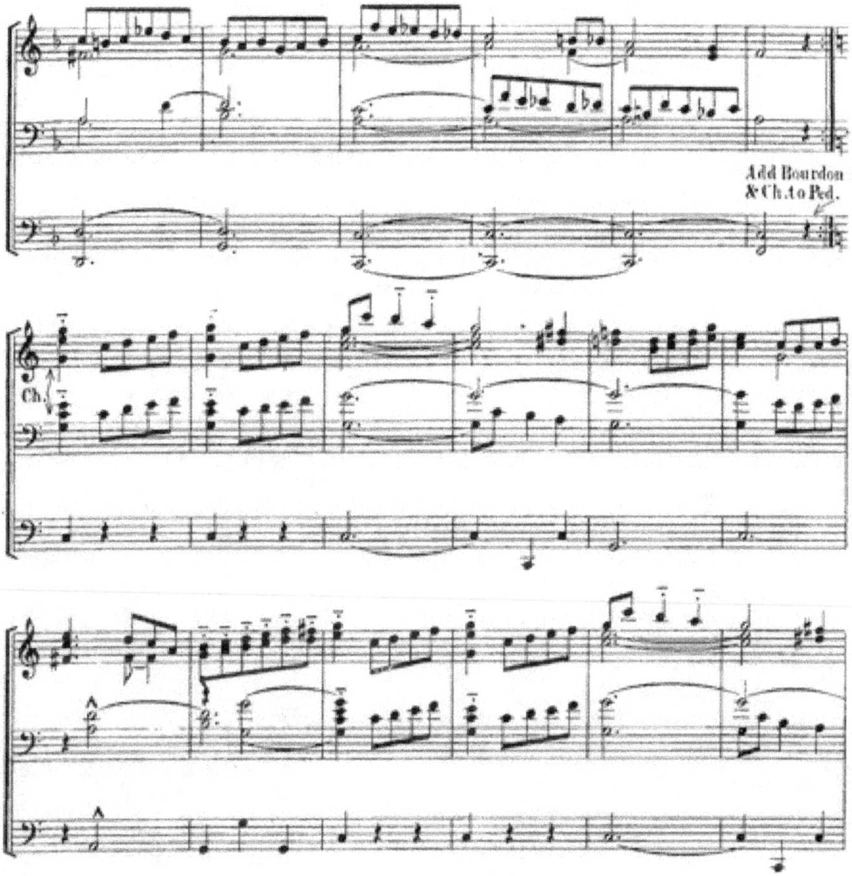
Add Bourdon
& Ch. to Ped.
Ch.
Gt.
Gt. to Ped.

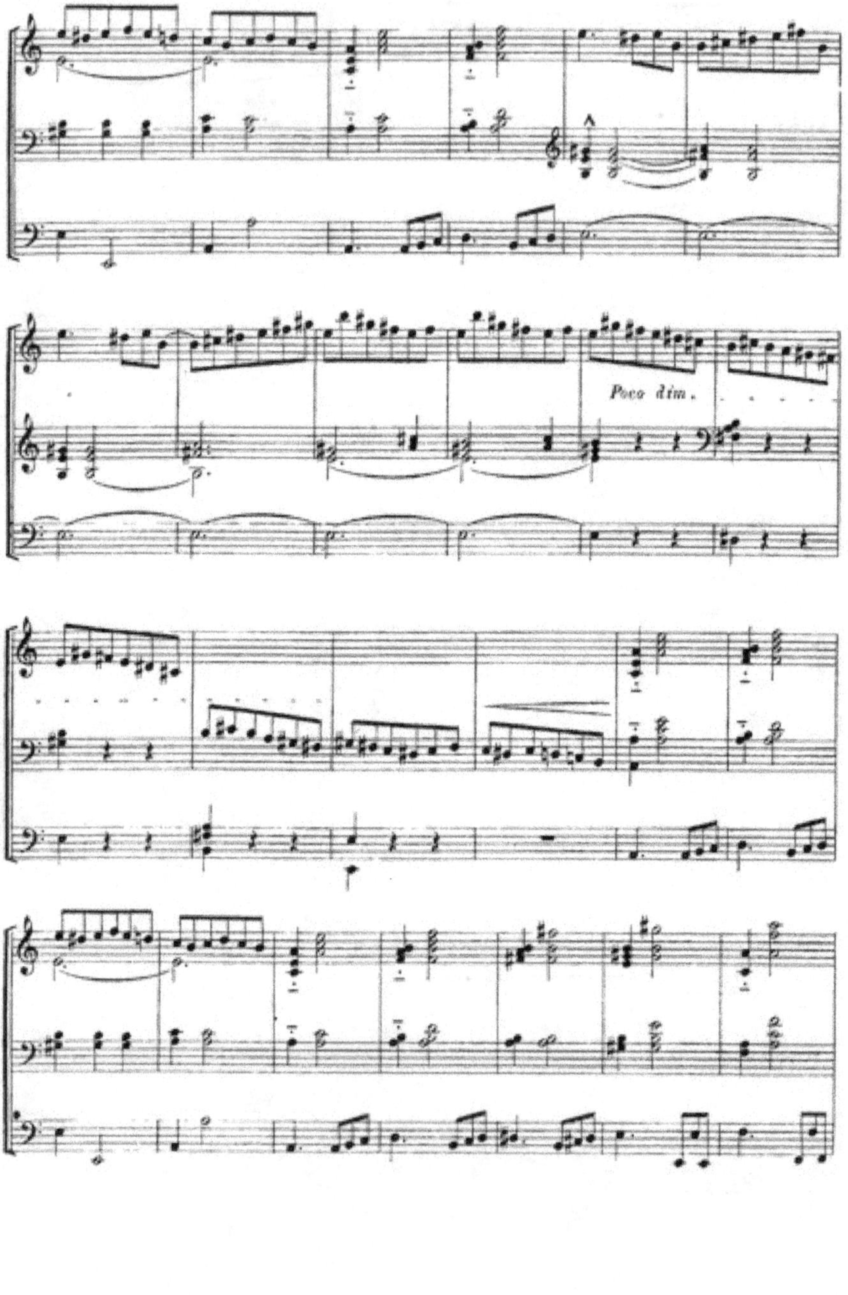
Poco dim.

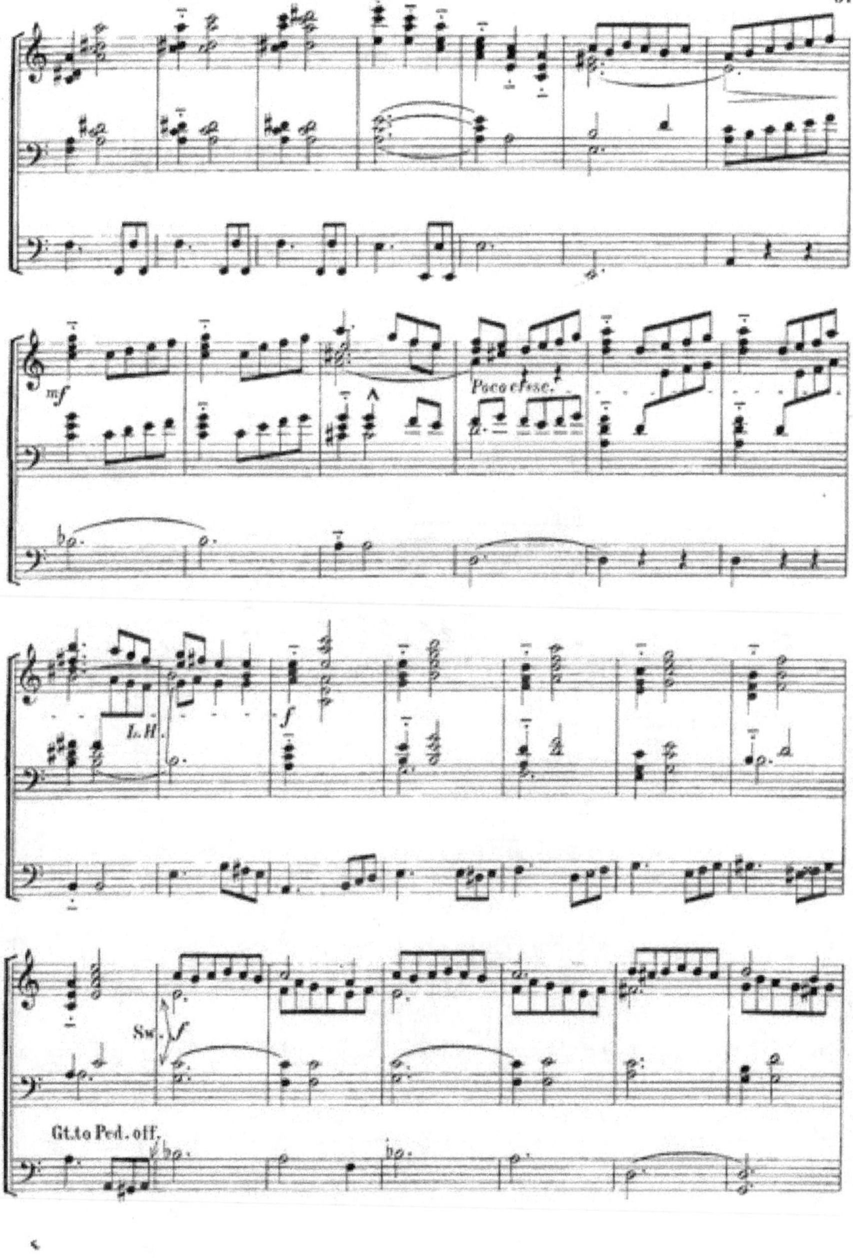
mf
Poco cresc.
L.H.
f
Sw.
f
Gt. to Ped. off.

88

CHICAGO AND WORLD'S FAIR NEWS.

MANY Chicagoans and visitors to this city are gratified at the completion of the great organ at the World's Fair. The builders, Messrs. Farrand & Votey, have had a big force of their most experienced workmen working day and night the past two months in the erection of this great instrument. Though not in the best position, acoustically speaking, the organ has an immense building to flood with its tone, the seating capacity of the hall alone being in the neighborhood of six thousand. In speaking with Mr. Eddy a few hours since, he said he had told the voicer that he wanted the organ powerful enough to raise the roof at the opening recital. This recital will probably be given by Mr. Eddy about the first of August.

With the exception of the Guilmant recitals, which take place the last Thursday, Friday, and Saturday in August, no other definite dates have as yet been set for organ recitals. Mr. Guilmant will sail on August 16, and will give his first recital in Chicago, which will be upon the great Farrand & Votey instrument, with the full Theodore Thomas Orchestra. He will doubtless give six organ recitals in this city, and then give recitals in some of the principal cities of this country and Canada. A hope is also expressed that this great master will give some recitals upon the great Auditorium Organ.

On July 5 Mr. Clarence Eddy dedicated a large three-manual, thirty-six stop Vocalion Organ in the Women's Building at the World's Fair. The organ numbers were Fantasie on Themes from Faust, Gounod-Eddy; Nuptial Song, Dubois; Nuptial March, Guilmant; Fantasie De Concert, Op. 33, Lux; Last Sleep of the Virgin, Massenet; Allegretto, from Serenade, Op. 63, Volkmar; Variations on "Annie Laurie," Buck; and the Offertoire to Saint Cecilia, No. 1, Batiste. The vocal numbers by Mlle. Nikita were Qui La Voce ("I Puritania"), Bellini; and "The Soul's Awakening," by Haddock.

He who said there was nothing new under the sun evidently had not seen some of the recent appliances on American organs before he made the remark. Had he examined some of these instruments he doubtless would not have left such a monument of his ignorance. He might have helped out a certain organ-builder and organist in this city, a few days ago, in determining why a certain organ would not be coaxed to even whisper. The man from the factory had been called to do a little tinkering, as it might be termed; everything being put in "press the button" order, the organist thought he would give the organ a trial, to see if all was satisfactory. Imagine the surprise of both when, after striking a few chords, not a sound was obtainable. Stops were drawn, electric switches were turned and returned, couplers were drawn, combination pedals were thrown off and on, every stop, button, and mechanical accessory in that organ was tried, still no sound. The tall, weird organ pipes stood like sentries over this dead king. Nothing broke the silence of that scene except the heaving of the motor below, and the deathlike little puffs of the pneumatics. A thousand memories rose in that organist's mind. He thought of the time when he, with a couple of brother organists, went to hear the great centennial organ which is in the Buffalo Cathedral. Having a letter of introduction to one of the prominent members of the Musical Committee of the Cathedral, everything pointed to a great treat. This gentleman kindly escorted the party to the organ loft. Starting the motors, one of the party was asked to play. A similar case, — no sound. Peering through the side of the organ it was discovered that two large bellows were not working. Four men were brought to work these emergency bellows, but still no sound. Finally it was decided that the organist who manipulated that mighty instrument would be found at the organ recital given that afternoon by Eugene Thayer in a distant part of the city. This proved to be true; and that organist, coming to his instrument, soon pointed out

the whys and the wherefores, and quickly dashed the tones of that masterwork into spray among the distant arches. But the Chicago organ was not going to give up the struggle so easily. The organist and builder vowed to stop all night, rather than to give in. Finally the trouble was discovered,—some one had dropped a toothpick, which had lodged beneath a lever below the manuals. That organist does not care to hear anything now about toothpicks, but he has not found out the use of said lever as yet. It has been suggested that its use is for substitutes, who, being very nervous, fail on the keys and slip off the bench on the pedal-board. The non-depression of this lever cuts the wind off from the valves, and therefore saves considerable discord heretofore coming from the organ during the sermon.

At the World's Fair informal organ recitals are given daily at two, half-past four, and seven P. M. upon the three-manual organ by Henry Pilcher's sons, of Louisville, Ky. This instrument is placed in the south-east end of the Liberal Arts Building. This building is 1,687 feet long, 787 feet wide, 245 feet high, and has a floor area of 44 acres. When one hears that 150,000 people had been within its walls at one time, and yet room left for 100,000 more, he begins to think how an organ would sound in such a structure. The organ would be fully as effective in the open air.

We feel sorry such an organ was not placed in a more appropriate building, as the instrument is one of special interest to organists. The stops are domino-shaped tablets placed over the swell keyboard, a slight touch on either the bottom or top of the tablet throws the stop on or off as desired. Many organists seem to think that this system of stops will soon supersede the old-fashioned draw-stop system, as this new system is quicker and easier manipulated than the old.

This organ is of fifty stops, thirty-seven of this number being speaking-stops, including a grand crescendo for the whole work. In its mechanism is used Pilcher's patent tubular pneumatic wind-chests, patent pneumatic key action, patent tubular pneumatic couplers, and patent register and combination action.

One special feature in this organ which doubtless will command much praise from visiting organists, is the combination movements. These adjustable combination movements are operated by pistons, placed below their respective manuals, great, swell, and choir organ, and are very comprehensive. They enable the organist to "set" any desired combination of stops on the manuals and the pedal, which combination is brought on at pleasure by the touch of the piston, and does not interfere with the movement of the "register keys." A Ross water motor, which is seen from the outside of the organ, is used for operating the feeders.

This organ shows in every respect superior workmanship. Mr. Pilcher, Jr., one of the members of the firm, is at the organ, and never tires in explaining the system to any who are interested.

Mr. Clarence Dickinson, organist of the Church of the Messiah, has given twenty-nine recitals upon this instrument. His selections included many of the most important organ works. Mr. James Watson of this city has also given recitals.

On Thursday, July 13, Mr. H. O. Farnham of Louisville, Ky., gave two recitals. One programme consisted of Allegro in G-minor, Haris; Allegro in C, Wood; Wedding March, Mendelssohn. Only thirty minutes are allowed the organ-builders at this hour, hence the shortness of the programme. At seven P.M. Mr. Farnham's programme consisted of Processional March, Whitney; Capriccio, Wély; Fantasia, Haris; Toccata, Mailly; and Dudley Buck's Variations on the "Star Spangled Banner."

Mr. Clarence Dickinson will give the recitals upon this organ the last two weeks of July.

Dr. J. H. Gower, organist of the Church of the Epiphany, gave a recital upon the Farrand & Votey organ in the above church Monday evening, July 3, performing Overture to Händel's "Occasional Oratorio;" Schumann's Traumerie;

The "Giant" Fugue, Bach ; Sacred March of the Priests,
Chauvet ; Concerto in G, Händel ; Overture, "Midsummer
Night's Dream," Mendelssohn ; "Pilgrim's Song of Hope,"
Batiste ; and Grand Offertoire in C-Minor, Batiste. The
vocal numbers by Miss Mary Neilson of Denver, Col., were
Händel's "Angels Ever Bright and Fair," and Gounod's
"There is a Green Hill Far Away." Notwithstanding the
heat of the evening, and the fact that the concert had not
been advertised, a large audience assembled to witness Dr.
Gower's ability as a concert organist. The applause that
evening alone was enough to convince one that Dr. Gower
is an organist of more than ordinary ability. The vocalist is
a stranger to Chicago audiences ; but the marvellous power
and quality of her voice, and the manner in which she sang
her numbers, go far in indicating that she has a great future.

The following Thursday evening Dr. Gower gave a recital
in the Episcopal Cathedral, Denver, Col., playing : The
Overture to "Samson," Händel ; Concerto in G, Händel ;
Sixth Sonata, Mendelssohn ; Batiste's Offertoire in F ; "The
Storm Fantasie," Lemmens ; Toccata in D, Bach ; "Pilgrim's Song of Hope," Batiste, and the Overture to "Semiramide," Rossini. Dr. Gower has been in Chicago only a
month, and it is truly wonderful what a number of people
go to hear his organ playing. He is one of the very few
organists who have the ability of making a great deal out of
a church service. Therefore, it is no wonder that his absence
from his organ one Sunday caused the question to be asked
by so many heretofore not so interested in organ playing,
"When will Dr. Gower return?"

During the heated term Mr. Archer's choir has been reduced to a quartet. During the month of August it is his
intention to take a vacation in the wilds of Northern Michigan.

Mr. Harrison M. Wild is spending his vacation in Minnesota. He looked very much fatigued after his winter's work,
and no one has earned the much-needed rest more than he.
Giving from fifty to seventy lessons a week, playing an organ
Sundays, a weekly organ recital, and much concert work
thrown in, is more than an ordinary man can stand. We
hope to see Mr. Wild come back with his old-time grip and
enthusiasm for his World's Fair Recitals.

Mr. Moore of St. Louis is now organist of the Cathedral
of the Holy Family, of this city, and is doing much to raise
the standard of music in this cathedral. This organ is the
largest in any church of this city. It was built, some twenty
years ago, by Mitchell of Montreal, Can. Recently it has
been overhauled by Roosevelt. It is of three manuals,
seventy-six stops, and has two 32-ft. pedal stops. One of
these is a Bombard, and was a 32-ft. striking reed, the tongue
of the reed being leathered to deaden the vibrations. The
Roosevelts changed this to a free reed. The other 32-ft.
stop is an Open Diapason, and in itself is a study for those
who tramp around seeing and hearing organs. It would be
hard to find another pipe on so large a scale, the measurement across the mouth of big C being twenty-eight inches,
and the measurement around the same being one hundred
and fifteen inches. These pipes are of two and one-half
inch stock, and each side is of one piece of timber. Owing
to the insufficiency of wind, it is said these pipes stood for
years without speaking. The organ is very powerful, and
Mr. Moore delights in making it known.

VOX HUMANA.

Mr. W. T. Best, having recovered from his recent illness, has returned
to his post in Liverpool, and has given the following recitals in St. George's
Hall : On July 1, Overture, Op. 15, Spohr; Alla Pastorale, H. Smart;
Concert Fugue, Krebs; Allegro, "Fiat Lux," Dubois; Caprice, "La
Chasse," Funagalli; and Fantasia on Chorals, Best.   On July 8th, Over-
ture, "Leon," Fétzelin; Légende, Hart; Toccata and Fugue in C-minor,
Bach; Andante, Villars; Tempo di March, Spohr.   On July 15th,
Toccata in A, Best; Siciliana and Intermezzo, Mascagni; Concerto No. 8,
Händel; Chant Pastorale, Dubois; and Selection from "War, Tell,"
Rossini.

PORTABLE PIPE ORGAN.

THE Portable Pipe Organ of the W. W. Kimball Company
is one of the most remarkable instruments now before the
public. It is a real pipe organ, having six stops in the manuals and two in the pedal, as follows :—

GREAT ORGAN : Open Diapason, metal (lower 12 wood)	61
Dulciana, metal	46
Cornopean (impinging reeds)	46
SWELL ORGAN : Viola di Gamba, metal	46
Stopped Diapason, wood	61
Flute, wood (4 feet)	61
PEDAL ORGAN : Bourdon, 16 feet (reeds with qualifying tubes)	31
Open Diapason, 16 feet (reeds with tubes)	31
COUPLERS : Great to Pedal,	
Swell to Great,	
Swell to Pedal,	
Octaves.	

Here is an instrument of eight real stops (not half-stops),
with two in the pedal. The pipes are all of the usual church
scales, and the instrument has the same power as any well-
made pipe organ of six manual stops, and more of manly
effect than most, because, of these manual stops, five of the
six are eight feet, and there are very rarely any organs of
one manual containing more than three stops of eight feet.
Moreover, this organ possesses the following advantages
which no other small organ has possessed : All the pipes
stand on the same wind-chest, and are all enclosed in a
swell. Hence, when the keyboards are coupled, you have a
single manual organ of four eight-feet flues, one brilliant reed,
and one four-feet, obtaining more brilliancy by means of the
octave coupler, if desired. Hence, it has a full organ effect
equal to that of the usual pipe organ of fifteen or eighteen
stops. On the other hand, using the manuals separately for
trio effects and the like, it has quite a good range, and is
available for many legitimate organ effects which usually are
impossible upon small instruments. It has a full pedal.
The vibrators in the pedal stops are free reeds, blown by
pressure, exhausting into qualifying tubes, which impart the
soft, distant, and pervading effect proper to a pedal, without
leaving anything perceptible of the flabby tone usual to pedal
reeds. This is one of the many novelties which combine to
render this instrument possible.

From a mechanical point of view the Kimball Portable
Pipe Organ is one of the most remarkable instruments to be
found. All the action, draw-stop and key, is pneumatic.
Every key has its valve or little pneumatic bellows. These
operate upon a new principle, and cannot get out of order or
cipher. All the pneumatics are carried by a six-inch wind.
The pipes are blown by a three-inch wind.

All of the organ above described is brought within a compass of six feet wide, three feet, six inches deep, and seven
feet high. The pedal keys project in front enough to make
the total floor space required six feet square. The organ is
packed by removing the pedal-board, which requires to turn
one button and raise the board off the two dowells which
hold it in place, then the entire keyboard and stop action
come off by removing four screws. All the action detaches
without unfastening anything beyond the button and the four
screws above mentioned. The part remaining with the pipes
and bellows is then six feet wide, seven feet high, and three
feet, six inches deep. It can be boxed in a plain box, laid
down upon its side, and even ended upon its head, without
loosening or disarranging the pipes or any part of the action.
Hence, it will go through any door or window affording a
space three feet six, by six feet. It requires no expert to set
it up.

The most remarkable point in this instrument, aside from
those mentioned above, is the wind supply, which is ample
under all circumstances. The tone is full, pervading, firm,
and steady. Here we have two wind supplies, one of six
inches and one of three, all within a compass mentioned
above, yet enough to run eight stops, with octave coupler,
under all circumstances. This is, perhaps, the greatest
marvel of all. It is done by a new system of feeders, and
by putting the bellows of the heavy wind inside that for the

light wind. The six-inch wind exhausts into the three-inch bellows, and, coming under less pressure, expands, and thus enables the supply to be kept up by feeders which, if operated upon a three-inch pressure, would be wholly incapable of doing the work.

This instrument has a history. Its conception dates back to a time before the great fire. There was a firm of organmakers, Decker & Feldgruacher, which tried to overcome the difficulties inherent in this condensation of the pipe organ. They used an action substantially like that of the usual church organ, with trackers, roller-boards, etc.; and this alone greatly enlarged the space required over the present instrument. But even then they found the wind pressure impossible to provide by any bellows that could be condensed into the space. This firm and others sank something like $250,000 in experiments and unsuccessful work. Still Mr. Kimball, who had undertaken the agency, believed that with proper skill all the difficulties could be overcome. At intervals after the failure of the old firm he talked with organbuilders. Everyone said that it was impossible. He offered two different experts a salary to enter his employ and experiment; but they declined upon the ground that the search was impossible, and they would be taking his money and rendering no return. Organists admitted the great importance of the idea. Everybody knows that there is a limit which reed organs cannot pass. Moreover, there is too great a break in price between the largest effective reed organ and the cheapest pipe organ. No pipe organ answers the demands of a good organist unless it has at least two manuals and five or six stops of eight-feet tone. This means ordinarily an expense of from $1,500 to $1,800.

At length Mr. Kimball heard of an organ-builder in St. Paul who was at work upon the same idea. He had invented an instrument of this kind. It had the bellows at the top and the pipes inverted. This conception was immediately rejected, on account of certain impracticable consequences appertaining, and a new beginning was made under Mr. Kimball's incisive criticism and suggestion. Finally, one instrument was turned out which began to look like the long sought ideal. It had a few minor imperfections; but it came so near the idea that it immediately sold, and has done good service ever since. Another was made a little better; it sold. Another still a little better, which also sold, until now, without having advertised these instruments, or having made any kind of promises concerning them, the firm is turning out five a month. All the mechanical difficulties have been so far overcome that the firm now expects to be able to send out a portable pipe organ without hearing any more complaint of it for keys sticking, or something of that kind, than they do from their reed organs, of which they send out twenty thousand without a single complaint.

Organists do not believe that the Kimball firm will find it practicable to stop at the point now reached. They believe that the plan on which these instruments are constructed presents so many advantages over those generally used by organbuilders, even the best of them, that eventually they will find it better to cover all sizes of organs that can be sold for less than $2,000. This would necessitate about four sizes of instruments, and perhaps the capacity of divisions between the bellows and wind-chest might have to be divisible. But the idea is practicable; and upon this system a pipe organ, usually costing $3,000, could be erected in church for less than $2,000, and be in no single respect inferior. On the contrary, the new style would have a vastly less liability to get out of order.

W. S. B. MATHEWS in *Music.*

Lone Organ in the Chicago Art Palace (Mason & Hamlin Makers).

SPECIFICATION.

GREAT ORGAN.

Clarinet	16 Ft.
Corno	16 "
Diapason	8 "
Gamba	8 "
Flute	8 "

SWELL ORGAN.

Salicional	8 Ft.
Keraulophon	8 "
Dolce Tremulant	8 "
Wald Flöte	4 "
Flauto Dolce	4 "
Æolian Harp	2 "

PEDAL ORGAN.

Bourdon	16 Ft.
Bourdon Dolce	16 "
Violoncello	8 "

MECHANICAL.

Octave Coupler.
Swell to Great.
Swell to Pedal.
Great to Pedal.
Full Organ Pedal.

OUR PARIS LETTER.

PARIS, 22 June, 1895.

On the 8th and on the 15th of this month were given the third and fourth Trocadéro recitals. The programme of the third consisted of the following numbers :—

Marche Gothique	Theo. Salomé.
Ode Funèbre (Trauer Ode) jane Audition	J. S. Bach.
Méditation	P. de Bréville.
(Orgue et Orchestre.)	
Trio de l'Oratorio de Noël	Saint-Saëns.
Deux Motets.	
a. O quam Gloriosum est Regnum (à 4 voix)	Vittoria.
b. Sanctus (à 4 voix)	Palestrina.
(Les Chanteurs de Saint-Gervais.)	
5th Concerto en fa	Händel.
I. Larghetto. II. Allegro. III. Alla Siciliana	
IV. Presto.	
Récit. et Arioso du Miracle de Naim	H. Maréchal.
Deux chansons françaises	Roland de Lassus.
a. Mon cœur se recommande à vous.	
b. Fuyons tous d'amour le jeu.	
(Les Chanteurs de Saint-Gervais.)	
Finale de la Seconde Sonate	Alex. Guilmant.

As will be seen, Mons. Guilmant was assisted by several vocal soloists, and by Les Chanteurs de Saint-Gervais, a choral club of mixed voices devoted to rendering the works of the old masters. The Bach Trauer Ode was by far the most interesting number of the programme. It is a rather long work, consisting of two parts, which comprise about fifteen separate pieces. It was composed, it seems, at the death of Christiane Eberhardine, Queen of Poland, and was performed for the first time at her funeral, held at Leipsic, in October, 1727. The work is scored for an orchestra of two flutes, two hautbois, two violes de gambe, two luths, and a quintette à cordes. It consists mostly of recitatives and arias, interspersed with magnificent chorals. Some of these chorals were grand beyond description, and seemed to me even finer than those in the "St. Matthew's Passion." Salomé's March was interesting, and Guilmant played his finale, from his own sonata, with a great amount of dash and vigor.

The programme of the fourth and last recital was as follows :—

Intra-bataca et Pavanelle (à l'Op. 132)	Rheinberger.
Mons. Werner, Organiste à Baden-Baden (élève de	
M. Guilmant.)	
Marche élégiaque	Alex. Guilmant.
(Orgue et Orchestre.)	
Méditation Religieuse	Fernand le Borne.
(Mons. Mancury de l'Opéra.)	
Prélude et Fugue en la mineur	J. S. Bach.
Hymne Nuptial (1re Audition)	Theo. Dubois.
Adagio pour flûte	Mozart.
(M. A. de Vroye.)	
7th Concerto en si bémol	Händel.
I. Andante. II. Largo e piano. III. Bourrée.	
Air d'Iphigénie en Aulide	Gluck.
(Mons. Mancury.)	
Sinfonia (overture) de la 35e Cantate	J. S. Bach.
(Orgue et Orchestre.)	
Finale de la 4e Sonata	Mendelssohn.

This programme was not as interesting as some of the others, although everything was well given, the Bach Sinfonia and the Händel Concerto being worthy of especial mention. Mons. Widor tells me that he is working at a grand organ concerto to be given for the first time at Geneva this coming autumn.   OUTRE MER.

REVIEW OF NEW ORGAN MUSIC.

PUBLISHED BY EDWIN ASHDOWN.

Grand Chœur in G . . . . . J. W. Hinton, Mus. Doc.

This composition (No. 4 of Four Movements for the Organ, by the organist of St. Matthew's, Westminster, London, has for a principal theme the opening phrase of "Rejoice Greatly," by Händel, and a choral for the second theme, both themes being combined at the end of the composition.

MIXTURES.

(FOUR RANKS.)

MESSRS. HOOK & HASTINGS have placed a two-manual organ having twenty-two registers in the new M. E. Church of Carbondale, Pa., and a three-manual organ of thirty-two registers in the United Presbyterian Church, Braddock, Pa. Both instruments are blown by a water motor.

The salary of the Melbourne City organist has been reduced from $1,500 to $1,000, on account of the financial depression in Australia.

Hook & Hastings have just finished an organ in the Roman Catholic Cathedral of Alton, Ill., having two manuals and twenty-seven registers, and blown by a water motor. The action is extended and reversed.

Mr. Walter J. Clemson, organist of St. Thomas' Church, Taunton, Mass., is having electric action attached to the organ in the church. He has received a Hope-Jones movable console, which is being attached to the organ.

There is a church in Brooklyn, N.Y., of which the pastor, the superintendent of Sunday-school, the director of the choir, the organist, the soprano, the alto, the tenor, the bass, and the sexton all live on the same street, and the church is located on a corner of the same street.

Mr. Edward E. Howe gave an organ concert in the Presbyterian Church, Hazleton, Pa., June 20, playing Marche de Rakoczy, Berlioz; Offertoire, "St. Cecilia," Batiste; Overture, "Rienzi," Wagner; and Overture to "Masaniello," Auber. Mr. Howe also played several piano solos, and a duct (with Mrs. Howe) for organ and piano.

Mr. Clarence Eddy performed the following programme at Springfield, Mass., Meriden, Conn., and Massillon, Ohio, the last of June: Fantasia and Fugue in G-minor, Bach; Romance, "Evening Star," and Pilgrim's Chorus, Wagner; Andantino, Chauvet; Gavotte, Martini; St. Cecilia Offertory, No. 1, Batiste; Lamentation, Guilmant; Allegretto, Foote; A Royal Procession, Spinney; Largo, Händel; Schiller March, Meyerbeer; Variations on "Home, Sweet Home," Flagler; and Overture to "William Tell."

A new organ (built by Mr. George S. Hutchings) in the Church of the Independent Christian Society, Gloucester, Mass., was inaugurated July 11, when Mr. Fred N. Shackley, organist of St. John's Church, Cambridge, Mr. William L. Estes, organist of the church, and Mr. Homer A. Norris, organist of the Ruggles-street Church, Boston, assisted by the Ruggles-street Male Quartet rendered the following programme: Overture to "Poet and Peasant," Suppé; Toccata and Fugue in D-minor, Bach; Serenade, Gounod; Offertoire, Wély; Variations on a Familiar Melody; Schiller March, Meyerbeer; Adoration, Dubois; Marche Militaire, Gounod; and several solos and quartets.

Mr. H. J. Proctor, formerly organist of a church in Minneapolis, is dead.

Mons. Ch. M. Widor, organist of St. Sulpice, Paris, and Mons. Clément Loret, another French organist, have each been created "Chevalier de l'ordre de Léopold."

Mr. Geo. S. Hutchings is building a two-manual organ with thirteen registers for the Masonic Hall, Brockton, Mass.

Mr. Dudley Buck has been appointed examiner and lecturer at the Utica, N.Y., Conservatory of Music.

Dr. Wm. Spark, the well-known Leeds organist, is announced to give a series of organ recitals in St. George's Hall, Liverpool, during the absence of Mr. W. T. Best.

The organ in the Cathedral at Bangor, Wales, is blown by two girls.

Messrs. Cole and Woodbury are building a two-manual organ with twenty-six registers for the First Universalist Church, Chelsea, Mass., where Mrs. Eugene Guelpa is organist.

Mr. Clarence E. Reof assisted at a recital given by his pupil, Miss Mabel F. Wood, in Asbury Temple, June 22, by playing the following organ numbers: Fantasia in E-flat, Rink; Adagio in B-flat, Haydn; Harvest Thanksgiving March, Calkin, and the orchestral parts of Beethoven's C-minor Concerto.

Mons. G. Schmidt, organist of St. Joseph's, Paris, has received the second prize of the Academy of Music, Toulouse, for an Offertoire to the organ.

It is reported in the *Musical Visitor* that Mr. S. P. Warren, probably the best organist in New York, took a lesson of Mr. Dudley Buck, for the purpose of obtaining a correct interpretation of one of the latter's compositions, and after the lesson handed Mr. Buck the customary five dollars.

The Americans are certainly more clever in getting money for some definite object than we are. It seems, in a chapel in Missouri, it was necessary to make a special appeal to obtain funds to buy an organ, and so a "Hugging Society" was introduced, to raise the cash. The following was put out on the scale of prices:—

"Girls under sixteen, twelve cents for a hug of two minutes, or ten cents for a short squeeze; from sixteen to twenty, twenty cents; from twenty to twenty-five, seventy-two cents; schoolmarms, forty cents; another man's wife, one dollar; widows, according to looks, from ten cents to three dollars; old maids, three cents a piece, or two for a nickel, and not any limit of time. Preachers are not charged. Editors pay in advertisements, but are not allowed to participate until everybody else is through, and even then they are not allowed to squeeze anything but old maids and schoolmarms." — *London Musical News.*

Miss Elfrida Andrée, the organist of the Cathedral of Gothenburg, Sweden, has composed a symphony which has been performed at the local opera house. The work was well received, and continued calls for the lady were heard.

Programme of the two last recitals given in St. Paul's Cathedral, Melbourne, Australia, by Mr. Ernest Wood, May 16 and 16: Prelude and Fugue in A-minor, Bach; Pastorale in E, Tombelle; Andante in G, Wesley; Finale in D, Lemmens. At the second recital, Prelude and Fugue in D-minor, Mendelssohn; Solitude, Goddard; Homage a Mendelssohn, Calking Offertoire in D, Batiste. Concerning these recitals the Melbourne *Argus* says: " The attendances at Mr. Wood's recitals have, during the past eighteen months, gone on steadily increasing, until they have now become quite phenomenal, so far as Melbourne is concerned. Surely such a trustworthy indicator of the trend of public opinion, in the matter of organ music and the performance of it, should be allowed to influence the future arrangements of those who wish to keep in accord with the spirit of the times."

CIPHERINGS.

OUR BLOWER. (From "Our Choir," by C. G. Bush.)

Copyright, 1883, by G. P. Putnam's Sons.

NEW ORGANS:

ST. PAUL'S UNIVERSALIST CHURCH, MERIDEN, CONN.

New Organ built by Messrs. Johnson & Son.

GREAT ORGAN.

Bourdon	16	Ft.
Open Diapason	8	"
Viola di Gamba	8	"
Doppel Flöte	8	"
Octave	4	"
Flauto Traverso	4	"
Twelfth	2⅔	"
Super Octave	2	"
Mixture	III. Rks.	
Trumpet	8	Ft.

CHOIR ORGAN.

Geigen Principal	8	Ft.
Melodia	8	"
Dulciana	8	"
Fugara	4	"
Flûte d'Amour	4	"
Clarinet and Fagotto	8	"
The usual couplers.		

SWELL ORGAN.

Lieblich Gedeckt	16	Ft.
Open Diapason	8	"
Salicional	8	"
Dolcissimo	8	"
St. Diapason	8	"
Violin	4	"
Flûte Harmonique	4	"
Flautino	2	"
Cornet Dolce	III. Rks.	
Cornopean	8	Ft.
Oboe and Bassoon	8	"

PEDAL ORGAN.

Double Open Diapason	16	Ft.
Bourdon	16	"
Violoncello	8	"

PEDAL MOVEMENTS.

F., MF., and P., Great Organ.
F., and P., Swell Organ.

¹ By kind permission of Messrs. G. P. Putnam's Sons.

NEW ORGAN IN PARK CONGREGATIONAL CHURCH, ST. PAUL, MINN.

Built by Mr. George S. Hutchings.

GREAT ORGAN.

Open Diapason	16	Ft.
Open Diapason	8	"
Viola di Gamba	8	"
Doppel Flöte	8	"
Octave	4	"
Flûte Harmonique	4	"
Octave Quinte	2⅔	"
Super Octave	2	"
Mixture	III. Rks.	
Trumpet	8	Ft.

PEDAL ORGAN.

Open Diapason	16	Ft.
Bourdon	16	"

PEDAL MOVEMENTS.

F., MP., and P., Gt.
F., MP., and P., Sw.
Gt. to Ped. Coupler (Reversible).
Sw. Tremolo.
The usual couplers.

SWELL ORGAN.

Bourdon (Treble and Bass)	16	Ft.
Violin Diapason	8	"
Salicional	8	"
Æoline	8	"
Stopped Diapason	8	"
Flauto Traverso	4	"
Fugara	4	"
Dolce Cornet	III. Rks.	
Cornopean	8	Ft.
Oboe	8	"

CHOIR ORGAN.

(In Separate Swell-box.)

Geigen Principal	8	Ft.
Dolcissimo	8	"
Flûte d'Amour	4	"
Violina	4	"
Piccolo Harmonique	2	"
Clarinet	8	"

ST. DOMINIC'S CHURCH, PORTLAND, ME.

New Organ built by Messrs. Hook & Hastings.

GREAT ORGAN.

Open Diapason	16	Ft.
Open Diapason	8	"
Viola da Gamba	8	"
Doppel Flöte	8	"
Octave	4	"
Twelfth	2⅔	"
Fifteenth	2	"
Mixture	III. Rks.	
Trumpet	8	Ft.

CHOIR ORGAN.

Geigen Principal	8	Ft.
Dulciana	8	"
Melodia	8	"
Flûte d'Amour	4	"
Piccolo	2	"
Clarinet	8	"
The usual couplers.		
Action watched and reversed.		
Water motor.		

SWELL ORGAN.

Bourdon	16	Ft.
Open Diapason	8	"
Viola	8	"
Stopped Diapason	8	"
Flauto Traverso	4	"
Violina	4	"
Flautino	2	"
Cornopean	8	"
Oboe and Bassoon	8	"

PEDAL.

Open Diapason	16	Ft.
Bourdon	16	"
Violoncello	8	"

PEDAL MOVEMENT.

Forte and Piano Gt.
Gt. to Ped. (reversible).

NEW ORGAN IN ST. MARY'S ROMAN CATHOLIC CHURCH, MASSILLON, OHIO.

Built by the Wirsching Church Organ Company.

GREAT ORGAN.

Open Diapason	8	Ft.
Viola di Gamba	8	"
Dulciana	8	"
Doppel Flöte	8	"
Flûte d'Amour	4	"
Octave	4	"
Octave Quinte	2⅔	"
Super Octave	2	"
Trumpet	8	"

PEDAL ORGAN.

Double Open Diapason	16	Ft.
Bourdon	16	"
The usual couplers.		

SWELL ORGAN.

Bourdon (Treble and Bass)	16	Ft.
Violin Diapason	8	"
Stopped Diapason	8	"
Salicional	8	"
Flûte Harmonique	4	"
Gemshorn	4	"
Cornet	III. Rks.	
Oboe and Bassoon	8	Ft.

PEDAL MOVEMENTS.

Full Organ.
Gt. to Ped. (Reversible.)

PNEUMATIC PISTONS.

F., MF., and P., Gt.
F., MF., and P., Sw.

NEW ORGAN IN BAPTIST CHURCH, WHITESBORO, N. Y.

Built by Messrs. Morey & Barnes.

GREAT ORGAN.

Open Diapason	8	Ft.
Dulciana	8	"
Melodia	8	"
Principal	4	"
Flûte Harmonique	4	"
Super Octave	2	"

PEDAL ORGAN.

Bourdon	16	Ft.

SWELL ORGAN.

Open Diapason	8	Ft.
Æoline	8	"
St. Diapason	8	"
Octave	4	"
Piccolo	4	"
Oboe and Bassoon	8	"

PEDAL MOVEMENTS.

F. and P., Gt. Organ.
The usual couplers.

VOL. II. No. 5.   SEPTEMBER, 1893.   WHOLE No. 17.

BACH

YEARLY SUBSCRIPTION $2.00.   SINGLE COPIES 25 CTS.

THE ORGAN

DEVOTED TO

A MONTHLY JOURNAL

THE KING OF INSTRUMENTS

RHEINBERGER

GUILMANT

FRESCOBALDI

BUXTEHUDE

MERKEL

BEST

EVERETT · E · TRUETTE ·
EDITOR & PUBLISHER
149 A. TREMONT ST. BOSTON.

HANDEL

THE ORGAN.

VOL. II. BOSTON, SEPTEMBER, 1893. No. 5.

THE ORGAN.

BOSTON, SEPTEMBER, 1893.

Published the first of every month. Subscription price $1.00 per year (European countries 10s. 5d.), payable in advance. Single copies, 15 cents.

Subscribers will please state with which number they wish their subscription to begin.

Remittances should be made by registered letter, post-office order, or by check payable to Everett E. Truette.

Correspondence, to secure notice, must in all cases be accompanied by the name and address of the writer, not for publication, but as a guarantee of good faith.

Advertising rates sent on application.

Address all communications,

THE ORGAN, 149 A Tremont Street, Boston, Mass.

Single copies of THE ORGAN can be procured of

NOVELLO, EWER, & Co.	New York.
G. SCHIRMER	New York.
OLIVER DITSON CO.	Boston.
L. H. ROSS & Co.	Boston.
N. E. CONSERVATORY	Boston.
H. B. STEVENS Co.	Boston.
LYON & HEALY	Chicago.
THEODORE PRESSER	Philadelphia.
WM. H. BONER & Co.	Philadelphia.
TAYLOR'S MUSIC HOUSE	Springfield, Mass.
GALLET & METZLER	Hartford, Conn.
RICHAULT & Co.	Paris.

CONTENTS:

No definite announcement can be made, as yet, with regard to Mons. Guilmant's recitals in Boston, beyond the dates which have been selected (September 25 and 26). Every effort to secure the use of a church with a good organ has thus far met with a refusal. A circular will be sent to the New England readers of THE ORGAN as soon as definite arrangements can be made.

Now that the organ in Festival Hall, at the World's Fair, is completed, it is hoped that regular recitals by the best organists of the country will be given until the fair is closed. Thousands of people will visit the fair and see this organ who have never heard a concert piece played on an organ of any size, and good organ music will be a revelation to them. If the standard indicated by the three or four opening recitals is kept up till the end, there will be no cause for the complaint that the organ and organ music have not received their share of patronage.

ORGANISTS who, after the past season of diligent work, have been rusticating on the ocean, in the woods, at the Fair, at the mountains, seashore, or elsewhere, are returning to their organ benches with their heads full of lofty plans and schemes for the coming season.

THE organ-tuner is greatly in demand, and open fourths and fifths are floating out through the open windows of our churches, as the temperament is being adjusted preparatory to the annual tuning of the organ.

A FEW extra hours work of the tuner in adjusting and correcting seemingly slight defects will save double the amount of expenditure later in the season, and prevent many vexatious mishaps.

THE old method of "letting the organ alone" as long as possible, sending for a tuner only when there was a cipher or a break-down, has been the ruination of some excellent instruments.

EVEN new organs require attention, and at least once or twice a year should be looked over and thus kept in a perfect condition. At the end of a decade an organ which is taken care of in this manner will be as good as new, and will have required less expenditure for repairs than another instrument which was "fixed only when necessary."

TAKE a case not far from the Boston Common. The church had the gift of a $10,000 organ. It was built by one of the best builders in the country, and the society understood that they possessed a fine instrument. Being a first-class piece of work, they agreed that, like a marble statue, it ought not to require any repairs or attention.

At the end of the first year the organist suggested that a tuner should be engaged to adjust a few minor defects, and tune the reeds as well as a few pipes which were "out of unison." The directors buttoned up their coats over their pocket-books, and said "the organ was as good as could be built, and had cost $10,000. We guess it will wear more than one year." Thus they refused to have even a drop of oil put on the motor bearings. This policy was continued for a few years, till the climax came one Saturday night after choir rehearsal.

The organist had looked after the occasional ciphers, had soiled his "Prince Albert" several times just before service, and had noticed that the block on which one of the pulleys of the motor chain was fastened had cracked, owing to careless adjustment of the man who attached the motor, and half cut loud he remarked that it would come down "one of these fine days." Sure enough, it did come down; and, as is customary with such accidents, it occurred at a time when it would be the most annoying. The organ was all right at the choir rehearsal; but Sunday, A.M., another story was to be told. The unsuspecting organist turned on the water, (the church was partially filled with the congregation) when, horrors! A cat-fight on the great organ keys, with full organ drawn, would not have produced a greater pandemonium of discord.

The aforesaid block, which, with the iron pulley, must have weighed five pounds, became detached during the night, and fell about seven feet, striking on the trackers of the swell organ. These little ribbons of pine wood offered no resistance; and the block went through, treating the trackers of the great organ in a similar manner, bringing up on the bellows after it had served the pedal organ likewise. The trackers of the choir organ escaped, as they were in another part of the instrument.

Twenty-seven trackers were broken, and it lacked but five minutes before the hour of service. The organist secured a hammer and a few crooked nails, with which he fastened the block in place so that the motor would work, after which he was obliged to play the whole service on the melodia in the choir organ.

Moral! Keep your organ in a good condition, and it will rarely "go back on you."

TUBULAR PNEUMATIC ACTION.

IN response to many requests we give herewith an illustration of the principle governing tubular pneumatic action which is engaging the attention of nearly every organ-builder in this country at the present time.

In the accompanying drawing, f is that portion of the wind-chest or sound-board which contains a body of *compressed air* supplied from the bellows. From this wind-chest the com-

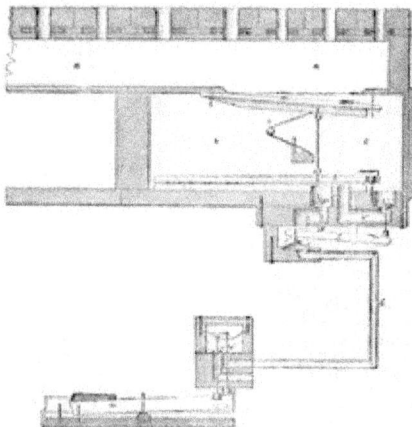

pressed air is admitted to the pipes by opening the valve m, there being one to each key. The pressure upon this valve with that of the spring t below, which is necessary to sustain it when the wind is "on," causes it to cling to its seat tenaciously in proportion to the wind pressure. The aggregate of the resistance of all the valves of a large organ when "coupled" amounts to too many pounds, and would soon weary a muscular performer. To overcome this the *pneumatic motor* is introduced, and is connected directly with the valve.

This pneumatic motor consists of a bellows within a reservoir of compressed air like the valve m, and is in this case located directly under it. This bellows is distended in its

normal condition, but in the accompanying cut the bellows is "exhausted" or shut.

It is evident that an orifice under this bellows into the outer atmosphere shown at o will cause the bellows to instantly collapse, dragging down and opening the valve m, provided that the superficial area of this bellows is greater than the opening covered by the valve. The bellows will remain "exhausted" as long as this orifice is open and the pipes will sound. But to get the bellows back to its position, and allow the valve to close in the same fraction of time, is the pneumatic problem which it is doubtful if anyone has yet solved. This duty is left to the spring t alone. It also follows that the bellows must be filled with compressed air like that upon its exterior. We must not only close the exit to the outside atmosphere, but we must open another orifice from the reservoir, or the "recover" would be too slow for use. This orifice is shown at o. The see-saw motion of the lever g will cause this alternating motion at the will of the performer.

There is now only left the means to operate this lever. This is shown at e, and is another bellows, which is in turn larger in area than the valve h, and is called a *diaphragm valve*,—a simple piece of thin leather glued over a circular depression. From the bottom of this depression leads the tube, varying in length from one to fifty feet, which gives the name *tubular pneumatic*.

Another reservoir of compressed air, adjacent to the keyboard, containing a valve representing each key and opening into its respective tube, will enable the player to send an "impulse" of compressed air through the tube, inflating the diaphragm e, raising the "poppet" valve h, closing its companion h at the other end of the lever, and exhausting the bellows h, thus pulling down the valve m, allowing the compressed air to pass to the pipes and causing them to speak. This is the general principle upon which all tubular pneumatic action is constructed, although each builder has his own specialities in detail, many of which are covered by patents, and which are of greater or less excellence.

THEORY OF THE ORGAN.

IT is rapidly becoming an acknowledged fact, that a thorough acquaintance with the construction of the organ is indispensable to every organist who cares to do more than "play a little;" and a brief consideration of the above subject may not come amiss.

Firstly, then, the mechanism of the organ must necessarily be considered, as it is variable in different organs; and the person who understands the "modus operandi" necessary to produce speech from the pipes can adapt his touch or handling of the keys, stops, pedals, etc., to any peculiarity of the instrument he may chance to perform upon. Secondly, any organ is liable to have a cipher occur, a pin drop out, a suit slip, a reed choke up with dirt or insects. A builder or tuner can suggest remedies for these mishaps to any person who has a mind to rectify the trouble, so that in many cases a service or performance would of necessity stop but for the tact of some person who can step inside and right the difficulty. Thirdly, if an organist understands the internal arrangement of the organ and its intricate mechanism, he can better appreciate how much strain is necessary to push or pull a stop-knob, or press a key, pedal, or any mechanical movement, and thus possibly save much wear and tear of the organ, as well as the organist.

Under the first head, we note the object of the key pressure is to open the valve which admits the wind to the cell or channel over which the pipe is situated. In the ordinary wind-chest or sound-board of our American organs, there is of necessity a feeling of resistance when the valve first starts, which is partially overcome as soon as it leaves its seat. This renders necessary what we may term the true organ touch, which may be called a firm attack when the key is first struck, which relaxes into simply a firm pressure of the key the instant the first attack is made. Any organist, who cares to look into a wind-chest and note how the valves are seated, will perceive how this applies; and when once the mind is firmly given to the pipes, the simple holding of the keys gives the effect. It is likewise equally desirable to let go the keys with equal decision. It therefore applies that good Manual technique consists in putting the keys down correctly as well as putting down the right key.

As to the second point, if a player is sufficiently informed as to be able to restore a dropped pin, slipped nut, or choked reed, very likely the matter of judgment in using the different parts of the organ will be helped, so that the pounding of keys and jumping and squirming upon the seat will be dispensed with in many instances, and two very important requisites, viz., deliberate but decisive movement, will succeed the flurry and haste which often produce more noise of keys, stops, and pedals (whether key or composition) than musical effect. This point also serves in considering the third point.

The matter of pedal technique is of great importance, but a few hours study of the construction of the action connections and of the pedals themselves would be a very valuable lesson. The composition or combination pedal, the stops, knobs, or registers, the management of even the swell pedal, surely need a technique; and the knowledge of what transpires when you "push the button" is of as much importance to the organist as it is to the photographer or the electrician, and it is very easily acquired. "The greatest player for effect" (said Mr. Geo. E. Whiting to the writer) "that I ever heard was the late Dr. J. H. Willcox." Whoever heard Dr. Willcox play will second the statement; and let me close by saying that Willcox knew the construction of the organ from A to Z; and if he could not or would not confine himself to legitimate organ music always, he most assuredly "pressed the buttons" in a legitimate manner.

GEO. H. RIDER.

CIPHERINGS.

LITTLE Edith had just been to church for the first time.
"And what did you think of it?" asked her mother.
"I didn't like the organ very well," she replied.
"Why not?"
"'Cause there wasn't any monkey with it." — *Harvard Lampoon.*

JOSIAH. I noticed a powerful smell of smoke in church, did you?"
MANDY. Law, Mr. Josiah, don't you know all these city churches use pipe organs. — *Chicago Inter-Ocean.*

BARTLETT. I hear that your next door neighbors have a new organ. Do you know how many stops it has?
JACKSON. Only about three a day, and those are only for meals. — *Ex.*

A YOUNG lady organist in a church in Colorado was somewhat captivated with the young pastor of the church in the next street, and was delighted to hear one week that by an exchange he was to preach the next Sunday in her own church.

The organ was pumped by an obstreperous old sexton, who would often stop when he thought the organ voluntary had lasted long enough.

This day the organist was anxious that all should go well, and as the services were about to begin she wrote a note intended solely for the sexton's eye.

He took it, and in spite of her agonized beckoning carried it straight to the preacher. What was that gentleman's astonishment when he read —

"Oblige me this morning by blowing away till I give you the signal to stop." — *Youth's Companion.*

NOTABLE ORGANS.

XII.

ST. BAVON, HAARLEM.

THE celebrated organ in Haarlem was commenced in 1735 and finished in 1738, and was built by Christian Müller. Appended is the specification.

GREAT ORGAN. 16 Stops.

Prestant	. . . . 16 Ft.	Quint Prestant	. . . 1⅓ Ft.
Bourdon	. . . . 16 "	Tertian	. . . II. Rks.
Octaav	. . . . 8 "	Mixture VI., VIII., and X. "
Roer-fluit	. . . . 8 "	Trompette	. . . . 16 Ft.
Viola di Gamba	. . . . 8 "	Trompette	. . . . 8 "
Roer-quint	. . . . 5⅓ "	Hautbois	. . . . 8 "
Octaav	. . . . 4 "	Trompette	. . . . 4 "
Gemshoorn	. . . . 4 "		

CHOIR ORGAN. 14 Stops.

Prestant	. . . . 8 Ft.	Sesquialtera II., III. and IV. Rks.
Quintadena	. . . . 8 "	Mixture VI., VII. and VIII. "
Hohl-fluit	. . . . 8 "	Cimbal	. . . . II. "
Octaav	. . . . 4 "	Cornet	. . . . V. "
Fluit-douce	. . . . 4 "	Fagot	. . . . 16 Ft.
Speel-fluit	. . . . 2⅔ "	Trompette	. . . . 8 "
Super Octaav	. . . . 2 "	Regal	. . . . 8 "

ECHO ORGAN, 15 Stops.

Quintadena	16 Ft.	Flageolet	4½ Ft.
Principal	8 "	Sesquialtera	II. Rks.
Bourdon	8 "	Mixture	IV. V. and VI. "
Quintadena	8 "	Cimbal	IV. "
Octav	4 "	Schalmei	8 Ft.
Flag-flöt	4 "	Dulcian	8 "
Nasard	2⅔ "	Vox Humana	8 "
Nacht-horn	2 "		

GREAT PEDAL, 15 Stops.

Sub-Principal	32 Ft.	Hohl-flöt	2 Ft.
Principal	16 "	Rausch-quint	V. Rks.
Sub-Bass	16 "	Busain	32 Ft.
Quinte	10⅔ "	Busain	16 "
Octav	8 "	Trompete	8 "
Hohl-flöt	8 "	Trompette	4 "
Quinte	5⅓ "	Clang	2 "
Octav	4 "		

THE ORGANIST'S RETROSPECT.[1]

BY HORATIO CLARKE.

CHAPTER V.

AMONG my schoolmates, Alfred Vane became my most intimate associate, and our friendship continued until his death. He was the only son of the village sexton, and not only had a musical nature, but was a rare mechanical genius. He also played the violin; and as often as possible we spent the evenings in playing duets together in the shop where the coffins were trimmed, and one of these, standing on horses ready for use on the following day, would serve as a table for our music-racks.

With many other of these tenements of death arranged in frames on the sides of the room, with their odor of varnish and tar, the lugubrious and dimly lighted surroundings served to impress gloomy and morbid thoughts upon my young mind which have ever since haunted my dreams; and in my wakeful hours on dreary nights, those dismal dark-stained coffins, wide at the shoulders and narrow at the feet, would often seem to be present at my bedside as fearful phantoms, especially on the night following my playing the organ at a funeral service in after years, until I would be compelled to arise and keep a light burning to drive them from my imagination.

Alfred was an adept in the use of tools, and was always engaged in constructing some experimental machine, or clock-work, with an intelligence far beyond his years. He was of great assistance to his father in many ways, and always seemed to anticipate his wishes without being told, manifesting a filial affection which is seldom witnessed. He despised all sham and affectation, and was so particular in all things of a mechanical nature and in his dealings with others, that the boys nicknamed him as "Old Accurate." He was an unselfish boy, and had an opinion of his own upon all subjects in which he was interested.

His father had the care of the Unitarian church. Alfred did the weekly sweeping and dusting. As often as I had time I would assist him, in return for which he would blow the organ for me, as the key-board was always left open. It was an old style "G" instrument in a dark mahogany case with gilded front pipes, but had no pedals. It had one man-

[1] Copyright, 1891, by Everett E. Truette.

-ual with part of the stops enclosed in a swell-box. It was a rich treat for me to press those keys and bring to remembrance the chords which I had practised in my early home.

From the friendship between us came the means of my getting together the first money toward the purchase of the coveted melodeon. It was then the custom to announce the death of any person in the parish, by at once having the age slowly tolled upon the bell of the church, whether in the night or daytime. The bell was also tolled for a few minutes one hour before the funeral. It was again tolled at the appointed hour, and finally, as the procession started from the house and rested at the grave. The tolling was done by a smaller rope operating a mechanism which carried the tongue against the bell, waiting each time between the striking until the sound had entirely died away. When tolling for the procession as it left the house, it was the custom to mount to the belfry and there watch for the cortège and toll the bell from this elevated position, until the mourners had passed out of the cemetery.

Unless the residence was at a distance from the village, the broken-hearted and their friends walked behind the hearse to the cemetery, and frequently the bearers carried the coffin on a bier through the streets, covered with a black velvet pall. As Alfred was needed to assist his father at the funerals, I was hired to toll the bell on all such occasions, and became a factor in the announcement of sorrow and woe in the ears of the quiet community, always bringing to my own mind the words of the familiar hymn,

' Oh as the bell with solemn toll
Speaks the departure of a soul,
Let each one ask himself, ' Am I
Prepared, should I be called to die?' "

It was a gloomy occupation, but I had a cheerful object in view.

At this time a new church had been built in an adjoining factory village, and I was hired to play the first violin in the choir at a small salary. These two sources of an income gave me a basis for calculation that at the end of a year I should have sufficient means to pay for a melodeon. With this prospect in view I became very hopeful, and my home trials seemed lighter, as I had learned to expect them as a part of my daily existence.

I did not neglect any duties which were required of me, for it has always been my method to first attack the most disagreeable things and have them disposed of. In sawing my daily stint of wood, I chose the heaviest and most knotty sticks first, and began with the largest end while my strength was the freshest. In this way, things to be done seem to lighten in their progress.

In my violin practising I worked upon the most difficult passages until they were mastered, which made lesser obstacles more easily overcome. I practised two hours each day in my room; went to school six hours; did my daily home work early in the morning, and always carried two aged and infirm people in the neighborhood pails of fresh water in addition to any other errands which might comfort them, for my good mother used to say, " Ernest! always have your eyes open to see if you can help anyone who is feeble, while you are young and strong, so that your life may be a blessing to others, but do not speak of it."

Those who have money can do their part in relieving suffering with what is in their power; but I had been taught that the spirit of love, or goodness, may be shed abroad at all times without riches, in the form of a kind word or deed at the right time, when our sympathy or aid is needed.

I generally spent a few minutes after school in the coffin-shop with Alfred, who was always busy at that hour, either in trimming or engraving a metal plate with the name and age of some one deceased, to be fastened upon the lid. Or now and then we would discuss things beyond our finite natures in the old graveyard, while he would be cutting an additional name on some family tombstone. Even as a boy he could not accept any theory of a life beyond these graves

PROCESSIONAL MARCH.

C. E. REED.

Gt. to Octave.

Sw. 8 & 4 Ft.

Ped. 16 & 8 Ft.
Gt. & Sw. to Ped., Sw.
to Gt.

Gt.

Copyright, 1893, by Everett E. Truette.

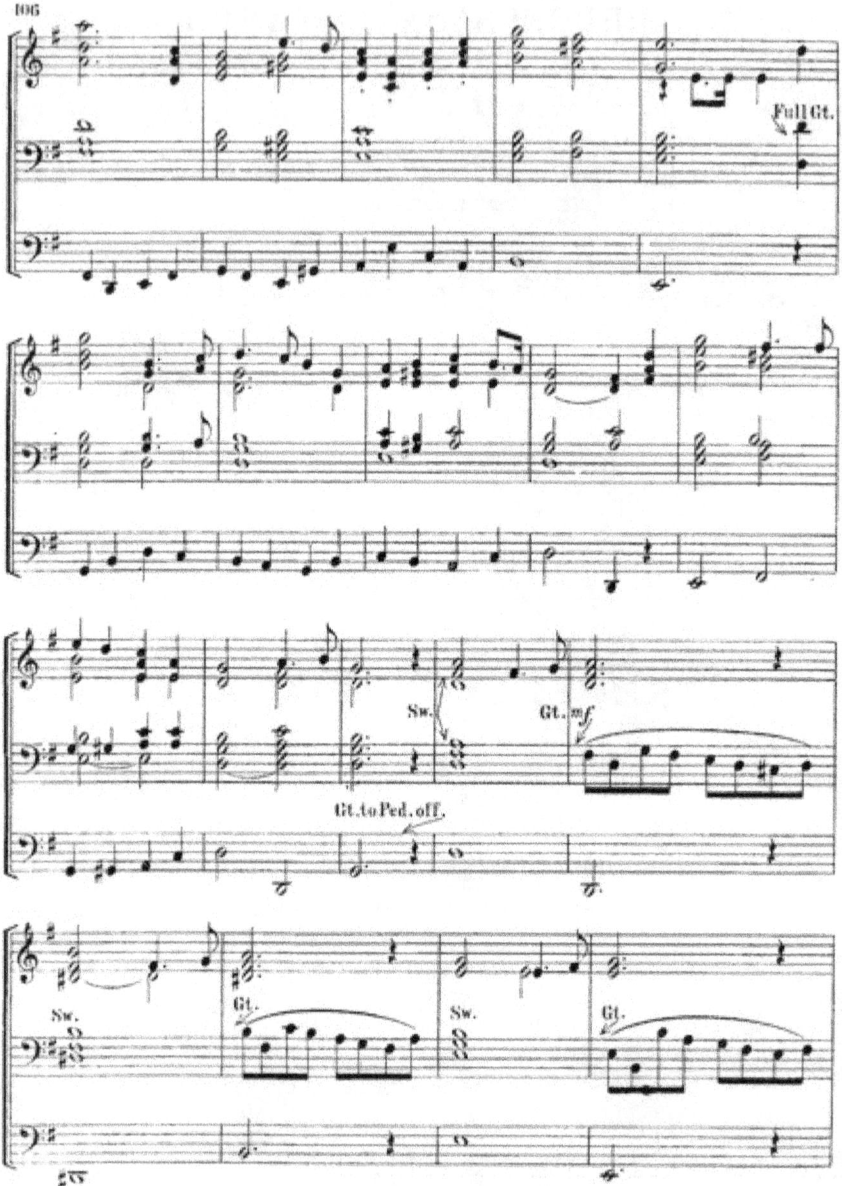
Full Gt.
Sw.
Gt. mf
Gt. to Ped. off.
Sw.
Gt.
Sw.
Gt.

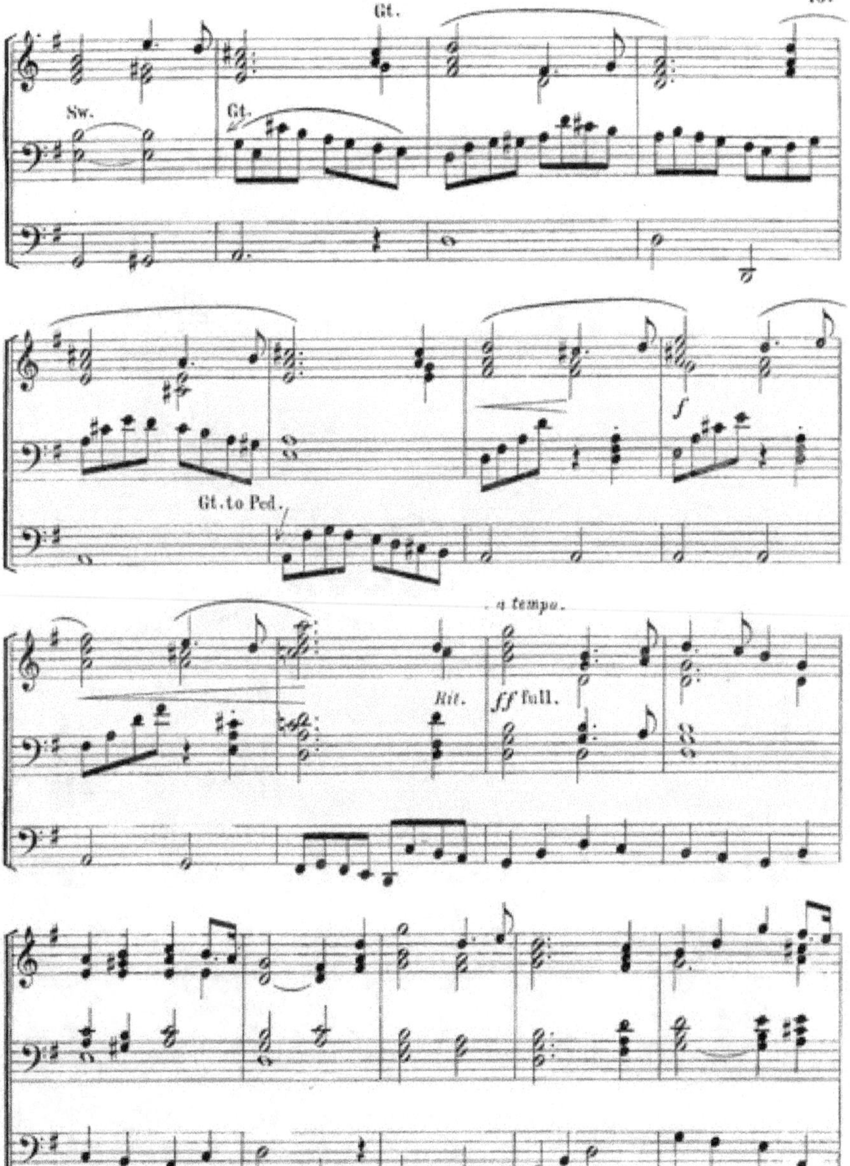
Gt.
Sw.
Gt.
Gt. to Ped.
a tempo.
Rit.
ff full.

1ˢᵗ Time. R.H. Ch. with Dulciana, Melodia & Flute 4 Ft. Coup. to Sw. L. H. Sw. Salicional, St. Diap.
2ᵈ Time. R.H. Gt. Doppel Flöte, Coup. to Sw. L. H. Full Sw.

Ped. 1ˢᵗ Time. Bourdon & Flute 8 Ft. Gt. to Ped.
2ᵈ Time. Add Op. Diap. 16 Ft.

Op. Diap., & Flute 4 Ft.

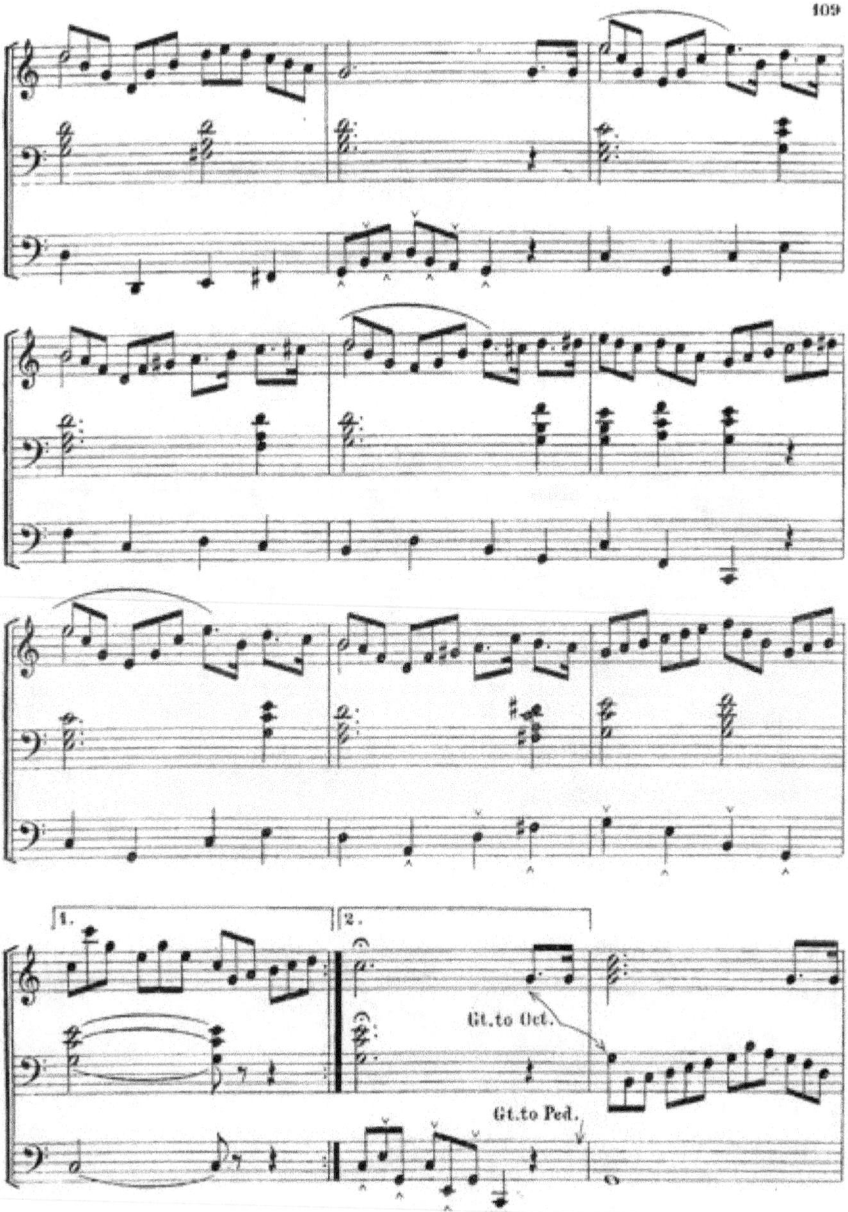
1.
2.
Gt. to Oct.
Gt. to Ped.

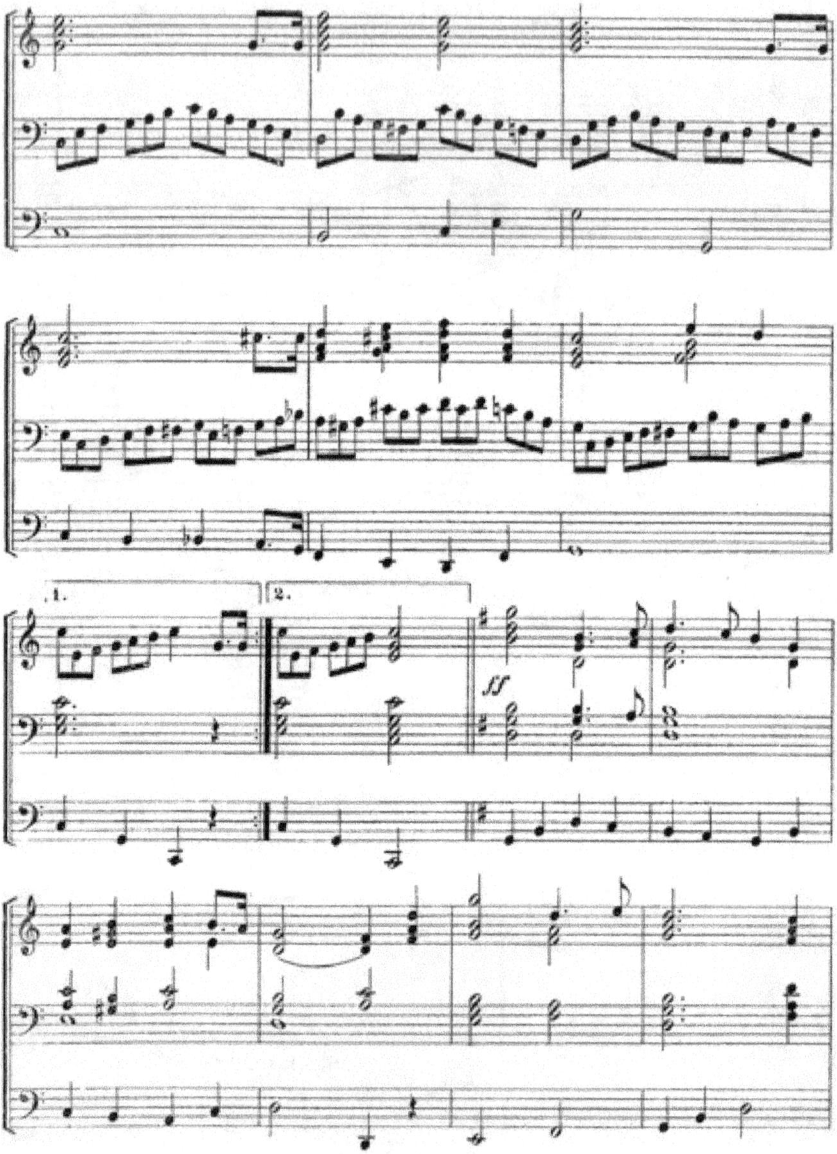
1.
2.
ff

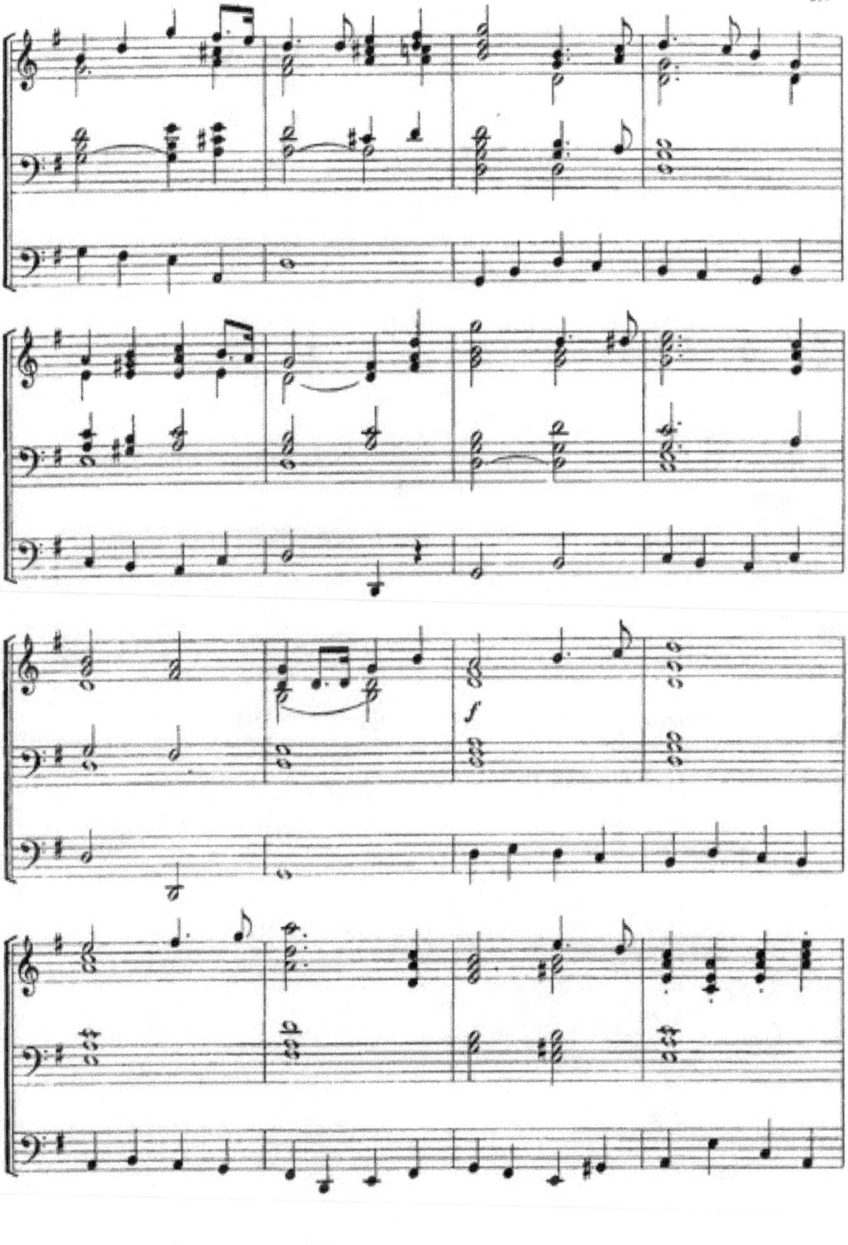
f

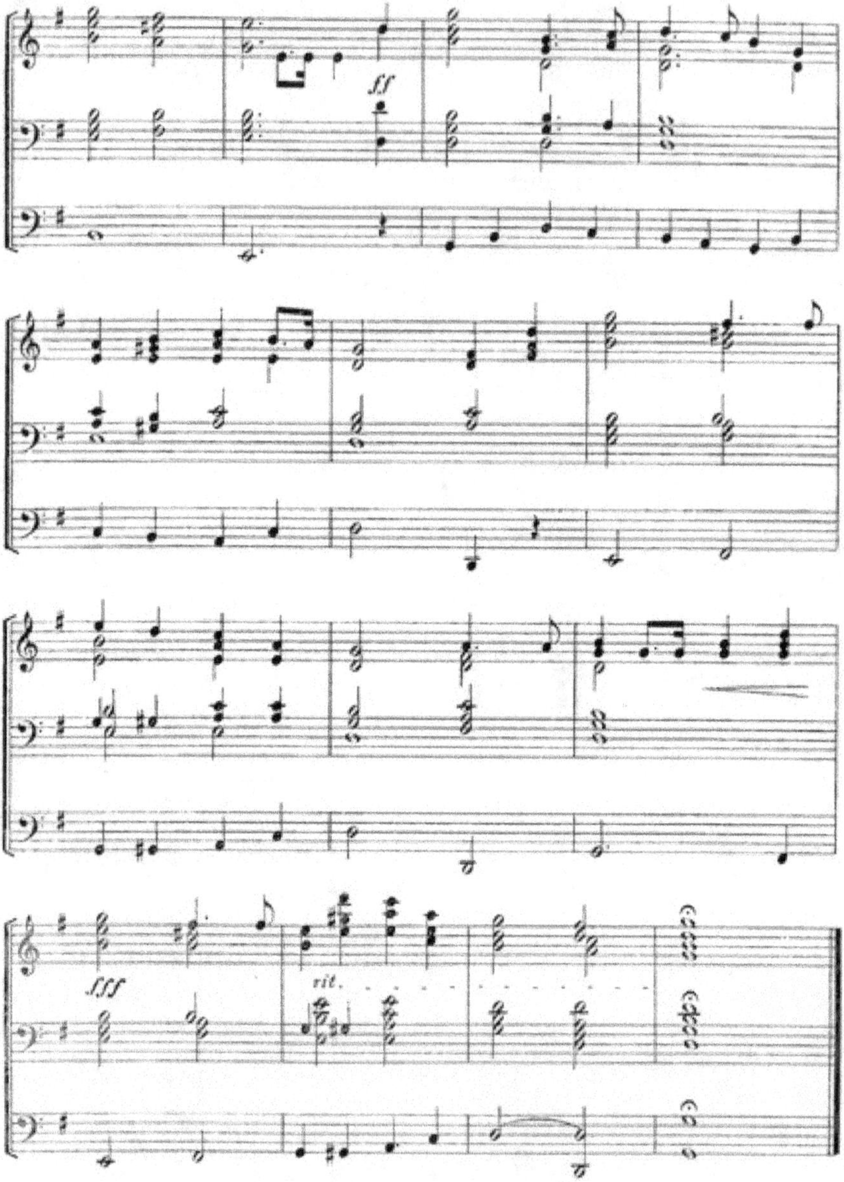
ff
fff
rit.

in which he had helped to lay away so many in their eternal rest. He wanted some tangible evidence to satisfy him that there is any possibility of another stage of existence, as a matter of justice to himself as a created being, and not based upon the conjectures of the ministers; while I then felt what seemed to be the reality of a spiritual world of personal identity, because the memory and influence of my father and mother were so vividly active in my mind,

The Sunday service in the factory village church was not so formal as in the old meeting-house. The minister was an energetic but uncultured Scotchman, who possessed a natural gift of eloquence. His sermons were unwritten; but as the words came spontaneously to his lips, he warmed up with such an impassioned excitement, that his audience became infused with the same spirit. He had been an intemperate man in the early days of his manhood, and was now an ardent reformer against the use of intoxicating liquors, to which in his later years he unfortunately yielded again.

On the heated Sundays in summer, as he became fired with his subject, it was his custom to set aside public conventionality, and take off his coat so as to gesticulate with greater freedom. If he observed any whisperings among the singers, he would stop immediately in his sermon and pray for their conversion.

At one time there had been some disaffection in the choir, which resulted in their determination not to sing together on the following week. It was a hot Sunday when the minister walked up the pulpit steps, took off his coat, and laid it over the back of the sofa. After he had announced the opening hymn, a determined voice from the opposite gallery spoke out:

"There'll be no singing to-day, for the singers are not here to sing?"

The minister quickly arose and sharply replied,

"Very well! there'll be no preachin' to-day, for I'll not be here to preach!"

Without further comment he put on his coat and walked out of the church, leaving the congregation to adjust the musical differences in the most satisfactory manner. On the following Sunday there was a full choir, and the preaching went on as usual.

This minister made quite a number of converts during the winter revival seasons; and it was his glory to have the ice cut in the factory pond on the coldest Sundays, and thoroughly immerse those who were thus incited to make a public profession of their conversion. I was frequently approached at such times and was earnestly labored with, being assured that I could not honestly read the scriptures without doing likewise.

But these rites had no lodgment in my nature, and I felt a repugnance in associating any religious motives with such forms. The simple principles of a true life which my parents had inculcated were at this time sufficient illumination for my guidance, independent of all rites and ceremonies: and the memory of their words and actions were my oracle for upright conduct.

(To be continued.)

CHICAGO AND WORLD'S FAIR NEWS.

(*Special correspondence to The Organ.*)

THE great organ built for Festival Hall, World's Fair, by Farrand and Votey, of Detroit, Mich., was finished and in excellent condition for the inauguration recital, Monday, July 31st. The instrument is a good one, the mechanism more than satisfying the numerous organ critics and organists who have tested it.

The voicing is very smooth and velvety, showing the most artistic workmanship. The pedal organ is somewhat weak; but this is owing to the position of the instrument, the four swell-boxes, going close against the roof, walls out its power. This failure cannot be overcome till the instrument

has fulfilled its mission at the Fair, and is moved to a proper organ gallery.

There are several parties after the builders with the hope of purchasing the organ, among them the Chicago University people. Many Chicagoans are expressing the hope that this organ will be purchased by the Art Institute, and erected in their hall, which is located in the central part of the city.

Chicago has no hall with a satisfactory organ where weekly organ recitals can be given at a low cost. At present writing, Mr. Frederic Archer is looking for a hall in a central part of this city, where he can erect an organ for weekly recitals this coming winter. The Festival Hall organ is just the instrument if a suitable hall could be secured for its erection.

In its present position the Auditorium organ is not effective enough for recitals, and the managers of the same do not care to use the hall unless they can fill it with six thousand people at one dollar a head.

On the afternoon of July 31st, Mr. Clarence Eddy drew a good audience to hear the inauguration concert upon the Festival Hall organ. The following programme was performed by this celebrated organist, in his usual scholarly manner:

Toccata in F	J. S. Bach.
Variations on the " Star-Spangled Banner "	Buck.
" A Royal Procession "	Spinney.
" Pilgrims' Chorus "	Wagner.
" Funeral March and Seraphic Song "	Guilmant.
" Saint Cecilia " Offertoire in C minor	Batiste.
Fantasie in F minor, " The Storm "	Lemmens.
Overture to " Oberon "	Weber.

On the following afternoon, at three o'clock, Mr. Geo. E. Whiting, of Boston, gave the following recital:—

Andante from Symphony No. 4	Beethoven.
Toccata and Fugue, in D minor	Bach.
Organ Symphony, No. 5 (first movement)	Widor.
Vorspiel, " Lohengrin "	Wagner.
Two Concert Etudes, A minor and B flat major	Whiting.
Selection from " The Flying Dutchman "	Wagner.
a, Introduction (Act III.); b, Senta's Ballad; c, Chorus of Sailors.	

In this recital Mr. Whiting made the fatal mistake of wishing to do things in the good old way. Mr. Whiting did not wish to be shown, or even learn, the mechanical accessories of the instrument. Pistons he did not wish to use, simply caring to adhere to the combination levers.

Therefore, when he desired to change his registration, he had to make long stops, which marred the unity of the numbers. If he had set his stops to his suiting on the combination pistons, which was the work of a few minutes, he would have saved himself much unnecessary trouble.

As seen, Mr. Whiting's programme was not by any means a drawing one, but in the second programme he made amends and was more like himself. It was as follows:—

Concert Overture	Hermann Wetzler.
Prelude and Fugue in C minor	Mendelssohn.
Sanctus from " St. Cecilia " Mass	Gounod.
Barcarolle	Sterndale Bennett.
Organ Sonata in A minor (first movement)	Whiting.
Pontifical March	Lemmens.
Finale, Symphony, No. 5	Beethoven.

At a reception given by Colonel and Mrs. Nicholas Senn of 532 Dearborn Avenue, this city, a few evenings since, Mr. Louis Falk, organist of the Union Congregational Church, surprised many of our younger organists in the rendition of the following programme on a Pelonbet organ:—

Torchlight March	Meyerbeer.
Overture, " Light Cavalry "	Suppe.
Chant Nuptiale	Lemaigre.
Méditation	Lemaigre.
Fanfare	Lemmens.
Overture, " William Tell "	Rossini.
Improvisation on National airs	Falk.
Schiller March	Meyerbeer.
Spring Song	Mendelssohn.
Cantilène	Grison.
March in E flat	Welp.

Although Mr. Falk boasts of having the finest church organ in Chicago, we are grieved to state that the said gentleman has within the last few years become quite a back number as regards an organist. Like many others who wander around in hearing organs and organists, we have many times been bitterly disappointed in only hearing Mr. Falk play a few chords for a concluding voluntary. We still cherish a hope that he will sometime gather himself up for a great effort.

Great organs always possess the magnetism necessary in drawing to their shrine not only celebrated organists but organ enthusiasts. Just as the great World's Fair organ was nearing "press the button" order we fortunately met at its keyboard Mr. G. Waring Stebbins, organist of Emmanuel Baptist Church, Brooklyn, N.Y. Mr. Stebbins having wandered in many lands, has a broad knowledge of many noted organs, therefore he is intensely interesting. At the time of Mr. Stebbins's visit this organ at the Fair was not completed; but by picking out a chord here and there, we got the full organ, which thoroughly convinced Mr. Stebbins that the instrument was a great surprise.

Mr. W. C. Carl, organist of the First Presbyterian Church, New York, gave three recitals on the Festival Hall organ during the second week of August. The programmes were:

Pastorale	Geo. McMaster.
Toccata in F	Bach.
March de la Symphonie, "Ariane"	Guilmant.
Organ Concerto in D-minor, No. 10	Händel.
Noel (new), dedicated to Mr. Carl	Th. Dubois.
Finale, from the Fifth Organ Symphony	Widor.
Festival March, "The Trumpeter," transcribed by Mr. Carl	Nessler.

This programme, with the exception of the Toccata and Fugue, was well rendered, the tempo of the former being painfully slow.

The second recital brought the following programme:—

Toccata and Fugue in D-minor	Bach.
Communion	Guilmant.
Marche Funèbre et Chant Séraphique	Guilmant.
Wedding Pastorale	Th. Dubois.
Pastorale (new)	Paul Wachs.
Variation on a Scotch Air	Dudley Buck.
March Triomphale	Henri Deshayes.

The programme rendered at Mr. Carl's third recital was:—

Overture, "Euryanthe"	Weber.
Visions	Rudolph Jüld.
Nuptial March	Baron F. de la Tombelle.
Suite for Organ	Deshayes.
Morceau Symphonique (new)	Guilmant.
Valse d'Amour	Th. Salomé.
Schiller March	Meyerbeer.

On the whole, Mr. Carl proved himself to be one of the best organists Chicago has been favored with. It is our hope to hear him again ere long.

A few Sundays since, at the First Presbyterian Church, this city, there happened to be three organists of the three First Presbyterian Churches of the three principal cities of the Union. Mr. W. C. Carl, First Church, New York; Mr. R. H. Woodman, First Church, Brooklyn, N.Y., and Mr. Clarence Eddy, First Church, Chicago. Mr. John H. Brewer of the Lafayette Avenue Presbyterian Church, Brooklyn, N.Y. also accompanied this blue concourse. Sunday evening, August 13 Mr. Henry Huntington Woodman of Brooklyn, N.Y. played the following organ numbers during service at the First Presbyterian Church, of which Mr. Clarence Eddy is organist. Opening Voluntary, "Allegretto," from the fourth Sonata, Mendelssohn, and Meditation, Woodman; the closing Voluntary being Fantasie in E-flat, Saint-Saëns. There being a great number, as when Felix Mendelssohn once played the organ in St. Paul's, London, who would not leave the church, Mr. Woodman, at the request of Mr. Eddy, played three numbers more, among them the first three movements of Mendelssohn's First Sonata.

Mr. Woodman gave three recitals this past week upon Festival Hall organ, World's Fair, with the following programmes:—

FIRST RECITAL:

Fourth Sonata (three movements)	Mendelssohn.
Allegretto, B-minor	Guilmant.
Overture in D	Henry Smart.
Pastorale in F	Kullak.
Concerto No. 2 (first movement)	Händel.
Paraphrase, "I am the resurrection"	Tombelle.
Marche Pontificale	Widor.

SECOND RECITAL:

Passacaglia	Bach.
Sonata in C-minor (first movement)	Th. Salomé.
Bridal Song	Jensen.
Pièce Héroïque	C. Franck.
Marche Religieuse	Guilmant.
Pastorale	Arthur Foote.
Christmas Offertoire	Jules Grison.

THIRD RECITAL:

Gothic March	Th. Salomé.
Carmène Pastorale	Grison.
Fantasie in E-flat	Saint-Saëns.
Organ Concerto, No. 1	Händel.
Marche Funèbre et Chant Séraphique	Guilmant.
Andante, with variations	Calkin.
Toccata	Tombelle.

As Mr. Woodman stands in the front rank of our American organists, it seems unnecessary to remark that he acquitted himself as a master.

Mr. Otto W. G. Pfefferkorn, organist of the great organ in Trinity Methodist Church, Denver, has exchanged places with Mr. Walter F. Skeele, organist of Plymouth Church, this city, for the month of August.

Mr. Davis, Chicago agent for Roosevelt and the Farrand and Votey Organ Company, is at his home in this city, quite sick from overwork, and many friends hope soon to see him around again.

Mons. Alex. Guilmant sailed from Havre, Saturday, August 19th, and will give his first recital in this country on the Festival Hall organ, World's Fair, Aug. 31st, also playing upon the same, Sept. 1st and 4th. Mr. Eddy is taking this year's vacation in working hard in arranging concerts throughout this country and Canada for Mons. Guilmant.

Following Mr. Woodman, Mr. Eddy gave the three following recitals at Festival Hall, Aug. 17th, 18th, and 19th.

Toccata in A (new)	W. T. Best.
Gavotte in F	Martini.
Funeral March of a Marionette	Gounod.
Largo	Händel.
"By the Sea"	Schubert.
"The Song of Spring"	Mendelssohn.
Overture to "William Tell"	Rossini.
"The Holy Night"	Buck.
Concert piece in C-minor	Thiele.

The numbers of the SECOND RECITAL were:—

Sonata in C-minor op. 70 (new)	Wermann.
Allegretto (dedicated to Clarence Eddy)	Arthur Foote.
Gavotte from Mignon	Thomas.
Overture to "Stradella"	Flotow.
Allegretto, op. 65	Volkmann.
"Harvest Home"	Walter Spinney.
"Festival March"	George Carter.
Theme, Variations, and Finale	Thiele.

THIRD RECITAL:—

Triumphal Fantasie	Dubois.
Prayer in G-flat	Lemaigre.
Fantasie de concert, on prayer from "Der Freischütz"	Liss.
Scherzo Symphonique	Guilmant.
Pastorale from Organ Suite	Oliver King.
Variations on "Austrian Hymn"	Astrap.
March in E-flat	Wely.
Concert Piece in E-flat minor	Thiele.

Mr. Walter E. Hall of Pittsburg, Pa., will be the performer preceding Alex. Guilmant.

VOX HUMANA.

MIXTURES.

(FOUR RANKS.)

The Bergstrom Organ Manufacturing Company of Minneapolis have failed for about $12,000. The largest creditor is Samuel Pierce, pipemaker, Reading, Mass.

Mr. Clarence Eddy inaugurated a three-manual Vocation Organ at the World's Fair with the following programme: Fantasia on themes from "Faust," Gounod-Eddy; Nuptial Song, Dubois; Nuptial March, Guilmant; Fantasie de Concert, Op. 33, Lux; The Last Sleep of the Virgin, Massenet, Allegretto, Op. 63, Volkmann; Variations on "Annie Laurie," Buck; Offertoire to St. Cecilia, No. 1, Batiste.

Mr. George S. Hutchings is building a two-manual organ of twenty-five registers for the First Baptist Church, Waltham, Mass.; one of twenty-four registers, for the Dorchester, Mass., Temple Baptist Church; one of nineteen registers, for the First Baptist Church, Johnstown, N.Y.; and one of twenty-two registers, for the Masonic Hall, Roxbury, Mass.

Mons. Alex Guilmant sailed for this country Aug. 29. He is expected to perform at the World's Fair, Aug. 31, Sept. 1, and Sept. 4, after which he will make a concert tour over the eastern half of this country.

A two-manual organ, built by Mr. George S. Hutchings, was dedicated in the New Hancock Church, Lexington, Mass., Aug. 23, with the following programme: Overture to "Stradella," Flotow-Buck; Allegretto, Tours; Elevation, Guilmant; Triumphal March, Buck; Pilgrims' Song of Hope, Batiste; Fantasia in C, Tours; Largo, Händel; Marche Funèbre et Chant Séraphique, Guilmant; Pastorale in C, Wely; Reverie, Meyer-Helmund; Schiller Festival March, Meyerbeer.

Mr. W. T. Best gave the following programme at his organ recital in St. George's Hall, Liverpool, Aug. 12: Overture "Rosamunde," Schubert; Romanza, "Deep in the Leafy Grove," Spohr; Organ Sonata, No. 2, A. L. Peace; Andante in A-minor, Smart; Benediction Nuptiale (" L'Orgue Moderne," No. 4), Villac; Marche from Saibe, Lorebire.

With reference to a note in our last number to the effect that Dr. Spark of Leeds was announced to give organ recitals at St. George's Hall, Liverpool, we are informed that this is not the fact. Although the report has been circulated in more than one London musical journal, it is entirely without foundation. Dr. Spark did not play at St. George's Hall, as Mr. Best resumed his duties several weeks ago.

We have read with no little surprise the opposition of the clergy, in many of the Scotch churches, when an attempt was made to introduce organs into their houses of worship, a half century ago; but the following letter from a Western pastor to a well-known firm of organ builders was written on July 14, 1893:—

"DEAR SIRS,—Yours of July 8 is at hand. I would first say we do not desire a pipe organ in our new church. We have no place for one. We are not quite ready to sell our birthright to heaven yet. We are commanded to make melody in our hearts to the Lord not on pipe-organs, or horns or fiddles. There is more glory to God in the music of a chorister on an old nail, caused by the wind that God causes to blow, than there is on ten thousand pipe-organs. God is now displeased with manufactured wind worship. Read Amos vi. 1-6; Eph. v. 19; Col. iii. 16. God bless you. I hope you will give this matter some serious thought in the light of Jesus and the Judgment. If you do, God will lead you out of the business."

A NEW ELECTRIC ORGAN.

A NEW organ, the gift of a lady member of the congregation, has just been erected in the church of St. John, Ponymynydd, near Mold. The console, which is portable, is connected with the organ by a flexible cable thirty feet in length, and can be moved to any part of the church. The stops are operated by electric buttons placed immediately over the manuals, requiring but the merest touch of the finger to work them. Part of the instrument stands in the chancel and part in the nave. Both organ and console are contained in oak cases of tasteful design. The interior of the church is very beautifully decorated, and the work occupied upwards of twenty years. The church is situated in the Rectory of Hawarden, Mr. Gladstone on Friday last visited the church, and tried the instrument, expressing himself as highly pleased with it. The opening services took place on Whit Sunday, when Mr. Robert Hope-Jones, the inventor of the system, presided at the organ, and displayed to the full the beauties of the organ under its improved conditions.

One object which attracted Mr. Gladstone's particular attention was the electric organ which is being erected by the inventor, Mr. Hope-Jones of Birkenhead, the keyboard of which was at least twenty yards from the organ itself, with which its only communication is a wire. Mr. Gladstone expressed himself delighted with the instrument, and played a few notes to test its tone, with which also he seemed much pleased. During the interview Mr. Gladstone put a lot of questions to the organ builders as to the method and material used in the construction of the organ, and everything was explained to his satisfaction save one point. The Premier was anxious to know what metals the pipes were made of; and being told tin and zinc, he asked: "Why those two in preference to any other two metals?" The organ builder, after a long pause, was only able to say, "I really can't say, unless it is because they are the best."

A VISIT TO A FAMOUS ORGAN.

(Written for The Organ.)

WE were making a short stay at Berne one beautiful summer, when it was suggested that Freiburg and its organ were within easy distance of us, and both of them well worth a visit. Some of our party were musical, and all ready for a run in any direction that might be pointed out, so we started. An hour's journey by rail, and — there we were! A quaint old place is Freiburg, and it looked very fair and picturesque as we entered it that lovely afternoon. It was market-day, and the blue blouses of the men, the clean, bright dresses of the women, and the chatter and the bustle, were pleasant in the ancient town as it lay in the sun, its remnants of long-disused fortifications appearing here and there, and its lines of houses plunging down the side of the ravine, then straggling up irregularly, like the few survivors of a broken but still advancing column, on the other side; for I should tell you the old Freiburgers saw fit to build their habitations on the sides of a cleft, or gorge, through which a river runs, called, if I remember rightly, the Sarine. Well, quaint and pleasant was Freiburg, and quaint and pleasant was the hostelry to which we were directed, where we were to spend the night.

The room in which we assembled for dinner opened upon a terrace, from which we looked down upon the river as it issued from the gorge, and down upon the curious old streets and houses that lay below, and felt ourselves to be in a sort of serene and virtuous elevation, above " the smoke and stir of this dim world." When "the business of the table " was over, we beguiled the time partly with gazing at the portrait of an intelligent-looking old gentleman, said to be the maker of the famous organ we had come to see.

At last the moment came for us to set out for the music. Ticket in hand, — for tickets had been distributed with the cherries and ices, — we wended our way to the Cathedral, a building in the Gothic style, plain, plainer, indeed, than most of the churches we saw in our tour, with little ornamentation or color about it, but large and imposing. We were told to go to the end of the seats, as far as possible from the organ, and we did so.

Presently little groups of people dropped in, until we mustered some thirty in all, and there we sat, in hushed and reverent stillness, waiting for what was to come. It was about eight o'clock, and still day; but we noticed that just three lamps, and those not very large, had been lighted in different parts of the area of the cathedral. Why so few and so scattered we discovered afterwards. Then the hour struck; there was the sudden ringing of a little bell, and immediately afterwards the tones of the great organ came rolling and crashing through the great cathedral — " The Hallelujah Chorus," and rather carelessly played, too. "The man is out of temper because there are so few hearers, and will not put out his strength." So we thought; and our first feeling, we must confess, was one of disappointment. A short pause ensued, and then followed a piece which made amends. This organ has one of the best Vox Humana stops in the world, and, in fact, the most noted, and this piece was obviously written and performed for the purpose of displaying its power and beauty. First, what seemed a human voice — "seemed!" nay, you would have said what must have been a human voice, sweet and clear, yet too far off for the words to be heard — broke gently and tremulously upon the ear; then another voice joined in the strain, and presently the harmonies of an orchestral accompaniment pealed forth in full flood. It was simply exquisite, and we all sat as if entranced. After this a Bach Fugue; then the well-known air from Judas Maccabæus, "See the Conquering Hero Comes," in which the voices of the Virgins were beautifully rendered by means of the lovely Vox Humana, and at last the organist gathered himself up for his grand and final effort.

By this time the shades of evening were gathering in, and the cathedral was filled with a gradually deepening gloom, to which the faint lights of the three lamps lent a picturesque effect. Overhead, in the organ-loft, the tall metal pipes of the instrument towered ghastly and grim, their apathetic stillness contrasting strangely with the volumes of sound they poured forth, and a red light began to glow beneath them, where the player sat amidst his curtains like an enchanter in his cave. We are going to have "The Storm." Hark! a village choir singing vespers in a church in the mountains. How beautifully that stop comes in! We hear the choristers; one, two,—then other voices joining, as the full anthem rises and swells, and the service goes on. Presently the regular beat of a bell. What is it? Is it a bell calling to the service, or a bell announcing the approach of a storm? If the latter—here comes the storm, muttering in the distance, gathering strength and rolling on; and at last, after a sudden crash, which makes you fancy you can almost see the zigzag lightning plunging its sharp lance points into the earth, we hear a terrible peal of thunder bursting through the aisles of the cathedral, and shaking the very walls, and making the lady who sits not far from us clutch her husband's arm in most unaffected terror. It is an absolutely perfect imitation. That organist must have studied storms. Even two of us who have dabbled considerably in organ playing, glance hastily to the windows to look for the storm-clouds. Half ashamed of the involuntary movement, we turn back and gaze at the tall weird organ-pipes, and at the glow beneath, and listen. The storm rages as storms do, and sometimes we hear through its bursts the village choir, with its wonderful voices, singing their hymns. The storm rolls and dies away in the distance, as storms do, and the anthem grows clearer and more triumphant. But it too dies away at last, and leaves nothing but a stillness in your ear.

A moment's pause; the little bell rings again, and all is over.

As we go out of the cathedral we find it is not by any means dark outside — not so dark as we should have expected from the interior gloom of the building. Nevertheless, an official of the hotel was waiting for us with a couple of candles in an old-fashioned square lantern. He goes before us, punctiliously showing us the way home, and as punctiliously blowing out the candles when we arrive at the door of the hotel. This is obviously part of the programme; and it is clear from our friend's manner that if the sun were blazing full in the sky he would still go before us with his candle, his countenance immovable as that of one who is rigidly performing his duty, showing us the way. The next day, on leaving the quaint old town, we cannot but take one last look at the cathedral where we had so much pleasure the evening before. Some will say our pleasure was derived from an illegitimate use of the instrument. Perhaps so. But the performance was exceedingly effective, and our party, at least, will not easily forget it.

W. G. PEARCE.

THE GUILMANT ORGAN RECITALS.

PROGRAMME No. 1.

1. Toccata in F	J. S. Bach (1685–1750)
2. Offertoire in D-flat (Op. 8)	Th. Salomé
3. Sonate Pontificale	Lemmens (1823–1881)
I. Allegro Moderato. II. Adagio. III. Marche Pontificale.	
IV. Fugue. Fanfare.	
4. { a. Invocation in E-flat { b. Finale in A-flat	Alex. Guilmant
5. Cantabile in A-flat	Samuel Rousseau
6. 3d Sonata in A. I, Con Moto Maestoso. II. Andante Tranquillo.	Mendelssohn (1809–1847)
7. Funeral March and Hymn of Seraphs	Alex. Guilmant
8. Chant in B-minor	R. Schumann (1810–1856)
9. Toccata in G	Th. Dubois
10. Improvisation on a theme to be given.	
11. March for a Church Festival	W. T. Best

PROGRAMME No. 2.

1. 2d Sonata in C-minor	Mendelssohn (1809–1847)
I. vivace, Adagio. II. Allegro Maestoso, Vivace. III. Fuga.	
2. Meditation in A-flat	Moritz Klein
3. 4th Sonata	Guilmant
I. Allegro. II. Andante. III. Menuetto. IV. Finale.	
4. Piece in F-sharp-minor	S. S. Wesley (1810–1876)

5. { a. Pastorale in F { b. Andantino in D-flat	Lemmens (1823–1881) A. Chauvet (1837–1871)
Transcribed by Guilmant.	
6. Prelude and Fugue in A-minor	J. S. Bach (1685–1750)
7. L'Adieu des Bergers (transcribed by Guilmant) Berlioz (1803–1869)	
8. { a. Fugue in C { b. Communion in A { c. Gavotte in F	D. Buxtehude (1635–1707) Eng. Gigout Padre Martini (1706–1784)
9. Improvisation on a theme to be given	
10. Fugue in D	Alex. Guilmant

PROGRAMME No. 3.

1. 1st Sonata	Th. Salomé
I. Andante, Maestoso, Allegro risoluto. II. Andante. III. Allegro Con Moto, Fuga.	
2. Ciacona in A-minor	D. Buxtehude (1635–1707)
3. { a. Elevation in A-flat { b. Nuptial March	Guilmant
4. 1st Sonata in F. Allegro Moderato. II. Adagio. III. Andante Recit. IV. Allegro vivace.	Mendelssohn (1809–1847)
5. Adagio in D-flat	F. Liszt (1811–1886)
6. Toccata et Fuga in D-minor	J. S. Bach (1685–1750)
7. Caprice in B-flat	Alex. Guilmant
8. Pilgrims' Chorus (Arranged by Liszt)	R. Wagner (1813–1883)
9. Improvisation on a theme to be given.	
10. Finale in D	Lemmens (1823–1881)

PROGRAMME No. 4.

1. 10th Concerto in D	G. F. Händel (1685–1759)
(Arranged with Cadenza by Alex. Guilmant.)	
I. Adagio. II. Allegro. III. Aria. IV. Allegro.	
2. Soeur Monique, Rondo. (Arr. by Alex. Guilmant.)	F. Couperin (1668–1733)
3. Prelude and Fugue upon B-A-C-H	Liszt (1811–1886)
4. Lamentation	Alex. Guilmant
5. Pastorale in E	César Franck (1822–1890)
6. Fantasia et Fuga in G-minor	J. S. Bach (1685–1750)
7. Offertoire upon two Christmas Themes	Alex. Guilmant
8. { a. Romance in F { b. Fanfare	A. Chauvet (1837–1871) Lemmens (1823–1881)
(Transcribed by Alex. Guilmant.)	
9. Improvisation on a theme to be given.	
10. Choral Song	S. S. Wesley (1810–1876)

PROGRAMME No. 5.

1. Religious March upon a theme of Händel	Alex. Guilmant
2. 6th Sonata in D-minor	Mendelssohn (1809–1847)
I. Choral with variations. II. Fuga. III. Finale Andante.	
3. Finale in B-flat	César Franck (1822–1890)
4. Pastorale in E	F. de la Tombelle
5. Cantabile in B-minor	Lemmens (1823–1881)
6. Prelude and Fugue in F-sharp	J. S. Bach (1685–1750)
7. { a. Consolation, Andante { b. Symphonic Movements	Alex. Guilmant
8. Chorus in B	R. Schumann (1810–1856)
9. Scherzo—Fanfare	Clement Loret
10. Improvisation on a theme to be given.	
11. Gothic March	Th. Salomé

The above programmes are copied, to use the phrase, to the letter from Mons. Guilmant's own writing, now on file among the correspondence of the former, to Mr. Clarence Eddy, Chicago, and doubtless will be found correct. Mons. Guilmant will probably play Programmes Nos. 1, 2, and 3 upon the World's Fair organ, which recitals take place August 31, Sept. 1, and Sept. 4. The improvisation will be given upon a suggested theme. At his last recitals in England Mons. Guilmant extemporized upon such themes as "God save the Queen," "The Marseilles Hymn," "Oh had I Jubal's Lyre," etc. Mr. Eddy is hard at work arranging recitals for this distinguished Parisian organist, having so far arranged some twenty recitals. Among the cities in which Mons. Guilmant will be heard are the following:—

Chicago, 3 recitals with the probability of 6; St. Louis, two, Sept. 11 and 12; Cleveland, Oct. 4; Toronto, Canada, Sept. 19 and 20; Montreal, Sept. 21 and 22; Hamilton, Ontario, Sept. 18; Northampton, Mass., Sept. 27; Detroit, Sept. 15; Rochester, N. Y., Oct. 7; Boston, Sept. 25 and 26; Cincinnati, Oct. 6 and 7; Brooklyn, N.Y., Oct. 12; New York, Oct. 13 and 14, sailing same day. Mr. Eddy has whole control in the contracting of these concerts, and the enthusiasm he is giving to the work cannot fail in making them a marked success. Those who have heard this celebrated performer express themselves as having listened to the finest exhibition of organ playing.

CORRESPONDENCE.

TWO DEBUTS.

To the Editor of THE ORGAN. I have just read, with much interest, my old friend Mr. Tilton's "Two Debuts," in THE ORGAN for July. In regard to the first occasion which Mr. T. mentions, I cannot speak; but for the second, the opening of the large organ in Dr. Neale's church on Somerset St. (now owned by Boston University and going by the name of Sleeper Hall), I can bear him out, and "go him one better," as I "assisted" on that occasion. Mr. F. F. Müller, then a leading pianist and teacher in the city, organist of the Händel and Haydn Society, etc., was to play "A Concert on a Lake, interrupted by a Thunder Storm!" written by the Chevalier Sigismund Neukomm. I was in the employ of the builder of the organ, in the capacity of tuner, and, known to have some knowledge of music, was selected by Mr. Simmons, at the request of Mr. Müller, to assist him in changing the registers. At certain points in the composition, mutterings of distant thunder were to be produced. The organist would place his foot upon the low C and C♯, and I was to draw the Double Open Diapason in the Pedal, until the proper amount of rumbling was heard, when the stop was shut off, to be drawn a little farther next time as the storm approached. At last, the storm being at its height, a rapid passage on the upper part of the manual came to suggest the blinding flash, followed immediately by the deafening crash, produced by the player laying *both arms* for a moment down upon the keys with his feet upon as many pedals as they would cover. The atmosphere thus cleared, the "Concert" proceeded to its conclusion. On that occasion Mr. Müller and Mr. S. A. Bancroft played a four-hand piece by Adolph Hesse.

The other members of that choir were Mr. Charles R. Adams, tenor and chorister, and Miss Jennie Twitchell, alto. This choir, during the time previous to the completion of the church, while the congregation worshipped in the vestry, used to spend an evening in the week in singing from "The Opera Chorus Book," at that time new to music lovers. These were very delightful occasions.

An incident connected with this matter of the new organ may serve to point a moral. The old organist had served satisfactorily enough in the old church, and on the old, not large, two-manual organ. He labored hard to secure this new and splendid instrument, but it was too much for him. In the classic language of the plains, he had bi—— but no matter. On the evening of the opening he was assigned the part of playing, as the final number, Old Hundred for the congregation to sing; but when the time came he could not be found. The next Sunday he floundered around with the 16-foot Pedal Trombone (there were three 16-foot stops on the Pedal and no others), and then gave place to his successor, poor man!

MORAL. A new organ will not make a good player out of a poor one. The improvisations and modulations will be the same, and whatever charm of novelty comes from new combinations will soon wear off, and it will be the same old story over again. I have observed it too many times to be in any doubt.

BOSTON, July 1893. O. B. BROWN.

NEW ORGANS.

NEW ORGAN IN BALTIMORE MASONIC TEMPLE.

Built by Messrs Hook & Hastings.

GREAT ORGAN.			SWELL ORGAN.		
Open Diapason	8 Ft.		Bourdon	16 Ft.
Dulciana	8 "		Violin Diapason	8 "
Melodia	8 "		Salicional	8 "
Flûte Harmonique	4 "		St. Diapason	8 "
Trumpet	8 "		Æoline	8 "
			Gemshorn	4 "
PEDAL ORGAN.			Violina (Blank)	4 "
Open Diapason	16 Ft.		Flautino	2 "
Bourdon	16 "		Dolce Cornet	III. Rks.
			Oboe and Bassoon	8 Ft.
PEDAL MOVEMENTS.				
Forte and Piano Comb., Gt.			Sw. to Gt. super-octave in addition
" " " " Sw.			to the usual couplers.
Gt. to Ped. (reversible).				

NEW ORGAN IN ST. STANISLAUS CHURCH, BUFFALO, N.Y.

Built by Messrs Johnson & Son, of Westfield, Mass.

GREAT ORGAN.			SWELL ORGAN.		
Double Open Diapason	8 Ft.		Bourdon	16 Ft.
Open Diapason	8 "		Open Diapason	8 "
Spitz Flöte	8 "		Salicional	8 "
Viola da Gamba	8 "		Æoline	8 "
Rugged Flute	8 "		Gedeckt	8 "
Octave	4 "		Quintadena	8 "
Flûte Harmonique	4 "		Flauto Traverso	4 "
Quinte	2⅔ "		Gemshorn	4 "
Super Octave	2 "		Flautino	2 "
Mixture	IV. Rks.		Cornet	III. Rks.
Trumpet	8 Ft.		Cornopean	8 "
			Oboe and Bassoon	8 "
CHOIR ORGAN.			Vox Humana	8 "
Geigen Principal	8 Ft.			
Dolce	8 "		PEDAL ORGAN.	
Melodia	8 "		Double Open Diapason	16 Ft.
Fugara	4 "		Violone	16 "
Flauto Amabile	4 "		Bourdon	16 "
Piccolo	2 "		Quint Bass	10⅔ "
Clarinet and Fagotto	8 "		Flauto	8 "
6 Couplers			Violoncello	8 "
11 Ped. Combination Movements.			Octave Bass	8 "
Pneumatic Action.			Trombone	16 "
Extended Action; reversed keyboards.				
Relief pallets in wind-chests.				

NEW ORGAN IN FIRST PRESBYTERIAN CHURCH, YONKERS, N.Y.

Built by Mr. George S. Hutchings.

GREAT ORGAN.			SWELL ORGAN.		
Violone	16 Ft.		Bourdon (Treble and Bass)	16 Ft.
Open Diapason	8 "		Open Diapason	8 "
Open Diapason	8 "		Stopped Diapason	8 "
Gamba	8 "		Salicional	8 "
Doppel Flöte	8 "		Æoline	8 "
Octave	4 "		Flauto Traverso	4 "
Flûte Harmonique	4 "		Fugara	4 "
Twelfth	2⅔ "		Super Octave	2 "
Fifteenth	2 "		Cornopean	8 "
Trumpet	8 "		Oboe	8 "
			Clarion	4 "
PEDAL ORGAN.			Vox Humana	8 "
Contra Bourdon	32 Ft.			
Open Diapason	16 "		CHOIR ORGAN.	
Bourdon	16 "		Dulciana	8 Ft.
Flöte	8 "		Geigen Principal	8 "
			Hohl Flöte	8 "
PEDAL MOVEMENTS.			Flûte Harmonique	4 "
F., MF., and P. Comb. Gt. Organ.			Violina	4 "
F., MF., and P. " Sw. "			Piccolo	2 "
Gt. to Ped. (reversible).			Cor. Anglais	8 "
Tremolo.				
(The usual Couplers).				

NEW ORGAN IN FIRST UNIVERSALIST CHURCH, CHELSEA, MASS.

Built by Messrs. Cole & Woodberry.

GREAT ORGAN.			SWELL ORGAN.		
Open Diapason	8 Ft.		Bourdon (Treble and Bass)	16 Ft.
Dulciana	8 "		Violin Diapason	8 "
Melodia	8 "		Salicional	8 "
Octave	4 "		Vox Celestis	8 "
Flûte d'Amour	4 "		St. Diapason	8 "
Twelfth	2⅔ "		Flauto Amabile	4 "
Fifteenth	2 "		Violin	4 "
Trumpet	8 "		Dolce Cornet	2 Rks.
			Flautino	2 Ft.
PEDAL MOVEMENTS.			Oboe	8 "
Forte and Piano Gt.				
Forte and Piano Sw.			PEDAL ORGAN.	
The usual couplers.			Open Diapason	16 Ft.
Gt. to Pedal (reversible).			Bourdon	16 "

During the past month Hook & Hastings have finished six two-manual Organs as follows: Brooklyn, N.Y., New Masonic Hall, Amsterdam, N.Y., Reformed Church, Augusta, Me., Christ Unitarian Church, Penn, Ill., Methodist Episcopal Church, Lynn, Mass., Freewill Baptist, Baltimore, Md., Grand Masonic Temple of Maryland. Among their present contracts are large three-manual Organs for Syracuse, N.Y., Park Central Presbyterian Church, Philadelphia, Pa., St. Anne's Church, East Boston, Mass., Church of the Sacred Heart.

GEORGE S. HUTCHINGS,

Church Organ Manufacturer,

23 TO 27 IRVINGTON STREET,

BOSTON, MASS.

Builder of some of the most famous organs in the country, among which may be mentioned The New Old South, Emmanuel, Second Church, Park St. Church, St. Paul's, Spiritual Temple, and Church of the Advent, all of Boston; also South Congregational Church, Middletown, Conn., New York Avenue M. E. Church, Brooklyn, N. Y., St. Paul's School, Concord, N. H., and All Saints Church, Worcester, Second Congregational Church, Holyoke, Mass., Grace Church, Providence, R.I., Plymouth Church, Minneapolis, First Congregational Church, Omaha, Neb., First Congregational Church, San Francisco, Cal., Independent Presbyterian Church, Savannah, Ga., and many others.

Send for catalogue.

S. ELLIOTT,

MANUFACTURER OF ACTIONS FOR

PIPE ORGANS.

WINCHESTER, - - MASS.

WOODBERRY & HARRIS,

399 ALBANY STREET,

BOSTON, MASS.

(Next building to West End Power Station.)

Builders of the following named organs, in White's Church, Savannah, N. Y., Fourth Church, Binghamton, N. Y., Grace Chapel, St. Louis Ch. Epis., Trinity M. E. Church, Salem, Mass., First Baptist Church, Chester, Ill., All Saints, etc.

Church, Chamber, and Chapel Organs.

Old Organs rebuilt, enlarged and revoiced; also, organs tuned and repaired by competent workmen. Motors for blowing organs furnished and applied.

Organists and Church Committees

ARE CORDIALLY INVITED TO EXAMINE THIS NEW MODEL.

LISZT ORGAN. Style 804.

This new and improved model is attracting wide attention among church committees and organists. It is decidedly superior to small Pipe Organs, and is unquestionably the most perfect instrument of its class. Send for specification. Sent free to any address.

ORGANS ALSO RENTED.

MASON AND HAMLIN ORGAN AND PIANO CO.

154 & 155 TREMONT STREET, BOSTON, U.S.A.

Branches: { 158 Fifth Avenue, New York. { 185 Wabash Avenue, Chicago.

ANNOUNCEMENT.

VOLUME II. OF THE ORGAN

COMMENCES

❋   MAY 1, 1893.   ❋

THE ORGAN.

Vol. II.   BOSTON, OCTOBER, 1893.   No. 6.

THE ORGAN.

BOSTON, OCTOBER, 1893.

Published the first of every month. Subscription price $2.00 per year (European countries 10s. 9d.), payable in advance. Single copies, 25 cents.

Subscribers will please state with which number they wish their subscription to begin.

Remittances should be made by registered letter, post-office order, or by check payable to Everett E. Truette.

Correspondence, to secure notice, must in all cases be accompanied by the name and address of the writer, not for publication, but as a guarantee of good faith.

Advertising rates sent on application.

Address all communications,

THE ORGAN, 149 A Tremont Street, Boston, Mass.

Single copies of THE ORGAN can be procured of

NOVELLO, EWER, & CO.	New York.
G. SCHIRMER .	New York.
OLIVER DITSON CO.	Boston.
L. H. ROSS & CO.	Boston.
N. E. CONSERVATORY	Boston.
H. B. STEVENS CO.	Boston.
LYON & HEALY .	Chicago.
THEODORE PRESSER	Philadelphia.
WM. H. BONER & CO.	Philadelphia.
TAYLOR'S MUSIC HOUSE .	Springfield, Mass.
GALLUP & METZGER	Hartford, Conn.
RICHAULT & CO.	Paris.

CONTENTS:

WE go to press two days later than usual in order to contain an account of Mons. Guilmant's concerts in Boston.

INASMUCH as only one composition has been received for our second organ music competition, we are obliged to withdraw our offer.

LOVERS of organ music in Boston, as well as other cities, may read with envy of the success attending the regular organ concerts of Mr. W. T. Best in St. George's Hall, Liverpool. These concerts are given on Thursdays, Saturdays, and on alternate Sundays, through a large part of the year. A small admission fee is charged on week-days, while, if we are not mistaken, the Sunday concerts are free. The attendance is always large, and even in August an audience of a thousand is a common occurrence.

WE were under the impression that the greatest fugue writer the world ever saw died in 1750, till we read the following in a Western paper: "It is now probable that criminal proceedings will be instituted against J. S. Bach, the owner of the Prairie City Bank, which made an assignment a few days ago."

THE "great and only musical journal in the world," known as the *Musical Courier*, announces that "the first appearance in the East of Alexandre Guilmant will be in Newark, Oct. 11." He performed in Boston Sept. 25 and 26, and in Northampton Sept. 27. Evidently "the East" ends at New York, and all cities *east* of New York are "not in it."

AN Australian paper thus describes the effect that the Overture to "William Tell" had on the writer's brain. " In the earlier portions, which simulate the rising of the storm in the Alps, the organist's manipulation of his instrument was extremely clever, *the crisp crash of the organ, if it is possible for sound to render the effects of sight, the blinding flashes of lightning that preceded the thunder crash.*"

Too much credit cannot be given to Mr. Clarence Eddy for the successful consummation of the greatest concert tour ever planned for an organist. But for his energetic efforts it is doubtful if Mons. Guilmant would have crossed the Atlantic this summer. To have secured engagements for this artist for over thirty organ recitals, to be given within a period of less than eight weeks, has been no small task, and its successful termination will mark an epoch in the history of the organ in this country. It was Mr. Eddy's first intention to secure Mr. W. T. Best also for a similar tour, but the arrangements failed to mature. We will hope that ere long England's noted organist will visit our country for just such a tour as Mons. Guilmant is now making.

THE "Organists' Association for the City of Wakefield," England, now in its fourth year, has fifty-three members, all of whom hold organist's appointments in or near the city of Wakefield. The objects of the association are friendly intercourse, and hearing and discussing papers on musical subjects. Such an association in this country — in Boston, New York, or Chicago, for instance — would have a salutary effect on all who joined the association. In this country there seems to be a hundred different methods and a hundred different ideas on the same subject with every hundred organists. Social intercourse and friendly discussion are comparatively rare among our organists, and any movement which will tend to remove the existing barriers will be hailed with delight.

A SHORT time since, when we were canvassing the different churches for the purpose of obtaining the use of a good organ for the organ recitals of Mons. Guilmant, we stumbled upon an example of how superior some people consider the organist of their own church to any other living organist, regardless of the world-wide fame of some other players. In this case a member of the standing committee was enlarging on the beauties of the organ in his church, — an organ of more than ordinary beauty, by the way, — and in the course of his remarks went on to say that, "We have a fine instrument in our church; in fact, we consider it the finest in the city. Its beauties would not be discovered by an ordinary organist, or by one unfamiliar with this particular instrument; and if Mons. Guilmant should attempt to play it, I think it would be a good plan to have *our organist instruct him* on the beauties which it contains. In a half day no doubt our organist could show him the beauties of our organ so that he [Mons. Guilmant] could do justice to the instrument." We should enjoy being a fly on the wall when "our organist *instructs*" Mons. Guilmant how to bring out the beauties of this organ, or of any other organ.

FOR THE PROTECTION OF ORGAN BUILDERS.

It is natural that an organ builder should experience a feeling of elation as each new specification is accepted and the contract is received, duly signed. But sometimes there are cases in which his anticipated prosperity meets with a barrier on some technical point which turns his joy to sorrow.

A case illustrating the object of this article was recently experienced by an organ builder of long-established reputation. He had received the award of a contract for a large organ from the committee thus appointed from a church in a wealthy Western city. The design for the case was received from the architect through this committee. The organ was faithfully built according to every detail of its specific construction. It was completed by the required date, and was forwarded to its destination.

On receiving notification that the organ had been shipped to the church, the trustees of the society sent a formal notice to the builder to the effect that the organ committee who signed the contract had no authority from the trustees to make such an order, and that they should not permit this organ to be placed in the church for which it was built. The organ committee would not hold themselves responsible for the transaction as individuals, and the result was that all the expense of construction and transportation, as well as legal expenses, had to be borne by the unfortunate builder.

In signing a contract, the builder has everything at stake with his investment, while the churches assume no risk whatever; and when there are mean-spirited men managing their affairs, as frequently occurs, for the chief manager is often a sharp man of means who will take advantage of any apparent flaw in a contract, through his inhumanity, the church thus receives the benefit of what an honest man loses by some sneaking subterfuge in the form of a compromise.

The writer is not an organ builder, and is not in the employ of any manufacturer on one side, nor church corporation on the other side, but simply makes this suggestion to all the organ builders in the United States, for their individual protection;—

To agree not to sign any contract as the "Party of the First Part," unless, in addition to the signatures of the organ committee as the "Party of the Second Part," there shall be a statement accompanying the signatures of the organ committee certifying that they are authorized to make this transaction, signed by the Board of Trustees, or legal managers of the society or corporation, whether they are the officers of a church or music hall, with the names of the chairman, secretary, and treasurer, as such.

An organ committee is generally a sub-committee appointed to attend to the details of procuring an organ; and unless it is distinctly stated that they are authorized to contract for an organ by the legal managers of a society, a builder may be placed in the unenviable position as in the illustration cited.

An organ builder has rights, and should stand up for them at the beginning of his negotiations. No honest organ committee will object to the certificate of their authority from the legal representatives of the society.

It sometimes occurs that after work has been begun upon an organ, a notice countermanding the order is received, in which the builder finds no redress for the loss on the work begun, and especially where prospective contracts have been deferred on account of the organ which has been ordered.

Organ builders have a sensitive feeling for which there is no ground, — that they are so dependent upon the popular favor and influence of a religious society for their future business, that they are often loath to assert themselves in demanding what is morally and legally their just due.

Financially, a church corporation is not always a reliable institution, although religiously it may consider itself sound to the core; but it is an organization which is supported by voluntary contributions, with a treasury in which there is seldom a surplus of funds. For this reason, an organ contract should not only have the signatures of the trustees of a society, in addition to the organ committee, but there should also be a guaranty that provision has been made for the payment of the contract when the builder's part has been fulfilled.

It is often the case that a contract is signed before the money for the payment thereof has been obtained, the committee trusting to luck or Providence in the expectation that some scheme for raising the funds will be developed in the interim while the organ is being constructed.

I once knew a minister who, as the one most interested, assumed to run the finances of his church, who told me that when he incurred any expense, such as the purchase of an organ, or the engaging of a high-priced organist, he went right ahead and entered into debt, using the members of his committee as figure-heads, without having the least idea of how the pecuniary obligations were to be met, as he left that part to his committee, and gave himself no further anxiety.

Sometimes during the building of an organ, the edifice in which it is to be placed is destroyed by fire; and in such a case, unless a special proviso is made, the builder is obliged to wait until another structure is completed before he can receive payment for his work. In order to guard against such an occurrence, a proviso should be made to the effect that on the completion of the organ in the manufactory, if there is a delay in the construction of the church, or if destroyed by fire, the organ should be paid for, deducting the expenses of shipment and erection in the church.

In illustration of this subject; a contract was closed by a builder with a church in Ohio for a large organ with an elaborate Gothic case and intricate action-work. While the organ occupied a capacious recess in the rear of the pulpit, the key-desk was located in one corner of the church, on the main floor, on one side, the mechanism running to the centre under the platform, and then branching into the organ at right angles. On the completion of the organ in the church, the committee desired the builder to furnish an organist at his own expense for an opening concert, for the benefit of the funds of the society. When this was acquiesced in, he was requested to furnish an organist for three more concerts before they could pay him. Being in need of the money due him, he provided for the three additional concerts. Then a meeting of the trustees was held, at which he was present, in the expectation of receiving the cash payment which was stated in the contract. The document was read through. The chairman of the committee was a rich man. He tried in every way to raise objections, in order that the other members should decide not to accept the organ; but when it was proved that the contract had been more than fulfilled, he coolly stated that the money had not been raised, and that no payment should be made at that time, when the organ builder, in addition to the amount invested in the instrument, had been the means of raising through those four concerts about one thousand dollars toward the organ fund, and had paid the concert organist and all his expenses. As he went to the railway station on his return home without his payment, for the small margin of profit on the organ would not admit of a law-suit, the secretary of the society came to him and apologized for the shabby treatment, but explained that the wealthy chairman ruled all their affairs, and that he had succeeded in making the pew builder, upholsterer, and building contractor compromise on their contracts, at a great sacrifice, in order to effect a settlement. He stated that this chairman was so mean in his dealings, that if a carpenter did any work for him at his residence, he always rejected the work, in order to get it for nothing, or at a compromise, and that the church affairs were controlled by him on the same basis, to the injury of the reputation of the members. This apology was intended as an overture to a compromise to which the honest builder would not yield, and it was more than a year before a settlement was effected, after many expensive visits to that city.

There are many points of mutual interest which organ builders should unite upon and agree together to pursue in their contracts with churches, which would be for their reciprocal benefit. Although in competition there is work enough for all, and with established standards in regard to contracts and many details, each would be the gainer if a convention of organ builders could be held in Boston on a date near at hand, which would result in the better protection of their interests.

The suggestion is therefore made that a convention of organ builders be held in Boston at the call of a committee who will organize for such a purpose, and present many matters for discussion and mutual agreement.

OPEN DIAPASON.

NOTABLE ORGANS.

XIII.

ABBEY CHURCH, WEINGARTEN.

ONE of the most remarkable organs in Europe is that in the Benedictine Monastery, Weingarten, Suabia, which was built by Joseph Gabler of Ochsenhausen, and finished in 1750. The shabby treatment which the builder received from the convent, during the construction of the instrument, reduced him to absolute poverty, from which he died soon after the completion of the instrument.

The organ contains 76 stops and 6,702 pipes, is 27½ feet wide, 30 feet deep, and 50 feet high. The paucity of reeds

and the superabundance of mixture work should be noted. Appended is the specification:—

GREAT ORGAN. 16 Stops.			
Prestant	16 Ft.	Quer-flöte	4 Ft.
Principal	8 "	Hohl-flöte	2 "
Rohr-flöte	8 "	Super-octave	2 "
Piffaro	8 "	Sesquialtera	VIII. Rks. 2¾ "
Quintaton	8 "	Mixture	XX. " 2 "
Octave	4 "	Cornet	VIII. " 2 "
Rohr-flöte	4 "	Trompeten	8 "
Flauto Dolce	4 "	Cymbelsbaun.	

CHOIR ORGAN. 12 Stops.			
Bourdon	16 Ft.	Salicional	8 Ft.
Principal	8 "	Octave Douce	4 "
Violoncello	8 "	Viola	4 "
Coppel	8 "	Nasat	2 "
Hohl-flöte	8 "	Mixture	XXI. Rks. 4 "
Unda Maris	8 "	Cymbal	II. " 2 "

ECHO ORGAN. 13 Stops.			
Bourdon	16 Ft.	Piffaro	4 Ft.
Principal	8 "	Super-octave	2 "
Quintaton	8 "	Mixture	XII. Rks. 2 "
Viola Douce	8 "	Cornet	IV. " 1 "
Flauto	8 "	Clarinet	8 "
Octave	8 "	Carillon	
Hohl-flöte	4 "		

POSITIV. 12 Stops.			
Principal Douce	8 Ft.	Rohr-flöte	4 Ft.
Violoncello	8 "	Quer-flöte	4 "
Quintaton	8 "	Flageolet	2 "
Flöte Douce	8 "	Cornet	XII. Rks. 2 "
Piffaro	4 "	Hautbois	8 "
Flauto Traverso	4 "	Voix Humaine	8 "

PEDAL ORGAN. 17 Stops.			
Contra Bass	32 Ft.	Sesquialtera Bass,	
Sub-Bass	32 "	II. and III. Rks. 2⅔ Ft.	
Octave Bass	16 "	Mixture Bass	V. Rks. 8 "
Violin Bass	16 "	Bombarde Bass	32 "
Quintaton Bass	16 "	Fagotto Bass	8 "
Super Octave Bass	8 "	Trompette Bass	8 "
Flöte Douce Bass	8 "	Cornet Bass	4 "
Violoncello Bass	8 "	Carillon Pedal.	
Hohl-flöte Bass	4 "		

ACCESSORIES.	
Coupler Echo to Great.	Rossignol.
Tremulant.	Cymbels.
Cuckoo.	La Force.

The compass of the manuals is forty-nine notes, and of the pedal organ twenty notes. "La Force" is a mechanical stop connecting forty-nine pipes with the lowest pedal key.

SHOULD A MUSIC TEACHER BE AN ORGANIST AS WELL AS A PIANIST?

BY ALBERT W. BORST.

ALL knowledge being additional power gained, the reply to the above question would, to a general observer, be altogether in the affirmative. The pianist, especially such an one as intends to be a specialist, may, however, look at the matter from this light: Can I get a better return by spending part of my time and money in studying the organ? Let us look into some of the special advantages offered to an organist. If the advantages prove to be so many as to be a fair offset to the expenditure, and assuming that the study of this instrument be not detrimental in any way to progress on the other instrument, then the answer is self-evident.

1. By reason of the sustaining tones of the organ, we are better able to acquire a strict *legato* touch. As it is now admitted by all first-class teachers that the singing tone on the piano is that which is most difficult to learn, our first point seems a strong one.

2. For the same cause as just named, students are taught accuracy, especially with regard to the duration of note values in the polyphonic style.

3. An organist is generally a more cosmopolitan musician than he who is merely a pianist : many branches of the musical art which are part of his calling are seldom offered to

the latter. For example, he has constant practice in accompanying both solo and chorus voices. He has to undertake the drilling of said voices. He is frequently called upon to exercise the gifts of extemporization and transposition.

4. The organ affords a great variety of tone-coloring, second only to that of the orchestra.

5. The music written for the instrument being chiefly of a broad, dignified, massive character, the study of such acts as a check on the taste of so many pianists who spend so much of their efforts on the technical difficulties of the modern brilliant school.

6. There is still another argument in favor of combining the two instruments, which ought not to be omitted, although it is one that will not meet with universal acknowledgment. Many young students, especially such as have spent a good deal of time in such European cities as Paris, Leipsic, Berlin, etc., are from their environment, as well as from motives of ambition, tempted to regard their art solely from the Bohemian side. Now, as one of the greatest missions of music is to transport us into a more elevated atmosphere, then a close relation with some church will often be of the highest advantage. Hegel says that "religion elevates the thoughts of artists; so that we expect a *higher revelation* of beauty than were otherwise possible."

7. To the country teacher, the part of organist is generally the main stepping-stone for his upward path. He has opportunities for being heard, both on the piano and organ, and so getting a teaching connection which the pianist might easily envy.

Audi alteram partem. One of the standard objections against studying the two instruments together is, that the firm touch of the one is antagonistic to the light touch requisite for the other. In olden times, when digital force was necessary to make the keys of the church "Kist o' whistles" consent to utter a tone, there was undoubtedly some justification for this objection. But the weight of finger pressure in our improved modern instruments assimilates so exactly with that of the piano, that the old argument must be ruled out of court. In evidence of this, we find artists, from Mendelssohn to C. Saint-Saëns, equally at home on both instruments.

To many the additional expense is an item for serious consideration. It is often possible for a teacher to make some concession when he finds a willing pupil who candidly states his difficulties. At least some portion of the time might be taken from that meted out for the piano instruction, equally as a comparatively short period suffices for a good pianist to have a working knowledge of the organ. And it cannot be too widely known that a good grounding of the piano must precede all instruction on the latter instrument. On the principle that "it is only by knowing other things that we know any one thing," as well as that it proves financially a sound investment, we advocate that the pianist should, sooner or later, make friends with the organ. — *The Etude.*

THE ORGANIST'S RETROSPECT.[1]

BY HORATIO CLARKE.

CHAPTER VI.

At the end of this year, when I was thirteen years of age, I had earned the money required to purchase a piano-cased melodeon, which Mr. Rodman brought out from the city with his own team. To my surprise, Mrs. Rodman consented to have it placed in her front room, providing that I would keep the curtains down and always wear my slippers on entering.

I had carefully learned the correct fingering of all the scales from my father's teaching, the memory of which quickly returned, and my lessons were now transferred from the violin to the new instrument. My first study was to play through all the tunes of "The Modern Harp," a good book of church music which was then very popular. The music

[1] Copyright, 1893, by Everett E. Truette.

was played from four staves, with the tenor at the top, transposing the notes of that part an octave lower than written; and the practice obtained from playing these hymn-tunes in this way fitted me for readily reading all church music at sight.

Enterprising members of the Orthodox congregation now began agitating the subject of the introduction of an organ in the place of the time-honored orchestra; and a second-hand instrument of one and a half manuals was found, and was placed in the arch in the rear of the choir gallery. It was a very old organ, with a mahogany case and gilded front pipes, the upper key-board ending with tenor F, the lower keys running down to GGG, and the pedals simply coupling to the keys as a more modern attachment, without separate sub-bass pipes.

My teacher was engaged to play this instrument; and his efforts underwent severe criticism from the ignorant censors, who said that he played too much like a pianist, when, in fact, he had a true organ touch.

I now began my practice in Rinck's "Organ School." From the beginning I was charmed with this composer. There was a peacefulness resulting from a communion with his thoughts which imparted a serenity of mind, encouraging me to extemporize in a similar style, and I soon found that I possessed the gift of improvisation. My teacher occasionally gave me lessons on the organ at the church, and I was permitted to practise there; but the want of money to pay for blowing was a hardship which many young organ students have to contend with.

As often as I could get a schoolmate to pump the bellows by doing him some favor in return, I revelled in the combinations which even this incomplete instrument afforded, and made a special study of registration, — the art of combining stops, or registers, so as to produce a pleasing variety in the quality of the tone, and the adaptation of these contrasts to phrases and sections of organ music. I first learned to associate the individual quality of each separate stop with its name, and then the various combinations which were practical and euphonious.

These qualities were so impressed upon my memory that I was soon able to practise upon the instrument without any blower, playing correctly upon the manuals and pedals without eliciting a sound, a technical practice heard only by the mental ear, but productive of excellent results in the way of discipline. I learned to see in my mind the relative positions of the manuals and pedals, so that I could read the music without looking at my hands or feet. This attainment is one of much importance in the early accomplishment of involuntarily measuring the distances of all intervals in fingering, as if the eyes were fixed upon the keys and fingers.

This method is necessarily followed by those who are deprived of sight, and my own experience proved its efficiency in the more rapid progress which I was thus enabled to make. The position of the pedal keys was easily found and fixed in the mind by simply touching the sides of the sharps in their relation to the other keys. In this way I readily learned to use the pedals without confusion.

I now used all my influence to induce the people of the factory village church to procure some kind of an instrument for the choir which would give the harmony, as we had only a violin and double-bass to support the voices. I had seen a French harmonium in a music store in the city, which was an instrument of real merit, but the price was beyond the means of the society.

In due time a second-hand American harmonium was rented and placed in the choir gallery. It was a very poor instrument compared with those of French manufacture. Instead of drawing, the stop-knobs revolved half way around, and there were no means of expression. Moreover, any attempt to increase the power by blowing with more force, always caused the valves to sound notes which were not voluntarily played. It also had a transposing key-board intended to simplify the art of playing, which I did not use.

(Continued on page 137.)

MELODY AND INTERMEZZO.

Moderato ma con moto.

JOHN S. CAMP, Op. 3 No. 2.

Gt. Doppel Flöte
& Gamba.

Sw. 8 & 4 Ft.
Ch. Melodia &
Dulciana.

Ped. Bourdon.
Sw. to Gt. & Sw. to Ch.

appassionata.

Poco

a tempo.

dim. Poco Rit.

Poco Rit.
Piu mosso e deciso.
Gt.to 15th
Sw. Full.
Gt.
Ped. f
Gt.to Ped.
1.
2.

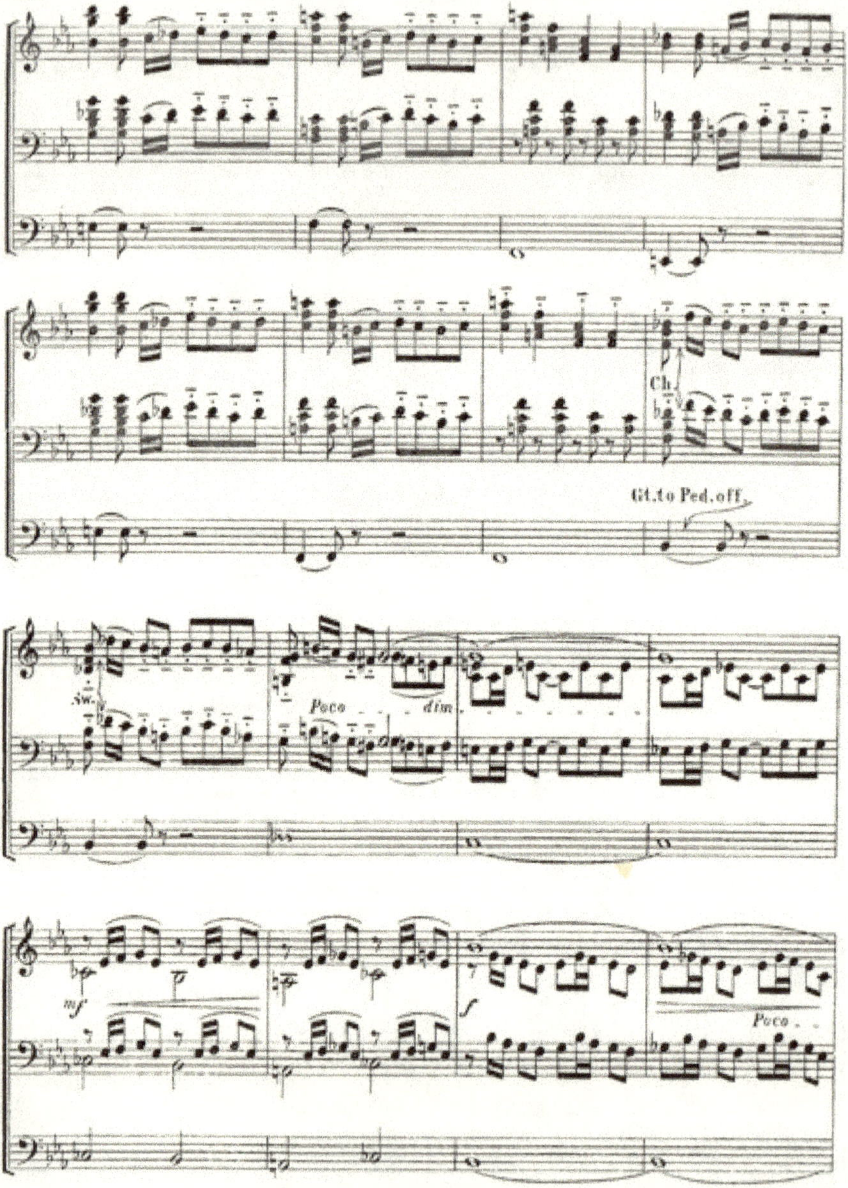
Ch.
Gt. to Ped. off
Sw.
Poco
dim.
mf
f
Poco . .

Tempo deciso.

Tempo come prima.

(Gradually reduce Sw. to 8 & 4 Ft. *mp*)

Roll.

Ch. *f*

Sw. Add Cornopean & Tremulant.

(Sw. to Ch. off.)

Gt.

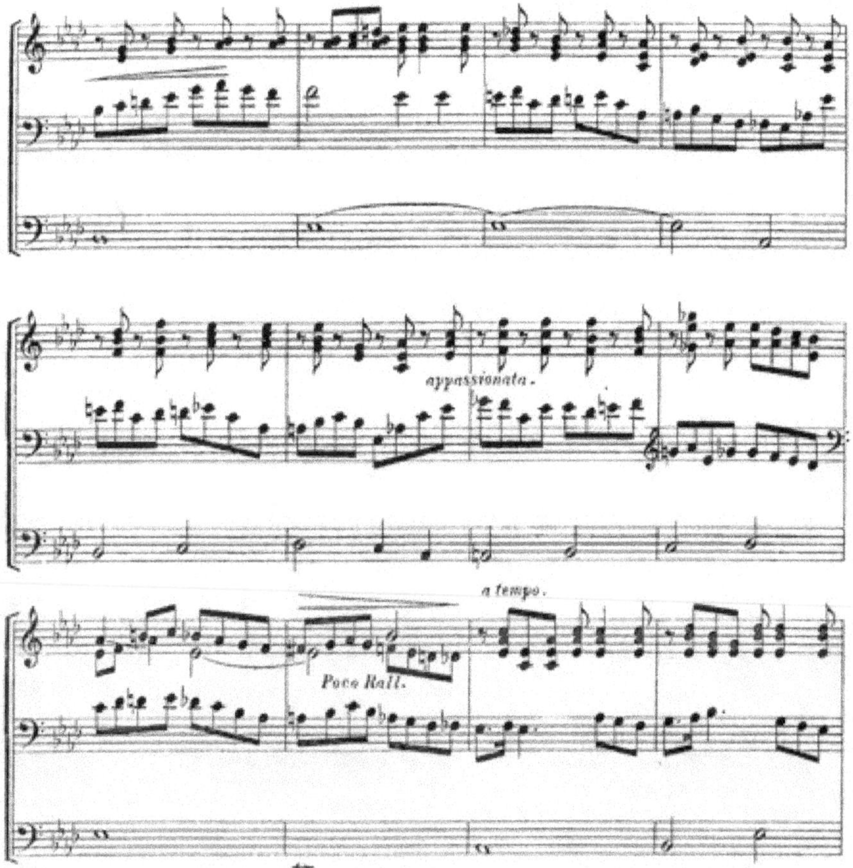
appassionata.
a tempo.
Poco Rall.

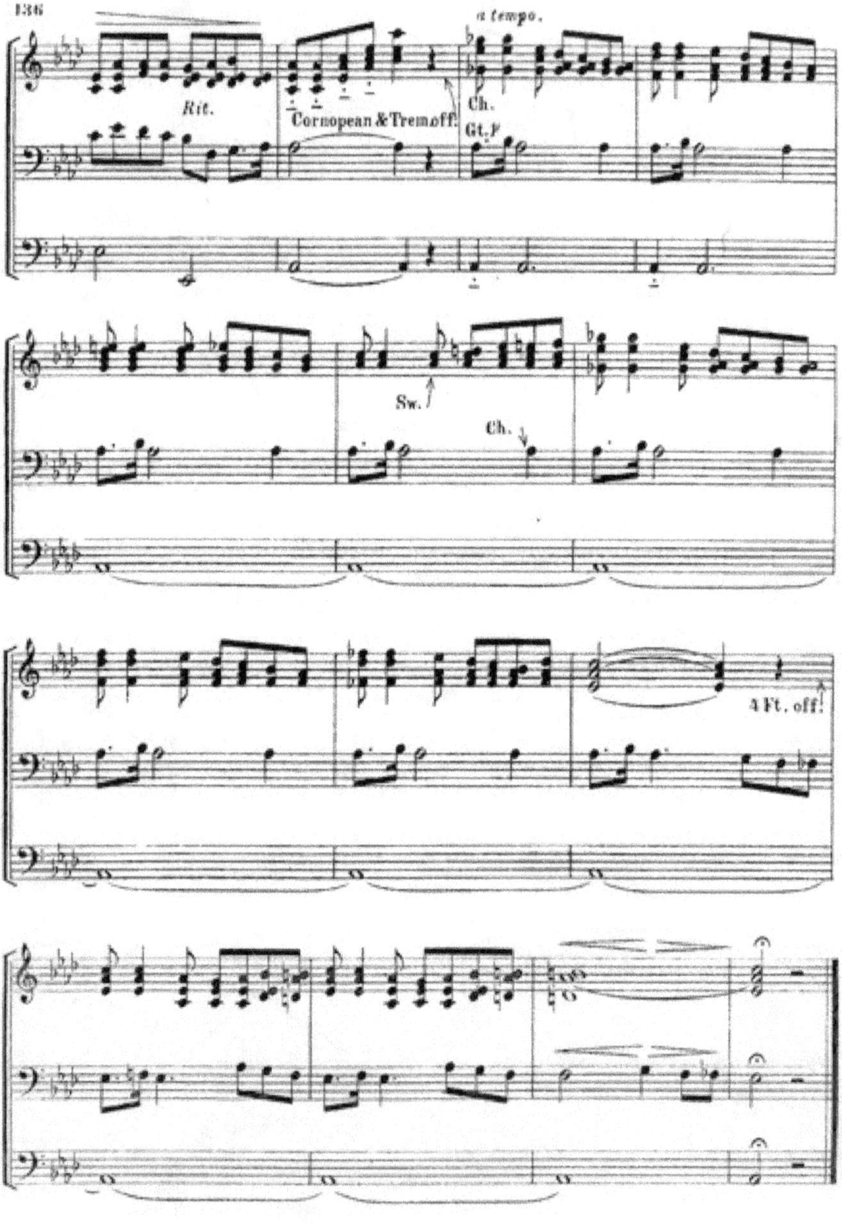
a tempo.
Rit.
Cornopean & Trem. off.
Ch.
Gt. P
Sw.
Ch.
4 Ft. off.

THE ORGANIST'S RETROSPECT.

(*Continued from page 128.*)

We used mostly the music of the old "Carmina Sacra" in the choir, and this crude instrument gave me a needed experience ; but the access to the pipe organ in my practising had excited a longing for tones in comparison with which the feeble sounds of the wheezy harmonium were but an aggravation.

In order to secure the regular attendance at church of a new family that had moved into the neighborhood, the minister invited the father, who played a little on the flute, to bring his instrument to church and accompany the harmonium. He owned a good flute, but did not blow it in tune, and I was obliged to tolerate an abomination which quite drove me distracted. However, the device of the minister secured the attendance of the new family, and illustrated what seems to be the especial use of either good or poor music in many American churches, an allurement to make the service more attractive, and to help enliven the dull order of ceremonies.

At the end of my fifteenth year, Mr. Rodman procured for me a situation in a large music store in Boston, at my earnest request. The instruments displayed in the show window had excited my fancy, which nothing would satisfy excepting contact with a larger musical world. It did not take long to learn that a music store is of all places one of the most unmusical. Music and merchandise belong to two distinct worlds of art and matter.

One or two of the clerks who were above me in my department were young men of immoral principles, whose presence was a continual torture to me. The proprietor was a stockholder in the large theatre; and this store was the headquarters for the sale of tickets for the performances, especially during the opera seasons, and for the old Music Hall concerts. All the noted actors and musicians assembled here for mutual intercourse, so that I had a near view of many celebrities. Much of my time was employed in acting as a messenger between the store, the theatre, and the Music Hall ; and from this connection I had a free pass to all performances in both places. But I had no inclination to avail myself of these opportunities, as I preferred to go out to my home in the country, where I could spend my limited time in practising ; for the store hours were long, and starting from home before six in the morning, I did not get back until nearly nine in the evening.

The owner of the store wished me to become fitted for a salesman at the front retail counter, and desired me to so familiarize myself with all the music which was then in vogue, that I might know the name of any piece which a customer should ask for by his humming or whistling the melody ; for the other clerks were not musical, and this was the only value that my musical culture could possibly have in this store.

My first duties each day were to get out the wholesale orders which came by mail, a labor which included the climbing of ladders and taking down large and heavy folios, which gave me plenty of exercise and dusty weariness, with many a fall. Being firm and unyielding in what I considered my own principles of integrity, I was constantly reviled by the other clerks, who placed every obstacle in the way of my work ; and they tried to bring obloquy on everything I did, so that the dealer might treat me with disfavor, and thus prevent my promotion.

My severe home discipline had taught me how to be silent, and I kept my own affairs to myself. But I was kept back from making any advancement ; and my wages were not increased to above two dollars a week all the time of my service, which was hardly sufficient to pay my carfare.

I had access to all the organ music which was kept in stock, both home and foreign publications. I was permitted to take this music home for inspection and study, and from a careful perusal I was enabled to make up a catalogue for a repertoire which should contain only compositions of merit ;

and this was the only musical advantage which my connection with this store afforded me.

There was then living in Boston an old man of nearly ninety years, bent with his age, who built small pipe organs in his house, using his parlors for the finished organs, and doing the work in the basement. As often as possible I would hurry to his place in my noon hour, and delight in playing the instruments over which he was enthusiastic. Many years before this time he had invented an instrument which he called the "Apollino," which produced the characteristic qualities of twenty-eight different instruments, in imitation of a large orchestra. In addition to its manuals and pedals, it also had a mechanism for performing musical arrangements automatically. It contained an imitation of the French horn and the bugle, with a mechanical embouchure, instead of using brass reeds ; and this was considered a remarkable invention. There were also drums and other accessories. This instrument was yet preserved, and was in playing order, after having been for many years on exhibition in the larger cities of the country.

(*To be continued.*)

CHICAGO AND WORLD'S FAIR NEWS.

(*Special Correspondence to* THE ORGAN.)

At present everything with us is Guilmant. This celebrated composer and organist arrived in Chicago Aug. 30, and at once took quarters at the Hotel Windemere, near the World's Fair, that he might be within easy access to Festival Hall and its organ. On the Atlantic Mr. Guilmant kept very closely to his berth, as to him such an expanse of water was as one great dose of ipecac. Mr. Guilmant was not long in Chicago before he went to the organ. In fact, he is very methodical, and loses very little time. With the exception of filling a few invitations, and one day at sight-seeing, Mr. Guilmant, while in Chicago, spent most of his time either writing or at the organ.

The first three recitals drew great audiences ; but owing to some mistake in advertising the hour, the fourth recital was not so largely attended.

The programmes were played in the order given in the last edition of THE ORGAN. Programme No. 3, which begins with the Salomé First Sonata, proved the most interesting. In this recital Mr. Guilmant had gained complete control of the instrument. His playing of the Marche Funèbre et Chant Séraphique, the Nuptial March, Caprice in Bflat, Fugue in D, Mendelssohn's First Sonata, Lemmens's Fanfare of Trumpets, and Bach's Toccata and Fugue in D-minor, was masterly and never to be forgotten.

Though we cannot rave over this master's technique, we are carried away by the wonderfully clean and neat treatment of all his numbers. The breadth and truly marvellous conception of whatever he undertakes are indeed wonderful.

In his improvisations we expected more dash than was given ; but a tone-poet, like a word-poet, is not always inspired. Surroundings have much to do with this, and Festival Hall, like the Paris Trocadéro, with confusion on the exterior and the tramp of feet of late comers on the interior, does not create in the artist the proper elements necessary for extemporaneous organ playing. Mr. Guilmant chose for themes, "Hail Columbia," "The Suwanee River," "Marseillaise Hymn," and "John Brown's Body."

In all his numbers Mr. Guilmant was *encored* and *re-encored*, and in some instances had to get off the organ bench twice, and even three times, before he was allowed to proceed.

On Sunday evening, Sept. 3, the announcement that Mr. Guilmant would play the closing voluntary for Mr. Eddy, packed the church, and many could not obtain standing-room. The evening was very warm, and the length of the service failed to make any one leave the church until Mr. Guilmant was about through. It was a grand sight, and one not often seen. The first number was extempore, followed by Prelude and Fugue in D-major, Bach; Andante in E, Guilmant; and ending with this composer's Marche Religieuse on Händel's theme, "Lift up your Heads." There were many in that audience who looked as if they would stay all night if Mr. Guilmant would only keep on playing.

Mr. Guilmant expressed a wish that Mr. Eddy would play for him, which he did on Saturday evening, Sept. 9, at Festival Hall. Mr. Eddy played Oscar Wermann's First Sonata, Dudley Buck's Variations on the "Star Spangled Banner," Spinney's Grand Processional March, Pilgrim's Chorus, Wagner, and Thiele's Theme and Variations in A-flat. Owing to a chorus rehearsal, no more numbers could be played. Mr. Guilmant was very enthusiastic in his applause after each number, and the pieces were all well played.

On Thursday, Sept. 7, at the request of Mr. Eddy, Mr. Guilmant was invited to try the Auditorium organ. After Mr. Guilmant got the position of the stops, and set and looked the combination pistons, which involves some time on an organ of one hundred and twenty-five stops, he began with his Grand Chœur in D, followed by Improvisation introducing the bells, Prayer in F, and Marche Religieuse.

Monday, August 21, Mr. Walter E. Hall of Pittsburgh, Pa., gave an organ recital in Festival Hall. This performer's thoughtful registration, coupled with agreeable smoothness and brilliancy of technique, went far toward making the recital an interesting one. His numbers included an attractive Manuet and Gavotte of his own composition, Frederick Archer's "Triumphal March" in E-flat, Flotow's "Martha" Overture, and, among other things, a dignified and tasteful performance of the Andante from Beethoven's Fifth Symphony.

The following day Mr. Hall gave his second recital, the programme being as follows:—

Festival March for Thanksgiving Day, W. E. Hall; Larghetto, Symphony No. 2, Beethoven; Overture, "Bluff King Hal," Stewart; Peer Gynt, E. Grieg; Air with Variations in A, Henry Smart; Festival March, Henry Smart.

The numbers of Mr. Hall's third and final recital were:— Coronation March, Meyerbeer; Andante from Symphony No. 1, Beethoven; Allegro (Eighth Concerto), and Allegro, "Cuckoo and Nightingale," Handel; Overture, "Merry Wives of Windsor," Nicolai; Bridal Song, McMaster; Allegretto, "The Hymn of Praise," Mendelssohn; Allegro in D, W. T. Best. Mr. Hall proved himself to be one of the best organists who has yet played in Festival Hall.

The recital following those given by Mr. Hall was given by Mr. A. S. Vogt, a Canadian organist, with the following programme:—

St. Anne's Fugue, Bach; Andante Grazioso, Smart; Sortie in D, Guilmant; Berceuse, Spinney; Allegretto Recitative, Finck; Romanza, Petrali; Vorspiel, "Lohengrin," Wagner-Sulze; Marche Militaire, Gounod-Archer.

Mr. Vogt showed study and ability, but lacked the snap and warmth needed in some of his numbers.

The following day at noon Mr. Henry Gordon Thunder of Philadelphia gave an exhibition of his power as a concert organist, giving the following programme:—

Fantasia and Fugue in G-minor, Bach; Introduction to third act, "Lohengrin," Fire Charm, "Die Walküre," Pilgrim's Chorus, "Tannhäuser," and Excerpt from third act, "Siegfried," by Wagner; Nuptial March, Guilmant; Allegretto in A, Tours; Offertoire in E-flat, Batiste; Nocturne in E-flat, Chopin; Schiller March, Meyerbeer.

Many agree that in the rendition of the above programme Mr. Thunder showed himself to be one of the best performers who has played on Festival Hall Organ.

The next recital in Festival Hall was given by the well-known Boston organist Mr. B. J. Lang, who played the following selections:—

Fantasie in G-major, Bach; Andante in C-major, Bach; Pastorale in F-major, Bach; Fugue on "B-A-C-H," Schumann; Overture, "Midsummer Night's Dream," Mendelssohn; Improvisation; Overture, "Egmont," Beethoven.

Owing to Mr. Lang's not familiarizing himself with this instrument, he made hard work for himself, and not until his improvisation was he like himself. It was a pleasure to us that Mr. Lang realized this, even after his recital, in saying that he had undertaken too big a task. Cheer up, Mr. Lang! It was Mr. Best who once said, "I have now been playing St. George's Hall organ five years, and have yet much to learn in the handling thereof." Even Mr. Guilmant, after giving four recitals and putting in many hours of practice on the same instrument, did not know until he was told that the organ possessed a grand crescendo pedal.

Mrs. Lizzie Bristliff, organist of the Leavitt Street Congregational Church of this city, has resigned her post to accept the position of teacher of music in Olivet College, Olivet, Mich. Mrs. Bristliff is a good performer; and her monthly Sunday evening organ recitals at the above church last winter always filled the church, her programmes being of a high order. This change may be so her a gain; to us it is a loss.

Miss Annie E. Tennent, a pupil of the above, gave the following well-selected programme on a two-manual Woodberry & Harris organ, in the Fourth Baptist Church of this city, Saturday afternoon, Sept. 2: Triumphal March, Buck; "Allegretto Grazioso," Tours; "Cavatina," Raff; Largo, Händel; "Air de Louis XIII.," Gyhs; "Offertoire in E-minor," Batiste; "Twilight Picture," Shelley; Postlude in F, Gade. Being at Mr. Guilmant's recital, we did not hear Miss Tennent's, but from hearing her play one or two numbers while practising, we judge she must have given her hearers a rare treat.

After a month's vacation Miss Helen Wheeler, organist of the Third Presbyterian Church, has returned to her organ. To lovers of the organ her presence at the keyboard is a pleasure. While many of our gentlemen organists doze and dream over some "squib" composition, Miss Wheeler treats her hearers to the chief works of Bach, Lemmens, Guilmant, etc., in a manner that solicits our highest praise. It is no wonder that in the Third Church, Chicago boasts of one of its best organists.

At Mr. Guilmant's recitals we were much pleased to meet Miss Helen Bain, a Kenosha, Wis., organist, and some time a pupil of Mr. Guilmant. Ere long she hopes to return to study with this same master. Miss Bain is a bright little woman, and her conversation on Mr. Guilmant and the organ is more than interesting.

Frederick Archer was billed to play Tema con Variazioni, Moszowski-Archer, and Overture "Guillaume Tell," Rossini, at Festival Hall at the Catholic Congress, Sept. 4; but Mackisne's tonic air and Mr. Archer's hayfever prevented his appearing. Mr. Harrison M. Wild substituted. We feel doubly sorry at Mr. Archer's not coming, as Mr. Guilmant expressed a wish to hear him.

Mr. Otto W. G. Pfefferkorn of Denver has been appointed organist of Plymouth Congregational Church, this city. Mr. Pfefferkorn is an excellent musician, and will be quite an acquisition to Chicago.

Mr. Davis, of Farrand & Votey Co., though still confined to his bed, is improving, and many express the hope of seeing him around again ere long with his old-time push and vigor.

VOX HUMANA.

ALEXANDRE GUILMANT IN BOSTON.

This noted French organist, who is creating a profound sensation in so many of our American cities, gave two recitals in the New Old South Church, Boston, Sept. 25 and 26, with the following programmes:—

PROGRAMME OF SEPTEMBER 25.

Toccata in F . . . . J. S. Bach.
Offertory in D-flat, Opus 8 . . . . . . Salomé.
Sonata Pontificale . . . . Lemmens.
a. Invocation in B-flat }
b. Finale in E-flat } . . . . . Alex. Guilmant.
c. "Funeral March and Hymn of Seraphs" }
Canon in B-minor . . . . Schumann.
Pastorale in E . . . . de la Tombelle.
Toccata in G . . . . Dubois.
Improvisation on a Theme to be given.
March for a Church Festival . . . . . Best.

PROGRAMME OF SEPTEMBER 26.

First Sonata . . . . Alex. Guilmant.
Andantino in D-flat . . . . Chauvet.
Gavotte in F-major . . . . Padre Martini.

(Transcriptions by Alex. Guilmant.)

Prelude and Fugue in A-minor . . . . . J. S. Bach.
a. Caprice in B-flat }
b. Elevation in A-flat } . . . . Alex. Guilmant.
c. Nuptial March }
First Sonata . . . . Mendelssohn.
Improvisation on a Theme to be given.
Finale in D-major . . . . Lemmens.

We doubt if Mons. Guilmant will create a greater furor in any city in this country than he has here in Boston. Five thousand people endeavored to secure the twenty-two hundred tickets which were issued, and the capacity of this beautiful church was the only thing which controlled the number of tickets.

The audience at both recitals contained many of the prominent musicians of this city and surrounding cities, while vocalists and violinists vied with organists in manifesting their appreciation.

Mons. Guilmant has raised organ playing to a point of virtuosity equal to the work of the celebrated pianists, and with him there is no chance to grumble at the "impossibilities of the organ." His playing of the above programmes was magnificent. In the two compositions of J. S. Bach there were excellent examples of his unique method of phrasing a subject or fragment, no matter in which voice it occurs, so that it always stands out prominently. On the piano this is much easier, as a little additional force will give prominence to the subject, but with the organ it is a different and difficult matter.

Mendelssohn's Second Sonata took the audience by storm, the slow movements being beautifully registered, and the last movement being played with a rapidity which would be ruinous with most organists.

Mons. Guilmant seemed to be a trifle nervous in the first movement of his own sonata; but more exquisite treatment of the pastorale we have never heard. The last movement was taken at a remarkable *tempo*, and was a revelation to the audience.

Some very dainty work was done in Salomé's Offertoire, Tombelle's Pastorale, and the Chauvet Andantino. The Toccata of Dubois roused the audience to a pitch of excitement which did not subside till Mons. Guilmant had bowed his acknowledgment three times. Such lightning staccato, and at the same time perfect phrasing and cleanness, we have never heard.

Schumann's Canon and the Caprice in B-flat were played very beautifully, as was the Nuptial March, while Martini's Gavotte, played mostly on the reeds, was very graceful.

Mons. Guilmant's improvising is even more wonderful than his staccato work. The subjects selected for him were "Jerusalem the Golden" and "See, the Conquering Hero Comes." To improvise a double fugue seems to require no effort on his part, while the audience listen in wonder.

Guilmant's advent in this country is proving to sceptics that the organ is a concert instrument, and that organ recitals will draw as large and enthusiastic audiences as the best orchestras; but comparisons must not be made between poor organ playing and good orchestral work.

A word should be said about the organ used on this occasion. Built seventeen years ago by Mr. Geo. S. Hutchings, it has always been considered one of our best instruments. With all respect to the late Eugene Thayer, under whose guidance it was constructed, we must protest against the relative position of the manuals, the great being the lower manual, and the choir the upper. This arrangement proved more annoying to Mons. Guilmant than any peculiarity with which he has met this side of the water, and we cannot conceive of a reason for the arrangement.

The instrument has fifty-five speaking stops and twelve composition pedals. The voicing of the organ is exceptionally fine, albeit the fact that the organ has not been retuned since it was constructed till just before these concerts was not in its favor. The tone of the Diapasons is solid, the flutes are all very good, and the Clarinet, Vox Humana, and Physharmonica are beautiful. The Clarinet is a free reed (tuned with a sliding wire), and has wooden pipes. The effect of the full organ is solid and impressive. We have never heard a larger number of effective combinations produced on any one organ than Mons. Guilmant showed us with this organ.

An informal reception was given to Mons. Guilmant by the Harvard Musical Association after the second concert; and before the concert he paid a visit to the New England Conservatory, playing for the students in Sleeper Hall.

As we go to press, Mons. Guilmant is probably displaying his talents to an audience in Smith College in Northampton, Mass.

MIXTURES.

(FOUR RANKS.)

It is announced that Mons. Alphonse Mailly will make a concert tour the coming season, visiting London, Paris, Amsterdam, and several German cities.

We have been informed that Mr. Charles Harris has withdrawn from the firm of Woodberry & Harris, organ builders, Boston.

The Broad Street Conservatory of Music has just issued an illustrated catalogue showing the building, several class-rooms, and some of the instructors. The organ department is in the hands of the Director, Mr. Gilbert E. Combs, and Mr. John W. Pommer, Jr.

The Carl Barckhoff Organ Co. are building two four-manual organs and several small organs. One of the former is for Brooklyn (see New Organs, this issue), and the other is for Philadelphia.

Mr. Arthur Rayns and gave an organ recital at the Unitarian Church, Wilton, N.H., the last week in August, performing March, "Queen of Sheba," Gounod; Overture, "Semiramide," Rossini; Offertoire, Wely; March from "Tannhäuser," Wagner; Overture to "William Tell," Rossini; First Organ Sonata, Thayer.

The Lancashire-Marshall Organ Co. have just erected a three-manual organ in the Congregational Church, Elgin, Ill., and are building organs for the M. E. Church of Waukesha, Wis.; Presbyterian Church, Portage, Wis.; M. E. Church, Bluffton, Ind.; and Lutheran Church, Loganville, Wis. The dull times do not seem to have affected the business of this firm.

Mr. Harry Golder gave an organ recital in the Presbyterian Church, Muncy, Pa., Sept. 4, which was pronounced a "grand success" by the local press. Appended is the programme: Pilgrim's Chorus, Wagner; Kyrie and Gloria, from Fourth Mass, Gänsel; Funeral March, Chopin; Impromptu, Leschetizky; Intro. and Gavotte, Allen; Swedish Wedding March, Söderman; Andante in F, Wely.

Mrs. A. W. Armstrong, assisted by Miss Carrie L. Shepley, gave an organ recital in the Baptist Church, W. Acton, Mass., Aug. 24, with the following programme: Jubilee, Overture, Weber; Variations on Scotch Air, Buck; Air de Louis XIII., Ghys; Pastorale, MacMaster; Marche Cortège, Gounod. Mme. Sophie Cortese and Mr. Edgar H. Hall sang several songs.

Mr. W. H. Donley inaugurated a new Möhler organ in the First Presbyterian Church, Indianapolis, Ind., Aug. 25, with the following programme: Overture, "Merry Wives of Windsor," Nicolai; Andante con Moto (Fifth Symphony), Beethoven; Extase, Lefébure-Wély; La Prayer and Cradle Song, Guilmant; Marche Cortège, Gounod; L'Invitation, Op. 65, Weber; Adagio (Seventh Symphony), Haydn; Allegro Moderato, Wely; Variations on an American Air, Flagler; Vorspiel, "Lohengrin," Wagner. Local papers speak well of the recital.

NEW ORGAN MUSIC.

Evening Song	M. E. Bossi
Idyl	" "
Allegretto	" "
Elegy in D Minor	Thomas
Elegy in F Minor	" "
Sonata No. 2	H. Fährmann
Bridal March (Organ and Orchestra)	C. Antony
Minuet	Hamilton Clarke
Six Pieces	Alfred Rotherl

The Sunday organ recitals in the People's Palace, London, were to be resumed Sept. 3, with afternoon and evening recitals to be given by Mr. B. Jackson.

The organ in Albert Palace, London, has been sold at auction for $5,125. This instrument was originally built by Messrs. Bryceson Bros., from the design of Mr. W. T. Best, for "The Hall," a private residence in the south-western part of the city, where Mr. Best and Mons. Guilmant, as well as other organists, were frequently invited to give performances. Financial difficulties caused the sale of the instrument, and it was erected in the Palace. It has now been sold a second time, Mr. Charles Henry Walter being the purchaser. The organ stood about 50 feet high, was 30 feet wide, about 30 feet deep, and cost in the neighborhood of $40,000. An echo organ was located at the other end of the hall.

Organ recital at the Queensland National Association Exhibition, July 24, by Mrs. Willmore; Overture to "Stradella," Flotow; Torine Song, Sonati; Serenade, Jenssen; Offertoire in D, Batiste; Toccata (Fifth Symphony), Widor; Andantino, Chauvet; Transcription, "Sing, Sweet One," Gounod; Postlude in E-flat, Wely.

Mr. Seymour Becker also gave the following programme July 31: Finale of Military Festival Te Deum, Grand Dances and Water Music from "Incidental Music to Shakespeare's Henry VIII," "The Lost Chord," and Fantasia, "The Gondoliers," all by Arthur Sullivan; Offertoire in C-Minor, Batiste; Prayer and Melody, Guilmant; Selection from "Faust," Gounod.

Mr. Hatley G. Fuller, organist of the Brighton Unitarian Church, died Sept. 4.

It is again necessary to remind our readers that they should send in programmes and specifications which they wish mentioned in THE ORGAN earlier. We cannot undertake to "notice" recitals given five or six months ago.

The regular weekly organ recitals at the Bow & Bromley Institute, London, were to be resumed Sept. 30. These concerts have been given for about fifteen years.

Verily there is, after all the fuss to the contrary, some attention in organ recitals. Note the crowds who have listened to the Guilmant recitals. Would the piano ever have been a popular concert instrument with us, if the world's greatest pianists had never given concerts in our cities?

Several changes and additions have been made in the schedule of Mons. Guilmant's concerts in this country. The demand for this artist has far exceeded the expectations, and the date of his return to Paris has been postponed to Oct. 21. Appended is a list of the concerts already given and to be given: Aug. 31, Sept. 1, 2, and 4; World's Fair; Sept. 12 (two concerts), St. Louis; Sept. 25, Detroit; Sept. 18, Hamilton; Sept. 19 and 20, Toronto; Sept. 21 and 22, Montreal; Sept. 23, Quebec; Sept. 25 and 26, Boston; Sept. 27, Northampton; Sept. 28, Utica; Sept. 29, Syracuse; Oct. 1, Oswego; Oct. 2, Rochester; Oct. 3, Buffalo; Oct. 4, Cleveland; Oct. 5, Delaware, O.; Oct. 6, Oberlin, O.; Oct. 7, Cleveland; Oct. 9, Pittsburgh; Oct. 11, Newark (with a reception Oct. 12); Oct. 13 (two concerts), New York; Oct. 16, Philadelphia; Oct. 17, New York; Oct. 18, Brooklyn. The first concert in New York will be at the Old South Church (Madison Avenue and 38th Street) in the afternoon, followed by another in the First Presbyterian Church (Fifth Avenue and 12th Street) in the evening. The third concert (Oct. 17) will be at St. Joseph's Church. The Brooklyn concert will be given in the N. Y. Avenue M. E. Church.

Mons. Guilmant performed in the Cathedral, Montreal, the 21st and 22d of September, before an audience of over five thousand, giving the same programmes as in Boston.

Organ recital at Montpelier, Vt., September 20, by Mr. Henry M. Dunham: Sonata No. 1, Mendelssohn; In Memoriam, Dunham; Cantilène Nuptiale and Grand Chœur, Dubois; Variations in C, Rinck; Prayer and Castle Song, Guilmant; Sonata in A-minor (first movement), Whiting; Theme Duo for Piano and Organ, Widor. Mr. D. S. Hampel played the piano parts.

Mons. Alexandre Guilmant will be in New York City about the middle of October. He gives a recital in the Old South Church on the afternoon of Oct. 13, under the direction of Mr. Gerrit Smith, and at the First Presbyterian Church in the evening of the same day, under the direction of Mr. Wm. C. Carl. On October 10 the Manuscript Society will render him

a reception at the Fifth Avenue Hotel, and on the 12th Miss Charlotte Walker and Mr. Wm. C. Carl, former pupils of Mons. Guilmant, will tender him another reception.

Organ Recital in First Presb. Church, Hazelton, Pa., Sept. 26, by Mr. Edward E. Howe. Programme: March from "Aida," Verdi; Aria from "Rinaldo," Handel; Hymn of Nuns, Wely; Cradle Song, Heller; First Movement of the "Unfinished Symphony," Schubert; Requests; Overture to "Zampa," Hérold.

Programmes of Mr. W. T. Best's regular organ recitals in St. George's Hall, Liverpool: Sept. 2: Allegro Symphonique, Salomé; Andante from Concerto in G-minor, Mendelssohn; Fugue in C, Best; Pastorale in G-minor, Guilmant; Fantasia, "The Storm," Lemmens; Overture, "Prociosa," Weber. Sept. 9: Sorabande (Cinq-Mars), Gounod; Andante, Smart; Sonata No. 3, Mendelssohn; Scherzo Symphonique, Guilmant; Selection from "Dinorah," Meyerbeer. Sept. 16: "Concertstück," Tople; Prelude in D-flat, Chopin; Choral March, Rossini; Toccata and Fugue in D-minor, Bach; Allegretto Cantabile, Salomé; Selection from the Water Music, Handel.

The firm of John W. Steere & Sons, pipe organ builders, Springfield, Mass., has been dissolved by the retirement of John S. Steere, and has been reorganized as John W. Steere & Son. The dissolution is due to family disagreements, brought about by the 1892 business in 1887. John S. Steere, who goes out, associates himself with George W. Turner, who was formerly a member of the original Steere & Turner firm, and the new house will assume that title. Mr. Turner started the pipe organ business with John W. Steere in Westfield in 1867, and in 1879 the business was removed to Springfield. — *Musical Courier.*

QUESTIONS AND ANSWERS.

E. C. H. A. Will you tell me through your "Questions and Answers" where I can find the Andantino in D-flat of Chauvet? I have sent to several publishers, and they know nothing of the piece.

ANS. Transcribed by Alex. Guilmant, and published by Hartmann, Paris.

J. H. R. If a student has played the third, fourth, and fifth books of Rinck fairly well, would you advise the immediate use of Mendelssohn's Sonatas?

ANS. We think it advisable to use Lemmen's Organ School, Part 2, before Mendelssohn's Sonatas.

CORRESPONDENCE.

A WORK ON ORGAN BUILDING.

BRISBANE, AUSTRALIA, *Aug. 17, 1893.*

To the Editor of THE ORGAN:

Do you not think it is about time that a modern treatise upon the organ should be issued, in view of the wonderful strides organ building has made?

A handbook of the organ was announced to be published by Sampson Low of London as far back as 1888, Mr. G. A. Audsley being the author, and judging from the prospectus, would have treated the subject exhaustively. The only book published of late years is "L'orgue ancien et moderne, par l'abbe van Counenbergh," J. van In & Co., Lierre, Belgium, which is unfortunately in French. It contains much valuable information concerning modern organists, or a short bibliography of the organ, while a chapter is devoted to American organ building, English work receiving scant notice; but in a recent music paper in London, reference was made to "Dr. Hopkins' forthcoming book," so let us hope for the best.

If a book were to be put forth, even in America, it would be well received without a doubt, the plan of the work to consist of a history of the organ from the *beginning of the present century,* tracing the various developments, and giving due prominence to such matters as pneumatic action, electric action, combination pistons (how many organists or students understand their principle, or could explain their working? yet they are dismissed in Stainer's and Archer's books with a few words), English, American, and Continental modern practice in organ building, with a biographical dictionary of modern organists. Some of the best books extant upon the history and construction of the piano have issued from America, why not one for the "King of Instruments"?

Trusting that some of your many readers will take this matter up,

I am, yours faithfully,

E. S. JONES.

[Such a work as the above has been partially prepared by a practical builder, and we are considering the advisability of publishing it, hesitating in view of demand for such a work being doubtful.—ED.]

CIPHERINGS.

AN organist who was presented with a handsome gold scarf-pin instead of cash for performing at a church wedding in April, has not yet been able to decide whether he is flattered or angry. The novelty of the presentation is said to have taken his breath away for at least a couple of hours.—*Ex.*

"WHAT's the subscription price of your new paper?"
"Two dollars a year."
"Is it intended for any particular class of readers?"
"Yes; it's for those who have two dollars."—*Ex.*

EXTRACT from "A New Dictionary of Music by Diogenes":—

Gamba is a stop in an organ, derived (*lucus a non lucendo*) from "gamba," Italian for leg, because it is impossible to play legato (leg or toe) passages upon it: it is not quick of speech, being often "slow, but not sure." The substitution in old organs of a German gamba for a good old English open diapason, opens the door to the remark that it must be one of the many gambols of the modern organ builder. The gamba sounds, when it does sound, somewhat like a certain kind of horn; hence a witty and learned organist (not Harris of Brookwall) observed, "*Nihil tetigit quod non (h) ornavit;*" that is, he never touched it because it never spoke like a horn, and we think he was right. "Viol di gamba" may be rudely translated "a vile dear gamba," which as put into some of the old organs it has certainly proved. Abel was a celebrated performer on the viol da gamba, the instrument from which the stop has taken its name; but time has put a stop to poor Abel, who was in truth a very able executant on the nasal-toned and now obsolete member of the viol tribe. See "Burn his History," also "Buzz-bee on Music."—*Musical Standard.*

NEW ORGANS.

FIRST CONGREGATIONAL CHURCH, PROVIDENCE, R.I.

(*New organ built by Mr. George S. Hutchings.*)

GREAT ORGAN.		SWELL ORGAN.	
Open Diapason	16 Ft.	Bourdon (Treble and Bass)	16 Ft.
Open Diapason	8 "	Open Diapason	8 "
English Open Diapason	8 "	Salicional	8 "
Viola di Gamba	8 "	Æoline	8 "
Doppel Flöte	8 "	Stopped Diapason	8 "
Flûte d'Amour	4 "	Wald Flute	4 "
Octave	4 "	Violina	4 "
Twelfth	2⅔ "	Octave	4 "
Fifteenth	2 "	Flautino	2 "
Mixture	IV. Rks.	Dolce Cornet	IV Rks.
Trumpet	8 Ft.	Cornopean	8 Ft.
		Oboe	8 "
PEDAL ORGAN.		Vox Humana	8 "
Open Diapason	16 Ft.		
Bourdon	16 "	CHOIR ORGAN.	
Violoncello	8 "	Open Diapason	8 Ft.
		Dulciana	8 "
PEDAL MOVEMENTS.		Melodia (Stopped Bass)	8 "
F. MF., and P. Comb. Great Organ.		St. Diapason	8 "
F. MF., and P. Comb. Swell Organ.		Celestina	4 "
F. and P. Comb. Choir Organ.		Flute	4 "
Gt. to Ped. (reversible).		Piccolo	2 "
Tremolo, Swell.		Clarinet	8 "
The usual couplers.			

CHURCH OF ST. JOHN THE BAPTIST, BROOKLYN.

(*New organ built by the Carl Barckhoff Organ Co.*)

GREAT ORGAN.		SWELL ORGAN.	
Open Diapason	16 Ft.	Bourdon	16 Ft.
Open Diapason	8 "	Open Diapason	8 "
Viola di Gamba	8 "	Violin Diapason	8 "
Germshorn	8 "	Stopped Diapason	8 "
Doppel Flöte	8 "	Salicional	8 "
Quint	5⅓ "	Quintadena	8 "
Octave	4 "	Principal	4 "
Hohl Flöte	4 "	Harmonic Flute	4 "
Twelfth	2⅔ "	Flageolet	2 "
Fifteenth	2 "	Cornet	III. Rks.
Mixture	IV. Rks.	Fagotto	16 Ft.
Cymbal	III. "	Cornopean	8 "
Harmonic Trumpet	8 Ft.	Oboe	8 "
		Vox Humana	8 "

CHOIR ORGAN.		PEDAL ORGAN.	
(*In a Swell Box.*)		Sub Bass	32 Ft.
Geigen	16 Ft.	Resultant	32 "
Dulciana d'Amour	8 "	Grand Open Diapason	16 "
Dulciana	8 "	Violon	16 "
Melodia	8 "	Bourdon	16 "
Violina	4 "	Violoncello	8 "
Flûte d'Amour	4 "	Flute	8 "
Piccolo Harmonique	2 "	Trombone	16 "
Clarinet	8 "		

SOLO ORGAN.	
Melodia	16 Ft.
Stentorphone	8 "
Concert Flute	8 "
Viola Pomposa	8 "
Hohl Flöte	8 "
Tuba Major	16 "
Tuba Mirabilis	8 "

COUPLERS (reversible piston knobs).
Super-Octave Sw. to Gt.
Sub-Octave Ch. to Gt.
Octave Pedal Coupler.
Octave Great Coupler.
In addition to the eight usual couplers, all of which are tubular pneumatic.

COMBINATION PISTON KNOBS.
Six for Great.
Six for Swell.
Six for Choir.
Six for Solo.

Six double acting Combination Pedals. Twelve additional pipes to all the pedal stops to complete the octave coupler, which is tubular-pneumatic. In operating, the octave key does not move, but the coupler opens the valve direct, thus duplicating the stops of the pedal organ. Bellows operated by two Electric Motors.

FIRST PRESBYTERIAN CHURCH, INDIANAPOLIS, IND.

(*New organ built by Mr. M. P. Möller.*)

GREAT ORGAN.		SWELL ORGAN.	
Open Diapason	8 Ft.	Violin Diapason	8 Ft.
Dulciana	8 "	St. Diapason	8 "
Doppel Flöte	8 "	Æoline	8 "
Flûte d'Amour	4 "	Flauto Traverso	4 "
Principal	4 "	Violina	4 "
Twelfth	2⅔ "	Flautino	2 "
Fifteenth	2 "	Oboe and Bassoon	8 "
PEDAL ORGAN.		PEDAL MOVEMENTS.	
Bourdon	16 Ft.	F. and P. Comb. Great.	
Lieblich Gedeckt	16 "	F. and P. Comb. Swell.	
The usual couplers.		Water Motor.	

GRACE CHURCH, SANDUSKY, OHIO.

(*New organ built by Messrs. Johnson & Son, Westfield, Mass.*)

Compass of Manuals, 61 keys; of Pedals, 30 keys.

GREAT ORGAN.		SWELL ORGAN.	
Open Diapason	8 Ft.	Bourdon (Treble and Bass)	16 Ft.
Viola da Gamba	8 "	Open Diapason	8 "
Doppel Flöte	8 "	Salicional	8 "
Octave	4 "	Æoline	8 "
Twelfth	2⅔ "	Stopped Diapason	8 "
Super Octave	2 "	Quintadena	8 "
Trumpet	8 "	Flute Harmonique	4 "
CHOIR ORGAN.		Violin	4 "
Geigen Principal	8 Ft.	Flautino	2 "
Dulciana	8 "	Dolce Cornet	III. Rks.
Melodia	8 "	Oboe and Bassoon	8 Ft.
Flûte d'Amour	4 "		
Piccolo	2 "		
Clarinet and Fagotto	8 "		
PEDAL ORGAN.		4 Combination Pedals.	
Open Diapason	16 Ft.	Gt. to Ped. (Reversible.)	
Bourdon	16 "	Reversed keyboards.	
Violoncello	8 "	Relief pallets in windchests.	
		The usual Couplers.	

VOL. II. No. 8. DECEMBER, 1893. WHOLE NO. 20.

BACH

YEARLY SUBSCRIPTION $2.00. SINGLE COPIES 25 CTS.

THE ORGAN

DEVOTED TO

A MONTHLY JOURNAL

THE KING OF INSTRUMENTS

RHEINBERGER

GUILMANT

FRESCOBALDI

BUXTEHUDE

MERKEL

BEST

EVERETT · E · TRUETTE ·
EDITOR & PUBLISHER
149 A. TREMONT ST. BOSTON.

HANDEL

The New England Conservatory of Music.

CARL FAELTEN, DIRECTOR.

The Organ Department

offers unsurpassed facilities for acquiring a thorough and practical education in the art of Organ Playing. The course of study, which may be pursued either in class or by private instruction, is very complete and comprehensive. The early grades embrace work in Pedal Obligato Playing, Hymn Tunes, and Chorales, with Interludes and Modulations. In the medium grades are studied Organ works of polyphonic character, Anthems and Improvisations, and by the more advanced students the works of all the great writers for the Organ, together with the study of Masses, Oratorios, etc.

The Department is provided with fourteen Pedal Organs for practice, several of which possess three manuals each.

Those students who have acquired sufficient ability are aided in securing Church positions by the *Conservatory Bureau*. A large number of students have already been placed in lucrative positions by the Bureau.

TUITION: CLASSES OF FOUR, TERM OF TEN WEEKS, $20.00.

BOARD OF INSTRUCTION.
- GEORGE E. WHITING.
- HENRY M. DUNHAM.
- ALLEN W. SWAN.

- Organ Practice, 10 cents per hour and upwards.
- Pupils may enter at any time.
- School Year from Sept. 7, '93 to June 21, '94.

Address, FRANK W. HALE, General Manager, Franklin Square, Boston, Mass.

THE ORGAN.

VOL. II.   BOSTON, DECEMBER, 1893.   No. 8.

THE ORGAN.

BOSTON, DECEMBER, 1893.

Published the first of every month. Subscription price $1.00 per year (European countries 10s. 5d.), payable in advance. Single copies, 25 cents.

Subscribers will please state with which number they wish their subscription to begin.

Remittances should be made by registered letter, post-office order, or by check payable to Everett E. Truette.

Correspondence, to secure notice, must in all cases be accompanied by the name and address of the writer, not for publication, but as a guarantee of good faith.

Advertising rates sent on application.

Address all communications,
THE ORGAN, 149 A Tremont Street, Boston, Mass.

Single copies of THE ORGAN can be procured of

NOVELLO, EWER, & CO.		New York.
G. SCHIRMER		New York.
OLIVER DITSON CO.		Boston.
L. H. ROSS & CO.		Boston.
N. E. CONSERVATORY		Boston.
H. B. STEVENS CO.		Boston.
LYON & HEALY		Chicago.
THEODORE PRESSER		Philadelphia.
WM. H. BONER & CO.		Philadelphia.
TAYLOR'S MUSIC HOUSE		Springfield, Mass.
GALLUP & METZGER		Hartford, Conn.
RICHAULT & CO.		Paris.

CONTENTS:

M. ALEX. GUILMANT is again at his own organ bench. His trip across the pond was extremely pleasant, and this time he was free from *mal de mer*.

WE have received from Mr. Samuel Pierce of Reading a set of sixteen specimen organ pipes. Each pipe belongs to the key "Middle C," and the stops represented are Open Diapason, Gamba (two specimens), Melodia, Doppel Flöte, Dulciana, Quintadena, Rohr Flöte, Gemshorn, Flauto Traverso, Oboe, Trumpet, Clarinet, Fagotto, and Vox Humana. The pipes are excellent examples of the superior workmanship of this pipe-maker, whose work is distributed all over this country and in many other countries.

THE following is worth recording. Messrs. X & Co. advertise in THE ORGAN. An agent for a certain New York paper — a useful paper, which is doing its share of good work — called on Messrs. X & Co., a few weeks ago, to solicit an ad. for the New York periodical. Mr. X. declined to advertise, not because he did not appreciate the value of said periodical, but simply because he did not care to place any more funds on the advertising account. The agent was invincible, and Mr. X was out of patience. Said the agent: "You advertise in THE ORGAN?"

Mr. X. "Yes."

AGENT. "That paper is no good. Its circulation is less than three hundred, and your ad. will not benefit you a particle."

Mr. X. *(who had other business awaiting him)*. "Maybe you are right, but see here! it is raining like thunder, and if you want to borrow an umbrella I will lend you one, but I'll be hanged if I will advertise in your paper. Good-morning."

THE HOPE-JONES SYSTEM OF ELECTRICAL ORGAN CONTROL.

IV.

IN our last article we promised our readers some particulars relating to the "Console" used by Mr. Hope-Jones for controlling his Electric Organ; and in so doing we would refer to the large three-manual organ in the East Parish Church, Scotland, which was some time since rebuilt by the Hope-Jones Electric Organ Company Limited of Birkenhead, England. The pipework in this instrument is very old; but the tone has been so greatly improved by the additional flush and attack of the wind given by the electric action, that it has been mistaken for a new organ.

The console is movable, and is connected with the organ by some seventy feet of flexible cable. This console was the first fitted by Mr. Hope-Jones's Company with "second touch" on both manuals and pedals. The object of this second touch is to give to the organ keys and pedals, as far as possible, the individual expressiveness of the pianoforte. Under ordinary circumstances the key falls about a quarter of an inch, and comes to rest on a felt cushion in the usual manner, sounding the notes of whatever stops are drawn. If, however, it be pressed more firmly, a spring underneath suddenly gives way, and it drops another sixteenth of an inch. This brings into action the pipes belonging to any other stops that may be drawn on the second touch, while those on the first touch still continue to speak. The method by which the stops or couplers are drawn on the second touch is as follows: certain of the stops and couplers are provided with a double movement; that is to say, they will, on being touched, spring either half on or full on. If requiring the stop on the ordinary touch, the organist will press the key in the usual way, when it will spring full on. If, however, he wants the stop on the second touch only, he presses more gently, thus throwing the stopkey but half-way on. In reference to the "double touch" as fitted to this instrument, the organist of the East Parish Church, Perth (Dan Wylie, Esq., of the firm of Paterson, Son & Company, Princess Street, Perth), writing on the 12th of July, says.—

"The double touch, I firmly believe, will have the effect of immensely extending and developing organ playing in such a way as to make it appeal far more to general music lovers than it has ever done hitherto."

Dr. A. L. Peace, the organist of Glasgow Cathedral, a well-known authority on organ mechanism, after testing the working of this console, wrote to Mr. Hope-Jones on the 15th of August as follows :—

"The repetition of the touch was equal to that of a grand pianoforte. The potentialities of your electric system appear

to be almost endless, and its application to organ building must not only effect a complete revolution in its construction (doing away with all its old cumbrous mechanism), but must also inevitably lead to a revolution in organ playing."

The stop-keys, a full-sized illustration of which will be given in a later article, consist in this particular console of ivory domino-shaped tablets one and three-fourths inches long by three-fourths wide. These are peculiarly formed to accommodate the finger, and are pivoted in the centre in such a manner that they may readily be thrown backward or forward, so as to bring the stops on or off, and to show the organist which position the slider occupies. Small colored buttons are placed on the name tablet, just above the stop-keys. These are variously colored, to denote the class of tone, — the flue stops white, reed stops red, and couplers black. A light touch of the finger suffices to make the stop-keys spring on or off. We may mention that these stop-keys, and also each row of manual keys, are separately hinged, and can consequently be easily lifted, their action being in no way affected by their position. The pedal board is arranged simply to slide into place, and is not fastened in any way. By this arrangement all the contacts on the console are readily accessible.

In the centre is placed a blank vulcanite stop-key known as the "stop-switch." The office of this switch is to cut the electric current off, or switch it on to the stop-keys. The stop-switch rests nominally in its open position, and need never be used. If, however, an organist, on commencing to play, having arranged the stops for his first movement, chooses to close the stop-switch, he may, either beforehand or whilst playing, after the position of the stop and coupler keys without affecting the combinations sounding on the various organs. Directly he touches his stop-switch again, either

by foot or by hand, the whole of the organ is instantly changed, and the new arrangement of stops and couplers brought into force. The stop-switch can be thrown on by a pedal.

This console, though not possessing all the latest developments of the Hope-Jones system, is fitted with a "Sforzando Pedal," which upon depression instantly throws on the whole of the stops and couplers. These remain on so long as the pedal is held down, but go off the moment it is liberated. This device also has a double touch, so that when the pedal is lightly depressed, it comes to rest on a strong spring, in which position only a certain number of the stops and couplers are brought into play. On pressing harder, the spring gives way, and the full organ is instantly obtained. The response of the stops is so instantaneous that the full organ can be thrown on and off several times in a second; in fact, more quickly than the foot can be moved.

This console is fitted with the usual composition pedals and combination pistons (the latter for the control of the pedal stops). These have some special features peculiar to the Hope-Jones system. The combination of stops affected by each composition pedal are arranged behind the stop-keys, so that if the organist desires he may easily alter the combinations. In each department the couplers are controlled by compound pedals, so that they may be operated in either direction simultaneously with the speaking-stops of the organ.

In our illustration we show a movable console built by the Hope-Jones Electric Organ Company Limited for the organ in the Church of St. Thomas, Taunton, Mass., U. S. A. The action for this instrument was put in hand by Mr. Hope-Jones long before the formation of his Company's Factory, and is not of recent design. The console, however, is of later date, and possesses the "second touch" and other improvements. This latter console, we understand, has just reached this country, and will be fitted shortly.

(*To be continued.*)

FREDERIC ARCHER.

Mr. Frederic Archer, the celebrated English virtuoso, was born in the classical old city of Oxford, England, on the

16th of June, 1838. A distinguished London critic, who has watched his career since childhood, says, "It is frequently supposed that men celebrated in literature and art derive

their intellectual gifts rather from the mother than from the father; but in this case it was otherwise. Mr. Archer's mother possessed no musical taste; and if the subject of this brief memoir owed anything to his parentage, the debt must be ascribed to the father, who was a sound theoretical and practical musician.

Not until he had reached his eighth year did our subject show any marked taste for music, when suddenly he gave unmistakable evidence of the possession of musical talents of the highest order. His father subjected him to a course of rigid elementary instruction; and within six months he could play any composition at first sight that was within the scope of his childish fingers, besides which he exhibited extraordinary power in the art of improvising.

About this time, Sir Henry Bishop (then musical professor of the University of Oxford) was introduced to Mr. Archer's father. Sir Henry played several pianoforte duets with the boy, who fulfilled his portion of the task at first sight in a manner that called forth the enthusiastic admiration of the eminent composer. Elementary studies were pursued with his father for some six months longer, when he became a chorister at Margaret Chapel, London, at that time celebrated for its daily musical services. The day before he left Oxford to enter on his new duties, he for the first time saw an organ key-board, having been taken to Magdalen College Chapel by the organist. He was not long at Margaret Chapel before he officiated as organist, though he had never received an organ lesson.

This young genius now made rapid strides. His next appointment was that of organist of St. Clement's, Oxford, about the same time becoming organist at Merton College, holding the two appointments simultaneously.

A few years later we find Mr. Archer travelling on the Continent, giving exhibitions of his marvellous skill as an organist. On his return to London he received his first important public appointment, as organist to the Panopticon. Here, with a concert instrument of exceptional size and excellence, he soon distinguished himself, and at once gained the name of one of the best among contemporary organists.

In May, 1875, the new organ in Alexandria Palace was completed. This instrument is one of the famous organs of the world, having four manuals and eighty-nine stops. It was built by Mr. Henry Willis of London, and is considered to be the masterwork of that eminent builder. On this instrument Mr. Archer has given upwards of two thousand recitals, never repeating a programme; his marvellous power of sight-reading, either from full orchestral score or other scores, renders his repertoire practically inexhaustible. His readiness and tact are indeed remarkable. He rarely looks at an organ before undertaking a recital thereon, and any one who has had an opportunity of noting the ingenuity with which he will conceal a "cipher," or other similar accident that may befall an instrument when under his control, will bear witness to his unique skill.

Mr. Archer is of the finest physique, and his appearance before the king of instruments is very imposing. Some of the effects which he succeeds in producing we have never heard accomplished by any other organist, for the simple reason that he has been gifted by nature with fingers of unusual length. Availing himself of this advantage, he frequently plays on two, and occasionally three, manuals, with the same hand, having educated one hand to do the work of two when required. His executive facility, both with hands and feet, is marvellous; passages of enormous difficulty and rapid tempo are played by him without the slightest apparent effort.

In 1880 Mr. Archer came to America, first settling in Boston, then going to Brooklyn. He accepted the position of organist and director at Henry Ward Beecher's Church, and later at Dr. Storrs's church in New York, which he left to become organist of the Church of the Incarnation, at the same time assuming the editorship of the *Keynote*. At present, Mr. Archer is organist of St. James R. C. Church, Chicago. As a concert organist, this virtuoso has been heard in nearly every city in Canada and the United States, and we feel safe in stating that he is one of the great organists of the world.

W. G. PEARCE.

COMPARATIVE TABLE OF THE LARGEST ORGANS IN THE WORLD.

Location.	Manuals.	Speaking Stops.	Mechanical Stops.	Pedal Movements.	Piston Combinations.	Pipes.	Great.	Swell.	Solo.	Fifth Manual.	Echo Manual.	First Pedal.	Second Pedal.	Compass Manuals.	Compass Pedal.	Flue Stops.					Reeds.				Ranks of Mixtures.	Bells.	Erected.	Builder.
Town Hall, Sydney, N. S. W.	5	128	18								10		29													1889	Hill & Son.
Cathedral, Riga, Russia.	4	124	19																							1883	Walcker & Son.
Cathedral, Garden City.	4	135	18							7			59													1887	Roosevelt.
Albert Hall, London.	4	111	11										21														Willis.
Auditorium, Chicago.	4	109	18							11	19															1889	Roosevelt.
St. Sulpice, Paris.	5	100	18							20			12													1862	Cavaillé-Coll.
Cathedral, Ulm, Germany.	5	100	9										24													1856	Walcker & Son.
St. George's Hall, Liverpool.	4	100	10										17													1867	Willis.
Town Hall, Leeds, England.	4	93	17								9		16													1878	Gray & Davidson.
Music Hall, Boston.	4	89	4										20													1863	Walcker & Son.
Alexandra Palace, London.	4	88	15										16														Willis.
Cathedral, Magdeburg.	5	86	9										18														Reubke & Son.
Notre Dame, Paris.	5	86	14										14													1868	Cavaillé-Coll.
St. Bartholomew's, N.Y.	4	86	26										15													1893	Hutchings.
Parish Church, Doncaster.	4	84	7								8		35													1863	Schulze.
Calvary Church, New York.	3	84	16										13													1888	Roosevelt.
Nicholai Kirche, Leipsic.	4	84	12										19													1862	Ladegast.
Marien Kirche, Lubeck.	4	82	15										16													1853	Schulze.
Music Hall, Cincinnati.	4	83	15								7		16													1878	Hook & Hastings.
Cathedral, Merseburg.	4	81	19										29													1855	Ladegast.

[1] 11 stops in Stage Organ, 8 in Echo Organ.
[2] Reconstructed.
[3] Mechanical stops and pedal movements combined.
[4] In Pedal Organ.
[5] One stop in Gt., others in Ped.

THE ORGANIST'S RETROSPECT.[1]

BY HORATIO CLARKE.

(AN AUTOBIOGRAPHY OF EVENTFUL NERVES)

IN TWENTY-FIVE CHAPTERS.

CHAPTER VIII.

During this year an incident occurred which nearly terminated my musical progress, and illustrated a mysterious and inexplicable phase of human nature.

In the adjoining residence there lived a good man and his wife, who had an only son two years my senior, of rare capabilities, noble in form, and fair of face. He had been brought up in the ways of uprightness, was surrounded with good influences at home, and was a leader among the pupils at school. But, as he was utterly unmusical, we had nothing in common sympathy with each other.

Beneath his attractive exterior and charming manners, unknown to his parents, there was a vein of insidious corruption and defilement. I was astonished at the revelation of bad principles which he frequently thrust upon me in the hope of uprooting my standard of morality. During the past year he often wickedly boasted of the number whom he had led astray from the paths of virtue. He exulted in his knowledge of the Scriptures, which he said he had read through for the sake of the reward his father had offered him for the task.

I was yet required to saw and split the wood for each day. The chopping-block was a section of a large log, and stood on a little elevation about thirty feet from the barn. One morning when I was splitting hard wood with a heavy axe, this schoolmate came into the yard and began to tempt me to an evil course of life.

Strength to resist temptation is given to those who sincerely desire not to yield to iniquity.

His propositions were so vile that I firmly told him that I would hear no such wicked suggestions. He turned white with rage, and, with an oath, hissed through his set teeth: —

"I would kill you, Osborne, if I was sure I could escape being hung for it!"

I started to go down toward the barn, and had got half way, when he shouted, —

"Stop, Osborne, where you are!"

I turned toward him, as he threatened, —

"I am going to roll this chopping-block on you, and if you dare touch it, to stop it, I will fling this axe at you and kill you!"

I would not run from such a bullying spirit, and stood my ground. He gave the log a hard push, and sent it rolling toward me. In order to save being knocked to the earth and having my limbs broken, as it reached the place where I was standing, I turned it from its course with a desperate kick, and it rolled down the declivity.

At this moment he seized the axe with both hands, and hurled it at me with all his strength. Fortunately, in its motion it made a revolution, so that only the handle struck my shoulder as I dodged the murderous missile, and it dashed against the barn a rod below with such force that the weather-boarding was shattered.

There being no witnesses to this frightful attack, I said nothing, and went into the barn as he left the yard. After this display of enmity I feared to meet him alone. But this apprehension was of short duration, for within a month he was taken with a serious illness, resulting from his irregular habits.

His disease made such rapid progress, that on my first call to inquire after his health, a neighbor came to the door and said that he had passed a very poor night, and seemed very low. Hearing our voices, his mother came to the door and said that he was dying, and that he wanted to see me. Although dreading such a scene, I entered the darkened room, where the afflicted parents stood weeping at the bed-

side. I went at once to him. He reached for my hand, which I gave, as he faintly uttered, —

"I am dying, Ernest! I am very happy, and am going to heaven! Good-by, Ernest!"

And then he gasped, —

"Receive — my — spirit! — Lord — Je — " and he breathed no more.

I took my hand from his, and left the room in the greatest conflict of mind which I had ever experienced. For I had been taught in the Sunday-school that the end of the wicked was fearful; but here was a peaceful deathbed, closing an impure life, with no evidence of repentance, sorrow for sin, nor conversion, which the prevailing religious teachings sternly proclaimed as essential, and I could not reconcile such a happy frame of mind with the knowledge which I possessed concerning his recent course of life.

The large funeral at the church was one of more than usual solemnity, the entire school attending in a body, and walking in the long procession. No higher eulogies could be given than were contained in the words spoken on that occasion by pastor and teachers, in which he was held up as an example for imitation to all the young people of his acquaintance.

I was one of the bearers, and as we lowered his body into the earth, my clothing in some way became entangled with the rope, and I was drawn into the grave, and fell upon the coffin, with no other injury than bruising the shoulder which was yet lame from the blow given by the handle of the axe. But my mind was bewildered with the confliction arising from the tributes of praise which I had just heard, contrasted with what I knew concerning the life of one who, dying at the age of eighteen, was a libertine, and in spirit a murderer.

· · · · · · · · · · · ·

My musical interest increased as I kept up my daily practising, and I obtained a number of pupils on the melodeon, giving the lessons at their homes. Thus far I had confined my studies exclusively to organ music, and had gone through with a course of thorough-bass and harmony; but having decided to become a teacher of music, it was necessary that I should also become proficient in pianoforte playing.

In various ways I had saved money enough to purchase a piano, and I began a series of valuable lessons with that devoted disciple of classical music in Boston, the late Otto Dresel, whose taste was of the most refined nature, and whose criticism was severe and unyielding.

I was not attracted toward the pianoforte, for to my mind its music simply represented a skeleton framework which the imagination fills out in form. Yet as an instrument for developing a facility of technique, it is more useful than the grasping and firm pressure which the organ keys require. The organ is played with fixed wrists, and with a legato touch made by the substitution of the fingers on the keys, while the piano touch requires great flexibility of the wrist, finger, and elbow joints.

Within a few weeks after I had taken up my piano scales and arpeggios, I found that I could play the organ with greater ease and facility, without detriment to the legato touch. In addition to my regular pianoforte practice, I played through the accompaniments of the standard oratorios and masses, and committed the principal choruses of the "Messiah" and "Creation" to memory.

The members of the Unitarian parish now began the agitation of the purchase of a new organ which should in every way be superior to any instrument in the other churches, and, after a few lively parish meetings, it was voted to have one built in Boston, which should be completed by the end of the year. This decision was doubtless of greater interest to me than to any other person, for I determined to make such progress that I might be able to obtain the position of organist.

I at once began a series of regular visits to the organ factory, where I watched the process of the building of this instrument from the very first stage. The builder, Mr. Sherburn, treated me with the utmost courtesy, giving me free

LIEBESLIED.

Allegretto sostenuto e amoroso.

A. HENSELT.

Gt. Doppel Flöte & Gamba.

Sw. 8 & 4 Ft. with Cornopean.
Ch. Melodia, Dulciana & Flute 4 Ft.

Ped Bourdon.
Ch. to Ped.

Ch.

Gt.

Ch. Flute 4 Ft. off.

Sw. Tremulant.

Ch. Add Flute 4 Ft.

Gt.

Tremulant off.

con espress.

Con anima.

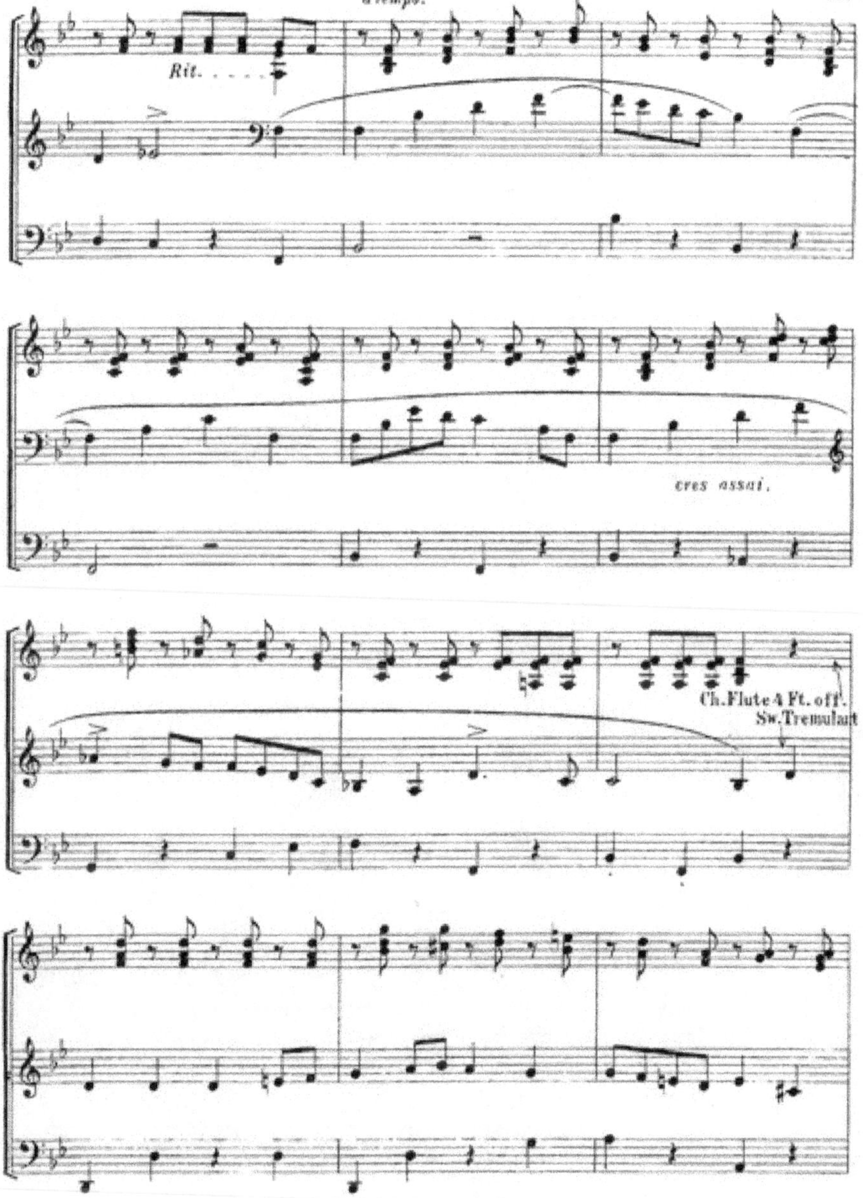
a tempo.
Rit. . . . .
cres assai.
Ch. Flute 4 Ft. off.
Sw. Tremulant

cres assai

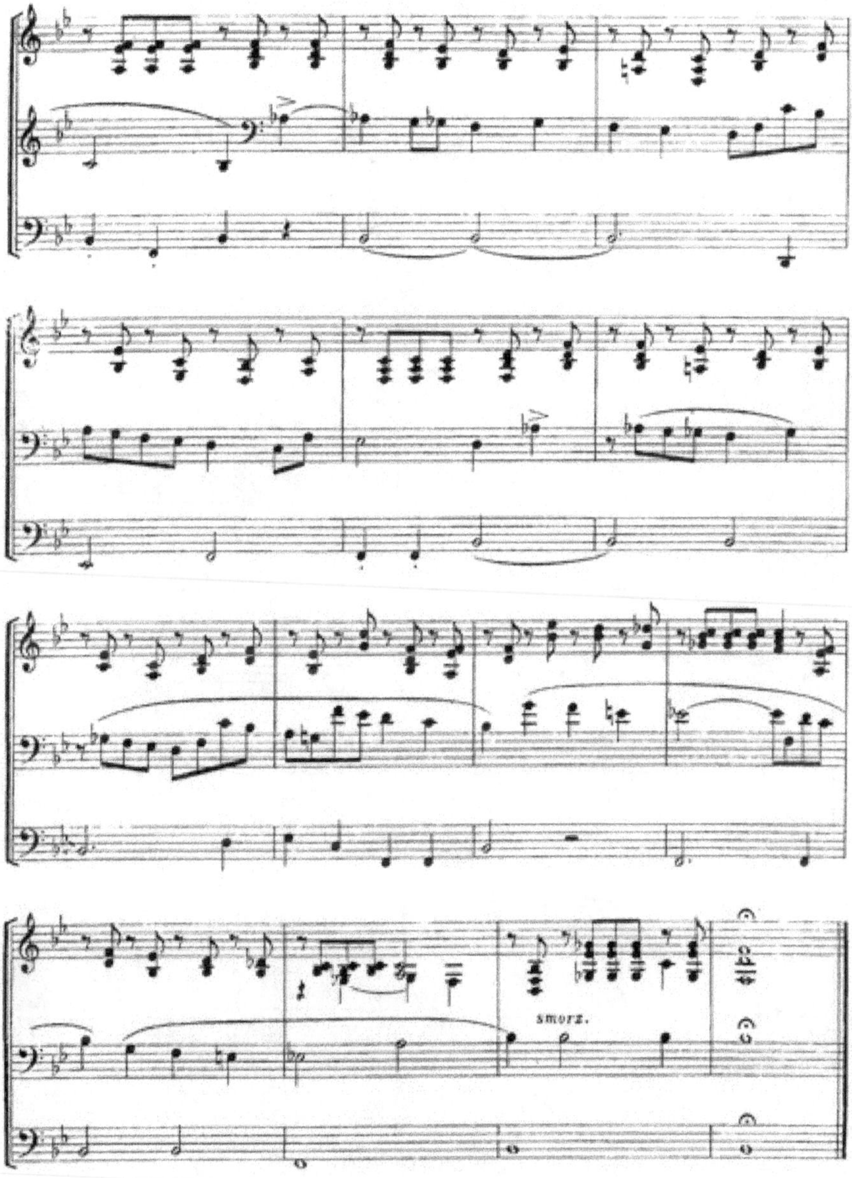
smorz.

ANDANTE IN A.

Dr. W. VOLCKMAR.

Gt.(or Ch.) Melodia & Dulciana.

Sw. Oboe. St. Diap. and Violina.

Ped. Bourdon. Sw. to Gt. & Sw. to Ped.

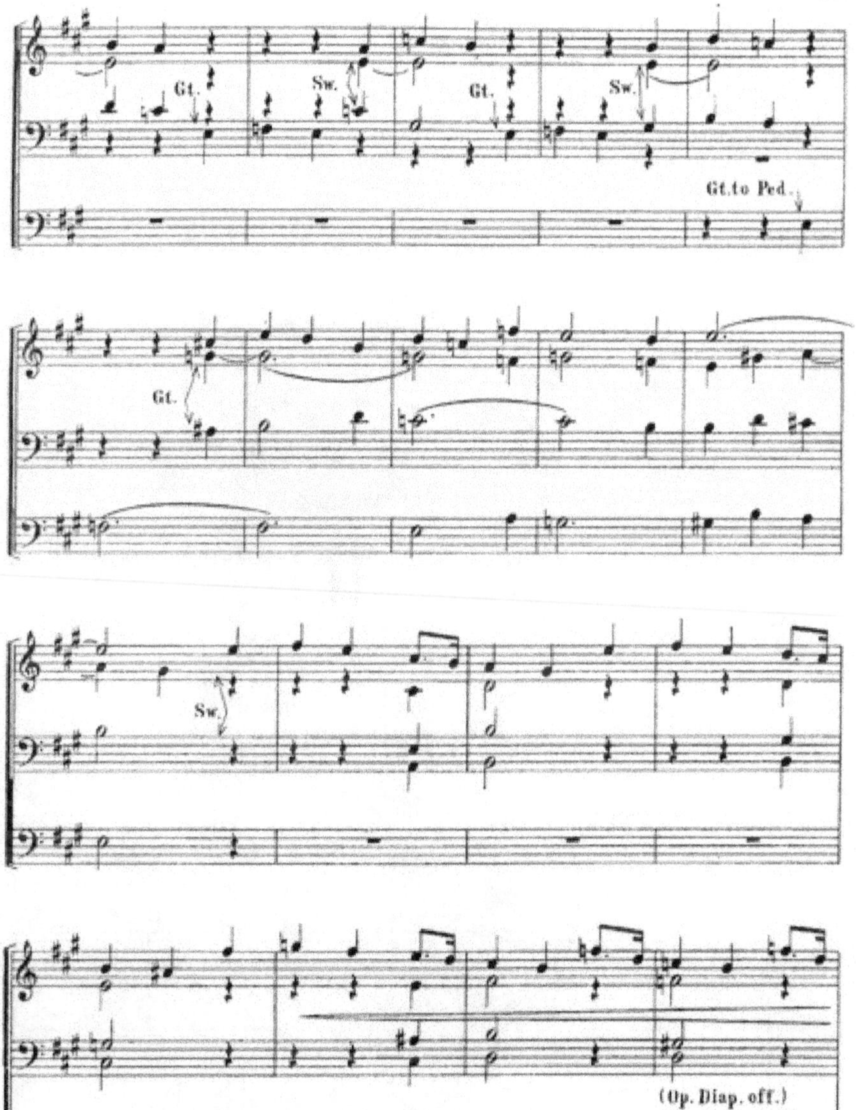
Gt.
Sw.
Gt.
Sw.
Gt. to Ped.
Gt.
Sw.
(Op. Diap. off.)

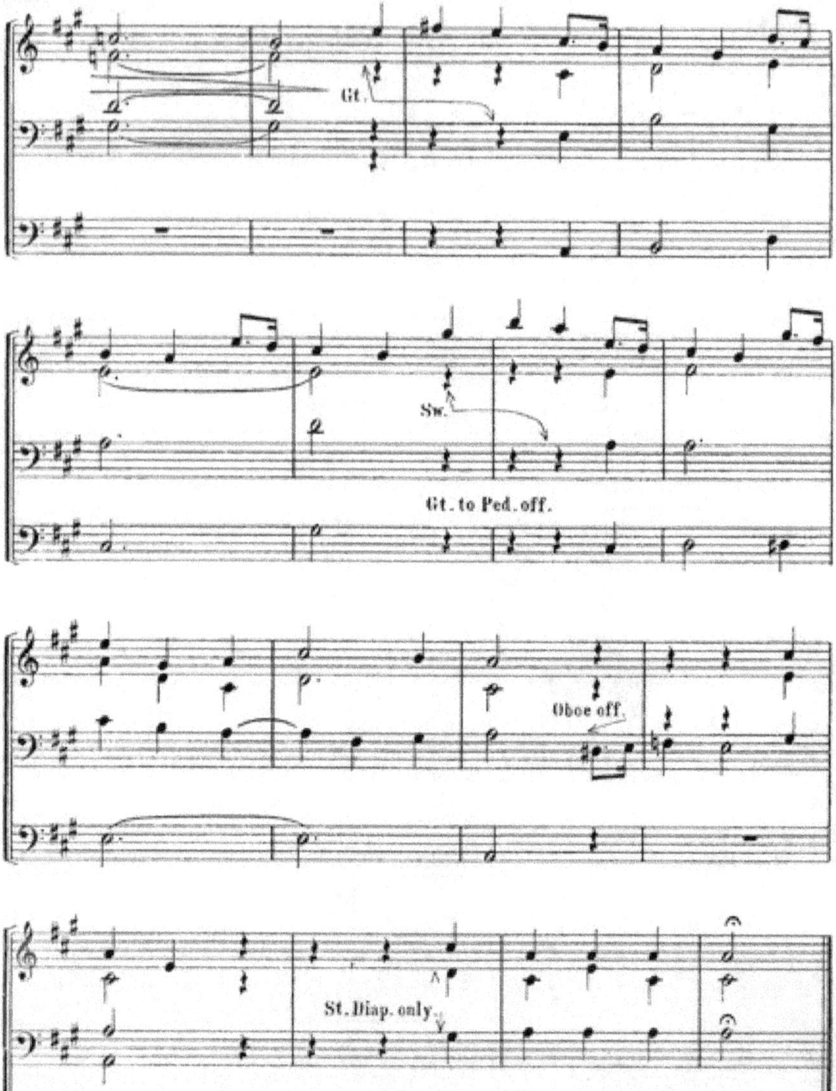
Gt.
Sw.
Gt. to Ped. off.
Oboe off.
St. Diap. only

range in each department of the factory, and initiated me into the principles of the voicing of the pipes, which is generally held in a halo of mystery. Every question which I asked was kindly answered and practically illustrated, the appreciation of which I did not forget in after years.

There was not a portion of this instrument which I did not understand, and long before it was completed I had every detail fixed in memory. I had a diagram of the order of stops in their actual distances apart, and was so conversant with the position of each, that I could make any desired combination, or place my hand on any name, with my eyes closed. Thus I had a complete mastery of the registration before any pipes were in the organ. I committed a number of excellent organ pieces so thoroughly to memory, that when lying awake in the night time I could mentally play them note for note, with the combinations I should use.

Meanwhile, I had sent a formal letter of application to the music committee of the church, and was one of several competitors for the position.

When the organ was finished at the factory, there was an exhibition of its capacities by eminent organists, and on that occasion Mr. Sherburn kindly arranged that at the proper moment I should be invited to take my place at the instrument for an improvisation.

With a rapidly beating heart I went to the key-desk, and, being familiar with every detail, my thoughts were expressed without restraint, and with much freedom in the use of the stops.

Having previously learned what melodies were favorites of the music committee, I wove them in as themes, but was careful on this occasion not to intrude my presence upon them, keeping myself in quiet reserve, and did not respond to the applause of the audience which followed my unexpected efforts.

(*To be continued.*)

OUR CHICAGO LETTER.

CHICAGO, Nov. 20, 1893.

AFTER giving recitals throughout Canada, Mr. Frederic Archer has returned to this city, where he has several recitals planned for the coming season. On the Sunday following Gounod's death, the entire musical services in the morning at St. James' Church, under his supervision, was devoted to Gounod's compositions.

At the performance of "Elijah," to be given by the combined Episcopal choirs of this city in the Auditorium on Nov. 23, Dr. Gower is to preside at the organ.

Mr. Clarence Dickinson, organist of the Church of the Messiah, and a pupil of Mr. Harrison M. Wild, has just begun Sunday evening recitals in the above church. Mr. Dickinson's ability as a concert organist is above the average, and he doubtless has a great career ahead of him. Many, no doubt, recall the stir his playing from memory created last season.

The organ recitals at the Church of the Epiphany, given by Dr. John H. Gower, still draw audiences that fill the church. This is no surprise, as Dr. Gower ranks high as a church and concert organist. At present writing, Messrs. Farrand & Votey are putting in their electric key contact in the Epiphany organ, which will doubtless prove satisfactory to Dr. Gower.

Dr. Gower's last programme, Nov. 2, contained the following : —

Overture, "Midsummer Night's Dream," Mendelssohn; Berceuse, Beaumont; Allegro con brio, Handel; Funeral March, Chopin; Fantasia and Fugue in G-minor, Bach; Offertoire in D, Batiste; Improvisation on theme selected by the audience; Fourth Sonata, Mendelssohn.

Mr. Harrison M. Wild's Sunday evening organ recitals prove as interesting as ever, and large audiences congregate to hear this well-known concert organist. The following programmes will doubtless be of great interest to lovers of the noble instrument : —

RECITAL No. 138, Nov. 12 : —

Prelude, Op. 32, No. 1, and Fugue, Op. 36, No. 3, H. W. Parker; Sonata, Op. 2 (MS.), Frederic Grant Gleason; Serenade, Bragg-Shelly ; Gavotte, Schumann-Shelly; Invocation, Op. 18, No. 2, Guilmant; Polish Dance, Scharwenka-Wild; Vienna March, Scotson Clark.

RECITAL No. 139, Nov. 19 : —

Prelude and Fugue in C, Bach; Sonata No. 5, Op. 50, S. D. Lampe; Cradle Song in A, Kroeger; La Tambourin, J. P. Rameau; Processional March, Op. 41, No. 5, Guilmant; Overture to "The Daughter of the Regiment," Donizetti.

Our last month's letter closed with the forty-third organ recital given upon the World's Fair Festival Organ. From this recital to the close of the Fair, which brought the sixty-first recital, with four exceptions, Mr. Eddy was the solo organist.

RECITAL No. 45 was given by Mr. N. J. Corey of Detroit, Mich., who gave the following programme : —

Fantasie in D-minor, Merkel; St. Ann's Fugue, Bach; Allegretto, Foster; Adoration et Vox Angelica, Dubois; Allegro Symphonique, Salomé; Idylle, Godard-Guilmant; Prayer in A, Marche aux Flambeaux, Guilmant.

RECITAL No. 49. By W. S. STERLING, Cincinnati, Ohio.

Prelude and Fugue in E-minor, Bach; Meditation, Medley; March of the Cavaliers, from "St. Elizabeth," Liszt; Allegro Cantabile, from Organ Symphony, No. 5, Widor; Toccata in F-flat, Seixas; Rhapsodie, No. 3, Saint-Saëns; Improvisations showing some resources of the organ; Allegro Symphonique, Salomé; Overture in E-minor, Morandi.

On Sunday, Oct. 22, the organ was used in a recital for the first time on a Sunday. The performer was Mr. J. Frederick Wolle of Bethlehem, Pa. The programme was a Bach one; and, as most of Chicago's organists were at their own organs, we fear Mr. Wolle's audience consisted of a delegation from the German Village.

Fantasia and Fugue in G-minor; Passacaglia and Fugue in C minor; Chorale in G, "Alle Menschen müssen sterben;" Prelude and Fugue in G; Aria in F; Toccata and Fugue in C; Fugue in G-minor; Fugue in D.

RECITAL No. 56, Oct. 23, was given by Mr. C. A. W. HOWLAND, organist of the First Unitarian Church, Detroit, Mich. Of all the recitals given at the Fair, this one deserves more than special mention. In the first place, this young organist is totally blind. In the second place, on account of the hall being so much used, the performer only had forty minutes to familiarize himself with the instrument. This is remarkable ; for M. Guilmant, with all his years of practice, snatched every available minute at this organ, even practising after dark and on Sunday for his recitals. In the third place, in the face of all obstacles, he handled the organ far better than the majority of the organists who gave recitals on the instrument. One naturally asks how he set his pistons. His plan was, in brief, to set the desired combination on each piston, after which he would try all the pistons, learning by tone and running his hands over the draw-stops what each piston included. Mr. Howland is ambitious. He has been abroad, and studied under Rheinberger, and now contemplates studying under M. Guilmant. The following is his programme, which was well played : —

Toccata in F, Bach; Offertory in D-flat, Op. 8, Salomé; Sonata in D-minor, Op. 42, Guilmant; Postludium in G, Whiting; Intermezzo and Fugue, Op. 88, Rheinberger; "Festival March" in D, Smart.

The concluding recitals given at the Fair by Mr. CLARENCE EDDY were as follows : —

RECITAL No. 44 : —

Fantasia and Fugue in G-minor, Bach; March of the Magi Kings, and Toccata in G-major, Dubois; Concert Adagio in E, Op. 35, Merkel; Peasants' March, Fumagalli; Third Sonata in C-minor, Guilmant; Offertory in F-major, Op. 36, Batiste; Chromatic Fantasia and Fugue, Thiele.

RECITAL No. 45 : —

Prelude and Fugue in G-major, Bach; Vorspiel to "Lohengrin," Wagner; Sonata in C-minor, No. 2, Op. 77, Dudley Buck; Variations on "Home, Sweet Home" (MS.), Flagler; Nuptial Song, Dubois; Marche Celebre, Lachner; Chorus in D-major, Guilmant; Saint Cecilia Offertory in D-major, Batiste.

RECITAL No. 46 : —

Prelude and Fugue in B-minor, Bach; Contemplation, Lemaigre; Sonata in D-minor, No. 1, Guilmant; Pastorale, Whiting; A Russian Romance (arranged by H. M. Eddy), Hoffman; Gavotte de Louis XV., Maurice Lee; Allegretto Expressivo, Op. 116, H. N. Bartlett; Coronation March (arranged by Best), Meyerbeer.

RECITAL No. 48 :—

Prelude and Fugue in A-minor, Bach; Romance, "Evening Star," Wagner; Sonata in G-minor, No. 2, Merkel; "Home, Sweet Home," and Triumphal March, Bach; Lamentation, Guilmant; Fantasie on the Portuguese Hymn, Jules Grison; Overture, to "Euryanthe" (arranged by S. P. Warren), Weber.

RECITAL No. 50 :—

Prelude and Fugue in E-minor, Bach; Prayer and Cradle Song, Guilmant; Sonata in D, No. 15, Op. 168, Rheinberger; "In Paradise," and "Alleluia," Dubois; "O Sanctissima," Liss; Melody and Intermezzo, H. W. Parker; Pontifical March, F. de la Tombelle.

RECITAL No. 51 :—

Prelude and Fugue in C-minor (Book 2), Bach; Traumerei and Romance, Schumann; Sonata in E-minor, Op. 19, A. G. Ritter; Night Song, Vogt; Fantasie on themes from "Faust," Gounod-Eddy; Introduction and Bridal Chorus from "Lohengrin," Wagner; Fragment Symphonique, Lemaigre; Jubilee Overture, Weber.

RECITAL No. 53 :—

Toccata and Fugue in D-minor, Bach; Offertory in D-flat, Op. 8, Salomé; First Sonata, Mendelssohn; Pastorale, Op. 47, MacMaster; Grand Chorus, Op. 48, MacMaster; Prayer in F, Guilmant; Fantasie in A-minor, Lemmens; Alla Marcia, Best.

RECITAL No. 54 :—

Second Sonata, Mendelssohn; Melody in C, John A. West; Fugue in G-minor (the lesser), Bach; Nuptial March, Guilmant; Pastorale (from the Second Symphony), Widor; Spring Song and Scherzo, Shelley; Schiller March, Meyerbeer.

RECITAL No. 55 :—

Toccata in A-flat, Hesse; Elevation in E, Saint-Saens; Third Sonata, Mendelssohn; Fugue in E-flat (St. Ann's), Bach; Marche Funèbre, and Grand Choeur Dialogue, Gigout; Romanza, Op. 22, No. 2, J. H. Brewer; Processional Grand March, S. B. Whitney.

RECITAL No. 57 :—

Prelude and Fugue, Bach; Idylle, "At Evening," Barth; Fourth Sonata, Mendelssohn; "Elsa's Bridal March," from "Lohengrin," Wagner; Prelude in A-major, Op. 40, No. 1, Chopin; "Religious March," Guilmant; Méditation in A-flat, Klein; Finale in D-major, Lemmens.

RECITAL No. 58 :—

Prelude and Fugue in A-minor, Eddy; Aria in D, Bach; Fifth Sonata, Mendelssohn; Fantasie, "Drowning Dagman," Matthison-Hansen; Fantaisie in D-major, Lemmens; Christmas Pastorale, Whiting; Variations on a Scotch Air, Buck; Grand March from "Rienzi," Wagner.

RECITAL No. 59 :—

Prelude and Fugue in C-major, Bach; Romanza, "O Cessate di Pearganni," Scarlatti; Sixth Sonata, Mendelssohn; Capriccio in F-major, Lemaigre; "Festival March," Best; Adagio in D-major (from Sixth Organ Symphony), Widor; "Daybreak," Spinney; "Torchlight March," Guilmant.

RECITAL No. 60 :—

Toccata and Fugue (Doric) Bach; "Ave Maria," Widor; Offertory on Two Christmas Hymns, Guilmant; Communion in F, Op. 58, Grison; Rondo Caprice, Op. 55, Buck; Pastorale in G, Best; Variations on "God Save the King," Hesse; Echo, and Méditation, F. de la Tombelle; "Pontifical March," Lemmens.

RECITAL No. 61 :—

Prelude and Fugue in D-minor, Mendelssohn; Funeral March, Chopin; Etude in C-sharp minor, Op. 46, No. 4, Chopin; Theme Variations and Finale (by request), Thiele; Grand Solemn March, Smart; Christmas Chimes, Cole; Concert Fugue in C-major, Hempel; Finale, Allegro Maestoso, Whiting.

FINAL RECITAL, No. 62, Tuesday, Oct. 31.

Festival Overture, Op. 31, on "A Strong Castle is Our Lord," Nicolai; "War March of the Priests" ("Athalie"), Mendelssohn; Variations on "The Last Rose of Summer," Buck; Tenth Sonata, Op. 146, Rheinberger; "Epithalame," Op. 58, No. 2, Guilmant; Concert Fugue in G Major, Krebs; "Triumphal March," Lemmens.

The above recital closed the series of World's Fair organ recitals held in Festival Hall. These recitals were listened to by persons from all parts of the world. The organ was praised by nearly all who heard it. As yet this instrument is unsold, and there remains a glorious chance for some large church or cathedral to obtain an instrument that has gained the highest praise from the severest critics. We hope that it will remain in Chicago.

The organ in the great Manufacturers' Building, by Pilcher & Sons of Louisville, Ky., gained a diploma from the Fair authorities. The builders also received a very highly complimentary letter from M. Guilmant, who tried the organ, and was greatly pleased with its tone and mechanism. This instrument has been sold to Trinity Church, Pittsburg, Pa., of which Mr. Walter E. Hall is the organist. We congratulate this church on securing such an excellent instrument for the small consideration of $12,000.

Many will be grieved to hear of the death of William J. Davis, which occurred at his residence in Chicago at midnight, Monday, Nov. 6. Mr. Davis was connected with the Roosevelt Organ Company for about eight years, the first half of this time as the Philadelphia representative, and the remainder as their Chicago representative. Previous to his being with the Roosevelt firm, he built organs in Buffalo, N.Y., and many Eastern organs bear his name and show his excellent workmanship. As a boy, he grew up in the organ business with Johnson & Sons. Mr. Davis's death was due largely to overwork. Burning the candle of life at both ends laid him too low for any medical aid. After supervising the construction of the great World's Fair Organ, and before its completion, he went to his residence, never to hear the tones of the organ which has thrilled thousands of listeners. Mr. Davis was well known to organists and organ builders all over the country, and had a broad knowledge of the organ. The funeral service, held at his late residence Thursday afternoon, Nov. 9, was attended by many friends, among them many prominent organists and organ builders. The body was taken to Hartford, Conn., for interment. Mr. Davis leaves a wife, who has the sympathy of many friends.

VOX HUMANA.

CORRESPONDENCE.

THE MODERN ORGAN.

To the Editor of THE ORGAN:

SIR, — If any proof could be needed that we are far behind the European standard in the model organ of the day, the playing of Mons. Guilmant at the Church of the New Old-South must have afforded that proof.

I anticipate the reply which would doubtless be given, — that this particular organ is *not* a modern one, — by saying that it differs in no respect from the organ of the day in general plan of construction, while in detail it is in many respects superior.

All the organs in this country are built as psalm-tune organs, — as such many are, in detail, musical, as this particular instrument certainly is; beyond this point of requirement they will not bear testing. They behave remarkably well so long as the player keeps to the jog-trot, London cab-horse pace, but beyond that you cannot go without developing asthmatic symptoms, — the panting and gasping for breath of an instrument inadequately winded.

Witness, for instance, the effect of the last movement of Mendelssohn's First Organ Sonata under the fingers of Mons. Guilmant — not half the notes sounded which were touched, and in every rapid passage the effect was as if the full organ had been suddenly shut off and brought on again with each chord.

Had a less celebrated player been at the keys, he would doubtless have been blamed and the organ excused. As the representative organist of Europe, but one conclusion is admissible.

I am not finding fault with this particular instrument. I am speaking in general terms in saying that the accepted model of the day is on similar lines of construction entirely defective, — primitive to a degree; for we find better method adopted as early as 1559 in the celebrated organ in Lubeck.

The first consideration with European organ builders is to provide adequate wind supply; the application of mechanical details, pneumatic or otherwise, is quite an after-consideration. In this country the order is entirely reversed. The fad of the day is the imitation of a new pneumatic motor, while the whole seasoning of the instrument which is the model does not lie in this detail as a primary thing, but in its perfectly supplied and steady wind, which is ignored.

Let any of my readers visit the organ factories, and they will see scores of instruments, big and little, all supplied from single wind reservoirs, — organs for which thousands are to be paid, with a couple of wind reservoirs as an unusual and liberal supply.

I know one "celebrated" organ which cost some $23,000, which is referred to as "extra fine." It possesses but three reservoirs, and is as asthmatical as the others when measured by Mons. Guilmant's test.

Organ builders are entitled to some excuse, for there are those who maintain that the organ should not be taken out of the sphere of its sacred usefulness, while an overwhelming majority regard the instrument merely as a piece of church furniture, which has to be decent looking, and — well, if it performs the functions for which it was erected it fulfils the conditions which bind the organ builder.

In Europe the requirements of the instrument are of a different standard. The services of the church demand a much more perfect instrument, and it is largely used for solo purposes. In this city, in particular, no interest is felt in the organ, and consequently I may presume there is not much prospect of improvement, — the old school rules.

It is rumored, I know not on what authority, that the old organ is to be re-erected in the new Music Hall; and the probability is that the work of its reconstruction will be carried out on the old lines. Elsewhere there is better prospect, and ere long organists and others will have the opportunity to judge of the merits of a large organ built on really modern lines for a city not a great way from Boston!

Yours, CARLTON C. MICHELL.

THE HOPE-JONES STOP KEYS.

BIRKENHEAD, ENG., Oct. 2, 1893.

To the Editor of THE ORGAN:

DEAR SIR, — As an interested reader of your paper, I have not failed to notice that the Hope-Jones Stop Keys (patent applied for in 1891) have been appropriated and fitted by certain builders to organs in the States, notably to one of the instruments exhibited at the World's Fair, and that the words describing the same, published in my pamphlet of December, 1890, have also been adopted.

I am, dear sir, Yours faithfully,

ROBT. HOPE-JONES, M.I.E.E.

THE INDISTINCTNESS OF ORGAN TONE.

UP to the present time, organ builders have followed a stereotyped form of tone combination in the composition of specifications, and the question arises, —

"Can there be an improvement in this respect ?"

I have been led to open the discussion of this important subject from the effect of listening to the programs of Mons. Guilmant in Boston, particularly in regard to the last movement of Mendelssohn's First Organ Sonata, which was rendered at the second recital. I am familiar with each note of this sonata, and have heard it performed by many eminent players in Europe and in this country; and with as many organs of various builders, the effect of this last movement has always been very unsatisfactory.

The renowned organist who has so recently interested our Boston musicians, gave this movement with remarkable spirit, with its runs and arpeggio form of chords, which my ear failed to recognize in their individual voices, and I should like to know if others have experienced the same impression.

The distinguished player omitted no notes, but the general indistinctness of tone has led me to reflect upon this subject, and to incline to the opinion that there is either a fault in the make-up of the chorus-work of organs in general, or that there is a limit to the style of the composition of music for the organ, even in classical form.

In choral passages and harmonic progressions, the full organ is majestic in its tone; but when there is an interpretation of florid and intricate movements in the interior and pedal parts, there is an indistinctness which causes the hearer to lose interest in the music unless the eye follows the score at the same time. Even when a choral is played with the full organ, the preponderance of the mixtures and super-octave stops renders the melody somewhat indistinct. This result is produced on account of each part having the same octave and mutation stops, which absorb the distinctness, and obscure the melody, or upper part.

In an orchestra, the different parts are executed with an individuality of instrumentation and consequent tone-quality, which preserves the distinctness, and the melody is re-enforced with instruments of a decided character. The indistinctness of the organ is not so marked when a single positive stop or a combination of 8ft. stops is used.

In order to open a discussion of this subject, I will close with two questions which I hope will be answered by a number of practical adepts.

1. Is there a fault in the construction of organ wind-chests, either with separate valves to each pipe, or in the ordinary method of manufacture ?

2. Can a better scheme of tone distribution of the chorus-work of organs be devised, wherein the 8ft. tone shall be more predominant ?

MILDOES.

MIXTURES.

(HOPE RANKS.)

Messrs. Hook & Hastings have just finished a two-manual organ in the Methodist Church of Cedar Sandwich, N.H., containing sixteen registers and five pedal movements.

Mr. Carl G. Schmidt, organist of the New York Ave. M. E. Church, Brooklyn, is giving a series of illustrated piano lectures at his residence on every other Wednesday afternoon.

Mr. George S. Hutchings is building a two-manual organ for St. Margaret's Church, Dorchester, Mass., which will have twelve registers. Another organ of the same size will go to the Belmont School, Belmont, Mass.

The Farrand & Votey Organ Co. are about to build a three-manual organ for Pilgrim Cong. Church, Cleveland, Ohio, and a two-manual organ for the new Fourth Presb. Church, New York.

Mr. Chas. Harris, late of Messrs. Woodberry & Harris, has associated himself with Messrs. Jas. E. Treat & Co., Methuen, Mass.

Mr. Clarence Eddy gave twenty-one organ recitals at the World's Fair, playing one hundred and sixty-eight compositions.

Mr. J. Warren Andrews, organist of Plymouth Church, Minneapolis, is giving a series of monthly special programmes, selected from the music of "The Messiah," at the regular evening services on the first Sunday of each month.

The large two-manual organ now being finished in the First Presbyterian Church of Galesburg, Ill., is from Hook & Hastings, and has thirty registers. It is blown by an electric motor. This firm have also shipped to Trinity P. E. Church, Hamilton, Ohio, a new organ displaying two fronts showing through arched openings. The organ contains two manuals and eighteen registers.

Mr. Will D. Belknap, a pupil of Mr. Clarence Eddy, is giving a series of organ recitals at the Stewart Ave. Universalist Church, Chicago. His programme for Nov. 5 contained: Sonata, Op. 70, Weimann; "A Evening," Bach; Berceuse, Spinney; Prelude and Fugue in D minor, Bach.

Mr. J. J. Miller gave the following programme at his regular organ recital at Christ Church, Norfolk, Va., Nov. 6: Concerto in F, Handel; Choral, Bache; Prayer and Cradle Song, 20th Funeral March and Seraphic Song, Guilmant; Triumphal March, Bach. Mr. Miller is doing good work in his district in creating a love for a good class of organ music.

Mr. Clarence Eddy has placed his concert business in the hands of Mr. A. B. Way, 403 Chamber of Commerce Building, Chicago, to whom applications should be made for dates. Mr. Eddy's time is always well filled, and it is necessary to book dates some time ahead.

Mr. Alex. Guilmant, while in Chicago, wrote the following letter to Messrs. Farrand & Votey: —

TRANSLATION.

It is with great pleasure that I have played the organ constructed for "Festival Hall," Chicago, by Messrs. Farrand & Votey. This instrument is excellent; it possesses stops of a charming quality (timbre); it has great power, and, besides, the sonority is expressive of it. The pistons, by which one can, at will, change the combinations, afford valuable resources to the organist for obtaining varied and instantaneous effects. I examined the interior of the organ, and I found the arrangement of it perfect; the work is executed with the greatest care and with excellent materials. It is an instrument of the first order. (Signed)

ALEX. GUILMANT.

CHICAGO, Sept. 9, 1893.

Mr. W. E. Fairclough, F. C. O., gave an organ recital at All Saints' Church, Toronto, Nov. 3, with the following programme: Trio Sonata in D minor, No. 3, J. S. Bach; Andante Grazioso in G, E. J. Hopkins; Sonata No. 3, in A, Mendelssohn; Fantasie in F, W. T. Best; Offertory in D flat, Th. Salomé; "Vision," Op. 22, H. W. Parker; Finale in E flat, Alex. Guilmant.

The Farrand & Votey Organ Co. are now erecting two-manual organs in the following churches: St. George's P. E. Church (Sunday-school room), New York; Trinity Cong. Church, E. Orange, N.J.; St. John's P. E. Church, Waterbury, Conn. (chorale chancel organ); St. Michael's P. E. Church, Brooklyn; First M.E. Church, Millville, N.J., and a large three-manual organ in First M.E. Church, Scranton, Pa.

Mr. H. C. Macdougall gave his 40th and 41st organ recitals in Central Baptist Church, Providence, R. I., Nov. 4 and 11, with the following programmes: Nov. 4 (4 weeks of Richard Wagner); Overture to " Die Meistersinger"; Introduction to Third Act, and Bridal Chorus from " Lohengrin"; Pilgrim's Chorus and March from " Tannhäuser." On Nov. 11, the programme, devoted to American composers, was as follows: Fugue, Ernest Krueger; Religious Air with Variations, G. E. Whiting; Processional March, S. B. Whitney; Eclogue, Chadwick, and Fugue, H. W. Parker; " Holy Night," and " On the Coast," Dudley Buck.

Mr. Letaine Holloway, F. C. O., gave an organ recital in Asbury Hall, Waltham, Mass., Oct. 16, with the following programme: Allegretto, Lemmens; Finale in G, Capocci; Intermezzo, Mascagni; Toccata and Fugue in D-Minor, Bach; Gavotte, " Mignon," Thomas; Jubilate March, Seanor.

Mr. Carl G. Schmidt is giving organ recitals on the first Saturday afternoon of each month at the New York Ave. M. E. Church, Brooklyn. The following programme selected from the works of Alex. Guilmant, was given Nov. 4: Fugue in F-Major (dedicated to Carl G. Schmidt); Cradle Song; Pastorale from the First Sonata; Ave Maria (Miss Marian Walker); Mascagni; Second Sonata; Soprano Solo, Tu lo sai superbetta, Pesch; Nuptial March; Meditation.

Mr. Gerrit Smith resumed his weekly organ recitals at the South Church, New York, Monday, Oct. 30, with the following programme: Prelude and Fugue in E-Minor, Bach; Melody in D, Guilmant; Thème Provençal, Vardi, Chant, Pastorale, and Cortège Funèbre, Dubois; Fantasia, Op. 103, Boëllmann; Canzonetta in E-Flat, Thomé; Allegro Moderato in F, Pastorale in E, and Bridal Chorus in D-Flat, Guilmant.

Mr. Samuel Pierce of Reading, Mass., shipped pipes and action for two organs to South America last month. These pipes were packed in small boxes, and went by steamer to the coast of Colombia, S.A., where they were transferred to another vessel and conveyed for ten days up the river. They then will be loaded on mules' backs, and conveyed one hundred and twenty miles over the mountains.

In spite of the financial depression, there seems to be a fair amount of business in the pipe-organ track. Most of the builders have considerable work on hand, though future contracts may be few. Mr. Samuel Pierce, pipe-maker, has just supplied pipes for two large four-manual organs, and for several good-sized three-manual organs. During the fall he has furnished no less than nine 16-ft. trombones for pedal organs.

Messrs. Mason & Hamlin have received the following letter regarding the Last Church Organs from Monsieur Alexandre Guilmant:—

TRANSLATION.
New York, Oct. 21, 1893.

I thank you very much for showing me your excellent instruments. I have experienced great pleasure in playing your organs, the instrument (Liszt Organ) with two manuals and pedals, is of beautiful tone and will be very useful to persons wishing to learn to play the Great Organ.

Accept my hearty congratulations, and allow me to express my best sentiments. Very sincerely yours,

ALEXANDRE GUILMANT.

Mr. Robert Hope-Jones delivered an interesting lecture on his system of Electrical Control, in Wakefield, England, in October.

Messrs. Gilbert & Butler are building a two-manual organ for the new Emmanuel Church, West Roxbury, Mass.

Mr. E. J. Macphblick gave a memorial service in memory of Gounod, at St. Patrick's Church, Boston, Nov. 17.

Mr. S. J. Gilbert, organist of Grace Church, Memphis, Tenn., has been arrested, accused of setting fire to the church. He was discharged from his post, and soon after the church was burned to the ground.

The organ in the Town Hall, Manchester, England, has recently been reconstructed by M. Aristide Cavaillé-Coll of Paris, and now contains four manuals, fifty-one speaking-stops, and twenty pedal movements.

Mr. Thomas Hill, the head of the firm of Messrs. Hill & Son, organ-builders, of London, died Oct. 22, at the age of seventy-two.

Mr. Charles Brindley, of the firm of Brindley & Foster, organ-builders, of Sheffield, England, died his month at the age of sixty.

Herr S. de Lange has been appointed a professor of the Stuttgart Conservatory.

During the absence of M. Guilmant from La Trinité, Paris, M. Regnault fulfilled the duties of sub-organist. Mr. Sabatol is the organist and choir-master at the choir, and when M. Guilmant is at his post at the gallery organ, very beautiful effects are produced with the two organs.

A new organ (Samuel Bishop) was inaugurated in St. James Church, Olney, Philadelphia, Nov. 16, by Mr. David D. Wood, who played: Favorite Overture, Auber; Largo and Minuet, Handel; Offertoire to St. Cecilia, Batiste; Andante and Minuet, Mozart; Torchlight March, Meyerbeer; Impositions; Overture to " William Tell," Rossini.

Mr. Fred L. Clark gave an organ recital in the Congregational Church of Houstonville, Mass., Nov. 16, playing Fantasia in C, Tours; " At Evening," Bach; Cantilène in A-minor, Salomé; Processional March, Whitney; Adagio in A-flat, Diemel; Vesper Bells, Spinney; Grand Chorus, Salomé; Overture to " Stradella," Flotow.

The firm of Hook & Hastings, organ-builders, has been organized into a stock company, with capital stock of $100,000, to be known as the Hook & Hastings Company. The officers are F. Warren Hastings, president; F. H. Hastings, treasurer; and Charles S. Hammer, secretary.

Mr. Fred L. Clark gave his sixteenth recital in Payson Church, Easthampton, Mass., Nov. 16, playing Sonata No. 2, Mendelssohn; Andante Cantabile, Tschaikowski; Scherzo, Lemaigre; Cantilène Nuptiale, Dubois;

Pastorale in G, Rheinberger; Concert Piece No. 2, Parker; March in E-flat, Wély.

Mr. Edward E. Howe gave his third organ recital in the First Presb. Church, Harleem, Pa., Nov. 14, with the following programme: A Polish Dance, Scharwenka; Theme and Variations, Hesse; Nocturne, Mendelssohn; Overture to " Wm. Tell," Rossini; Offertoire in A-flat, Read (Mr. A. M. Amey, 390th of Mr. Howe); St. Cecilia Offertoire, Batiste; Intermezzo, Mascagni; Finale, " Song Unto God," Handel.

Any singing-class teacher, organ teacher, or choir leader who will send his or her address to Filmore Bros., 143 W. Sixth Street, Cincinnati, or to 40 Bible House, New York, will receive, free, a copy of the December number of *The Musical Messenger*, with its interesting reading and Christmas music.

Mr. Wm. C. Carl gave the first of two organ recitals at the Drexel Institute, Philadelphia, Nov. 16, with the following programme: First Sonata, Salomé; Communion and March from " Ariane," Guilmant; Concerto in D-minor, Handel; Vision, Biel; Suite for Organ (MS.), Deshayes; Pastorale, MacMaster; Toccata from Fifth Symphony, Widor.

Mr. Herve D. Wilkins of Rochester, N.Y., inaugurated a new organ (Wm. King & Son) in the State Reformatory Chapel, Elmira, N.Y., Nov. 13, with the following numbers: Grand Chorus in D, Guilmant; Murmuring Zephyrs, Jensen; Auld Lang Syne, Wilkins; Funeral March and Seraphic Song, Guilmant; " At Evening," Bach; The Storm Fantasia, Lemmens; Home, Sweet Home, Wilkins; Scene Militaire, Wilkins.

An attempt was made a short time ago to burn the Trinity Episcopal Church in Chicago. The incendiary had piled a lot of music, which he had previously saturated with kerosene, inside the organ, and ignited it. A prayer-meeting was being held in the chapel, and the fire was discovered in time to prevent serious damage.

Excellent photographs of M. Guilmant may be ordered of W. G. Pearce, 52 Ogden Place, Chicago, Ill. Large size (8x10), one dollar; cabinet size, fifty cents; before the keyboards, fifty cents. Mr. Pearce also has some good photographs of Mr. Eddy. Large size (8x12), two dollars; cabinets, fifty cents; M. Guilmant and Mr. Eddy together, fifty cents.

LETTER FROM AUSTRALIA.

BRISBANE, Sept. 9, 1893.

MONSIEUR WIEGAND, the city organist of Sydney, gave five recitals on the organ by Willis in the Exhibition Building, Brisbane.

The second programme consisted of Sonata No. 1, Mendelssohn; Elevation in F. Batiste; Andante (Fourth Symphony), Haydn; Concert Study, Lacombe; Fugue in D, Bach; Fantasia on " Les Huguenots," Meyerbeer; Song without Words, Wiegand; Funeral March and Seraph's Song, Guilmant; Triumphal March in F, Grison. The third programme was, Sonata No. 4, Mendelssohn; Prayer, Lemaigre; Pastorale in A, Guilmant; Les Courriers, Ritter; Fugue in G-minor, Bach; Fantasia in " Carmen," Bizet; Ave Maria, Schubert; Cantilène, Grison; Offertory in B-flat, Guilmant; Marche Américaine, Widor.

The occasion was one of great interest to organists and musicians, his fame as an organist being widely known and having preceded him. The items specially worth mentioning were his performances of the First, Fourth, and Sixth Sonatas of Mendelssohn, in which faultless execution both in manual and pedal was displayed; on the other hand, his rendering of Bach's Toccata and Fugue in D-minor, great G-minor Fugue, and Toccata in F were open to criticism, not being at all in accordance with the traditional reading. The remainder of the programmes consisted of light operatic selections and piano music. An exceptionally fine rendering of Guilmant's Marche Funèbre and Chant Séraphique must be noted. In the opinion of connoisseurs, Mr. Wiegand's playing was marred by an excessive use of the Vox Humana, it being introduced into almost every piece, as also a prominent pedal being employed in soft passages; but, on the whole, it may be said that his performances were greatly appreciated, displaying his own remarkable powers as a player and the many beauties of the instrument. Concerning the Toccata in F, a local paper has discovered that " its lack of form is amply compensated for by minor changes." We live and learn.

The organist of Melbourne Cathedral intends giving a series of recitals shortly, when the scheme will comprise works of Hatton, Smart, Archer, Wély, Tombelle, Guilmant, Vilboe, etc., Merkel, Lux, Morandi, and Capocci, representing the modern English, French, German, and Italian schools of organ music, while Bach and Mendelssohn represent the classics.

E. P. JONES.

NEW ORGANS.

ST. PETER'S CATHEDRAL, MONTREAL.

(New organ built by Casavant Bros.)

GREAT ORGAN.

Montre	16 ft.
Montre	8 "
Bourdon	8 "
Kerataphone	8 "
Salicional	8 "
Flûte Traversière	4 "
Flûte Harmonique	4 "
Prestant	4 "
Nazard	2⅔ "
Doublette	2 "
Mixture	V. Rks.
Bombarde	16 ft.
Trompette	8 "
Clarinette	8 "
Clairon	4 "

SWELL ORGAN.

Gambe	16 ft.
Principal	8 "
Mélodie	8 "
Viole de Gambe	8 "
Voix Céleste	8 "
Flûte Octaviante	4 "
Octave	4 "
Octavin	2 "
Mixture	III Rks.
Cor Anglais	8 ft.
Voix Humaine	8 "
Hautbois-Basson	8 "
Trompette	8 "
Clairon	4 "

CHOIR ORGAN.

Quinston	16 ft.
Principal	8 "
Bourdon	8 "
Flûte Harmonique	8 "
Dulciana	8 "
Flûte	4 "
Violina	4 "
Piccolo	2 "
Cromorne	8 "
Musette	8 "

PEDAL ORGAN.

Flûte (Acoustic Bass)	32 ft.
Flûte Ouverte	16 "
Principal	16 "
Violon Basse	16 "
Bourdon	16 "
Grosse Flûte	8 "
Violoncelle	8 "
Flûte	4 "
Bombarde	16 "
Trompette	8 "
Clairon	4 "

COMBINATION PISTONS, ETC.

Five to Gt., Five to Sw. Three to Ch.

Four automatic adjustable Comb. Pedals.

Pedal Ventil to reduce Pedal to one stop.

Full Organ Pedal.

Sw. to Gt., Super and Sub-Octaves, in addition to the usual couplers.

Electro-pneumatic Action.

Electric motor.

This instrument was inaugurated by M. Alex. Guilmant, Sept. 21 and 22, before an audience of over five thousand.

PARK CENTRAL PRESB. CHURCH, SYRACUSE, N.Y.

(New organ built by Messrs. Hook & Hastings.)

GREAT ORGAN.

Open Diapason	16 ft.
Open Diapason	8 "
Viola da Gamba	8 "
Doppel Flöte	8 "
Flûte Harmonique	4 "
Octave	4 "
Twelfth	2⅔ "
Fifteenth	2 "
Mixture	III Rks.
Trumpet	8 ft.

CHOIR ORGAN.

Geigen Principal	8 ft.
Dulciana	8 "
Melodia	8 "
Flûte d'Amour	4 "
Piccolo	2 "
Clarinet	8 "

PEDAL ORGAN.

Open Diapason	16 ft.
Bourdon	16 "
Violoncello	8 "

SWELL ORGAN.

Bourdon (Treble and Bass)	16 ft.
Open Diapason	8 "
Salicional	8 "
Æoline	8 "
Stopped Diapason	8 "
Flauto Traverso	4 "
Violina	4 "
Dolce Cornet	III Rks.
Vox Humana	8 ft.
Cornopean	8 "
Oboe (with Bassoon)	8 "

PEDAL MOVEMENTS, ETC.

F., Mf., and P., Comb. Great.
Gt. to Ped. (reversible) Swell.

The usual couplers.

Electric motor.

CHURCH OF OUR LADY OF THE ROSARY, HOLYOKE, MASS.

(New organ built by Mr. George S. Hutchings.)

GREAT ORGAN.

Double Open Diapason	16 ft.
Open Diapason	8 "
Melodia	8 "
Viola di Gamba	8 "
Dulciana	8 "
Doppel Flöte	8 "
Flûte	4 "
Octave	4 "
Twelfth	2⅔ "
Fifteenth	2 "
Mixture	IV. Rks.
Trumpet	8 "
Clarinet	8 "

SWELL ORGAN.

Bourdon (Treble and Bass)	16 ft.
Open Diapason	8 "
Stopped Diapason	8 "
Keraulophon	8 "
Viola	8 "
Æoline	4 "
Flûte Harmonique	4 "
Piccolo	2 "
Mixture	III. Rks.
Cornopean	8 "
Oboe and Bassoon	8 "

PEDAL ORGAN.

Open Pedal Bass	16 ft.
Bourdon	16 "
Violoncello	8 "

PEDAL MOVEMENTS, ETC.

F., Mf., and P., Comb. Great. Swell.
Gt. to Ped. (reversible).

The usual couplers.

Pneumatics to lower 24 notes of Great.

Compass of Manuals, 61 notes; Pedals, 27 notes.

CHAPEL, NEW YORK STATE REFORMATORY.

(New organ built by William King & Son.)

GREAT ORGAN.

Open Diapason	16 ft.
Open Diapason	8 "
Gamba	8 "
Melodia	8 "
Octave	4 "
Harmonic Flute	4 "
Twelfth	2⅔ "
Fifteenth	2 "
Mixture	II Rks.
Trumpet	8 ft.

SWELL ORGAN.

Bourdon	16 ft.
Violin Diapason	8 "
Salicional	8 "
St. Diapason	8 "
Flautino	4 "
Fugara	4 "
Horn Trumpet	8 "
Flautino	4 "
Oboe and Bassoon	8 "

CHOIR ORGAN.

Keraulophon	8 ft.
Dulciana	8 "
Clarabella	8 "
Violina	4 "
Flûte d'Amour	4 "
Clarionet	8 "

PEDAL ORGAN.

Double Open Diapason	16 ft.
Grand Bourdon	16 "
Violoncello	8 "

PEDAL MOVEMENTS. *(Double-acting.)*

Full Great Organ.
S. ff. and p. B. Stops.
Gamba and Melodia.
Full Swell Organ.
Salicional and St. Diapason.
Great to Pedal (Reversible).
The usual couplers.
Electric Motor.

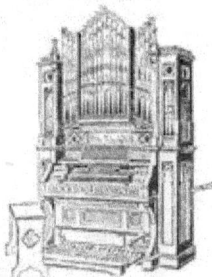

Letter from Alex. Guilmant to Farrand & Votey Organ Co.

[Handwritten letter in French, reproduced in facsimile]

C'est avec grand plaisir que j'ai touché l'Orgue construit pour la "Festival Hall" à Chicago par M. M. Farrand & Votey. Cet instrument est excellent; il possède du jeu d'un timbre charmant, il a de la puissance et en outre, la sonorité en est expressive. Les Pistons dont on joue à son gré

Changer les mélanges, offrent de précieuses ressources à l'organiste pour obtenir des effets variés et instantanés. J'ai visité l'intérieur de cet Orgue et j'en ai trouvé la disposition parfaite, le travail est exécuté avec le plus grand soin et avec d'excellents matériaux. C'est un instrument de premier ordre.

Alex. Guilmant

Chicago 9 Septembre 1893

[TRANSLATION.]

"It is with great pleasure that I have played the organ constructed for "Festival Hall," Chicago, by Messrs. Farrand & Votey. This instrument is excellent; it possesses stops of a charming quality (*timbre*); it has great power, and, besides, the sonority is expressive of it. The pistons, by which one can, at will, change the combinations, afford valuable resources to the organist for obtaining varied and instantaneous effects. I examined the interior of the organ, and I found the arrangement of it perfect; the work is executed with the greatest care and with excellent materials. It is an instrument of the first order."

(Signed)   ALEX. GUILMANT.

VOL. II. No. 9.   JANUARY, 1894.   WHOLE No. 21.

BACH

YEARLY SUBSCRIPTION $2.00.   SINGLE COPIES 25 CTS.

THE ORGAN

DEVOTED TO

A MONTHLY JOURNAL

THE KING OF INSTRUMENTS

RHEINBERGER

GUILMANT

FRESCOBALDI

BUXTEHUDE

MERKEL

BEST

· EVERETT · E · TRUETTE ·

EDITOR & PUBLISHER

149 A. TREMONT ST. BOSTON.

HANDEL

The New England Conservatory of Music.

CARL FAELTEN, Director.

The Organ Department

offers unsurpassed facilities for acquiring a thorough and practical education in the art of Organ Playing. The course of study, which may be pursued either in class or by private instruction, is very complete and comprehensive. The early grades embrace work in Pedal Obligato Playing, Hymn Tunes, and Chorales, with Interludes and Modulations. In the medium grades are studied Organ works of polyphonic character, Anthems and Improvisations, and by the more advanced students the works of all the great writers for the Organ, together with the study of Masses, Oratorios, etc.

The Department is provided with fourteen Pedal Organs for practice, several of which possess three manuals each.

Those students who have acquired sufficient ability are aided in securing Church positions by the *Conservatory Bureau.* A large number of students have already been placed in lucrative positions by the Bureau.

TUITION: CLASSES OF FOUR, TERM OF TEN WEEKS, $20.00.

BOARD OF INSTRUCTION.
{ GEORGE E. WHITING.
HENRY M. DUNHAM.
ALLEN W. SWAN. }

{ Organ Practice, 10 cents per hour and upwards.
Pupils may enter at any time.
School Year from Sept. 7, '93 to June 21, '94. }

Address, FRANK W. HALE, General Manager, Franklin Square, Boston, Mass.

THE ORGAN.

Vol. II.   BOSTON, JANUARY, 1894.   No. 9.

THE ORGAN.

BOSTON, JANUARY, 1894

Published the first of every month. Subscription price $2.00 per year (European countries 10s. 9d.), payable in advance. Single copies, 15 cents.

Subscribers will please state with which number they wish their subscription to begin.

Remittances should be made by registered letter, post office order, or by check payable to Everett E. Truette.

Correspondence, to secure notice, must in all cases be accompanied by the name and address of the writer, not for publication, but as a guarantee of good faith.

Advertising rates sent on application.

Address all communications,

THE ORGAN, 149 A Tremont Street, Boston, Mass.

Single copies of THE ORGAN can be procured of

NOVELLO, EWER, & Co.	New York.
G. SCHIRMER	New York.
OLIVER DITSON Co.	Boston.
L. H. ROSS & Co.	Boston.
N. E. CONSERVATORY	Boston.
H. B. STEVENS Co.	Boston.
LYON & HEALY	Chicago.
CLAYTON F. SUMMY	Chicago.
THEODORE PRESSER	Philadelphia.
WM. H. BONER & Co.	Philadelphia.
TAYLOR'S MUSIC HOUSE	Springfield, Mass.
GALLUP & METZGER	Hartford, Conn.
RICHAULT & Co.	Paris.
NOVELLO EWER & Co.	London.

CONTENTS:

"How can I do a decent amount of organ practice in the church during the cold weather?" is a common question just now. We recommend the plan originated by one ingenious organist whose zeal and wits overcame the obstacle of a cold church. He took an old-fashioned folding clothes-horse, and tacked cloth on its four sections. Having made a fifth section, also covered with cloth, he enclosed his organ bench and console within the clothes-horse, placing the fifth section on top for a roof. With a kerosene lamp burning on the floor, the thermometer within this miniature studio was raised from 26° to 65° in ten minutes, and his practice was never afterward a trial in cold weather.

This is the season when the electric motor smiles at its twin sister, the water motor. The thermometer at zero has no effect on the former, but is very trying to the latter if it happens to be in a cold corner. One water motor in Boston, in trying to keep out the cold, imbibed too freely, and became a little dazed. When being thawed out it burst, and, instead of sending the wind up into the organ, and the water down into the cellar, it sent a stream of water up into the organ, and the wind was nowhere. The sexton, who received some of the aforesaid water in the eye, placed an additional item on his bill to the church, "Laundry, 14 cents."

ONE of the most complete and satisfactory features of the music at the World's Fair was the series of organ recitals given in Festival Hall. A *résumé* of these recitals may prove of interest to readers of THE ORGAN. The organ built by Messrs. Farrand & Votey was formally opened July 30, by Mr. Clarence Eddy, from which time to the close of the fair, Oct. 30, 62 recitals were given by 21 organists. The 62 programmes contained 507 compositions (including repetitions), of which 464 were organ compositions, and 43 were "arrangements." This latter fact speaks well for the taste of our organists, who evidently prefer the legitimate organ music. Of the 507 compositions, 62 were composed by Bach, 43 by Guilmant, 8 by Merkel, 6 by Rheinberger, 5 by Best, 6 by Batiste, 3 by Wély, and 22 by Dudley Buck. Bach's Toccata and Fugue in D-minor was given 10 times, the Toccata in F, 9 times, and the Fantasia and Fugue in G-minor, 7 times. 49 numbers were sonatas, complete or in part, and 53 were fugues. 176 compositions were by German composers, 159 by French, 28 by English, 53 by American, and 91 by miscellaneous composers. The lion's share of the recitals was given by Mr. Clarence Eddy, who gave 21 recitals. Mr. Guilmant gave 4 recitals, which were naturally the most noteworthy. Mr. R. Huntington Woodman, of Brooklyn, gave 4 recitals; Messrs. G. E. Whiting, Walter E. Hall, Wm. C. Carl, S. A. Baldwin, Harrison M. Wild, Wilhelm Middelschulte, and Frank Taft each gave 3 recitals. Mr. J. F. Wolle gave 2 recitals, and 1 recital was given by each of the following organists: Messrs. B. J. Lang, H. G. Thunder, A. S. Vogt, Thomas Radcliff, George W. Andrews, Louis Adolph Coene, Otto Pfefferkorn, N. J. Corey, W. S. Sterling, and C. A. W. Howland.

AN ORGANIST AND A PIANIST.

THE question whether or not one person can be an organist and a pianist is at present receiving considerable notice in the musical press. Many writers claim that the action and necessary manipulation of the keys is so dissimilar in the two instruments, that practice on one instrument is injurious to a perfect technique at the other instrument. Other writers enthusiastically point to our improved organ action, claiming that the one obstacle is now removed; that organists no longer require "the grip of a giant" to play their instrument, and hence organ practice and piano practice are nearly similar.

It seems to us that both sides are right to a certain extent, but that two important points, which have as much influence on the question as the stiffness of the action of an organ, are apparently overlooked by every writer who has thus far expressed himself on the subject.

Can any one conceive of a Guilmant and a Paderewski combined in one person? And yet these two artists have many characteristics in common, and both are artists of the very front rank.

The question whether one person can be both a good pianist and a good organist depends solely upon the interpretation of the word *good*, for a reply. That he never could be a Guilmant and a Paderewski no one will deny. Life is too short. There is a period in the progress of every student, toward the attainment of that degree of proficiency necessary to become an artist, when he practises daily just as many hours as physical endurance will allow. Pianists practise from six to ten hours, and organists devote four to six hours to their instrument (we are considering only those who are on the road to an artistic career); but who could endure eight hours' piano practice and five hours at the organ, six days a week for forty weeks?

Look at the other interpretation of the word *good*. A man may play the piano fairly well, and likewise the organ fairly well. He practises the piano four hours, and the organ three hours, each day. This is about all the average man can endure, considering that one hour at the organ is as fatiguing as two at the piano. When will he become an artist at both instruments? Probably not before he is ninety-three.

M. Guilmant, who is one of the leading organists of the world, plays the piano? Yes! Effectively? Yes! A great pianist? Never!

The most objectionable features of the piano playing of organists are attributed to the stiffness of organ action, while we claim that to-day this has almost nothing to do with it.

When an organist plays on the organ *fortissimo*, he uses full organ, and, if the instrument is large, the volume of tone is immense — five times as much as five pianists could produce with five pianos. When he sits at the piano and attempts to play *fortissimo*, he endeavors, from force of habit, to produce the same volume of tone. It is impossible, and yet he strives for it, producing the harsh tones which are so objectionable, and are characteristic of the piano playing of organists. This can be overcome to a certain extent, but we doubt if years of labor would entirely eliminate it.

Another point of difference is the legato playing. It is claimed that legato playing on the organ assists the pianist to acquire a legato touch at the piano. So it does in one respect. It schools the mind to watch for the legato all the time, as its absence at the organ is more prominent than at the piano; but beyond this point it renders little assistance to the pianist.

To play legato on the organ, every key must be held down till the next key is depressed, *but not a fraction of a second longer*, else a disagreeable lack of clearness will be the result. Consequently, organists carry the fingers high, and move them instantly, when changing from one note or chord to another, securing a "crisp legato." Now, this "crisp legato" playing is useful in playing the piano at certain times, but it is not the embodiment of pure legato playing for that instrument. A slight overlapping of the tones, — a moulding, as it were, of one chord into the next, — so essential in artistic piano playing, requires just the opposite treatment; and herein lies another objectionable feature of the piano playing of organists. A pianist who has acquired the perfect legato touch (of the piano), when playing the organ, overlaps the keys in the same manner, and thus his playing is "muddy and disagreeable."

There is undoubtedly a great deal of unnecessary prejudice against one person playing both piano and organ, as any energetic student may play both organ and piano "fairly well;" but if he aims to be an artist, he must remember that an artistic career at either instrument will require a lifetime, and its attainment will be sufficient reward for the work of a lifetime.

> There was a young girl in the choir
> Whose voice rose higher and hoir,
> Till it reached such a height,
> It was clear out of seight,
> And they found it next day in the spoir.
> *Detroit Free Press.*

ELIAS HOOK.

ELIAS HOOK, the founder of the well-known firm of organ builders, E. & G. G. Hook, later Hook & Hastings, and now Hook & Hastings Company, the oldest establishment of organ builders in this country, was born in Salem, Mass., in 1806. He was apprenticed to Wm. M. Goodrich, a prominent organ builder, about 1824. In 1827, with his brother George, he established a factory in Salem, their first organ being erected in the Unitarian Church, Danvers, Mass. From these small beginnings the firm rapidly grew to importance, and in 1830 moved to Boston. Their sign, a miniature pipe-organ, which stood over their door on Friend Street, will be well remembered by the older citizens of Boston, and, though grim with age, it now reposes on one of the walls of the finishing hall, in the present factory at Kendal Green. In 1831 the firm moved to Cornhill, and later to Leverett Street, where they remained till 1853.

Elias Hook

The business had grown to such an extent that it was again necessary to seek larger quarters, and they moved to a large factory on Tremont and Ruggles Streets. In this factory many notable organs were constructed, among which may be mentioned those in Cincinnati Music Hall; Cathedral of the Holy Cross, Church of the Immaculate Conception, and Tremont Temple, Boston; St. Francis Xavier and St. Luke's, New York; Plymouth Church, Brooklyn; Industrial Exposition, Milwaukee; Cathedral, Denver, Colorado; St. Joseph's Cathedral, Buffalo; Yale College, New Haven; Unity Church and Union Park Cong. Church, Chicago, and Mechanics Hall, Worcester.

Elias Hook was a man of intensely amiable qualities; always gentle in manner and refined in tastes, he made friends at every turn. Being appreciative, he always enjoyed organ music, but never was much of a performer; though it is said that he composed a little. The death of his wife was a serious blow to him, and for a long time crippled him, as he was by nature dependent on the companionship and affection of one so near and dear.

Somewhat later he became attached to John Wilcox, and spent much of his time in the company of this organist, who owed most of his success to the influence of the genial organ builder.

Elias Hook died of apoplexy, June 15, 1881, at the age of seventy-six, just nine months after the death of his brother George.

FOR BEGINNERS IN PEDAL PLAYING.

It is the compass and capacity of the pedal section of an organ which give the instrument dignity, and cause it to be unapproachable by any other musical instrument. In this respect even a grand symphony orchestra is always lacking, compared with the deep and pervading bass of the organ. In legitimate organ music, the pedal part has its own distinct *voice*, independent of the manual parts.

The attainment of the use of the pedals is not so difficult as it seems, providing one has previously obtained perfect control of manual technique; and the object of this brief article is to afford encouragement to beginners, in giving a few preliminary rules in relation to the use of the pedals.

The organ seat should be at such a height above the naturals that the sole of the foot will hang from its own weight, without any lifting of the knee, at a short distance above the natural key, almost touching it, without resting on it, so that the toe or heel moving from the ankle-joint, *without lifting the knee*, will depress the pedal.

The first exercises in learning to play the pedals are to find the precise location of each key on the pedal clavier without looking at the feet. The position of each key may be firmly fixed in the mind, so that there will not be the slightest danger of a mistake, by first locating the relative position of the sharp with the natural keys which are adjacent.

The lowest C always being found without hesitation, the octave above, or the middle C of the key-board, may at once be found by lightly touching the toe of either foot against the left side of C sharp. This should be practised with both feet until the natural key may be touched without the least hesitation, and then the C of the higher octave should be found in the same manner.

Next should be found the position of the lowest E and the octave above, by touching the toe lightly on the right side of D sharp.

Next, the position of the lowest F and the octave above, by touching the left side of F sharp.

Next, the position of the lower B and the octave above, by touching the right side of A sharp.

Next, find the more difficult letters of D, G, and A, which are located within the position of the sharps, but which must be found by their relation to the adjacent sharps.

The novitiate in pedal playing can now write a series of original pedal exercises embodying these simple rules for finding the keys.

The next exercises should be a sequence of alternate fifths, as C for the left foot, G for the right foot, D [left], A [right] and so on, ascending and descending the compass of the keyboard.

Next, a succession of fourths in the same manner.

Next, a succession of thirds in the same manner.

Next, a succession of sixths in the same manner.

Next, a succession of octaves.

Next, these exercises should be repeated in all the keys with the toe.

Next, these exercises should be repeated in the key of C, using first the toe and then the heel upon the same note, striking it twice, as C [toe], C [heel], in order to give freedom to the motion of the ankle-joint without depressing the knee, or causing any motion of the torso, or upper part of the body.

Having thus located the position of each key with the proper motion of the ankle-joint, it will be an excellent practice to take a hymn-book and play through the bass parts alone with both feet, using the heel when required, until the relative position of each key of the clavier is firmly fixed in the mind.

The student will now be prepared to take up progressive studies in pedal playing, which should be marked with all the indications for the use of all the movements of the feet.

HORATIO CLARKE.

THE ORGANIST'S RETROSPECT.

BY HORATIO CLARKE.

(AN AUTOBIOGRAPHY OF ERNEST OSBORNE)

IN TWENTY-FIVE CHAPTERS.

CHAPTER IX.

The new organ was finished in the church at the contracted time, and it was played the first Sunday by an organist from the city. During the coming week the regular organist was to be chosen by the committee. The decision rested between a former organist and myself. He was an active member in the parish, and was a teacher in one of the public schools. He had canvassed the whole society, and had obtained the signatures of a large number in the parish to a petition in favor of his receiving the appointment, while I solicited no person to speak a word in my behalf.

In order to cause me to withdraw my application, my competitor showed me his petition, with its numerous signatures, so that I might feel conscious that I had no friends in the society.

When the decision was made, I was chosen as the organist of the church, and I accepted the position with undemonstrative but inward joy. The organ was of more than usual excellence, and it was an inspiration to play it. My competitor was a talented and critical musician. At the first service after my appointment, he took his position in a pew in the side gallery, where he could overlook my management of the keys and stops, and he kept up this critical inspectorship every Sunday during the year.

While it destroyed much of my freedom, it made me very careful in the rendering of my organ selections and improvisations. It was a severe ordeal, to be conscious that in every succession of notes played, in each pedal key touched, and in the changes of the stops, there was an unfriendly critic present, watching for mistakes, so that a plea of my incompetency might be presented to the music-committee, and he thus be installed in my position.

This unpleasant discipline had such an effect upon me, that, in all my succeeding hours of study, I practised as though an enemy were behind me, watching my defects, and it ever haunted me through all my public playing.

Looking back upon this period after more than thirty subsequent years of arduous musical study and practising, I have not been called upon for any higher grade of performance in any church position than in the music which I rendered when I was seventeen years of age.

Had I then realized the fact that no greater appreciation by churches or the general public would ever be given to my progress in organ music, I should have saved my nervous system from much wasted anxiety and future delusion, the hard work of succeeding years simply resulting in an unsatisfactory effort to attain a more advanced proficiency in my chosen art, as far as there has been any recognition from those who have not had practical acquaintance with the structure of organ music.

While I grew in favor as an organist and teacher, my home life became more intolerable in the humiliating experiences which I was obliged to suffer. Mr. Rodman felt much pride in my musical progress, and did all in his power to encourage me.

But it exasperated the jealous nature of Mrs. Rodman to such a degree, that I daily had to bear the meanest invective in false and wicked accusations, with threats of exposing faults to others of which I was unconscious.

She was determined to break up my "foolish pride," as she termed my dignified self-respect, and to put an end to my musical progress. She was vehement in her declaration that I should be put to learn the trade of a blacksmith, and that my ideas of a professional life should be crushed.

She at last forbade my practising any more in her house. But Mr. Rodman was my true friend, and provided a way in which my musical studies could be continued. His office was in a neat building which was detached from the factory; and to this place he moved my piano and melodeon. It was a good room twenty-five feet square and twelve feet high, with a smooth floor of hard wood, and was only occupied by his desk. As I gave my lessons at the residences of pupils in the evening, this arrangement for practising was better than at the house, and I arranged my time so as not to interfere with the business affairs of the office.

I was yet attending school, and practised five hours daily, besides giving two or three lessons each evening. As I was now earning my own living and paid for my board, I was released from all work about the house. Why I remained an inmate of such a suffering house as Mrs. Rodman made for me, now seems unaccountable; but Mr. Rodman helped me to advantages which would not have been possible elsewhere.

My visits to the organ factory had awakened a deep interest in the structure of the instrument, and, having every facility for doing any kind of work in Mr. Rodman's manufactory, I longed to use my constructive ability in this direction. Mr. Rodman was a very ingenious mechanic, and readily granted me permission to occupy one corner of his office for a pipe organ, with the promise of his own help in fitting the various parts.

I determined to make a small organ of two manuals, with a full set of pedals, with independent sub-bass pipes, and to enclose it in one corner of the room, so that it would occupy a space of ten feet in width and eight feet in depth. The capacity of an organ of one manual is too limited for the rendition of organ music, and is only an aggravation to a student.

On mentioning my desire to Mr. Sherburn, the organ builder, he said that I would be welcome to any old materials which he had on hand in the way of one or two old organs which he had stored away, as he would not have use for them in the construction of new instruments. I selected two fine wind-chests, as well as a set of double-banked keys, and bellows, with portions of wind-trunks and action work. There was just the quantity of wood pipes for all my requirements excepting the sub-bass pipes; but the metal pipes had all been melted, with the exception of a reed stop, which had been carefully packed away.

In addition to the gift of all this material, my good friend said that if I needed any new work to complete my plan, he would furnish it at the actual cost of labor and stock.

Mr. Sherburn was a man of broad and true principles in his organ building. He had a hearty recognition for all merit, whether emanating from his own factory or from that of a competitor. His word was as good as a signed contract, and every detail of construction was sure to be faithfully executed. He was a staunch friend through my entire musical life, and the establishment which he founded has the reputation of being the highest in the art.

Having selected the materials, I drew my own plans for the location of every part, and Mr. Sherburn gave me a scale for the construction of the pedal wind-chest and its pipes, which were to be made by Mr. Rodman. I decided not to have any case with front pipes, but to place both manual chests upon the same level, and instead of having the pipes of the upper manual enclosed in a separate swell-box, to sheathe in the entire instrument with matched stock, having swell folds in the front over the key-desk, thus rendering the whole organ expressive.

Before giving in my order for the new metal pipes, I had a number of experimental pipes made having the pitch of Middle C. Among these was one of a small diameter, less than an inch. In experimenting with this pipe I obtained a quality of tone partaking somewhat of the nature of a stringed instrument as well as of an orchestral oboe, and I had a stop made from this sample which I named "Obolette."

The specification of my studio instrument contained the organ, flute, string, and reed quality of tone, with twenty draw-stops, including the three usual couplers and " Tremolo."

I carried my sample string-toned pipe to several different organ builders, hoping to interest them in the introduction of such a stop, but in nearly all cases they were not musicians,

and gave me clearly to understand that they did not deviate from their established routine of constructing either pipes or mechanism, and that they should make no innovations unless forced to protect themselves when in competition with others, or until they should be obliged to yield to a very strong demand for greater improvements than the trade yet required.

It is the lack of a thorough musical education which places many organ builders at a disadvantage in important particulars which only an organist appreciates. A builder possessing a progressive spirit and not being an adept in musical science and the possibilities which a cultivated player perceives, is obliged to depend on others for suggestions in regard to many details essential to progress, upon which, there being no standard of co-operation, even organists do not agree.   *(To be continued.)*

MIXTURES.

(FOUR RANKS.)

Mr. B. J. Lang, organist of King's Chapel, Boston, has given two very interesting illustrated lectures on pianoforte touch in Chickering Hall during the past month.

Mr. Allen W. Swan gave one of his interesting organ recitals in the Unitarian Church, New Bedford, Mass., Dec. 17, with the following programme: Prelude to "Lohengrin," Wagner; Sonata Pontificale, Lemmens; Pastorale in E, Tombelle; Cujus Animam, Rossini; Fra; Salome; Pastorale, Wély; Grand March from " Aïda," Verdi.

Mr. Wm. C. Carl opened a new Farrand & Votey organ in the First M. E. Church, Scranton, Pa., Dec. 7, playing Toccata in F, Bach; Introit, MacMaster; Gavotte, Nesvadba; Finale, Fifth Symphony, Widor; Concerto No. 10, Handel; Vision, Bird; Marche de la Symphonie, "Arione," Guilmant; La Consummant, Mailer; Fanfare (3183) Dubois; Valse d'Amour, Salome; Schiller March, Meyerbeer.

Mr. J. Warren Andrews gave an organ recital at the Park Cong. Church, Minneapolis, Nov. 27.

The College of Organists, London, has received a Royal Charter, which was signed by the Queen, Nov. 23, and hereafter will be called the Royal College of Organists.

A new organ, built by the Hook & Hastings Co., for the M. E. Church, Centre Sandwich, N.H., was inaugurated Nov. 30.

Messrs. Wm. King & Son of Elmira, N.Y., are building two-manual organs for M. E. Church, Troy, Pa., and Westminster Presbyterian Church, Harrisburg, Pa.

Sexton : A London Church.   *Parson and Choir disagreed.*

Parson : I claim to direct, and only the theological aspirations of the congregation, but the drudi-soul-quavers, sharps and flats of the choir as well.

Choir : We won't stand for, confine yourself to dogma, and leave music to those who know something about it. We strike.

Parson : I shall fill all your places.

Choir : And we will go to another church.   *(I vacant severally.)*

Mr. Homer W. Parker gave an organ recital in Trinity Church, Boston, Dec. 13, with the following programme: Sonata in F minor, Rheinberger; Offertoire in D-flat, Salome; Caprice in B-flat, Guilmant; Fireside and Fugue in G minor, Bach; Concert Piece in B, Minor, Miss Jeannie M. Crocker sang arias of Mendelssohn and Parker.

The organ in Trinity Church has been re-voiced, the pitch being changed to the French pitch, and several minor alterations have been made.

Mr. W. H. Donley gave his fourth organ recital (third series) in Plymouth Church, Indianapolis, Dec. 2, with the following programme: Overture in C, Mendelssohn; Larghetto from "The Power of Sound," Spohr; Pastorale, Louis XV, Archer; Selection from " Der Freischütz," Loss; March from "Lohenra Symphony," Raff; Prayer and Barcarolle, Meyerbeer; Gavotte, Nesvadba; Love-Duo (Messe de Mariage), Dubois.

Mr. George S. Hutchings is placing a two-manual organ with twenty-two registers in Grace Episcopal Church, Madison, N.J., and one with seventeen registers in the First Independent Cong. Church, Meadville, Pa.

" Mons. Alex. Guilmant, when in New York, was invited by the reverend Fathers of St. Francis Xavier Church to play their large organ, built in Boston. This he did, and after the trial he remarked to the priests that it was the finest organ that he had played in this country. The organ was built by Hook & Hastings."

The Music Trades of New York announces that the Farrand & Votey Organ Co. are to build a two-manual organ for the Jay Gould Memorial Church, Roxbury, N.Y.

Theodore Dubois, organist of La Madeleine, Paris, has composed an opera for the Opéra Comique, which, it is expected, will be produced next season.

A large two-manual organ (thirty speaking-stops), built by Mr. John Brown, of Wilmington, Del., has been erected in the Gaston Temple Memorial Church, Washington, D.C., and was formally opened last month by Messrs. Chas. S. Elliott, and James Gastfield.

GRAND CHOEUR.

HENRI DESHAYES.

Moderato 120 = ♩

Gt. to Octave.

Gt.

Sw. 8 & 4 Ft. (f)

Ped. 16 & 8 Ft. (f)
Sw. to Gt. & Gt. to
Ped.

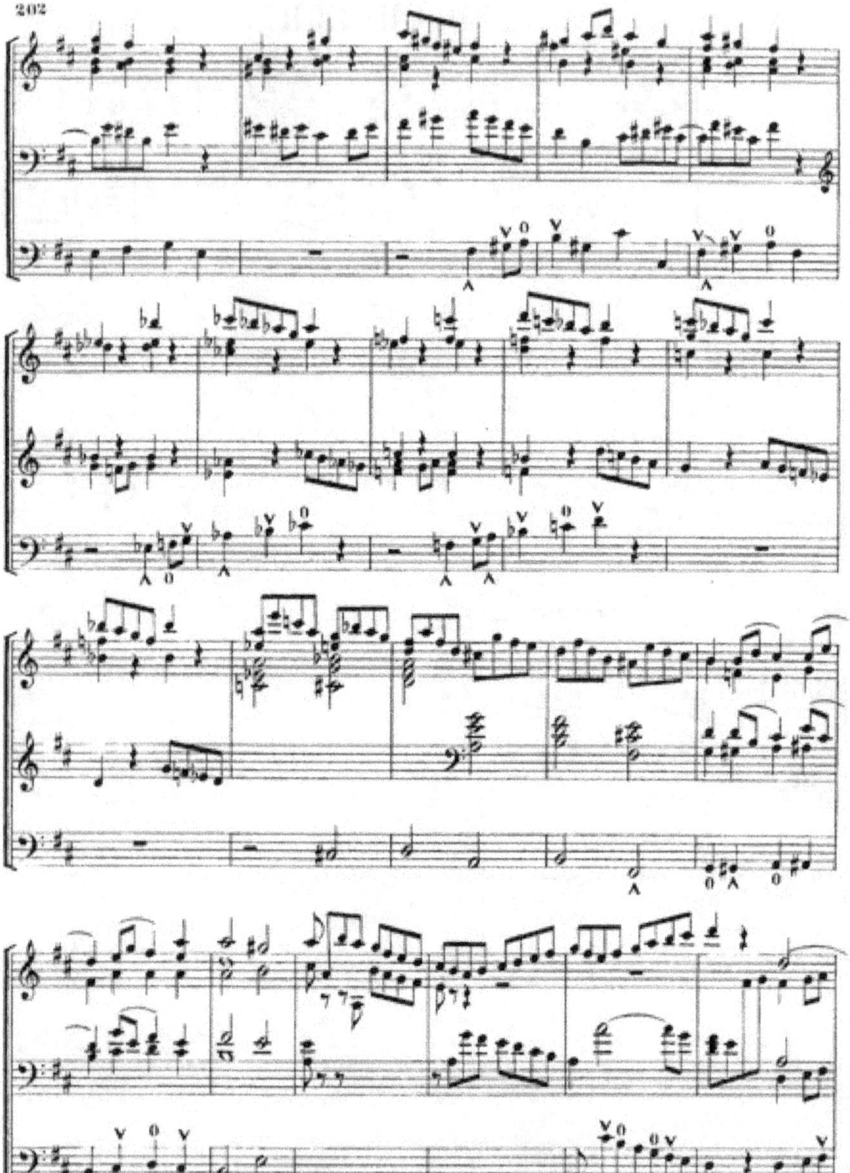

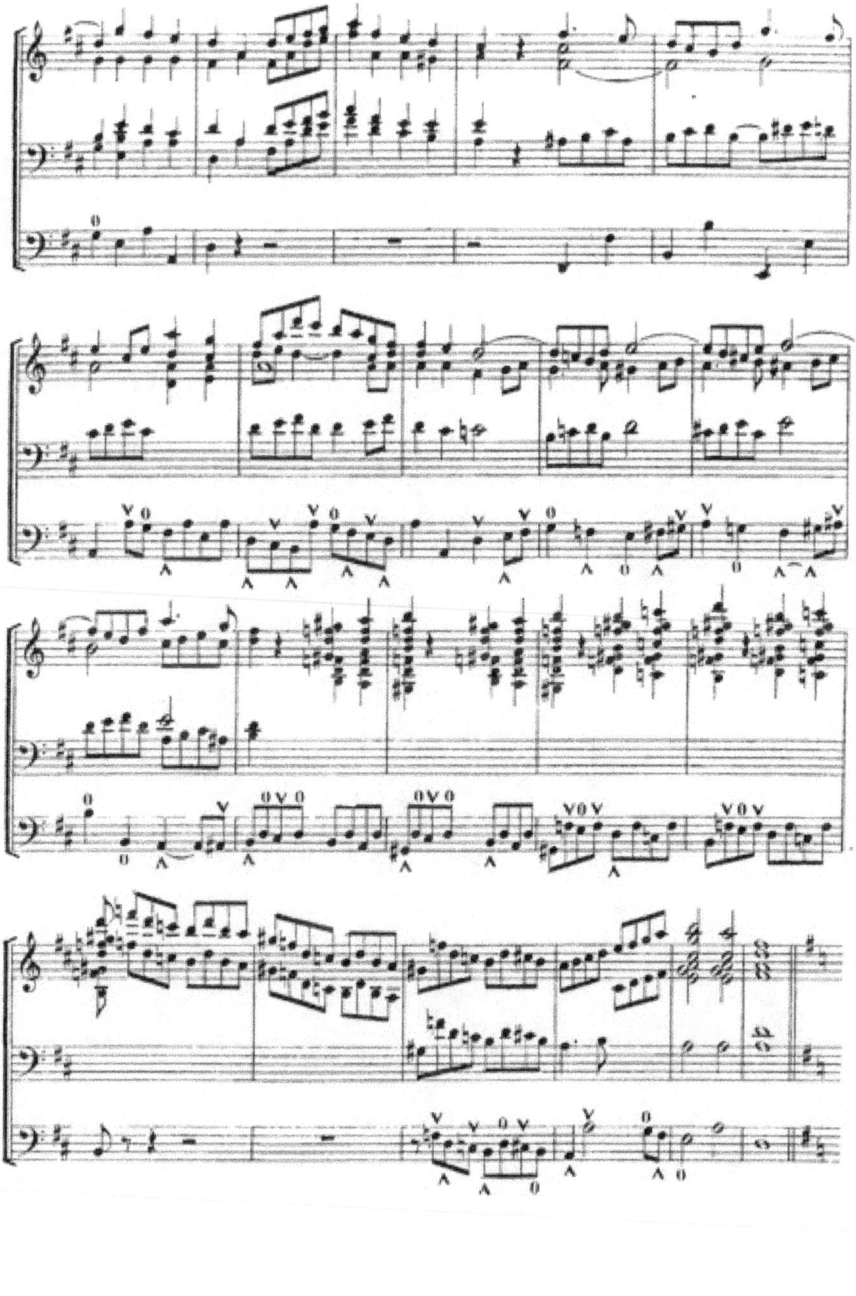

PRAYER.

L'istesso tempo.

Sw. St. Diapason, Violin & Trem.

Reduce Ped. to Bourdon.

Add Flute 4 Ft.

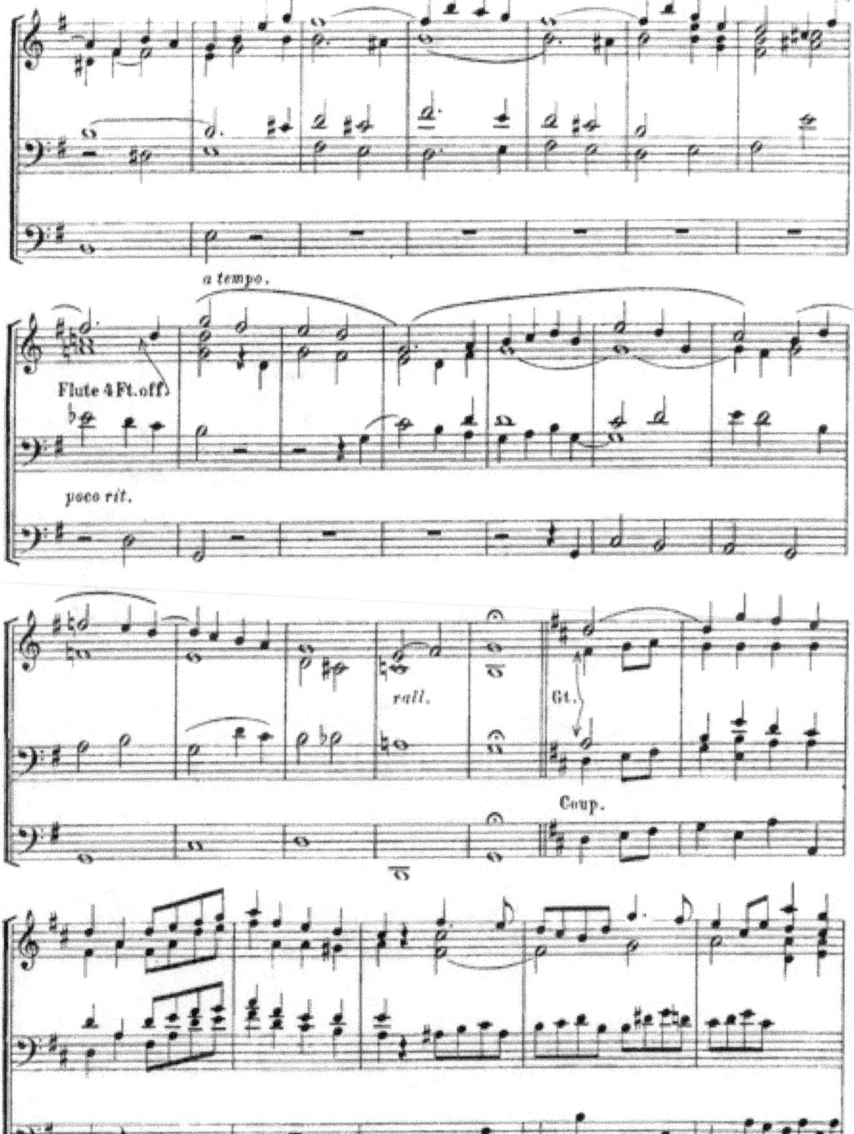
a tempo.
Flute 4 Ft. off)
poco rit.
rall.
Gt.
Coup.

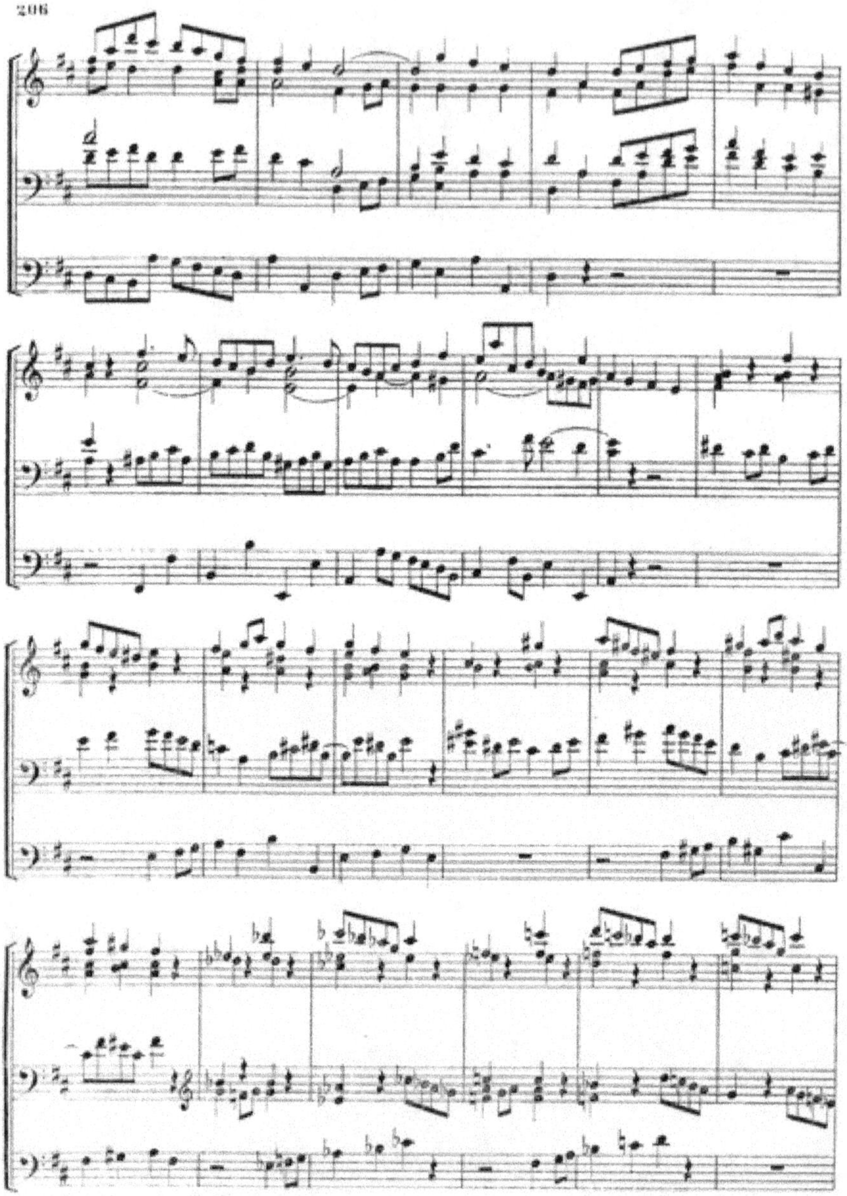

Full Organ.

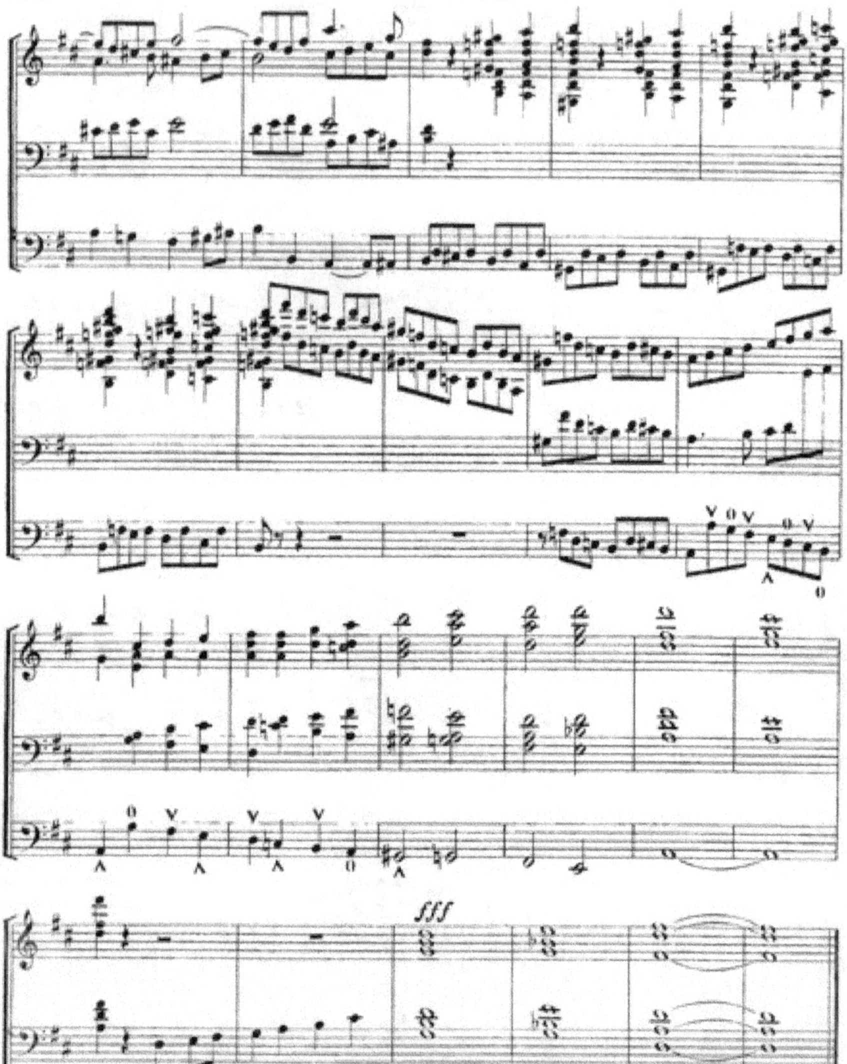
fff

Mr. Wm. C. Carl gave his second organ recital at the Drexel Institute, Philadelphia, Nov. 16, when he presented the following very interesting programme: First Sonata, Salome; Communion (dedicated to Mr. Carl) and Marche de la Symphonie "Ariane," Guilmant; Concerto, No. 10, in D minor, Händel; Visions, Bird; Suite for Organ (written for, and dedicated to, Mr. Carl), Deshayes; Pastorale, Mac Master; Toccata from Fifth Symphony, Widor.

Mr. David D. Wood gave an organ recital in the Tabor Presb. Church, Philadelphia, Dec. 1., inaugurating a new organ (built by Mr. John Brown, Wilmington, Del.) having two manuals, twenty-two speaking stops, and five pedal movements. Mr. Wood's programme consisted of Triumphal March, Roeske; Offertoire in G, Wely; Larghetto and Minuet, Mozart; Wedding March, Mendelssohn; Improvisation on Popular Airs; Overture to Semiramide, Rossini.

The Church of the Sacred Heart, East Boston, Mass., dedicated its new organ on Christmas. It is a large two-manual instrument, built by the Hook & Hastings Co. It has a massive quartered oak exterior, showing large 16 ft. open metal pipes on the front. It has two manuals, thirty registers, and is blown by a water motor.

Mrs. A. W. Armstrong, assisted by her pupils, Miss Hettie A. Davis, Miss Carrie L. Shapley, and Miss Jennie F. Kractzer, gave an organ recital in the Baptist Church, W. Acton, Mass., Nov. 25, when the following organ numbers were given: March from Leonore Symphony, Raff; Grand Chorus in D, Guilmant (Miss Shapley); Variations on an American Air, Flagler (Miss Davis); St. Cecilia Offertory No. 2, Batiste; Melody and Intermezzo, Camp (Miss Kractzer); "The Storm," Lemmens (Miss Shapley).

Guilmant at St. George's Church, — by invitation of Mr. W. S. Chester, the organist, Mr. Guilmant, accompanied by Mr. Carl, tried Jardine's grand organ in the above church, and was more than delighted with its volume of tone and beautiful solo stops, and highly complimented Mr. Jardine, saying it was as effective as the grand instruments of Cavaille of Paris. After playing it he asked Mr. Chester to play it, and went to the centre of the church to judge of the effects. Notwithstanding that one section of the organ is in the chancel and the other section in the gallery, nearly 200 feet apart, it is readily played at the console in the chancel by an electric action, giving the organist instant control over its 160 stops and 5,000 pipes, the longest of which is the CCC 32 feet.

Musical Courier.

FROM AUSTRALIA.

Mr. Ernest Wood gave the following programme at St. Paul's Cathedral, Melbourne, Oct. 19: Prelude and Fugue in F minor, Bach; Air and Variations, Hatton; Cantilène Pastorale, Guilmant; Shepherd's Song and Idyl, Merkel; Offertoire, Grison. On the same evening Mr. J. Albert Mallinson gave a recital in St. George's Church, St. Kilda, Melbourne, in which he played: Prelude and Fugue in A minor, Bach; Pastorale in E, Tombelle; Romance, Mallinson; and Toccata in D, Dubois. On Oct. 21, Mr. S. Disker gave a recital at Wesleyan Church, Brisbane, playing Pastorale from a Suite, Hampton; Andante in E minor, Batiste; Andante from Kreutzer Sonata, Beethoven-Batiste; Elegie, Silas; Selections from the "Redemption," Gounod. The last two numbers were in memoriam of Ch. Gounod.

E. S. Jones.

Mr. R. Huntington Woodman gave two organ recitals at the New York Ave. Church, Brooklyn, Nov. 16 and 23, with the following very interesting programmes: Passengha Fugue, Bach; Pastorale, Foote; Fourth Symphony (last movement), Widor; Andante con Variations, Calkin; Cantilène in A minor, Grison; Second Concerto (first movement), Handel; Prière and Canzona, Guilmant; Marche Cortège, Gounod. Nov. 22: Fourth Sonata (last movement), Mendelssohn; Scotch d'Amour, Klein; Sing unto God, Handel-Woodman; Christmas Offertory, Grison; March of the Three Kings (by request), Dubois; Traumerei "I am the Resurrection and the Life" (MS.), written for Mr. Woodman, de la Tombelle; Communion, Saint-Saëns; Marche Religieuse, Guilmant; Cantabile (Fourth Symphony), Widor; Concert Variations on "The Star Spangled Banner," Buck.

A series of five miscellaneous concerts, under the direction of Mr. J. Warren Andrews, were given by the Plymouth Church Choral Society at that church during the past month. At each recital Mr. Andrews performed one or more organ numbers, the principal works being: Prelude and Fugue, Op. 37, Mendelssohn; Schüler March, Meyerbeer; Second Sonata, Bach; Caprice in B-flat, Guilmant; Vesper Hymn, Variations, Andrews; Second Concerto, Handel; Largo (with string orchestra), Händel; and Sonatas Op. 88 and 98, Rheinberger.

Mr. Wm. C. Hammond gave his eighty-second organ recital at the Second Congregational Church, Holyoke, Mass., Nov. 20, with the following programme: Vorort, Titcombe; Postlude, Dumbris; Overture in D, Mehul; Sonata No. 4, Guilmant; Melody in C, Salome; Funeral March in B-flat, Guilmant; Andante Cantabile (from String Quintet), Tchaikovsky. Mr. Hammond's organ recitals have long been the leading musical attraction in Holyoke, and large audiences are the rule. The concerts are given every Monday during the musical season, and the programmes contain many works seldom, if ever, heard in other organ recitals. The organ has recently been rebuilt, and is now one of the best in the State. Tubular-pneumatic action has been applied, and the console has been extended.

Mr. W. T. Best gave four organ recitals in St. George's Hall, Liverpool, early in November, just before the fall term of the Assize, during

which term the recitals are discontinued. The programmes were: Nov. 4, Fantasia Chromatica, Thiele; Pastorale, Kullak; Variations on a Russian Hymn, Freyer; Scherzo in F-sharp minor, Hutton, Dict.; "La Pesca" (Scènes Musicales No. 20), Rossini; Ave Maria, Best, Nov. 9; Rigaudon, Lulli; Andante in G, Smart; Concerto No. 8 in A minor, Händel; Elegy, Op. 51, Bargiel; Overture composed for the opening of the London Exhibition, 1862, Auber. Nov. 11: Overture in C, Lindblad; Andante and Variations, Op. 83, Mendelssohn; Marcia Eroica and Finale, Best; Allegro Cantabile (Fifth Symphony), Widor; Selection from "Fidelio," Beethoven. Nov. 12: Offertoire, Batiste; Rhapsodie sur Cantiques Bretons, Saint-Saëns; Fantasia and Chorale, Smart; Motet, "Incense et vanae cura," Haydn; Air, "Sanctum et terribile," Pergolesi; Marche Solennelle, Villac.

Mr. J. J. Miller gave his twenty-first organ recital in Christ Church, Norfolk, Va., Dec. 4, with the following programme: Toccata in F, Bach; Larghetto from the "Water Music," Händel; Christmas Pastorale, Merkel; Serenade, Gounod; Christmas March, Le Blanc. The printed programme of this recital contains an article on "The Use and Misuse of the Organ in Public Worship," written by Mr. J. V. Flagler, which contains some sound advice to young organists. The article, which is copied from a New York periodical, is too long to be copied; but the closing words should be taken to heart by many of the vocalled organists who are pianists from noon Sunday till 10.30 the following Sunday, and in truth are still pianists while on the organist's bench. "The constant use of the swell-pedal by the right foot, while employing the left foot for playing or thumping the pedals, is a decidedly bad habit, unfitting the player for performing legitimate organ music, where smooth pedalling is necessary, and inducing the habit of using the swell in a dangerously monotonous manner. Such organists are called 'wood sawyers,' from the position they occupy on the organ stool."

Programme of Mr. Wm. C. Hammond's eighty-third organ recital, in the Second Cong. Church, Holyoke, Mass.: Canzona, Gabrilli; Romanza, Scudianti; Andante Cantabile, from Quintet in D, Haydn; Sonata, No. 2, Merkel; Melody in G from String Quartet, and Pièce Symphonique, Op. 14-2, Grieg.

Mr. Stanley Addicks gave an organ recital in the Drexel Institute, Philadelphia, Nov. 21, before an audience of fifteen hundred people. Programme: Prelude and Fugue in A minor, Bach; Coronation March, Svendsen; Fourth Sonata, Mendelssohn; Offertory in D-flat, Salome; "The Death of Ase" (from "Peer Gynt"), Grieg; Postlude in E-flat, Wely.

The Hook & Hastings Co. has just finished an organ in the North Presbyterian Church of Allegheny, Pa., having two manuals, twenty-two registers, and blown by a water motor; also an organ for St. Brendan's Church, Berlin, N.H., which has two manuals, and thirteen registers.

Messrs. Johnson & Son have recently placed two-manual organs in the following churches: First M. E. Church, Merrillville, N.Y.; Mt. Auburn M. E. Church, Cincinnati, Ohio; Congregational Church, Bound Brook, Conn.; First M. E. Church, Northampton, Mass.; Ravenswood M. E. Church, Chicago, Ill. (this organ opened by Louis Falck, Dec. 12); and are building for the following churches: First M. E. Church, Flint, Mich.; Congregational Church, Housatonic, Mass.; Trinity Church, Mendham, N.J.

Mr. Fred L. Clark gave an organ recital in Emanuel Memorial Church, Sherburne Falls, Mass., Dec. 7, when he played Marche Religieuse, Guilmant; Offertory in D-flat, Salome; Andante from Fifth Sonata, Merkel; "Tannhauser" March, Wagner; Vesper Bell, Spinney; Andante Cantabile, Tschaikowsky; Offertory in D minor, Batiste; Cantilène Nuptiale, Dubois; Largo, Handel; Finale in D, Lemmens.

Mr. S. Clarke Lord gave an interesting programme of organ music at the Asylum Hill Cong. Church, Hartford, Conn., Nov. 17, performing: the Fourth Sonata, Mendelssohn; Pastorale in D-flat, Foote; Allegretto in B minor, Pastorale in A, and Marche Religieuse, Guilmant; Gavotte, Thomas; Pièce Symphonique, Grieg.

An organ recital was given in All Saints' Church, Toronto, Dec. 2, by Mr. W. E. Fairclough, F. C. O., with the following numbers: Prelude and Fugue in G, Bach; Melody and Intermezzo, Parker; Marche de Fête (dedicated to Mr. Fairclough), Wm. Reed; Variations on Theme from Bach's B minor Mass, Liszt; Andante from First Symphony, Mendelssohn; Chanson in A, Durand; Toccata in A-flat, Hesse.

Mr. Frank Treat Southwick gave an organ concert in St. Andrews Church, New York, Nov. 21, playing: Chromatic Fantasia, Thiele; Sonata No. 3, Guilmant; Rhapsodie on Breton Melodies, Saint-Saëns; Allegretto, Lemmens; Marche Pontificale, Widor; Siegfried's Funeral March, Wagner; Les Préludes, Liszt.

Mr. Clarence Eddy gave the following programme of organ music at the N. Y. Ave. M. E. Church, Brooklyn, N.Y., December: Prelude and Fugue in A minor, Bach; Am Meer, Schubert; Pilgrim's Chorus, Wagner; Romanza, Op. 22, No. 2, Brewer; Spring Song and Scherzo, Shelley; Melody and Intermezzo, Parker; The Holy Night, Buck; Toccata in A, Best; Gavotte from "Mignon," Massenet; Lamentation and Scherzo Symphonique, Guilmant; Offertoire in C minor, Batiste.

A new Hook & Hastings organ in Park Presbyterian Church, Syracuse, N. Y., was inaugurated Dec. 21 by Dr. G. A. Parker, with the following programme: Toccata, Bach; Offertoire, Salome; Pilgrim's Chorus, Wagner; Capriccio, Lemaigre; Andante Cantabile, Tschaikowsky; Communion, Batiste; Sonata No. 2, Mendelssohn; Overture to "Mignon," Thomas; March of the Magi Kings and Toccata, Dubois.

CORRESPONDENCE.

FREDERICK ARCHER.

To the Editor of THE ORGAN :—

CHICAGO, ILL., Dec. 4.

SIR. —In this month's issue of your paper I read with interest Mr. Pearce's remarks on Mr. Frederick Archer.

By way of an appendix I would like to ask the following questions : —

1. If it was it that Mr. Archer — the greatest exponent of modern organ playing — did not give any recitals on the organ in the Festival Hall at the World's Fair?

2. Was he asked to do so by the authorities?

A large number of organists from all parts of the country gave three recitals each, whilst M. Guilmant was heard four times, and Mr. Eddy twenty-one times, I believe ; but Mr. Frederick Archer (admittedly the greatest of all) did not give even one recital, although he resides within easy walking distance of the Festival Hall.

Your obedient servant,

JOHN N. GOWER, *Mus. Doc., Oxon.*

KEYS INSTEAD OF STOP KNOBS.

To the Editor of THE ORGAN :—

OBSERVING in your November number a notice of a new organ built in Boston with such an application, brings to my mind that such a method was advocated by Mr. H. W. Nichol, a talented New York organist, at least twenty years ago, in a pamphlet which he then published.

In 1877 a Western organ builder obtained a patent for operating the stops of an organ by using two sets of natural keys, the lower key to bring on the stop, and pressing the key above to release it. A second patent was obtained by the same builder, simplifying the method, using a single natural key with the bevelled front reversed, on which the name was engraved. The key was pressed to bring on the stop, and it was released by simply touching the front of the key, pneumatic stop-action being used in both of these cases.

At this same time an organ was built for the Elm-street Methodist Church in Toronto, Canada, by Messrs. Warren & Son of that city, in which the stops were brought on by natural keys, and released by an adjacent ebony sharp key. These are historical facts which illustrate that new inventions in organ-building do not always originate in Boston.

B. ALGY.

NEW YORK, Dec. 19, 1893.

To the Editor of THE ORGAN : —

IN the December number of your paper I noticed a communication from Robert Hope-Jones, in which he stated that his stop keys have been appropriated, and fitted by certain builders to organs in the States ; notably to one of the instruments exhibited at the World's Fair.

As Mr. Jones has made this claim and statement, and limits himself to the date of his application for a patent, 1891, he has no right to claim this as his invention ; and having no right to this claim, the organ builders of the United States who have used the Tablet, Domino, Register, or Stop Key Action, cannot be charged with appropriating his invention.

In proof of my statement I shall offer in evidence the patent granted Gustave Sander, Aug. 2, 1887, No. 367,666, entitled, " Pneumatic Action for Organs."

In this patent there are five sheets of drawings. On sheet three, Fig. 6 and 7 ; sheet four, Fig. 12 ; and sheet five, Fig. 13, these stop or register keys are fully illustrated.

Commencing with line eighty-seven, page four, he describes the register key as a lever pivoted in the middle. To press on the lower end brings the stop on, pressure on the upper end shuts it off.

These stop-keys are all arranged in a row over the manuals, and do away with the stops at the sides of the key-boards. This row of stop keys he called the balanced register clavier.

After the description of his invention, follow his claims. Claim two, page six, line fifty-eight, is the " balanced register clavier," consisting of the register keys (18), and their connections. As Sander's application for a patent was filed Feb. 7, 1887, that of Hope-Jones of England four years later, 1891 (according to his own statement), the invention is clearly that of Sander.

In Topfer's Orgelbau (1888 edition), page seven hundred, this patent is described ; and on table forty-three, Fig. 9 and 10 of the Atlas, are drawings of the same, as this work has found sales in Germany, England, and America. Possibly Mr. Hope-Jones may have seen this work some time previous to his application for a patent in 1891.

Who can tell?

IRA BASSET.

CHICAGO, Dec. 11, 1893.

" INDISTINCTNESS OF ORGAN TONE."

To the Editor of THE ORGAN :—

SIR, — " Melodia," in his letter under the above heading in your last issue, invites reply to the following questions :

1. " Is there a fault in the construction of organ windchests, either with separate valves to each pipe, or in the ordinary method of manufacture ? "

2. " Can a better scheme of tone distribution of the choruswork of organs be devised, wherein the 8ft. tone shall be more prominent ? "

Following, as these queries do, my letter on the modern organ in the same issue of your paper, touching the defects to which " Melodia " calls attention, it may not be impertinent if I try to reply.

1. To diagnose the disease and practically reply to both questions, I might sum up the matter as the country doctor did when asked of what his patient had died, and say, " Want of breath." That is the exact reply to " Melodia's " query No. 1.

2. A better scheme in every way has long ago been devised. Organ builders have to make a living, and the commercial side of organ building must be considered as well as the artistic side. When committees, and private individuals as well, expect for a sum of three or four thousand dollars an organ which, if properly constructed, ought to cost half as much again, there can be but one reply to all concerned : The coat must be cut according to the cloth. It may, however, have a modern fashion about the cutting.

When it comes to the expenditure of large sums of money, which not infrequently happens, conditions all round are changed : the whole exigencies of the case demand different treatment. It is because the same lines are adhered to that the faults exist which " Melodia " and every sound expert condemns — for which there is no excuse but custom. Every stop in these large organs is panting for breath, like goldfish crowded in a glass bowl, with their mouths at the surface, struggling for air, which they cannot obtain beneath. And this is not the exception, it is the rule, — the inevitable outcome of huge sound-boards, which are constructed to supply through a single pallet ten, twelve, fourteen stops, — or more.

It is of little avail that the organ builder displays his immense wind reservoir and large wind trunks — they are so much jelly, all the more easily shaken ! He has found it so, and applies concussion bellows, or *winkers* as he happily terms them, all over the organ, which in certain usage by the player exaggerate the evil — though they may save a full chord. So when a Guilmant or a Best essays a programme, the famous organ fails, and appears what it is, — a poor, lungless invalid !

The European organ builders years ago adopted better methods. When the super work of their organs is drawn, the foundation stops are not robbed of their wind tension ; moreover, in regulating their stops the life is not knocked out of the trebles in favor of a prominent tenor range, as is the custom here, so that their mixtures, which are much brighter than ours, and, by the way, are differently treated by players, do not overpower the foundation stops, which are prominent under all conditions of use.

Hear Guilmant on his own organ, or on the splendid instrument at the Trocadéro Palace ; or Best on his organ in St. George's Hall, Liverpool, nearly forty years old ; or any one of the modern organs of Willis of London or Cavaillé-Coll of Paris, and you will listen in vain for any of the defects named. They are splendidly prompt of tone in attack, and beautiful in detail.

To this we must come — we are fast coming, in fact. Demand for something better is springing up in the country, and a year or two — probably less as we move here — will work all the changes which "Melodia" seeks.

Yours,   CARLTON C. MICHELL.

BOSTON, Dec. 2, 1893.

THROUGH CANADA WITH ALEX. GUILMANT.

DOUBTLESS M. Guilmant uttered a sigh of relief in getting away from the din, push, and pull of a great city, coupled with the excitement of a World's Columbian Exposition. Leaving Chicago close on midnight, brought us to Detroit about eight the following morning. Meeting at the station Mr. Farrand of the Farrand & Votey organ system, and Mr. York, some time a pupil of M. Guilmant, we drove to the hotel. After breakfast we were joined by Mr. Votey, and took a drive through this beautiful city of homes.

After M. Guilmant had tried some of Detroit's best organs, we were driven to the immense organ plant of Messrs. Farrand & Votey. Lack of space prevents any description of this great factory, where all the latest and best machinery is to be seen, turning out the most artistic work. Some organs just finished surpassed in excellence of workmanship and mechanical accessories those finished ten years ago, as far as the Pullman vestibule train at the Columbian Exposition surpassed the John Bull train. A beautiful pedal reed organ, a gift to M. Guilmant, and bearing his name, stood ready to be shipped to his Meudon home. In the afternoon M. Guilmant spent the usual two hours in familiarizing himself with the organ and the programme of the evening — I might add that this custom he observed throughout all his trip. The *Chicago Tribune* of Monday, August 1, said of M. Guilmant's practising. "As the church-bells were ringing Sunday morning, Alexandre Guilmant, the great Parisian organist, stole into Festival Hall by the rear entrance, and for two hours made the building tremble with grand music. The melody floated out over the silent Park, attracting the attention of several hundred visitors. They rattled at the door of the hall, and sought entrance by the windows, but were warned away by the guards. Then they sat on the steps, and heard what they could of the glorious music, and made significant inquiries as to the motives for locking the doors." The recital in Detroit was well attended, as were all the concerts given by this artist. After bidding adieu to many kind friends, we left Detroit the following morning for Niagara Falls. After a charming ride through gorgeous scenery, we arrived at Niagara about seven in the evening. We took a short walk through the village, M. Guilmant wishing to obtain some souvenirs of the Falls. We soon returned to the hotel, the air being somewhat humid, a shower having fallen during the day. Here was a glorious opportunity to enjoy the company of a great artist — no reporters to ask questions, no organists asking information or autographs. M. Guilmant spied a piano, such as generally adorn hotels, with squeaky dampers, and an action that needed hours of regulating. Piled high on the instrument was the average hotel repertoire; but among it a copy of Mendelssohn's "Elijah." This M. Guilmant took up, and first played that ever lovely air, "O Rest in the Lord," which he followed by one or two airs of the same oratorio. These, with one or two of his own compositions, with a fugue *extempore*, constituted the list which he played.

Sunday morning came, and with it the glorious sunshine. A short walk and we were ready for breakfast, after which we crossed to the American side. We reached the Park. What a glorious day ! — none better could be wished. When we reached the edge of the Falls, every other word from M. Guilmant was, magnificent ! charming ! extraordinary ! etc. Upon reaching the Canadian side he walked about ten yards, and, rubbing his hands, exclaimed, "Very charming ! magnificent ! I thank you very much for bringing me to such a treat. I will not forget it, and will go home to Meudon delighted."

But to change the theme, I turned to the subject of the organ every available chance, and these following lines will be of interest at least to the admirers of M. Guilmant : —

"How do you like Batiste, monsieur ?" — "Very much, very much." — "But you do not play his compositions much !" — "No ; but I do not know why. His Offertoires in C-minor and E-minor are charming, very musical, with charming flute passages, but he lacks solidity." — "Do you admire Wély ?" — "I prefer Wély to Batiste. He was the finest extemporaneous player on the organ that France has produced. Extemporaneous players are rare. M. Lemmens could not extemporize at all." At this point I asked at length about his own compositions. "The Allegretto in B-minor was about my first composition." — "Do you write quickly ?" I inquired. "Yes ; at times. My Fugue in D I wrote in one evening, and the Second Meditation, with which you seem to be very familiar, I wrote one morning before breakfast. Having two melodies running through my head, I jotted them down upon paper." — "Do you have to make many changes ?" — "No ; seldom any." At this point he withdrew from his pocket a small blank note-book, and asked me to see for myself. This little book, purchased in France, had the staff running the length of the book. I had frequently seen him jotting down composition in spare moments ; and as we sat in the coach, waiting for the train to start, he composed a little prayer, and, tearing out the leaf, said, "Here is a souvenir for you."

I asked him several questions about his Marche Funèbre, and if his mother admired it ; to which he replied : "Yes, very much. She frequently asked me to play it for her. That is the reason I played it at her death. . . . No, she was not a musician, though she had a good voice and sang well."

When asked if any other members of his family were musicians, he replied : "I have one brother a professor of languages in a university in the south of France, another brother a French professor in Repton College, Repton, England. I have one son a civil engineer, who plays violoncello ; and three daughters, one unmarried at home who plays the piano, one married to a civil engineer, and the eldest, who can play Bach well (on the organ), is married to an electric engineer."

With regard to the American edition of his compositions he said : "I have not received a penny for them, not even a copy. The American edition abounds in errors and alterations."

A few of many questions regarding organs will doubtless be acceptable. "No," said he, "I prefer the organ in Notre Dame to that of St. Sulpice. Notre Dame has the advantage for acoustics, and, though not as large an organ as that of St. Sulpice, it has sixteen stops on the pedal, while St. Sulpice has but ten. The Trocadéro organ, like the one in the Royal Albert Hall (London), is in a poor building for effect."

I asked several questions regarding some of the famous Continental organs, of which we read so much in the glowing accounts of travellers. "Oh," said he, "I prefer Berne to Freiburg, but there are many better organs in France and England. There is little progress in organ building in Germany and the Netherlands."

"But now, sir, how about organ playing abroad ?" — "Oh, I think your organists in America are just as good as abroad, and young organists have the same advantage here. To me it seems a mistake in their going abroad. . . . I use Lemmens's organ school ; I prefer it to Rinck. It is more modern. . . . I only teach ten hours each week. I devote most of my time to composition, business, etc. . . . Yes,

I think Wesley the best composer of the English school. I concertize in England each autumn and spring, but on account of my American trip I must forego the autumn one this season." — "Will you return to America again?" — "Well, no; it is too far, and takes too much time. I must confine myself to England and France. . . . I play at two services Sundays in my church, the morning service being from nine till ten, at which I play three numbers (opening voluntary, the offertory, and the closing voluntary), and again at vespers, which are from three till four P.M., or till five, when there is a sermon, M. Salomé playing the chancel organ."

An hour's ride from Niagara Falls brought us to Hamilton, Ontario, where we were met by Mr. Aldous, a former Parisian organist. After dinner we visited Mr. Aldous's church, and at the close of the service M. Guilmant played his Marche Religieuse. The following day, after a drive through this beautiful city, M. Guilmant took his usual practice, and gave his evening recital. The following day we reached Toronto, where we were met by Mr. Risch of the firm of Mason & Risch. After a visit to Mr. Torrington's College of Music, we were driven through the city by Mr. Torrington, after which came the practice and evening recital. After the recital M. Guilmant was tendered a banquet by the College of Music. This was a very elaborate affair, which closed with many speeches, one in French by M. Guilmant. The following day, after a luncheon tendered by Mr. S. Nordheimer at the Toronto Club, we were accompanied on a drive by Mr. W. E. Fairclough, a Toronto organist, to Glenedyth, Mr. Nordheimer's home. This is a charming home, almost a castle, which stands a mile back from the gate. After passing over dale and fen, and over brooks and rustic bridges, we arrived at this castle, and were shown through a home fit for a king. At five o'clock M. Guilmant gave his twilight recital—and we were off for Montreal. In the afternoon we were at the new organ of St. Peter's Cathedral, a grand instrument in a great cathedral, the latter which is just completed, after twenty years' work. On the great cathedral and upon bill-boards we read the following advertisement of the concert:—

INAUGURATION DE L'ORGUE.
Nouvelle Cathédrale.
Canon Dominoy.
PAR ALEXANDRE GUILMANT.
21 AND 22 SEPT., 8 P.M.

The great cathedral was crowded,—over five thousand persons, many standing. So great was the crowd, that at the other end of the cathedral only the full organ could be heard. This sometimes caused applause in the middle of a number. The second night drew as large an audience as the first.

The day following the first recital ushered in bright and pleasant, but ere the hour of mid-day a slight rain began to fall. Knowing that M. Guilmant would be occupied in the morning, I walked across the Park from the hotel to take another look at the great cathedral of St. Peter's, where so many had enjoyed the concert the evening previous. A walk of about three-quarters of an hour from this cathedral, through many quaint old streets where one hears little English but much French spoken, brought me to Notre Dame.

Facing Place d'Armes is the noblest ecclesiastical structure in Canada, which bears the name of Notre Dame Cathedral, but in reality is only the parish church of the Sulpicians. The building itself is in the Gothic style, and is much admired for its plain and single stateliness. It has actually contained fifteen thousand people. The carved woodwork around the choir is particularly fine, representing the sacrifice of Christ, but the interior decorations are somewhat florid. The tower of the church contains ten bells besides "Le gros Bourdon," called Jean Baptiste, weighing twenty-four thousand pounds, the largest in America. An elevator carries passengers up to these bells at a fee of twenty-five cents. But within the last two years Notre Dame has acquired an additional interest from its great organ, which for the first time resounded through the church on Easter Day, 1891, and in the following May was formally inaugurated by Mr. Frederic Archer, who gave three recitals before an audience of thirty-five thousand people.

The builders of this magnificent instrument are Messrs. Casavant Bros. of St. Hyacinthe, Quebec. And, as it now stands, it perhaps rivals any organ that has been erected. There is no organ in this country to compare with it, and it is only equalled in size by the one in the Auditorium in Chicago. Of the European organs, the one with which it may be compared is that of *Notre Dame de Paris*.

The builders spent years in preparation for the work. The order was given in 1885. Between that time and the completion of the instruments the two brothers travelled through Europe and worked in the factories of England, Holland, Austria, and Belgium. There they acquired a general knowledge and a practical experience which they have brought to bear without stint in the execution of their work. The original cost was thirty thousand dollars; but by the characteristic liberality of this church, they were given *carte blanche* to add everything which would make their undertaking a success.

The instrument is placed in the second or upper gallery, and towers forty feet. Its depth from the key-board is fifty feet, and its breadth fills up nearly the whole width of the edifice. It is erected over an archway, through which the light streams upon the choristers: this sacrifice has spoiled the lower part of the noble instrument. It has five thousand seven hundred and seventy-two pipes, from the size of a quill to those monsters thirty-two feet long. The stops number one hundred, besides many mechanical appliances. The mechanism is all electric, being worked by five cells of Champeron battery.

At the arrival of M. Guilmant and the builders of the organ we mounted to the organ loft. What a glorious console! What beautiful and artistic workmanship! Doubtless M. Guilmant felt at home before the console, as every stop bears French tabulation, plates bearing the names of the different manuals being placed over the different groups of stops; as, "*Positif*," "*Grand Orgue*," "*Récit*," "*Expressif*," "*Solo Expressif*," "*Accouplements et Régistres Accessoires*." M. Guilmant first drew his favorite stop, "Ze Gambo," as he terms it; and after trying it a few minutes he rubbed his hands and said, "Very good, very good." He now began in a quiet strain; and as the first few notes went pulsing and waving through the air, their wonderful sweetness was apparent. He now began increasing the tone, until the chords of the full organ went crashing and echoing through the lofty arches of the great cathedral. This instrument is one of only three or four in America which possess the "cathedral roll."

The organ of Notre Dame is certainly wonderful,—worth even a long journey. It is an organ worth hearing, and well worth remembering. The whole cathedral seemed filled with heavenly tones, and the lofty arches rang with harmony. Chord after chord went echoing and repeating themselves in the distance, only to burst into spray and fade into silence; I had been hearing M. Guilmant; now I was hearing M. Guilmant and a great organ. Desiring to be alone, and enjoy the instrument in undisturbed solitude, I left the key-board and went to the farther end of the gallery which runs to the altar. Here I could enjoy the sweetest of sweet compositions of the performer, with their enchanting melodies and masterly accompaniments. Never shall I forget them as they floated through the cathedral, gathering sweetness as they went.

Now the performer changes his theme, and launches out into more spirited music: "See, the Conquering Hero Comes," etc. Now we are again hearing the full organ, a voice with the very reverberation of thunder. Louder and louder, peal upon peal, flash upon flash, thunder upon thunder, pealing, rolling, reverberating, crashing across continents and seas. All heaven joining in the chorus, all the world's great master organs joining in the great amen!

I could have sat and listened for hours to the master performer, and never have thought of earthly cares, but it came to an end at last. The last chords died away, and we descended to the main floor. Never shall I forget that organ nor its performer. "One hour of glorious life is worth an age without a name."　　　　　　　　WILLIAM GEORGE PEARCE.

NEW ORGANS.

ELIADAH GRAND LODGE OF PERFECTION, CLEVELAND, OHIO.

(New organ built by Messrs. Johnson & Son.)

GREAT ORGAN.		
Double Diapason	16	Ft.
Open Diapason	8	"
Viola da Gamba	8	"
Dulciana	8	"
Melodia	8	"
Octave	4	"
Flauto Traverso	4	"
Twelfth	2⅔	"
Super Octave	2	"
Mixture	III.	Rks.
Trumpet	8	Ft.
Clarinet	8	"

SWELL ORGAN.		
Bourdon (Treble and Bass)	16	Ft.
Open Diapason	8	"
Salicional	8	"
Æoline	8	"
Vox Celeste	8	"
Stopped Diapason	8	"
Quintadena	8	"
Flûte Harmonique	4	"
Fugara	4	"
Flautino	2	"
Dolce Cornet	III.	Rks.
Cornopean	8	Ft.
Oboe and Bassoon	8	"

PEDAL MOVEMENTS, ETC.

Three Comb. Pedals for Great.
"   "   "   " Swell.
Gt. to Ped. (reversible).
The usual couplers.
Compass of Manuals, 61 notes.
"   " Pedals, 30 notes.

GRACE CHURCH, LOCKPORT, N.Y.

(New organ built by Mr. George S. Hutchings.)

GREAT ORGAN.		
Open Diapason	16	Ft.
Open Diapason	8	"
Viola di Gamba	8	"
Doppel Flöte	8	"
Octave	4	"
Flûte Harmonique	4	"
Octave Quinte	2⅔	"
Super Octave	2	"
Mixture	III.	Rks.
Trumpet	8	Ft.

SWELL ORGAN.		
Bourdon (Treble and Bass)	16	Ft.
Open Diapason	8	"
Salicional	8	"
Æoline	8	"
Stopped Diapason	8	"
Flauto Traverso	4	"
Fugara	4	"
Flautino	2	"
Dolce Cornet	III.	Rks.
Cornopean	8	Ft.
Oboe	8	"

CHOIR ORGAN.		
Enclosed in a Swell Box.		
Geigen Principal	8	Ft.
Dolcissimo	8	"
Concert Flute	8	"
Flûte d'Amour	4	"
Piccolo Harmonique	2	"
Clarinet	8	"

PEDAL ORGAN.		
Open Diapason	16	Ft.
Bourdon	16	"
Violone	16	"
Octave (from Open Diapason)	8	"
Violoncello (from Violone)	8	"
Quinte (from Bourdon)	10⅔	"

PEDAL MOVEMENTS.

F., MF., and P. Comb. for Gt.
"   "   "   " Sw.
Gt. to Ped. (reversible).
The usual couplers.

PARK CONGREGATIONAL CHURCH, WORCESTER, MASS.

(New organ built by J. W. Lane, Waltham, Mass.)

GREAT ORGAN.		
Open Diapason	8	Ft.
Dulciana	8	"
Melodia	8	"
Octave	4	"
Twelfth	2⅔	"
Fifteenth	2	"
Trumpet	8	"

SWELL ORGAN.		
Bourdon (Treble and Bass)	16	Ft.
Salicional	8	"
Æoline	8	"
Stopped Diapason	8	"
Flûte Harmonique	4	"
Flautino	2	"
Dolce Cornet	III.	Rks.
Oboe and Bassoon	8	Ft.

PEDAL ORGAN.		
Bourdon	16	Ft.
Open Diapason	8	"

The usual couplers.
Ross water motor.

PEDAL MOVEMENTS.

F. & P. Comb. Great.
"   "   " Swell.
Gt. to Ped. (Reversible).

CHURCH OF THE SACRED HEART, EAST BOSTON.

(New organ built by the Hook & Hastings Co.)

GREAT ORGAN.		
Open Diapason	16	Ft.
Open Diapason	8	"
Viola da Gamba	8	"
Dulciana	8	"
Melodia	8	"
Flûte d'Amour	8	"
Octave	4	"
Twelfth	2⅔	"
Fifteenth	2	"
Mixture	III.	Rks.
Trumpet	8	"

SWELL ORGAN.		
Bourdon	16	Ft.
Open Diapason	8	"
Salicional	8	"
Viola	8	"
Stopped Diapason	8	"
Flûte Harmonique	4	"
Violina	4	"
Flautino	2	"
Dolce Cornet	III.	Rks.
Cornopean	8	Ft.
Oboe (with Bassoon)	8	"

PEDAL MOVEMENTS, ETC.

F. & P. Comb. Great Organ.
"   "   " Swell.
Gt. to Ped. Reversible.
The usual couplers.

PEDAL ORGAN.		
Open Diapason	16	Ft.
Bourdon	16	"
Violoncello	8	"

Console, extended and reversed, with pneumatic action. Water Motor.

CIPHERINGS.

AN EPITAPH ON CHRISTOPHER SCHRIDER.

(Found in Webb's Collection of Epitaphs.)

" HERE rests the musical Kit Schrider,
Who organs built when he did bide here,
With nicest ear he tuned 'em up :
But death has put the cruel stop :
Tho' breath to others he convey'd,
Breathless, alas ! himself is laid,
May he who us such keys has given,
Meet with St. Peter's Keys of Heaven !
His Cornet, Twelfth, and Diapason
Could not with air supply, he reasoned ;
Bass, Tenor, Treble, Unison,
The loss of tuneful Kit bemoan."

ONE of the well-known Boston organists, who officiates at one of the Unitarian churches, was taken suddenly ill just before Christmas Sunday. He sent his son to the house of Mr. X, another well-known organist, who had always played in an Episcopal Church, and was a staunch Episcopalian himself. As Mr. X had resigned his position, Mr. A thought he could be prevailed upon to substitute in such an emergency. Mr. A Jr. rang the bell at the house of Mr. X, but unfortunately Mr. X was out. Mr. A Jr. was received by one of the ladies of the house, and after stating that he called to see if Mr. X would be kind enough to substitute for Mr. A Sr., in consideration of the latter's illness, he received this characteristic reply : "Do you suppose for a moment that Mr. X would put his foot inside any *Unitarian* church, and on Sunday too ?"

ORGAN MUSIC

Published and Imported by EVERETT E. TRUETTE & Co., 149A Tremont Street, Boston.

VOL. II. No. II.   MARCH, 1894.   WHOLE No. 23.

BACH

YEARLY SUBSCRIPTION $2.00.   SINGLE COPIES 25 CTS.

THE ORGAN

DEVOTED TO

A MONTHLY JOURNAL

THE KING OF INSTRUMENTS

RHEINBERGER

GUILMANT

FRESCOBALDI

BUXTEHUDE

MERKEL

BEST

· EVERETT · E · TRUETTE ·
EDITOR & PUBLISHER
149 A. TREMONT ST. BOSTON.

HANDEL

THE ORGAN.

VOL. II. BOSTON, MARCH, 1894. No. 11.

THE ORGAN.

BOSTON, MARCH, 1894

Published the first of every month. Subscription price $2.00 per year (Foreign countries $2.50), payable in advance. Single copies, 25 cents.

Subscribers will please state with which number they wish their subscription to begin.

Remittances should be made by registered letter, post-office order, or by check payable to Everett E. Truette.

Correspondence, to secure notice, must in all cases be accompanied by the name and address of the writer, not for publication, but as a guarantee of good faith.

Advertising rates sent on application.

Address all communications,

THE ORGAN, 149 A Tremont Street, Boston, Mass.

Single copies of THE ORGAN can be procured of

NOVELLO, EWER, & CO.	. . .	New York.
G. SCHIRMER	. . .	New York.
OLIVER DITSON CO.	. . .	Boston.
L. H. ROSS & CO.	. . .	Boston.
N. E. CONSERVATORY	. . .	Boston.
H. B. STEVENS CO.	. . .	Boston.
LYON & HEALY	. . .	Chicago.
CLAYTON F. SUMMEY	. . .	Chicago.
THEODORE PRESSER	. . .	Philadelphia.
WM. H. BONER & CO.	. . .	Philadelphia.
TAYLOR'S MUSIC HOUSE	. . .	Springfield, Mass.
GALLUP & METZGER	. . .	Hartford, Conn.
RICHAULT & CO.	. . .	Paris.
NOVELLO EWER & CO.	. . .	London.

CONTENTS:

IMPORTANT NOTICE.

WE regret to announce that in all probability the issue of THE ORGAN will be *suspended* after the next number (the end of Vol. II.). Our reasons for discontinuing the publication are several. The field in which we labor is not a popular one, and we must look for support almost entirely to those who are interested in the pipe organ.

A large amount of time and capital has been expended in an effort to awaken more interest in this instrument; to bring before organ students and amateurs material both interesting and valuable; to interest professional organists in some of the shortcomings of the instrument, and to invite their co-operation in recommending improvements; to bring before organ builders as forcibly as possible the needs of a modern organist, and to chronicle important items of news throughout the organ world.

That we have received a fair amount of encouragement we admit. Nearly all the prominent organ builders have responded with subscriptions, advertisements, and hundreds of encouraging letters. Most of the leading organists of this country, and many of those countries where the English language prevails, are on the subscription list, and their number is rapidly increasing. We are daily in receipt of complimentary and encouraging letters from both subscribers and non-subscribers. However, after all has been said, the total amount of patronage is insufficient to warrant a continued outlay of time and capital.

The continued financial depression has made collections bad. Many of our subscribers and advertisers are in arrears. We have willingly given our time and thought without expecting any immediate return, and have been satisfied to receive a new dollar for an old one; but we will not, in addition to this, continue to put our hands in our pockets to pay the cost of publication for the benefit of the large number who are more than anxious to receive the advantages of the journal, but who are inexcusably tardy in their remittances.

We have been unable to keep all our promises, with regard to contributed articles, of a year ago. We have the written pledges of a large number of organists who agreed to furnish us with essays, compositions, etc., for which we promised to pay a reasonable sum, but no amount of urging has brought a fulfilment of these pledges.

It is with no little regret that we lay down the pick and shovel (our enemies will say, synonymous terms for scissors and glue-pot), for we have made hosts of stanch friends, but under existing circumstances no other course is inviting. All subscribers whose subscription does not expire on or before our next issue will receive a check for the balance of their subscription.

THE February number of the *London Musical Herald* contains, among other interesting matter, a biographical sketch of Mr. J. K. Strachan, organist of the Free College Church, Glasgow. Mr. Strachan was at one time a pupil of Mons. Guilmant, and thus expresses himself on organ matters in general: —

"If the organ is ever to become a popular concert instrument, our leading organ builders must make it possible for a solo-player to produce his effects promptly, neatly, and artistically. . . . Great players cannot afford to stay three or four days in a certain town to try to get mastery over a series of blunders specially prepared for him by celebrated patentees. . . . The best concert organs in England and Scotland are all defective in the *pedal organ*. . . . There are three or four stops on a pedal organ which are of little use, and three or four most necessary stops are not there. For example, why have builders so much antipathy to put a soft 8-ft flute on the pedal organ? You can always find a roaring reed or two, but a soft 8-ft flute seems beneath their notice."

The pedal organs of most of our American organs have this same fault. Mons. Alex. Guilmant, on his recent visit to this country, complained not a little of our "incomplete pedal organs," there being no stopped 8-feet bass. A Violoncello requires less room and costs considerable less than an 8-ft. flute, which undoubtedly explains the presence of the former instead of the latter in nine out of ten of our organs; but for utility there is no 8-ft. stop for the pedal which will compare with an 8-ft flute.

We present to our subscribers in this issue the first of a set of five organ compositions by M. Aloys Claussmann. organist of the Cathedral of Clermont-Ferrand, France, which were composed expressly for THE ORGAN. The second of the set will appear in our next issue, and all five will be pub-

lished in sheet form. Our subscribers will appreciate this opportunity of obtaining entirely new organ music of more than ordinary interest. The five compositions are Marche de Fête, Prière, Pastorale, Élévation, and Marche Religieuse, and are inscribed to Messrs. Clarence Eddy, S. P. Warren. R. Huntington Woodman, S. B. Whitney, and Wm. C. Carl.

THE miniature organ, a cut of which may be found on another page, which was constructed by Mr. James E. Treat when only a lad of thirteen, must have proved to the boy's parents, beyond a doubt, the natural bent of that young mind. Imagine a lad just entering his teens constructing a two-manual pipe organ with a Dulciana in the swell (it really had a swell pedal too), a Stopped Diapason in the great, a swell to great coupler, and a Tremulant! The organ contained but an octave of keys, but each key had its own pipe, and all the pipes sounded. Young James constructed every part of this miniature instrument except the pipes. Placed beside the larger instrument just finished by this builder, the miniature organ was an object of no little interest.

THE organ which has been built for Grace Church, San Francisco, Cal. (the gift of Mr. Edward F. Searles, in memory of Mrs. Searles), by Messrs. James E. Treat & Co., was publicly exhibited at the factory in Methuen, Mass., Feb. 26, 27, and 28. A number of prominent organists of New England accepted the invitation of the builders and examined the instruments.

The construction of this organ has been something unique in the history of organ building in this country. Nothing that money and skilled workmen could accomplish has been omitted, and the result is an instrument which is a credit to any builder in the world.

A detailed description of the organ may be found in another column, but we would call special attention to the combination movements. There are no adjustable combination movements, but a series of twenty-four individual set combinations, divided between ten double-acting pedals which do not affect the draw-stops, and fourteen piston-knobs which move the draw-stops. The advantages of each system of combination movements are increased by the presence of the other system, and the disadvantages are materially reduced. It will be patent to every organist that it is well nigh impossible to place an organ of this size more under the control of

the performer than by means of these twenty-four combination movements.

The voicing of the individual stops is specially pleasing ; and the *ensemble* effects are well balanced, albeit, a "setting-up room" is not conducive to a critical examination of the tone of loud combinations. The solidity and absolute absence of any roughness in the tone of the reeds is very noticeable. The diapasons, of which there are five, are rich, and present charming gradations of the foundation tone.

This organ will be shipped to California at once, and will prove a beautiful memorial, erected to the memory of a former resident of San Francisco — one whose noble and generous deeds were numerous and unrecorded.

JAMES E. TREAT.

MR. JAMES E. TREAT, of the firm of James E. Treat & Co., builders of the Memorial Organ for Grace Episcopal Church, San Francisco, Cal., fully illustrated and described in this issue, was born in New Haven, Ct., in 1837. At the age

of thirteen years, interest in the pipe organ was shown by the construction of the model of a two-manual organ 2 ft. 2 in. high, 1 ft. 8 in. wide, and 1 ft. 4 in. deep, having great and swell with unison coupler, a cut of which is here given. This

crude attempt was remarkable when it is known that at that time a wished-for view of the interior of an organ had not been obtained. Verbal description and books were his only aid. The little organ secured for him favorable notice from several builders, with offers of instruction and employment.

Accepting that from Westfield, Mass., he was apprenticed in March, 1855, to Wm. A. Johnson during his minority, the indenture being signed and sealed in due form, now in the possession of Mr. Treat.

Beginning at the work-bench, and ending apprenticeship and engagement as voicer and tuner, in 1860 he accepted a position with Henry Erben of New York, then in the zenith of his fame. The magnitude, thorough and substantial character of the work, purity of tone, and generous use of the 16 ft. octave by this builder, filled him with admiration. He was placed in the "voicing-room," in charge of Mr. Berry, and shortly sent South to erect several organs. Although considered foolhardy by his relatives, for it was a serious thing for a Yankee to be found in that section, he placed instruments in Atlanta and Columbus, Ga., and performed work in Alabama and other Southern States, being in Montgomery during the inauguration of Davis. Ready to return, he found nearly all the transportation companies withdrawn. The Confederacy having made it treason to pay any Northern debt, he was forced to borrow sufficient money from a committeeman to defray travelling expenses; and, passing through many exciting scenes, he reached New York June 1, 1861. Upon his assertion that the South was fixed for a fight, the cordial reception was followed by a general frigidity, which proved a loyalty to the Stars and Stripes.

An interest in other business induced him to make Boston his residence in 1862; but the demands of a service in setting up and finishing the work of other builders made extensive travel a necessity, covering the country from east to west, and including the Bahamas and Cuba, and furnishing that most valuable experience, an inspection of the works of the different makers while adjusting and tuning the same.

Being satiated with travel, and desiring to investigate the "free" reed principle as applied to the cabinet organ, he entered the tuning department of George Woods & Co. in 1871, and with the assistance of pipe-organ experience rapidly rose to the manipulation of the highest class of work in that branch. In 1875 he formed a co-partnership with Mr. John P. Richardson for the manufacture of cabinet organs, of which a few superior instruments were produced. Becoming satisfied that the profit was in the cheaper grades, and impressed with the limited resources of the free reed, he disposed of his interest, and accepted an engagement with Hutchings, Plaisted, & Co. in 1876, a voicer, tuner, and finisher, finally making all the reed work for this house.

In 1881 he went to Philadelphia to develop the Schmole Electric Patents in the interest of New York capitalists, building two electric manual and mechanical organs, which were favorably received. Negotiations between the principals failing, after obtaining and assigning to them various patents relating to the same, he returned to Boston, and re-entered the employ of Hutchings & Plaisted in 1885.

Receiving in 1886 a commission to build the organ for Kellog Terrace Music Hall, Great Barrington, Mass., of three manuals and fifty-three registers, declared by experts to be the most costly and effective instrument in private hands in this country, he equipped a manufactory in Boston, and with a small but select corps of skilled workmen built the organ, completing it in 1888, the hall being then ready to receive it. During this time also was built a two-manual instrument of the same high character of construction, and placed in the Methuen home of Mr. E. F. Searles. A two-manual instrument of thirty stops was then constructed and placed for exhibition in the Old South Meeting-House, and a series of recitals given upon it, beginning Dec. 26, 1889, for which ten thousand gratuitous tickets were issued, to the satisfaction of many patrons.

He then went abroad for study of foreign organs, a large part of the year being spent in England and on the Continent, returning in December, 1890.

Mr. Treat says: "In my opinion the best organs of England are better than those of any other country. It is a religious instrument, and owes its exalted position there to the Church of England. Here it is regarded as a piece of church furniture — a mystery — opened with great éclat, praised for its push-knobs, and allowed to go to ruin."

Mr. Treat further says: "The cost of a properly built American organ of to-day is out of all proportion to the price received for it. I look to electricity of the future to equalize this. Under this system the organist can be satisfied with pedal and piston mechanism, and some of the appropriation will be left for the pedal organ and the builder."

NOTABLE ORGANS.

XV.

SCHWEINFURT.

The above cut is copied from an old engraving of the front of an organ which at one time stood in the church at Schweinfurt, Bavaria, but has long since been removed.

ORGANS AND ORGAN TEACHING AT THE NEW ENGLAND CONSERVATORY OF MUSIC.

The organ department of this institution, after a period of more than twenty years' successful development, presents many features which will undoubtedly be of interest to our readers. Originally the entire equipment for both practising and teaching purposes consisted of several Mason & Hamlin reed organs, having two banks of keys, twenty-seven notes on the pedals, and each blown by hand. The number of organs necessary for the wants of the institution was increased gradually during the years when the school was located in a portion of Boston Music Hall building, and it was during this period that the first pipe organ was added.

In the year 1882, the institution, having outgrown its quarters in the Music Hall building, bought and took possession of what was originally the St. James Hotel, and rearranged the rooms so as to permit a very large number of class and practice rooms as well as a home for three hundred and fifty lady students. The organ department at present employs for lessons and practice two three-manual pipe organs, two two-manual pipe organs, and two two-manual reed organs. Ten reed organs were added last year to replace old ones, and were manufactured by the Estey Company expressly for the Conservatory, upon specifications arranged especially for the needs of pipe-organ students. The wind for all these organs is supplied by a single Sturtevant rotary blower, the motive power being furnished by a steam-engine.

The organ pupils taught by the Conservatory during this long period of its career number many thousands. They are to be found filling important positions in every State in the Union and in Canada, while in the city of Boston and the surrounding towns it is safe to say that a large majority of the best players were educated in this school. The lessons are given in classes of four, or privately, as the applicant chooses. Among the free advantages available for organ students in particular, may be mentioned a class in choir accompaniment, conducted by either Mr. G. E. Whiting or Mr. H. M. Dunham; and a class preparatory to improvisation, under the instruction of Dr. Percy Goetschius, late of the faculty of the Stuttgart Conservatory. The course preparatory to improvisation covers a period of two terms, and is formed at the beginning of the first and third terms of the year.

An interesting and extremely useful class, which is available for all organ pupils, is that instituted for the purpose of teaching the general principles of organ construction and tuning. A pipe organ having two manuals, a full compass of pedals, and nine speaking-stops has been erected in the Conservatory for the special use of this class. The lessons given are object lessons of the most practical kind. There being no case to the organ, the explanations made by the teacher are easily understood. It is not intended, by the means of this class, to make professional organ tuners or builders, but to familiarize the student with the interior of the organ, which to many organists is as a sealed book; and, furthermore, to enable them to remedy the many minor defects and accidents to which all organs are liable.

THE FUTURE OF THE ORGAN.

MUSICIANS have smiled contemptuously at the insignificant organette, the more elaborate orchestrion, and the many mechanical devices for the playing of instruments automatically. But these toys have simply been the forerunners of what is to be a fundamental principle in the structure and use in the organ of the future, which will be presented to the musical public at no distant date.

The recent introduction of electricity in a way which gives each stop or set of pipes its own independent wind-chest and valves, now presents a field for musical composition far in advance of what has been thought of in the past, and which will afford surprising results, which will be truly musical and artistic.

Since each stop has its own valves and electric wires, as many separate parts may be written as there are stops, if need be, each part having its own individuality of tone, as in the orchestra, which will be distinguishable, whether running above or below another quality of tone.

For this instrument a new score notation is to be used, written with an ink of such a nature that it will conduct the current of electricity through the written notes, when the manuscript shall be placed in its moving receptacle.

The concentration of the numerous electrical wires renders the mechanism very compact for translating the written copy into musical sound. Not only will the notes be perfectly executed, but the registration and expression will all be carried out as existing in the mind of the composer, even to the ritards and holds. The effect will not be so mechanical as in the old way of manipulating the keys, while the field for variety and elaborate composition will be wonderful.

The score will be as elaborate as that used by an orchestral conductor, and the future organist will be a composer in the highest sense of the word. He will be encouraged to write even compositions in the symphonic form, because he can then have them performed according to his ideal, with no expense in the production.

This new instrument will also have manuals and pedals for the use of those who are not able to compose the more intricate music. Compared with what will be accomplished through this great advance in musical development, the present style of organs in vogue will seem but tame and unwieldy instruments, which in due time will be relics of the past.

LE PROPHÈTE.

THE ORGANIST'S RETROSPECT.[1]

BY HORATIO CLARKE.

(AN AUTOBIOGRAPHY OF ERNEST OSBORNE.)

IN TWENTY-FIVE CHAPTERS.

CHAPTER XI.

I WAS now eighteen; and, in order to devote my time exclusively to my musical improvement, I ceased attending school. I had every facility for practising, and made the best of this opportunity. It was one of my rules to thoroughly learn each organ piece before attempting a new one. During this year I committed to memory each of Mendelssohn's Organ Sonatas and his Three Preludes and Fugues.

Our talents are developed by persistent efforts in accomplishing what we undertake. For the encouragement of true growth in any mental attainment, there should be not only the power to communicate, but also a recipient state should exist in the minds of those who are acted upon. In the musical world this is not often the condition, especially in the experience of an organist. With his education in the classical forms of his art, his listeners in the Sunday services are not in a state of musical culture to receive his best thoughts; and in his efforts to reach and please them he is often obliged to lower his own standard and introduce melodies with which they are familiar.

For a special occasion I had prepared a pleasing theme, consisting of a simple melody with its chords for the left-hand on the upper manual, while the right-hand gave an ornate flute obligato on the lower manual. At the close of the service an influential lady of the congregation came to the organ gallery and highly complimented me on the rendition of the piece, rapturously expressing her delight, and ending her words of praise by telling me how much it made her think of a hand-organ.

An organ fugue can be enjoyed and appreciated only by one who has followed its symmetrical structure by either practising it himself, or looking at the score when it is being played. Organ music is for organists, rather than for the unmusically educated masses who support religious services.

In one of the churches in which I have since acted as the organist, there was a generous-hearted banker whose emotional nature was easily excited by a familiar melody; and on more than one occasion I have known him to come up to the organ at the close of the exercises, and, touching my shoulder, say, —

"Osborne, the piece you played at the collection cost me a five-dollar bill !"

One Sunday after service I told him that I wanted him to listen to a classical organ piece. I selected that graceful Prelude of Bach, No. 7, in the Second Book of the "Peter's Edition," and played it with a pleasing combination of stops. He listened patiently through it, and at its close I asked him how he liked it? Looking somewhat bored, he answered: —

"Well, Osborne, to tell you the truth, it sounded to me

(Continued on page 283.)

MEMORIAL ORGAN

FOR

GRACE EPISCOPAL CHURCH,

SAN FRANCISCO, CAL.

BUILT BY

JAMES E. TREAT & CO., METHUEN, MASS.

·NEW·ORGAN·GRACE·CHVRCH·
·SAN·FRANCISCO·

SCHEME
OF THE
MEMORIAL ORGAN
FOR
GRACE EPISCOPAL CHURCH . . . . . . SAN FRANCISCO, CAL.
BUILT BY
JAMES E. TREAT & CO., METHUEN, MASS.

Great Organ	CC to C⁴ 61 notes	12 stops	884 pipes
Swell Organ	CC to C⁴ 61 notes	16 stops	1,120 pipes
Choir Organ	CC to C⁴ 61 notes	11 stops	671 pipes
Pedal Organ	CCC to C¹ 30 notes	8 stops	240 pipes
Mechanical Registers		10	
Total		**57 stops**	**2,921 pipes**
Combination Pistons		14	
Combination Pedals		10	
Mechanical Movements		7	

GREAT ORGAN.

		PIPES.
1. Open Diapason	16 ft.	61
2. Open Diapason, 1st	8 ft.	61
3. Open Diapason, 2d	8 ft.	61
4. Gemshorn	8 ft.	61
5. Viola da Gamba. Proof tin	8 ft.	61
6. Doppel Flöte	8 ft.	61
7. Octave. Proof tin	4 ft.	61
8. Flûte Harmonique, 3d and 4th oct. har.	4 ft.	61
9. Twelfth	2⅔ ft.	61
10. Fifteenth. Proof tin	2 ft.	61
11. Mixture. Proof tin	3 Ranks.	183
12. Trumpet. Proof tin bells, 4th oct. har.	8 ft.	61

CHOIR ORGAN.

13. Lieblich Gedeckt	16 ft.	61
14. Open Diapason	8 ft.	61
15. Viola Dolce	8 ft.	61
16. Dolcissimo	8 ft.	61
17. Melodia. 4th and 5th oct. har.	8 ft.	61
18. Quintadena. Proof tin	8 ft.	61
19. Violin. Proof tin	4 ft.	61
20. Flûte d'Amour	4 ft.	61
21. Piccolo Harmonique. 3d and 4d oct. har.	2 ft.	61
22. Contra Fagotto	16 ft.	61
23. Clarinet. (Fagotto Bass.)	8 ft.	61

SWELL ORGAN.

		PIPES.
24. Bourdon Treble	16 ft.	61
Bourdon Bass		
25. Open Diapason	8 ft.	61
26. Flûte Harmonique, 3d, 4th, and 5th oct. har.	8 ft.	61
27. Salicional. Proof tin	8 ft.	61
28. Dolcissimo	8 ft.	61
29. Stopped Diapason	8 ft.	61
30. Octave	4 ft.	61
31. Flûte Flute. 3d and 4th oct. har.	4 ft.	61
32. Gemshorn. Proof tin	4 ft.	61
33. Flautino	2 ft.	61
34. Mixture	4 Ranks	244
35. Trumpet	16 ft.	61
36. Cornopean. Proof tin bells, 4th oct. har.	8 ft.	61
37. Oboe and Bassoon. Proof tin bells	8 ft.	61
38. Vox Humana. Proof tin	8 ft.	61
39. Clarion. Proof tin bells, 3d oct. har.	4 ft.	61

PEDAL ORGAN.

40. Grand Bourdon	32 ft.	30
41. Double Open Diapason	16 ft.	30
42. Double Gamba	16 ft.	30
43. Double Dulciana	16 ft.	30
44. Bourdon	16 ft.	30
45. Flute	8 ft.	30
46. Violoncello	8 ft.	30
47. Trombone	16 ft.	30

MECHANICAL REGISTERS
(OVER KEYS)

48. Great to Pneumatic.	53. Swell to Pedal.
49. Swell to Great.	54. Choir to Pedal.
50. Choir to Great.	55. Swell Tremolo.
51. Swell to Choir.	56. Choir Tremolo.
52. Great to Pedal.	57. Blowers' Signal (Contingent).

COMBINATION PISTONS
(UNDER THEIR MANUAL AND NUMBERED FROM THE LEFT.)

GREAT.

No. 1. 4, 6.
No. 2. 6, 2, 3, 4, 6.
No. 3. 1, 2, 3, 4, 5, 6, 7, 8, 9, 10.

CHOIR.

No. 1. 16, 17, 20.
No. 2. 17, 18, 20.
No. 3. 13, 17, 20, 21.

SWELL.

No. 1. 27, 29.
No. 2. 38, 55.
No. 3. 25, 26, 27, 28, 29, 31.
No. 4. 25, 26, 29, 35, 36, 37, 39.
No. 5. 24, 25, 26, 27, 28, 29, 30, 31, 32, 33, 36, 37.

PEDAL (Under Great Manual).

No. 1. 43.
No. 2. 44, 45.
No. 3. 41, 42, 44, 45, 46.

COMBINATION PEDALS
(DOUBLE-ACTING AND NUMBERED FROM THE LEFT.)

MECHANICAL MOVEMENTS

No. 1. Great to Pedal (Reversible).
No. 2. All Couplers.
No. 3. Swell Tremolo (Reversible).
(The above are 2d tier.)

No. 4. Balanced Swell Pedal.
No. 5. Crescendo and Diminuendo.
No. 6. Crescendo Indicator [1] (Right.)
No. 7. Wind Indicator [2] (Left.)

MEMORANDA.

THE Organ is placed in the North Chancel aisle, one front facing the transept, the other the chancel, occupying a floor space of 17 x 28 ft., with key desk and choir gallery in the transept, elevated 3 ft. from auditorium floor. The organ chamber has a height of 35 ft.

The Case, of pure Gothic order, from design by Mr. Henry Vaughan of Boston, is of quartered oak, dark finish, exceeding rich in detail, with displayed pipes of burnished proof tin, 102 in number.

The Key Desk [3] is of improved construction. A system is introduced by which the registers most used are placed nearest the performer. The Pneumatic Motor [4] is applied to the Great and its couplers, and to the lower octave of the Swell, Choir, and Pedal organs. The Register action is Tubular Pneumatic. [5] There are three wind reservoirs, aggregate capacity 135 square ft. All the manual chests are on a level, insuring equal temperature. The Swell Box is 12 x 12 ft. 6 in., and 16 ft. high, with double louvers. A separate box with adjustable front is located in the rear, within, for the Vox Humana. The Organ is blown by a powerful hydraulic engine, operating duplex feeders underneath, throwing 50 cubic feet of compressed air drawn from the interior of the organ exclusively at each movement of its piston. There are two distinct systems of combination movement, — by pistons under their manual, affecting the drawstops, throwing on the combination and taking off all others; and by the usual double acting pedals not affecting them, making in all 24 fixed combinations, each different from the other. These systems can be used jointly or severally, the changes made with the greatest speed and ease.

All the stops are full compass of the keyboard. The Reed 16 ft. octaves are full length. The pitch is 435 A.

The instrument is notable in that it was built by the day, by a corps of skilled workmen, and from selected and kiln-dried (slow process) woods and the best material in all departments, a combination rarely established in organ building. Hard woods and iron contribute to a permanent construction.

The highest consideration has been given to the tonal department, which determines the real value of the organ; and harmonics, the purest of tones, freely used. The Diapasons are dignified and mellow, and the 16 and 8 ft. "flue" stops maintain their strict character, and are graded to combine and solidify the tonal pedestal, upon which is placed the Reed and compound work. The voicing throughout, the construction as well, has been under the personal supervision of Mr. Treat, and the reed stops by him exclusively.

It has been the fixed intention of the builders, by the elimination of sensational features and a careful attention to details, to construct an instrument eminently fitted for use in divine service; to make it a memorial in fact as well as name, and they submit it as an absolute art production.

[1] Patented by James E. Treat. Owned and used exclusively by this house.

a Monsieur R. Huntington Woodman.

PASTORALE.

Aloÿs Claussmann.
Op. 26, N.º 3.

Con moto. 104 : ♩

Récit. Fonds de 8 et 4 (boite ouverte)
Positif. Fonds de 8 et 4.
G.O. Fonds de 8 et 4.
Ped. Fonds de 8 et 16.
Récit et Pos. accouplés au G.O.

Sw. 8 & 4 Ft. (Box open.)
Ch. 8 & 4 Ft.
Gt. 8 & 4 Ft.
Ped. 16 & 8 Ft.
Sw. & Ch. to Gt. Gt. to Ped.

G.O.
Gt.

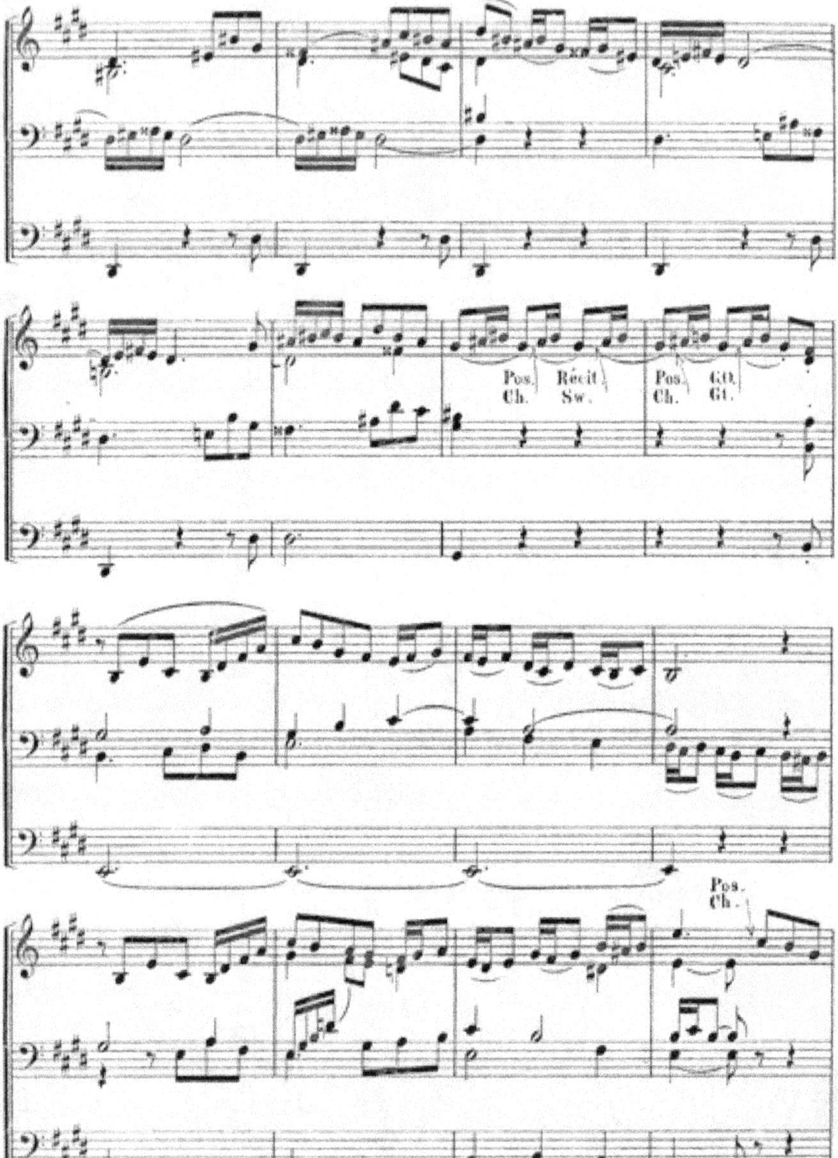
Pos. Ch.
Récit Sw.
Pos. Ch.
G.O. Gt.
Pos. Ch.

Récit.
Sw.

dim. e roll.

Pos.
Ch.

Pos.
Ch.

Récit.
Sw.

Pos.
Ch.

Otez les accouplements.
Sw. & Ch. to Gt. off.

Otez la Montre du Pos. et le 4 p.
Reduce Ch. to Flute 8 Ft.

dim.   *rit.*

Récit.
Sw.

Récit. Hautbois et Flûte de 4. (trémolo ad libitum)
Pos. Bourdon et Salicional de 8.
G. O. Flûte de 8.
Ped. Bourdons de 8 et 16.

Sw. Oboe, Flute 4 Ft. & Tremulant.
Ch. Melodia & Dulciana.
Gt. Doppel Flöte.
Ped. Bourdon & Flute 8 Ft.

Andantino 63 = ♩.

mf

Pos.
Ch.

pp

f

Récit.
Sw.

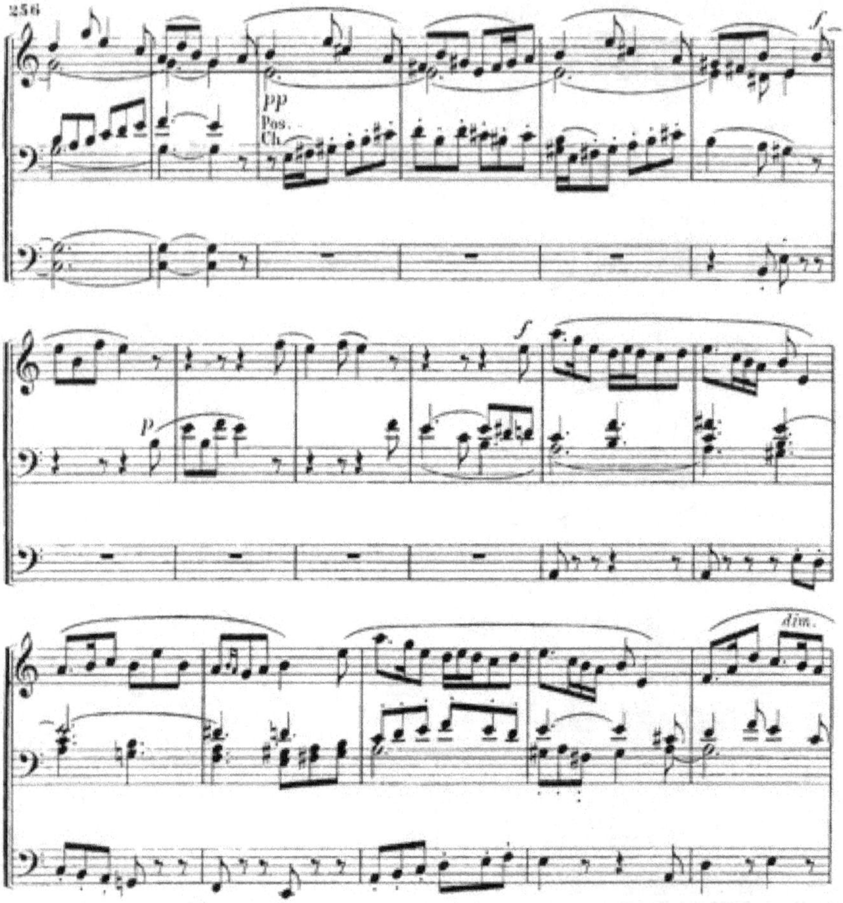
pp
Pos.
Ch.
f
p
f
dim.
poco rit.
G.O. Flûte solo.
Gt.

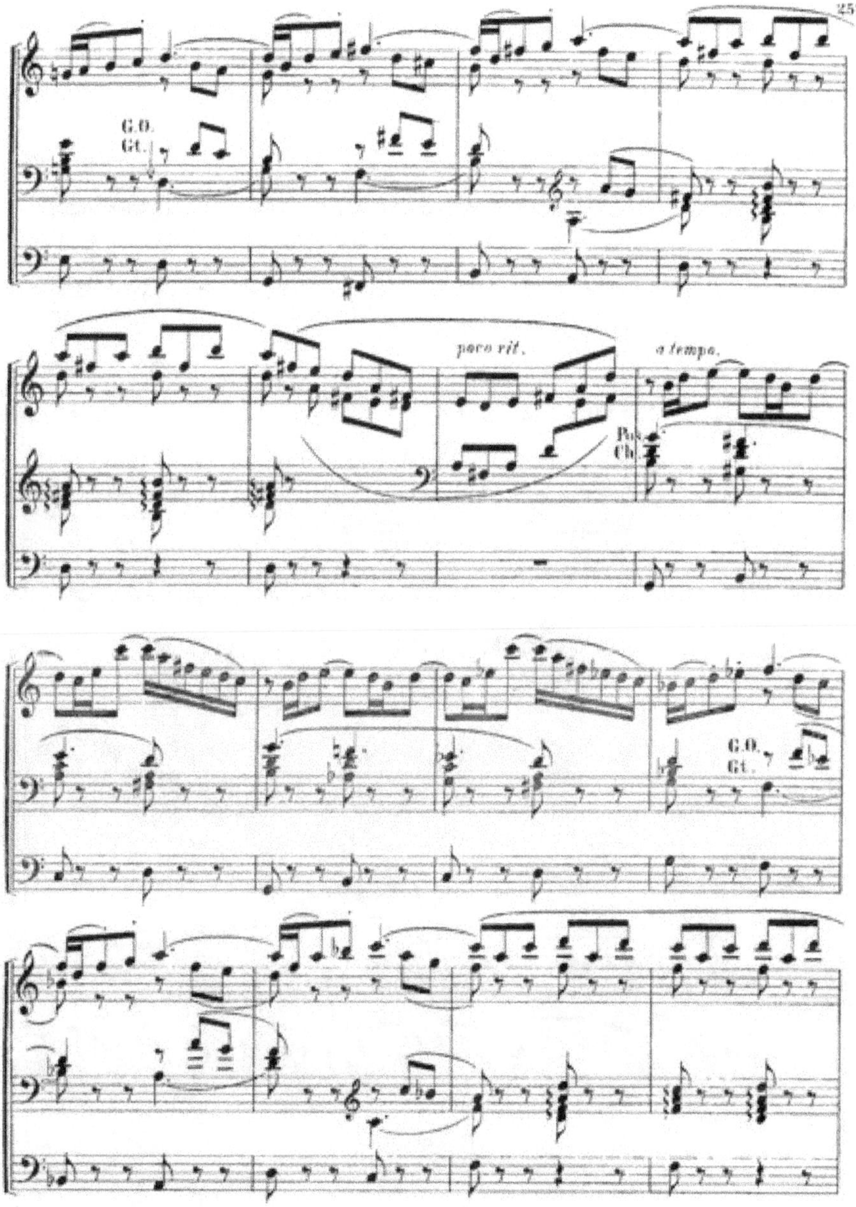
G.O.
Gt.
poco rit.
a tempo.
Pos.
Ch.
G.O.
Gt.

Pos.
Ch.
Accouplez Pos. au G.O.
Add Ch. to Gt.
G.O.
Gt.
cresc.
dim.
Pos.
Ch.
G.O.
Gt.
Pos.
Ch.
G.O.
Gt.
rit.
Récit.
Sw.
a tempo.
Pos.
Ch.

Otez Hautbois et Flute de 4 au Récit.
Mettez Bourdon 8 Gambe et Voix Céleste.
Ajoutez la Montre de 8 au Pos.
Otez l'accouplement du Pos. au G.O.

Sw. St. Diap., Salicional, Violin & Tremulant.
Ch. Add 8 Ft. stops.
Ch. to Gt. off.

cresc
Pos.
Ch.
G.O.
Gt.
Pos.
Ch.
Récit
Sw.
Pos.
Ch.
G.O.
Gt.
molto rall.
a tempo.
Pos.
Ch.
Récit
Sw.
PP
Accouplez Récit au G.O.
Add Sw. to Gt.

G.O.
Gt.
f
Pos.
Ch.
Otez l'accouplement du Récit au G.O.
Sw. to Gt. off.
G.O. Flûte.
Gt.
pp
Otez les jeux du Récit et mettez Hautbois seul, avec trémolo.
Reduce Sw. to Oboe & Tremulant.
Récit.
Sw.
p
G.O.
Gt.
Otez la montre du Pos.
Reduce Ch. to Melodia.
rit.

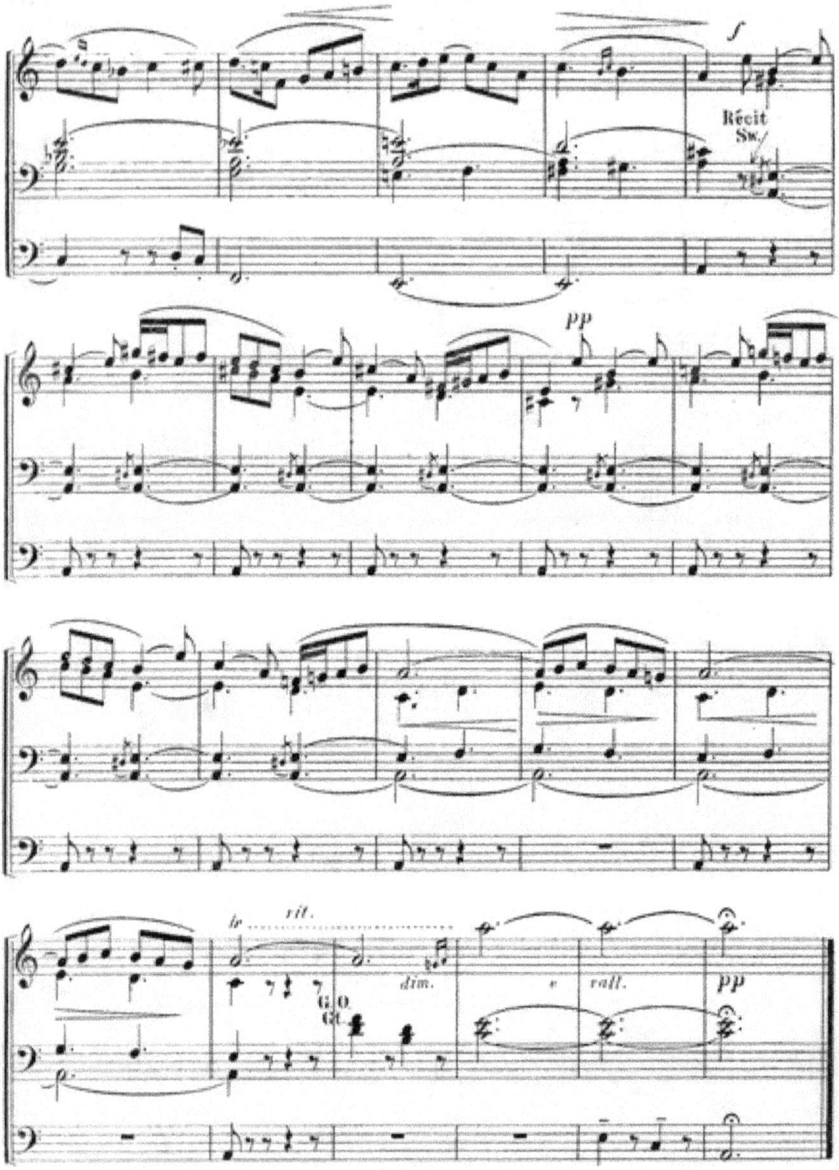
Récit
Sw.
pp
rit.
dim.
G.O.
Gt.
rall.
pp

(Continued from p. 248.)

like stirring a pail of oatmeal mush around and around with a stick."

As introductory to a mental experience which occurred this year, I am led to record that the human body has within it a vital nervous or electrical force which proceeds from the life which enters the brain. This force is latent until it is excited into activity by an internal energy.

Without constantly replenishing this vital force by full and deep breathing, with nourishing food, and requisite physical exercise, there will occur an exhaustion which can be replenished in no other way, and which sooner or later will develop in some chronic disease or nervous prostration, which will not only tend to shorten life, but will render existence a burden.

When engaged in the intense application of practising technical exercises on the organ or pianoforte, — in the study of hard passages, — or in the rendition of any piece which requires fixed attention, there is a tendency to withhold the action of the lungs in breathing. Any player may observe this fact in his own experience; and it is an important point, to which the notice of young musical students is seldom directed, and which they should strive to avoid, and thus prevent the seeds of future suffering being sown.

> " Rare talents, luxuries, and wealth
> Afford him joy where reigns not health;
> But deeply breathing purest air
> Revives the heart, and frees from care.
> Thus dark foods entrance from its Source,
> Prolongs the years in happy course;
> Bars dread disease from left encroach,
> And Death delays his grim approach."

In addition to this deleterious habit of suspending the breathing, there is a waste of much nervous force through the motions of the fingers when practising, and more especially when playing in public. In the sphere of an audience, whether in religious services or at concerts, the mental concentration required in such efforts is often extremely exhausting.

Each Sunday I was afflicted with severe headaches, which rendered the day intolerable. The debility which follows public playing with nervous temperaments often leads to the use of stimulants, but fortunately in my own experience no such habit was formed. As stated in an early chapter, my meal times were not surrounded with cheerful influences, and I always hurried through them as moments which I dreaded, being glad to get away from the table; and I now spent no other hours in the house, excepting to sleep.

The effect of home influences rendered my social nature undeveloped; and in my ambitious plans I was absorbed with one object, which was both my profession and recreation, without a change or thought. Such a temperament is inclined to oscillate to extremes, and become eccentric or visionary. I was of an enthusiastic and excitable disposition in all things which interested me. With many hours spent in practising each day with a suspension of free and natural breathing, and with the nervous exhaustion resulting from this steady routine of work, I was quite ready for a state of reaction.

The church where I was the organist was more than a century old, and up in the mossy garret beneath the heavy hewn timbers were stored away many relics of past generations. There were old foot-stoves, lamps, candle-racks, music-books, hymn-books, and works of a dead and discarded theology. I was always interested in things of the past, which excited my imagination with melancholy thoughts, in which I revelled.

I was naturally concerned with religious matters, my life being in harmony with the moral code which the Unitarian preaching so earnestly inculcated. But my mind was now beginning to seek the unfathomable mysteries of the supernatural. I was led into a train of thought which for a number of years prevented my further mental development, and brought me into very narrow ideas of life and uncharitable judgment, which retarded my musical progress for a while.

From among the old books in the garret of the church I selected an old worm-eaten volume published a hundred years before, with its *f*'s for *s*'s, and catch-words at the bottom of the page. I took it with me up the ladder leading to the belfry, and up yet higher, above the bell which I had so often tolled for funerals, into a shadowed room in the spire, where I opened the book and began earnestly to read. It was Doddridge's " Rise and Progress of Religion in the Soul."

I was in that morbid state of mind in which this spirit of the past had power to take control of my thoughts; for a book is a materialized spirit, and in his thoughts doth reside the life of the man who wrote it. It is thus that we are able to converse with the spirits of departed men. Every precept and exhortation in this book had full sway over me, and all things of this world became dark and more gloomy. I felt myself a deeply convicted sinner, guilty of playing the organ in a Unitarian Church whose very roof had sheltered this sacred volume.

The Orthodox Church near by now seemed enshrouded with a halo of the true light, and I hastened to accept its tenets. I read Baxter's " Saints' Rest," Baxter's " Village Sermons," and studied theological works, besides spending hours in prayer in the little spire-room of the church, far above the vain world, preparing myself to proclaim the true gospel. I talked with all my acquaintances on the subject of the salvation of their souls according to the strict Calvinistic doctrines. Now and then I would secure a prospective convert, and take him with me up into the spire and pray with him, and read him one or two frightful sermons on escaping from hell. In my own mind, destruction awaited every person who refused to accept my creed.

I kept a long list of names of persons for whose conversion I daily prayed, and tried to establish neighbourhood prayer-meetings for those of my own age. I became an ascetic of the severest type. Life had no beauty, but all was vanity, and only the elect were the favored ones, among whose numbers I felt certain that I was counted.

I listened to the Unitarian sermons with a critical search for heresy. I looked upon the hours of playing the organ on Sunday as spent in sin, and frequently during the sermon I would steal out and hasten to the doors of the Orthodox Church, so that I might come within the sound of a few sentences of holy inspiration. It is even now a wonder to me how in this state of religious frenzy I could make any acceptable music as an organist. How I longed for my engagement to end, so that I might find a position in an evangelical church where only the truth would be preached.

I now felt it my duty to unite with the Orthodox Church, and made a public profession of my faith in quite the spirit of a martyr; but after getting safely within the fold, I was amazed to find such an amount of indifference manifested by this sedate body of worshippers, in regard to the spiritual interests of their neighbors and acquaintances. But, like the old worm-eaten volume, there was a possibility of my having been a hundred years behind the times, of which I did not then seem to be aware.

My Unitarian friends certainly treated me with the utmost kindness, doubtless interpreting my fervor as the result of a diseased mental condition; for although I had violated the rules of courtesy by ignoring every interest of the society employing me, they patiently bore with my erratic condition, and retained me as their organist until an opening occurred for me in the city, which I then firmly believed was a direct answer to my earnest prayers.

(To be continued.)

MIXTURES.

(FOUR RANKS.)

Mr. B. J. Lang and Mr. Howard M. Dow gave an organ concert at the Second Unitarian Church, Boston, January 31. The recital was under the auspices of the Woman's Alliance, and Miss Carrie Dulce, violinist, assisted.

The Hook & Hastings Co. have recently shipped organs to St. Mark's Church, Richmond, Va.; Presb. Church, Tallahassee, Fla.; Trinity Episcopal Church, St. Augustine, Fla.; Christian Church, Rushville, Ind.; and Cong. Church, Lisbon, N.H. Each of these organs had two manuals. This company claims to produce a $3,000 organ per week the year around.

Mr. George S. Hutchings is building a large two-manual organ for the Congregational Church, Elkton, Fla.

Mr. R. J. Gillert, for twenty-five years organist of the Prospect-street Church, Cambridge, Mass., died February 5.

The organ in the Central Cong. Church, Boston, is being moved from its present location in the chancel to a chamber at the right of the chancel by the builders, Hook & Hastings Co.

Mr. George S. Hutchings is building an organ for the residence of Mr. George A. Stearns, Watertown, Mass., which will contain two manuals and thirteen registers.

Mr. J. J. Miller gave an organ concert in Christ Church, Norfolk, Va., February 5, playing Toccata in D minor (chorus), Aria in D, and Fugue in G-minor, Bach; Cujus Animam, Rossini; Sonata No. 2, Mendelssohn; Allegretto, Merkel; Ave Maria, Schubert; Marche Caprice, Mendelssohn. Mrs. William T. Brooke, soprano, assisted.

Mr. Auguste Wiegand gave the following programme at the Town Hall, Sydney, Australia, November 11: Schiller March, Meyerbeer; "Le Chemin du Parade," Rheinenthal; Entr'acte, "La Colombe," Gounod; Romance in A flat, Mozart-Martin; Overture "Semiramis," Rossini; "L'Extase, Adam-Wiegand; Marche Eternel Voyageur, Keller; Vogue Léger Zephir, Mendelssohn; Sydney March in E, Wiegand.

Mr. Ernest Wood's programmes for his recitals in Melbourne (Victoria, Australia) at intervals, during the month of November have just reached us. The last recital consisted of Sonata No. 6, Merkel; Meditation sur le Stabat Mater, Guilmant; Communion in F, Batiste; Alla Marcia, Best. The principal works at the other recitals were: Fantasia, Lux; Sonata Pontificale, Lemmens; Prelude and Fugue in B-minor, Bach; Fourth Sonata, Mendelssohn; Rhapsodie No. 3, Saint-Saëns.

Mr. Fred L. Clark gave his seventieth recital in Payson Church, Easthampton, Mass., January 26, with the following programme: Fantasia and Fugue in G-minor, Bach; Offertory in D-flat, Salomé; Serenade, Taft; Marche Célèbre, Lachner; Pastorale, Foote; Andante in E-flat, Mozart; Finale in D, Lemmens. Mrs. J. E. Lander, contralto, assisted.

Mr. Harrison M. Wild's 142d organ recital on Sunday afternoon, January 20, given in the Unity Church, Chicago, consisted of the following numbers: Prelude and Fugue in G, Bach; Sonata No. 3, Mendelssohn; Elegy, Chauvesne; Cantona, Wolstenholme; Soldiers' Chorus, "Faust," Gounod-Hall; Offertoire, Op. 7, Batiste. The quartet of the church assisted.

Mr. S. Clarke Lund gave an organ recital, January 26, at the Asylum Hill Cong. Church, Hartford, Conn., with the following programme: Sonata Pontificale, Lemmens; Aria in D, Bach; Evening Quiet, Rheinberger; Intermezzo, Mascagni (by request); Pastorale in A, Deshayes; Finale from Second Symphony, Widor; Festival March, Smart. Mr. Clinton H. Newton, baritone, assisted.

The Hook & Hastings Co. of Boston have just furnished the First Presb. Church of Lockport, N.Y., a very large two-manual organ, containing thirty-one registers and nine pedal movements. It is operated by pneumatic action, both the keys and registers, and contains the Hook & Hastings Grand Crescendo and Decrescendo Pedal. It is blown by a water motor.

Mr. Wm. C. Hammond's ninetieth recital at the Second Cong. Church, Holyoke, Mass., brought out the following compositions: Toccata in F, Speth; Bourrée from Third Violoncello Sonata, Bach; Adagio Cantabile, from String Quartette in D, Haydn; Sonata No. 5, Rheinberger; Offertoire in F-minor, Canon in C-minor, Cantilene in A-minor, and Grand Chorus in A, Salomé. At the ninety-first recital Mr. Hammond was assisted by two of his pupils, Miss Katharine M. Fales and Miss May E. Stetson, who played works of Rheinberger and Guilmant.

Mr. S. B. Whitney has recently given organ concerts as follows: at Waltham, Mass., now Hutchings organ in the Baptist Church; at Arlington, in the new Unitarian Church, Cole & Woodberry organ; and at Gloucester, on the Emmons Abbott Memorial organ, for the purchase of which Miss Abbott made provision in her will. At each of these concerts Mr. Whitney was assisted by three soloists from the choir of the Church of the Advent, Boston. Later, Mr. Whitney gave a second recital in Gloucester, and conducted the fifteenth Vermont Choir Festival at Rutland, of which the local papers spoke in the highest terms of praise.

In the sketch of Mr. Geo. S. Hutchings in the last issue of THE ORGAN, the number of organs which Mr. Hutchings has erected was wrongly stated as 275. The number should have been 350.

Mr. M. E. Wesley, who has been treasurer of the Royal College of Organists since the formation of the society, has resigned the position.

The Albert Palace organ, which cost nearly $40,000 when constructed, was sold a short time ago for about $1,600, and is again for sale, as the palace is to be torn down.

Mr. W. E. Fairclough, F.C.O., gave the following programme at his fifth recital in All Saints' Church, Toronto, Feb. 3: Concerto No. 6, Handel; Melody in C, Silas; Two Choral Preludes, Bach; Air with Variations, and Finale Fugato, Smart; Canon in B-minor, Schumann; Allegro Cantabile, Widor; Triumphal March, Lemmens; Fantasia on two English Melodies, Guilmant.

It has been rumored for some time that the Wirsching Organ Company of Salem, which has been shut down for quite a while, would not re-open their factory. It is understood that the company has gone out of business.

Programme of organ music given by Mr. Wm. C. Hammond at the Second Cong. Church, Holyoke, Mass., Feb. 21: Overture in D, Arne; Gavotte in A, Gluck; Andante and Variations from the Septette, Beethoven; Isolde's Lament and Death, "Tristan and Isolde," Wagner; Andantino in D-flat, Chauvet; Canon in B-minor, Schumann; Offertoire in C-minor, Grison.

On Jan. 26 a number of organists from Boston and vicinity, in response to an invitation from Mr. Walter J. Clemson, visited St. Thomas' Church, Taunton, Mass., to inspect the electric action and movable console constructed by the Hope-Jones Electric Organ Co. of England, which has been recently attached to this organ (built by Hook & Hastings).

Mr. Clemson accompanied his choir in a couple of anthems and a hymn, after which the console was moved down the centre aisle of the church as far as the flexible cable (100 ft.) would permit.

Mr. Clemson carefully explained the peculiarities of the movable console, which can be placed anywhere within the length of the cable (the cable itself containing four hundred wires), the stop keys, stop switch, storznardo pedal, "double touch," and electric swell pedal. After several of the organists had examined the console, a visit was made to the interior of the organ, and the electric connections were inspected. Mr. Clemson then entertained the visitors at his own house near by. The refreshments were very acceptable, and it was noticeable that the "second touch" was still "on." However, nothing "ciphered," and the 10.20 train brought the happy company back to the city. A vote of thanks was extended to the host, and all voted that the Hope-Jones console had received a notable send-off.

The principal feature of this console which interested the visitors was the "second touch," as movable consoles, flexible cables, stop keys, and stop switches (another form of changeable combination pedals) are no novelties this side of the pond. The "second touch" is practically a coupler which does not work when pressing the keys lightly, but which "couples" when the keys are played firmly. For instance, "second touch" in the swell is a great to swell coupler. If the keys are depressed lightly the coupler does not work; but if one or more notes are played firmly, they bring on the corresponding keys of the great. A melody can thus be emphasized in any voice or part by playing with a firmer touch. This undoubtedly has its advantages, but some skill is required to avoid bringing on the second touch on the wrong keys. The point which pleased us the most was the facility of repetition with this electric action, which was remarkable. Mr. Clemson exhibited one of the four little dry cells, which will supply electricity for full organ for twenty minutes running, and after a pause of a minute will have accumulated power enough for another twenty minutes. Some of the visitors complained at the idea of the power giving out at the end of twenty minutes; but it seems to us that any organist who will play on full organ for twenty minutes ought to have the power give out, to bring him to his senses.

A perfect familiarity with the different features of this console would, of course, give one a better idea of the value of the innovations than could be obtained in one short examination.

Mr. Jonathan Carl Woodman, at one time an organist in Brooklyn and New York, the father of the well-known organist, Mr. R. Huntington Woodman, died last month in Brooklyn. He was over eighty years old.

Since the death of Mr. Thomas Hill the Liverpool Road Factory (London) has been closed, and several organs which were on hand were sold at a ridiculously low figure. According to the London Musical Opinion and Music Trade Review, a chamber organ by Hill was sold for $200; an exquisite little Sweetler for $85. Another two-manual organ brought $250; while a stock organ having two manuals and sixteen stops sold for $400.

Mr. W. H. Donley opened a new Hook & Hastings organ (two manuals and twenty-two speaking-stops) in the Main-street Christian Church, Rushville, Ind., Feb. 7, with the following programme: Overture, "Semiramis," Rossini; Andante, Fifth Symphony, Beethoven; Fête Bohème, Gounod; Prayer and Cradle Song, Guilmant; Gavotte from "Mignon," Thomas; March in E-flat, Wely; L'Invitation, Weber; Vesper Bells, Spinney; Intermezzo, Gautier; Variations on a Scotch Air, Bach; Overture "La Bayadère," Auber. Mrs. Lavona Posey, Mrs. Nell McVay, and Miss Shadey Sleeth assisted with several songs.

The Farrand & Votey Organ Company have issued their seventh annual memorandum calendar, which has been sent to the patrons of this house. The inside cover is graced with a commendatory letter from Mr. Clarence Eddy, praising the famous organ in Festival Hall, World's Fair. The calendar reached us too late for us to insert the whole letter, but we copy one paragraph which shows the tone of the whole letter:—

"Musically this organ is worthy of rank among the few great organs of the world, while from a technical standpoint it occupies a supreme position."

The Möller Organ Company of Hagerstown, Md., is apparently doing a good business this year, having erected a large two-manual organ in the Epworth M. E. Church, Wilmington, Del.; one in the Fresh Church of Stroudsburg, Pa.; and another in St. Paul's P. E. Church, Smithsburg, Md. This company have on hand orders for organs for St. Paul's M. E. Church, Hagerstown; First M. E. Church, Martinsburg; M. E. Church, Spartanburg, S.C.; Zion M. E. Church, Washington, D.C.; Holy Trinity P. E. Church, Baltimore; St. Mary's P. E. Church, Columbus, Ga.

During the holidays Dr. Gerrit Smith of N.Y. gave a recital in St. Paul's M. E. Church, Hagerstown, and spoke in the highest terms of the new Möller organ.

Mr. Wm. C. Carl gave the last two of his "Afternoons of Organ Music" at the First Presb. Church, N.Y., on Jan. 31 and Feb. 7. The programme of Jan. 31 was: Toccata and Fugue in D, Bach; Méditation (new), Klein; Gavotte (*dans le style ancien*), Neustedt; Preislied, "Die Meistersinger" (violin and organ), Wagner; Theme and Variations, "The Harmonious Blacksmith," Handel; Recit. and Aria from "Don Munio," Buck; Scherzo in E, Gigout; Prélude (MS.) (*see time*), Guilmant (composed expressly for Mr. Carl during M. Guilmant's American Tournée); Andante from Concerto in E-minor (violin), Mendelssohn; Wedding March, de la Tombelle. Mr. Hubert Arnold, violinist, and Mr. George L. P. Butler, tenor, assisted.

Mr. Carl's last recital was of special interest, as, by request, he gave one of the programmes which he performed at the World's Fair: viz., Toccata in F, Bach; Concerto in A-minor; Marche de la Symphonie "Ariane," Guilmant; Song, "Spring Voices," Carl; Noël, Dubois; Concerto in D-minor (with Cadenzas by Guilmant), Handel; Finale from Fifth Symphony, Widor; "A May Song," Carl; Allegretto (composed specially for Mr. Carl), Salomé; Quartet, "Honor and Glory," Costa. Mr. Carl was assisted by the quartet of the church.

Mr. Harrison M. Wild gave his 150th organ recital in Unity Church, Chicago, Feb. 18, with the following programme: Prelude and Fugue on B.A.C.H., Liszt; Wedding Music, Dubois; The Egyptian's Lament ("Ben Hur") (MS.), Stern; Fantasia on "Eventide" (MS.), Rohner; Toccata from Fifth Symphony, Widor. The compositions by Messrs. Stern and Rohner are dedicated to Mr. Wild.

Mr. Chas. H. Morse gave the following programme of organ music at Plymouth Church, Brooklyn, Feb. 15: Andante Cantabile in F (Fourth Symphony ?), Beethoven; Bénédiction Nuptiale, Dubois; Offertoire in D-flat, Salomé; Pastorale in A, Deshayes; Gavotte from an Overture, Bach; Élégie in F-minor, Rousseau; Caprice in B-flat, Guilmant; Marche Cortège, Gounod. This recital is the first of a series to be given during Lent.

Messrs. Cole & Woodberry have just erected an organ in the Church of the Sacred Heart, Roslindale, Mass. It contains two manuals and eighteen stops. This firm are building an organ (two manuals and seventeen stops) for the Church of Our Saviour, Roslindale; one for Church of St. Peter, Boylston Station, and one for Cushing Academy, Ashburnham, Mass. The last named will contain twenty-five stops.

Mr. Edward E. Howe gave an organ recital in the First Presb. Church, Harlem, Pa., Feb. 14, with the following programme: Marche Militaire, Schubert; Sonata No. 1, Mendelssohn; Offertoire in D-flat, Salomé; Andantino, Chauvet; Caprice, Guilmant; Overture to "Wm. Tell" (by request), Rossini; Carillon de Louis XIV., Neustedt; Overture to "Masaniello," Auber.

Another effort is being made by the Musical Society of the Ann Arbor, Mich., University to raise funds to purchase the Farrand & Votey organ in Festival Hall, at the World's Fair. The organ is offered for $15,000, one-half its original cost.

The fifth and last concert given in Plymouth Church, Minneapolis, under the direction of Mr. J. Warren Andrews, by the Plymouth Choral Society, Feb. 21 (postponed from Jan. 31), was devoted exclusively to works of Chas. Gounod. Mr. Andrews played the following arrangements for the organ: Marche Militaire, Funeral March of a Marionette, and Marche Cortège.

During the months of February and March, Mr. Andrews is illustrating, with organ selections, a series of lectures given by Rev. Geo. H. Wells, D.D., on the subject of the "Lower Rhine."

CIPHERINGS.

THE following afflatus of an inspired reporter, describing an organ placed in a chapel, has been brought under my notice:—

"THE ORGAN AND PLATFORM.

"The organ itself has a very imposing appearance as witnessed from the opposite side of the chapel, and is an instrument which reflects the highest credit on the builders, ..., whose reputation has long borne a place in the first rank of musical circles for their efficiency in placing before the public instruments which could compete with any in the world. The great organ has six stops: principal, stopt diapason (treble), stopt diapason (bass), open diapason, mixture (two ranks), and dulciana. The swell organ consists of five stops, namely: cornopean, flute d'amour, liebich, bourdon, principal, and open diapason. There are also two coupler stops: swell to great, and great to pedals; and one pedal bourdon—making

a total of fourteen stops. The framework immediately connected with the finger-board is made of walnut, *finely polished in French*, and underneath are arranged *two* distinct sets of pedals, of two octaves each, with *a varrating* pedal-board, constructed upon an *approved Parisian principle*. There are *two compasses* on the great organ, which comprises 56 notes, while the swell organ has 44 notes, and the compass of the pedal organ is CCC to C—making 25 in all. Of the tone of the instrument too much could not be said: it contains that mellowness which could not possibly be excelled by instruments of greater power. *Every note is in perfect unison*, while the power of the stops is in every way admirable, not deteriorating, but adding considerable sweetness *to the natural tone*. The whole is encased in a beautiful panelled framework of yellow pine, which is polished in its natural color, and thus exhibits a fine contrast between the framework and the pipes (25 in number) in front of the organ, which are of a very light blue-lavender, and which are to be, as soon as time allows, diapered and flowered in gold in a manner which will materially enhance their appearance. *The swell pipes* are fitted up on each side *of the curtain*, and are made of the kind of material and polished as is the framework."
— *Ex.*

CORRESPONDENCE.

"THE INDISTINCTNESS OF ORGAN TONE."

To the Editor of THE ORGAN: —

"MELODIA" seems to have awakened much interest in this important subject concerning organ music, and I hope that the discussion will not degenerate into personalities.

There is a vast field for improvement in the structure of specifications, which in their present conventional form appear to be founded upon a commercial basis. The advancement in this respect would involve so much additional expense in the construction, that the art would be carried far beyond the realm of competition.

In the introduction of his subject, I discover not the least intention on the part of "Melodia" to cast disparagement upon the work of any builder, but rather to invite attention to principles of musical vibrations.

While it is positive that organ music has its limitations, it must be admitted that the human ear, *per se*, as a receptacle of vibrations which produce there what is termed sound, also has its limitations. It can only perceive vibrations of a limited rapidity or slowness. The lower tones in organ music require a certain amount of time for the sound waves to be formed before they can be impelled forward for the ear to interpret into musical sound. Hence quickly moving passages in the lower tones can never become satisfactorily distinct to any ear.

We often read in favorable criticisms of the playing of concert organists, that their rapidity of pedal execution is wonderful? Facility in the use of the pedals is commendable; but speed of execution, as far as the effect of the 16' or 32' registers is concerned, beyond the capacity of their speech, is wasted muscular exercise.

Music for the pedal department should be written according to the law of vibrations; and it is not in harmony with the dignity of the art if this law is violated, whether by Mendelssohn in the Finale of the First Organ Sonata, or by any other composer.

Many organists who read THE ORGAN were once pupils of the distinguished Haupt of Berlin; and they will remember his careful injunctions in guarding them against the too rapid playing of organ music, especially fugues. He himself used to play Bach's Greater G-minor Fugue at a speed of about 90 M.M. to the *eighth* note! He was accustomed to maintain that a quicker tempo was entirely destructive to clearness. This will hardly be credited by American organists who work this fugue up to a speed of 100 M.M., and are disappointed in the indistinctness of the pedal pipes when taken upon the organ at this railroad velocity, in which there is neither art nor dignity.

I hope other organists will communicate their experience on this subject, and let us hear from organ builders also.

PHILOMEL.

THE ORGAN IN TEWKESBURY ABBEY.

To the Editor of THE ORGAN :—

THIS organ was built in 1885 by Messrs. Michell & Thynne. In an elaborate description of this instrument which I have, the credit for the superior claims of this organ is given to Mr. Thynne, who was admitted into the intimate confidence of Schulze, the noted German organ builder of Paulinzelle, near Erfurt, who taught Mr. Thynne how to use his scales.

The description says that, by a special method of voicing, Mr. Thynne has preserved power without harshness. In reference to the most modern method of voicing string-toned stops, the description says, " The Gamba, or rather ' Viole d'Orchestre,' as Mr. Thynne has called it, to distinguish it from the ordinary Gamba stop, also treated in a special manner, a secret of Mr. Thynne's, produces a marvellous effect, resembling a violin as it has never been produced before."

As Mr. Michell, who is now in Boston, U.S.A., has expressed himself very positively in your columns in relation to improvements in organ building, I would like to know if in this published description of the organ in Tewkesbury Abbey, an injustice has not been done him in the omission of giving him credit for what is attributed to Mr. Thynne? Perhaps Mr. Michell will explain this matter?

CHELTENHAM.

ELECTRO PNEUMATIC ORGANS.

To the Editor of THE ORGAN :—

IN your December issue Mr. Hope-Jones notes that an American builder uses stop keys, and describes them in his (Mr. Hope-Jones') own terms. He has found some one to copy him in his turn, and one finds his remarks most interesting. The paradoxical phenomenon of Satan rebuking sin is always so.

As, however, Mr. Hope-Jones considers the *ipsissima verba* in which inventions are described to be also of interest to your readers, I give two descriptions of electro pneumatic stop keys. The pamphlet of Monsieur Dryvers was widely circulated in Great Britain.

DRYVERS, 1887.

Des leviers fort agiles, disposés à proximité de l'organiste, font obtenir instament l'effet désiré. De sorte que sans abandonner le clavier, sans interrompre le jeu, l'exécutant n'a qu'à effleurer du doigt un ou plusieurs de ces leviers, pour obtenir les timbres et groupes de jeux les plus caractéristiques.

JONES, 1891.

These tablets x x are actuated by the lightest touch of the performer's finger, without his having to raise his hands from the keys. A *glissando* movement of the finger across them will bring on or silence the full organ, or any portion of it, instantaneously.

LONDON, 18 *Jan.*

THOMAS CASSON.

OAKLAND, CAL., Feb. 14, 1892.

To the Editor of THE ORGAN :—

You will confer a great favor by answering the following questions:—

1. What are those pages printed in fine type in the first part of each volume of Peters' edition of Bach, headed " Variante "?

2. Did any such person as Ernest Osborne ever exist, or is he a creation of Mr. Clarke?

W. B. K.

Ans. 1. In his efforts to find the most perfect expression of his ideas, the immortal Bach made several copies of some of his works, each copy being more or less varied. These

variations have been preserved, and are published in the Peters' edition of his works.

Ans. 2. Every character mentioned in " The Organist's Retrospect " is taken from life (with names changed to avoid personalities), and every incident mentioned is founded upon fact.

ED.

NEW ORGANS.

RESIDENCE OF MR. J. M. SEARS, BOSTON.

(New organ erected by Mr. George S. Hutchings.)

COMPASS OF MANUALS, 61 KEYS; OF PEDALS, 30 KEYS.

GREAT ORGAN.		
Open Diapason (7 lower notes wood)	Metal,	16 Ft.
Open Diapason	"	8 "
Viola di Gamba . Pure Tin,		8 "
Gemshorn	Metal,	8 "
Doppelflöte	Wood,	8 "
Flauto Traverso	"	4 "
Octave	Metal,	4 "
Super Octave	"	2 "

SWELL ORGAN.		
Lieblich Gedeckt (treble and Bass)	Wood,	16 Ft.
Open Diapason	Metal,	8 "
Spitzflöte	"	8 "
Salicional	80% Tin,	8 "
Aeoline	Metal,	8 "
Vox Celestis	"	8 "
Stopped Diapason	Wood,	8 "
Flûte Harmonique,	Metal,	4 "
Violina	"	4 "
Flautino	"	2 "
Oboe	"	8 "

PEDAL ORGAN.		
Contra Bourdon (18 notes from 16 ft. Bourdon)	Wood,	32 Ft.
Violone		16 "
Bourdon		16 "
Flöte (from 16 ft. Bourdon)		8 "
Violoncello (from 16 ft. Violone)		8 "

SOLO ORGAN.		
Geigen Principal .	Metal,	8 Ft.
Dulciana	"	8 "
Concert Flute	Wood,	8 "
Viola d'Concerto, Pure Tin,		8 "
Flûte d'Amour	Wood,	4 "
Fugara	Metal,	4 "
Clarinet (Fagotto Bass)	"	8 "
Blank (for a future addition).		

COUPLERS (PISTON KNOBS).
Ch. to Gt. Sub. Octave.
Sw. to Ch. " "
In addition to the usual couplers.

COMBINATION PEDALS.
1. Great operating on Great and Pedal Stops.
2. Great operating on Great and Pedal Stops.
3. Great operating on Great and Pedal Stops.
4. Great (Full).
5. Great and Pedal Stops off.
6. Swell operating on Swell and Pedal Stops.
7. Swell operating on Swell and Pedal Stops.
8. Swell operating on Swell and Pedal Stops.
9. Swell (Full).
10. Swell and Pedal Stops off.
11. Choir operating on Choir and Pedal Stops.
12. Choir operating on Choir and Pedal Stops.
13. Choir (Full).
14. Choir and Pedal Stops off.
15. Great to Pedal Reversible.
16. Swell to Great at Octaves.
17. Balanced Swell Pedal for operating Choir Swell.
18. Balanced Swell Pedal for operating Swell.
19. Pedal Stops off.
20. Balanced Pedal for Grand Crescendo, the latter so arranged that all the stops can be brought on instantaneously, so as to be used as a Sforzando pedal, or very gradually for the crescendo.

The Combination Action is of novel construction, there being two rows of piston knobs placed in parallel lines over the swell keys, one piston to each stop; the name of the stop is engraved on an ivory tablet placed between the upper and lower pistons; and by means of these pistons any stop upon the manual can be made to operate on any combination pedal, together with any pedal stop that may be required. In operating the combination pedal these pistons are moved inward or outward, as the case may be, showing what stops are on and those which are off (the combinations being double acting). The registers themselves are in no way affected, so that any combinations which may have been prepared previously by means of the registers are not disturbed.

The key-desk is reversed, and stands away from the front of the organ case just far enough to allow good comfortable room for the performer.

The case and key-desk of the instrument are made of quartered oak, very elaborately and beautifully carved, and finished very dark, resembling English oak. The front or display pipes are made of pure block tin, and are not polished as usual, but have a dead finish like that of frosted silver; this, together with the rich dark finish of the case, makes a very beautiful and imposing appearance.

The main bellows is placed in a room built expressly for it in the basement, three stories below the organ room, and has six feeders, driven by a two-horse power electric motor. The Choir manual is enclosed in a swell-box with double shades, as well as the Swell manual.

The action of the instrument is electric throughout, and is capable of repeating to a very marked degree of rapidity. In fact, to us the most commendable features of the organ are the action (keys) and the voicing. The individual stops have a distinct character of their own, while the *ensemble* is remarkably pleasing for a house organ. The acoustic properties of the music room are such as to enhance the effect of tonic combination without rendering them offensive, while there is an entire absence of the deadening effects usually found with an organ placed in a private residence.

FIRST PRESBYTERIAN CHURCH, LOCKPORT, N.Y.

(New organ built by the Hook & Hastings Co.)

GREAT ORGAN.

Double Open Diapason	. 16	Ft.
Open Diapason	. 8	"
Viola di Gamba	. 8	"
Dulciana	. 8	"
Doppel-flöte	. 8	"
Octave (Principal)	. 4	"
Flûte d'Amour	. 4	"
Twelfth (Octave Quint)	. 2⅔	"
Fifteenth (Super Octave)	. 2	"
Trumpet	. 8	"

PEDAL MOVEMENTS.

F., MF., and P. Comb. to Gt.
"   "   "   "   " Sw.
Gt. to Ped. (reversible).
The usual couplers.
Water Motor.

SWELL ORGAN.

Bourdon (Treble & Bass)	. 16	Ft.
Open Diapason	. 8	"
Salicional	. 8	"
Stopped Diapason	. 8	"
Aeoline	. 8	"
Vox Celestis	. 8	"
Flauto Traverso	. 4	"
Violina	. 4	"
Mixture	. III.	Rks.
Cornopean	. 8	Ft.
Oboe & Bassoon	. 8	"
Vox Humana	. 8	"

PEDAL ORGAN.

Double Open Diapason	. 16	Ft.
Bourdon	. 16	"
Violoncello	. 8	"

(Third Division, Echo Organ.)

(IN A SWELL-BOX.)

Echo Salicional (new form)	8	Ft.
Quintadena	8	"
Flûte Octaviante	4	"
Clarinet	8	"
Tremulant		

MECHANICAL.

Ch. to Gt. Sub. Octave.
Sw. to Gt. Unison.
Sw. to Gt. Octave.
7 Combination Pistons placed beneath Great Keyboard.
7 Special Pedals.

PEDAL ORGAN *(North Side.)*

Great Bass	. 32	Ft.
Open " (new form)	. 16	"
Great Flute	. 8	"
Bombard	. 16	"

(South Side.)

Sub. Bass	. 16	Ft.
Flûte d'Amour	. 8	"

CHOIR ORGAN.

Viola	. 8	Ft.
Echo Viola (new specialty)	8	"
Flûte Traversière (new form)	8	"
Salicet	. 4	"
Flûte d'Orchestre (new form)	4	"
Piccolo Harmonique	. 2	"
Orchestral Oboe	. 8	"
Sw. to Choir.		
Sub. Octave (in itself).		
Tremulant.		

The organ is divided into two parts (fifty feet apart).

A Ross water motor operates the four square feeders in the basement. The action is Tubular-pneumatic.

NOTE.—This organ was on exhibition at the factory two afternoons, and we regret that imperative engagements prevented our examining the instrument.

ST. LUKE'S CHURCH, GERMANTOWN, PA.

(New organ built by Messrs. Cole & Woodberry, in conjunction with Mr. Carlton C. Michell.)

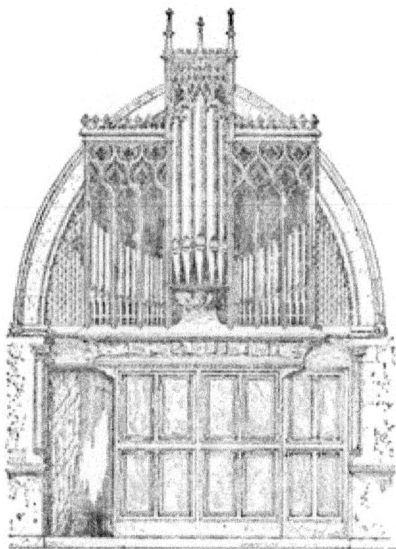

GREAT ORGAN.

(First Division.)

Bourdon (special form)	. 16	Ft.
Principal Diapason	. 8	"
Small Diapason	. 8	"
Flûte Harmonique	. 4	"
Octave	. 4	"
Octave Quinte	. 2⅔	"
Super Octave	. 2	"

(Second Division, Trumpet Organ.)
(ON HEAVY WIND AND IN SPECIAL BOX.)

Trombone	. 16	Ft.
Tromba (Harmonic)	. 8	"
Clarion	. 4	"
Mixture (15, 19, 22, 26, 29)	V. Rks.	

SWELL ORGAN.

Geigen Diapason	. 8	Ft.
Viole d'Orchestre (new)	. 8	"
Viole Céleste	. 8	"
Rohr-flöte (new form)	. 8	"
Octave	. 4	"
Mixture (15, 19, 22)	III. Rks.	
Contre Posaune	. 16	Ft.
Cornopean	. 8	"
Oboe	. 8	"
Vox Humaine	. 8	"
Unison.		
Octave (on itself).		
Tromblom (light wind).		
" (heavy wind.)		

GEORGE S. HUTCHINGS,

Church Organ Manufacturer,

23 TO 27 IRVINGTON STREET,

BOSTON, MASS.

Builder of some of the most famous organs in the country, among which may be mentioned The New Old South, Emmanuel, Second Church, Park St. Church, St. Paul's, Spiritual Temple, and Church of the Advent, all of Boston ; also South Congregational Church, Middletown, Conn., New York Avenue M. E. Church, Brooklyn, N. Y., St. Paul's School, Concord, N. H., and All Saints Church, Worcester, Second Congregational Church, Holyoke, Mass., Grace Church, Providence, R.I., Plymouth Church, Minneapolis, First Congregational Church, Omaha, Neb., First Congregational Church, San Francisco, Cal., Independent Presbyterian Church, Savannah, Ga., and many others.

Send for catalogue.

ORGAN MUSIC

Published and Imported by EVERETT E. TRUETTE & Co., 149A Tremont Street, Boston.

Capocci, F. Allegretto,		$ .40
Clausmann, Aloys. First Collection, in Six Parts—		
Part I. { Fantasia in C-minor. / First Meditation in B. / Andante in D.		1.80
Part II. { Scherzo in B-minor. / First Elevation in D-flat. / Cantilène in E-minor.		1.00 / .60 / .50
Part III. { First Offertory in E. / Second Elevation in A-minor. / Communion in D.		1.00 / .80 / .60
Part IV. { Pastorale in D. / Elegie in C-sharp minor. / Grand Chœur in C.		1.00 / .80
(To be completed.)		
Dallier, H. Six Grand Preludes. Complete,	net,	1.60
Decq, A. Méditation Religieuse		.80
Prayer		.80
Deshayes, Henri. Grand Chœur in D		.75
Dubois, Theo. Twelve Pieces, complete	net,	$3.20
Prelude in F. / Offertory in E. / Toccata in G. / Verset in D. / Offertory in E-flat. / Verset (Choral).	Fantaisie in E. / Meditation in E-flat. / March of the Magi Kings. / Offertory in E-flat. / Cantilène in A flat. / Grand Chœur in B-flat.	
Dubois, Theo. Messe de Mariage	net,	3.20
Entrée du Cortège. / Bénédiction Nuptiale.	Offertoire and Invocation. / Laus Deo.	
Dubois, Theo. Grand Chœur in B-flat		.50
Offertory in E-flat		.50
Fink, C. Adagio (Sonata in G-minor)		.25
Gigout, Eugene. Ten Pieces, complete	net,	3.20
Gigout, Eugene. Six Pieces.		
1. Prelude and Fugue		1.50
2. Andante and Allegro Con Moto		1.50
3. Fantasia		1.30
4. Andantino		1.20
5. Larghetto		1.30
6. Andante Sostenuto		1.20
Grison, Jules. First Collection of Organ Pieces, in Eight Parts.		
Part I. St. Cecilia Offertory, No. 1		1.00
Part II. St. Cecilia Offertory, No. 2		1.00
Part III. St. Cecilia Offertory, No. 3		1.00
Part IV. First Offertory for Palm Sunday		1.00
Part V. Second Offertory for Palm Sunday		1.00
Part VI. Communion		.80
Part VII. Christmas Offertory		1.00
Part VIII. Grand Triumphal March		1.20

Grison, Jules. Second Collection of Organ Pieces, in Six Parts.		
Part I. { Grand Chœur in F. / Cantilène Pastorale. / Christmas Offertory in C.		$1.60
Part II. { Christmas Offertory in F. / Communion in G.		2.00
Part III. { Marche Funèbre. / Les Cloches.		2.00
Part IV. { Fantasia. / Fugue.		2.00
Part V. { Toccata in F. / Meditation in E. / Festival March.		2.40
Part VI. { Festival Offertory. / Meditation in B. / Fantasia on the Portuguese Hymn.		2.40
Gounod, Ch. Serenade		.50
Guilmant, Alex. Pastorale, Op. 26, for Piano and Organ		1.50
Hesse, Adolph. Andantino		.35
Larghetto in B-flat		.25
Lemaigre, Ed. Twelve pieces. Complete	net,	2.40
Solemn March. / Meditation. / Pastorale. / Alla Fuga.	Elegy. / Caprices. / Prayer. / Melody.	Andante Religioso. / Two Preludes, in Form of a Canon. / Scherzo.
Lemaigre, Ed. New Compositions, in Six Parts.		
Part I. { Fragment Symphonique (Allo Polacca) / Andantino. / Intermezzo.		1.50
Part II. { Cantabile. / Prelude, Grand Chœur.		1.50
Part III. { Magnificat in F. / Magnificat in D.		2.40
Part IV. { Offertory. / Contemplation. / Prelude.		1.50
Part V. { Stabat Mater. / Cantena Pastorale.		2.00
Part VI. { Elegy (March). / Elevation. / Kyrie. / Five Versets.		2.00
Lemmens, J. Adoration		.25
Liszt, Fr. Adagio in D-flat		.25
MacMaster, Georges. Prelude in A-flat		.60
Mendelssohn, Felix. Adagio (First Sonata)		.25
Merkel, Gustav. Prelude in F		.25
Prelude in A-minor		.20
Allegretto in A		.50
Andantino in F		.25
Canon in F-sharp		.30
Osborne, Ernest. Melody		.25
Parisot, Octave. Elevation		.90
Reed, C. E. Fantasia in C		.75
Processional March		.75

VOL. II. NO. 12.　　　　APRIL, 1894.　　　　WHOLE NO. 24.

BACH

YEARLY SUBSCRIPTION $2.00.　　　　SINGLE COPIES 25 CTS.

THE ORGAN

DEVOTED TO

A MONTHLY JOURNAL

THE KING OF INSTRUMENTS

RHEINBERGER

GUILMANT

FRESCOBALDI

BUXTEHUDE

MERKEL

BEST

·EVERETT·E·TRUETTE·

EDITOR & PUBLISHER

149 A. TREMONT ST. BOSTON.

HANDEL

THE ORGAN.

Vol. II. BOSTON, APRIL, 1894. No. 12.

THE ORGAN.

BOSTON, APRIL, 1894.

Published the first of every month. Subscription price $1.00 per year (European countries 101. 36.), payable in advance. Single copies, 15 cents.

Subscribers will please state with which number they wish their subscription to begin.

Remittances should be made by registered letter, post-office order, or by check payable to Everett E. Truette.

Correspondence, to secure notice, must in all cases be accompanied by the name and address of the writer, not for publication, but as a guarantee of good faith.

Advertising rates sent on application.

Address all communications,

THE ORGAN, 149 A Tremont Street, Boston, Mass.

Single copies of THE ORGAN can be procured of

NOVELLO, EWER, & CO.	. . . . .	New York.
G. SCHIRMER	. . . . .	New York.
OLIVER DITSON CO.	. . . . .	Boston.
L. H. ROW & CO.	. . . . .	Boston.
N. E. CONSERVATORY	. . . . .	Boston.
H. B. STEVENS CO.	. . . . .	Boston.
LYON & HEALY	. . . . .	Chicago.
CLAYTON F. SUMMY	. . . . .	Chicago.
THEODORE PRESSER	. . . . .	Philadelphia.
WM. H. BONER & CO.	. . . . .	Philadelphia.
TAYLOR'S MUSIC HOUSE	. . . . .	Springfield, Mass.
GALLUP & METZGER	. . . . .	Hartford, Conn.
RICHAULT & CO.	. . . . .	Paris.
NOVELLO EWER & CO.	. . . . .	London.

CONTENTS:

As announced in our last number, the further issue of THE ORGAN is suspended with this number. Since our announcement we have received hundreds of letters from subscribers and non-subscribers, from advertisers, and from dealers, besides numerous letters from contemporary editors, urging in the strongest terms a continuance of the publication. We beg permission to acknowledge with thanks the receipt of all the letters mentioned above, and regret to say that we are still convinced that the demand for THE ORGAN is too limited to warrant its continuance. Reminding our subscribers that in the course of a month they will receive a remittance for the balance of their subscription, we close the mucilage pot, hang up the scissors, and say au revoir.

IN response to several inquiries, we would state that we have a few copies left of the first volume (unbound) of THE ORGAN, and about twenty-five copies of volume two, besides a number of copies of several issues, which we offer to the public at our regular rates, viz., twenty-five cents per single number, or two dollars for twelve issues.

THE plans for rebuilding Tremont Temple, Boston, are nearly completed, and our attention naturally turns to the proposed organ for the hall. With their proverbial liberality (?) the architects at first allotted a space *three feet deep* for the organ. (How many people still think that an organ consists of a row of displayed pipes and a console!) We understand that a few more *inches* in depth have been allotted to the organ, that the instrument will be corbelled out over the choir seats; that the action will be extended, and that all this shall cost but $5,000. There is not a small prospect in "The Hub" of any competition between organists and hand-organ grinders. The latter still have the field to themselves.

IT is with no little regret that we announce the retirement of Mr. W. T. Best, for nearly forty years organist of St. George's Hall, Liverpool. For some time past Mr. Best has been in very poor health; even as long ago as 1884, when the writer frequently met him in Liverpool and London, his health was not such as to encourage the most arduous concert work. It is greatly to be regretted that he was unable to visit this country last summer; that the concert tour which was partially planned for him was unavoidably abandoned.

Mr. Best has for years occupied one of the pinnacles of the tower of organ fame, and very few organists have attained such a world-wide reputation as a concert player.

The hundreds of arrangements from the scores of the great masters which Mr. Best has given to the world besides his original compositions, are well known in this country; but perhaps his greatest reputation has been won as an executant, than whom none is superior.

SAMUEL PIERCE.

Mr. Samuel Pierce was born in Hebron, Conn., in 1819, but he is a son of Massachusetts by adoption, at least; for he came to Reading in 1837, and has carried on business there for nearly half a century. He has been prominent in public as well as in business life, having served on the Reading Board of Selectmen, and represented the town in the Legislature. He began the business in a small way in the ell part of his house, and gradually developed it until, as a manufacturer of metal and wood organ pipes and organ material, Mr.

Pierce is unquestionably almost universally known, not only because his business was established away back in 1847, but also because it is of great magnitude, he carrying on the largest factory for the production of organ pipes in this country. But its output is even more remarkable for its quality than its quantity. From the very first, Mr. Pierce has made it an invariable rule to furnish only the very highest grade of work; and the uniform excellence of it has gained for it so high a reputation, that the simple fact that organ pipes or material were made by him is accepted as satisfying evidence that they are, to say the least, equal to the best the market affords. His productions are shipped to all parts of the Union; to Canada, Jamaica, and South America. The metals used are zinc and a composition of pure tin and lead, never being adulterated with other metals. All the pipes are of good weight, special care being taken to have the thickness suited to the requirements of the tone in the various stops. The workmanship is the very best in every respect, and the voicing is done by men of great experience and skill, who have not only the ability, but the determination, to meet the tastes and requirements of even the most critical as regards quality and strength of tone. The wood pipes manufactured by Mr. Pierce are made of thoroughly seasoned, assured, clear Michigan pine, shellacked, and every detail of the workmanship is thoroughly first-class. Some eighteen years ago, Mr. Pierce began to make a specialty of supplying nearly all kinds of pipe-organ materials, such as keys, pedals, various action parts, tapped and plain wires, tuners' tools, etc., and has built up a very

extensive business in this department alone. A specialty is also made of the gilding, silvering, bronzing, and decoration of front pipes, and the results attained are such as to give entire satisfaction to even the most critical. Mr. Pierce employs more than fifty experienced men, the majority of whom are skilled workmen; this fact, taken in connection with the magnitude and complete equipment of his factory, which is two and three stories, affording about 14,000 square feet of floor space, goes far to explain his success in filling orders at comparatively short notice, despite the extent and variety of his business. Mr. Pierce has been ably assisted in the development of his business by Mr. Thomas R. Todd, who has had charge of the correspondence and office work for more than twenty-one years. The foregoing sufficiently indicates how prominent and important a factor Mr. Pierce and his enterprise has been to the growth and development of the town of Reading.

From "Reading: Its Representative Business Men."

NOTABLE ORGANS.

XVI.

PALACE OF THE TUILERIES, PARIS.

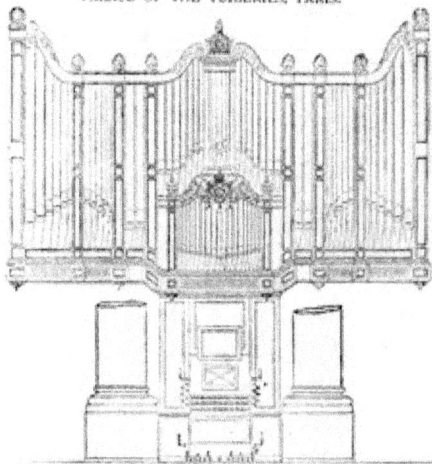

THE organ formerly in the Tuileries Palace was constructed in 1827 by Sebastian Érard, partially destroyed in the famous political events of July, 1830, and reconstructed in 1835 by P. Érard, a nephew and successor of Seb. Érard. In 1870 the palace and its contents were destroyed by fire at the time of the communistic demonstrations. The instrument comprised three manuals of fifty-nine keys and a pedal.

Appended is the specification:—

GREAT ORGAN.	SWELL ORGAN.
(*Lower Keyboard.*)	(*Middle Keyboard.*)
Bourdon,	Bourdon,
Flûte,	Prestant,
Prestant,	Flûte Harmonique,
Nasard,	Trumpet,
Fifteenth,	Hautbois,
Fourniture (III Rks.),	Bassoon,
Trumpet.	Voix Humaine.

There were no separate stops for the pedal, and the upper keyboard was fitted with but one set of pipes, having a special contrivance for varying the power of any one note or combination of notes. This set of pipes was called "*jeu expressif,*" and was the invention of Seb. Érard.

Mr. W. Starles, who has been organist of Kirkstall (England) Church for nearly forty years, has resigned his position, and will receive a retiring pension.

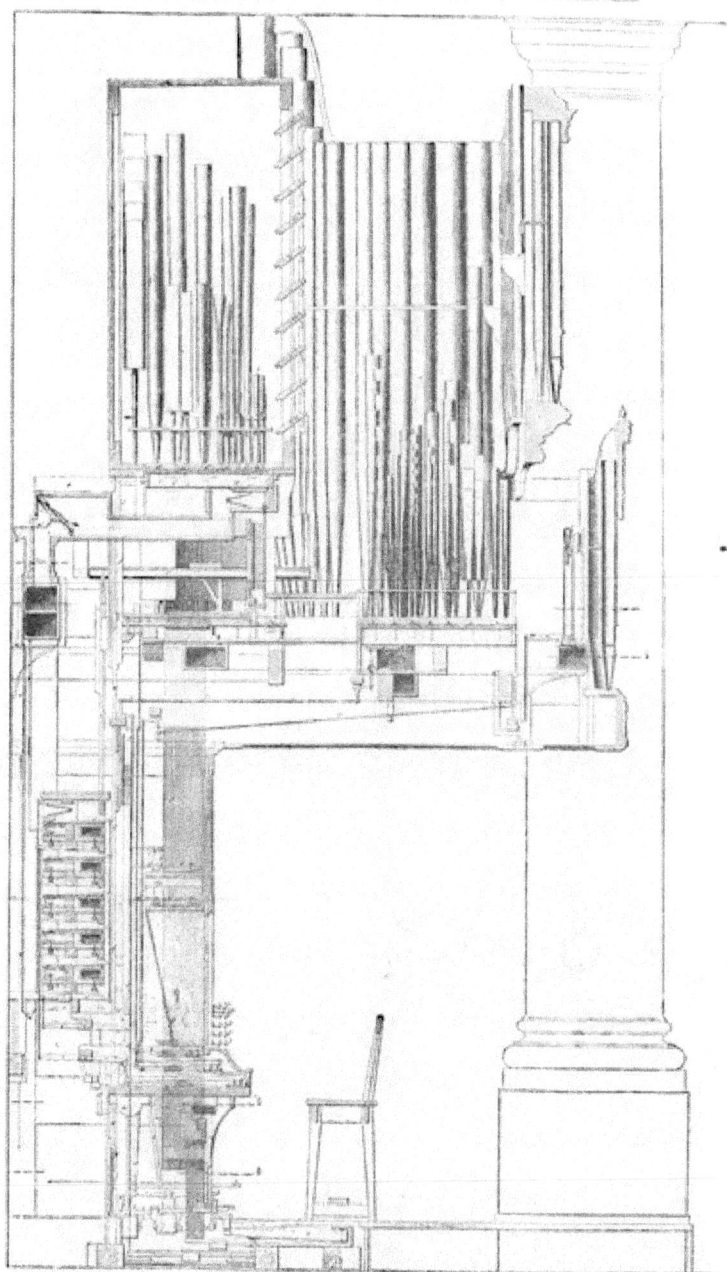

VERTICAL SECTION OF THE ORGAN FORMERLY IN THE TUILERIES PALACE, PARIS.

METHODS OF ORGAN BLOWING.

The mechanical arrangements for supplying organs with the necessary wind have, on the whole, fairly kept pace with the improvements effected in other departments of organ construction.

Nearly all the old treatises upon the organ state that the first pipe organ of which there is any record in this country, was that erected in Winchester Cathedral (*circa* A.D. 950). This organ, it is averred, possessed *only* forty "keys," but needed seventy blowers. Considering that for some centuries after the date named, the "keys" were rude beams of timber pushed so as to admit of being struck with both fists, and that consequently *only one was used at a time*, the blowing arrangements must have been singularly defective.

It is one of the writer's early recollections how, when he and a friend were but very youthful music students, they were permitted by Mr. Richardson, the then organist of Salisbury Cathedral, to practise upon the cathedral organ — which they did, *blowing one for the other* alternately, about half an hour at a time. From the seventy men toiling at the organ with forty keys, to the striplings blowing singlehanded a three-manual FFF organ, a great advance in bellows construction and arrangement is apparent. But when modern improvement introduced heavier wind pressure, and especially since wind came to be used expensively (as steam) to move heavy swell shutters, to draw stops, couplers, and composition movement, absolutely new methods of blowing became necessary.

First of all, the bellows itself had to be strengthened, and the action governing it modified. Where a wooden bar and a few tapes sufficed to regulate the folds, strong middle frames and iron regulators with double-leathered gussets were needed.

With a view to obviate the disadvantages inherent to bellows with folds, cases working like gasometers, with elaborate counterpoises, have been tried, but apparently without much success.

To overcome the friction of feeder actions, — always a prominent cause of wasted power, — numberless contrivances have been introduced, none perhaps more ingenious than the variety known as "centrifugal feeders;" the weight attached to each feeder supplying the force *both* to drive out the wind and to open the bellows ready for work.

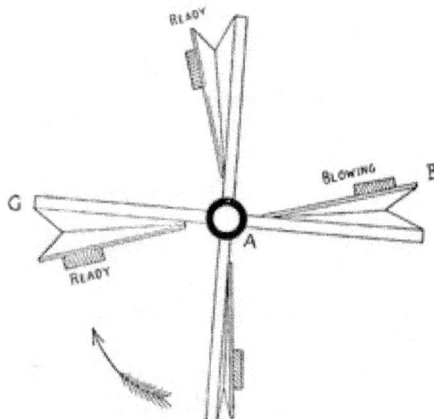

From a glance at the rough diagram illustrating the principle of this discovery, it will be seen if the four bellows are made to revolve on the centre A, that as each successive bellow comes to B, the weight will cause it to discharge, and as it comes up towards C the same weight will draw it open.

To work such a system of feeders, a heavy fly-wheel is obviously needed.

Of more practical service are the different forms of French double-acting feeders, which undoubtedly lend themselves best to the requirements of high-pressure organs. No absolute rules can be laid down as to the best system of planning organ bellows and blowing methods. All depends upon the size of the organ, the wind pressure, and the special features and circumstances of each particular case.

Human power, as applied by the means of the ordinary bellows handle, is used under conditions singularly wasteful. If the muscular power of a man is to be fully available, it can only be when pulling horizontally, as in rowing, and then he must have firm back and firm rest. But if the resistance in pounds to be overcome is less than the weight of his body, utilizing his weight upon a treadmill action has been over and over again proved to be the method by which a man can exert the most power *for the longest time*, besides commanding the advantages of perfect steadiness. Whatever be the motive power, and whatever the action, handles, treadmill, or crankshaft, the all-important and first consideration is to determine the size and shape of feeders suited to the particular instance.

The considerations involved in the case of an ordinary hand-blown organ will sufficiently illustrate the general principle. Let us imagine two organs, each having bellows surface of 7 ft. by 4 ft. The first instrument for a church, the second for a school, study, or music chamber. What are the conditions special to each?

The first, or church organ, will be principally used for services at stated times, when a regular adult blower will be in attendance; and, again, seldom will it play for more than ten or fifteen minutes continuously.

The second instrument will play at irregular hours, sometimes for a long time continuously, and may be needed suddenly when no strong man is at hand, but only the young people, whom it may even be more convenient to employ habitually.

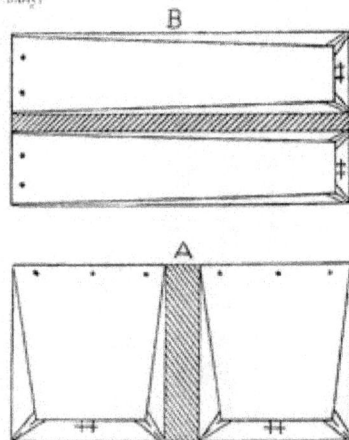

In the diagram, A represents the arrangement of feeder for the church organ, B, that for the other instrument. A will give steady wind, brief intervals of rest being needed by the blower, who must be an adult. B will give wind somewhat less steady, from the greater rapidity of strokes needed, but requiring no great exertion.

Now, whatever the motive power, the same problem must be solved; and in the case of engine power the size and shape of feeders must be governed by the nature of the motive

(*Continued on page 287.*)

à Monsieur Clarence Eddy.

MARCHE DE FÉTE.

Récit. Fonds et Anches de 8 et 4.
Pos.   Fonds et Anches de 8 et 4.
G.O.   Grand Choeur.
Ped.   Fonds et Anches de 8,4 et 16.
Tous les claviers accouplés.

Sw. 8 & 4 Ft. with reeds.
Ch. 8 & 4 Ft.
Gt. Full.
Ped. 16, 8 & 4 Ft.
Sw. to Gt. & Gt. to Ped.

Aloÿs Claussmann, Op. 26, No. 1.

Ôtez Tirasse
et Anches de la Ped.
Gt.to Ped.off.

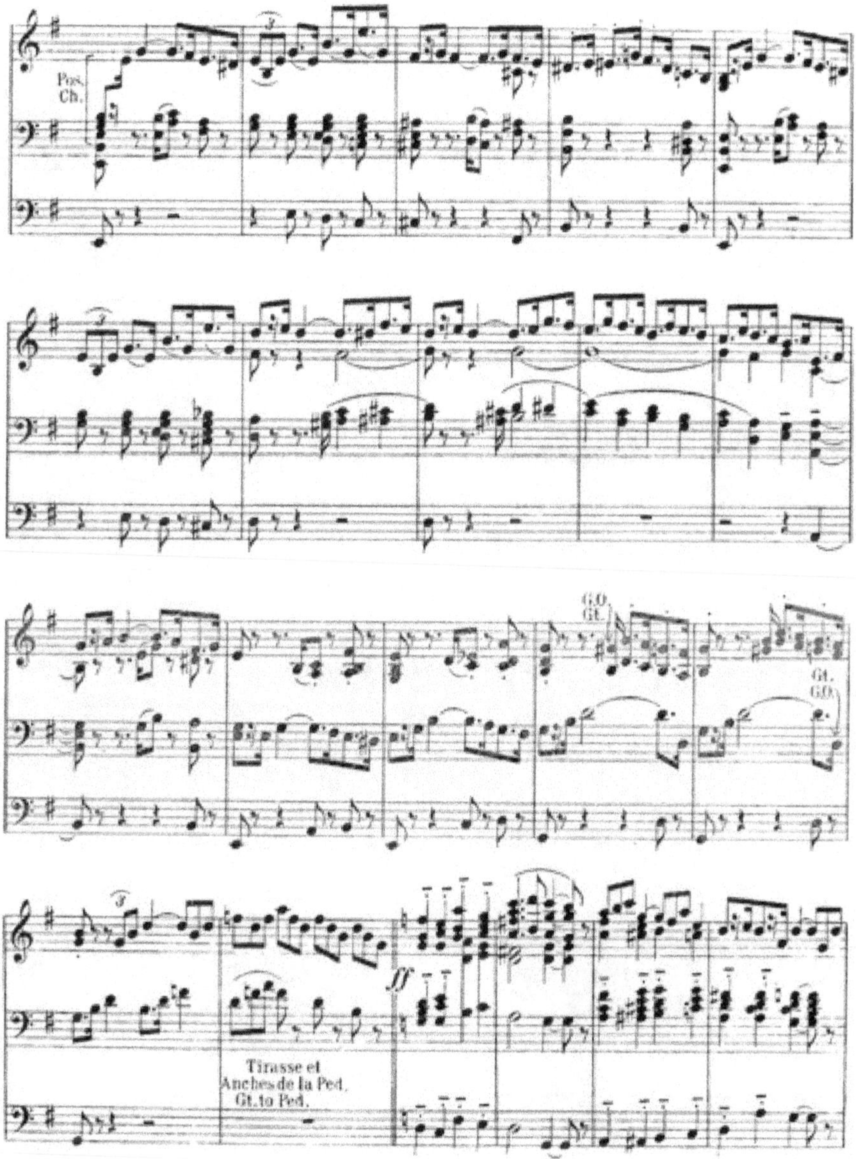

Pos.
Ch.
G.O.
Gt.
Gt.
G.O.
ff
Tirasse et
Anches de la Ped.
Gt. to Ped.

Ôtez les
Anches à tous
les claviers
Ne laissez
au G.O. au Pos
et au Récit.
que les fonds
de 8 & 4 p.
Ôtez Tirasse.

Reduce Gt.Ch
& Sw.to foun-
dation Stops of
8 & 4 ft.
Gt.to Ped.off.

G.O.
Gt.

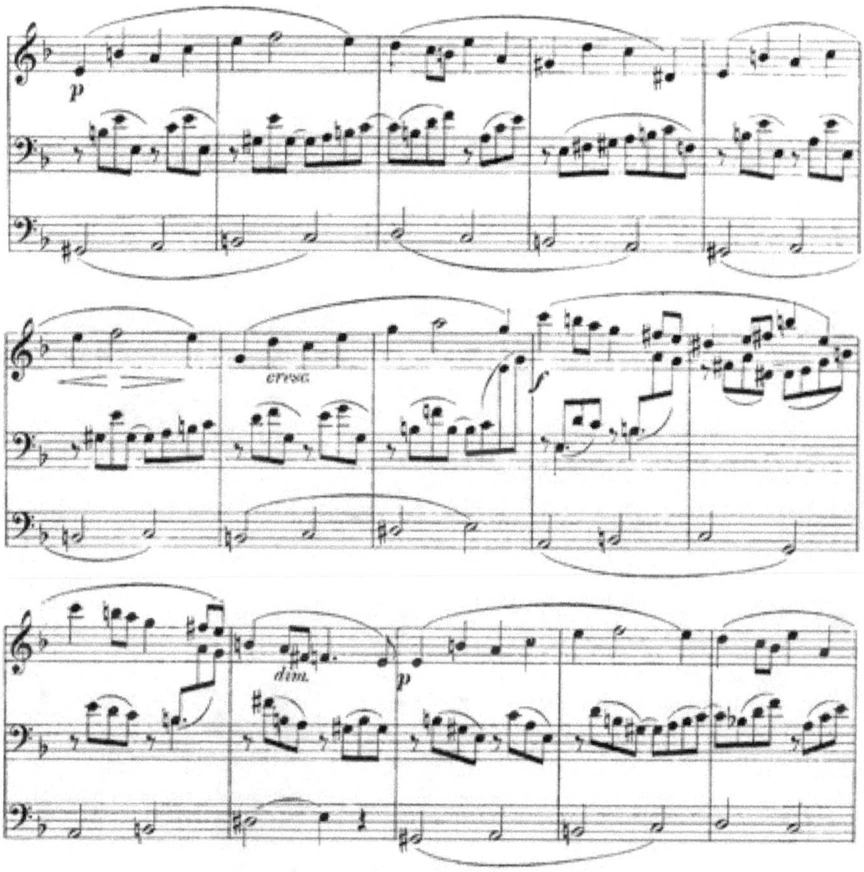
p
cresc.
dim.
p
cresc.

poco rit
f
dim.
GD.
Gt.
(Anches du Récit (boite fermee.)
(Add Sw. reeds (box closed.)
Récit
Sw.
Tirasse.
Gt. to Ped.

mettez Anches du Pos.
Add Ch. reeds.
Pos.
Ch.
Anches du G.O. et fonds de 16 p.
Add Gt. reeds & 16 Ft.
G.O.
Gt.
Anches de la Ped.
Add Ped. reeds
rit.
cresc. molto
Tempo I.
ff Full Organ
3

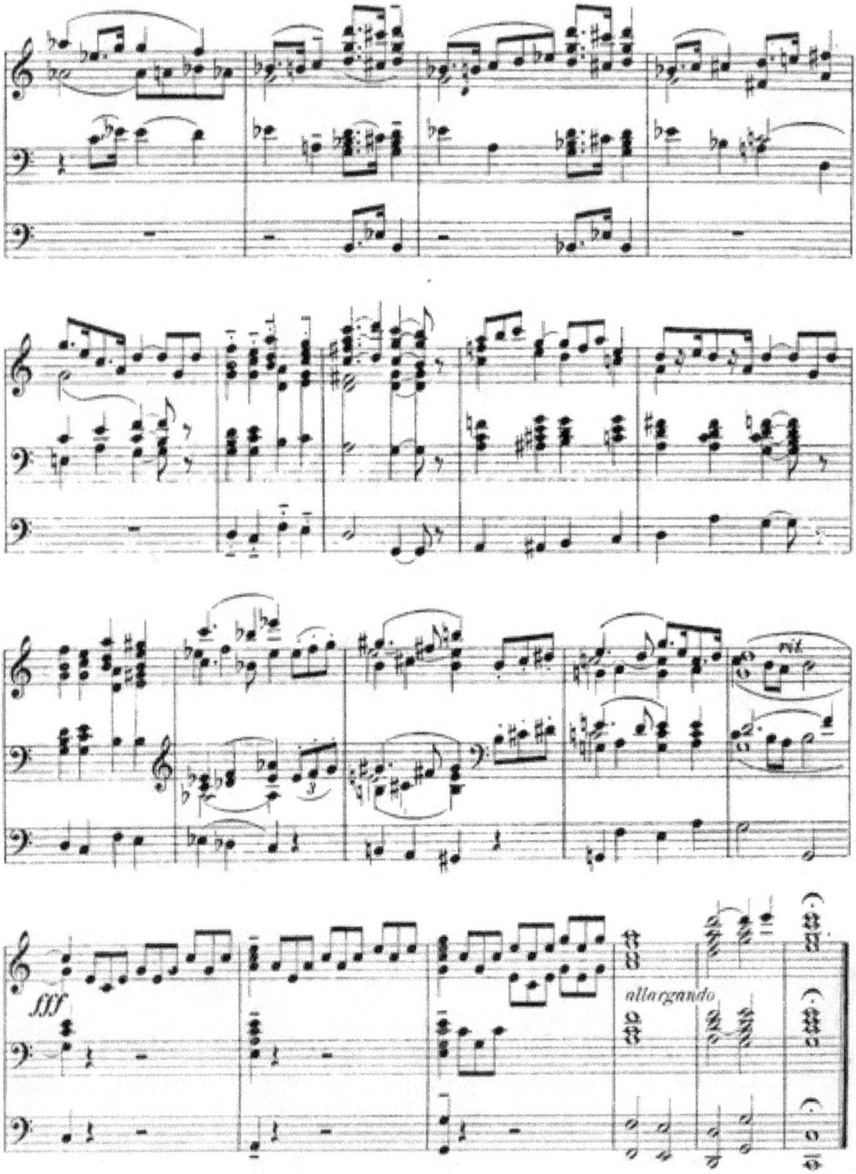
rit.
fff
allargando

(*Continued from page 270.*)

force, according as it works best when the piston surface is increased and stroke diminished, or *vice-versa*. So important are these considerations, that *in almost every instance* where any of the accredited mechanical motors prove a failure, it may clearly be traced to an unintelligent "setting out" of the feeders or action. Water power under average conditions appears to be the best agent for driving the bellows in large organs, but this remark is without prejudice to some other excellent motors in use. When gas engines are *perfectly* silent, and when oil engines are finally perfected, both cannot fail to be largely used in cases where water is not available. Electricity also is being pressed into the service; but any detailed consideration of the merits of these systems would carry beyond the scope of the present contribution.

J. W. HINTON, M. A. *Mus. Doc.*

THE ORGANIST'S RETROSPECT.[1]

BY HORATIO CLARKE.

(*AN AUTOBIOGRAPHY OF LENOX OSBORNE.*)

IN TWENTY-FIVE CHAPTERS.

CHAPTER XII.

EARLY one morning Mr. Rodman came to my door and informed me that there was an advertisement in one of the Boston daily papers for an organist, and that he thought I would be interested in answering it. I accordingly went immediately into the city to the place indicated, and learned that there was a large number of applicants who had already sent in their names and recommendations. The advertiser was the director of music for a society about to build a church at the South End of the city. Having sold their down-town edifice, they had leased a large hall, since used as a theatre, in which there was then a large organ with three manuals.

On learning that no organist had been engaged for the following Sunday, I asked for the privilege of playing on that day, which was readily granted; as I preferred to rest upon my fitness for the position rather than to depend upon testimonial letters. I then went to the hall, and familiarized myself with the instrument, which was enclosed within an ornamental screen, instead of displaying front pipes, and the stop-knobs had various-colored ivories for each section of the organ.

The choir consisted of a quartet, which met at the residence of the director on Saturday evening for rehearsal, so that my first Sunday with the large organ was without any previous adaptation to the voices; but at the close of the evening service I was engaged as organist for the ensuing year, at an increased salary compared with what I had been receiving.

The change from a rural neighborhood to contact with the activity of a busy city, gave me another impulse in my musical progress, and made a decided change from the monotonous and rigid associations of the past year. Although the denomination was that towards which my religious thoughts had been led, I found the members less narrow in expressing their opinions, and more social with each other. The change was so much in contrast, and so unlike the Sundays in the country, that I soon began to doubt whether I had not exposed myself to greater worldly temptations in accepting this more advanced position?

However, I continued with this society while the new edifice was building, and was successful in having a large three-manual organ built for it. The contract was given my friend Mr. Sherburn; and from the beginning to its completion, I spent many hours in the organ factory. The specification was of my own preparation, and the first "Vox Humana" of the builder was placed in the Swell as a 16 ft. register, an octave lower than the diapason pitch. This was done for the reason that the imitative quality of this stop loses its characteristic effect when used above the range of the tenor notes,

either in solos or chords. A German "Gamba," with its beautiful mouth, was also placed in the Choir, which was so slow of speech that a St. Diapason slide drew with it as a "helper."

The church and organ were completed just at the beginning of the Civil War, when the tide of popular feeling was patriotic and national music prevailed. The organ was opened with an elaborate programme, given by the most noted players in the city, illustrating the varied capacities of the instrument. My numbers were a brilliant overture and the primo of a four-hand piece arranged from one of Handel's choruses. Although the concert was under my direction, I have not yet forgotten the shrinking I then felt in making an exhibition of my own attainments in comparison with the other talented organists.

The pastor of the church was an ardent lover of organ music, and in the Sunday services there was a happy sympathy between us. Just before entering the pulpit, he would often send me a little note, to the effect that there were certain afflicted ones in the congregation to whom he hoped that I would direct my musical thoughts, so as to afford them comfort; for he believed in the power which was given me to reach the hearts of the listeners. On entering a church to render my services as organist, I have always felt the sphere of an audience, so that my improvisations would be adapted to their thoughts. Sometimes when I would see a certain face, I would endeavor to touch that individual's heart with good impressions; and many times have I received kindly letters conveying expressions of the consolation which had thus been afforded, even from strangers whom I have not since personally met.

The members of this society treated me with unusual kindness in every way. They fitted up a special music-room in the edifice for my use, in which I now had a pedal piano-forte, which I found more beneficial in technique than in using the large organ.

I spent the requisite time in studying the violoncello, in order to take the part in a string quartet which met weekly in my room, to play the beautiful quartets of Mozart and Haydn and the more modern composers. Although I had not kept up my violin practice, yet I felt the good effects of my early studies in forming my taste for melodic passages in my organ improvisations. I also found that the study of the violoncello was of much assistance in my pedal playing, as it enabled me to carry the bass more distinctly in my mind in organ music, causing me to phrase all the pedal movements as if bowed and accented, in my mental conception.

In addition to my Sunday engagement, my services were often in requisition for lectures and other occasions at the old Tremont Temple, for which I prepared a large repertoire of overtures and entertaining music, not considered classical. I was also frequently employed by organ builders to exhibit their new instruments, when finished, in the churches throughout the New England States. I began to obtain many pupils in the city, and was fairly on the avenue of musical and financial prosperity. But my nervous organization was not strong, and was soon put to a decided test.

I had carefully prepared and announced a programme of classical organ music, to be given in the church. The selections were from Bach's Preludes, Fugues, and Trio Sonatas; Mendelssohn's Sonatas and Fugues, and Variations by Hesse. There was no admission fee, and the audience was made up of many organists and musical critics.

On taking my place at the organ, I was so affected with nervous excitement that I could scarcely breathe, knowing that the attention of other minds who were familiar with the music would be fixed upon every note, and that some would doubtless have the score of the pieces before them, in order to observe if I should make any errors.

The opening number was the Fourth Organ Sonata by Mendelssohn; but when I began playing, my excitement was so intense that I could not feel one key from another, and it seemed as if I should swoon away in a fainting-fit. I perceived that I had no control of myself, and that I was not breathing. I knew that my reputation as an organist was at stake, and, having brought this recital upon myself as a free-will offering, I determined to conquer. Recognizing my confused condition as I attempted the first brace, I resolved to make a prelude in this style until I should become calm, by obtaining control of my breathing, so that a circulation of the blood was restored. I was then able to play through the piece without mistakes, but with a mental agony which I have never forgotten, and which has ever since come upon me in the attempt to render similar pieces in the presence of a musical audience.

Although I kept control of myself through the remainder of the programme, the suffering which I endured on that evening was so indelibly impressed upon my mind, that I have not since experienced the least ambition to appear in such a position before a critical audience as the hero of such an occasion, for the romance had forever departed.

The next day I was so feeble that I could not raise my feet to step upstairs, and I was a number of weeks in recovering my wonted energy. I presume that my condition was not noticed, but that my nervous tension was so magnified that my defects were more apparent to my own perceptions, yet I carefully refrained from looking at the newspapers, so that I should not be irritated by any criticisms; and thus my musical conceit was effectually cured.

In playing in church, or at organ exhibitions, or entertainments where the music was in the Free Style, I had no such experience; and although I kept on with my studies in the classical compositions of the masters, I knew that I was not physically able to maintain myself where I should be subject to adverse criticisms, and governed myself accordingly.

This unfortunate condition was a direct result from the close application of previous years; and it was not until it was quite too late to be of use to me, that I ascertained how to counteract this nervous tendency, and to keep entire control of myself before an audience, and also how to practise daily without injury to my health, by simple exercises in physical culture directed to this end. From the experience here described, I decided not to again appear in public in a strictly classical programme while subject to such nervous prostration, although I had the ability to render this music when alone.

Soon after this event the music committee desired me to organize a new choir, and increased my salary to double the previous amount, and I was also engaged to act as the director, as well as being organist, the music in my previous situations having been in the charge of others.

THE VOLUNTEER ORGANIST.

The great big church was crowded full uv broadcloth and uv silk,
An' satins rich as cream that grows on our ol' brindle's milk;
Shined boots, biled shirts, stiff dickeys, and stove-pipe hats were there,
An' doods 'ith trouserloons so tight they couldn't kneel down in prayer.

The elder in his pulpit high, said, as he slowly riz —
"Our organist is kep' to hum, laid up 'ith rheumatiz,
An' as we hev no substitoot, as Brother Moore ain't here,
Will some 'un in the congregation be so kind's to volunteer?"

An' then a red-nosed, drunken tramp, of low-toned, rowdy style,
Give an introductory hiccup, an' then staggered up the aisle.
Then tho' that holy atmosphere there crep' a sense uv sin,
An' thro' thet row uv sanctity the odor uv ol' gin.

Then Deacon Purington, he yelled, his teeth all sot on edge —
"This man perfanes the House er God! W'y this is sacrilege!"
The tramp didn't hear a word he said, but staggered 'ith stumblin' feet,
An' sprawled an' staggered up the steps, an' gained the organ seat.

He then went pawrin' thro' the keys, an' soon there rose a strain
Thet seemed to jest bulge out the heart, an' lenrify the brain;
An' then he slapped down on the thing 'ith hands an' head an' knees,
He slam-dashed his full body down keatin' up on the keys.

The organ roared, the music flood went sweepin' high an' dry,
It swelled into the rafters, and bulged out into the sky;
The ol' church shook an' staggered, an' seemed to reel an' sway,
An' the elder shouted "Glory!" an' I yelled out "Hooray!"

An' then he tried a tender strain thet melted in our ears,
Thet brought up blessed memories, an' drenched 'em down 'ith tears;
An' we dreamed uv ol'-time kitchens, 'ith Tabby on the mat,
Uv home an' love an' baby-days, an' mother, an' all that!

An' then he struck a streak uv hope — a song from souls forgiven —
Thet burst from prison-bars uv sin, an' stormed the gates uv heaven;
The mornin' stars they sung together — no soul was left alone —
We felt the universe was safe, an' God war on His throne!

An' then a wail uv deep despair an' darkness come again,
An' long, black crape hung on the door uv all the homes uv men;
No love, no light, no joy, no hope, no songs of glad delight,
An' then — the tramp he staggered down an' reeled into the night.

But we knew he'd tol' his story, tho' he never spoke a word,
An' it was the saddest story that our ears had ever heard;
He hed tol' his own life history, and no eye was dry thet day,
When the elder rose an' simply said: "My brethren, let us pray."
                                                    Yankee Blade.

CIPHERINGS.

The following must surely have been written by an American organist from his own practice: —

"'Rooles for Playin' Onto a Organ into Meetin':' When the preacher cums in and neels down in the pulpit, pull out all the stoppers. That's wot the stoppers is for. When a him is gave out to be sung, play over the wheat toon before singin', but be sure to play it so that they can't tell whether it's that toon or some other toon. It will amouse the people to gess. When you play the interloods, sometimes pull all the stoppers out, and sometimes pull them all in. The stoppers is made to pull out and in. Play the interloods about twice as long as the toon. The interloods is the best part of the newsie, and should be the longest. Play from the interloods into the toon without letting them kno when the toon begins. This will teach them to mind thare biznes. Always play the interlood's faster or slower than the toon. This will keep it from bein' the same time as the toon. If the preacher give out five verses, play four. Too menny verses is teejus. Doorin' the sermon go out of the church, and cum back in time for the next toon. This will show you doant mean to be hard on the preacher by havin' too menny listenin' to him at wunst.'" — *Ex.*

DE GUSTIBUS NON EST DISPUTANDUM.

TO THE EDITOR OF THE "MUSICAL STANDARD."

SIR, — It is singular to observe that a paid organist always upholds the *voluntary* principle.

Though he earns his living as a *pedlar*, yet he looks upon himself as a most respectable member of society.

He uses many *pipes*, but no tobacco. If he wants to increase the sound he puts a *stop* to it.

Bellows are as indispensable to him as to the minister of a raming congregation.

On his general appearance, we may say that he has abundance of (h) *air*, a well-made *chest* (which however contains nothing but wind.)

His *feet* are not confined to two, but men are to be found possessing eight, sixteen, or even thirty-two. One gentleman of our acquaintance has three and one-third — a most peculiar *foot.*

He cannot trust much to his eyesight, as he is always employing *trackers* to do his work.

For a powerful motive his coign of vantage is tin.

He is fond of a good reed, but does not care for books. He also enjoys a smart *march*, but a quick walk is insufferable to him.

Overtures he regards as undignified, save when he is desirous of *coupling* himself to some fair one possessing the sweetest of Vox Humana's or Vox Angelica's.

In that case (and that only) he often longs for a *cipher*, but likes it to be on a right hand of £500, in which case he soon becomes a *great* man, and generally assumes the *hairy swell.*

He has a partiality for *compositions* — except such as he sometimes receives from the estate of A. B., a bankrupt.

He is often sharp (♯), more rarely (perhaps he should say

more *accidentally*) double sharp (X), and still more rarely (of course) relishes a little XX.

But, after all, he will even be found a man of upright *principal.*

I remain, sir,

Your obedient servant,

A. Bray.

Foxs Asylorum. *Musical Standard.*

A Handy Music Lexicon, based upon the learned and thorough work of the late Professor Kalauer, has been edited by Peter Sebastian Dommerwetter, and published in Boston by Dole & Praetsch (50 cts.): The work is genuinely American: one might say it is a merry kind. One can perceive that the editor has solved the problem of how to convey the medium of knowledge in the sugar coat of amusement. Glancing at the pages of this little work, one finds that Bach owes his fame chiefly to the fortunate circumstance that he was commissioned to write the accompaniment to a celebrated melody by Gounod. Out of prodigious self-conceit, he published the former without the melody, as a so-called prelude, together with other pieces, under the title of "The Well Tempered Clavichord;" but it found small sale among the admirers of the "Ave Maria." Turning to "Organ" we read: "A newspaper; also a wind instrument run by a crank. It was while seated at an organ that Sir Arthur Sullivan bewailed the 'Lost Chord.'" Of "Coloratura" it says, "The chromatic coloring of a composition; the faster the colors are, the more they run." This little work will find a ready sale among those who care to smile.

MIXTURES.

(FOUR RANKS.)

Mr. Philip Wirsching, late of the Wirsching Organ Co., has become connected with the Farrand & Votey Organ Co.

Mr. W. O. Wilkinson is giving a series of Lenten organ recitals in St. Michael's P. E. Church, N.Y.

Mr. Wm. E. Mulligan gave his fourth recital at St. Mark's Church, N.Y., March 4.

Mr. John Henry Cornell, at various times organist of St. Paul's Church, the Old Brick Church, and St. John's Chapel, New York, died in that city March 1, in the age of sixty-six.

Mr. L. V. Flagler inaugurated a new Hook & Hastings organ in the First Presb. Church, Lockport, N.Y., Feb. 27, when he performed the following composition: Improvisation; Prelude and Fugue in A-minor, Bach; Idylle and Toccata, Rheinberger; Selections from "Tannhäuser," Wagner; Scene in the Alps, Flagler; Minuetto, Salomé; Concert Variations on "America," Flagler.

The pupils of Mr. J. Warren Andrews gave a recital at his studio, Plymouth Church, Minneapolis, March 19. Miss Bertha Bradish played Toccata and Fugue in D-minor, and Vorspiel, "Wir glauben All," Bach; and Miss Evelyn Mealy played Priere in G-flat, L'ouvigne.

Mr. Alex. S. Gibson performed the following organ selections at the fourth concert of the People's Course, at the First Cong. Church, Waterbury, Conn., March 2: Overture, Spark; Gipsy Dance, Scharwenka-Gibson; Variations, "Jerusalem the Golden," Spark; Pastorale in E, de la Tombelle; Toccata in G, Dubois; Nuptial March, Guilmant.

Mr. J. J. Miller gave his twenty-fourth recital (requested) in Christ Church, Norfolk, Va., the last of February, playing: Concerto in F, "The Cuckoo and the Nightingale," Handel; March of the Magi Kings, Dubois; March: Funebre, Chopin; Am Meer, schubert; Storm Fantasia, Lemmens; March and Chorus from "Tannhäuser," Wagner.

Mr. Harrison M. Wild performed the following programme at Unity Church, Chicago, March 4: Prelude and Fugue, Op. 37, No. 3, Mendelssohn; Variations on Theme by Beethoven, Merkel; Fantasia on Church Chimes and Romanza, Harriss; Scene Orientale (MS.), dedicated to Mr. Wild, Kroeger; Concert Variations on "Star Spangled Banner," Buck.

Mr. Fred L. Clark gave his eighteenth organ recital in Payson Church, Easthampton, Mass., March 2. The programme was: Sonata in G-minor, Merkel; Cavatina, Saint-Saëns; Wedding Song, Parker; Pastorale, Wachs; Invocation, Dubois; Marche Pontificale, Lemmens; Entrée du Cortège, Dubois.

"In one of the leading Minneapolis churches it is the custom of a large portion of the congregation to remain after the evening service, to listen to the organ, which is usually played twenty minutes or so, according to the disposition of the organist. To this custom the sexton seriously objects, declaring that the committee, in their great zeal in preparing the spe-ci-tion of stops for the organ, had utterly overlooked the most important of all stops, the *stop o'clock stop.*"

A good story is told of the elder Jardine, who was lately inspecting a modern organ, with its abundance of lead pipe for tubular action, when he remarked, "Humph—well—a man must be a blamed plumber nowadays to be an organ builder."

Organ recital in Unity Church, Chicago, Feb. 25, by Mr. Harrison M. Wild: Toccata in F, Bach; Sonata Op. 21, Ritter; Serenard Chant, Wirsching; Walter's Prize Song, Wagner; Damnos Triumphal March, Costa; Scherzo in D, Capocci.

Mr. Alfred Pennington gave an organ recital in Warner Hall, Oberlin, Ohio, March 18, playing Fantasia and Fugue in G-minor, Bach; Canon in B-flat and Sonata in C-minor, Guilmant; "The Holy Night," Buck; Legende et Finale Symphonique, Op. 71, Guilmant; Transcription, "On the Wings of Song," Mendelssohn; Concert Variation on Austrian Hymn, Pride.

During the past month the Hook & Hastings Co. have finished organs in the Horace Memorial Free Baptist Church, Chelsea, Mass., having two manuals; in First M. E. Church, Knoxville, Tenn., with two manuals and eighteen registers, having the action extended; and in the First Presb. Church, Muncie, Ind., having two manuals and twenty-nine registers, with extended action.

Mr. Harrison M. Wild played the following pieces at his organ recital March 10, in Unity Church, Chicago: Military Overture, Mendelssohn; Sonata Op. 25, Salomé; Variations, Best; Allegretto, Archer; Pontifical March, Lemmens; Fantasia in C, Tours.

Miss Fay Simmons is giving a series of Lenten organ recitals in St. James' Church, Cambridge, Mass. The recital for March 10 consisted of Cantilène, Rheinberger; Sonata No. 1, Bach; Serenade, Schubert; Overture to "Masaniello," Auber; Fantasia, Tours; Offertoire in D-flat, Salomé; Nearer my God to Thee (Transcription), Simmons; Offertory to St. Cecilia, Batiste.

Miss Luella M. Pollardee gave an organ recital in Warner Hall, Oberlin, Ohio, March 28, with the following programme: Prelude and Fugue in G-minor, Bach; Sonata No. 2, Mendelssohn; Canzonetta, Rheinberger; Theme and Variations in A-flat, Hesse; Adagio in E for Violin and Organ, Bach; Nuptial Postlude, Guilmant. Mrs. H. M. Rice, soprano, and Mr. F. G. Doolittle, violinist, assisted.

Mr. Samuel P. Warren gave his 230th and 231st organ recitals in Grace Church, New York, March 1st and 8th, with the following programmes: Passeoglia, Fresobaldi; Trio Sonata, No. 6, Bach; Six Pieces from op. 172, Rheinberger; Fifth Symphony, Widor. March 8: Concerto in C, Handel; Adagio in C, Hopper; Sonata No. 2, Bargiel; Scottish Eclogue and Wedding Hymn, Salomé; Chant du Soir, Bossi; Prelude and Fugue in E, A. C. H., Liszt.

Mr. Henry M. Dunham gave a very enjoyable organ recital at the Shawmut Church, Boston, March 15, when he presented the following programme: Prelude and Fugue in A-minor, Bach; Andante Cantabile, Tschaikovsky-Morse; In Memoriam, Dunham; Pastorale, Op. 20, Foote; Coronation March, Meyerbeer-Best. The most pleasing number was Mr. Dunham's In Memoriam, which was very effectively given, and was encored. Mr. Wm. H. Dunham sang.

The Providence (R.I.) Music Hall is to be reconstructed into business offices, and the large three-manual organ which it contains is for sale. The Hook & Hastings Co., who built the instrument about twenty years ago, are prepared to place this organ in any hall or church for a very low figure. The organ has an imposing exterior, and contains a large number of stops. This company purchased the instrument recently, and will make it practically as good as new. Here is an opportunity for some society or corporation to secure a bargain.

Mr. Robert Ross, of the Ross Valve Co., of Troy, New York, manufacturers of the Ross water motor, was, not long since, brutally murdered by one of the political thugs who control the ballot box in that city. Mr. William Ross, brother of the murdered man, was seriously injured in the attempt to render assistance to his brother.

The Ross brothers were, among other law-abiding citizens, stationed at the polls, at the recent election, to insure honest voting, and to prevent "repeating." About one o'clock a gang of thirty thugs, headed by "Bat" Shea, attempted to do some illegal voting, and a general fight ensued, in which the said Shea drew a revolver and shot Robert Ross in the head, killing him instantly. William Ross was shot down and seriously wounded.

Mr. Geo. S. Hutchings is now constructing a three-manual organ with 32 registers for the Unitarian Church, Medford, Mass.; a two-manual organ with 12 registers for St. Mary's Church, Dedham; a two-manual organ with 27 registers for Second Cong. Church, Attleboro; a two-manual organ with 17 registers for the M. E. Church of Lisbon, N.H.; a two-manual organ with 20 registers for Presb. Church, Cambridge, Ohio; and a two-manual organ with 29 registers and tubular pneumatic action for St. Luke's Church, Jamestown, N.Y.

Mr. Wallace P. Day is giving a series of weekly organ recitals, Sunday evenings, at Grace Church, Jacksonville, Ill. Two of the latest programmes were: Adagio in A-flat, Volckmar; Overture to Occasional Oratorio, Handel; Fantasia on a Welsh March, Best; Prayer in F and Allegro in F-sharp Minor, Guilmant. The second: Barcarolle, Hoffman; Schiller Festival March, Meyerbeer; St. Cecilia Offertory, Batiste; Christmas Pastorale, Merkel.

The late August Hamann left a very valuable collection of vocal, instrumental, and orchestral music, most of which cannot be obtained in this country. This music will be sold for one-third of its value. Send for catalogue to Mrs. Elizabeth Hamann, Cor. Summer and Cedar Streets, West Somerville, Mass.

The London *Musical News* announces that the Albert Palace Organ has been purchased by the Benedictine community of Fort Augustus, N.B., for the use of the pro-Cathedral, Oban.

The Music Trades announces the incorporation of the Maryland Church Organ Co. of Baltimore, Md., and the Kilgen Church Organ Co. of Chicago. The capital of the latter is $3,500, and Charles C. Kilgen, Henry Kilgen, and Geo. E. Kilgen are the incorporators.

Trinity P. E. Church of Shamokin, Pa., will open a new Hook & Hastings Co. organ on Easter Sunday. It is built into a chamber prepared for it by the side of the chancel, and will prevent to view the fronts, — one toward the chancel, the other toward the nave. Wind will be furnished by a water motor. This firm has just finished a two-manual organ in the Calvary Presbyterian Church of West New Brighton, Staten Island, N.Y.

A new organ for St. Patrick's Church, Sydney, Australia, has been constructed by Messrs. Aristocen in France from specifications furnished by M. Auguste Wiegand. The instrument was to have been inaugurated by M. Wiegand on St. Patrick's Day.

Mr. Harrison M. Wild gave his one hundred and fifty-third organ recital in Unity Church, Chicago, March 11, with the following programme: Solemn March, Smart; Sonata, Op. 88, Rheinberger; Pastorale, Wachs; "Home, Sweet Home," Buck; Menuet Gavotte, Thomas—Westbrook; Canzonetta del Salvator Rosa, Liszt-Westbrook; March and Chorus from "Tannhäuser," Wagner.

The Sydney (Australia) *Daily Telegraph* announces that during the year 1893, M. Auguste Wiegand, the organist of the Town Hall (containing the biggest organ in the world), performed seven hundred and eighty-six compositions, of which three hundred and twenty-seven were French, sixty-eight English, two hundred and thirty-four German, seventy-six Belgian, fifty-nine Italian, and twenty-two of other nationalities. It would be interesting to know how many of the seven hundred and eighty-six compositions were *organ compositions*.

Mr. W. C. Carl gave another recital at the Drexel Institute, Philadelphia, the last of February, with the following programme:— Overture to "Euryanthe," Weber; Minuet, Neustedt; Scherzo, Gigout; "Messe de Mariage," Dubois; La Cinquantaine, Marie; Intermezzo, Salomé; Fugue in D, Guilmant; Prélude for Organ (MS. dedicated to Mr. Carl), Guilmant; Prélude Nuptiale, Guilmant; Mr. Carl also opened a new Hook & Hastings organ in Cong. Church, St. Albans, Vt., March 8.

During the month of January organ recitals were given on the exhibition organ of the Queensland (Australia) National Association. Two programmes given by Mrs. Willsone have just arrived. The first (Jan. 10) consisted of a March in E-flat, Wély; Andante in E-minor, Batiste; Toccata in G, Dubois; Marche Religieuse, Chauvet; Andante from Second Symphony, Weber; Grand Chœur, Guilmant; Fugue in G-minor, Bach; Communion in E, Grison; and Marche Militaire, Gounod.

The large $10,000 organ for St. Mary's Church, Newton, Conn., has just been shipped from the factory of the Hook & Hastings Co. It will be in position in time for the formal opening Easter Sunday. It has three manuals, forty-nine registers, and will be blown by a water motor. The first M. E. Church, Dallas, Texas, will open the new organ, also built by the Hook & Hastings Co., on Easter Sunday. It has two manuals, eighteen registers, and is blown by a water motor. The M. E. Church South, of Fredericksburg, Va., has just received a new two-manual organ from the same house. It stands in the corner of the auditorium, and shows two fronts.

Mr. Clarence Eddy has returned to Chicago from his California trip. While away he gave organ recitals in the Cong. Church, Colorado Springs; First Cong. Church, and the Tabernacle, Salt Lake City; First Cong. Church, Riverside, Cal.; Westminster Presb. Church, St. Joseph, Mo.; First Cong. Church, Pasadena, Cal.; and Immanuel Presb. Church, Los Angeles. The principal works performed were: Prelude and Fugue in A-minor, Bach; Pontificale Sonata, Lemmens; Selections from the "Messe de Mariage," Dubois; Fugue in D, and Lamentation, Guilmant; Fantasia and Fugue in G-minor, Bach; and Concert Piece, Op. 35, Law. Mr. Eddy expects to return to California for the Musical Congress, to be held in May.

Mr. Chas. H. Morse gave his second Lenten Organ Recital in Plymouth Church, Brooklyn, the last of February. The programme was: Fragment Symphonique, Lemaigre; Slumber Song, Schumann; Christmas Musette, Mailly; Military March, Schubert; Sonata No. 6, Mendelssohn; Méditation in A-flat, Klein; and Overture to Zanetta, Auber. At the third recital, March 5, Mr. Morse played: Sonata in F-minor, Ritter; Cantabile, Rousseau; Intermezzo, Mascagni; Choral Prelude, Bach; Evening Reverie, Saint-Saëns; "Soeur Monique," Couperin; and Grand March from "Leonore Symphony," Raff.

At the Church of the First Religious Society, Roxbury, the wind is supplied by the labor of two "gentlemen of mahogany complexion." One Sunday Mr. Philip Hale, the organist, had decided to play the Toccata in F, of Bach, which requires considerable wind, and does not come under the head of "short and easy compositions." It was a warm day, and the blowers worked hard. When the composition was ended, one of the "mahogany gentlemen" puffed, mopped his face, and broke out: "For de lan', sake! has dat organist been laying down on dem keys?"

CORRESPONDENCE.

To the Editor of THE ORGAN :—

Mr. CARLTON C. MITCHELL, the writer of the very uncomplimentary letter in the December number of THE ORGAN concerning our American organ builders and their work, has so far modified his views of American ideas, that he has appropriated for his own use the combination of a valve, a following lever, and a pneumatic bellows, in a pneumatic swell pedal, of which I am the inventor and, with one other, own the exclusive right to use, as Mr. Mitchell is aware.

Peradventure, if Mr. Mitchell ever has an idea of his own, he will know better how to respect the effort and expense contingent upon securing a United States patent, and give at least the courtesy of an interview to those of whom he wishes favors.

Respectfully,

ERNEST M. SKINNER.

23 IRVINGTON STREET, BOSTON, MASS.

AN IDEAL ORGAN.

To the Editor of THE ORGAN :—

A NUMBER of your correspondents have spoken of an "ideal organ." What constitutes an ideal organ is largely a matter of opinion; but I think a majority would find a near approach to their idea of perfection in an organ built from the following specification. The points considered in this specification are a complete tonal resource; a perfection of touch, repetition, and response; an absence of duplication in the stops (for use in combination); an increase in combination possibilities, by a new stop-action system in swell and choir organs; a simplicity of arrangement in key, draw-stop, and combination action; and an expense within reasonable limits — in short, a *practical* organ, which is suitable in every way for any purpose for which a pipe organ can be utilized.

GREAT ORGAN.

Open Diapason	16 Ft.	metal.
Open Diapason, American type	8 "	
Open Diapason, English type	8 "	
Open Diapason, Small	8 "	
French Horn	8 "	
Violoncello	8 "	
Gemshorn	8 "	
Harmonic Flute (large scale)	8 "	wood.
Harmonic Flute	4 "	metal.
Octave	4 "	"
Quinte Flute	2⅔ "	"
Fifteenth	2 "	"
Mixture	IV. Rks	
Trumpet	8 Ft.	

SWELL AND CHOIR (OR SECOND ORGAN).

One wind-chest enclosed in swell-box, and controlled by the swell and choir keys. Every stop can be drawn upon either or both manuals, the couplers working as in the old stop system: for instance, if the Oboe, St. Diapason, and Salicional be drawn upon the swell manual, the same Salicional may be drawn upon the choir manual, in combination with any or all other stops on the swell and choir chest, and the swell to pedal, choir to pedal, choir or swell to great, and swell to choir will bring into effect such stops as are in use, on the manuals affected by the couplers drawn. The "second" organ is a combination of the common type of swell and choir organs now in use, without duplication of stops and with a few additions which would be acceptable.

Gedeckt	16 Ft.	wood.
Contra Salicional	16 "	metal and wood.
Contra Dulciana	16 "	"
Open Diapason	8 "	metal.
Geigen Principal	8 "	"

Spitz-flöte	8 Ft.	metal.
Salicional	8 "	"
Voix Céleste	8 "	"
Viol d'Orchestra	8 "	"
Æoline	8 "	"
Concert Flute	8 "	wood.
Stopped Diapason	8 "	"
Dulciana	8 "	metal.
Quintadena	8 "	"
Violina	4 "	"
Octave	4 "	"
Salicet	4 "	"
Flauto Traverso	4 "	wood.
Flûte d'Amour	4 "	"
Dolce Cornet	IV Rks	metal.
Piccolo	2 Ft.	"
Saxophone	8 "	
Oboe	8 "	
Orchestral Oboe	8 "	
Clarinet	8 "	
Cornopean	8 "	
Contra Fagotto	16 "	

ECHO ORGAN (VENTIL), FROM GREAT MANUAL.

Vox Humana	8 Ft.	wood.
Echo Flute	8 "	"
Echo Voix Céleste	8 "	"
Quintadena	8 "	"

PEDAL ORGAN.

Bourdon	32 Ft.	metal.
Bourdon	16 "	"
Open Diapason	16 "	"
Violone	16 "	"
Dulciana	16 "	"
Flute	8 "	"
Gedeckt	8 "	"
Dulciana	8 "	"
Quinte	10⅔ "	"

COUPLERS.

Swell on itself at 8vs.
Swell to Great (unison).
Swell to Great at 8vs. (pedal).
Choir to Great (unison).
Choir to Great Sub-Octave.
Swell to Choir (unison).

Great Separation.
Great off, Echo on.
Swell to Pedal.
Choir to Pedal.
Great to Pedal (reversible).
Pedal on itself at 8vs.

Stop and Combination Action.

Every stop on the second organ has two registers, — one for the upper, and one for the lower keyboard. The second organ contains twenty-seven stops; but in combination possibilities it is equivalent to two separate organs of twenty-seven stops each, every stop being characteristic, and all together representing all qualities and grades of organ tone.

GREAT ORGAN.

Combination, 1, 2, and 3 . . . set.
" 4, 5 . . . . . adjustable.

SECOND ORGAN, UPPER MANUAL.

Combination, 1, 2, 3, 4, 5, 6 . . adjustable.

SECOND ORGAN, LOWER MANUAL.

Combination, 1, 2, 3, 4, 5, 6 . . adjustable.

All combinations control pedal stops and suitable couplers, and move registers, and are so comprehensive in arrangement that a few moments' inspection will make their operation clear.

Tremolo, upper manual.
" lower manual.
" Echo Organ.
Grand Crescendo (balance pedal).
Full Organ with Couplers.
All Couplers (locking pedal).
Balanced Swell (Second Organ).
Tubular pneumatic or electric action throughout.

Greatest wind pressure necessary for pipe work, 4 inches; and for mechanism, 3 inches.

I have long believed that the combining of the swell and choir manuals, in the manner suggested here, would meet with favor, and take this opportunity of offering it for criticism. It is not what might be called a colossal organ in its number of stops, nor in its number of manuals.

It may be thought that an ideal organ should have four or five manuals, but this is written in the belief that three manuals, under proper control, make the most convenient form of console.

Hoping that THE ORGAN will live and grow, and that this will be thought worthy of your consideration, I am,

Very truly yours,

ERNEST M. SKINNER.

23 IRVINGTON STREET, BOSTON, MASS.

NEW ORGANS.

FIRST CONG. CHURCH, ELDORA, IOWA.
(*New organ built by Mr. Geo. S. Hutchings.*)

GREAT ORGAN.		SWELL ORGAN.	
Open Diapason	8 Ft.	Bourdon, Treble and Bass	8 Ft.
Dolcissimo	8 "	Violin Diapason	8 "
Melodia (Stopped Bass)	8 "	Salicional	8 "
Octave	4 "	Æoline	8 "
Octave Quinte	2⅔ "	Stopped Diapason	8 "
Super Octave	2 "	Flûte Harmonique	4 "
Trumpet	8 "	Violina	4 "
		Oboe and Bassoon	8 "

PEDAL MOVEMENTS.
F. and P. Comb. to Gt.
" " " " Sw.
Gt. to Ped. (reversible).
Tremolo.
The usual couplers.

PEDAL ORGAN.
Bourdon . . . . . . 16 Ft.
Flute . . . . 8 "

TRINITY, P. E. CHURCH, ST. AUGUSTINE, FLA.
(*New organ built by the Hook & Hastings Co.*)

GREAT ORGAN.		SWELL ORGAN.	
Bourdon	16 Ft.	Viola	8 Ft.
Open Diapason	8 "	Stopped Bass	8 "
Dulciana	8 "	Flûte Harmonique	4 "
Melodia	8 "	Violina	4 "
Octave	4 "	Oboe and Bassoon	8 "
Twelfth	2⅔ "	
Fifteenth	2 "	

The usual couplers.
F. and P. Comb. to Gt.
Water Motor.

PEDAL ORGAN.
Bourdon . . . . . 16 Ft.
Open Diapason . . . 16 "

FIRST BAPTIST CHURCH, PORTLAND, OREGON.
(*New organ being constructed by Mr. Geo. S. Hutchings.*)

GREAT ORGAN.		CHOIR ORGAN.	
Open Diapason	16 Ft.	Lieblich Gedeckt	16 Ft.
Open Diapason	8 "	Geigen Principal	8 "
Gamba	8 "	Melodia	8 "
Viola di Gamba	8 "	Dolcissimo	8 "
Doppel Flöte	8 "	Flûte d'Amour	4 "
Flûte Harmonique	4 "	Piccolo Harmonique	2 "
Octave	4 "	Clarinet	8 "
Octave Quinte	2⅔ "	
Super Octave	2 "	PEDAL ORGAN.
Mixture	IV Rks.	Open Diapason	16 Ft.
Trumpet	8 Ft.	Violone	16 "
		Bourdon	16 "
SWELL ORGAN.		Quinte	10⅔ "
		Octave	8 "
Bourdon, Treble and Bass	16 Ft.	Violoncello	8 "
Open Diapason	8 "	Gedeckt	8 "
Salicional	8 "	
Æoline	8 "	PEDAL MOVEMENTS.
Stopped Diapason	8 "	Full Organ (with all Couplers).
Quintadena	8 "	F., MF., and P., Comb. for Great.
Fugara	4 "	" " " " " Swell.
Flauto Traverso	4 "	F. and P. Comb. " Choir.
Flautina	2 "	All couplers.
Dolce Cornet	V. Rks.	Gt. to Ped. (reversible).
Cornopean	8 "	Grand Crescendo.
Oboe	8 "	Octave Coupler (Sw. to Gt.).
Vox Human	8 "	Tremolo (Swell).
		The usual couplers.

The compass of the manuals will be 61 notes, and of the pedals, 30 notes. Tubular pneumatic action is used throughout all the manuals and pedals, with pneumatic stop action.

ORGAN MUSIC

Published and Imported by EVERETT E. TRUETTE & Co., 149A Tremont Street, Boston.